OLD TESTAMEN

ISAIAH 40-66

EDITED BY

MARK W. ELLIOTT

GENERAL EDITOR

THOMAS C. ODEN

IVP Academic

An imprint of InterVarsity Press
Downers Grove, Illinois

InterVarsity Press
P.O. Box 1400, Downers Grove, IL 60515-1426
ivpress.com
email@ivpress.com

InterVarsity Press® is the book-publishing division of InterVarsity Christian Fellowship/USA®, a movement of students and faculty active on campus at hundreds of universities, colleges, and schools of nursing in the United States of America, and a member movement of the International Fellowship of Evangelical Students. For information about local and regional activities, visit intervarsity.org.

The Scripture quotations quoted herein are from the Revised Standard Version of the Bible, copyright 1946, 1952, 1971 by the Division of Christian Education of the National Council of the Churches of Christ in the U.S.A. Used by permission. All rights reserved.

Selected excerpts from Fathers of the Church: A New Translation, ©1947–. Used by permission of The Catholic University of America Press, Washington, D.C. Full bibliographic information on volumes of Fathers of the Church may be found in the Bibliography of Works in English Translation.

Selected excerpts from The Works of Saint Augustine: A Translation for the Twenty-First Century, Part 3, translated by Edmund Hill, edited by John E. Rotelle, ©1990-1997. Used by permission of the Augustinian Heritage Institute, Ardmore, Pennsylvania.

Selected excerpts from John Chrysostom, Old Testament Homilies, translated by Robert Charles Hill, ©2003. Used by permission of Holy Cross Orthodox Press, Brookline, Massachusetts.

Selected excerpts from The Ascetical Homilies of Saint Isaac the Syrian, ©1984. Used by permission of Holy Transfiguration Monastery, Boston, Massachusetts.

Selected excerpts from Cyril of Alexandria, translated by Norman Russell, ©2000. Used by permission of Taylor & Francis Books, London.

Selected excerpts from John Cassian, The Conferences, translated and annotated by Boniface Ramsey, OP, copyright ©1997 by Boniface Ramsey, OP; Cassiodorus: Explanation of the

Psalms, 3 vols., translated and annotated by P. G. Walsh, copyright ©1990-1991 by P. G. Walsh; Gregory of Nyssa: The Life of Moses, translation, introduction and notes by Abraham J. Malherbe and Everett Ferguson, preface by John Meyendorff, copyright ©1978 by Paulist Press, Inc.; Origen: An Exhortation to Martyrdom, Prayer and Selected Writings, translation and introduction by Rowan A. Greer, preface by Hans Urs von Balthasar, copyright ©1979 by Paulist Press; Pseudo-Dionysius: The Complete Works, translation by Colm Luibheid, foreword, notes and translation collaboration by Paul Rorem, preface by Rene Roques, introductions by Jaroslav Pelikan, Jean Leclercq and Karlfried Froehlich, copyright ©1987 by Paulist Press; Symeon the New Theologian, The Discourses, translation by C. J. de Catanzaro, introduction by George Maloney, SJ, preface by Basile Krivocheine, copyright ©1980 by Paulist Press. Reprinted by permission of Paulist Press, Inc. <www. paulistpress.com>.

Selected excerpts from The Sermons of St. Maximus of Turin, translated and annotated by Boniface Ramsey, OP, copyright ©1989 by Boniface Ramsey, OP; Origen, Prayer; Exhortation to Martyrdom, translated and annotated by John J. O'Meara, copyright ©1954 by Rev. Johannes Quasten and Rev. Joseph C. Plumpe; John Cassian, The Institutes, translated and annotated by Boniface Ramsey, OP, copyright ©2000 by Boniface Ramsey, OP; Theodoret of Cyrus: On Divine Providence, translated by Thomas Halton, copyright ©1988 by Rev. Walter J. Burghardt and Thomas Comerford Lawler; St. John Chrysostom: Baptismal Instructions, translated and annotated by Paul W. Harkins, PhD, LLD, copyright ©1963 by Johannes Quasten and Rev. Walter J. Burghardt, SJ; Newman Press, an imprint of Paulist Press, Inc., New York/Mahwah, N.J. Reprinted by permission of Paulist Press, Inc. <www.paulistpress.com>.

Selected excerpts from St. Basil the Great, On the Holy Spirit, translated by David Anderson, ©1980; St. Cyril of Alexandria, On the Unity of Christ, translated by John A. McGuckin, ©2000; Melito of Sardis, On Pascha: With the Fragments of Melito and Other Material Related to the Quartodecimans, translated by Alistair Stewart-Sykes, ©2001. Used by permission of St. Vladimir's Seminary Press, 575 Scarsdale Road, Yonkers, N.Y. 10707.

Selected excerpts from Faith Gives Fullness to Reasoning: The Five Theological Orations of Gregory Nazianzen, introduction and commentary by F. W. Norris, ©1990. Used by permission of Koninklijke Brill.

Cover design: David Fassett
Images: silver texture background: © Katsumi Murouchi / Getty Images
        stained glass cathedral window: © elzauer / Getty Images
        gold texture: © Katsumi Murouchi / Getty Images
        abstract marble pattern: © NK08gerd / iStock / Getty Images Plus

ISBN 978-0-8308-4346-6 (paperback)
ISBN 978-0-8308-1481-7 (hardcover)
ISBN 978-0-8308-9736-0 (digital)

Printed in the United States of America ∞

InterVarsity Press is committed to ecological stewardship and to the conservation of natural resources in all our operations. This book was printed using sustainably sourced paper.

Library of Congress Cataloging-in-Publication Data
A catalog record for this book is available from the Library of Congress.

P 32 31 30 29 28 27 26 25 24 23 22 21 20 19 18 17 16 15 14 13 12 11 10 9 8 7 6 5 4 3 2 1

Y 47 46 45 44 43 42 41 40 39 38 37 36 35 34 33 32 31 30 29 28 27 26 25 24 23 22 21 20 19

Contents

INTRODUCTION TO ISAIAH 40-66

Isaiah has been the scene of many battles in the struggle for a Christian reading of the Bible.[1] From as early as disputes about the identity of the virgin, or young girl, of Isaiah 7:14[2] to that of the Servant in the Servant Songs of the latter part of the book, one fact remains undisputed, captured by Sirach: "By [Isaiah's] dauntless spirit he saw the future and comforted the mourners in Zion."[3] His vision focuses on the sweeping course of salvation in God's unfolding of his covenantal faithfulness and loving triumph within history, set against a sober background of judgment and the grim realities of faithlessness.

Metaphor, History and God's Revelation of Himself

The heavy use of metaphor in this second part of Isaiah is breathtaking. In reading the text, we are almost swept away by the sheer force of the rhetorical torrent that washes over our imagination. We are struck as we read how God takes sides, how his passion burns against evil and duplicity and how, with even more intensity, he promises faithfulness and salvation. However, the ancient Christian writers in interpreting these actions of God never reduce God simply to the content of metaphors. For instance, when Isaiah refers to God as a woman who could never forget her nursing child,[4] he is not saying that God *is* a woman, a mother. However if we look for God as he is, then there is no sense of God being other than what he says and does in the world, in history and in Israel's witness. But once the metaphorical is taken into account, while fully realizing that these metaphors do not express the fullness of God's existence, God is then seen as both mysterious and as *the* only true reality that exists in this world.[5] God, not metaphor or language, is

---

[1]Brevard Childs, *The Struggle to Understand Isaiah as Christian Scripture* (Grand Rapids: Eerdmans, 2004).
[2]See Adam Kamesar, "The Virgin of Isaiah 7:14: The Philological Argument from the Second to the Fifth Century," *Journal of Theological Studies* 41 (1990): 51-75.
[3]Sir 48:24.
[4]Is 49:15.
[5]According to John Milbank, either we believe in an endless semiosis of language or a theological account of meaning. In *The Word Made Strange* (Oxford-Malden: Blackwell, 1997), 106, Milbank writes: "If metaphor is fundamental, then religion ceases to be a mystery in addition to the mystery of humanity itself. . . . Instead, original metaphor implies either a primal personification of nature ('paganism') or else a primal response to nature as a personal address ('monotheism')." A. C. Thiselton has described the task of the biblical interpreter as going beyond explanation to understanding, beyond significance to application. In his essay " 'Behind' and 'in Front of' the Text: Language, Reference and Indeterminacy" in *After Pentecost*, ed. C. Bartholomew, C. Greene and K. Möller (Grand Rapids: Zondervan, 2001), 97-120, he writes: "If God is more than an existent object within the world, such poetic creative hymnic form as 'Holy, holy, holy is the Lord of hosts; the earth is full of his glory' (Is 6:3) tran-

both the ground and mystery of the world. His creation is permeated with "the grandeur of God."[6] Any subsequent application of how we talk about him, then, is predicated on the notion that the subject matter of the Bible is the God who teaches us theology, teaching us, in effect, how to think and speak of him.

It is common to patristic commentators, especially Cyril of Alexandria and Theodoret of Cyr, however, to also speak of the obscurity of Scripture, which is the whole reason for commenting on it. Theodoret of Cyr was sometimes happy to paraphrase a text if its meaning is clear enough; he did not try to explain everything. Both Cyril and Theodoret of Cyr were aware of a special vocabulary of the Septuagint and its rhetoric—its use of figures and metaphor—but not of any particular grammatical style.[7] Metaphor was Scripture's *lingua franca*. The two differ in that only Cyril will speak of the metaphorical sense as something "mystical." Also, the Alexandrian used shadow as well as type, while Theodoret of Cyr used only type. Augustine was famously aware how all language pointed to a reality that is ultimately higher than, but in no sense lesser than, the reason of language and the intimations of sense.

Today symbol has taken the place of sacrament in a culture of meaning. The signified and the sign are tied together as equal partners. This is how it operated in the days of Gnostic myth in which meaning was at most the next step up from the mere sign. Only later at the hands of the Neoplatonists and Christians did myth come to be seen as pointing to a meaning distinct from the story and poetry itself, and thus also higher than those.[8]

How do the metaphorical and the poetic relate to real life if it is all about a new world of meaning of its own? The Gospel parables and the prophetic metaphors of bride and groom, of a mother in labor, of a trampler of the wine press are all in touch with the world of creation and ordinary life. It is not a different world but the same seen with new significance. Is that not what revelation is about? For Jerome, who reflected as much as anyone on these things and whose conclusion is reminiscent of that of Thomas Aquinas, metaphor seems a bridge between literal and spiritual meanings. The metaphor demands opening up to the spiritual.[9]

The Patristic Commentaries' Contribution to Exegesis

Through various genres, the church fathers—those orthodox Christian theologians of the patristic period from the early centuries of the church—aid our awareness of God's revelation of himself to his world. Theological treatises, such as Basil's *On the Holy Spirit* and Augustine's *On the Trinity*, or works of spiritual edification, such as Gregory of Nyssa's *On the Life of Moses* and John Cassian's *Conferences*, are quite adept at creating this awareness. Of course, these latter genres rely heavily on key passages of Scripture that strike fatal blows to any competing doctrinal positions. In contrast to the theological treatises, the patristic commentaries on Scripture are not always as focused, although, at times, they can present short, pithy *scholia* on particularly relevant passages, or questions on difficult texts[10] or summaries of works or discourses. This brevity brings with it a newfound delight—until we realize that these abbreviated thoughts are sometimes

---

scends representational, referential, single meaning. In Tillich's use of the term, we enter the realm of double-edged symbol, which opens up both reality and our own self-hood" (p. 110).

[6]From "The Grandeur of God," Gerard Manley Hopkins.

[7]Jean-Noel Guinot, *L'exégèse de Théodoret de Cyr*. Theologie historique 100 (Paris: Beauchesne, 1995), 60.

[8]Jean Pépin, *Mythe et Allégorie: Les origins grecques et les contestations judéo-chrétiennes* (Paris: Aubier, 1958), 79.

[9]P. Jay, *L'exégèse de saint Jérôme d'après son commentaire sur Isaie* (Paris: Études augustiniennes, 1985), 159-60.

too short to provide the insight we were looking for to begin with![11]

One of the main contributions the church fathers have provided the church in its reading of Isaiah is enabling the people of the church to receive the message of Isaiah in the light of its fulfillment. The Fathers help us to see the nature of the trinitarian God reflected in the verses of the Old Testament. Does this mean they were reading in[12] that content from the New Testament as interpreted by the church? At times, yes. But patristic biblical interpretation is at its best when it is metaphorically treated, as mentioned above. We are told, for instance, to flee unbelief—not Egypt. It is less plausible when it is so keen to actualize the text that it makes the referent of idolaters in Isaiah 44, for instance, the Jews of post-Constantinian times. The words of the prophets are dressings on the wounds that are meant to heal the people of God at all times and in all places, and for that reason the theological reading of the Fathers allows room for today's readers to provide their own interpretation as applied to their own situation.

For the same reason, the Fathers are not all that interested in questions about authorship, as to whether the Isaiah of Jerusalem who wrote Isaiah 1-39 is the same person who wrote Isaiah 40-66. Most likely, if they asked themselves such questions, they would have answered in the affirmative.[13] But from their way of operating, it is not a question in which they seem much interested. These are living oracles of the living God, from everlasting to everlasting.

In summary, the Fathers encourage us to read against the grain, to read closely and to read for profit. Their commentary is especially useful when it brings theological, moral and spiritual help mediated through Christian doctrine to the fore.[14] We have made selections for this commentary that demonstrate this usefulness, having principally chosen four major commentators: Eusebius of Caesarea, Jerome, Cyril of Alexandria and Theodoret of Cyr. Of these four, the first has a commentary that can at times be fascinating but at other times is not much more than a mere paraphrase of the Scripture verses. In these instances, its chief benefit is its identification of the translation choices of the three main Jewish translators[15] from Hebrew to Greek whose main mission was to provide a different translation once the Christians had expropriated the Septuagint. The last of the four, Theodoret of Cyr, wrote short *scholia*—or at least these are what remain of his work.[16] The second, Jerome, at times provides illuminating historical and parallel back-

---

[10]Mario Girardi, *"Catechesi ed esegesi nel monachesimo antico"* in *Esegesis e catechesi nei Padri (saec. IV-VII)*, Biblioteca di scienze religiose 112, ed. Sergio Felici (Rome: Libreria Ateneo salesiano, 1994), 19-20. He argues that our commentaries grew out of the earlier genre of "difficult passages" as practiced in monastic circles. But the Alexandrian approach of Origen seems to have been one of continuous verse-by-verse commentary of whole books of Scripture.

[11]Theodoret of Cyr's *Commentary on Isaiah*, for example, has this nature. J.-N. Guinot argues that Theodoret was sharply pointed for good pastoral reasons; J.-N. Guinot, *L'exégèse de Théodoret de Cyr* (Paris: Beauchesne, 1995), 807.

[12]Otherwise known as eisegesis.

[13]See, for instance, the opening passages on Is 40:1 where they wrestle with the question of why the words, "Comfort, comfort my people" are recorded immediately after Hezekiah's prayer in Isaiah 39. The Septuagint is key in providing a helpful referent for these words in the priests of the temple which it brings into the text at Is 40:2. Thus, Isaiah is addressing these words to the priests who are to offer comfort to the people since Hezekiah's prayer did not.

[14]A paper by Mark Sheridan on usefulness in patristic exegesis has helped me to appreciate this.

[15]Aquila, Symmachus and Theodotion. There was also a Lucian text based in Antioch that formed the basis for much of that area's interpretation of the Old Testament.

[16]We are tremendously fortunate in having major scholarly studies on all four of these. These four major studies are Hollerich [M. Hollerich, *Eusebius of Caesarea's Commentary on Isaiah: Christian Exegesis in the Age of Constantine* (London and New York: Oxford University Press, 1999)]; Jay (see n. 9); Fernández Lois [A. Fernández Lois, *La Cristologia en los Commentarios a Isaias de Cirilo de Alejandra y Teodoreto de Ciro* (Roma: Pontificio Istituto Biblico, 1998)]; and Guinot (*L'exégèse de Théodore de Cyr*). (This last deals with more than just his commentary on Isaiah but at 879 pages gives a

ground material for the prophecies while often looking forward to their New Testament fulfillment, while Cyril's commentary often focuses on christological emphases that reach their eschatological fulfillment ultimately in the final judgment.

The Centrality of Soteriology

Is it justified to read the book of Isaiah christocentrically, or even messianically? Yes and no. No, if we mean that the prophet knew about a figure called Jesus Christ who seems to be much more than anything that the prophet ever imagined. In fact, Isaiah's prophecy speaks more of God in action, of one who is a living and active presence, than of any one specific, embodied person in history. The answer is yes, if we mean that Jesus Christ is a remarkable fulfillment of not just one isolated prophetic passage but of many passages within the book of Isaiah, especially Isaiah 40-66. There is less christocentrism in the patristic commentaries than one might expect. This is true in spite of all the similarities between the person of Isaiah, the prophet-martyr, and Jesus Christ, as seen in early Christian theology from *The Ascension of Isaiah* onwards,[17] especially the clear correspondences between Jesus and the "suffering servant" of Isaiah 53. The message of Isaiah concerns the outworking of redemption, even though the foundations of that salvation are presupposed to be in Jesus, as they would be from at least Irenaeus onward. Thus, to allege that the Messiah, as understood through the church's christological interpretations, is one of the main characters in the book of Isaiah, is to be overly bold. Also, it is overly bold to assert, as John F. A. Sawyer does, that, "there is a great deal in the book about [Jesus]."[18]

As interpreted by the leading patristic writers, the message of Isaiah 40-66 is soteriological rather than christological, that is, focused relatively more on the process of God's salvation than on the identity of the Savior. Indeed, God's work in judgment and salvation is perhaps the key to almost all the patristic treatments of Isaiah. Perhaps this emphasis was inspired, at least in part, by the theological tendencies of the Greek translation of Isaiah in the Septuagint (LXX). As Eugene R. Ekblad has said, "The LXX appears to emphasize a greater distance between servant Israel and the Lord than is present in the MT." Nevertheless, the Septuagint favors the nations as receiving salvation mediated through Israel.[19] Ekblad gives two examples. First, unlike in the Masoretic Text, in Isaiah 41:1 (LXX) the Lord does not threaten judgment on the nations. Instead, the nations declare judgment on the gods and call for counsel[20] from the Lord. Second, the Septuagint uses *doulos*, which means "servant" or "slave," instead of *pais*, which means "servant" or "son." In some parts of the New Testament, *pais*, like *amnos* ("lamb"), is used to reinforce the humiliation and functional nature of Christ, as if the Son's person was almost effaced by his function. Although it is possible that this verbal detail we have briefly rehearsed may not have any significance, it is commonly noted in Isaianic

lot of discussion to that work!) Concerning Cyril, we should not ignore A. Kerrigan's classic *Cyril of Alexandria, Interpreter of the Old Testament* (AnBib; Rome: Pontificio Istituto Biblico, 1952) or the helpful recent essay by Robert Wilken, "Cyril of Alexandria as Interpreter of the Old Testament" in *The Theology of Cyril of Alexandria: A Critical Appreciation*, ed. Thomas Weinandy and Daniel G. Keating (London and New York: T&T Clark, 2003), 1-22.

[17]These points are made in the first chapter of John F. A. Sawyer, *The Fifth Gospel* (Cambridge: Cambridge University Press, 1998). *The Ascension of Isaiah* is a first- to second-century Christian work.

[18]Ibid., 102.

[19]E. R. Ekblad, *Isaiah's Servant Poems According to the Septuagint: An Exegetical and Theological Study* (Louvain: Peeters, 1999).

[20]Gk *boulai*, Is 41:21.

studies that the "suffering servant" seems to change character between Isaiah 42 and Isaiah 53, from being strongly identifiable with Israel to becoming more distinct from Israel. Certainly, by Isaiah 49, the way of the servant seems to be rougher, reaching its nadir in Isaiah 53, of course.

Many of the Fathers[21] identify a new theme with the start of Isaiah 54: the beginning of the church. It is plausible, therefore, to speak of Isaiah 54-66 in terms of restoration and judgment, including ethical teaching, as analogous to motifs of the cross, the resurrection and the ascension in the New Testament. The descent metaphors of later Christology are anticipated before Isaiah 54, and the ascent metaphors after. The Fathers seem very aware of these affinities.[22] Isaiah 40-66, on the whole, provides us with perhaps the closest thing that the Old Testament has to offer regarding a primitive systematic theology. The point is, however, that a distinct christological and ecclesiological interpretation seems to emerge slowly and gradually as one progresses through the patristic comments on Isaiah 40-66 in this volume.

The Text of Isaiah

The distinct nature of the biblical text that many of the Fathers commented on depends on a Greek translation that diverges from the standard Hebrew Masoretic text, on which the Revised Standard Version and other standard, modern translations are based. The Septuagint has readings that seem on the way to a more universal and Logos-centered religion. It would indeed seem, as A. van der Kooij and others have observed,[23] that there is some, even if not an abundance, of eschatological and at times messianic translating in the Septuagint. There was clearly "actualization" going on in the work of the translator, perhaps about a high priest who would teach the law properly.[24]

Famously, Jerome insisted on the "Hebrew truth" (*hebraica veritas*). Consequently, he usually gives us a Latin translation based first on the Hebrew text and only secondarily on the Septuagint.[25] Perhaps he felt that he was getting closer to the original meaning this way. It is not that he thought that the Septuagint was only a spiritual rendering of the prophet's words; rather, perhaps he thought that the Hebrew provided depths that a church that knew only the Septuagint would miss. In the case of Isaiah 40-66, however, Jerome often works directly out of the Septuagint.[26]

Unlike Jerome, Eusebius seems to have known no Hebrew; therefore, he was grateful for the help of the Greek translator Symmachus, whose translations retained much of the Hebrew character of the text. At times, Eusebius offers these riches to his inheritors, namely, Cyril of Alexandria and Theodoret of Cyr. For example, Eusebius comments on the translation of Isaiah 46:11, which reads, "the man of my counsel [*andra boulēs mou*] from a far country." The Septuagint has "and from the distant land about which I have

---

[21]Such as Chrysostom, Jerome and Theodoret.

[22]Notably, Jerome, Theodoret, Ambrose and Cyril of Alexandria.

[23]For a more sober estimation, see the work of Johan Lust, *Messianism and the Septuagint*, Bibliotheca Ephemeridum Theologicarum Lovaniensium 178 (Louvain: Peeters, 2004), and the caution in Karen Jobes and Moisés Silva, *Invitation to the Septuagint* (Grand Rapids: Baker Academic, 2000), 297-300.

[24]A. van der Kooij, *Die alten Textzeugen des Jesajabuches: Ein Beitrag zur Textgeschichte des Alten Testaments* (Freiburg-Göttingen: Universitätsverlag-Vandenhoeck & Ruprecht, 1981), 33.

[25]Jay, *L'exégèse de saint Jérôme*, 142ff., suggests that *hebraica veritas* meant more than just a translation from the Hebrew. It also provided a Jewish way of interpreting the history of Israel, a view of truth revealed in history, that complemented that given by the Septuagint mediated through the church.

[26]E.g., Jerome on Is 51:4 [*AGLB* 35:1464], where he is explicit that the LXX gives us help in spiritual application of the meaning.

decided." The alternative translation (that of Symmachus), which is closer to the Hebrew, nicely sets up a christological interpretation. Eusebius comments:

> "A man of his counsel." Who else can this be than his Christ, who, it says, has been called from a distant land, that is, from the innermost part of Hades. All the things which I have announced before his time I will bring into action through him.[27]

It is likely that Eusebius (as well as Procopius) used the "lost" exegesis of Origen on Isaiah; yet it seems clear that the lost commentaries of the Alexandrian master got no further than Isaiah 30, and thus it is difficult to speak of an Origenian interpretation of Isaiah 40-66. While Ziegler is right to maintain that Eusebius used and reused Origen's favorite words and phrases, Eusebius was on his own when it came to the exegesis of Isaiah 40-66.[28] In fact, Manlio Simonetti has established that Eusebius distanced himself from the Alexandrian method of interpreting every passage in Scripture with both a literal and an allegorical meaning. He preferred instead to divide the Bible, specifically the prophecies of Isaiah, into historical, messianic and allegorical passages.[29] As Simonetti admits, Eusebius did not always stick to this plan; nevertheless, a good part of the text of Isaiah is thought by Eusebius to refer to the historical Israel, up to the times of the emperors Vespasian and Hadrian. At this point, the newly "grafted" branch of the Gentiles (Rom 11:17) inherits God's promises and Spirit. Eusebius preferred a "communal" Christology in which the Logos is not joined to an individual soul but to the Word's influence on the church, which had grown to extend throughout the empire. And yet, this is conceived of in very spiritual and theological terms. In fact, there is a constant movement in his Isaiah commentary to a spiritual, "heavenly" interpretation, not unlike that of Origen.[30]

Theodoret of Cyr, for all his supposed Antiochene foundations, is not totally uncritical of the hallowed Antiochene Septuagint. While Cyril of Alexandria hardly mentions any variants, Theodoret mentions variants by Symmachus (e.g., Is 42:19), and the three[31] (e.g., Is 42:4). He does so only in the case of an omission or variation from the Hebrew text,[32] and not, like Eusebius, when he wants to suggest an interesting interpretation. One sees no reason to doubt that Theodoret of Cyr has the use of Origen's Hexapla, which listed the various translations of Aquila, Symmachus and Theodotian. By the time we get to the early sixth century, Procopius of Gaza was more interested in summarizing and presenting the varieties of interpretation, not the various textual variations.[33] He preserves the anonymity of the interpreters by using the phrase "some say."

Christian exegetes assume that the Bible is prophetic enough in its inspiration to have more than one

---

[27]*Commentary on Isaiah*; GCS 57(9):300.

[28]GCS 57(9):xxxi. Cf. Michael J. Hollerich, who argues that Eusebius consulted Origen as an authority; *Eusebius of Caesarea's Commentary on Isaiah: Christian Exegesis in the Age of Constantine* (New York: Oxford University Press, 1999), 47.

[29]M. Simonetti, "Uno squardo d'insieme sull'eseges: patristica d: *Isaia* fa IV e V secolo" *Annali di Storia dell'Esegesi* 1 (1984): 9-44.

[30]F. Young, *Biblical Exegesis and the Formation of Culture* (Cambridge and New York: Cambridge University Press, 1997), 122-29.

[31]Aquila, Symmachus and Theodotion.

[32]As Robert Hill puts it in his introduction to FC 101:12, "[Theodoret] made use basically of his Antiochene form of the LXX and referred to alternative Greek versions available in a copy of the Hexapla, not so much for critiquing his LXX text paleographically as for explicating the many semantically challenging phrases any commentator encounters."

[33]Even so, he makes some references to Symmachus in particular.

meaning, such that what was said in criticism of the people of Israel is somehow a word for the church and what is said of salvation in such universal terms can only be fulfilled in the church. In a similar way, Franz Rosenzweig held that Judaism was the "fire of the Star" and Christianity "the rays of the Star."[34] To see the prophets as finding fulfillment need not mean that there was and remains no fulfillment for them in terms of Israel, in the light of Romans 9-11. One of the shared features of Alexandrian and Antiochene Christian interpretations alike is the awareness of the second advent as being just as strong a theme as the first, even though they might understand both advents in different ways. And yet, of course, because God's intervention on earth in Christ is central to the faith, no church father will allow us to think that God's words have no impact on concrete history. Rather, they speak to historical situations.

History and Prophecy

Jerome insists that there can be no figurative exegesis that does not base itself on a historical reality. The type does in fact do something to history such that it prepares the way for the future action. For Jerome, living only a generation after the emperor (Julian) who denied the link between the events of the Old and those of the New Testament, there was an intimate connection between the type and its historical reality.[35] Jerome and the Antiochenes, quite possibly owing to their christological emphases, stress that, in general, God has dealt with the human soul from the beginning of time and that the history of Israel is to be read not allegorically in the sense of providing timeless truths but as a historical education, or *paideia*, of the human race as it co-operates in faith, and this in a way analogous to the all-important Luke 2:52, "And Jesus increased in wisdom and years and in divine and human favor." The line of David represents humanity, and the New Testament or Covenant arises from that line. Jerome even suggests that it was the universal sinful soul with whom God first had dealings before deserting it at the fall to spend time with Israel as a kind of provocation to the human race as a whole.[36] Yet the point is that God acts through human souls.

Simonetti has noted that Jerome adds two themes to what he received from Eusebius's scheme: heresy and the Christian soul's (and humanity in general's) relationship with Christ. But the Christology is also intriguing. Jay also shows that for Jerome, if all prophecies are not completely fulfilled, all are well underway. Jerome starts, albeit cautiously, the dominantly Christocentric interpretation of Isaiah that Cyril of Alexandria will take over and expand. But Jerome loved the prophets perhaps more than the New Testament (on this Simonetti and Jay are agreed). His commentaries on the three major prophets form the crowning glory of his career. As F. M. Abel showed, Cyril was influenced strongly by Jerome.[37] Yet in comparison, Cyril seems more to emphasize God's action in Christ's church. He is decidedly centered in Christ in the church. There is only a remnant left, and the preparation that is done in the Old Testament seems almost to have been a waste of time and effort, for God in the New Testament will be doing a new thing.[38] Yet, on closer inspection, it is because judgment has been poured out on humankind in the Old Testament and taken up by

---

[34]Franz Rosenzweig, *The Star of Redemption*, trans. William W. Hallo (Notre Dame, Ind.: Notre Dame Press, 1985).

[35]See Jay, *L'exégèse de saint Jérôme*, 263ff.

[36]Theodoret on Is 55:4 (SC 315:180); Jerome on Is 54:6 (*AGLB* 35:1544).

[37]"Parallélisme exégétique entre s. Jérôme et s. Cyrille d'Alexandrie," *Vivre et Penser* (1941): 94-119, 212-30. Abel's case has been strengthened by the work of Fernandez Lois: see also, in summary form, Norman Russell, ed., *Cyril of Alexandria* (London and New York: Routledge, 2000), 70-71.

[38]Cf. Wilken, "Cyril as Inerpreter," 20: "Cyril is fascinated by the theme of 'newness' in Christ."

Christ that there can be a hope for a brighter future for the human race, one that is held out by the church.

We now have opportunity to consider a specific example of how the Fathers treated history and prophecy. Isaiah 46:10-11 reads in the Septuagint: "My counsel shall stand, and I will accomplish all my purpose, calling a bird of prey from the east, and from a far country [a man] concerning which [pl.] I have willed." Eusebius was grateful for the help Symmachus gave him, which we noted above.[39] Theodoret, by contrast, avoids the precise referent of the bird of prey, since the point of the metaphor is to signify the speed of the return from exile. But this of course implies that in Theodoret's view the bird of prey is Israel.[40] A third possibility emerges when Guinot, the editor of Theodoret, tells us that Cyril of Alexandria, with a nod to Ezekiel 17:2-6, concludes that the bird is Cyrus. However, on close inspection Guinot's note is not quite accurate. Cyrus does not qualify for the epithet "bird of prey," but the Babylonian (Nebuchadnezzar) does, and the memory of such a nasty bird (eagle) in Ezekiel clinches it. Cyril writes:

> We take the bird that is called from the east and from a far land to be the Babylonian, which scorched all the territory of the Jews and took Jerusalem and broke up the temple among them. And they pulled out both the ordinary flock and the leading birds among them, and forced them into the region and land of the Persians and subjected them to a yoke of harsh imprisonment. This becomes clear from what God said to Ezekiel (Ezek 17:2-6).[41]

This interpretation, however, does not square with the Eusebian reading of the following line: "a man of my own counsel." However because the standard Septuagint does not have that, but rather has the phrase "about which I willed,"[42] Cyril, loyal to the Septuagint, is able to change the meaning of the verse away from a christological referent to a historical one, but one in which Cyrus has been left behind in Isaiah 45. God is not to be trifled with. Of course the issue of context matters. The Septuagint translates the preceding verse, Isaiah 46:10, as "I declare the last things (*eschata*) before they happen and they are immediately accomplished." This is already slightly different from the Hebrew text: "I declare the following things from the beginning and from ancient times what is not yet done." This means that the reader should be aware that it is not always exactly the same text as is rendered in the RSV or other modern translations that the Fathers were working from. Also, it becomes clear how the text of the Bible encouraged the Fathers to think in terms of the biblical prophets as speaking of the end times and fulfillment of salvation history in Christ.

The question of whether an interpretation can still be edifying even when obviously exegetically strained or uncertain is one that would have troubled the Fathers. Spirituality is always guided and driven by theology for the Fathers, and theology has to have good exegetical foundations. They did not believe they were free to take liberties with the text or to engage in reader-response interpretation or spiritual interpretations just for the sake of being somehow more "spiritual."

In fact, in an age when people made no great distinction between the word and the things, the *realia* that that word represented, it is not altogether helpful to speak of some Fathers as being more spiritual than others in what they took Scripture to be talking about.[43] The Fathers tended to see concrete things, rather than

---

[39]See p. xxii.
[40]SC 315:47.
[41]PG 70:997.
[42]Gk *peri hōn bebouleumai.*
[43]Ernst Dassmann has brought attention to this in *Augustinus, Heiliger und Kirchenlehrer* (Stuttgart: Kohlhammer, 1993).

events and histories, as types, just as words were the focus, not sentences. Young rightly sees sacrament rather than historical narrative as the central issue for the Fathers.[44] Yet, she then goes on to suggest that the Antiochenes, such as Theodoret of Cyr, were more interested in morals that one can gain from stories. Both the Alexandrian and Antiochene schools were united in seeing morality as the central thrust of Scripture and sanctification as its end product. Perhaps the difference between the two was that while Origen, an Alexandrian, saw that the words of Scripture were like jars of clay—[45]to be broken—the Antiochenes refused to regard the earthly realities as merely symbolic. They applied a sacramental principle instead. Christian spirituality follows an ascending, descending and reascending pattern.

For Theodoret of Cyr, the fuller, spiritual sense of an Old Testament passage (*kata tēn dianoian*) corresponds to the spiritual vision (*theoria*) of a prophet, who could himself see no further ahead than the obvious fulfillment of his prophecy within the history of Israel. Theodoret of Cyr is anti-Platonic and biblically eschatological in intent when he writes on Isaiah. We get an unusually full and helpful insight into his overall hermeneutic in his comment on Isaiah 60:1:

> This prophecy has three subjects: the first is the rebuilding of Jerusalem, portrayed as in a sketch, which took place at the time of Cyrus and Darius; the second shows more precisely the lines of truth—the shining brightness of the holy church—portrayed as if in an icon "written" with many colors. And finally, it portrays the archetype of the icon, that is, the life to come and the citizenship in heaven. The divine Paul taught this distinction: "The law contained the shadow of things to come and not the image of the realities."[46] And he calls the things to come the immortal and pain-free existence, the life unsullied by worry; whereas the image of the realities is the ecclesiastical commonwealth and its existence that is like a model of the things to come.... For the painters have the reality that they copy to make their picture, drawing a sketch first before filling in the shadow with colors.... The prophetic words apply to the church of God, which has received the light of the knowledge of God and is encircled by the glory of the Savior.[47]

Like a picture or an icon, the Old Testament is a sketch of the New Testament, which in turn is the representation of the final heavenly reality. But there is also a sense in which the Old Testament excites the reader's imagination in a way that deepens and stretches spirituality, adding fullness to the lived faith, especially when the reading is viewed in the light of the New Testeament perception of future realities.

For Theodoret of Cyr, the fullness of the prophecy is seen in its application to the fullness of truth in Christ. This application is more than an accidental correspondence. The act of perceiving this is something intended by the Holy Spirit in his communication to the prophet. In other words, the later interpretations are part of the effect of the prophecy.[48] The prophecies are each taken up and fulfilled in the coming of Christ ("the organizing principle of history"[49]) and in the "apostolic" events thereafter and in the dawning end times. Thus, no prophecy is superfluous, even when it cannot be entirely applied to Christ. Or, perhaps

---

[44]Young, *Biblical Exegesis*, 117.
[45]According to Origen's *Commentary on John*, book 4, section 2; GCS 4:98.
[46]Heb 10:1.
[47]SC 315:238-40.
[48]A. Vaccari made this point long ago in "La θεωρία nella scuola esegtica di Antiochia," *Biblica* 1 (1920):3-31.
[49]Ibid., 4.

Theodoret of Cyr wants Christ's work to be viewed in the past and the time "to come," as well as a reality in the present. Thus, when Theodoret treats Isaiah 49:1-5, he easily shuttles between speaking of "Christ is" and "Christ was," since, sacramentally speaking, the past and present become one.[50] Furthermore, the close attention to moments in history makes the prophesied narrative different from mythical stories.[51] Poetic oracles, such as Isaiah 40-66, hit their targets not in the place and times of the prophet but in the real events on the earth with the coming of God's new work on a clearly defined world stage. For this reason, Theodoret of Cyr reveals his love for place names and other geographical details. This could be interpreted as either a love for precision or a predilection for the marginal.[52]

Theodoret is, however, most keen to insist that through the coming of Christ, the blessing of salvation is transferred to the nations. This metaphor is part of the intention of the original prophecy. Clearly, when the text talks of Jerusalem, it cannot be principally about the literal Jerusalem, although we can learn a lot about Christ and his church from the character of Zerubbabel.[53] Of course, some prophecies can be in large part fulfilled within the events of the history of Israel. The fact that the temple was literally rebuilt once is but one example. In any case, Theodoret of Cyr was concerned to write a commentary for his own generation, which was the fuller meaning of reading Isaiah *sub specie novi testamenti*—in the light of the New Testament.[54]

Theological Interpretations

John Sawyer has raised alarm at the treatment of Isaiah at the hands of Chrysostom and his contemporaries. There are many patristic interpreters who seem too ready to use the Bible more as a club than as a revelation of God's will for humanity. There are, for example, the comments on Isaiah 60:9, which in the hands of the tradition of interpretation encouraged missionaries to take the gospel to all the nations in a way that was strong on persuasion but weak on dialogue; or Isaiah 56:10, which, according to Chrysostom, meant that all the Jews at all times in all places are rightly called "dogs"; or, as he claims from Isaiah 49:6 ("I will give you as a light to the nations, that my salvation may reach to the end of the earth"), the church was told to turn its back on Jews and attend to the Gentiles. What about persistent hellfire (Is 66:24)? "The saints will come out, and they will see the corpses of people who rebelled against me. Their worm will not die, and their fire will not be extinguished, and they shall be as a vision for all flesh." This was interpreted hyperliterally by Basil of Caesarea *inter alia*.

Isaiah has given us much that is positive to Christian theology.[55] One could even speak about it in terms

---

[50]SC 315:74-76.

[51]Guinot, *L'exégèse*, 329-30.

[52]On Is 47:15, Theodoret of Cyr asserts that the reason for prophecies of doom was twofold: first, to warn the Israelites of the present and immediate future to repent; second, to show that catastrophe (whether in 587 B.C. or A.D. 70) is planned by God. Here are two sides of a theodicy: God gives them a warning, but he is ultimately the one who permits the harsh consequences of judgment. Likewise, when trying to show that the oracle of Is 47 came from God—as in the case of the prophecy of Samuel against Saul in 1 Sam 28—Theodoret of Cyr had to argue that the battle between Israel and the Philistines (1 Sam 28) did indeed take place the next day. See N. Fernandez Marcos and José Ramón Busto Saiz, *Quaestiones in Reges et Paralipomena Theodoreti Cyrensis; editio critica* Textos y estudios Cardenal Cisneros 32 (Madrid: Instituto Arias Montano, 1984), 56.

[53]E.g., Hag 2:21; Zech 4:6.

[54]Metropolitan Demetrios Trakatellis, "Theodoret's Commentary on Isaiah," in *New Perspectives on Historical Theology*, ed. B. Nassif (Grand Rapids: Eerdmans, 1996), 313-15, draws a parallel with John Chrysostom: "One could suggest however that Chrysostom's insistence on literal-historical exegesis also has to do with his intense socio-ethical sensitivities." Cf. J. Breck, *The Power of the Word: The Scriptures in Orthodox Interpretation, Confession and Celebration* (Crestwood, N.Y.: St. Vladimir's Seminary Press, 1987).

of the power of the word working on the church's theology through the ages. It is arguably more about the powerful effect of the Bible than what readers have done with it, along the lines of Isaiah 55:10-11: "My word . . . shall not return to me empty." Such passages as Isaiah 6, for instance, have contributed to the doctrine of the Trinity; Isaiah 7:14 was a seminal passage in working out the doctrine of virginal conception; Isaiah 9:1-6 speaks to the character of the Messiah and his kingdom; Isaiah 40 is a rehearsal of salvation history; Isaiah 45 confirms what came to be known as the *deus absconditus,* or the God who "hides himself"; the powerful imagery of Isaiah 53 speaks in specific terms of the atonement; Isaiah 61 anticipates the Holy Spirit's mission; and finally, Isaiah 66 portrays in vivid terms the eschatological final judgment.

With the last mentioned, Cyril of Alexandria is instructive here. Rather than viewing this chapter only as a promise of total destruction, he understands Isaiah 66 as referring to the Jews "who suffered at the hands of the Romans, namely, when the temple was destroyed."[56] In other words, for Cyril, it is the memory of the fate of the Jews that endures, not tormented suffering. In Cyril's defining or limiting the target of the threat of judgment, there is a humane reading at work. In any case, one should not see the theological tradition of interpretation, which contains both Basil's and Cyril's interpretations, as monolithic.

The different styles, principles and theological emphases of interpretation according to each interpreter are among the most interesting aspects of patristic commentary in this volume. We see this most vividly in their commentary on Isaiah 53. For many of our commentators, this was meant to be the high point or the fulcrum of the book to which Isaiah 40-51 looked ahead and on which Isaiah 54-66 proceeded as they outlined the life enabled by the new covenant in Christ's blood described in Isaiah 53.

For our purposes, we will focus on but one example: the first few verses of Isaiah 53. We note, first, that even Eusebius can wax theological on Isaiah 53, although the "theological yield of Eusebius' *Commentary on Isaiah* is rather slight. . . . The commentary is silent about the Arian controversy and the council. Their only reflection is the negative evidence of Eusebius' avoidance of calling the Logos a second God (*deuteros theos*)."[57] M. Hollerich's view is that Eusebius saw the incarnation in didactic terms of an ethical nature, since Jesus came to teach.[58] However, Eusebius does use Isaiah 53:1-4 to speak of Christ's origin from a virgin and loves to tie in what is said here with the earlier soteriological oracles of Isaiah 7:14 and Isaiah 11:1.

In commenting on Isaiah 53:2, for theological reasons, Jerome takes a slightly different tack. He chooses to focus on the beauty of Christ in response to the claim of the text that there was no beauty in the Servant.

> If he did not have beauty or glory, but his form was base and lacking before the sons of men or as the Hebrew has it, despised and least among people . . . how then can it be said in the psalms, "Gird your side with your sword, O mighty one, with your beauty and fairness"?[59] This can be easily solved. He was despised and base

---

[55]Childs (*Struggle,* x): "Sawyer's emphasis on the misuse of the book seems to drown out its major role as a truthful tradent of the gospel." In other words, there is something about the gospel in Isaiah that refuses to be silenced, no matter the cultural forces. In Childs's work, hermeneutical issues will be primary, but not in a purely critical way of showing how people misread; rather, they are to reveal how "the Bible continues to stimulate every new generation of serious readers in unexpected ways and in unlikely places. The power to transform lives, to open new vistas of hope, and to offer the gift of divine reconciliation are part of the unexpected surprises inviting its readers to an encounter with a gracious and forgiving God."

[56]PG 70:1450.

[57]ECCI 61.

[58]Cf. the Eusebian comments on Is 43:8-11.

[59]Ps 45:3 (44:3 LXX).

when he hung on the cross and was made for us a curse and carried our sins and said to the Father, "God, my God, why have you forsaken me?"[60] But he was glorious (*inclutus*) and fair in appearance when, at his passion the earth trembled, rocks were split and the elements were terrified at the sun's fleeing and the eternal night.[61]

Jerome solves the conundrum of the reference to beauty in Psalm 45[62] by having this reference to beauty refer to the pen of the scribe in the previous verse of the psalm, rather than to the person of Christ. Jerome prefers not to emphasize Christ's beauty because he sees his true beauty and glory revealed in the "ugliness" of his passion. Christ's glory and beauty were hidden for a time under the ugliness of the curse of our sin and the suffering that went along with it. His underlying glory and beauty appear only after his suffering and death for our sins is accomplished. God's beauty, not to mention also his strength,[63] is made perfect in weakness, and there is no place that weakness is more evident than on the cross. It is therefore on the cross that God's true beauty is made evident, albeit of a totally different sort than we would expect, since the inward beauty of the passion is concealed for a time by the outward ugliness involved in carrying it out. Its true beauty, however, would ultimately be revealed.

Cyril also comments on Isaiah 53:2:

> For human things are in every way small and cheap and worthless compared with the divine and highest eminence and outshining beauty of [his human] nature (*physis*). For it is said, "He is fair in beauty among the sons of men."[64] And [Isaiah 53:2] adds to this description: "He is more rejected than all men," that is, his appearance (form) is more rejected, as if to say: Among men of distinction some are seen as distinguished by their fine radiant appearance. But Emmanuel was not among them. Rather, his appearance was reduced to a lowly and despised level.[65]

Fernandez Lois claims that Cyril, uncharacteristically, is using the term *physis* to refer to the human nature. But it seems more likely that Cyril is referring to the humbling of Jesus' divine nature. Emmanuel, to which Cyril refers in this passage, is normally used when Cyril is speaking of the divinity, as Lois admits elsewhere. It is God who has become ugly even by human standards, although it only appeared that way. There was not total *kenosis*, according to Cyril's thought. To human beings, God does not seem attractive. Conversion, new eyes, a purification of the gaze is required in order to see his true beauty.

Likewise, Cyril's work, at its most creative, seems as much eschatological and to do with final judgment as it is christological, because judgment and salvation rather than the identity of Jesus are the central focus. To this extent one may need to nuance De La Margerie's interpretation of Cyril:[66] It is christological, in that it is understood that only Christ makes any interpretation for the present possible. It is not Christocentric, however, in the sense that the emphasis of the commentary is not on the Christ-event itself but on salvation

---

[60]Mt 27:46.
[61]*AGLB* 35:1513.
[62]Ps 44 LXX.
[63]2 Cor 12:9.
[64]Ps 45:3.
[65]PG 70:1171.
[66]B. de La Margerie, "L'exégèse christologique de Saint Cyrille d'Alexandrie," *Nouvelle Revue de Théologie* 102 (1980):400-425. Also his indispensable *Introduction à l'histoire de l'exégèse. 1, Les pères grecs et orientaux* (Paris: Cerf, 1980.)

history from start to finish. For the first advent came in the conditions of unbelief so that God had to appear in an unattractive form, just as he had at Sinai. The incarnation was the judgment on that unbelief. For faith, however, that lowliness is welcome, even familiar. The divine beauty is something visible only to the eye of faith; it is completely unlike human beauty, similar to what Jerome has said.

Theodoret's commentary on Isaiah 53:2-4 reads:

> And next [Isaiah] teaches the forms of dishonor and shame: "He was a man in sorrow." [Isaiah] points out the nature which received the suffering, for his body was nailed to the cross, but his divinity made the passion its own (*oikeiousthai*).[67]

Guinot notes that Cyril used the verb *oikeiousthai* in his Epistle 3.6 to Nestorius and that Theodoret is trying hard, after the Council of Ephesus of 431, to reconcile Antiochene two-natures Christology with the personal unity of Christ as demanded by Cyril. The context of the previous sentence of the above passage helps: "He points out *the* nature that received the suffering" (emphasis added). However, the very verb *oikeiousthai* means that while the body was nailed to the cross, only the divinity owned the passion:

> "And he was familiar with sickness." This was said about his humanity. For to be courageous and philosophical touches not the divine but the human nature. "For his face was turned away. It was not valued or appreciated. . . ." The three translators render it this way: "And like a hiding of the face (*prosōpou*) from him, he was made nothing and not appreciated." That is, he hid the divine energy, choosing suffering instead, and did not seek vengeance on those who did this to him.[68]

For Theodoret it is clearly the human in Christ who accepts the indignity. It is the *prosopon* of divinity that is hidden. This suggests that this *prosōpon* of the divinity might well be revealed, that it is in theory open to being seen by "all flesh."[69] For Theodoret the beauty of Christ is in the gentleness of his first coming when forgiveness and persuasion are offered, as opposed to him coming in the full force of his divinity and power.[70] G. W. Ashby argued that Theodoret of Cyr understood Isaiah to be predicting a new humanity of Israel, and thus he prophesies about the human nature of Christ only.

> The prophet predicts the passion accurately (*akribēsteron*). In fact, chapter 53 is very much applied to Christ as a prediction. . . . There are limits to a prophet's elasticity of mind. A man who one minute calls Israel a worm and implies that Israel needs rescuing will not be soon afterwards describing Israel as saving the world by his

---

[67]SC 315:148.

[68]SC 315:148-150.

[69]This reference to "all flesh" takes us back to the comments on Is 40:7, where there is some disagreement as to whether "all flesh shall see the glory of the Lord" refers to the universal second coming or to the experience of the church's faith.

[70]And yet we do find more of a sense that Christ was humanly beautiful in Augustine, based on the idea that the creation shares much of the essential but also apparent goodness of its creator. In Sermon 254 Augustine writes how it is mandatory that any sacrifice be without blemish. In Sermon 27 he speaks of how what Christ underwent was a deforming for our sake (an idea that is also to the fore in Hans Urs von Balthasar's work *The Glory of the Lord* (*Herrlichkeit*), which implies an original form of beauty. As Carol Harrison has argued, for Augustine, beauty is the most embodied of the three transcendentals. See Carol Harrison, *Beauty and Revelation in the Thought of Saint Augustine* (Oxford : Clarendon Press; New York: Oxford University Press, 1992). The "bride and bridegroom" theme appears in more than one of Augustine's psalm *Ennarationes*. In the exchange of his beauty for her ugliness, "the change to beauty in the bride is not automatic but in seeing how she has made him ugly she repents from her ugliness." In later exegesis, for example, on Ps 32:11, "it is the outward form of, for example, the face of an old person or a disfigured martyr . . . which does not simply point to a transcendent, divine beauty but rather reveals it precisely in that form" (Harrison, *Beauty*, 235, 237).

sufferings and death. Hence Theodoret of Cyr applies some sayings to a future liberation of Israel and some to the man who, according to his human nature was Israel.[71]

Like many of a former generation who classified Theodoret of Cyr as a (crypto-)Nestorian, G. W. Ashby, with the help of K. Jüssen, asserts that the human nature of Christ was "a personal individual manhood."[72] As Guinot notes, however, one finds throughout Theodoret's commentary a preference for speaking of Christ in the form of God and Christ in the form of a slave, which avoids the controversy that would have come had he spoken nonmetaphorically, with literal precision, e.g., in speaking of "God" and "the assumed man."[73]

In this brief rehearsal of patristic interpretation on the Servant's despised appearance in Isaiah 53:2, we saw how even one small phrase concerning his lack of beauty occasioned much theological rumination on the relation of the human and divine in Christ and the conundrum the relationship between the two sometimes occasioned among commentators. They sought to wrestle with the problems and questions the text posed to them, much as modern commentators do. Although they did not always get everything right, we, like Thomas Aquinas, assume that the church fathers still have the edge when it comes to scriptural exegesis in its application to the church and its faithful. Their holy minds were granted the gift and the task of unfolding the mysteries of the canonical texts.[74] In this, we see how the Roman Catholic and Orthodox churches understand the value of "from faith to faith." Those who acknowledged and in that sense fixed the canon and supplied a rule of faith for its interpretation had as much right to be honored as those who wrote the books that formed it.

---

[71]G. W. Ashby, *Theodoret of Cyrrhus as Exegete of the Old Testament* (Grahamstown: Rhodes University, 1972), 87-88.

[72]K. Jüssen, "Die Christologie des Theodoret," *Theologie und Glaube* 27(1935): 438-52.

[73]See J.-N. Guinot, "La place et le rôle de l'histoire evenementelle dans l'exégèse de Théodoret de Cyr," in *Historiographie de l'église des premiers siècles*, ed. B. Pouderon and Y.-M. Duval (Paris: Beauchesne, 2001), 329-48.

[74]See "Lo studio dei Padri della Chiesa nella formazione sacerdotale: Istruzione della Congregazione per l'educazione cattolica" (*Osservatore Romano* del 10.1.1990).

ISAIAH 40-66

40:1-2 COMFORT FOR JERUSALEM

[1]*Comfort, comfort my people,*
  says your God.
[2]*Speak* tenderly to Jerusalem,*
  and cry to her

that her warfare[n] is ended,
  that her iniquity is pardoned,
that she has received from the LORD's hand
  double for all her sins.

n Or *time of service* * LXX *Priests, speak*

OVERVIEW: It is difficult to understand why these words that call for comfort follow Hezekiah's request in the previous chapter that there be peace and righteousness in his days. His prayer there, however, was for himself and not his descendants—a prayer that God disapproved (EUSEBIUS). Therefore Isaiah, according to the Septuagint text, asks the priests to petition the Lord on behalf of the people since King Hezekiah had neglected them (EPHREM, CYRIL). This prayer is also addressed to leaders in the church, who need to offer appropriate comfort to their people who come to God in repentance and faith (CONSTITUTION OF THE HOLY APOSTLES).

When Israel's warfare is over, having received double for its sins, God offers special, tender comfort to its people, as a caring parent who is not afraid to correct his wayward children (GREGORY OF NAZIANZUS). Because God's justice is tempered by his mercy, the punishment inflicted is less than equal to the sin committed (THEODORET). The joy of salvation comes, then,

as blessed relief after the corrective work on the soul has been done (AMBROSE).

40:1 Comfort My People

GOD DISAPPROVES OF HEZEKIAH'S PRAYER.
EUSEBIUS OF CAESAREA: God did not approve of Hezekiah's proposal. The fact that he mentioned only himself in his prayer and not the people was blameworthy. That is why the prophet says in what follows, "Comfort my people, says the Lord." COMMENTARY ON ISAIAH 2.15.[1]

ON BEHALF OF HEZEKIAH'S DESCENDANTS.
EPHREM THE SYRIAN: Hezekiah offered prayers to God because he had been told that death was imminent, but he failed to pray that evil should be averted from his descendants. Hence Isaiah says, "Comfort, comfort my people, you priests." COMMENTARY ON ISAIAH 40.1.[2]

---

[1]AnBib 2:317*; GCS 57(9):247. [2]AnBib 2:317**; ESOO 2:86.

IN THE FACE OF CALAMITY, PRAY FOR OTHERS. CYRIL OF ALEXANDRIA: Hezekiah was at a loss for a defense. Since he could offer no excuse for his crimes, he said that God's word was good, even though it foretold things that should have made him shed tears. Then he asks for peace in his own days, bidding goodbye, as it were, to those who were to come after him and thereby neglecting his native land, his own city and his own race. But it would have been better for him to be sorry for the things that had been predicted and to ask God for mercy and happiness (not temporary and restricted) on behalf of those to come after him. COMMENTARY ON ISAIAH 3.4.40.1.[3]

BISHOPS BRING COMFORT WITH LAW AND GOSPEL. APOSTOLIC CONSTITUTIONS: Observe, you who are our beloved sons, how merciful yet righteous the Lord our God is; how gracious and kind to me. And yet most certainly "he will not acquit the guilty,"[4] although he welcomes returning sinners and revives them, leaving no room for suspicion to those who wish to judge sternly and reject offenders entirely, refusing to promise exhortations to them that might otherwise bring them to repentance. In contradiction to people like this, Isaiah says to the bishops, "Comfort, comfort my people, you priests. Speak comfortably to Jerusalem." It therefore behooves you, on hearing those words of his, to encourage those who have offended and lead them to repentance. Give them hope that it is not in vain that you enter into their situation of sin, because you love them. Readily receive those who are penitent and rejoice over them. Judge the sinners with mercy and compassion. For if somebody was walking beside the river and ready to stumble, and you pushed him and threw him into the river, instead of offering him your hand to help, you would be guilty of murdering your brother or sister. Instead, you should lend a helping hand when they're ready to fall. Otherwise they will perish without anyone to help. And you do this so that the people watching are warned and so that the offenders may not utterly perish. It is your duty, O bishop, neither to overlook the sins of the people nor to reject those who are penitent so that you may not unskillfully destroy the Lord's flock or dishonor his new name, which he has imposed on his people. And you yourself should also be above reproach as those ancient pastors were of whom God speaks to Jeremiah and others.[5] CONSTITUTIONS OF THE HOLY APOSTLES 2.15.[6]

40:2 Priests Speak Tenderly to Jerusalem

SPEAK, YOU PRIESTS, TO THE HEART OF JERUSALEM. THEODORET OF CYR: The God of the universe has left the king aside to invite the priests to give courage back to Jerusalem, as if the chastisement with which it had been threatened had already occurred. This is made clear in the passage to follow: "Comfort [Jerusalem], for its humiliation is accomplished." The words of the threat have received a perfect accomplishment. "[Its] sin is put away: for it has received of the Lord's hand double the amount of its sins." It is worthwhile to admire the kindness of the Master at this point: because he is good and his compassion is unfathomable, and although he inflicted a punishment less than equal to the sin, he says, by reason of great benevolence, that this lesser punishment is double the amount of the sin. Now that the chastisement was less than the sin, the same prophet has cried in testimony: "Your chastening was to us with small affliction."[7] Nevertheless, because he tempers his justice with infinite mercy, the lesson that the victims of the chastisement call small, the judge has called double [the amount of the sin]. Then he teaches the comforters the means of comfort. COMMENTARY ON ISAIAH 12.40.1-2.[8]

CORRECTION IS FOR THE SOUL'S GREATER BENEFIT. GREGORY OF NAZIANZUS: How is it that some receive at the Lord's hand double for their sins and the measure of their wickedness is

---

[3]AnBib 2:318*; PG 70:796-97. [4]Nah 1:3. [5]Jer 12:10; Zech 10:3; Mal 1:6. [6]ANF 7:402*. [7]Is 26:16. [8]ITA 570-71; SC 295:394-96.

doubly filled up, as in the correction of Israel, while the sins of others are removed by a sevenfold compensation?[9] What is the measure of the Amorites that is not yet full?[10] And how is the sinner either acquitted or chastised again, acquitted perhaps, because reserved for the other world, chastised because healed thereby in this? ON HIS FATHER'S SILENCE, ORATION 16.5.[11]

PUNISHMENT A BLESSING. AMBROSE: There is also another type of consolation to those who remove heavy punishments, as you have it written in the book of Isaiah: "Comfort, comfort my people," says the Lord. "Priests, speak to the heart of Jerusalem, comfort it, for its humiliation is complete, its sin is removed, for it has received from the Lord's hand double for its sins." Although faith was lacking, punishment makes good; those who are not absolved by the praise of merits are relieved by the removal of punishments. EXPOSITION OF PSALM 118.18.2.[12]

---

[9]Ps 79:12 (78:12 LXX). [10]Gen 15:16. [11]NPNF 2 7:249. [12]CSEL 62:496.

40:3-5 THE VOICE IN THE WILDERNESS

[3]*A voice cries:*
"In the wilderness prepare the way of the
    LORD,
    make straight in the desert a highway for
    our God.
[4]*Every valley shall be lifted up,*
    and every mountain and hill be made low;
the uneven ground shall become level,
    and the rough places a plain.
[5]*And the glory of the LORD shall be revealed,*
    and all flesh shall see it together,
    for the mouth of the LORD has spoken."

OVERVIEW: The way of the Lord is made straight in our hearts through true contemplation and those activities that follow from such contemplation. The Lord wants to find in us a path by which he can enter into our souls (ORIGEN), as he condescends to dwell in our hearts by meeting us through his Word (AMBROSE). The Word is united to the soul through the Spirit's election (CYRIL OF JERUSALEM). When Isaiah speaks of preparing a way, this concerns the preparatory work done by John the Baptist: God has to be allowed to come close in Christ before spiritual rebirth is possible. But it seems that Christ is now also the means of preparation (AUGUSTINE). John as a herald announces the incarnation of the Word (THEODORET). The prophecy will ultimately be fulfilled in the last times with an angel, not John, playing the announcer's role (JEROME).

Isaiah is declaring here the essential humility of the ministry as a lowly conduit to do God's work (CAESARIUS). Continuity between the penitent life and Christ's work of fulfilling the law can also be seen here (TERTULLIAN). Ultimately, Isaiah's prophecy concerns the cross of Christ. The way prepared is God's coming to the human heart in the incarnation (AUGUSTINE). The prophet prepares a way beforehand for souls to receive God (CHRYSOSTOM). The valleys are unbelievers and the mountains are demons, who are worshiped on the mountains (THEODORET). If one takes the filling of the valleys in a literal way, one might even say the valleys are full of holy ascetics who empty their hearts, only to be filled later with the presence of God (EPHREM). In the valleys, the Lord has prepared a smooth highway for us, although at times it may be felt as hard and rough (CASSIAN). The return from Babylon was not evident to all, but the story of the cross of Christ has been proclaimed to the ends of the earth (THEODORET). The Word assumed what is common to all humanity (MARIUS).Through him, the revelation of God's glory appears even in the humility of the incarnation (AMBROSE) as the Son reveals the Father's glory to the world (CYRIL).

40:3 Prepare the Way of the Lord

MAKING A PATH IN THE HEART FOR GOD TO FIND. ORIGEN: The Lord wants to find in you a path by which he can enter into your souls and make his journey. Prepare for him the path of which it is said, "Make straight his path." "The voice of one crying in the desert"—the voice cries, "prepare the way." HOMILIES ON THE GOSPEL OF LUKE 21.5.[1]

CONTEMPLATION FOLLOWED BY PRACTICE. ORIGEN: Now the way of the Lord is made straight in two ways: by contemplation, which is clarified by truth unmixed with falsehood, and by activity, which follows sound contemplation of the appropriate action to be taken, which is conformed to the correct sense of these things to be done. COMMENTARY ON THE GOSPEL OF JOHN 6.103.[2]

THE CONDESCENSION OF GOD. AMBROSE: God, indeed, never descends from any place, for he says, "I fill heaven and earth."[3] But he seems to descend when the Word of God enters our hearts, as the prophet has said, "Prepare the way of the Lord, make his paths straight." We are to do this, so that, as he himself promised, he may come together with the Father and make his abode with us.[4] ON THE CHRISTIAN FAITH 5.7.98.[5]

SPIRIT'S ELECTION ACCORDING TO FAITH. CYRIL OF JERUSALEM: While the heavenly powers rejoice, let the souls that are to be united to the spiritual bridegroom make themselves ready. For the voice is heard of one crying in the wilderness, "Prepare the way of the Lord." For this is no light matter, no ordinary and indiscriminate union according to the flesh but the all-searching Spirit's election according to faith. CATECHETICAL LECTURES 3.1.[6]

PREPARATION AND REBIRTH. AUGUSTINE: They were not reborn, those who were baptized by John's baptism, by which Christ himself was baptized.[7] Rather, they were "prepared" by the ministry of a forerunner, who said, "Prepare a way for the Lord"—for him in whom alone they could be reborn. ENCHIRIDION 14.49.[8]

THE INCARNATION IS THE WAY. AUGUSTINE: John [the Baptist] was filled with the Holy Spirit; and he had a baptism from heaven, not from human beings. But how long did he have it? He said, "Prepare the way for the Lord." But when the Lord was known, he himself became the way; there was no longer need for the baptism of John, by which the way was to be prepared for the Lord. TRACTATES ON THE GOSPEL OF JOHN 5.15.4.[9]

THE VOICE OF THE ONE CRYING IN THE WILDERNESS. THEODORET OF CYR: The true consolation, the genuine comfort and the real deliverance from the iniquities of humankind is the incarnation of our God and Savior. Now the first who acted as herald of this event was the inspired John the Baptist. Accordingly, the prophetic text proclaims the realities that relate to him in advance, for that is what the three blessed Evangelists have taught us and that the most divine Mark has even made the prologue of his work. As for the inspired John, whom the Pharisees asked whether he himself was the

---

[1]FC 94:90. [2]FC 80:197. [3]Jer 23:24. [4]Jn 14:23. [5]NPNF 2 10:296*. [6]NPNF 2 7:14*. [7]Mt 3:13. [8]LCC 7:368. [9]FC 78:123*. [10]Jn 1:23.

Christ, he declared on his part: "I am 'the voice of one crying in the wilderness, Make straight the way of the Lord'" as the prophet Isaiah said;[10] I am not God the Word but a voice, for it is as a herald that I am announcing God the Word, who is incarnate. Moreover, he refers to the Gentiles as the "untrodden [land]" because they have not yet received the prophetic stamp. COMMENTARY ON ISAIAH 12.40.3.[11]

PROCLAMATION OF FIRST AND SECOND ADVENTS. JEROME: In that the Word has now become flesh and dwelled among us, now there will not be in any way the voice of a prophet in the desert but the voice of the archangel, preparing the way for the one coming not in the humility of the flesh but for him who is with the Father. And in those days they were going out into the desert, so as to hear the forerunner of the assumed man and to see the sand perturbed by the wind. Letter 119.10.[12]

HUMILITY OF MINISTRY. CAESARIUS OF ARLES: "I am the voice of one that cries out in the desert." This means, I am not the Word that was with God from the beginning and that was God, but I am rather a voice; in other words, I am a minister of the Word, in order that through me he may reach the hearing and senses of [people]. For this reason the blessed Baptist exclaimed with equal humility, "He must increase, while I must decrease."[13] SERMONS 217.2.[14]

THE END OF THE LAW AND PROPHETS. TERTULLIAN: Since even then by Isaiah it was Christ, the Word and the Spirit of the Creator who prophetically described John as "the voice of one crying in the wilderness to prepare the way of the Lord." And [he] was about to come forth for the purpose of terminating from that point onwards the course of the law and the prophets: by their fulfillment and not their extinction. AGAINST MARCION 4.33.[15]

THE WORD COMING TO THE HEART. AUGUS-

TINE: There it is written, "a voice of one crying in the wilderness," the Word is conceived in the virgin's womb. If the voice is not the Word, it is then a loud clanging of metal.[16] For one then would not be able to say that every word is a sound but not every sound is a word. For it is not unfitting to take "the way" as that which came up to the very heart and filled us inwardly. Indeed, the heart became his place to which he comes and remains. SERMON 289.[17]

THE WORK OF PREPARATION. CHRYSOSTOM: Do you see that both by the words of the prophet and by his own preaching, this one and only thing is manifested, that he came, making a way and preparing beforehand, not bestowing the gift, which was the remission, but ordering in good time the souls of such as should receive the God of all? HOMILIES ON THE GOSPEL OF MATTHEW 10.3.[18]

40:4 Hills Brought Low

EVANGELICAL PROCLAMATION FILLS THE WHOLE WORLD. THEODORET OF CYR: He has clearly shown by these terms the facility of the evangelical proclamation: thanks to this facility, in a short time it filled the whole world. One should understand by "filled valleys" and "mountains and hills brought low" that literally it relates to a way that is level and cleared of all obstacles, but in a figurative sense, the souls of the unbelievers are the valleys, those who are lying in some way at the bottom of a pit and who do not have the intelligence to turn toward the heavens, while the mountains and the hills are the demons who are worshiped on the mountains and on the hills, whose deceit has been ended by the incarnation of our Savior. COMMENTARY ON ISAIAH 12.40.4.[19]

[11]ITA 571; SC 295:396. [12]CSEL 55:465. [13]Jn 3:30. [14]FC 66:121. [15]ANF 3:404. [16]1 Cor 13:1. [17]PL 38:1309. [18]NPNF 1 10:63**. [19]ITA 575; SC 295:396-98.

The Lord Saves and Fills the Valleys with Saints. Ephrem the Syrian: It is said that the valleys are filled, because the Lord has entered the world, and has redeemed all the peoples from the bondage of the devil, and brought them back to the faith and adoration of their Creator and has taught them to hope in eternal salvation. This is also said, because he has filled the deep valleys and the horrible and inhospitable caves with ascetics, who, after abandoning the cares of this world, exclusively devote themselves to honor and praise God. Commentary on Isaiah 40.4.[20]

The Way of the Lord. John Cassian: According to the plain teaching of the Lord, the king's highway is easy and smooth, though it may be felt as hard and rough. For those who piously and faithfully serve him, when they have taken on them the yoke of the Lord and have learned of him, that he is meek and lowly of heart, at once [they] somehow or other lay aside the burden of earthly passions and find no labor but rest for their souls, by the gift of the Lord. [To this] he himself testifies by Jeremiah the prophet, saying, "Stand on the ways and see, and ask for the old paths, which is the good way, and walk in it: and you shall find refreshment for your souls."[21] For to them at once "the crooked shall become straight and the rough ways plain"; and they shall "taste and see that the Lord is gracious."[22] And when they hear Christ proclaiming in the Gospel, "Come unto me, all you that labor and are heavy laden, and I will refresh you," they will lay aside the burden of their sins and realize what follows: "For my yoke is easy, and my burden is light."[23] The way of the Lord then has refreshment if it is kept according to his law. Conference 24.25.[24]

40:5 The Glory of the Lord

All Flesh Shall See the Salvation of God. Theodoret of Cyr: The one who has made these declarations, he says, is incapable of deceit. As for me, I am greatly astonished at those who think that the prophet has made these proph-

ecies on the subject of the return from Babylon; for they should have considered that the prophetic text has clearly proclaimed in advance that the salvation of God would be evident for all people, whereas this return [from exile] was not evident for all, while the cross of the Savior and the sufferings of the Master have reached even to the ends of the earth. Commentary on Isaiah 12.40.5.[25]

The Incarnation Where All Flesh Saw Salvation. Marius Victorinus: But when he took on flesh, he took on the universal logos of flesh. For he triumphed over the powers of all flesh in the flesh, and thus he came to the aid of all flesh, as is said in Isaiah, "all flesh will see the salvation of God," and in the psalms, "All flesh will come to you."[26] Against Arius 3.3.[27]

Revealed Glory in Ugliness. Ambrose: He [Christ] was a reproach but at the same time also the majesty of the Lord, as it is written, "And the glory of the Lord shall be revealed, and all flesh together shall see the salvation of God." What had he lost if he had nothing less? He had neither comeliness nor beauty, but he had not ceased to be the power of God. He appeared a man, but the divine majesty and glory of the Father shone on earth. Letter 27.[28]

The Lord of Glory Reveals the Father's Glory. Cyril of Alexandria: And this is the Lord of glory, and we too have come to know his glory. However, those of old did not see it when he showed himself during the dispensation in which he was made man, equal to God the Father in strength, operation and glory, bearing all things by the word of his power and with great tranquillity performing godly works, enhancing creation, raising the dead and performing other deeds of wonder effortlessly. For the glory of the Lord appeared, and all flesh saw the salvation of

[20]ESOO 2:86. [21]Jer 6:16. [22]Ps 34:8 (33:9 LXX). [23]Mt 11:28-30. [24]NPNF 2 11:543*. [25]ITA 575; SC 295:398. [26]Ps 65:2 (64:3 LXX, Vg). [27]CSEL 83 1:196. [28]FC 26:139.

God, that is, of the Father. For he has sent us his Son from heaven to salvation and redemption. For the law brings no one to perfection, for the sacrifices in prefigurative form were unable to deal with sin. But we have been perfected in Christ and reconciled from every fault as we have been honored with the spirit of sonship. COMMENTARY ON ISAIAH 3.4.40.3-5.[29]

[29]PG 70:804.

40:6-8 THE WITHERING GRASS

[6]*A voice says, "Cry!"*
  And I said, "What shall I cry?"
All flesh is grass,
  *and all its beauty is like the flower of
    the field.*
[7]*The grass withers, the flower fades,*
  when the breath of the LORD blows upon it;
  surely the people is grass.
[8]*The grass withers, the flower fades;*
  but the word of our God will stand for ever.

OVERVIEW: The voice of the Lord is not to be understood as audible but as an impression on the heart. The ephemeral nature of all those who neglect the Spirit is contrasted with the condition of those who attend to the Word and gain its everlasting qualities (EUSEBIUS). Just as all flesh is like grass, so also the fleeting nature of human life serves as a reminder of the Creator (BASIL, JEROME). Inherent in physical growth is also its decay; such is not the case with spiritual growth (JEROME). Our spiritual life is like a tree whose glory is hidden until late in the season, reminding us that the one who assumed from us what was lowly will not deny to us what is exalted (AUGUSTINE). First, however, our flesh must be considered like "grass" that needs to be kept underfoot (BEDE), as it needs to be checked by denying its desires (ORIGEN). In contrast with our flesh, the permanence of the divine Word is the most real entity there is (AUGUSTINE). Though the Word became mortal in order to raise humanity to immortality, the Word remained unchanged (ATHANASIUS). As it remains in us, it provides us with life, guarding our lives for eternity (CYRIL).

40:6 All Flesh Is Grass

THE VOICE OF THE LORD TO THE PROPHETS.
BASIL THE GREAT: "The voice of the Lord is on the waters."[1] In many places you might find the word *voice* occurring. Therefore, for the sake of understanding what the voice of the Lord is, we should gather, as far as we are able, from the divine Scripture what has been said about the voice; for instance, in the divine warning to Abraham: "And immediately the voice came to him: He shall not be your heir."[2] And in Moses: "And all the people saw the voice and the flames."[3] Again in Isaiah: "The voice of one saying, Cry." With us, then, voice is either air that has been struck or some form that is in the air against which he who is crying out wishes to strike. Now, what is the voice of the Lord? Would it be considered the impact on the air? Or air, which has been struck reaching the hearing of him to whom the voice comes? Or neither of these but that this is a voice of another kind, namely, an image formed by the mind of people whom God wishes to hear

[1]Ps 29:3 (28:3 LXX). [2]Gen 15:4. [3]Ex 20:18.

his own voice, so that they have this representation corresponding to that which frequently occurs in their dreams? Indeed, just as, although the air is not struck, we keep some recollection of certain words and sounds occurring in our dreams, not receiving the voice through our hearing but through the impression on our heart itself, so also we must believe that some such voice from God appeared in the prophets. HOMILIES ON THE PSALMS 13.3 (PSALM 28).[4]

THE EPHEMERAL FLESH AND THE ENDURING WORD. EUSEBIUS OF CAESAREA: This is the nature of all flesh and of the human who bears the image of the earthly; I mean the body-lover who lives according to the flesh. In like manner the grass of the earth and the beautiful flowers rise up and bloom for a short time, but soon they wither through their unstable nature.... The voice in the desert prophesying about God the Word is John teaching about Christ, as only from then on will it stand forever, and it guards those who stand with it and run with it as those who are becoming models of its salvation. COMMENTARY ON ISAIAH 2.16.[5]

CLEAR REMINDERS OF THE CREATOR. BASIL THE GREAT: I want the marvel of creation to gain such complete acceptance from you that, wherever you may be found and whatever kind of plants you may chance on, you may receive a clear reminder of the Creator. First, then, whenever you see a grassy plant or a flower, think of human nature, remembering the comparison of the wise Isaiah, that "all flesh is as grass, and all the glory of humanity as the flower of the grass." For the short span of life and the briefly enduring pleasure and joy of human happiness have found a most apt comparison in the words of the prophet. Today he is vigorous in body, grown fleshy from delicacies, with a flowerlike complexion, in the prime of life, fresh and eager, and irresistible in attack. Tomorrow that same one is piteous or wasted with age or weakened by disease. HOMILIES ON THE HEXAEMERON 5.2.[6]

LOSS OF BODILY STRENGTH IS A LOSS OF SELF. JEROME: We are still alive, but part of us has already perished in old age. Even though our soul is the same, nevertheless, we who suffer the loss of the pristine vigor of youth are, in a real sense, other than we were. HOMILIES ON THE PSALMS, ALTERNATE SERIES 67 (PSALM 89).[7]

FALSE AND TRUE GLORY. JEROME: Indeed, if anyone regards how weak the flesh is, that we wax and wane with the minutes of the clock and that we do not remain in the same state ... there can be no doubt that flesh is rightly called "grass" and its glory like the flower of the grass or the rushes of the fields. The one who was once an infant is suddenly a boy; the boy is suddenly a youth and up to old age is changed through stages. A beautiful woman who carries a train of young men behind her becomes wrinkled, her brow all furrowed; she who before was fit for love is afterwards fit for loathing.... But the one who has and guards the image of the heavenly, such humanity discerns the Lord's salvation, is renewed daily in knowledge after the image of the Creator and puts on an incorruptible and immortal body; it changes its glory but not its nature.[8] COMMENTARY ON ISAIAH 11.23.[9]

THE HOPE GIVEN TO OUR BODIES. AUGUSTINE: Wonder not that you will be a sharer of [Christ's] eternity. For he first became a sharer of your flesh, which is like grass. Will he who assumed from you what was lowly deny to you what is exalted with respect to you? ... How great, then, is the hope of the grass since the Word has been made flesh? He who abides forever has not disdained to assume grass, that the grass might not despair of itself. EXPLANATIONS OF THE PSALMS 103.19-21.[10]

---

[4]FC 46:199*. [5]GCS 57(9):251. [6]NPNF 2 8:76-77**. [7]FC 57:78. [8]This theme can also be found in Ambrose *Hexaemeron* 3:29. Basil *Homily* 5 (FC 46:69). [9]AGLB 30:1241-42**. [10]NPNF 1 8:509**.

THOSE PLANTED IN CHRIST ARE LIKE TREES YET TO FLOURISH. AUGUSTINE: So those flourishing, wicked people are like grass, sprouting in winter, drying up in summer. Take care that you, though, fix your roots in the Word of God, which abides forever, and that you are a tree living in a hidden way. "For you are dead, and your life is hidden with Christ in God."[11] That is where your root is; that is where you are alive. That, you see, is where you have placed your hope. . . . So do not let the winter time get you down. In the winter many prolific fruit trees lack the ornament of leaves and without the grace of fruit are like withered trees, and yet they are not in fact withered. When the grass is flourishing, they haven't even got leaves . . . the summer is the judge . . . the sun of justice is the judge. SERMON 25A.I.[12]

BE RENEWED BY HEAVENLY GRACE. BEDE: Let all who long to be refreshed by the sweetness of the living bread, all who love to be renewed by the banquet of heavenly grace, sit down on the grass. Let them trample on the bloom of the grass. Let them chastise the body and subject it to slavery.[13] HOMILIES ON THE GOSPELS 2.2.[14]

THE MIND OF THE FLESH. ORIGEN: And [Christ] commanded all the multitudes to sit down on the grass because of what is said in Isaiah, "All flesh is grass." That is to say, he commanded them to subjugate the flesh and to keep in subjection "the mind of the flesh,"[15] so that one might be able to partake of the loaves that Jesus blesses. COMMENTARY ON MATTHEW 11.3.[16]

THE UNCHANGABLE NATURE OF THE DIVINE WORD. AUGUSTINE: Both what is being thought of by intelligence and what is sounding out loud in speech is changeable and dissimilar. The first will not remain when you have forgotten it, nor will the second when you stop speaking. But "the Word of the Lord remains forever" and abides unchanged and unchangeable. SERMON 187.3.[17]

THE WORD REMAINS FOREVER. ATHANASIUS: What advancement, then, was it to the Immortal to have assumed the mortal? Or what promotion is it to the Everlasting to have put on the temporal? What reward can be great to the everlasting God and King in the bosom of the Father? Do you not see that this too was done and written because of us and for us, that the Lord, having become a human being, might make immortal us who are mortal and temporal and bring us into the everlasting kingdom of heaven? Do you Arians not blush, speaking lies against the divine oracles? For when our Lord Jesus Christ was among us, we indeed were promoted, as rescued from sin; but he is the same, nor did he change when he became man, but, as has been written, "the Word of God abides forever." Surely as, before he became human, he, the Word, dispensed to the saints the Spirit as his own, so also when made human, he sanctifies all by the Spirit and says to his disciples, "Receive the Holy Spirit." DISCOURSE AGAINST THE ARIANS 1.12.48.[18]

THE WORD REMAINS AS IT DWELLS IN US. CYRIL OF ALEXANDRIA: The Word of the Father dwells in our hearts through faith. When we receive the riches of his divine Spirit, then we have him in ourselves as that which is most worth having, since he is the giver of eternal life. For when the Word dwells in us, he remains there forever, sustaining and enlivening us. Now if anyone wishes to know from the Word of God his commandment, then we say that this is immeasurably useful. For God guards both the commandment and those who observe it for the life which is yet to come. As was said by the Lord himself, "Truly I tell you, that if anyone keeps my word, he shall not see death."[19] COMMENTARY ON ISAIAH 3.4.40.6-8.[20]

---

[11]Col 3:3. [12]WSA 3 2:88-89*. [13]1 Cor 9:27. Bede simply follows Origen here. [14]CS 111:18-19*. [15]Rom 8:6. [16]ANF 9:433*. [17]WSA 3 6:28-29*. [18]NPNF 2 4:334**. [19]Jn 8:51. [20]PG 70:805.

40:9-11 THE STRENGTH OF THE SHEPHERD

⁹*Get you up to a high mountain,*
O Zion, herald of good tidings;°
lift up your voice with strength,
O Jerusalem, herald of good tidings,ᵖ
lift it up, fear not;
say to the cities of Judah,
"Behold your God!"
¹⁰*Behold, the Lord GOD comes with might,*

and his arm rules for him;
behold, his reward is with him,
and his recompense before him.
¹¹*He will feed his flock like a shepherd,*
he will gather the lambs in his arms,
he will carry them in his bosom,
and gently lead those that are with young.

o Or O herald of good tidings to Zion   p Or O herald of good tidings to Jerusalem

OVERVIEW: The Christian life is an ascent (AM-BROSE) as we reach to the heights of doctrine and Christian living (GREGORY THE GREAT). This is what Peter preached at Pentecost when the type of this prophecy was fulfilled (CYRIL OF JERUSA-LEM). Isaiah exhorts those tempted to be afraid to trust in their God (THEODORET) and be zealous in doing good to bring honor to his name (CLEMENT OF ROME) in the awareness that God is fully cognizant of human works (ISHOʻDAD). The oracles of the prophet are in agreement with the Gospel (THEODORET). He knows our weakness and calls on us to trust the strength and authority of the arm of our Lord Jesus (CYRIL). He protects the souls of the lambs whose wisdom comes from their simplicity (APONIUS). Christ feeds his flock by the power of his teachings (THEODORET).

40:9 Go Up to a High Mountain

THE EFFORT AND ACHIEVEMENT OF ACTS OF DISCIPLESHIP. AMBROSE: Ascend this mountain ... not with physical steps but with more exalted deeds. Follow Christ so that you might be a mountain yourself, for there are mountains surrounding him. Look in the Gospel, and you will find that only the disciples went up the mountain with the Lord. EXPOSITIONS ON THE GOSPEL OF LUKE 5.41.[1]

REACH FOR THE HEIGHTS OF LOFTY PRAC-TICE. GREGORY THE GREAT: The high mountain is the summit of doctrine and practice. Let one rise up who hurries to anoint the king. Let him reach into the heights. Let him rise up in lofty practice, in lofty contemplation, in the wisdom of the Word, in the power of love. He who is the One anointed by preaching is so great that he can be scarcely reached, even by the highest places. ... The highest heights are the power of perfect conversation, and this is achieved by many perfectly. SIX BOOKS ON 1 KINGS 6.114.[2]

PETER'S GOOD TIDINGS TO JERUSALEM AT PENTECOST. CYRIL OF JERUSALEM: For in the power of the Holy Spirit, by the will of the Father and the Son, Peter stood with the Eleven and, lifting up his voice (according to the text, "Lift up your voice with strength, you who bring good tidings to Jerusalem"), captured in the spiritual net of his words about three thousand souls. So great was the grace that worked in all the apostles together, that, out of the Jews ... this great number believed, were baptized in the name of Christ and continued steadfast in the apostles' doctrine and in the prayers.[3] CATECHETICAL LECTURES 17.21.[4]

[1]CCL 14:149-50. [2]CCL 144:613-14. [3]Acts 2:42. [4]NPNF 2 7:129*.

THE CHORUS OF THE APOSTLES. THEODORET OF CYR: It is the chorus of the apostles that the prophetic text raises here. It is precisely for this reason that after expressing this exhortation in the singular the text shifts into the plural and says, "Lift up [the voice], do not fear." In the same way, in his turn, Christ our Master said to the apostles, "Do not fear those who kill the body but cannot kill the soul."[5] And again, after bringing them out from the prison, he bade them to proclaim quite freely the words of this life.[6] Moreover, he calls "mountain" the summit of the knowledge of God. COMMENTARY ON ISAIAH 12.40.9.[7]

40:10 Behold, the Lord Comes

BE ZEALOUS IN DOING GOOD. CLEMENT OF ROME: We must . . . be zealous in doing good, for all things are from him. [Isaiah] warns us, "Behold, the Lord comes, and his reward is before his face, to pay each person according to his work." He therefore urges us who believe in him with all our heart not to be lazy or careless in any good work. Let our glorying and our confidence be in him. Let us be subject to his will. 1 CLEMENT 34.2-5.[8]

EVIDENT TO GOD. ISHO'DAD OF MERV: "Behold, his reward is with him," that is, Behold, the works of each person are conspicuous before God, and he judges according to what each of us has done, by granting a reward to the good and by abandoning the evil to punishment. COMMENTARY ON ISAIAH 40.10.[9]

THE SECOND COMING OF THE SAVIOR. THEODORET OF CYR: These words are a glimpse of the second coming of the Savior. It is then that he will give the laborers their reward. "He will reward each according to his works,"[10] according to the word of the apostle. "For the Day," he says, "will declare it, because it will be revealed by fire; and the fire will test each one's work, of what sort it is."[11] This is the proclamation that the Lord has

ordained to the holy apostles to make in their turn. "Go," he has said, "to the lost sheep of the house of Israel. And as you go, preach, saying, 'The kingdom of heaven is at hand.'"[12] One can therefore see that the oracles of the prophet are thus in agreement with the words of the Gospel. COMMENTARY ON ISAIAH 12.40.10.[13]

AUTHORITY OF CHRIST. CYRIL OF ALEXANDRIA: For our Lord Jesus Christ showed himself to us having divine strength, and his arm with authority, that is, with power and dominion. LETTER 1.31.[14]

40:11 He Will Feed His Flock

TRUE PHILOSOPHERS ARE NOT SOPHISTICATED. APONIUS: I say that these [lambs] are the souls of those who are truly made heavenly philosophers, rejecting the world with its delights and false show and who prefer to dwell in the desert rather than in royal palaces. EXPOSITION OF SONG OF SONGS 2.3.[15]

THE SHEPHERD SENDS HIS FLOCK. THEODORET OF CYR: Of this prophecy also let us observe the fulfillment in the exact way and in truth in the holy Gospels. In the first place, the Lord has said, "I am the good shepherd, and I know my sheep and am known by my own . . . and [I] lay down my life for the sheep."[16] Moreover, he has likewise gathered the lambs with his arms, [that is to say] by the power of his teachings. For soon he said to the fishermen, "Follow me, and I will make you fishers of men [people]."[17] Presently he called the publicans and ate with them.[18] Again, another time, he allowed even a woman who had led an evil life to shed tears at his feet.[19] He has likewise comforted pregnant women with the thought that they

---

[5]Mt 10:28. [6]See Acts 5:17-20. [7]ITA 578*; SC 295:400-402. [8]FC 1:36*. [9]CSCO 303(128):43. [10]Mt 16:27. [11]1 Cor 3:13. [12]Mt 10:6-7. [13]ITA 579; SC 295:402. [14]FC 76:27; PG 77:32. [15]CCL 19:38. [16]Jn 10:14-15. [17]Mt 4:19. [18]See Mt 9:9-10. [19]See Lk 7:36-50.

would give birth for salvation.[20] As they learned of the destruction of death and the hope of the resurrection, they possesed sufficient solace for their pains in the expectation of the benefits that had been announced. Finally, while the holy Virgin still carried him in her womb, he filled Elizabeth, who was with child, with joy. COMMENTARY ON ISAIAH 12.40.11.[21]

---

[20]See Lk 1:39-45. [21]ITA 580*; SC 295:402-4.

40:12-14 GOD UPHOLDS THE UNIVERSE

[12]Who has measured the waters in the hollow
    of his hand
    and marked off the heavens with a span,
enclosed the dust of the earth in a measure
    and weighed the mountains in scales
    and the hills in a balance?

[13]Who has directed the Spirit of the LORD,
    or as his counselor has instructed him?
[14]Whom did he consult for his enlightenment,
    and who taught him the path of justice,
and taught him knowledge,
    and showed him the way of understanding?

OVERVIEW: All things are sustained by God (GREGORY OF NYSSA), who is too profound to be reduced to truths comprehensible to the human intellect (AMBROSE). And yet, God may express himself to us in terms we can understand (HILARY) even though he encompasses the universe (CYRIL OF JERUSALEM). God is active everywhere, not just in special places (JEROME). As magnificent as he is, he can make himself small for his creation (EPHREM), although human language still finds its limits in speaking about God. Thus, for instance, the Lord is not literally seated at the right hand of the Father (AUGUSTINE). Human perception also had difficulty with the incarnate Son who was wrongly seen by human eyes as not amounting to much (HIPPOLYTUS). But this is because ultimately only God, the author of all things, understands God (AMBROSE). Father, Son and Spirit share their counsel and understanding among one another (JEROME). Isaiah's rhetorical question here, then, as to who could possibly know the mind of the Lord or serve as his counselor is ultimately answered by the New Testament: it is the Son who does these things (BASIL).

40:12 Who Has Measured the Waters?

GOD SUSTAINS CREATION. GREGORY OF NYSSA: For this cause [God] comprehends in himself all the intelligible creation, that all things may remain in existence controlled by his encompassing power. AGAINST EUNOMIUS 2.11.[1]

THE CLEAR LIMITATIONS OF HUMAN KNOWLEDGE. AMBROSE: Who, then, ventures to consider his knowledge on the same plane with that of God? Does any person presume to know what God has sealed with his own oracular and majestic pronouncements? SIX DAYS OF CREATION 6.2.7.[2]

GOD ENCLOSES ALL. HILARY OF POITIERS: The

---

[1]NPNF 2 5:120. [2]FC 42:231**.

words "I AM THAT I AM" were clearly an adequate indication of God's infinity. But, in addition, we needed to apprehend the operation of his majesty and power. For while absolute existence is peculiar to him who, abiding eternally, had no beginning in a past however remote, we hear again an utterance worthy of himself issuing from the eternal and holy God, who says, "who holds the heaven in his palm and the earth in his hand," and again, "The heaven is my throne and the earth is the footstool of my feet. What house will you build me or what shall be the place of my rest?" The whole heaven is held in the palm of God, the whole earth grasped in his hand.

Now the word of God . . . reveals a deeper meaning to the patient student. . . . This heaven that is held in the palm of God is also his throne, and the earth that is grasped in his hand is also the footstool beneath his feet. This was not written that . . . we should conclude that he has extension in space, as of a body. . . . It was written that in all born and created things God might be known within them and without, overshadowing and indwelling, surrounding all and interfused through all, since palm and hand, which hold, reveal the might of his external control, while throne and footstool, by their support of a sitter, display the subservience of outward things to One who, himself outside them, encloses all in his grasp. . . . Being infinite, he is present in all things. In him who is infinite all are included. ON THE TRINITY 1.6.[3]

GOD ENCLOSES THE UNIVERSE. CYRIL OF JERUSALEM: Now this Father of our Lord Jesus Christ is not circumscribed to some place, nor is there heaven beyond him, but "the heavens are the work of his fingers,"[4] and "the whole earth is held in the hollow of his hand." He is in everything and yet nothing contains him. CATECHETICAL LECTURES 4.5.[5]

CHRIST CANNOT BE CONTAINED. JEROME: He [Christ], who . . . balances the universe, cannot

be contained in a single sepulcher. HOMILY 87, ON JOHN 1:1-14.[6]

THE LIMITLESS CREATOR TOOK ON CREATURELY MEASURE. EPHREM THE SYRIAN: Let the great sea praise the hands of the Son that measured it, and was astonished. . . . Blessed be his noble act! HYMNS ON THE NATIVITY 13.15.[7]

WE MUST NOT THINK OF GOD IN PHYSICAL TERMS. AUGUSTINE: God sits in heaven and measures the heaven with his palm. Does the same heaven become broad when God sits in it and narrow when he measures it? Or, when God is seated, is he no wider than the palm of his hand? If this is the case, then God has not made us to his own likeness, for with us the palm of the hand is much narrower than the bodily part on which we sit. So, if God is just as broad in the palm of his hand as when he is seated, he has made our members quite different. Not in this does the likeness consist. For shame! SERMON 53.14.[8]

SPACE AND PLACE ARE METAPHORS. AUGUSTINE: Although these things seem illogical when heard by us according to our human capacity, nevertheless we are moved by them to think of spiritual things in an ineffable manner. Hence, even if we think that the body of the Lord, which when raised from the grave into heaven was not without human form and did indeed have bodily members, nevertheless he is not to be thought of as sitting on the right hand of the Father, as if the Father could be seen sitting on his left. In that blessedness indeed that surpasses all human understanding, "the right" is the name of that same blessedness. LETTER 120.3.[9]

A MERE DROP FROM THE BUCKET. HIPPOLYTUS: [Christ] . . . is of no reputation in the world but of illustrious fame in heaven, being betrayed by those who are ignorant [of his perfections] to

---

[3]NPNF 2 9:41**. [4]Ps 8:3 (8:4 LXX). [5]LCC 4:101. [6]FC 57:219.
[7]NPNF 2 13:248**. [8]WSA 3 3:73**. [9]CSEL 34 2:716.

those who know him not, being accounted as a drop from a cask. We, however, [Isaiah] says, are spiritual, who, from the life-giving water of Eu phrates, which flows through the midst of Baby-lon, choose our own peculiar quality as we pass through the true gate, which is the blessed Jesus. THE REFUTATION OF ALL HERESIES 5.4.[10]

40:13-14 *Who Has Directed the Spirit of the Lord?*

THE FATHER AS AUTHOR OF ALL THINGS. AMBROSE: "Yet to us there is but one God, the Father, of whom are all things, and we to him; and one Lord Jesus Christ, through whom are all things, and we through him."[11] . . . The apostle says according to the prophecy of Isaiah, "Who has known the mind of the Lord, or who has been his counselor?" And he added, "For him and through him and in him are all things," which Isa-iah said of the artificer of all, as you have it. "Who has measured the water with his hand, and the heaven with his palm?" And the apostle has added, "For of him and through him and in him are all things." What is "of him"? That the nature of all things is of his will, and he is the author of all things that come into existence. "Through him" means what? That establishment and con-tinuance are seen to have been bestowed on all things through him. "In him" means what? That all things by a certain wonderful desire and inef-fable love look on the Author of their lives and the minister of their graces and functions, accord-ing to what is written: "The eyes of all hope in you," and "You open your hand and fill every liv-ing creature with your good pleasure."[12] ON THE HOLY SPIRIT 2.9.85, 90-91.[13]

TRINITARIAN COUNSEL. JEROME: Symmachus translated, "Who has prepared the Spirit of the Lord and who has shown to him the man of his counsel? With whom has he entered into counsel

and has given him understanding and has taught him the path of justice and instructed him in knowledge and has shown the way of wisdom to him?" In this translation it appears more clearly that the one whom the Spirit prepared or founded is he about whom the apostle says, "The Lord is the Spirit" and "On him the Spirit rested, the Spirit of wisdom and understanding." And further on, "The Spirit of the Lord is on me, wherefore he has anointed me."[14] For the same Spirit of the Lord is "the man of his counsel," in whom "dwelled all richness of divinity in bodily manner." With that one he entered into counsel about whom we said above, "wonderful counse-lor," and in Proverbs it is written, "God founded the earth with wisdom; he prepared the heavens with foresight."[15] Moreover, the Septuagint said, "Who has known the mind of the Lord and who has been his counselor," meaning it to be under-stood that the mind and reason and sense of God through which all things were made and without whom nothing was made is he about whom it is sung in the Psalms, "The heavens were prepared by the Word of the Lord, and all their power by the Spirit of his mouth."[16] COMMENTARY ON ISA-IAH 11.25.[17]

WHO COUNSELS THE FATHER BUT THE SON? BASIL THE GREAT: "Who has known the mind of the Lord or who rather has been his counselor?" This passage is not merely a rhetorical question. If it were, "who" could not possibly refer to any-one. Rather, the use of "who" indicates a rare per-sonage. . . . All these questions . . . have the same answer: "For the Father loves the Son and shows him all that he himself is doing."[18] ON THE HOLY SPIRIT 5.7.[19]

---

[10]ANF 5:57-58. [11]1 Cor 8:6. [12]Ps 145:15 (144:15 LXX). [13]NPNF 2 10:125-26**. [14]Lk 4:18. [15]See Prov 8:22-27. [16]Ps 33:6 (32:6 LXX, Vg). [17]AGLB 30:1249-50. [18]Jn 5:20. [19]OHS 23.

40:15-24 PROVIDENCE RULES THE VASTNESS OF CREATION

¹⁵*Behold, the nations are like a drop from a bucket,*
and are accounted as the dust on the scales;
behold, he takes up the isles like fine dust.
¹⁶*Lebanon would not suffice for fuel,*
nor are its beasts enough for a burnt offering.
¹⁷*All the nations are as nothing before him,*
they are accounted by him as less than nothing and emptiness.

¹⁸*To whom then will you liken God,*
or what likeness compare with him?
¹⁹*The idol! a workman casts it,*
and a goldsmith overlays it with gold,
and casts for it silver chains.
²⁰*He who is impoverished^q chooses for an offering*
wood that will not rot;
he seeks out a skilful craftsman

to set up an image that will not move.

²¹*Have you not known? Have you not heard?*
Has it not been told you from the beginning?
Have you not understood from the foundations of the earth?
²²*It is he who sits above the circle of the earth,*
and its inhabitants are like grasshoppers;
who stretches out the heavens like a curtain,
and spreads them like a tent to dwell in;
²³*who brings princes to nought,*
and makes the rulers of the earth as nothing.

²⁴*Scarcely are they planted, scarcely sown,*
scarcely has their stem taken root in the earth,
when he blows upon them, and they wither,
and the tempest carries them off like stubble.

q Heb uncertain

OVERVIEW: The resources of the entire world would not be enough to satisfy the sacrifice God requires (EUSEBIUS). The heavens themselves were made to show God's harmony of diversity as well as to provide for the protection of the earth (AMBROSE). Humanity, by contrast, fashions idols, false gods, out of creatures (JEROME). God has made the world vast in its extent and insignificant in each part to illustrate the infinite character of the Divine, although there is no art that could depict the one who is without limit. Those who make idols try to capture the essence of God but will fail because they are trying to produce them from a source outside of God. Instead of the weakness of idols, however, they should look to the one who laid the foundations of the earth (THEODORET). When Christ came, he initiated the first of the many attacks the saints would make against the falsehood of idolatry (CYRIL).

In attempting to understand the earth, help can be found by contemplating the heavens (BASIL). We also begin to get a sense of the strength and grandeur of God when we contemplate his creation (THEODORET), which he made with such consummate ease (CHRYSOSTOM). The creation itself is not the limit of God's power; rather, he has accomplished what he deems to be best (THEODORET).

40:15-18 *The World Is Not Enough*

**WE COULD NEVER OFFER SUFFICIENT SACRI-
FICE.** EUSEBIUS OF CAESAREA: He teaches, therefore, that all of this service through blood and
sacrifice is no longer appropriate for God. Neither someone offering all the four-footed creatures of the earth nor all of Lebanon and all the
matter produced in it as sacrifices would be worthy before God. "All the nations are as nothing,
and are reckoned as nothing." What kind of clinging to idolatrous straying did God not know
about? COMMENTARY ON ISAIAH 2.18.[1]

**THE HEAVENS ARE A HARMONIOUS CRE-
ATION FOR OUR PROTECTION.** AMBROSE: Their
pleasure lies rather in their admiration of this
most beautiful fabric of the world, this accord of
unlike elements, this heaven that is "spread out
like a tent to dwell in" to protect those who
inhabit this world. SIX DAYS OF CREATION 3.1.5.[2]

40:19 *The Idol*

THE MEANING OF IDOLATRY TODAY. JEROME:
According to the moral sense we can say that the
leaders of the heretics flourish, inventing different idols from their heart or by the charm of
speech, which is what silver means, or by the
splendor of gold, which appeals to the senses, or
by the fine wood—these are the more vile teachings and are thought everlasting by those who
invent them and are strengthened by dialectical
skill lest they move and decay. Instead, they
"stand fast" with a solid root. COMMENTARY ON
ISAIAH 11.26.[3]

THE VAST SCALE OF CREATION AND HISTORY.
JEROME: For if we consider the different nations
in all the world, from ocean to ocean, that is,
from the Indian Sea to Brittania, and from the
Atlantic up to the northern ice cap where the
waters congeal and fine amber is frozen, we see
that every race of human being lives like locusts
within it. . . . Are we not amazed at the relative

smallness of human beings whose bodies are like
locusts when you consider their minute movements in the grand scheme of things? . . . The
Lord is the one who stretched out the heavens
and increased them so that the multitude of
angels could live above them and the human race
could dwell below as a house fit to contain all the
reasonable creatures he had made. . . . Greek and
Roman history tells of so many kings. Where is
that uncountable army of Xerxes? Where is the
Israelite host in the desert? Where is the incredible power of kings? What shall I say about those
long ago? For present examples teach us that leaders are next to nothing, and the rulers of the earth
are considered empty. The princes and judges of
the earth[4] . . . are neither sown nor planted nor
fixed with a stable root. They are carried off at
the command of God in an instant and perish like
the blade of grass taken by the wind and storm,
just as it is written, "And I crossed over, and he
was not there; I sought him, and his place was not
found."[5] COMMENTARY ON ISAIAH 11.27.[6]

THE DIVINE CAPACITY IS INFINITE. THE-
ODORET OF CYR: At the moment when he gave
the law, the God of the universe transmitted his
commands in these terms: "You shall not make
for yourself an image or likeness of any thing,
whether of things in the heaven above, and in the
earth beneath, and in the waters under the earth
. . . for I am the Lord your God."[7] That is to say, of
the God whose appearance you have not seen.
Here also the prophetic text, while denouncing
the lack of sense of those who fabricate idols and
who worship them, strives to show the infinite
character of divine capacity; but in [Isaiah's]
inability to teach people another way, he sets out
the creation to indicate [its] extraordinary measure; that which, he says, is a drop in the bucket,
a turning of a balance, or spittle, so much is all
the human race in relation to that ineffable and
unlimited power. Then [Isaiah] teaches that the

---

[1]GCS 57(9):255. [2]FC 42:69. [3]AGLB 30:1253. [4]Jerome: "or, as others
reckon, the heavens." [5]Ps 36:36 Vg. [6]AGLB 30:1255-58. [7]Deut 5:8-9.

collection of all kinds of beasts is a small thing and not enough for an offering in honor of the divine magnificence, and that [even] all the forests of Lebanon are incapable of satisfying the fire lit [on the altar of sacrifice]. What image could you, therefore, fashion that would be equivalent in nature? COMMENTARY ON ISAIAH 12.40.18.[8]

ART CANNOT IMITATE THE DIVINE IMAGE.
THEODORET OF CYR: What art can produce an imitation of him who precisely is boundless? COMMENTARY ON ISAIAH 12.40.19.[9]

40:20 Wood That Will Not Rot

THE ARTIST CREATES AN IMAGE, NOT REALITY. THEODORET OF CYR: On the subject of the God of the universe, [Isaiah] has expressed himself in the following manner: "Lebanon is not enough to burn," while here, to mock the feebleness of idols, he makes it obvious that the artisan has a need for wood to give form to the pretended god. Not only, [Isaiah] says, does he borrow its essence and its appearance from an outside source, but he even calls for much artfulness in order to obtain an image and to keep it from being moved. COMMENTARY ON ISAIAH 12.40.20.[10]

40:21 Told to You from the Beginning

WHERE WE FIND TRUE STABILITY. THEODORET OF CYR: From the beginning, [Isaiah] says, have I not taught you the weakness of the idols? Do you not know who it is who set the earth on its foundations with a view to assuring its stability? COMMENTARY ON ISAIAH 12.40.21.[11]

THE TRUTH EXPOSES DECEPTION. CYRIL OF ALEXANDRIA: The divinely inspired Scripture was not silent. For the knowledge of the truth from above was veiled through the patriarchs, through the law and the prophets. But this was not the case when the only-begotten Word of God came among us as a man to illuminate those on the earth. This was the last days when the

leader of those who oppose spiritual deception came. It was the first of the attacks on idolatry. For the choir of the saints never stops attacking such deception, showing how loathsome it is while at the same time making known the [true] Maker and Lord of the universe. COMMENTARY ON ISAIAH 3.5.40.15-21.[12]

40:22-23 He Stretches Out the Heavens

THE HEAVENS HELP TO EXPLAIN THE NATURE OF THE EARTH. BASIL THE GREAT: "He that stretches out the heavens as a vaulted ceiling." These same thoughts, let us also recommend to ourselves concerning the earth, not to be curious about what its substance is; or to wear ourselves out by reasoning, seeking its very foundation; or to search for some nature destitute of qualities, existing without quality of itself; but to realize well that all that is seen around it is related to the reason of its existence, forming an essential part of its substance. HOMILIES ON THE HEXAMERON 1.8.[13]

THE TENT'S FLOOR IS THE EARTH, ITS ROOF IS THE SKY. THEODORET OF CYR: It is he, [Isaiah] says, who has caused the earth to appear; it is he who holds it in his hand and who directs it. As for human beings, they are no different from grasshoppers if one compares them with divine power. Then [Isaiah] teaches that God is not only the Maker of the earth but also the Creator of the heavens: "He that set up the heaven as a chamber and stretched it out as a tent to dwell in." For since the earth is like the ground floor of a house and the sky simulates a roof in the form of an arch and dome, [Isaiah] has aptly compared it with a tent. And after having shown us the God of the universe as Creator, the prophetic text indicates to us his ineffable providence. COMMENTARY ON ISAIAH 12.40.22.[14]

---

[8]ITA 583-84**; SC 295:406-8. [9]ITA 584; SC 295:408. [10]ITA 584; SC 295:408. [11]ITA 584; SC 295:408. [12]PG 70:813. [13]NPNF 2 8:56**. [14]ITA 584*; SC 295:408-10.

GOD'S EASE IN MAKING CREATION. CHRYSOS-TOM: When he spoke of the heavens, Isaiah said, "It is he who set up the heaven as a vaulted chamber and stretched it out as a tent over the earth." And he said of the earth, "It is he that comprehends the circle of the earth and made the earth as if it were nothing," even though the earth is so great and vast. . . . Despite the fact that the earth is so great and so vast, God made it with such ease that the prophet could find no fitting example. So he said that God made the earth "as if it were nothing." AGAINST THE ANOMOEANS, HOMILY 2.24-25.[15]

GOD'S WILL IS THE MEASURE. THEODORET OF

CYR: It is thus he has brought down Sennacherib, Nebuchadnezzar and thousands of others. "And has made the earth as nothing." For the power of the Creator does not even have the object of his creation as a measure, but only his will: "Our God has done in heaven and on earth whatsoever he has pleased,"[16] not all that he has the power [to do] but all he pleases: for he would be capable [of accomplishing] works many times greater, but God has accomplished what he judges to be best. COMMENTARY ON ISAIAH 12.40.23.[17]

---

[15]FC 72:80-81. [16]Ps 115:3 (113:11 LXX). [17]ITA 585; SC 295:410.

40:25-31 NO ONE IS COMPARABLE TO GOD

[25]To whom then will you compare me,
    that I should be like him? says the Holy
      One.
[26]Lift up your eyes on high and see:
    who created these?
He who brings out their host by number,*
    calling them all by name;
by the greatness of his might,
    and because he is strong in power
    not one is missing.

[27]Why do you say, O Jacob,
    and speak, O Israel,
"My way is hid from the LORD,
    and my right is disregarded by my God"?

[28]Have you not known? Have you not heard?
The LORD is the everlasting God,
    the Creator of the ends of the earth.
He does not faint or grow weary,
    his understanding is unsearchable.
[29]He gives power to the faint,
    and to him who has no might he increases
      strength.
[30]Even youths shall faint and be weary,
    and young men shall fall exhausted;
[31]but they who wait for the LORD shall renew
      their strength,
    they shall mount up with wings like eagles,
they shall run and not be weary,
    they shall walk and not faint.

* LXX *He who brings forth by number the order of the cosmos*

OVERVIEW: God is beyond comparison with any other being (THEODORET), so any analogy we

might use will always be deficient (TERTULLIAN). Since God is the maker of all things he knows everything about each component of that creation (THEODORET). Isaiah tells us to lift up our eyes and contemplate this creation. When we take the time to do this, we see the ordered seasons and the greatness and glory of God, which, in turn, causes us to think of higher things (ORIGEN). Creation itself is a witness to the power, strength and greatness of God (JEROME). And yet, amid the vastness of this world, nothing escapes his view, including humanity's rebellion against him. Isaiah calls on humanity to remember that it is the eternal one who spoke to Moses with whom they are dealing (THEODORET).

Some use this passage to denigrate the Son. God has made everything in creation; he did not make a son and delegate the rest of creation to him (ATHANASIUS). In exalting the poor and lowly, he enacts the words of Hannah (THEODORET). When Christ takes us up into the clouds with him, we will soar like eagles as we become young again with the immortal bodies he will give us (JEROME), being able to flee from and above earthly suffering (THEODORET).

40:25 To Whom Will You Compare Me?

HOW CAN ONE COMPARE? THEODORET OF CYR: To him who has performed works, to him who has accomplished these works and who continually goes on performing them, to whom do you compare him? What mark of respect do you offer to him that is worthy of him? COMMENTARY ON ISAIAH 12.40.25.[1]

ANALOGIES REFERRING TO GOD ARE ALWAYS DEFICIENT. TERTULLIAN: God is one thing, and what belongs to God is another thing. . . . How will you employ in a comparison with God an object as your example, [such as a king] which fails in all the purposes that belong to a comparison? Why, when supreme power among kings cannot evidently be varied but only unique and singular, is an exception made in the case of him (of all others) who is King of kings, and (from the exceeding greatness of his power and the subjec-

tion of all other ranks to him) the very summit, as it were, of dominion? AGAINST MARCION 1.4.[2]

40:26-27 Lift Your Eyes

GOD'S ALL-ENCOMPASSING POWER. THEODORET OF CYR: [Isaiah] says, look at the sun, the moon, the movement of the stars, the cycle of the year, the changing of the seasons, the regular succession of night and day. For this is what [Isaiah] has added: "He who brings forth by number the order of the cosmos." For he calls the setting in order of creation "the cosmos." "He shall call them by names." He is ignorant of nothing, [Isaiah] says, but he knows all things with clarity, since it is he who has given a name equally to each and every thing. "By means of the greatness of [your] glory and by the power of [your] might nothing has escaped you." He has power above all, he is able [to do] all, he is ignorant of nothing that exists, and he knows the very thoughts of people. COMMENTARY ON ISAIAH 12.40.26.[3]

THINK OF HIGHER THINGS. ORIGEN: "Lift up your eyes" occurs in many places in Scripture when the divine Word admonishes us to exalt and lift up our thoughts, to elevate the insight that lies below in a rather sickly condition, and is stooped and completely incapable of looking up, as it is written, for instance, in Isaiah: "Lift up your eyes on high and see. Who has made all these things known?" COMMENTARY ON THE GOSPEL OF JOHN 13.274.[4]

CREATION'S GREATNESS ATTESTS GOD'S MIGHT. JEROME: Since so great is the power and majesty of the Creator, to which likeness do you compare God, thus failing to understand the founder from the greatness of creation? If you do not believe the words, at least believe your eyes and recognize the power of the Lord from the service all heavens and elements give him, who

---

[1]ITA 585; SC 295:410. [2]ANF 3:273-74*. [3]ITA 585*; SC 295:410-12. [4]FC 89:125.

"leads out their army by number," that is, the heavens, about which in the psalms it says, "Who numbers the host of stars and calls them all by name." Or we can call the army of heaven angels and all the companies of heaven.... For the greatness of the strength of God made all to serve him in order ... but he knows their way and reasons and course in his majesty as the Creator.[5] COMMENTARY ON ISAIAH 11.27.[6]

NOTHING ESCAPES GOD'S NOTICE. THEODORET OF CYR: Do not think that I ignore the designs of your souls, God says through Isaiah, and do not believe that you escape my view when you hold perverse reasonings. This passage lets [us] see clearly that he has also thrown the accusation of polytheism against Israel itself. COMMENTARY ON ISAIAH 12.40.27.[7]

40:28-30 Power to the Faint

I AM THE ETERNAL GOD. THEODORET OF CYR: Then he recalls the truths that he has often taught: "[I am an] eternal God." This is what the blessed Moses has also said: "I AM WHO I AM."[8] As for the blessed David, he in his turn addresses himself to him in these terms: "But you, Lord, endure forever, and your remembrance to generation and generation."[9] Or again: "But you are the same, and your years shall not fail."[10] COMMENTARY ON ISAIAH 12.40.28.[11]

GOD NOT SO WEAK THAT HE COULD ONLY MANAGE TO MAKE THE SON. ATHANASIUS: If they shall assign the toil of making all things as the reason why God only made the Son, the whole creation will cry out against them as saying unworthy things of God; and Isaiah, too, who has said in Scripture, "The everlasting God, the Lord, the Creator of the ends of the earth, does not faint, neither is he weary: there is no searching of his understanding." And if God made the Son alone, as not lowering himself to make the rest but committed them to the Son as an assistant, this on the other hand is

unworthy of God, for in him there is no pride. No, the Lord reproves the thought when he says, "Are not two sparrows sold for a farthing?"... If then it is not unworthy of God to exercise his providence, even down to things so small, a hair of the head and a sparrow and the grass of the field, also it was not unworthy of him to make them. For what things are the subjects of his providence, of those he is Maker through his proper Word. No, a worse absurdity lies before the people who speak this way; for they distinguish between the creatures and the framing and consider the latter the work of the Father, the creatures the work of the Son; whereas either all things must be brought to be with the Son, or if all that is originate comes to be through the Son, we must not call him one of the originated things. DISCOURSE AGAINST THE ARIANS 2.17.25.[12]

THE WORDS OF HANNAH. THEODORET OF CYR: This is what the admirable Hannah has also said: "The Lord makes poor and makes rich; he brings low, and he lifts up."[13] COMMENTARY ON ISAIAH 12.40.29.[14]

40:31 With Wings Like Eagles

THE SAINT WILL BE MADE YOUNG AGAIN. JEROME: We have said that the old age of eagles is revived by a change of their wings and that they alone who see the brilliance of the sun and the radiance of its splendor are able to gaze with gleaming eyes; and they test their young ones to see whether they are of noble birth by this same test. In the same way the saints are made young again as they put on their immortal bodies so that they no longer feel the toil of mortals but are taken up into the clouds before the face of Christ, and in no way (following the Septuagint) do they hunger, since they have the Lord present to them

---

[5]LXX has "nothing is hidden from you in glory and power." [6]AGLB 30:1258-59. [7]ITA 586*; SC 295:412. [8]Ex 3:14. [9]Ps 102:12 (101:13 LXX). [10]Ps 102:27 (101:28 LXX). [11]ITA 586*; SC 295:412-14. [12]NPNF 2 4:362*. [13]1 Sam 2:7 LXX. [14]ITA 586; SC 295:414.

as food. COMMENTARY ON ISAIAH 12.2-3.[15]

THE SPIRIT'S RENEWAL. THEODORET OF CYR: These things took place at the time of the Jews and the divine apostles. In fact, all those who did not believe were handed over to famine, disease, war and bondage. Those, however, who believed

were renewed by the All-Holy Spirit and so imitated the swift flight of eagles. They flew over all the earth, struggling in bodies so foreign to them. COMMENTARY ON ISAIAH 12.40.30.[16]

---

[15]AGLB 35:1293-95. [16]SC 295:414.

41:1-7 RENEWED STRENGTH

[1]Listen to me in silence, O coastlands;
    let the peoples renew their strength;
let them approach, then let them speak;
    let us together draw near for judgment.

[2]Who stirred up one* from the east
    whom victory meets at every step?
He gives up nations before him,
    so that he tramples kings under foot;
he makes them like dust with his sword,
    like driven stubble with his bow.
[3]He pursues them and passes on safely,
    by paths his feet have not trod.
[4]Who has performed and done this,
    calling the generations from the beginning?

I, the LORD, the first,
    and with the last; I am He. [†]

[5]The coastlands have seen and are afraid,
    the ends of the earth tremble;
    they have drawn near and come.
[6]Every one helps his neighbor,
    and says to his brother, "Take courage!"
[7]The craftsman encourages the goldsmith,
    and he who smooths with the hammer him
        who strikes the anvil,
saying of the soldering, "It is good";
    and they fasten it with nails so that it
        cannot be moved.

* LXX Who raised up righteousness   † LXX I AM the first, and I AM the future

OVERVIEW: Churches (THEODORET) and Christians are like islands in a sea of sin and persecution (THEODORET, AMBROSE) through which God calls his people to follow in his path of righteousness (EUSEBIUS), as he destroys the tyranny of sin through his Son (CYRIL). This is the righteousness Paul spoke about in the New Testament (THEODORET)—the righteousness of Christ that would not fail (JEROME). The righteousness God

calls for has always been the same in the Old and New Testaments (THEODORET).

When Isaiah speaks of the Lord who is the first and the future, he affirms the Son's coeternity with God (GREGORY OF NYSSA). Although the words ingenerate, unoriginate and immortal are not found here, they are definitely implied in the words and therefore cannot be considered unscriptural (GREGORY OF NAZIANZUS). The call of salvation here is a universal call to Christians, and to their neighbors as well, who witness the Christian's life and worship (EUSEBIUS). Once a person has experienced the glory of God, there is no way he or she wants to keep this hidden (THEODORET). The good news of the gospel also naturally leads to generosity of spirit (CYRIL). And yet, in the face of this good news, there are still those who make idols. They know they have made them with their own hands but still worship them (ISHO'DAD, THEODORET).

41:1 Coastlands

THE CHURCHES AS ISLANDS. THEODORET OF CYR: He calls the churches "islands," because they receive the assault of the waves of persecutors and because they are founded on the rock. He gives the title of "princes" to the heralds of truth, who have become changed from their [previous state] after their call: "Follow me," says [the Scripture] and I will make you fishers of men."[1] They have consequently taken on new strength: it was no longer fish drawn from a single lake, but humans drawn from the entire world that they made their catch. COMMENTARY ON ISAIAH 12.41.1.[2]

CHRISTIANS ARE LIKE ISLANDS IN SEAS OF SIN. AMBROSE: "Be you renewed, O islands," because, just like islands, we are surrounded on the sea of this world by waves of sin. These islands were renewed by the forgiveness of sins through the coming of the Lord. THE PRAYER OF JOB AND DAVID 4.9.34.[3]

41:2 Who Raised Up Righteousness

THE VICTORIOUS PATH OF SALVATION. EUSEBIUS OF CAESAREA: For it was a work of righteousness not only for the Jews but also for the other nations to be called to the knowledge of God. So who is raising up this righteousness from the dawn of the light? Who is calling all to follow him? Who is the one offering this to all the

peoples so as to shock the kings of the nations and to confound the foremost among them? God resists and tames those who attack this work, sweeping away the fighters with a word of righteousness, as they are conquered by the righteousness of God. It also serves to win over those who follow this word. He makes a rough way for the feet of the enemies of righteousness. He makes smooth a path for the feet of those who walk in peace. COMMENTARY ON ISAIAH 2.19.[4]

GOD DESTROYED THE TYRANNY OF SIN THROUGH CHRIST. CYRIL OF ALEXANDRIA: The wonder of God is not only found rightly in the magnificent work he did in the creation. For he has done nothing less than save the inhabitants of the earth, delivering the human race from death and destruction and the devil's snare. For he has condemned the sin that had become master through our sins, so that he has justified through faith those who are able to be with him. He became for us righteousness and redemption and sanctification before God the Father.[5] COMMENTARY ON ISAIAH 3.5.41.2.[6]

RIGHTEOUSNESS FOR BELIEVERS. THEODORET OF CYR: Of this righteousness, the blessed Paul has said in his turn: "It is from God that we have been given wisdom, righteousness, sanctification and redemption."[7] When this righteousness arose and pervaded the world, kings were dismayed, tyrants were conquered, all kinds of torments were suppressed; the persecuted overcame their persecutors, and, as if rejoicing in great peace, they ran the course that was set before them.[8] However, the words "it will not come" are not to be found in the Septuagint.... They show clearly that righteousness will not come for all but [only] for believers; for the ungodly did not even desire to pay attention to divine messages. COMMENTARY ON ISAIAH 12.41.2.[9]

---

[1]Mt 4:19. [2]ITA 598*; SC 295:416. [3]FC 65:417-18. [4]GCS 57(9):259. [5]See 1 Cor 1:30. [6]PG 70:828. [7]1 Cor 1:30. [8]See 2 Tim 4:1-8. [9]ITA 598-99*; SC 295:416-18.

41:3 His Feet Have Not Trod

THE INDEFATIGABLE SAVIOR. JEROME: "His feet will not trod the path," that is, he will not feel the labor of life or any fatigue from human weakness, but he "will drink from the torrent on the way, and therefore, will lift up his head."[10] . . . That which we interpreted as referring to the person of Christ, some refer to Cyrus, the king of the Persians, . . . while some of the Jews think this is said about Abraham. COMMENTARY ON ISAIAH 12.3.[11]

41:4 The "First" Has Called the Generations

GOD REMAINS THE SAME. THEODORET OF CYR: From the beginning, [Isaiah] says, God has made announcements concerning righteousness. He made the covenant with Abraham in these terms: "All the nations of the earth shall be blessed in your seed,"[12] and he [renewed] the covenant with Isaac, Jacob, Moses and David. This is what he has likewise announced through other prophets. "I, God, I AM the first, and I AM the future." The One who gave the Old Testament, he says, is not different from the One who established the New. The divine nature is one, always the same and unchanging. COMMENTARY ON ISAIAH 12.41.4.[13]

THE SON IS COETERNAL WITH THE FATHER. GREGORY OF NYSSA: "I, the Lord, the first, and with the last; I am he." There is no "God" "before" God, nor can we call "God" that which is "after" God. (For that which is after God is the creation, and that which is before God is nothing, and nothing is not God, or, one should rather say, that which is "before" God is God in his eternal blessedness, defined in contradistinction to nothing.) . . . . For if it is the Father who speaks in this way, he bears witness to the Son that he is not "after" himself. For if the Son is God and whatever is "after" the Father is not God, it is clear that the saying bears witness to the truth that the Son is in the Father and not after the Father. If,

[however,] one were to grant that this statement is of the Son, the phrase "no other has been before me" will be a clear allusion that he whom we contemplate "in the Beginning" is apprehended together with the eternity of the Beginning. AGAINST EUNOMIUS 5.1.[14]

IMMORTAL AND INDESTRUCTIBLE. GREGORY OF NAZIANZUS: [Where] do you get those fortresses of yours, "ingenerate" and "unoriginate," from— or where the term "immortal"? Show us the express words, or we cross them out as unscriptural, and you will be dead as a result of your own principles, since the words, the wall of defense you trusted in,[15] will have been destroyed. Is it not plain that these terms derived from passages that imply, without actually mentioning them? Which passages? What about "I am the first, and I am hereafter,"[16] and "Before me there is no other God and after me there shall be none,"[17] "for everything that exists" [God is saying] "is mine, without beginning or ending"?[18] You have taken the truths that there is nothing before God and that he has no prior case, and you have given him the titles "unoriginate" and "ingenerate." The fact that there is no halt to his ongoing existence means he is "immortal" and "indestructible." ON THE HOLY SPIRIT, THEOLOGICAL ORATION 5(31).23.[19]

41:6 Everyone Helps a Neighbor

GOD'S SALVATION EXTENDS TO CHARITABLE PAGANS. EUSEBIUS OF CAESAREA: You, Jacob, now ponder such things, the Savior of everything did not privilege you over the salvation of other human beings but chose the things that suited you, while to the rest of the nations he announced an exchange, summoning them all to knowledge of him. . . . He calls "islands" the churches from all the nations, since those par-

---

[10]Ps 110:7 (109:7 LXX). [11]AGLB 35:1296-98. [12]Gen 26:4. [13]ITA 599; SC 295:418. [14]NPNF 2 5:173*. [15]See Ps 31:2 (30:3 LXX). [16]Is 44:6. [17]Is 43:10. [18]Ps 50:12 (49:12 LXX). [19]FGFR 291.

tially submerged under the evil of life are like those islands in the sea. . . .

For it is not only those who are called who come to salvation, but also those nearby according to the laws of neighbor love (*philanthropy*). So they say these things to those worshiping God nearby, who would like to be their brothers and friends yet who are still "out of place." There was a time when our own craftsman prevailed, beating out idols, and the smith struck with a hammer his gods. But now we know that they are nothing and recognize the illusion of our forefathers. COMMENTARY ON ISAIAH 2.19.[20]

ONCE ENLIGHTENED, YOU CANNOT HIDE GOD'S GLORY. THEODORET OF CYR: Those who formerly have been in error, as soon as they have benefited from the light of the knowledge of God, cannot bear to hide his glory but call all people to participate in it. "And one will say," that is to say, one who is removed from the darkness of ignorance. COMMENTARY ON ISAIAH 12.41.6.[21]

THE REALIZATION OF GOD'S GENEROSITY. CYRIL OF ALEXANDRIA: The meaning of this is as follows: They have approached and come together, no longer staying apart, not alienated from each other through sin but as if brought close through spiritually taking possession, are joined into one faith and a common spirit. For once they tasted of the Lord and understood that he is good[22] and began to wonder at the beauty of

his truth, they did not only keep the gift for themselves but each one generously came to the aid of his brother and his friend. COMMENTARY ON ISAIAH 3.5.41.4-6.[23]

41:7 The Craftsman Encourages the Goldsmith

THE FOOLISHNESS OF IDOLATRY. ISHO'DAD OF MERV: By mocking those who make the idols, [Isaiah] says, "The craftsman encourages the goldsmith, who strikes with the hammer." That is, even though they know that their hands have made them and that "they fasten them with nails," they are not ashamed to adore them. COMMENTARY ON ISAIAH 41.7.[24]

THE CRAFTSMANSHIP OF THE ARTISANS. THEODORET OF CYR: Look, [Isaiah] says, what the newcomers to the truth say to those who are still held prisoner to the error of idols, to show them their impotence: idols can neither walk nor hold themselves up without being fastened with nails. As for the phrase "it is a piece well joined," the three interpreters have rendered it, "it is a joint well made"; that is to say, the joints are well fitted. It has been put together by craftsmanship. COMMENTARY ON ISAIAH 12.41.7.[25]

---

[20]GCS 57(9):258-60. [21]ITA 600*; SC 295:418. [22]Ps 34:8 (33:9 LXX). [23]PG 70:832-33. [24]CSCO 303(128):44. [25]ITA 600; SC 295:418-20.

41:8-16 ISRAEL MY SERVANT

[8]But you, Israel, my servant,
  Jacob, whom I have chosen,
  the offspring of Abraham, my friend;

[9]you whom I took from the ends of the earth,
  and called from its farthest corners,
saying to you, "You are my servant,

I have chosen you and not cast you off";
fear not, for I am with you,
be not dismayed, for I am your God;
I will strengthen you, I will help you,
I will uphold you with my victorious right
hand.

¹¹Behold, all who are incensed against you
shall be put to shame and confounded;
those who strive against you
shall be as nothing and shall perish.
¹²You shall seek those who contend with you,
but you shall not find them;
those who war against you
shall be as nothing at all.
¹³For I, the LORD your God,
hold your right hand;

it is I who say to you, "Fear not,
I will help you."

¹⁴Fear not, you worm Jacob,
you men of Israel!
I will help you, says the LORD;
your Redeemer is the Holy One of Israel.
¹⁵Behold, I will make of you a threshing sledge,
new, sharp, and having teeth;
you shall thresh the mountains and crush them,
and you shall make the hills like chaff;
¹⁶you shall winnow them and the wind shall
carry them away,
and the tempest shall scatter them.
And you shall rejoice in the LORD;
in the Holy One of Israel you shall glory.

OVERVIEW: The seed of Abraham to which Isaiah refers are those who in faith receive and pass on the Word of God. This happened in the New Testament among those apostles who were Jewish as well as Gentiles (EUSEBIUS, THEODORET). Though this seed is small in number, its message is powerful and will grow (EUSEBIUS) as God provides courage to strengthen the church (GREGORY OF NYSSA). The prophecy is fulfilled in the end of the Babylonian captivity and in the overcoming of the enemies of the apostles and martyrs (THEODORET).

Enemies of God's ministers will end up as though they never existed (CYRIL). The worm is a humble creature but effective in undermining error (THEODORET). It is not wrong to see the metaphor of the worm as anticipating the work of Jesus (EPHREM). The worm-church has a hidden, rapidly working power that burrows through adversity. Jesus experienced such adversity, being fully human just as Christians are (THEODORET). But he ultimately prevailed, and his humble church will prevail in the world as well (EPHREM). Its preaching will overcome the

opposition latent in our hearts (JEROME).

41:8-9 Israel My Servant

APOSTLES AS SERVANTS. EUSEBIUS OF CAESAREA: Since the seed of Abraham is spread over all the earth, he speaks about this. . . . In the same way Paul the apostle shows the Jews, "first it was necessary that the word be proclaimed to you, but since you turn away, we are going to the Gentiles."[1] Isaiah addresses those among them, therefore, who would obey the calling and the Gospel word that is handed on: "You whom I took from the ends of the earth and called from its farthest corners." Many from the Jews, during the apostolic times, handed on the word of Christ, not only to the land of Judah but also to the rest of the nations. For the seed of Abraham rises quickly, until the time when God remembers the election of the apostolic chorus, and he says to them, "you are my son," or, according to the other

[1]Loose rendering of Acts 13:46.

interpretations, "you are my servant; I have chosen you and not abandoned you." Probably the divine apostle equates the servant with himself, made present as one worthy of the honor of being a servant of the Savior, since also from the first the word proclaimed this, saying, "great to you are those called 'my servant.'"[2] COMMENTARY ON ISAIAH 2.20.[3]

BELIEVERS ARE DESCENDANTS OF ISRAEL. THEODORET OF CYR: To Israel [Isaiah] awards praise at one time, then later addresses accusations. Far from acting in a contradictory manner, he does things in consonance. For those who believe are descendants of Israel, as are also those who crucified Jesus. It is, therefore, natural that [Isaiah] should praise one and accuse the other. Here, in any case, he has recalled his promises and his benefits of former times: he led their patriarch [Abraham] out of the land of the Chaldeans. He delivered their whole race from the domination of the Egyptians; and he deemed them worthy of all kinds of attention. COMMENTARY ON ISAIAH 12.41.8.[4]

41:10 I Am with You

THE "WORM" JACOB. EUSEBIUS OF CAESAREA: He adds that he is to strengthen and sustain those undergoing afflictions at the hands of those [who oppose God] with the vision of the goal that awaits them. He encourages with good news of God speaking to you without deceit: "I am the Lord and God, and I strengthen your right arm," and I say to you, "Do not fear, I will help you." In the Septuagint, "I will help you, do not fear, you worm Jacob," does not appear. This one who was after the former people called "chosen" is now called worm through its worm-like subjection to the cities of the unbelieving nations and all of their polytheistic errors. In addition, what is perfect and special in the apostolic preaching will destroy and remove the demonic energies from the depth of human thinking. Indeed, the Savior called himself a worm, saying "I am a worm and

no man,"[5] a disgrace among people and an object of their contempt. Since there were only a few who were the Savior's disciples, there being twelve apostles, therefore the Septuagint says, "Israel, the very few." COMMENTARY ON ISAIAH 2.20.[6]

THE GOD OF COURAGE. GREGORY OF NYSSA: For to none other than to God does it belong to implant courage in the fearful, saying to the fainthearted, "Fear not, for I am with you, be not dismayed," as says the psalmist, "Yes, though I walk through the valley of the shadow of death, I will fear no evil, for you are with me."[7] AGAINST EUNOMIUS 2.15.[8]

41:11 Put to Shame

THE DELIVERANCE FROM BABYLON. THEODORET OF CYR: This is what already happened figuratively in the epoch of the Babylonians, since the God of the universe destroyed their empire, liberated the Jews from bitter servitude and brought them back to the land of their ancestors. However, this deliverance applies properly and truly to the holy apostles and to the victorious martyrs: their enemies are covered with shame, their persecutors have today disappeared and are unknown, whereas the defenders of the truth attract all the attention and are known by all. COMMENTARY ON ISAIAH 12.41.12.[9]

41:13 Holding Israel's Hand

DO NOT BE AFRAID. CYRIL OF ALEXANDRIA: There are many who think of the holy mysteries and the saving message in disrespectful ways, but they amount to nothing, and such impious adversaries will perish. For those who oppose the divine agents of preaching are doing no less than fighting against the teachings of godliness. . . .

---

[2]Is 49:6 LXX. [3]GCS 57(9):261. [4]ITA 600*; SC 295:420. [5]Ps 22:6 (21:7 LXX). [6]GCS 57(9):262. [7]Ps 23:4 (22:4 LXX). [8]NPNF 2 5:134*. [9]ITA 601*; SC 295:420-22.

For thousands will make war against God's ministers, but these will end up as though they never existed and will clearly be brought low, falling under the machinery of the wrath of God. [Isaiah] tells them to quit relying on human strength and their own foolhardiness, saying, "I am your God who strengthens your arm," that is, I am the one who supports you and makes you prevail in any test. I say to you, "Do not be afraid, O little Israel." COMMENTARY ON ISAIAH 3.5.41.11-14.[10]

CHRIST POSSESSES A HUMAN MIND AND SOUL. THEODORET OF CYR: When we hear the prophet say, "You, Israel, my child, Jacob whom I have chosen, the seed of Abraham, whom I have loved,"[11] we do not think, do we, that the Jews are only flesh and not complete human beings composed of bodies and rational souls? . . . And [don't we think] that the seed of Abraham is not without a soul and not without a mind but that it possesses everything that belongs to Abraham's nature? . . . We confess one Son, who, according to the divine apostle,[12] took hold of the seed of Abraham and brought about the salvation of human beings. DIALOGUE I.[13]

41:14 Jacob, the Worm

JESUS MAKES SENSE OF THE PROPHECY. EPHREM THE SYRIAN: The Spirit described his generation as a worm that was without meaning. The type that the Holy Spirit shaped attains its meaning. HYMNS ON THE NATIVITY 1.10.[14]

THE FOOLISH SHAME THE WISE. THEODORET OF CYR: This shows clearly that the prophetic text applies to those who have believed in the Lord. It is a small part of Israel that believed, while the major part refused to. That is why Paul said that even at the present time there

remains a remnant according to God's gracious election. . . .[15] As for the name "worm," it fits very well. In the first place, this remnants' appearance was contemptible. In fact, this is what the divine apostle meant when he said, "God chose the foolish of the world to shame the wise."[16] But Isaiah calls them worms for another reason. The worm that lodges in wood of poor quality will in a short time wear it down. Similarly, those who are athletes of the truth will, while hidden and imperceptible, destroy the error of the idols. COMMENTARY ON ISAIAH 12.41.14.[17]

ENCOURAGEMENT FOR THE PEOPLE OF ISRAEL. EPHREM THE SYRIAN: Therefore, you will subdue kings and kingdoms with your frailty and will overturn their schemes and proud designs. So [Isaiah] calls the Jews, about whom he is speaking here, "worm," in order that they may understand that they cannot rely on their strength; nonetheless, their weakness will not hinder them, since worms are able to consume hard wood, so that, in the future, they will destroy the pride and power of very strong kingdoms. COMMENTARY ON ISAIAH 41.14.[18]

THE CHURCH'S PREACHING. JEROME: "I have placed you like a new threshing wagon [sledge] with jagged wheels." . . . We can also say that the person of the church is in a new wagon with the jagged wheels of the preaching of the gospel, which cannot be worked at all in the old way of the letter but in the new way of the Spirit, and which wears away the hardest hearts of unbelievers, separating the wheat from the chaff. COMMENTARY ON ISAIAH 12.4.[19]

---

[10]PG 70:836-37. [11]Is 41:8. [12]Heb 2:16. [13]FC 106:37-38. [14]CSCO 186(82):2. [15]Rom 11:5. [16]1 Cor 1:27. [17]SC 295:422. [18]ESOO 2:88-89. [19]AGLB 35:1303.

41:17-29 THE MASTER OF IDOLS

¹⁷*When the poor and needy seek water,*
   and there is none,
   and their tongue is parched with thirst,
I the LORD *will answer them,*
   I the God of Israel will not forsake them.
¹⁸*I will open rivers on the bare heights,*
   and fountains in the midst of the valleys;
I will make the wilderness a pool of water,
   and the dry land springs of water.
¹⁹*I will put in the wilderness the cedar,*
   the acacia, the myrtle, and the olive;
I will set in the desert the cypress,
   the plane and the pine together;
²⁰*that men may see and know,*
   may consider and understand together,
that the hand of the LORD *has done this,*
   the Holy One of Israel has created it.

²¹*Set forth your case, says the* LORD;
   bring your proofs, says the King of Jacob.
²²*Let them bring them, and tell us what is to*
      happen.
Tell us the former things, what they are,
   that we may consider them,
that we may know their outcome;
   or declare to us the things to come.
²³*Tell us what is to come hereafter,*
   that we may know that you are gods;

do good, or do harm,
   that we may be dismayed and terrified.
²⁴*Behold, you are nothing,*
   and your work is nought;
   an abomination is he who chooses you.

²⁵*I stirred up one from the north, and he has*
      come,
   from the rising of the sun, and he shall call
      on my name;
*he shall trample*ʳ *on rulers as on mortar,*
   as the potter treads clay.
²⁶*Who declared it from the beginning, that we*
      might know,
   and beforetime, that we might say, "He is
      right"?
There was none who declared it, none who
      proclaimed,
   none who heard your words.
²⁷*I first have declared it to Zion,*ˢ
   and I give to Jerusalem a herald of good
      tidings.
²⁸*But when I look there is no one;*
   among these there is no counselor
   who, when I ask, gives an answer.
²⁹*Behold, they are all a delusion;*
   their works are nothing;
   their molten images are empty wind.

r Cn: Heb *come*   s Cn: Heb *first to Zion, Behold, behold them*

OVERVIEW: Prophetic speech about God is often metaphorical (TERTULLIAN). Isaiah's promise of pools in the desert, for instance, was literally offered to Gentile believers later in the Gospel of John (THEODORET). Trees denote people of a deepened understanding that arises out of their virtues (JEROME). Holy people are those who give true refreshment in this life (CYRIL). Not only does God show his supremacy over idols, but also he demonstrates that he is the master and lord even of the demons (JEROME). Idols obviously have no power to change anything in the real world (THEODORET), and following idolatrous conceptions of God ultimately leads to emptiness and judgment (JEROME). Thus, the reign of idolatry is attacked from all sides by God through his church as the oracles are silenced and truth reigns instead (THEODORET).

He who is the only incarnate Word of God is by divine nature and right king, but he is also said to be elected by his people (CYRIL). They, in turn, are encouraged by him to march through the church, which is the heavenly Jerusalem, to the heavenly position that he will give them as their only true comforter (EUSEBIUS). Idolatry is stupid as well as impious (THEODORET).

41:18 I Will Open Rivers

PROPHETIC SPEECH IS OFTEN METAPHORICAL. TERTULLIAN: God is not offering his services as a water manager or a farmer when he says, "I will open rivers in a dry land; I will plant in the wilderness the cedar and the box tree." AGAINST MARCION 3.5.[1]

POOLS IN THE DESERT. THEODORET OF CYR: He refers in this way to those who have been entrusted with the grace of instruction. For he has said in the holy Gospels: "He who believes in me, as the Scripture has said, out of his heart will flow rivers of living water."[2] "I will make the desert pools of water and a parched land springs." He gives the name "desert" to the Gentiles; this promise had been made to them similarly in the preceding passages. COMMENTARY ON ISAIAH 12.41.18.[3]

41:19 The Cedar and the Acacia

THE SYMPHONY OF THE VIRTUES IN THE LIGHT OF CHRIST. JEROME: All these [types of trees] are equally placed in solitude, lest even one chord from the harp of the Lord and any virtue of the graces of the church seem to be missing. They are planted in the desert so that all might understand and recognize with a common mind that

the hand of the Lord has accomplished all these things, so that in the desert of the nations there came rivers of virtues and in a land once a desert and full of salty water the cedar and cypress and other trees may grow, whose height and stature rush to the skies. The olive tree is the same tree that supplies both light and relaxation after working. COMMENTARY ON ISAIAH 12.5.[4]

HOLY PEOPLE BRING SPIRITUAL REFRESHMENT. CYRIL OF ALEXANDRIA: The water was not life-giving. For they were not able to satisfy those who longed for truth from their teachings. Their tongues remained parched from thirst. But I will hear them, says the God of Israel, and I will not abandon them. For he had mercy on the mass of those who strayed and did not leave them without gifts from above, but rather he gave to them in fullness, and this in such a way as is finely described in the verses that follow. . . . The desert and the land short of water is the region of the Gentiles. The desert that will run dry and barren of any flowering growth, meaning spiritual growth, is the way of shriveling, where the wild trees are those useful only for burning in fire. The water allows the nations to bear fruit. To those who were once thirsty he says, "I will make rivers flow on the mountains," that is, holy people who are enriched by the divine word from above and pour out like flowing streams to the thirsty. COMMENTARY ON ISAIAH 3.5.41.16-20.[5]

41:21 Bring Your Proofs

MOSES AND THE PROPHETS REVEAL PAST AND FUTURE EVENTS. THEODORET OF CYR: To the expression "your judgment draws near," Symmachus has given the following interpretation: "Present your case, the Lord has said; bring up your solid supports, the king of Jacob has said." Become judges, he says, between myself and the idols; produce your solid props or, according to

---

[1]ANF 3:324. [2]Jn 7:38. [3]ITA 602*; SC 295:424. [4]AGLB 35:1307. [5]PG 70:840-41.

Theodotion, "your firm supports," that is to say, the idols. Let them reveal the future; let them inform us of [the things] that have happened from the beginning. I, for my part, have not ceased to do the one and the other. Through my servant Moses, I have even taught what took place before the creation of humanity. As for the future, I have revealed it through [Moses] and through the other prophets. COMMENTARY ON ISAIAH 12.41.23.[6]

41:22 Tell Us What Is to Happen

GOD CONTROLS EVEN THE DEMONS. JEROME: "Tell us what is to come hereafter, that we may know that you are gods; do good or do harm, that we may be dismayed and terrified." . . . It is a further sign that the idols are not gods that they can do neither good nor evil. It is not saying that the idols or the demons inhabiting idols do not do evil frequently, but that unless God permits them to have power they cannot do so. So in the Gospel demons ask that they might have power over a herd of pigs,[7] and in Job we read that without the Lord's command the devil is not able to destroy livestock or goods.[8] COMMENTARY ON ISAIAH 12.6.[9]

IDOLS LACK POWER AND PRESCIENCE. THEODORET OF CYR: If you do not want to demonstrate your personal strength from your knowledge or prescience, then do so through a demonstration of your power. Demonstrate your power, whether it be kind or punishing. "It is I who will put to death and I who will bring to life, I who will strike down and I who will heal. There is no one who can deliver out of my hands."[10] But because you are lacking in knowledge and in power, I will now expose your emptiness. "They have dug you from the ground as an abomination." For whether they are wooden or from gold, silver or bronze, they all have their origin from the earth. COMMENTARY ON ISAIAH 12.41.24.[11]

41:25 One from the North

JUDGMENT ON THE EMPTINESS OF FALSE TEACHING. JEROME: This is spoken against the idols and those who after the coming of Christ still refused to abandon them but maintained them in their error. And he says that he will raise up a people of nations from the north. . . . But this will be the response of all, all those who follow vanity and winds and adore the works of their own hands. What we have said about the idols and the peoples we can refer to the teachings of corruption and to their princes, the heresiarchs, that when Christ announced peace to the church and showed it the way of truth, they followed error so as to be like wind and a whirlwind. COMMENTARY ON ISAIAH 12.7.[12]

THE DESTRUCTION OF THE IDOLS. THEODORET OF CYR: He threatens the idols with destruction. He calls "the one who comes from the east" the righteousness that has awakened, concerning which he had earlier said, "Who has roused righteousness from the east?"[13] And he calls the one from the north the church drawn from the nations, toward which came the one from Theman or from the "rainy country," according to the other translators. For God came from Theman,[14] that is, from the south. It is to this church that the Master Christ has revealed himself, finding it scattered by the deceit of the idols. He warmed [the church] with the southern rays and led it to life. Its leaders, priests and teachers have trampled the idols under their feet. COMMENTARY ON ISAIAH 12.41.25.[15]

41:26 None Declared It

THE ORACLES ARE SILENCED. THEODORET OF CYR: And what has been accomplished confirms the text: the oracles spread through all parts of the earth and of the sea have ceased to speak, and those who used to attend to them open-

---

[6]*ITA* 604*; SC 295:426-28. [7]Mt 8:31. [8]Job 1:12. [9]*AGLB* 35:1307, 1309-10. [10]Deut 32:39. [11]SC 295:428. [12]*AGLB* 35:1311-13. [13]Is 41:2. [14]See Hab 3:3. [15]SC 295:428-30.

mouthed have now turned away from them to learn the truth. COMMENTARY ON ISAIAH 12.41.26.[16]

THE MEANS OF CONSOLATION. CYRIL OF ALEXANDRIA: "I will give a leader to Zion, and I will console Jerusalem as I go." . . . Again the multitude of those going astray is promised the revealing of the Savior, through whom each one under heaven has been saved and is summoned to the recognition of the truth. So that we could have a guide who would be able and skilled to lead us along the path of salvation, the only-begotten Son of God became a human being. And though he was King by nature in that he is considered to be God and from God the Father and ruler of all things with all creation under his feet, he is said to be elected king among us. COMMENTARY ON ISAIAH 3.5.41.27-28.[17]

41:27-29 Good Tidings to Jerusalem

THE WAY OF ASCENT TO GOD. EUSEBIUS OF CAESAREA: I want you to know, God is saying, I have intended from the beginning of everything to give authority to my church over all things, and the authority of my kingdom I shall give to my Zion. And I shall stir up my Jerusalem, preparing it as the road on which are all those who labor in it towards the thrice-blessed goal—to the God over all and his heavenly kingdom. COMMENTARY ON ISAIAH 2.21.[18]

ISAIAH MOCKS IDOLS AND THEIR MAKERS. THEODORET OF CYR: It is in a perfectly appropriate way that he both shows the stupid nature of the idols and accuses of impiety those who have fashioned them. For if the idols are inanimate, their makers are full of stupidity and impiety. COMMENTARY ON ISAIAH 12.41.29.[19]

[16]ITA 605; SC 295:430. [17]PG 70:848. [18]GCS 57(9):267. [19]ITA 606; SC 295:432.

42:1-4 THE SERVANT OF JUSTICE

[1]Behold my servant, whom I uphold,
  my chosen, in whom my soul delights;
I have put my Spirit upon him,
  he will bring forth justice to the nations.
[2]He will not cry or lift up his voice,
  or make it heard in the street;
[3]a bruised reed he will not break,
and a dimly burning wick he will not
    quench;
  he will faithfully bring forth justice.
[4]He will not fail[t] or be discouraged[u]
  till he has established justice in the earth;
  and the coastlands wait for his law.

t Or burn dimly   u Or bruised

OVERVIEW: The messianic servant is of the seed of Abraham, which points to his full humanity as well as to his ultimate fulfillment of Israel's role as servant in God's plan (EUSEBIUS). As servant, he humbles himself to redeem (GREGORY OF NA-ZIANZUS) and rescue human nature (PSEUDO-DIONYSIUS). Those who have the serenity of the servant show they too are his servants (ATHANASIUS). The Word brings peace to all who are his, providing a place for all with their various weaknesses (HIPPOLYTUS). The highest one became the lowest (AUGUSTINE), offering healing instead of judgment to those who are his (EUSEBIUS). He offers a gentle and peaceful kingdom (IRENAEUS) to all among the nations who trust in his name (THEODORET). What was prophesied about the servant saints of the Hebrew Bible is then ultimately gathered up in Christ (JEROME), who sought to fan the flickering flame of Jewish faith (JEROME)—but with tenderness (BENEDICT). Thus, when the people are about to be extinguished, Christ offers a hope that will not fail (ISHO'DAD), sealed in his resurrection (EUSEBIUS).

42:1 Behold My Servant

CHRIST THE SERVANT. EUSEBIUS OF CAESAREA: Although this very great person is not the one who was in the mind of those hearing the prophecy the first time, he is not here called "Jacob" or "Israel" or "the seed of Abraham," so clearly the Christ of God is meant here, just as the Evangelist paid witness: "I have set my Spirit on him, and he will execute judgment on the nations."[1] And after many things have taken place in the nations, which were not made fit to be counted in the apostolic chorus, the nations will hope in him. But in Isaiah's prophecy the names of Jacob and Israel are missing. Who else could this be, the one called servant of God and his chosen one? Therefore it continues, "My soul delights in him." For only he is the chosen one of God, and the so-called soul of God was delighting in him. In a manner similar to referring to the feet, hands, fingers and eyes of God, Scriptures make use of the term "soul" in relation to God. ... He is "chosen," not in the same way as the apostles, since it is to him alone that it is said, "whom my soul esteems," but also "the Spirit of God was dwelling in him alone."[2] "For in him the fullness of the deity dwelled bodily."[3] For the Spirit is given to the one coming forth "from the root of Jesse,"[4] the unique Word of God, whom the apostle revealed saying, "The Lord is the Spirit."[5] For he alone, pouring out the Spirit of inheritance, worked all things

outwardly concerning the worldwide judgment on the nations, so that all would be prepared for the coming of God's verdict. COMMENTARY ON ISAIAH 2.22.[6]

CHRIST HUMBLES HIMSELF TO REDEEM HUMAN NATURE. GREGORY OF NAZIANZUS: Next is the fact of his being called Servant[7] and serving many well, and that it is a great thing for him to be called the Child of God. For in truth he was in servitude to flesh and to birth and to the conditions of our life with a view to our liberation, and to that of all those whom he has saved, who were in bondage under sin. What greater destiny can befall humanity's humble state than that it should be intermingled with God and by this intermingling should be deified, and that we should be so visited by the Dayspring from on high,[8] that even that holy thing that should be born should be called the Son of the Highest, and that there should be bestowed on him a name that is above every name?[9] And what else can this be than God?—and that every knee should bow to him that was made of no reputation for us, and that mingled the form of God with the form of a servant, and that "all the house of Israel should know that God has made him both Lord and Christ"?[10] For all this was done by the action of the Begotten and by the good pleasure of him that begat him. ON THE SON, THEOLOGICAL ORATION 4(30).3.[11]

THE GOODNESS OF GOD'S PROVIDENTIAL GIFTS. PSEUDO-DIONYSIUS: The goodness of the Deity has endless love for humanity and never ceased from benignly pouring out on us its providential gifts.[12] ... It made it possible for us to escape from the domain of the rebellious, and it did this not through overwhelming force, but, as Scripture mysteriously tells us, by an act of judgment accomplished in all righteousness. Benefi-

---

[1]Mt 12:18. [2]Is 11:2. [3]Col 2:9. [4]Is 11:10. [5]2 Cor 3:17. [6]GCS 57(9):269. [7]Cf. Is 49:6; 53:11. [8]See Lk 1:78. [9]Phil 2:9. [10]Acts 2:36. [11]NPNF 2 7:310*. [12]See Tit 3:4.

cently God's goodness wrought a complete change in our nature. It filled our shadowed and unshaped minds with a kindly, divine light and adorned them with loveliness suitable to their divinized state. It saved our nature from almost complete wreckage and delivered the dwelling place of our soul from the most accursed passion and from destructive defilement. Finally, it showed us a supramundane uplifting and an inspired way of life in shaping ourselves to it as fully as lay in our power. ECCLESIASTICAL HIERARCHY 3.3.11.[13]

THE PEACE OF THOSE WHO ARE GOD'S. ATHANASIUS: It is possible, with the help of God, easily to distinguish the presence of the good and the bad; a vision of the holy ones is not agitated. "He shall not protest and cry out; none will hear his voice."[14] It occurs so quietly and gently that joy and gladness and confidence are at once born in the soul.... The soul's thoughts remain untroubled and calm, so that, enlightened of itself, it contemplates those who appear. LIFE OF ST. ANTHONY 35.[15]

THE INCLUSIVITY OF THE WORD'S COMPASSION. HIPPOLYTUS: As the Word shows his compassion and his denial of all preferential treatment among all the saints, he enlightens them and adapts them to that which is advantageous for them. He is like a skillful physician, understanding the weakness of each one. The ignorant he loves to teach. The erring he turns again to his own true way. By those who live by faith he is easily found. To those of pure eye and holy heart, who desire to knock at the door, he opens immediately. For he casts away none of his servants as unworthy of the divine mysteries. He does not esteem the rich person more highly than the poor, nor does he despise the poor person for his poverty. He does not disdain the barbarian, nor does he set the eunuch aside as no man. He does not hate the female on account of the woman's act of disobedience in the beginning, nor does he reject the male on account of the man's transgression. But he seeks all and

desires to save all, wishing to make all the children of God and calling all the saints to one perfect human person. For there is one Son (or Servant) of God, by whom we too, receiving the regeneration through the Holy Spirit, desiring to come all into one perfect and heavenly human person.[16] ON THE ANTICHRIST 3.[17]

THE NAMES OF THE PATRIARCHS ATTEST CHRIST'S TRUE HUMANITY. AUGUSTINE: The passage reads, "Jacob, my son, I will uphold him; Israel, my elect, my soul has assumed him." ... It is true, indeed, that the Vulgate text has "my servant" in place of "Jacob" and "Israel," but the Septuagint translators preferred to make the meaning more explicit, namely, that the prophecy concerns the "Highest" insofar as he became the "lowliest," in the form of a servant. Hence they placed the name of that man from whose stock the "form of a servant" was assumed. It was to him that the Holy Spirit was given. CITY OF GOD 20.30.[18]

42:3 A Bruised Reed

GOD'S SILENT, COMPASSIONATE ROAD TOWARD JUDGMENT. EUSEBIUS OF CAESAREA: He does not say, "Jacob my son and Israel my beloved," but simply "Behold my son and my beloved." Hence, the names of Jacob and Israel are marked with an obelisk in the Septuagint, as if the prophecy were not in the Hebrew. And it is silently omitted by the other translators, as it is not found in the Hebrew.... Therefore, the prophecy does not apply either actually or figuratively to the Jews but only to the Christ of God, to whom clear evidence and the results bear witness. For Christ alone prophesied the future judgment to the Gentiles, quietly sojourning in human life and setting judgment on the earth. And not only did he not break the bruised reed, but so to say he bound it up, setting up and

[13]PDCW 220-21. [14]Is 42:2; Mt 12:19. [15]FC 15:167. [16]Eph 4:13. [17]ANF 5:205*. [18]FC 24:336.

strengthening the weak and the bruised in heart. And just as Christ did not neglect the sick and the corrupt, who needed his medicine, or bruise the repentant with harsh judgment, so he did not quench those who continued in evil and were smoking under the fire of passion by preventing their following their own choice; nor did he punish any of them before the time, reserving the time of their due chastisement for the general judgment. PROOF OF THE GOSPEL 9.15.[19]

A GENTLE AND PEACEFUL KINGDOM. IRENAEUS: By such means was the prophet—very indignant, because of the transgression of the people and the slaughter of the prophets—both taught to act in a more gentle manner, and the Lord's advent was pointed out, that it should be subsequent to that law that was given by Moses, mild and tranquil, in which he would neither break the bruised reed nor quench the smoking flax. The mild and peaceful repose of his kingdom was indicated likewise. For after the wind that rends the mountains, and after the earthquake and after the fire come the tranquil and peaceful times of his kingdom, in which the Spirit of God does, in the most gentle manner, vivify and increase humankind.[20] AGAINST HERESIES 4.20.10.[21]

THE NATIONS TRUST THE NAME. THEODORET OF CYR: [Isaiah] calls him "servant" or "slave," according to the other interpreters, in connection with his humanity. It is in relation to this that he has [also] given him the name of Jacob and Israel, seeing that it is from Jacob, who is also Israel, that [Christ] descended according to the flesh. In the same way he also receives the most Holy Spirit, not insofar as [he is] God—for he lacks nothing—but as man for the purpose of becoming the model for those who have believed in him. Of this gentleness both his words and his deeds give witness: "Learn from me," [Christ] says, "for I am gentle and lowly of heart."[22] Even when he received a blow to the face, he said to the one who struck him, "Friend, if I have spoken evil, bear

witness to the evil; but if well, why do you strike me?"[23] Although he could destroy those who unleashed rage against him by having lightning strike them immediately, he breaks them like a bruised reed and snuffs them like smoldering flax; he has borne their folly. For [Christ] was aware of the outcome of these events, and he knew that the truth would be manifested through them. It was likewise even after he had been delivered over to death; he shone forth anew, filled the earth with truth and had invited the Gentiles to put their hope in him. It is this that the prophetic text has said: "In his name the nations put their trust." COMMENTARY ON ISAIAH 12.42.4.[24]

IS THE SERVANT CHRIST OR JACOB? JEROME: It appears that Matthew the Evangelist did not by preferring the authority of the old interpretation ignore the truth of the Hebrew text. Rather, as a Hebrew among Hebrews and deeply taught in the law of the Lord, Matthew distributed his Hebrew learning to the nations. For if the Septuagint translators are accepted when they write, "Jacob my son, I will lift him up; Israel my chosen, my soul has lifted him up," then how can we understand the text fulfilled in Jesus, since it was obviously written about Jacob and Israel? We read that the blessed Matthew, not only in this verse but in another, has done this: "Out of Egypt I have called my son,"[25] while the Septuagint translated, "Out of Egypt he has called his sons."[26] LETTER 121.2.[27]

CHRIST, THE SPARK OF PURIFYING FIRE. JEROME: For after the coming of the Lord and Savior, who gave the spirit of the gospel interpretation, [Christ] rested in the death of the Jewish letter, with which all works are bruised. Christ did not snuff out the smoking wick, reducing it to ashes. Instead, he ignited a great flame from this little spark, a spark that had almost gone out. The

---

[19]POG 2:182-83. [20]See 1 Kings 19:11-12. [21]ANF 1:490*. [22]Mt 11:29. [23]Jn 18:23; Mt 20:13. [24]ITA 614-15*; SC 295:434. [25]Mt 2:15. [26]Hos 11:1. [27]CSEL 56:9.

result is that the whole earth was ablaze with the fire of the Lord and Savior. Letter 121.2.[28]

Discipline Requires Tenderness. Benedict: [The abbot] must be aware of his own frailty and remember that it is forbidden to break the already bruised reed. We do not mean that he should countenance the growth of vice but that he use discretion and tenderness as he sees it expedient for the different characters of his brothers. He is to endeavor much more to be loved than to be feared. Rule of St. Benedict 64.[29]

A Prophecy of Liberation in Christ. Isho'dad of Merv: "A bruised reed he will not break, and a dimly burning wick he will not quench," that is, [Christ] will not be hard or angered with those who have a feeble spirit. He will not render powerless that strength that is left to them, but he will lead them back to virtue with kindness. [Isaiah] calls a "dimly burning wick" the one whose oil is finished and where there is no greasy matter left. This means, when the people are about to be extinguished because of the afflic-

tion of captivity, he will make them shine against their hope. This is clearly said with regard to Zerubbabel but is evidently accomplished by our Lord, the Savior. Commentary on Isaiah 42.3.[30]

42:4 He Will Not Fail

God's Judgment Established. Eusebius of Caesarea: With truth and boldness to all, he proclaims the judgment of God, which has not ceased to operate. Rather, God's judgment is like light shining through the resurrection of the dead, which the prophetic word announced, saying, "He will give light and not be crushed." For those who planned Christ's death tried to crush him and extinguish him. For it is the nature of all mortal species to be crushed by death. But it did not crush *him*. Christ was the only person of all time who was shown to be stronger than death. Commentary on Isaiah 2.22.[31]

[28]CSEL 56:12. [29]LCC 12:332. [30]CSCO 303(128):44. [31]GCS 57(9):269.

42:5-9 THE NAME OF THE LORD

[5]Thus says God, the Lord,
who created the heavens and stretched them out,
who spread forth the earth and what comes from it,
who gives breath to the people upon it
and spirit to those who walk in it:
[6]"I am the Lord, I have called you in righteousness,
I have taken you by the hand and kept you;
I have given you as a covenant to the people,
a light to the nations,
[7]to open the eyes that are blind,
to bring out the prisoners from the dungeon,
from the prison those who sit in darkness.
[8]I am the Lord, that is my name;
my glory I give to no other,
nor my praise to graven images.
[9]Behold, the former things have come to pass,
and new things I now declare;
before they spring forth
I tell you of them."

Overview: Christ is worshiped as God due to his unique power and glory (Eusebius), which restores order to our body, soul and spirit (Tertullian). His Spirit is given to all who turn from earthly desires (Irenaeus, Origen). The Son and the Spirit work together with the Father as one God in the mission of our salvation (Ambrose) redeeming us from our prison-like state (Epistle of Barnabas) to true Christian freedom, which offers a much better existence (Lactantius). Those who are darkened in intellect and imprisoned by sin are blind (Theodoret). No longer ruled by the blindness of ignorance, we have our spiritual sight restored so that we now can see the Father through the Son (Clement of Alexandria). But God's being can never be reduced to or dependent on our perception of him, nor can it be diminished by comparison with any other being (Gregory of Nazianzus). His glory cannot be shared by idols; it is to be found, rather, "within the life of the Trinity" (Gregory of Nyssa). As the Son possesses the glory of the Father (Theodoret), being of one substance with the Father, the divine-human Christ not only shares in that glory but also shares it with us (Cyril). In this way, he fulfills his promise made to Abraham, Moses and the rest of the prophets (Eusebius) and brings to our humanity the gifts of the "new things" that his divine nature bestows on humanity (Cyril).

42:5 The Lord, the Creator

The Name, Glory and Power. Eusebius of Caesarea: The name by which he will be praised as the Lord and God of all, [Isaiah] says, "I will give to no other" but to you alone, whom I shall grant to be light to the nations. Hence, in the promise the Christ of God is called Lord and God by all the nations, the Father having granted him alone that glory. Next comes "nor will I give my powers to the carved images," or, according to Aquila, "my worship to carved images," or, with Symmachus, "my praise to carved images." . . . According to this, Christ alone is called God

since to him alone and to no other has God, who is above all things, given his glory and power. Commentary on Isaiah 2.22.[1]

Flesh Comes First, Then Spirit. Tertullian: And again, "who gave breath to the people on the earth and spirit to those walking on it." For at first the soul, that is, "breath," was given to the people who go around on the earth, that is, to those acting in flesh in a fleshly manner; then later the Spirit was given to those who walk on the earth, that is, those who subdue the works of the flesh, as the apostle affirms, "Not that which is spiritual first, but that which is animal and then that which is spiritual."[2] For although Adam from the beginning prophesied that great mystery in Christ and the church, "this is now bone of my bone and flesh of my flesh, on which account a man will leave his father and mother and cleave to his wife and they two will become one flesh,"[3] he was subject to a falling of the spirit. On the Soul 11.3-4.[4]

Those Who Turn from Earthly Desires. Irenaeus: The breath of life, which also rendered man [a person] an animated being, is one thing, and the vivifying Spirit another, which also caused him to become spiritual. And for this reason Isaiah said, "Thus says the Lord, who made heaven and established it, who founded the earth and the things therein, and gave breath to the people on it and the Spirit to those walking on it"; thus telling us that breath is indeed given in common to all people on earth but that the Spirit is theirs alone who tread down earthly desires. Against Heresies 5.12.2.[5]

The Universal Participation in the Spirit. Origen: It says, "He who gives spirit to the people who are on the earth, and spirit to them who walk on it." For undoubtedly every one who walks on the earth, that is, every earthly and

---

[1]GCS 57(9):271. [2]1 Cor 15:46. [3]Gen 2:23-24. [4]CCL 2:797. [5]ANF 1:537-38*.

corporeal being, is a partaker of the Holy Spirit that he receives from God.[6] ON FIRST PRINCIPLES 1.3.4.[7]

UNITY OF DIVINITY AND OPERATION. AMBROSE: The Son is both sent and given, and the Spirit also is both sent and given; they have assuredly a oneness of Godhead who have a oneness of action. ON THE HOLY SPIRIT 3.2.10.[8]

42:6 Given as a Covenant

THE LORD KEEPS THE COVENANT. EPISTLE OF BARNABUS: Moses received it, but they were not worthy. But how did we receive it? Learn! Moses received it as a servant, but the Lord himself gave it to us, that we might become the people of inheritance, by suffering for us. And he was made manifest in order that they might fill out the measure of their sins and we might receive the covenant through the Lord Jesus who inherited it, who was prepared for this purpose, in order that by appearing in person and redeeming from the darkness our hearts, which had already been paid over to death and given over to the lawlessness of error, he might establish a covenant in us by his word. For it is written how the Father commands him to redeem us from darkness and to prepare a holy people for himself. Therefore the prophet says, "I, the Lord your God, have called you in righteousness, and I will grasp your hand and strengthen you; and I have given you as a covenant to the people, a light to the nations, to open the eyes of the blind and to release from their shackles those who are bound and from the prisonhouse those who sit in darkness." We understand, therefore, from what we have been redeemed. EPISTLE OF BARNABAS 14.4-7.[9]

THE FULLNESS OF CHRISTIAN FREEDOM. LACTANTIUS: Since, therefore, we were as though blind before, and when we sat as though enclosed by the prison house of foolishness in the darkness, not knowing God and his truth, we were enlightened by him who adopted us by his gracious treatment (his will in our favor). And when he had freed us as from evils and bonds and brought us into the light of wisdom, he recognized us as the heirs of his heavenly kingdom. DIVINE INSTITUTES 4.20.[10]

42:7 Blind Eyes

THE BLINDNESS OF IGNORANCE. THEODORET OF CYR: He calls "blind" here those who are impaired in their intellectual vision; he calls the same people imprisoned by the bonds of sin and held by the darkness of error. After having delivered them from the murk of ignorance and having broken the bonds of sin, he has led them to the light of truth. COMMENTARY ON ISAIAH 12.42.7.[11]

BEHOLD THE FATHER THROUGH THE SON. CLEMENT OF ALEXANDRIA: "The opened eyes of the blind" means [Christ] provided clear knowledge of the Father through the Son. STROMATEIS 1.19.92.2.[12]

42:8 Glory Given to No Other

GOD'S NAMES DO NOT CIRCUMSCRIBE HIM. GREGORY OF NAZIANZUS: The same thing applies to the word *Lord*, which is also used as a name of God. "I am the Lord your God," he says. "This is my name," and "The Lord is his name."[13] But we are making deeper enquiries into a nature that has absolute existence, independent of anything else. The actual, personal being of God in its fullness is neither limited nor cut short by any prior or any subsequent reality—so it was, and so it will be. ON THE SON, THEOLOGICAL ORATION 4(30).18.[14]

GOD WILL NOT GIVE HIS GLORY TO IDOLS. GREGORY OF NYSSA: [Eunomius says,] Receiving

---

[6]Origen later restricts possession of the Spirit to those who are saints. See *On First Principles* 1.3.5-7. Here he is speaking of the common enlivening Spirit that is breathed into all human beings, as it was in Adam in Gen 2:7. [7]OFP 31-32*. [8]NPNF 2 10:137*. [9]AF 313. [10]FC 49:300*. [11]ITA 617; SC 295:438. [12]FC 85:93**. [13]Ex 15:3. [14]FGFR 274*.

glory from the Father, not sharing glory with the Father, for the glory of the Almighty is incommunicable, as [the Lord] has said, "I will not give my glory to another." Who is that "other" to whom God has said that he will not give his glory? The prophet is speaking of the adversary of God, yet Eunomius refers the prophecy to the only-begotten God himself! For when the prophet, speaking in the person of God, had said, "I will not give my glory to another," he added, "neither my praise to graven images." AGAINST EUNOMIUS 2.10.[15]

THE SON POSSESSES THE GLORY OF THE FATHER. THEODORET OF CYR: It is the Son who possesses the glory of the Father, and it is in the glory of the Father that he will manifest himself, for the divinity of the Son and of the Father is one. Thus, if God says that he will not give his glory to another and if the Son manifestly possesses the glory of the Father, it is evident that he is not another according to the essence but that [the Son] has the same nature as the Father. COMMENTARY ON ISAIAH 12.42.8-9.[16]

THE SON SHARES THE FATHER'S GLORY. CYRIL OF ALEXANDRIA: If he is properly and truly the only God, he may be said by us to be the Creator of all things. As the most wise Paul says, "Although there may be so-called gods in heaven or on earth—as indeed there are many 'gods' and many 'lords'—yet for us there is one God, the Father, from whom are all things and for whom we exist, and one Lord, Jesus Christ, through whom are all things and through whom we exist."[17] And since he has introduced himself to us as the author of great and marvelous things, he says that his glory, that is, the sum of virtues appropriate to God, is not to be given to lifeless idols or to any other created thing but is to be retained for himself alone. It follows from this that the glory of the Godhead may not fittingly be attributed to any other being that differs from him in essence but only to the ineffable and transcendent nature itself. Although he said that his

own glory is to be given to nobody, however, he gave it to the Son. For the Son has been glorified in the same way, indeed, as the Father too who is worshiped in heaven and on earth. How then did God give his glory to him, as to one who was not different from him in virtue of the consubstantiality, even though each was divided off into his own hypostasis? The nature of the supreme deity is one in three distinct hypostases, conceived of and worshiped as such by those who hold orthodox views. COMMENTARY ON ISAIAH 3.5.42.8.[18]

GOD MADE MAN BRINGS GOD'S GLORY TO US. CYRIL OF ALEXANDRIA: There was no other way to honor the slave [i.e., humanity] except by making the characteristics of the slave his very own so that they could be illumined from his own glory. What is preeminent will always conquer, and the shame of the slavery is thus borne away from us. He who was above us became as we are. He who is naturally free took on the limitations of our life. This was why honors passed even to us, for we too are called the children of God, and we regard his own true Father as our Father also. All that is human has become his own. And so, to say that he assumed the form of a slave expresses the whole mystery of the economy in the flesh. So, if [my opponents] confess one Lord and Son, the Word of God the Father, but say that a simple man of the line of David was conjoined as a companion of his sonship and his glory, then it is time for you to speak to people who choose to think like this. . . . It seems that they argue as though there are two sons unequal in nature and that a slave is crowned with the glory that is proper to God, that some bastard son is decked out with the selfsame dignities as the one who is really God's natural Son, even though God says quite clearly, "I will not give my glory to another." How can someone who has only been honored with a mere conjunction fail to be "other" to the true and natural Son when he has just been assumed

---

[15]NPNF 2 5:118**. [16]ITA 617; SC 295:438. [17]1 Cor 8:5-6. [18]COA 87-88*; PG 70:856.

for the office of servant, given the honor of sonship, just like us, and sharing in another's glory that he attains by grace and favor?

So the Emmanuel must not be separated out into a man, considered as distinct from God the Word? On no account. I say that we must call him God made man, and that both the one and the other are this same reality, for he did not cease to be God when he became man, nor did he regard the economy as unacceptable by disdaining the limitations involved in the self-emptying. ON THE UNITY OF CHRIST.[19]

42:9 Proclaiming New Things

NEW THINGS LIKE FIRST THINGS. EUSEBIUS OF CAESAREA: "Behold, the first things," he says, "came to pass. But I proclaim new things, and before they arise, I will cause these things to be heard by you."[20] Just as he says "the first things" would be fulfilled through my works, as I promised Abraham concerning his "seed," so indeed I acted. I fulfilled also those things foretold by Moses and the rest of the prophets; "now I promise to everyone what was proclaimed before" and to make them come to light through the prophecies, for "I caused these things to be heard by

you." COMMENTARY ON ISAIAH 2.22.[21]

INCORRUPTION, HOLINESS, RIGHTEOUSNESS ARE THE NEW THINGS. CYRIL OF ALEXANDRIA: When the prophet says, "Behold, the former things have come to pass, and new things I will now declare, and before I declare them they have been made known to you," he does not allow the word of the Savior to be disbelieved by us in any detail. For just as what was said from the beginning about his coming has come to fulfillment, he says, so too will what he calls the new things turn out to be true and will be revealed before they appear. What are these things? They are the eternal life that is to come, which our Lord Jesus Christ promised us, that is, the life of incorruption and holiness and righteousness, the kingdom of heaven, the glorious participation in spiritual good things, the fruits of forbearance, the rewards of piety, the crown of love for Christ. May we too attain them through his grace and loving kindness. COMMENTARY ON ISAIAH 3.5.42.8-9.[22]

---

[19]OUC 75-76; SC 97:368-70. [20]At the end, he joins Is 45:21 to Is 42:9. [21]GCS 57(9):272. [22]COA 88; PG 70:856-57.

42:10-17 SONG OF PRAISE TO THE LORD

[10]Sing to the LORD a new song,
  his praise from the end of the earth!
Let the sea roar[v] and all that fills it,
  the coastlands and their inhabitants.
[11]Let the desert and its cities lift up their
    voice,
  the villages that Kedar inhabits;
let the habitants of Sela sing for joy,

let them shout from the top of the
    mountains.
[12]Let them give glory to the LORD,
  and declare his praise in the coastlands.
[13]The LORD goes forth like a mighty man,
  like a man of war he stirs up his fury;
he cries out, he shouts aloud,
  he shows himself mighty against his foes.

¹⁴*For a long time I have held my peace,*
  I have kept still and restrained myself;
*now I will cry out like a woman in travail,**
  I will gasp and pant.
¹⁵*I will lay waste mountains and hills,*
  and dry up all their herbage;
I will turn the rivers into islands,
  and dry up the pools.
¹⁶*And I will lead the blind*
  in a way that they know not,
in paths that they have not known

I will guide them.
I will turn the darkness before them into light,
  the rough places into level ground.
These are the things I will do,
  and I will not forsake them.
¹⁷*They shall be turned back and utterly put*
    to shame,
  who trust in graven images,
who say to molten images,
  "You are our gods."

v Cn Compare Ps 96.11; 98.7: Heb *Those who go down to the sea* * LXX *I have kept silence; I shall not always keep silence and endure, shall I? I have been as patient as a woman in labor.*

OVERVIEW: A new spiritual beginning deserves a new song (ORIGEN), and the nations are the most ready to sing that song since they have been kept in bondage so long (EPHREM). The lyrics of this song are Christ the Word put to music (CLEMENT). He forms the *cantus firmus* on which the church is grounded (JEROME) but also allows us to soar with the melody of his wonderful acts and signs (CYRIL). This happens, for instance, when he takes special care of those who suffer (JEROME) or destroys the power of sin (THEODORET) about which he has chosen to remain silent no longer (BASIL). God is now gathering evidence in preparation for his verdict (AUGUSTINE), although he is patient and willing to indulge sinners for a season (GREGORY THE GREAT). God's patience is his justice surrounded by his compassion (AUGUSTINE) as he allowed himself to experience humiliating torment and even death (ALEXANDER). He did this in order to set us free from sin's power (THEODORET) by restoring us to his image through his love, which is like a transforming fire (LEO).

42:10 Sing a New Song to the Lord

A NEW SONG FOR A NEW BEGINNING. ORIGEN: You descend into the water and come out unimpaired, the filth of sins having been washed away. You ascend "a new person"[1] prepared to "sing a new song." HOMILIES ON EXODUS 5.5.[2]

THE SONG OF THE REDEEMED GENTILES.
EPHREM THE SYRIAN: Here [Isaiah] speaks again about the Gentiles and invites them to sing a new song to the Lord. Indeed, if the Jews, redeemed from captivity after seventy years, had to sing a new hymn to the Lord, their liberator, why should not the Gentiles do the same? And should they not burst out into a new song with much more good reason, since they have been delivered from a bondage of many centuries?

"His praise from the end of the earth," that is, it happens in a wonderful way that the salvation given by Christ to humankind is celebrated by the remotest nations with hymns and songs.

"The coastland and their inhabitants": those nations who submit to the waves of the sea with their ships will praise the Lord. Those who have considered the sea as a divinity and sacrifice to it will recognize, after being enlightened by faith, their true God, and they will consider and preach him as the Lord of the sea. COMMENTARY ON ISAIAH 42.10.[3]

CHRIST IS THE NEW SONG. CLEMENT OF ALEXANDRIA: Inasmuch as the Word was from the

---

[1]Eph 2:15; 4:24. [2]FC 71:283-84**. [3]ESOO 2:91.

first, he was and is the divine source of things. But inasmuch as he has now assumed the name Christ, consecrated of old and worthy of power, he has now been called the New Song. This Word, the Christ, the cause of both our being at first (for he was in God) and of our well-being, this very Word has now appeared as man. He alone is both God and man. He is the Author of all blessings to us. By him, we, being taught to live well, are sent on our way to life eternal. . . . This is the New Song, the manifestation of the Word that was in the beginning and before the beginning. The Savior, who has existed before, has in recent days appeared. EXHORTATION TO THE GREEKS 1.[4]

THE CHURCH IS NOT SUBMERGED. JEROME: Even as islands have been set in the midst of the sea, churches have been established in the midst of this world, and they are beaten and buffeted by different waves of persecution. Truly these islands are lashed by waves every day, but they are not submerged. They are in the midst of the sea, to be sure, but they have Christ as their foundation, Christ who cannot be moved. HOMILIES ON THE PSALMS 24 (PSALM 97).[5]

GOD SETS OUT SIGNS. CYRIL OF ALEXANDRIA: The word of the holy apostles and Evangelists about the Savior made visible the message of the glory of the Savior. At that time they wrote words concerning his ineffable divinity, and they hymned his transcendent virtue, not placing him among the things that are born but above those things that have been called into being and in such a nature he was placed beside God the Father. At that time their words set forth the divine signs that are beyond wonder and its explanation. COMMENTARY ON ISAIAH 4.1.42.11-12.[6]

42:13 God Mighty Against His Foes

THE SWEETNESS OF GOD IS MADE BITTER BY HUMAN SIN. JEROME: Also in Isaiah it says, "the Lord of powers will come out and wage war, and will rouse his zeal and will shout in triumph over his foes with strength." For God will come out from his place, once he is compelled to break his peace and gentleness and kindness for the sake of putting sins right, who, although by his nature is sweet, has been made bitter by our flaw, not in himself but in those suffering, to whom the torments are bitter. It is he who elsewhere spoke by the prophet, "I am God, and I do not change."[7] COMMENTARY ON ZECHARIAH 3.14.3-4.[8]

OUR ENEMIES DESTROYED. THEODORET OF CYR: It is [Christ] who has destroyed the power of death; it is he who has crushed the way of sin; it is he who has made the tyranny of the devil to cease; it is he who has put an end to the error of idols. COMMENTARY ON ISAIAH 12.42.13.[9]

42:14 I Have Held My Peace

GOD HAS PATIENTLY REMAINED SILENT UNTIL NOW. BASIL THE GREAT: Still, the saying of Isaiah has come to my mind: "I have kept silence; I shall not always keep silence and endure, shall I? I have been as patient as a woman in labor." May it be that we both receive the reward for our silence and acquire some power for refuting, so that, when we have given our proofs, we may dry up this bitter torrent of falsehood poured out against us. May we say, "Our souls have passed through a torrent,"[10] and, "If it has not been that the Lord was with us, when people rose up against us, perhaps they had swallowed us up alive, perhaps the waters had swallowed us up."[11] LETTER 223.[12]

GOD'S SILENCE COMES BEFORE HIS JUDGMENT. AUGUSTINE: The one who speaks is now keeping quiet. He speaks in commandments; he keeps quiet in judgment. . . . How has he kept

---

[4]ANF 2:173. [5]FC 48:192*. [6]PG 70:864-65. [7]Mal 3:6. [8]CCL 76A:879. [9]ITA 618; SC 295:442. [10]Ps 124:5 (123:5 LXX). [11]Ps 124:2-3 (123:2-3 LXX). [12]FC 28:127**.

quiet, seeing that he spoke to say this very thing? He says, "I have kept quiet," and yet he does not keep quiet, because just by saying "I have kept quiet," God has not kept quiet. So then, Lord, I hear you speaking in so many commandments, as many sacred signs, so many pages, so many books. And then I hear you saying this, "I have kept quiet, will I keep quiet always?" So how have you kept quiet? Because I am not yet saying, "Come, you blessed of my Father, receive the kingdom." And I am not yet saying to the others, "Go into the eternal fire that has been prepared for the devil and his angels."[13] And while I am not yet saying these things, I am already warning you that I am going to say them. Sermon 47.4.[14]

God Has Restrained His Anger. Gregory the Great: "I spoke as if giving birth." For as we already have said, giving birth with pain expels that which was developing deep within for a long time. The one who was always silent speaks out now like one giving birth, for the coming judge withheld revenge from being inflicted on humans for a long time; for he shows the extent to which he kept contained within the pressure of endurance, like a headache. So no one, when God hides this light, should despise him or criticize him when God flashes down from heaven to burn up those who have contempt for him. For the one who does not long for pardon then without a doubt he will burn as punishment. So we accept the time of calling through heavenly grace, while indulgence still prevails, and may we flee the wrath that is all around, making an improvement in our lifestyle. Morals on the Book of Job 10.31.[15]

God Will Not Always Remain Silent. Augustine: "Sweet and righteous is the Lord."[16] You love [him] because he is sweet. You fear [him] because he is righteous. In a gentle voice, he said, "I have kept silence." But as a just person, "shall I always be silent?" "A Lord compassionate and merciful."[17] Yes, indeed. Yet add, patient; yet

add, and very compassionate. Tractates on the Gospel of John 33.7.[18]

The Things Christ Suffered. Alexander of Alexandria: Christ suffered shame for humanity's sake in order to set people free from death. This he exclaimed, as in the words of the prophet, "I have endured as a woman in childbirth." In very deed Christ endured for our sakes sorrow, ignominy, torment, even death itself, and burial. For thus he says himself by the prophet, "I went down into the deep."[19] Who made him thus to go down? The ungodly. . . . They suspended him on the tree—the One who stretches out the earth. They transfixed him with nails who laid firm the foundation of the world. They circumscribed him who circumscribed the heavens. They bound him who frees sinners. They gave him vinegar to drink who has enabled them to drink of righteousness. They fed him with gall who has offered to them the bread of life. They caused corruption to come on his hands and feet who healed their hands and feet. They violently closed his eyes who restored sight to them. They gave him over to the tomb who raised their dead to life both in the time before his passion and also while he was hanging on the tree. Epistles on the Arian Heresy 5.5.[20]

42:16 Leading the Blind

The Blindness of Unbelief and Ignorance. Theodoret of Cyr: Again, God calls the people who suffer from unbelief and who are devoid of intellectual acuteness "the blind." He promises to guide their steps on the way they do not know, for they failed to recognize the path of the truth but followed on the paths of error. "I will turn darkness into light for them." After freeing them from their previous ignorance, I will deem them worthy of the knowledge of God, for ignorance is like darkness, whereas knowledge is

---

[13]Mt 25:34, 41. [14]WSA 3 2:299-300*. [15]CCL 143:577. [16]Ps 25:8 (24:8 LXX, Vg). [17]Ps 86:15 (85:15 LXX, Vg). [18]FC 88:57**. [19]Jon 2:4. [20]ANF 6:301*.

analogous to the light. "And crooked things into straight." For the difficult course of wisdom, of the governing of oneself and of justice, he has made an easy course, since he has attached the hope of future benefits to the efforts to claim virtue. "These are the words that I will fulfill for them; and I will not forsake them." I will not cease to judge them worthy of these benefits, and I will lavish all kinds of care, even to the future. COMMENTARY ON ISAIAH 12.42.16.[21]

GOD IS THE SOURCE OF LIGHT AND LOVE. LEO THE GREAT: The apostle John teaches how this is fulfilled: "We know that the Son of God came and gave understanding to us, that we might know the truth and be in his true Son."[22] And again, "Let us love, therefore, since God first loved us."[23] By loving us, God restores us to be his image, so that he might find the form of his own goodness in us. He grants that we ourselves might work what he works, indeed setting light to our minds and causing us to burn with the fire of his love, in order that we love not only him but also the things that he loves. SERMON 12.1.[24]

---

[21]ITA 619-20*; SC 295:444. [22]1 Jn 5:20. [23]1 Jn 4:19. [24]CCL 138:48-49.

42:18-25 ISRAEL BLIND AND DEAF

[18]Hear, you deaf;
    and look, you blind, that you may see!
[19]Who is blind but my servant,
    or deaf as my messenger whom I send?
Who is blind as my dedicated one,
    or blind as the servant of the LORD?
[20]He sees[w] many things, but does not observe
        them;
    his ears are open, but he does not hear.
[21]The LORD was pleased, for his righteousness'
        sake,
    to magnify his law and make it glorious.
[22]But this is a people robbed and plundered,
    they are all of them trapped in holes
    and hidden in prisons;
they have become a prey with none to rescue,

    a spoil with none to say, "Restore!"
[23]Who among you will give ear to this,
    will attend and listen for the time to come?
[24]Who gave up Jacob to the spoiler,
    and Israel to the robbers?
Was it not the LORD, against whom we have
        sinned,
    in whose ways they would not walk,
    and whose law they would not obey?
[25]So he poured upon him the heat of his anger
    and the might of battle;
it set him on fire round about, but he did not
        understand;
    it burned him, but he did not take it to
        heart.

w Heb *you see*

OVERVIEW: The handiwork of the invisible God is made visible in creation (ORIGEN), if we would only listen and see (BASIL). But we must also exercise our wills for grace to enable our seeing

(CASSIAN). Some could see and then know God's work but choose to look away (THEODORET). Spiritual tunnel vision is the result of a continuous refusal to believe (EUSEBIUS) and of bad choices made (THEODORET). God tests faith through what freedom suffers (CYPRIAN). Violent people will find themselves afflicted inside as well as out (EUSEBIUS), often producing most of their hardship and trouble themselves (FILASTRIUS).

42:18 Deaf and Blind

THE GRACIOUS GIFT OF SPIRITUAL SIGHT.
ORIGEN: Now the blind see when they see the world, and from the exceedingly great beauty of things that have been created they contemplate the Creator corresponding in greatness and beauty to them. And when they see clearly "the invisible things of God from the creation of the world, which are perceived through the things that are made,"[1] [then] they see and understand with attentiveness and clarity. COMMENTARY ON MATTHEW 11.18.[2]

LISTEN AND SEE. BASIL THE GREAT: It is evident, indeed, that some possess ears better able to hear the words of God. But to those who do not have those ears, what does he say? "Hear, you deaf, and, you blind, behold." Also, "I opened my mouth and panted,"[3] and "You have broken the teeth of sinners."[4] All these things were said in reference to the faculties that render service for spiritual food and spiritual doctrine. HOMILIES ON THE PSALMS 16.13. (PSALM 33).[5]

A LACK OF RECEPTIVITY IS A MATTER OF THE WILL. JOHN CASSIAN: "Who is deaf but my servant? And who is blind but the one to whom I have sent my messengers?" And so that no one would be able to ascribe this blindness of theirs to nature and not to will, he says elsewhere, "Lead out the people who are blind and who have eyes, who are deaf and who have ears."[6] And again he says, "You who have eyes and do not see, and ears and do not hear."[7] CONFERENCE 13.12.3-4.[8]

WILLFUL IGNORANCE. THEODORET OF CYR: Who is as blind as the one who has moved away? Symmachus translates, "Who is as blind as the perfect and as blind as the servant of the Lord?" He says that although the nations are just as much in error, they do not deserve the same accusation. For they did not have the prophets guiding them toward the truth and were not deemed worthy of such attention. "The one who is far off" has the same meaning; he who has been called by God has left the service of God, preferring the worship of idols. COMMENTARY ON ISAIAH 13.42.19.[9]

42:19-21 Good Teacher, Slow Student

YOU SEE BUT DO NOT OBSERVE. EUSEBIUS OF CAESAREA: He reports how they became the blind and dull by saying, "They see many things but do not observe." These things were previously communicated [in Isaiah]: "Keep listening, but do not comprehend; keep looking, but do not understand. Make the mind of this people dull."[10] . . . You see that all these things he says about the people, he means concerning those of the circumcision. But "the Lord was pleased, for his righteousness' sake, to magnify his praise." And they surrendered to those who made war on their souls and became "a people who have been torn in pieces, plundered and trapped in a secret room" of their souls, "and in their own homes as well." For these very reasons those who plotted with these thoughts that they hid from Christ were themselves caught in a "trap from which they could not be delivered," there being no "rescuer" and none to say, "Release them." COMMENTARY ON ISAIAH 2.23.[11]

42:22 All of Them Trapped

THE WAY OF DESTRUCTION. THEODORET OF CYR: He has taught us both the divine object and

---

[1]Rom 1:20. [2]ANF 9:448. [3]Ps 119:131 (118:131 LXX). [4]Ps 3:7 (3:8 LXX). [5]FC 46:272*. [6]Is 43:8. [7]Jer 5:21. [8]ACW 57:478-79. [9]SC 295:446-48. [10]Is 6:9-10. [11]GCS 57(9): 275-76.

the free will of the human creature. Although he desires, he says, that you be justified by choosing godliness, you have, on the contrary, taken the opposite way and reaped death. "For there is a snare in the secret chambers everywhere, and in the houses also, where they have hidden them." COMMENTARY ON ISAIAH 13.42.22.[12]

42:24 Who Gave Up Jacob?

GOD IS BEHIND ALL TESTING TIMES. CYPRIAN: In this part of the Lord's Prayer, [Christ] shows that the enemy is powerless against us without God's prior permission. During temptation, consequently, all our fear and devotion and attention should be focused on God, since evil has only such force as he himself permits.[13] . . . Moreover, evil is given power over us according to our [willful] sins. As Isaiah writes, "Who gave Jacob up to the looters and Israel to the ponderers." It was the Lord, against whom we sinned, in whose ways we would not walk and whose law we refused to obey. So he unleashed the fury of his anger against us. And again, when Solomon strayed from the precepts and paths of the Lord, it was recorded, "The Lord stirred up Satan against Solomon himself."[14] THE LORD'S PRAYER 25.[15]

THOSE WHO TURN A DEAF EAR. EUSEBIUS OF CAESAREA: Since God had been addressing people who could not hear him, he now speaks of them as helpless and weak. . . . For the outcome of the matter was no longer an issue but would be accomplished very soon. . . . He sent on them the fury of his anger, and battle overtook them. Those who were already wearied by war once more took it on themselves so as to hold on to Jerusalem and their rule over it. But war was unleashed on them, and not only in an external sense but also in that which afflicted their souls. COMMENTARY ON ISAIAH 2.23.[16]

HUMAN BEINGS PRODUCE HARDSHIP FOR THEMSELVES. FILASTRIUS: But Scripture declares that these evils are not by nature made by God but rather come from causes dwelling within humans. Sins against the Lord are the source of trials and pressures of various persecutions that with God's permission rise up against those sinning, as it is written, "who gives Israel up to the spoil." Is it not the Lord against whom they sinned and his ways in which they did not want to walk? For Scripture elsewhere states that God did not make evil things. In the book of Genesis, which speaks of the creation of the world, it states that all God made was very good. . . . So evils are not naturally caused by God's creating but by human will. BOOK OF HERESIES 79.2-5.[17]

[12]ITA 621-22*; SC 295:448. [13]See 1 Cor 10:13. [14]1 Kings 11:14. [15]ANF 5:454**. [16]GCS 57(9):276. Cyril points out that God is the only one who could have delivered the Jews over to their enemies since throughout the whole of their history, they were otherwise under his divine protection. See *Commentary on Isaiah* 4.1.42.24 (PG 70:880-81). [17]CCL 9:250.

43:1-7 NO FEAR

[1]But now thus says the LORD,
he who created you, O Jacob,
  he who formed you, O Israel:
"Fear not, for I have redeemed you;
  I have called you by name, you are mine.
[2]When you pass through the waters I will be with you;
  and through the rivers, they shall not overwhelm you;
when you walk through fire you shall not be burned,
  and the flame shall not consume you.

³*For I am the* LORD *your God,*
　the Holy One of Israel, your Savior.
I give Egypt as your ransom,
　Ethiopia and Seba in exchange for you.
⁴*Because you are precious in my eyes,*
　and honored, and I love you,
I give men in return for you,
　peoples in exchange for your life.
⁵*Fear not, for I am with you;*

I will bring your offspring from the east,
　and from the west I will gather you;
⁶*I will say to the north, Give up,*
　and to the south, Do not withhold;
bring my sons from afar
　and my daughters from the end of the earth,
⁷*every one who is called by my name,*
　whom I created for my glory,
　whom I formed and made."

OVERVIEW: Believers belong to a covenant of a better order, a new creation (PROCOPIUS), as they are sustained through the risky transition into new life (CLEMENT). One must actively practice virtue in order to keep Jesus as companion on the way (AMBROSE). There is a risk-taking confidence involved in faith (ISAAC), but we can be assured that the flames ultimately will not consume those who trust God (CAESARIUS). Faith also comes to realize that there is no need to search anxiously for God. He is already present in all things (PACHOMIUS), although it is particularly in his grace that he keeps the believer's head above the water (GREGORY THE GREAT). The believer also shares a supreme confidence that God will protect his garden of the faithful from fire (ORIGEN). God calls his people by name, and, because he loves them and has chosen them, they now have become respected and glorious as their offspring return from the east—a prophecy that literally received its fulfillment when Cyrus returned the Jews to Judea from Babylon (THEODORET). But it also pointed toward that time when Christians would be gathered into heaven (PROCOPIUS). His saints, in return, offer praise to him for the material and spiritual care he provides (DIDACHE). Christ, through Isaiah, intimates that these saints who have received his blessings will be called his name, referring to his own who would later be called Christians (EUSEBIUS).

43:1 Redeemed by the Lord

GOD REDEEMS HIS CREATION. PROCOPIUS OF GAZA: The things said here are of a quite different tenor from what was said in the previous passage about the people of the covenant, where he called them blind, deaf and plundered. Now the message here is of the better condition of those believers of the covenant who belong to a better order. For the former ones were those who were suffering. Here he addresses as "you" those who recognize their Creator and Maker. "Do listen to the one who keeps you an unblemished creation and product, for here you are fittingly called Jacob and Israel. For I made you in your soul, according to the image, and formed you, taking a body from the ground, and I provided my blood for you, buying back my own creation. You, being made worthy of these things, go by the road on which you are instructed to go and preach the good news. Although some will attack you, be encouraged that you are special. 'For behold, I am with you always, even to the end of the age.'[1] Be followers of me, the one who wished to give my blood of redemption for you, as atonement." . . .

"You are mine." For we are said to have been Christ's, even before the separation from God that occurred when we as sinners went out of the garden, though by nature we were always God's. But he has made us once more to be his own through the Holy Spirit making us strong through every trial. Rivers, water and flames denote the many channels of temptation. For it is written, "All who

---

[1] Mt 28:20.

wish to live godly lives in Christ Jesus will be persecuted."[2] And Christ says to those who believed in him, "You will have sorrow in the world."[3] Commentary on Isaiah 43.1-13.[4]

43:2 When You Pass Through the Waters

God Will Support Us. Clement of Alexandria: "Even if we cross over, they shall not slip, says the Lord." We shall not slip into corruption, we who are crossing over into incorruption, because he himself will support us. For so he himself has said and so he has willed. Christ the Educator 1.9.84.[5]

The Virtues of the Wayfarer. Ambrose: We are wayfarers in this life. Many are walking along this way. All need to make a good passage. The Lord Jesus is walking with one who is making a good passage. Thus we read, "When you pass through the waters, I will be with you, and the rivers shall not cover you, nor fire burn your garments when you shall walk through." But one who keeps a fire pent up in his body, the fire of lust, the fire of immoderate desire, does not pass through but burns the covering of his soul. A good name is more excellent than money, and above heaps of silver is good favor. Faith itself redounds to itself, sufficiently rich and more than rich in its possession. There is nothing that is not the possession of the wise person except what is contrary to virtue. Wherever he goes, he finds all things to be his. The whole world is his possession, since he uses it all as his own. Letter 15.[6]

Faith Scorns Natural Danger. Isaac of Nineveh: "If thou go through fire, thou shalt not be burned, and the rivers shall not flow over thee." Faith has many times worked such things before the eyes of all creation. If knowledge were given the opportunity to attempt such things, it would in no wise be persuaded. For it is by faith that men have entered into flames and bridled the burning power of the fire, walking unharmed through the midst thereof, and they have trodden upon the back of

the sea as upon dry land. All these are above nature and opposed to the modes of knowledge. Ascetical Homilies 52.[7]

The Flames Will Not Harm You. Caesarius of Arles: If you watch and seek, the Lord says, "Here I am,"[8] and "If you pass through fire," I am with you "and the flames shall not consume you." If you ask through prayer, you will find, and if you knock through giving to the poor, Christ opens the doors to you in order that you may enter and possess paradise. Now if you still think that anything will remain at the end of the world, consider your own end. Sermon 158a.1.[9]

God Is Present in All Places. Pachomius: Become guileless, and be like the guileless sheep whose wool is sheared off without their saying a word. Do not go from one place to another saying, "I will find God here or there." God has said, I fill the earth, "I fill the heavens,"[10] and again, "If you cross the water, I am with you." Instructions 1.25.[11]

Grace to Keep Our Head Above Water. Gregory the Great: For the rivers overflow those whom the active business of this world confounds with perturbation of mind. But one who is sustained in mind by the grace of the Holy Spirit passes through the waters and yet is not swamped by the rivers, because in the midst of crowds of peoples he so proceeds along his way as not to sink the head of his mind beneath the active business of the world. Letter 7.4.[12]

God Protects His Garden. Origen: What kind of fire? "He stationed the cherubim and the fiery sword, which turns about to protect the way of the tree of life."[13] Where the tree of life is, where the paradise of God is, where God the gardener is, where the blessed and the elect and the holy ones of

---

[2]2 Tim 3:12. [3]Jn 16:22. [4]PG 87:2381-85. [5]FC 23:75. [6]FC 26:81**. [7]AHSIS 255. [8]Is 58:9. [9]FC 47:363-64. [10]Jer 23:24. [11]CS 47:23. [12]NPNF 2 12:211. [13]Gen 3:24.

God reside, there the blessed await God's own way of handling affairs. HOMILY ON 1 KINGS 28.9.3.[14]

I HAVE CALLED YOU BY NAME. THEODORET OF CYR: Even when the compassionate God disciplines, he does not abandon mercy. . . . For, he says, "judge, consider, take heart." Now God strengthens those who were reduced to slavery in Babylon. And since they bore the title "the people of God," it was appropriate that God addressed the people in this way: "I have called you by your name. You are mine." He says, "You possess the name by which I have called you." COMMENTARY ON ISAIAH 13.43.1.[15]

43:4 I Give Men in Return for You

WITH GOD'S LOVE COME RESPECT AND GLORY. THEODORET OF CYR: God renders the summary of benefits in which they take pleasure. It is because I love you, he says, and because I have chosen you that you have become respected and glorious. "And I will give men for you, and princes for your life." He means to speak of the Babylonians, whom he has delivered over to Cyrus. COMMENTARY ON ISAIAH 13.43.4.[16]

43:5 Bringing Offspring from the East

BABYLON DEFEATED. THEODORET OF CYR: These predictions received their fulfillment after the defeat of the Babylonians, for Cyrus commanded [the Jews] to return to Judea. At the time the latter made [their] return from the east, those who had taken flight during the war and reached the west then [also] returned to the land, probably because they recognized the peace that had come on Judea. In any case, it is with truth and precision that the text clearly indicates the people that the holy apostles have called from the entire world and who have obtained salvation. For in every city the Jews were the first to whom the apostles offered the divine teachings. COMMENTARY ON ISAIAH 13.43.5.[17]

CHRISTIANS GATHERED INTO HEAVEN. PROCOPIUS OF GAZA: "I will destroy those warring with you on account of the gospel, both people and leaders." He encourages them in this way. "And your children, which you have sown by God and which you have begotten throughout the world, I will gather to my heavenly city, raising up those airborne, through the air, like birds made light by the winds," that is, the angelic forces. "I shall raise up your offspring to be my children through their being reborn in the church, and all those called by my name Christians are welcomed." For Christ prophesied these things through the godly prophet. COMMENTARY ON ISAIAH 43.1-13.[18]

43:7 Created for God's Glory

MATERIAL AND SPIRITUAL REFRESHMENT. DIDACHE: You, almighty Master, created all things for your name's sake and gave food and drink to people to enjoy, that they might give you thanks; but to us you have graciously given spiritual food and drink and eternal life through your servant. Above all we give thanks because you are mighty; to you be the glory forever. DIDACHE 10.3-4.[19]

CHRIST FORETELLS HIS FOLLOWERS WILL BE NAMED AFTER HIM. EUSEBIUS OF CAESAREA: If it is necessary for some to be marked by name, then I will make it clear to them all that they are now "those who have been called by my name." From where else did the name of Christians come than from the name of Christ? For it was he who foretold such a thing through the prophet. COMMENTARY ON ISAIAH 2.24.[20]

---

[14]FC 97:332**. [15]SC 295:450. [16]ITA 634; SC 295:452. [17]ITA 634-35*; SC 295:452-54. [18]PG 87:2384. [19]AF 263*. [20]GCS 57(9):278. Eusebius continues with a further textual analysis: "Instead of 'in my glory I have prepared him' the others translate 'I have created him for my glory' that is, 'I have created a new people for glory,' through whom I will be glorified. But 'I have fashioned it,' since it was unformed in its ways."

43:8-21 NO SAVIOR APART FROM GOD

⁸*Bring forth the people who are blind, yet
        have eyes,
    who are deaf, yet have ears!*
⁹*Let all the nations gather together,
    and let the peoples assemble.
Who among them can declare this,
    and show us the former things?
Let them bring their witnesses to justify them,
    and let them hear and say, It is true.*
¹⁰*"You are my witnesses," says the* LORD,
    *"and my servant whom I have chosen,
that you may know and believe me
    and understand that I am He.
Before me no god was formed,
    nor shall there be any after me.*
¹¹*I, I am the* LORD,
    and besides me there is no savior.
¹²*I declared and saved and proclaimed,* *
    *when there was no strange god among you;
and you are my witnesses," says the* LORD.
¹³*"I am God, and also henceforth I am He;
    there is none who can deliver from my hand;
I work and who can hinder it?"*

¹⁴*Thus says the* LORD,
    your Redeemer, the Holy One of Israel:

*"For your sake I will send to Babylon
    and break down all the bars,
    and the shouting of the Chaldeans will be
        turned to lamentations.*ˣ
¹⁵*I am the* LORD, *your Holy One,
    the Creator of Israel, your King."*
¹⁶*Thus says the* LORD,
    *who makes a way in the sea,
    a path in the mighty waters,*
¹⁷*who brings forth chariot and horse,
    army and warrior;
they lie down, they cannot rise,
    they are extinguished, quenched like a wick:*
¹⁸*"Remember not the former things,
    nor consider the things of old.*
¹⁹*Behold, I am doing a new thing;
    now it springs forth, do you not perceive it?
I will make a way in the wilderness
    and rivers in the desert.*
²⁰*The wild beasts will honor me,
    the jackals and the ostriches;
for I give water in the wilderness,
    rivers in the desert,
to give drink to my chosen people,*
    ²¹*the people whom I formed for myself
that they might declare my praise."*

x Heb obscure   * LXX *reproached*

OVERVIEW: Isaiah is amazed at God's action of bringing those who were formerly blind and gathering them into the church (EUSEBIUS). But he also notes the unique character of this saving God who has nothing "comparable to him." This also has implications for the Son's relationship to the Father. The Son is no "secondary God," nor can he properly be said to be merely a likeness of God (MARIUS) or a god who came after the Father in time since God says here that there was no God before or after him (CHRYSOSTOM). Isaiah's prophetic faith here envisions the future gathering of the blind into the light as if this has already happened (PROCOPIUS) in Christ, who has rescued his people as God's chosen one, the great "I AM" witnessed to throughout Scripture (THE-

ODORET). He is the only true God, who is perfectly divine with no deficiency in goodness, wisdom, power or anything else. Otherwise he would not be God (JOHN OF DAMASCUS). Not only is he God, but also he has shown Israel that he is their God and that he cares for them, even by his reproaches, as no one else would (THEODORET). He cares for all of his people, including the nations, who, too, will not be snatched from his hand (CYRIL).

God sent the runaway Medes to rescue the Israelites (ISHO'DAD) from the enslavement of the Babylonians, who were unwilling to recognize their victory only came about because he willed it (THEODORET). His destruction of Babylon was like that of long ago when he defeated the Egyptians, although he wants to direct Israel's attention to the new things he is doing among them (EUSEBIUS). Instead they are to look at the new path God is making for those in the church that he leads safely through the waters of trials and temptations (PROCOPIUS). They are to look to the new thing he is doing in his incarnation among his people (AMBROSE) and with the apostles who act as channels for the irrigation of the world with the knowledge of God (TERTULLIAN, CLEMENT, THEODORET). He assuages the thirst of his elect race, the Jews, with whom he himself identified fully, having become incarnate himself as a Jew from the tribe of Judah (THEODORET). Thus, he provides abundant waters in the wilderness for both Jews and Gentiles (CYPRIAN), providing them with a new covenant of freedom that is the "new thing" he is accomplishing for his people (IRENAEUS).

43:8-9 The Spiritually Insensitive

"BLIND" AND "DUMB" NATIONS DRAWN INTO THE CHURCH. EUSEBIUS OF CAESAREA: If they seemed to have the eyes of the soul and a human mind, they were still nonetheless blind to the deceit of idolatry. But what then happened to them provides the basis for Isaiah's message. For the former blind and deaf were gathered together into the church of God even as the rulers of the nations opposed the people of God. The prophet is amazed and tries to make sense of the prophecy that he is speaking, and so he calls out, saying, "Who can announce these things?" COMMENTARY ON ISAIAH 2.24.[1]

43:10 No God Was Formed Before God

THE SON IS NOT A COPY OF GOD. MARIUS VICTORINUS: If Christ is Son, Christ is certainly after God. But after God there is nothing comparable to him. Christ is therefore not comparable to God; or if he is not after God, certainly he is with God; for in no way can he be before God; therefore he is consubstantial (*homoousion*) . . . substance as substance, especially if it is a homogeneous substance that is realized in two or more individuals, which is said to be identical substance, not similar. AGAINST ARIUS 2.1.1.[2]

THE SON IS NOT YOUNGER THAN THE FATHER. CHRYSOSTOM: Still I would like to ask of our opponents what the words mean that were once uttered by the prophet, "Before me there was no God, and after me there is none." If the Son is younger than the Father, how can the Father say, "after me there shall be none"? You will not, therefore, also deprive the Only Begotten himself of his substance, will you? Indeed, you must dare to do this or else to accept the one Godhead with the distinct persons of the Father and the Son. HOMILIES ON THE GOSPEL OF JOHN 4.[3]

PROPHETIC FAITH SPEAKS OF FUTURE THINGS. PROCOPIUS OF GAZA: "I have glorified you in the world."[4] By this glory Christ has led the blind people into the light. For the sun of righteousness does not allow us to be children of the night and shadows but rather of day, as the divine apostle says. When Paul says, "They have been gathered,"[5] this in fact has not yet taken

---

[1]GCS 57(9):278. [2]FC 69:199*. [3]FC 33:48**. [4]Jn 17:4. [5]See Eph 5:8.

place, and he is obviously speaking prophetically, meaning "they will be gathered." For speaking of things to come as if they had happened is customary in the Scriptures; another example of such is "I have given my back to the rod"[6] and "they divided my clothing among them."[7] COMMENTARY ON ISAIAH 43.1-13.[8]

43:11 Besides Me There Is No Savior

SAVIOR AND GOD. THEODORET OF CYR: If you want to have me as a witness to your verdict, then be the first to render witness to my truth. In this case, I will not be alone in bearing witness, but there is also my chosen servant. Now it is neither Moses nor another of the prophets who is referred to here, but Christ our Master. And he calls him a [servant], not as God but as a human being; for it is as a human being that he has named him "chosen." . . . We likewise find in the holy Gospels this number of two witnesses. In the course of a conversation with the Jews our Master Christ in effect declared, "It is written in your law that the testimony of two persons is true. I bear witness concerning myself, and the Father who sent me bears witness."[9] . . . "I am, I am your God, and there is no other savior besides me." Again these words proclaim the one divinity. For our Master Christ is called "savior" throughout the holy Scriptures, as I think even the followers of Arius and Eunomius would concede. Now if apart from God there is no savior and if Christ is called "Savior," it is clear that he participates in the [divine] nature. If Christ does not, as the blasphemers allege, then he is not Savior. . . . But if he is Savior, then he shares the same essence to which alone belongs the faculty of saving.[10] COMMENTARY ON ISAIAH 13.43.10-11.[11]

THE IMPLICIT PERFECTION OF DIVINITY. JOHN OF DAMASCUS: It has been sufficiently demonstrated that God exists and that his essence is incomprehensible. Furthermore, those who believe in sacred Scripture have no doubt that he is one and not several. For the Lord says at the beginning of his lawgiving, "I am the Lord your God, who brought you out of the land of Egypt. You shall not have strange gods before me."[12] And again: "Hear, O Israel: the Lord your God is one Lord."[13] And through the mouth of the prophet Isaiah: "I am," he says, "the first God, and I am the last, and there is no God besides me. Before me there was no God, and after me there shall be none, and beside me there is none." And the Lord speaks thus to his Father in the holy Gospels: "This is eternal life: that they may know you, the only true God."[14] With those who do not believe in sacred Scripture we shall reason as follows. The Divinity is perfect and without deficiency in goodness or wisdom or power. He is without beginning, without end, eternal, uncircumscribed; to put it simply, he is perfect in all things. Now, if we say that there are several gods, there must be some difference to be found among them. For if there is no difference at all among them, then there is one God rather than several. But if there is some difference, then where is the perfection? For if one should come short of perfection in goodness, or power, or wisdom, or time or place, then he would not be God. The identity of God in all things shows him to be one and not several. ORTHODOX FAITH 1.5.[15]

43:12 No Strange God Among You

NO ONE ELSE CARES. THEODORET OF CYR: I not only made the predictions; I have also brought them to their conclusion. "I reproached, and then there was no strange god among you." The three interpreters have rendered the word "I have reproached" by the verb "I have made to understand," which comes back to saying, I have born witness. The verb "I have made reproaches" also has the same sense: it is because they do not cease to sin that they suffer reproaches. More-

---

[6]Is 50:6. [7]Ps 22:18 (21:19 LXX). [8]PG 87:2388. [9]Jn 8:17-18. [10]J.-N. Guinot comments (SC 295:458 n. 2) that Theodoret uses such rigorous syllogisms often in his writings against Arianism. To some the argument might seem more circular than deductive. [11]SC 295:456-58. [12]Ex 20:2-3. [13]Deut 6:4. [14]Jn 17:3. [15]NPNF 2 9:4**.

over, he then makes the following declaration: At the time when I gave the law, no strange god was present: "You are my witnesses, and I am the Lord God." Know clearly, he is saying, that no one else is concerned for you, but that you alone have benefited by my providence. COMMENTARY ON ISAIAH 13.43.12.[16]

43:13 No Frustrating God's Work

GOD SAVED THE WANDERING NATIONS. CYRIL OF ALEXANDRIA: "I will act, and who will hinder it?" For I have accomplished the calling of the nations, he says, that is, I have saved those who were led astray. And who can alter this, or who could change things so that they did not happen? The Savior himself assures us that no one can snatch those who are being saved from the hand of God. "For my sheep hear my voice, and I know them; and they follow me, and I give them eternal life."[17] COMMENTARY ON ISAIAH 4.1.43.11-13.[18]

43:14-15 I Will Send to Babylon

GOD WILL SEND THE MEDES TO DELIVER THE ISRAELITES. ISHO'DAD OF MERV: "I have brought down all the runaways and the Chaldeans," that is, "For your sake I will send you to Babylon" and will make the Medes rise, in order to deliver you from captivity. And when the Babylonians fly from you in every manner, through the land and the sea, they will be captured in "their ships" and be imprisoned. He calls "runaways" the Medes because of their previous weakness. COMMENTARY ON ISAIAH 43.14.[19]

A FAILURE TO RECOGNIZE GOD'S PROVIDENCE LEADS TO DISASTER. THEODORET OF CYR: [Isaiah] predicts the defeat of the Babylonians and the enslavement of the Chaldeans. They will suffer these misfortunes because of you, he says, since they were unwilling to recognize that their victory depended on my good will and that you were made prisoners because I rejected you. COMMENTARY ON ISAIAH 13.43.14.[20]

43:16 A Path in the Sea

GOD WILL DO SIGNS, AS HE DID BEFORE. EUSEBIUS OF CAESAREA: Although these things were done to the Babylonians and Chaldeans, prophetically speaking, the future things that are "not yet" shall be as if already accomplished. God has completed these by himself, comparing the present events with those that happened earlier: I showed my divinity to those in Egypt and led my people through the Red Sea. I made a way "in the mighty water" and a dry path through that same sea when I threw the chariots of Pharaoh and his forces into the sea to the bed prepared for them, sinking down to the abyss and no longer able to rise. They were like those of old who were bent like a snuffed wick in a burning flame. I worked such things among the ancients, who in turn passed on the memory of those wonders to those of old who followed. But for the present I command them no longer to be amazed at those deeds, neither those done in Babylon nor those in Egypt. COMMENTARY ON ISAIAH 2.25.[21]

GOD MAKES A PATH. PROCOPIUS OF GAZA: How has he led chariots and horses? It is clear that Pharaoh pursued Israel by his own decision, for God had already spoken in this way to him: "I have raised you up as to show my power in you and so that my name might be made known throughout the earth."[22] Thus in a marvelous way God saves those who are fleeing from the desire for earthly things as they are pursued by the devil. God shows them that the wild waves of the present life are passable and that they will not be overwhelmed by trials but will arrive securely in the desert with a stilled and purified mind. They will eat the heavenly bread and drink the water from the rock. This is to share in Christ and to go through the Jordan and gain the Promised Land. COMMENTARY ON ISAIAH 43.14-28.[23]

---

[16]ITA 638*; SC 295:458. [17]Jn 10:27-28. [18]PG 70:897. [19]CSCO 303(128):45-46. [20]ITA 638; SC 295:460. [21]GCS 57(9):280. [22]Ex 9:16. [23]PG 87:2393.

43:19-20 A New Thing

THE NEW CREATION REQUIRES UNEXPECTED MEANS.
AMBROSE: "Although he took a body, although he became man to redeem humanity and recall it from death, still, being God, he came to earth in an unusual way so that, as he had said, 'Behold, I make all things new,' he might thus be born from the womb of an immaculate virgin, and be believed to be, as it is written, 'God with us.'"[24] LETTER 44.[25]

THE SPIRITUAL IRRIGATION OF THE WORLD.
TERTULLIAN: For of this number I find figurative hints up and down the Creator's dispensation in the twelve streams of Elim.[26] . . . Now the same number of apostles was thus portended, as if they were to be fountains and rivers that should water the Gentile world, which was formerly dry and destitute of knowledge, as he says by Isaiah, "I will put streams in the unwatered ground." AGAINST MARCION 4.13.[27]

A NEW EYE IS REQUIRED.
CLEMENT OF ALEXANDRIA: The Word says, "Look, I am doing something new, which no eye has seen, no ear heard, no human heart felt."[28] These are to be seen, heard and grasped by a new eye, a new hearing and a new heart when the Lord's disciples speak, listen and act in the Spirit. STROMATEIS 2.4.15.3.[29]

THE NEW THINGS.
THEODORET OF CYR: What I am going to do, he says, merits still more admiration than the things done [in the past]. He adds what will be: "And I will make a way in the wilderness and rivers in the dry land." Some have thought that these declarations relate to the return from Babylon. This is wrong, for he did not favor them at that time, while they were returning from exile, either with a strange road or with rivers. But he is calling the Gentiles "the desert" [wilderness], and the preachings of the apostles "rivers" and the course that escapes error "the way." What he has added makes it equally obvious. COMMENTARY ON ISAIAH 13.43.19.[30]

THE JEWISHNESS OF JESUS' HUMANITY.
THEODORET OF CYR: "Because I have given water in the wilderness and rivers in the waterless land to assuage the thirst of my elect race; the people I have set aside for myself proclaim my virtues." The race that [Jesus] put on according to his human nature is human nature in its entirety, yet is nearer still to the Jewish race. For there is no doubting that our Lord came from Judah. COMMENTARY ON ISAIAH 13.43.21.[31]

GOD PROVIDES ABUNDANT WATERS OF REBIRTH FOR THE GENTILES.
CYPRIAN: But as often as water is named alone in the holy Scriptures, baptism is referred to, as we see intimated in Isaiah: "Remember not," says he, "the former things, and consider not the things of old. Behold, I will do a new thing. . . ." There God foretold by the prophet that among the nations, in places that previously had been dry, rivers should afterwards flow plenteously and should provide water for the elected people of God, that is, for those who were made children of God by the generation of baptism. Moreover, it is again predicted and foretold before, that the Jews, if they should thirst and seek after Christ, should drink with us, that is, should attain the grace of baptism. "If they shall thirst," he says, "he shall lead them through the deserts, shall bring forth water for them out of the rock. The rock shall be cloven, and the water shall flow, and my people shall drink,"[32] which is fulfilled in the Gospel, when Christ, who is the Rock, is cloven by a stroke of the spear in his passion; who also, admonishing what was before announced by the prophet, cries and says, "If anyone thirst, let him come and drink. He who believes in me, as the Scripture says, out of his belly shall flow rivers of living water."[33] And that it might be more evident

---

[24]Mt 1:23. [25]FC 26:226. [26]Num 33:9. [27]ANF 3:364. [28]Is 43:19; 64:4; 65:17; 1 Cor 2:9. [29]FC 85:167. [30]*ITA* 639*; SC 295:462. [31]SC 295:464. [32]Is 48:21. [33]Jn 7:37-38.

that the Lord is speaking there not of the cup but of baptism, the Scripture adds, saying, "But this spoke he of the Spirit, which they that believe in him should receive." For by baptism the Holy Spirit is received, and thus by those who are baptized and have attained to the Holy Spirit is attained the drinking of the Lord's cup. LETTER 62.8.[34]

43:21 They Might Declare My Praise

THE NEW COVENANT OF FREEDOM. IRENAEUS: God would make a new covenant with people,[35] not such as that which he made with the ancestors at Mount Horeb, and would give to people a new heart and a new spirit.[36] And again [it is written], "And do not remember the things of old: behold I make new things." [This] plainly announced that liberty that distinguishes the new covenant and the new wine that is put into new bottles,[37] [that is], the faith that is in Christ, by which he has proclaimed the way of righteousness sprung up in the desert and the streams of the Holy Spirit in a dry land, to give water to the elect people of God, whom he has acquired. [This is done] that they might show forth his praise but not that they might blaspheme him who made these things, that is, God. AGAINST HERESIES 4.33.14.[38]

---

[34]ANF 5:360. [35]Jer 31:31, 32. [36]Ezek 36:26. [37]Mt 9:17. [38]ANF 1:510-11.

43:22-28 THE ONE WHO BLOTS OUT TRANSGRESSION

[22]"Yet you did not call upon me, O Jacob;
  but you have been weary of me, O Israel!
[23]You have not brought me your sheep for burnt offerings,
  or honored me with your sacrifices.
I have not burdened you with offerings,
  or wearied you with frankincense.
[24]You have not bought me sweet cane with money,
  or satisfied me with the fat of your sacrifices.
But you have burdened me with your sins,
  you have wearied me with your iniquities.*

[25]"I, I am He
  who blots out your transgressions for my own sake,
  and I will not remember your sins.
[26]Put me in remembrance, let us argue together;
  set forth your case, that you may be proved right.†
[27]Your first father sinned,
  and your mediators transgressed against me.
[28]Therefore I profaned the princes of the sanctuary,
  I delivered Jacob to utter destruction
  and Israel to reviling."

---

* LXX.   † The LXX *lege sou tas anomias sou prōtos, ina dikaiōthēs* has more to do with confession than the (ironic?) Hebrew, which calls on Israel to "account for yourself that you may be justified" in an adversarial manner.

OVERVIEW: God did not save Israel from slavery only to elicit a response of worship focused on the sacrifice of bulls. The sacrifice he was looking for is a spiritual sacrifice of the heart (CYRIL). In fact, under the new covenant initiated by his servant when he called Israel, none of these sacrifices are mentioned (EUSEBIUS). He also wants to show his people here that grace is stronger than sin (AMBROSE). Coupled with this grace is a healthy spiritual discipline on our part to recall past sins (CHRYSOSTOM) that also leads to remembrance of God's past mercies (THEODORET). Confession is good for the conscience and spiritual combat (ORIGEN). Be honest about spiritual culpability—the sooner the better (AUGUSTINE, CASSIODORUS)! Contrition too is sacrificial and costly but also restorative (CHRYSOSTOM). Sin should be understood as a personal insult to God (PROCOPIUS). Not time, but sincere confession, restores God's favor immediately (CHRYSOSTOM). His mercy makes up for our incomplete repentance, supplementing our feeble and small efforts with his own measureless generosity in destroying our iniquities for his own sake (CASSIAN). Therefore, seek God's justifying grace, trusting that what we shall be thereafter is not for us to judge (CLEMENT). Justification is simultaneous with confession of sin (JEROME) and a strong condemnation of sins in oneself (CHRYSOSTOM). Sin is the reason for the Babylonian exile (THEODORET). Idolatry is an especially serious offense to God (EPHREM).

43:22-24 Bad Sacrifice and False Service

TRUE WORSHIP AND SACRIFICE. CYRIL OF ALEXANDRIA: In the previous passage, prophecies were made of the covenant of Christ and the graces bestowed by him, because he had promised that he would make a way in the wilderness and streams in the arid land, on account of which the beasts of the field would bless him.[1] This may be understood as the praise of spiritual sacrifice and the fruit of the new covenant in Christ. Here in the present passage, he tries to assure Israel that they have been ransomed out of Egypt and delivered from the grievous burden of slavery there—but not so that they would offer cattle to him and find access to God through blood and smoke! For such things are refuse in God's sight and are shadows rather than the truth itself.

He therefore says, "I have not now called you, O Jacob." The word *now* should be taken to mean "not when you were offering me sacrifice," that is, "I have not called you while you were sacrificing oxen and slaughtering sheep, so that you should not conclude that you had received deliverance as some kind of reward for the offering. On the contrary, it was while you were in sin and guilty of defilement, for you had worshiped the gods of the Egyptians, that I deemed you worthy of mercy and love." Therefore the gift is one of gentleness, and the fruit of loving kindness is grace, and the liberation is as if out of love. The sheep of your burnt offerings are nothing to me, he says, nor indeed have you glorified me with your sacrifices.[2] For how can that which is entirely unacceptable and offered in vain contribute to my glory? You have performed no service with your sacrifices. A person who pursues the good, he says, who achieves the moral character that leads to virtue, who submits to my will, who puts the teaching of the prophets into practice—that is the person who may be said to serve the God who rules over all. But a person who fills the holy tabernacle with the smoke of frankincense, who offers oxen or sheep or who has put on a fine show, will not render any genuine glory. Such a person has done absolutely nothing that pleases me. Therefore service does not consist in offering sacrifice. It consists in the readiness to submit a tender neck, a neck that needs, as it were, not so much as a touch to do the will of God.[3] . . . Everywhere he represents worship in shadows as rejected and the things in types as taken away, drawing us to the righteousness that is in Christ and teaching us to be refashioned according to the evangelical way of life, which is the only way

---

[1]Is 43:19-20. [2]Cf. Is 1:11; Jer 6:20. [3]He cites further examples, see Jer 7:21-22; 6:20; Ps 50:9.

that what is pleasing to God can be brought about, and in which we can arrive at the worship that is truly irreproachable and sincere, that is, the worship that is spiritual. "For God is spirit, and those who worship him must worship in spirit and in truth."[4] COMMENTARY ON ISAIAH 4.1.43.22-24.[5]

YOUR SACRIFICE DOES NOT SERVE ME. EUSEBIUS OF CAESAREA: For there was no mention at all of such things required from you in the laws of the new covenant that I established through my servant whom I chose. But you did not offer these things to me. If it had been necessary to say such things, you still probably would have done something contrary. "In your sins is your preference" or as the other interpreters put it, "in your sins and in your unrighteous acts you called on me." COMMENTARY ON ISAIAH 2.25.[6]

43:25 Transgressions Blotted Out

THE TRIUMPH OF GRACE. AMBROSE: You have blotted it out, indeed, in your hearts and minds, but the Word of God is not blotted out, the Holy Spirit is not blotted out but turns away from impious minds. It is not grace but iniquity that is blotted out; for it is written, "I am he, I am he who blots out your iniquities." ON THE HOLY SPIRIT 3.10.61.[7]

A HEALTHY SPIRITUAL DISCIPLINE. CHRYSOSTOM: We must always have these sins before our eyes, so we may be purified from them. And though God, by clemency, forgives you every sin, yet you, for the safety of your soul, must always have the sin before your eyes. For the memory of past sins hinders future ones; and one who is bitten by his past sins demonstrates the will to be steadfast about the next ones. For David says, "And my sin is ever before me,"[8] in order to have the past ones before his eyes and not to fall into future ones. That God demands this firm stance from us, listen to him say, "I am the one who blots out your sins, and I will not remember

them; you, however, remember them, and we shall settle accounts, says the Lord. First state your sin so you may be justified." . . . Time does not excuse; rather, the manner of the repentant individual erases the sin. HOMILIES ON REPENTANCE AND ALMSGIVING 7.4.11-12.[9]

CONFESSION WITH GRATITUDE. THEODORET OF CYR: Do not forget your errors, God says, but keep them firmly in your memory so that you will always recognize how great are my benefits. In this way you will avoid committing the same misdeeds. Now since he has mentioned judgment and that fear is an appropriate response, he teaches them who would learn the way of victory. "You be the first to confess your sins, so as to be justified." I do not want to overcome you, but rather I long for the opposite. Learn how it is possible for you to overcome; confess first your errors, and I will grant you pardon. I will judge you if you attempt to hide something from me. If you confess, I will forgive. COMMENTARY ON ISAIAH 13.43.26.[10]

CONFESSION PREEMPTS THE DEVIL'S ACCUSATION. ORIGEN: For now the devil urges us to sin and also accuses us when we do sin. If, therefore, in this life we anticipate him and are ourselves our own accusers, we escape the wickedness of the devil, our enemy and our accuser. . . . Does he [the prophet] not evidently show the mystery that we are dealing with when he says, "you speak first" to show you that you ought to anticipate him who was prepared to accuse you? HOMILIES ON LEVITICUS 3.4.5.[11]

STATE THE CASE FOR YOUR INNOCENCE. AUGUSTINE: All truth is justice. In the confessing of what is the case, there is justice. He speaks the truth, that sinners who justify themselves by their faults cannot be justified. And in this way

---

[4]Jn 4:24. [5]COA 88-90*; PG 70:909-12. [6]GCS 57(9):282. [7]NPNF 2 10:143-44**. [8]Ps 51:3 (50:5 LXX). [9]FC 96:95. [10]SC 295:466. [11]FC 83:61*.

one is called truly just in that confessing one's own sin, he asks them to be accounted to himself yet begs God for mercy. For he knows that it is stated in the law, "Confess your sins, and you will be justified." What does it mean "to confess at the start of speaking" unless "to speak freely and not just when forced to"? For who (even one who fears God) is without sin, since faults get mixed into thinking and unconsciously we sin in so many ways? QUESTIONS ON THE OLD TESTAMENT 30.[12]

THE ONLY WAY TO ACQUITTAL. CASSIODORUS: Though this type of argument seems without resort and bereft of human force in court trials here on earth, before God it is invested with invincible protection. Only confession of faith can acquit the person whom no arguments defend. Such a course is permitted to those who truly repent, who in seeking pardon for themselves strive instead to condemn their own actions. This is what Isaiah too advises: "Speak first of your iniquities that you may be justified." EXPOSITION OF PSALM 6.2.[13]

TRUE SACRIFICE TAKES PLACE IN THE HEART. CHRYSOSTOM: Groan bitterly, sacrifice confession (for, he says, "Declare first your transgressions that you may be justified"),[14] sacrifice contrition of heart. These victims turn not to ashes or dissolve into smoke or melt into air. They do not need wood and fire but only a deep-pricked heart. This is wood; this is fire to burn, yet not consume them. For one who prays with earnestness is burned yet not consumed, but like gold that is tested by fire becomes brighter. HOMILIES ON 2 CORINTHIANS 5.4.[15]

TRANSGRESSION IS DIRECTED AGAINST GOD. PROCOPIUS OF GAZA: Nature is too weak to gain righteousness by works. For the human disposition is inclined toward evil from an early age, as David clearly says, "If you kept record of our transgressions, who would stand? For with you there is atonement."[16] For I myself am merciful,

and I wish that those in trouble remember their Savior and give him thanks through all things. For this is what the saints do. . . . And do not be ashamed to confess your sins. For the Pharisee did not do so, and he was condemned. But the tax collector did so, and he was justified.[17] . . .

"You transgressed against me"—this is given great force. For it is not a transgression against humanity or created nature. For the idolater rejects the divine nature as he robs the same of its transcendence and glory, which are to be worshiped. As God says in Jeremiah, "Why have you spoken to me? You have all acted unrighteously and impiously toward me,"[18] says the Lord Almighty. COMMENTARY ON ISAIAH 43.14-28.[19]

TIME HAS NO BEARING ON FORGIVENESS. CHRYSOSTOM: God does not wait for time to elapse after repentance. You stated your sin, you are justified. You repented, you have been shown mercy. Time does not excuse; rather, the manner of the repentant individual erases the sin. One individual may wait a long time and not gain salvation, and another, who confesses genuinely, is stripped of the sin inside a short time. HOMILIES ON REPENTANCE AND ALMSGIVING 7.4.12.[20]

DO NOT BE STUBBORN IN THE FACE OF FORGIVENESS. JOHN CASSIAN: "Forgive us our trespasses as we forgive those who trespass against us."[21] Whoever, therefore, desires to obtain the forgiveness of sins should strive to use these methods. The obstinacy of a hardened heart should turn no one away from a salutary healing and from the source of so great mercy, for even if we did all these things they would not be ineffective for the expiation of our crimes unless the goodness and mercy of the Lord destroyed them. When he has seen the services of a devout effort rendered by us with a humble mind, he supplements these feeble and small efforts with his own

---

[12]PL 35:2232. [13]ACW 51:92. [14]Is 43:26 LXX. [15]NPNF 1 12:303-4**. [16]Ps 130:3-4 (129:3-4 LXX). [17]Lk 18:10-14. [18]See Jer 2:29. [19]PG 87:2397-2400. [20]FC 96:95. [21]Mt 6:12.

measureless generosity, as he says: "I am the one who destroys your iniquities for my own sake, and I will not keep record of your sins." CONFERENCE 20.8.8-9.[22]

43:26 State Your Case

WE SEEK JUSTIFICATION AND TRUST GOD FOR THE REST. CLEMENT OF ALEXANDRIA: And it is ours to flee to God. And let us endeavor after this ceaselessly and energetically. For he says, "Come to me, all who labor and are heavy laden, and I will give you rest."[23] And prayer and confession with humility are voluntary acts. Therefore it is enjoined, "First tell your sins, that you may be justified." What afterwards we shall obtain, and what we shall be, it is not for us to judge. FRAGMENTS 11.3.[24]

THE CONFESSING SINNER IS JUST. JEROME: We are just when we acknowledge that we are sinners, and our justice depends not on our personal merit but rather on the mercy of God, as holy Scripture says: "The just is an accuser of himself in the beginning of his plea."[25] And in another place, "State your sins, that you may be justified." AGAINST THE PELAGIANS 1.13.[26]

THE WAYS OF REPENTANCE. CHRYSOSTOM: Do you wish that I shall speak of the ways of repentance? They are many and various and different, and all lead to heaven. The first way of repen-

tance is condemnation of sins. "First declare your sins, that you may be justified." CONCERNING THE POWER OF DEMONS 2.6.[27]

43:27 Your Mediators Transgressed

DO NOT BLAME GOD FOR THE SINS OF YOUR ANCESTORS. THEODORET OF CYR: [The Lord] has proclaimed these words in addressing those who were in Babylon. It is not I, he says, who am the cause of these misfortunes, but your ancestors, and your priests, who have transgressed my laws. Their iniquity has transformed the renown of Israel to an object of shame. COMMENTARY ON ISAIAH 13.43.27.[28]

43:28 Princes of the Sanctuary

A CURSE ON THE HOUSE OF MANASSEH. EPHREM THE SYRIAN: "Your princes profaned the sanctuary." Those who were from the house of Manasseh profaned the sanctuary with the four-faced idol, which they placed inside the sanctuary. Because of those crimes, and in particular because of Manasseh's crime, "I have given Jacob to the curse, and Israel to reviling." COMMENTARY ON ISAIAH 43.28.[29]

---

[22]ACW 57:700-701. [23]Mt 11:28. [24]ANF 2:583*(Fragment 16. PG 9:761.) [25]Prov 18:17. [26]FC 53:247. [27]NPNF 1 9:190*. [28]ITA 643; SC 295:466. [29]SESHS 2:109.

44:1-5 SERVANT ISRAEL

[1]"But now hear, O Jacob my servant,
  Israel whom I have chosen!
[2]Thus says the LORD who made you,
  who formed you from the womb and will

help you:
Fear not, O Jacob my servant,
  Jeshurun whom I have chosen.
[3]For I will pour water on the thirsty land,

and streams on the dry ground;
I will pour my Spirit upon your descendants,
    and my blessing on your offspring.
⁴They shall spring up like grass amid waters,ʸ
    like willows by flowing streams.
⁵This one will say, 'I am the LORD's,'

another will call himself by the name of
    Jacob,
and another will write on his hand, 'The
    LORD's,'
    and surname himself by the name of Israel."

y Gk Compare Tg: Heb *They shall spring up in among grass*

OVERVIEW: Spiritual revival comes through hearing God's word (JEROME). This cannot happen, nor can any blessing be expected, unless the Holy Spirit is present (AMBROSE). This Spirit will be poured out not only on Israel but even on the descendants of Babylon (THEODORET). Those on whom the Spirit descends avoid the rivers of Babylon, which represent evil desires. They instead focus on the willow tree of chastity, whose flower, whenever it is steeped in water, is said to extinguish whatever kindles sensual desires and passion within us (METHODIUS). Willows are also a type of those who offer spiritual support to others as they are rooted in the streams of divine Scripture (CASSIODORUS). God's rich mercy extends to all who call on his name, despite whatever name they may use to describe their relationship to him (PROCOPIUS). Christians are free in the glory they derive from their name (THEODORET).

44:2 Chosen Jeshurun

TO SEE GOD IS TO HEAR HIS VOICE. JEROME: For "Jeshurun," a Hebrew word, the other translators translate *euthytaton* or *euthē*, that is, "most right" and "right," and only the Septuagint had "most loved" and connected it to "Israel." For according to the Hebrew and the faith of the Scriptures, "Israel" means "the sight of God," that is, a person who sees God, not in the natural things but in the sound of his voice. . . . Isaiah also compares those being reborn in baptism with flourishing plants and with the willow, which rises up near flowing water. Against the nature of

things the willow bears fruit, although it was previously barren or became barren because its seed was taken for food. COMMENTARY ON ISAIAH 12.17.[1]

44:3 God's Spirit Poured Out

THE HOLY SPIRIT IS VITAL FOR ALL BLESSINGS. AMBROSE: God himself testifies that the Holy Spirit presides over his blessings, saying, "I will put my Spirit on your seed and my blessings on your children." For no blessing can be full except through the inspiration of the Holy Spirit. ON THE HOLY SPIRIT 1.7.89.[2]

THROUGH ISRAEL BABYLON'S DESCENDANTS WILL BE BLESSED. THEODORET OF CYR: He does not cease to make mention of the creation and of his kindness after the creation. . . . You will not be alone in enjoying my benefits, he says, for the thirsty nations will also drink from the streams of salvation, thanks to your descendants. . . . He is addressing those who are in Babylon, yet it is not to them but to their descendants that he promises to give the grace of the Spirit. . . . Here the prophetic text, having promised to give water to those traveling through a dry land, has shown through whom he will give it. "I will set my Spirit on your seed and my blessing on your children." COMMENTARY ON ISAIAH 13.44.1-3.[3]

---

[1]*AGLB* 35:1348-49. [2]*NPNF* 2 10:105*. [3]*SC* 295:466-68.

44:4 Like Willows by Flowing Streams

As Willows on the Banks. METHODIUS: For everywhere the divine writings take the willow as the type of chastity, because when its flower is steeped in water, if it is drunk, it extinguishes whatever kindles sensual desires and passions within us, until it renders completely barren and makes every inclination to the begetting of children without effect, as also Homer indicated,[4] for this reason calling the willows destructive of fruit.... For as it is the nature of this tree to bud and grow to maturity when enriched by words, so it is the nature of virginity to blossom and grow to maturity when enriched by words, so that one can hang one's body[5] on it.

If, then, the rivers of Babylon are the streams of voluptuousness, as wise people say, which confuse and disturb the soul, then the willows must be chastity, to which we may suspend and draw up the organs of lust that overbalance and weigh down the mind, so that they may not be borne down by the torrents of incontinence and be drawn like worms to impurity and corruption. SYMPOSIUM OR BANQUET OF THE TEN VIRGINS 4.3-4.[6]

A Type of Faithful People. CASSIODORUS: The willow is a type of saintly and faithful persons. As Isaiah puts it, "There shall spring up, as it were, grass in the midst of water, and the willow in ever-flowing water." So it is on people like these that we hang our instruments, when we bestow them by sharing the grace from reading from the divine Scriptures. Our instruments are the means of bestowing the grace of psalmody and the cause of our joy when it is bestowed on us in turn. EXPOSITION OF PSALMS 136.2.[7]

44:5 Names That Will Identify One as the Lord's

Acknowledging God as Creator. PROCOPIUS OF GAZA: We have seen many of the saints themselves latch on to names of certain men. One calls himself Jacob, another Israel, others even call themselves Jeremiah and Isaiah and Daniel. Encouraged by these names, they give themselves over to martyrdom with enthusiasm. "Another will write with his hands, 'the Lord's.'" This signifies the marking that many have on their hands or arms, or it refers to those marked with the sign of the cross or the name of Christ. The portion or the inheritance of the name of God is implied by the use of the name derived from "Jacob" [i.e., "Israel"]. It signifies that those who have acted in a godly way will not be allowed to go to utter ruin, for he does not want to destroy the whole of Israel but turn them totally toward God. And he provides the way of salvation to those who believe in him.

He calls himself Lord and God, Creator and Framer—this is intended to show that they were in error when Israel gave the name of "god" to others who were not gods and forgot the one who was from the beginning the creator of humanity. They were honoring their parents as the ones who were responsible in the beginning and ignoring the Maker, as one of the prophets said: "The son gives glory to the father and the slave to his master,"[8] and "If I am the Father, then where is my glory?"[9] and "If I am the ruler of all, where is the fear of me?"[10] says the Lord. For [the Son] is the Lord who rules the creation by hand, but the Father is the one who made it. COMMENTARY ON ISAIAH 44.1-5.[11]

Total Freedom of Language. THEODORET OF CYR: The reality comes to confirm the prophecy: it is with total freedom of language that each of the believers calls herself a Christian and derives glory from this name. COMMENTARY ON ISAIAH 13.44.5.[12]

---

[4]*Odyssey* K 510. [5]Or, harp: *organon*. [6]ANF 6:324. [7]ACW 53:361**. [8]Deut 32:8. [9]Deut 32:9. [10]Mal 1:6. [11]PG 87:2401. [12]ITA 652; SC 295:468.

44:6-8 THE FIRST AND THE LAST

⁶*Thus says the* LORD, *the King of Israel*
    and his Redeemer, the LORD *of hosts:*
"*I am the first and I am the last;*
    besides me there is no god.
⁷*Who is like me? Let him proclaim it,*
    let him declare and set it forth before me.
Who has announced from of old the things to
    *come?*ᶻ

*Let them tell us*ᵃ *what is yet to be.*
⁸*Fear not, nor be afraid;*
    have I not told you from of old and declared
        it?
    And you are my witnesses!
Is there a God besides me?
    There is no Rock; I know not any."

z Cn: Heb *from my placing an eternal people and things to come*   a Tg: Heb *them*

OVERVIEW: There is a clear connection between God's presence that saves our souls and the understanding of who he is (PSEUDO-CLEMENT). It is unthinkable that God should be more than one (AMBROSE). The prophet can be trusted to anticipate just as much the mysteries of the Trinity as he does the mystery of the incarnation (GREGORY OF NYSSA). The Son and the Father share firstness and lastness together and equally (ATHANASIUS). An image of something that is of the same nature does not imply a double of it (BASIL). To be God and Savior, the Son has to be consubstantial with the Father (THEODORET), and through this consubstantiality, he acts to persuade and instruct the sinfully ignorant about what is true by tailoring his argument to their current situation of ignorance concerning him (CYRIL). God presents them with a rhetorical question about knowledge of the future, decisively demonstrating that no one but he could know such things because he is the first and the last (JEROME).

44:6 I Am the First and the Last

I AM THE FIRST AND THE LAST. PSEUDO-CLEMENT OF ROME: Things being as they are, we have chosen the best way to come to the understanding of the intelligible things—by coming to them with God. Thanks to him, we can advance without fear of danger, holding the immortal rudder of the soul and not allowing fleshly passion to erupt into this immortal and intelligible substance and reserving for each one of the intelligible as much honor as is allowed by the order that [God] willed, he by whom their very existence and rank was established. God is the noncreated, in fact the first of all, to which the prophets render acknowledgment. "I, God, am the first, and after me and outside of me there is no god." So we have to realize that he is without beginning and ungenerated. RECOGNITIONS 3.6.1-3.[1]

THERE ARE NOT THREE GODS. AMBROSE: I have not read of, or heard of or found any varying degree in God. Never have I read of a second, never of a third God. I have read of a first God; I have heard of a first and only God. ON THE CHRISTIAN FAITH 5.9.116.[2]

BESIDES ME THERE IS NO GOD. GREGORY OF NYSSA: "I am the first, and hereafter am I, and no God was before me, and no God shall be after me."[3] For knowing more perfectly than all others the mystery of the religion of the gospel, this great prophet foretold even that marvelous sign concerning the virgin, and gave us the good tid-

---

[1]Apocr 217. [2]NPNF 2 10:299. [3]Cf. Is 41:4; 44:6; 48:12 LXX.

ings of the birth of the Child and clearly pointed out to us that name of the Son. He, in a word, by the Spirit includes in himself all the truth, in order that the characteristic of the divine nature, whereby we discern that which really is from that which came into being, might be made as plain as possible to all. [Isaiah] utters this saying in the person of God: "I am the first, and hereafter am I, and before me no God has been, and after me is none." Against Eunomius 5.1.[4]

The Unique Nature Shared by Father and Son. Athanasius: For God is one and only and first. But this is not said to the denial of the Son; perish the thought. For he is in that One and First and Only, as being of that One and Only and First the only Word and Wisdom and Radiance. And he too is the First, as the fullness of the godhead of the First and Only, being whole and full God. Discourse Against the Arians 3.23.[5]

God Is Not Divisible into Numbers. Basil the Great: If we count, we do *not* add, increasing from one to many. We do not say, "one, two, three," or "first, second, and third." God says, "I am the first, and I am the last." We have never to this present day heard of two gods.... How does one and one not equal two gods? Because we speak of the emperor and the emperor's image— but not two emperors.... The image of the emperor is an image by imitation, but the Son is a natural image. On the Holy Spirit 18.45.[6]

Father and Son Share the Same Divinity. Theodoret of Cyr: "Thus says the Lord, the king of Israel, the God of hosts who has saved them: I am the first, and I remain after these things. Apart from me there is no God." If there is no God apart from him, the Son is not consubstantial with the Father, as the blasphemy of

Arius and Eunomius teaches. How, then, can they call him God? If the Son is God and the prophetic word is true that openly states there is no other God, the divinity of the holy Trinity is one, even if they do not admit this. Commentary on Isaiah 13.44.6.[7]

44:7-8 Who Is Like Me?

Changing Over to Knowledge of Truth. Cyril of Alexandria: Having made mention of the knowledge in Christ, recapping things for our benefit, he now turns his address to something else that is very necessary. For at the time when the godly prophet Isaiah composed the words about such things, offensive and irresistible temptations ruled over them. For what "God" and "honor" meant seemed to be up to the judgment of each individual. So God needs to provide them with some rousing encouragement and arguments tailored to their situation. He turns them away from polytheism and the sicknesses that troubled them and summons them through a change of mind to a knowledge of the truth and of his glory and brings them back to the awareness of his incomparable power. Commentary on Isaiah 4.2.44.6-7.[8]

God's Gifts of Freedom. Jerome: Who is like me? Let him call the things that are not as if they are and let him explain the order of my creation, by which reason I have set humans free in motion as I made them on the earth. And this is not all I will to do, but I also seek out for them knowledge of things to come. So you, Israel, whose king and redeemer I am, do not fear idols, which you have learned on Mount Sinai to be nothing. Commentary on Isaiah 12.18.[9]

---

[4]NPNF 2 5:173**. [5]NPNF 2 4:397**. [6]NPNF 2 8:28**. [7]SC 295:468-70. [8]PG 70:924. [9]AGLB 35:1353.

44:9-13 IDOLS ARE NOTHING

[9]*All who make idols are nothing, and the things they delight in do not profit; their witnesses neither see nor know, that they may be put to shame.* [10]*Who fashions a god or casts an image, that is profitable for nothing?* [11]*Behold, all his fellows shall be put to shame, and the craftsmen are but men; let them all assemble, let them stand forth, they shall be terrified, they shall be put to shame together.*

[12]*The ironsmith fashions it[b] and works it over the coals; he shapes it with hammers, and forges it with his strong arm; he becomes hungry and his strength fails, he drinks no water and is faint.* [13]*The carpenter stretches a line, he marks it out with a pencil; he fashions it with planes, and marks it with a compass; he shapes it into the figure of a man, with the beauty of a man, to dwell in a house.*

b Cn: Heb *an axe*

OVERVIEW: Isaiah prophesies of a future time when idol worshipers will be put to shame, but let us also listen to these words in our time and repent of our error (EUSEBIUS), because behind the attractive form of an idol lurks a demonic power (IRENAEUS). These idols are useless at anything other than deceiving their worshipers; they give no positive benefit (ATHANASIUS). That idols resemble their makers suggests they are far from divine (THEODORET). Idolaters look to idols to send them bodily goods, but in vain (ISHO'DAD).

44:9-10 Idol Worshipers Put to Shame

FUTURE AND PRESENT REPENTANCE. EUSEBIUS OF CAESAREA: Isaiah sees that in the ensuing time a very great number of people will arise who all "will be ashamed" and who will cease from their continual error. They will be ashamed and hide their faces. If they persist in their error, however, they will be given over to destruction at the time of judgment. But this word is also for those of us now in the present. COMMENTARY ON ISAIAH 2.26.[1]

44:11 The Artisans Are Human

THE MAKERS OF IDOLS ARE MERE MORTALS.

IRENAEUS: When, however, the Scripture terms them [gods] that are not gods, it does not declare them as gods in every sense but with a certain addition and signification, by which they are shown to be no gods at all, as with David, "The gods of the heathens are idols of demons"[2] and "You shall not follow other gods."[3] For in the fact that he says "the God of the heathen," yet the heathen are ignorant of the true God, and he calls them "other gods," he thereby bars their claim [to be looked on] as gods at all. But as to what they are in their own person, he speaks concerning them, "for they are," he says, "the idols of demons." And Isaiah says, "Let them be confounded, all who blaspheme God and carve useless things; even I am witness, says God." He removes them from [the category of] gods, but he makes use of the word alone, for this [purpose] that we may know of whom he speaks. AGAINST HERESIES 3.6.3.[4]

THE IRONY OF IDOLATRY. ATHANASIUS: How could he fail to pity them in this also, seeing that they worship them that cannot see. In hearing,

[1]GCS 57(9):285. [2]Ps 96:5 (95:5 LXX). [3]Ps 81:9 (80:9 LXX). [4]ANF 1:419**.

they pray to them that cannot hear. Born with life and reason, people, as they are, call gods things that do not move at all but do not even have life. Strangest of all, do they serve as their masters beings whom they themselves keep under their own power? Against the Heathen 13.4.[5]

44:12 The Ironsmith and the Idol

The Foolishness of Idolatry. Theodoret of Cyr: [Isaiah] has demonstrated that the production of these so-called gods relies on contributions. Their creator needs the blacksmith to prepare the tools and the whetstone for sharpening them; for his part, the bronzesmith needs coal and fire, while the constructor of the objects needs food and drink! It takes all this to prepare a god who is worshiped by these ignorant people. Isaiah is not finished mocking them. After choosing a log, the artisan immediately measures the so-called god. whereas the true God is immeasurable. He then shapes it with the appropriate tools, whereas the real God has no form or shape. . . . He does not copy divine characteristics but human ones; he shapes his human image and adores his own image as if it were divine. Commentary on Isaiah 13.44.12.[6]

The Artisans Make Idols to Satisfy Their Bodily Needs. Isho'dad of Merv: "He becomes hungry, and his strength fails." The first reason for the making of idols is the need of their makers. They are hungry and thirsty and have no food, and, therefore, they make idols, so that their need may be satisfied, thanks to what they themselves do. According to Henana,[7] it is with regard to the weakness of the idols that the prophet says that they cannot deliver anybody from these needs, when they hunger and thirst, not even the person who makes them and believes he has made a god. Commentary on Isaiah 44.12.[8]

---

[5]NPNF 2 4:11. [6]SC 295:472. [7]Henana (c. 545-610), a significant figure in Syriac literature who wrote many exegetical works on the Old and New Testaments. The majority of his writings are now lost, and fragments of them are preserved in the works of Isho'dad and other later Syriac authors. [8]CSCO 303(128):46.

44:14-20 WORSHIPING BLOCKS OF WOOD

[14]He cuts down cedars; or he chooses a holm tree or an oak and lets it grow strong among the trees of the forest; he plants a cedar and the rain nourishes it. [15]Then it becomes fuel for a man; he takes a part of it and warms himself, he kindles a fire and bakes bread; also he makes a god and worships it, he makes it a graven image and falls down before it. [16]Half of it he burns in the fire; over the half he eats flesh, he roasts meat and is satisfied; also he warms himself and says, "Aha, I am warm, I have seen the fire!" [17]And the rest of it he makes into a god, his idol; and falls down to it and worships it; he prays to it and says, "Deliver me, for thou art my god!"

[18]They know not, nor do they discern; for he has shut their eyes, so that they cannot see, and their minds, so that they cannot understand. [19]No one considers, nor is there knowledge or discernment to say, "Half of it I burned in the fire, I also baked bread on its coals, I roasted flesh and have eaten; and shall I make the residue of it an abomination? Shall I fall down before a block of wood?"

He feeds on ashes; a deluded mind has led him astray, and he cannot deliver himself or say, "Is there not a lie in my right hand?"

OVERVIEW: The reality is that idols are made out of all sorts of base materials in ways that befit their corruptibility (JUSTIN MARTYR). In contrast, God needs neither food nor drink (EUSEBIUS). The use of trees to make gods is a real confusion of what wood was intended for by the Creator (THEODORET). Idolatry is, in more recent times, to be found in those who worship the clever artifice of human teachings (JEROME). Heresies are usually related to the myths of the pagans (CYRIL). It is foolish to worship a piece of wood; is God fabricated in that way (THEODORET)?

44:15 *Then the Wood Becomes Fuel*

WOOD USED FOR FUEL, THEN FOR IDOLATRY. JUSTIN MARTYR: We do not honor with many sacrifices and garlands of flowers such deities as humans have formed and set in shrines and called gods. For we see that these are soulless and dead and do not have the form of God (for we do not consider that God has such a form as some say that they imitate to his honor). These are names and forms of those wicked demons that have appeared. For why need we tell you who already know, into what forms the artisans, carving and cutting, casting and hammering, fashion their materials? And often out of vessels of dishonor, by merely changing the form and making an image of the requisite shape, they make what they call a god; which we consider not only senseless but to be even insulting to God, who, having indescribable glory and form, thus gets his name attached to things that are corruptible and require constant service. FIRST APOLOGY 9.1-3.[1]

GOD DOES NOT HUNGER OR THIRST. EUSEBIUS OF CAESAREA: What do you think of them, and what is the nature of those who make gods from inanimate statues? For it is easy to see in the latter that they are works of artisans, prepared by axes and drills and such tools, the invention of skillful and industrious people, who through a need of food have found an instrument of leisurely falsehood. What do you think of the nature of God and about whether God needs our sacrifices and whether God is weak, as if according to Symmachus he is hungry and weak and feeble and cannot even drink water. The statement that God cannot drink water implies that he desperately needs liquid, while in fact God shares in no such thing, as though he were a dumb creature. COMMENTARY ON ISAIAH 2.26.[2]

A BLASPHEMOUS USE OF GOD'S CREATION. THEODORET OF CYR: The prophet proceeds to teach that the Creator gave the forests and woods on the mountains to supply food and fuel and for the sake of human bodies. They, however, take a holm oak, an oak or a cedar that God has planted and watered by providing rain for the benefit of human bodies and use these trees to create gods. COMMENTARY ON ISAIAH 13.44.13.[3]

44:18 *Lack of Discernment*

HERETICS FASHION DECEITS. JEROME: Whatever is said about idols can also be referred to the leaders of heresies, who form likenesses of their teachings with a heart of deceitful artifice and worship those things that they know to be facsimiles . . . and abusing the untrained minds of the common people with dialectical skill, just as with axes and files, with lines and planes they form their gods. The sweet talkers beat with a hammer and embellish with the fineness of their speech. COMMENTARY ON ISAIAH 12.18.[4]

THE FOOLISHNESS OF THE HERETICS. CYRIL OF ALEXANDRIA: The wise and eloquent people

[1]ANF 1:165**. [2]GCS 57(9):285-86. [3]SC 295:474. [4]AGLB 35:1355.

among the pagans are full of admiration for a well-turned phrase. One of their main preoccupations is with elegance of expression. They are filled with the greatest enthusiasm for good style and take great pride in verbal dexterity. The base material of their poets is merely lies fashioned in rhythms and meters for grace and harmony, but for truth they have little if any regard. I would say that they are sick from the lack of any true or proper notion of the nature and reality of God. ... And God said of them through the voice of Isaiah, "Know that their hearts are dust and that they have erred.".... As for the inventors of impure heresies, those profaners and apostates who have opened their mouths against the divine glory, "those who have uttered perverted things,"[5] we could accuse them of having slipped in their madness as low as the foolish pagans; perhaps they have slipped even lower, for it would have been better never to have known the way of sacred truth than once to have known it, to have turned away from the sacred commandment that was handed on to them. ON THE UNITY OF CHRIST.[6]

44:19 Wood for Warmth

WHY BURN THE LEFTOVER WOOD? THEODORET OF CYR: If it is a god, [Isaiah] says, the whole of the wood should be divine. Why, therefore, do you burn leftover parts of the wood and avail yourself of the fire to provide for your food, since at one time you bake bread, at another you boil and roast meat, and both eat and warm yourself and enjoy its light? Is not the wood that is put into the fire of the same kind as that which you worship? How, therefore, can you cast aside the one and adore the other? COMMENTARY ON ISAIAH 13.44.17.[7]

44:20 A Lie in My Right Hand

THE SPIRIT ENABLES SIGHT. THEODORET OF CYR: Foolishness has mastered them; they have lost the faculty of reasoning and are slaves to folly. This is why I will put my Spirit on your descendants, so that they will be delivered from error, for in no other way can they receive the truth. "See, you will not say, There is a lie in my right hand." The other interpreters join this passage to the one that precedes: "[Know] that no one is able to deliver his soul and no one says, is it a lie that you have in your right hand?" [Isaiah] has, therefore, said about the people who are in error that they do not recognize as a lie that which they are holding. But according to the Septuagint, this phrase, which is put into the mouth of God, should be understood thus: "Are my works," he says, "like those of a whetstone? Has a human made me? Am I an idol? Am I fabricated by cutting wood or stones of gold or silver?" COMMENTARY ON ISAIAH 13.44.20.[8]

---

[5]Acts 20:30. [6]OUC 49-50. [7]ITA 655-56; SC 295:474. [8]ITA 656*; SC 295:476.

44:21-24 THE SALVATION OF ISRAEL

[21]Remember these things, O Jacob,
  and Israel, for you are my servant;
I formed you, you are my servant;

O Israel, you will not be forgotten by me.
[22]I have swept away your transgressions like
  a cloud,

and your sins like mist;
return to me, for I have redeemed you.

[23]*Sing, O heavens, for the* LORD *has done it;*
   shout, O depths of the earth;
break forth into singing, O mountains,
   O forest, and every tree in it!
For the LORD *has redeemed Jacob,*

and will be glorified in Israel.

[24]*Thus says the* LORD, *your Redeemer,*
   who formed you from the womb:
"I am the LORD, *who made all things,*
   who stretched out the heavens alone,
   who spread out the earth—Who was with
   me?[c]*—"*

c Another reading is *who spread out the earth by myself*

OVERVIEW: God works in salvation to remove the colors of iniquity that prevent the divine light from shining through the soul (ORIGEN). Anticipations of pardon came before Christ, but only with the incarnation has full pardon come (THEODORET). The fullness of such salvation is reason for much rejoicing (PROCOPIUS). The whole creation, in fact, rejoices. The persons of the Trinity cooperated in creation (THEODORET, ATHANASIUS).

44:22 Transgressions Swept Away

THE SCRIPTURE CLEANSES THE SOUL. ORIGEN: It is as though a malicious painter brought together colors to paint an image of the earthly that God did not make in you. So you must now beg God, as the prophet says, "Blot out your iniquities as a cloud, and your sins as a mist." And when [God] has blotted out all those colors in you which have been taken up from the reddish hues of malice, then that image that was created by God will shine brightly in you. You see, therefore, how the divine Scriptures bring in forms and figures by which the soul may be instructed toward knowledge and cleansing of the soul. HOMILIES ON GENESIS 13.4.[1]

PARTIAL AND FULL FORGIVENESS. THEODORET OF CYR: God pardoned Israel's sins when he brought them out of the Babylonian captivity. But, really and truly, it was only after the incarnation that God forgave the sins of those who

believed in him. He removed the cloud of their sins and supplied them with eternal life. COMMENTARY ON ISAIAH 13.44.22.[2]

44:23 Depths of the Earth Shout

REASONS FOR REJOICING. PROCOPIUS OF GAZA: He calls "depths" what he once called "mountains." They excel in works and words.... For there is a great difference between grace and the law, since the law threatens punishments to those who transgress and calls out a command for repentance. Yet these heralds of grace, rejoicing, cry out proclaiming to the world the forgiveness of sins and justification by faith and the imparting of the Holy Spirit and the radiance of sonship [adoption], as well as the kingdom of heaven and the hope which will not pass away—good things beyond imagining....

The heralds of grace rejoice because Israel has been redeemed and the Son of God glorified. He is their kinsman by nature yet truly God. This moves the earth and its parts to praise. God, who has redeemed Jacob and Israel, will be glorified, or, as in the other translations, "He will be glorified in Israel."[3] COMMENTARY ON ISAIAH 44.6-23.[4]

CREATION REFLECTS THE WONDER OF THE TRINITY. THEODORET OF CYR: Again, the pro-

---

[1]FC 71:193-94**. [2]SC 295:476-78. [3]This translation of "the others," as also attested by Eusebius, is closer to the Hebrew. [4]PG 87:2412.

phetic text has made use of a personification. Just as when [Isaiah] accuses Israel, he has invited the heavens and the earth to serve as witness, so also when he announces benefits, he invites creation anew to partake in the joy; it is not as though the elements are animate, but when we are depressed, they seem somber to us, and when we are happy, they naturally seem more radiant. It is not the elements that have changed, but it is to us that they present this appearance. If, however, one desires to apprehend the celestial powers by the phrase "the heavens" and the holy prophets by "the foundations of the earth," with the thought that they are the ones who sustain [the benefits], one will not be far from the truth. For the Lord has said, "There is joy in the presence of the angels of God over one sinner who repents."[5] One can understand the mountains, hills and the woods in a similar fashion. After the return of Israel, they flourished again because they were cultivated and were the source of rejoicing on the mountains. COMMENTARY ON ISAIAH 14.44.23.[6]

44:24 The Lord Stretched Out the Heavens

THE ONE CREATOR IS FATHER, SON AND HOLY SPIRIT. THEODORET OF CYR: The text has presented, at the same time, a triple teaching: God is the creator, the master and the protector. For the term "Lord" demonstrates his sovereignty; the idea of "redemption," God's protection; and that of "formation," the creation. "I am the Lord who performs all these things." It is I who have sent you the sorrows and who will obtain the joys for you. Then God shows, by the events that have already happened, what he is able to do. "I alone stretched out the heaven and established the earth." This again serves to refute completely the madness of Arius and Eunomius, for who is the one who alone has created the elements? Is it the Father? Then the Son is not the Creator. Or is it the Son? Then the Father is not the Creator. But if it is the Father and the Son, how should we understand the term "alone"? Surely it is evident that we must understand it of the one divinity of

the Trinity. COMMENTARY ON ISAIAH 14.44.24.[7]

THE FIRSTBORN SON. ATHANASIUS: And when the prophet says concerning the creation, "That stretches forth the heavens alone," and when God says, "I only stretch out the heavens," it is made plain to everyone that in the "Only" is signified also the Word of the Only, in whom "all things were made" and without whom "was made not one thing."[8] Therefore, if they were made through the Word, and yet he says, "Only," and together with that Only is understood the Son, through whom the heavens were made, so also then, if it is said, "One God," and "I Only," and "I the First," in that "One" and "Only" and "First" is understood the Word co-existing, as in the Light the Radiance. And this can be understood of no other than the Word alone. For all other things subsisted out of nothing through the Son and are greatly different in nature, but the Son himself is natural and true offspring from the Father. And thus the very passage that these insensate have thought fit to adduce, "I the First," in defense of their heresy, does rather expose their perverse spirit. For God says, "I the first, and I the last"; if then, as though ranked with the things after him, he is said to be first of them, so that they come next to him, then certainly you will have shown that he himself precedes the works in time only; which, to go no further, is extreme irreligion. But if it is in order to prove that he is not from any, nor any before him, but that he is Origin and Cause of all things and to destroy the Gentile fables that he has said, "I the first," it is plain also that when the Son is called firstborn, this is done not for the sake of ranking him with the creation but to prove the framing and adoption of all things through the Son. For as the Father is first, so also is [the Son] both first, as image of the First, and because the First is in him, and also offspring from the Father, in whom the whole creation is created and adopted into sonship. DISCOURSE AGAINST THE ARIANS 3.24.9.[9]

---

[5]Lk 15:10. [6]ITA 658*; SC 315:12-14. [7]ITA 659*; SC 315:14. [8]Jn 1:3. [9]NPNF 2 4:398-99.

44:25-28 THE POWER OF THE WORD

²⁵*who frustrates the omens of liars,*
  and makes fools of diviners;
who turns wise men back,
  and makes their knowledge foolish;
²⁶*who confirms the word of his servant,*
  and performs the counsel of his messengers;
who says of Jerusalem, "She shall be inhabited,"
  and of the cities of Judah, "They shall be built,

and I will raise up their ruins";
²⁷*who says to the deep, "Be dry,*
  I will dry up your rivers";
²⁸*who says of Cyrus, "He is my shepherd,*
  and he shall fulfil all my purpose";
saying of Jerusalem. "She shall be built,"
  and of the temple, "Your foundation shall be laid."

OVERVIEW: The faithful do not look to the heathen world for their understanding of God (TERTULLIAN). To effect his will, they know that God only needs to speak (THEODORET). What is taught by God will endure time and judgment (BASIL). The sovereign God, who can give wisdom to a foreign king (JEROME), is ready and able to destroy demonic powers (EPHREM).

44:25 Making Knowledge Foolish

GOD MAKES THEIR KNOWLEDGE FOOLISH. TERTULLIAN: Remember that the "heart of humanity is ashes," according to the estimate of God, and that "the very wisdom of the world is foolishness."[1] . . . Then, if the heretic seeks refuge in the depraved thoughts of the vulgar or the imaginations of the world, I must say to him, "Part company with the heathen, O heretic!" For although you are all agreed in imagining a God, yet while you do so in the name of Christ, so long as you deem yourself a Christian, you are a different person from a heathen. So give the nonbeliever back his own view of things, since he does not himself learn from yours. Why lean on a blind guide, if you have eyes of your own? Why be clothed by one who is naked, if you have put on Christ? ON THE RESURRECTION OF THE FLESH 3.[2]

44:26 The Word of His Servant

THE PROPHET IS THE SERVANT. THEODORET OF CYR: Here he calls "servant" the very prophet who is exercising the ministry of these words. "And verifying the counsel of his messengers." Not only of this messenger, he says, but also that of all the others who transmit the divine word. Thus, it is not without forethought that he has made this declaration here but to give force to what is going to be said, for he prophesies in the next passage the royalty of Cyrus, who was the first to reign over the Persians, and the return of the people, the reconstruction of Jerusalem and the total defeat of Babylon. This is why he has prefaced it with "And confirming the word of his servant." "Who says to Jerusalem, you shall be inhabited; and to the cities of Judea, you shall be built, and its desert places shall spring forth." The text has shown the tremendous power of the Creator: I only have to speak, he says, and my will is accomplished; for it is by a word that I likewise effected the creation. COMMENTARY ON ISAIAH 14.44.26.[3]

44:27 Who Speaks to the Deep

---

[1]1 Cor 1:20. [2]ANF 3:547. [3]ITA 659-60*; SC 315:16.

ONLY REVEALED TEACHING WILL REMAIN.
BASIL THE GREAT: Yet there will be a time when
all things will be burned up by fire, as Isaiah says
when he addresses the God of the universe: [You]
"who say to the deep, 'Be thou desolate, and I will
dry up all your rivers.'" Casting aside, therefore,
the wisdom that has been turned into foolishness, receive with us the teaching of truth,
homely in speech but infallible in doctrine. HOM-
ILIES ON THE HEXAMERON 3.6.[4]

**THE DEMONIC RIVERS OF IDOLATRY WILL
DRY UP.** EPHREM THE SYRIAN: "I will dry up
your rivers," that is, he will extend his hand over
the Euphrates. In a different way, we may intend
that the Lord will destroy the devil and his
frauds, into which he plunges people as into a sea.
And the rivers, which he dries up, are the armies
of his iniquity. COMMENTARY ON ISAIAH 44.27.[5]

44:28 Cyrus Is My Shepherd

CYRUS WILL SHEPHERD THE PEOPLE TOWARD

GOD'S PURPOSE. JEROME: And he who attacks
Jerusalem and destroys Babylon, says also to
Cyrus the king of the Persians, who first
destroyed Babylon and the Chaldeans, "You are
my shepherd," or as the Septuagint translates,
"that you might be wise." The cause of this difficulty is clear. For the Hebrew word *ro'i*, if we read
a letter *res* (r), means "my shepherd," if with a letter *daleth* (d), then "knowing or understanding,"
whose similarity is only distinguished by a little
apex, and on account of this the two words are
often confused. It is written at the start of Ezra,
the prophet, that at the edict of Cyrus, the king of
the Persians and Medes, the captivity of the people of Israel was ended and those who wanted to
return were sent back to Jerusalem under
Zerubabel son of Salathihel and Hiesu the son of
Iosdech the high priest.[6] The Lord inspired Cyrus
to do his will and carry out his orders. COMMEN-
TARY ON ISAIAH 12.20.[7]

---

[4]FC 46:47. [5]SESHS 2:113. [6]Ezra 1. [7]AGLB 35:1360-61.

45:1-3 CYRUS THE DELIVERER

[1]Thus says the LORD to his anointed, to Cyrus,
　　whose right hand I have grasped,
to subdue nations before him
　　and ungird the loins of kings,
to open doors before him
　　that gates may not be closed:
[2]"I will go before you
　　and level the mountains,[d]

I will break in pieces the doors of bronze
　　and cut asunder the bars of iron,
[3]I will give you the treasures of darkness
　　and the hoards in secret places,
that you may know that it is I, the LORD,
　　the God of Israel, who call you by your
　　name."

d One ancient Ms Gk: Heb *the swellings*

OVERVIEW: Cyrus was chosen by God to fulfill a
function (THEODORET). In the work of Cyrus,

God shows his sovereignty over the world
(CYRIL). The figure of Cyrus foreshadows that of

Jesus Christ (TERTULLIAN). God has the power to make changes to the geological fabric of the earth (AMBROSE). The Lord has invested Cyrus with sovereignty (THEODORET). Knowing our God has such strength, not even death is to be feared, especially since we have more certainty about what lies beyond it than did those in Old Testament times (CHRYSOSTOM). Treasures now hidden will be revealed (BASIL). This showing of the divine treasures can happen anticipatively in this life through the spiritual reading of the Scriptures (ORIGEN, GREGORY OF NAZIANZUS). Or the treasures in the deep could be the patriarchs who waited for Christ in hell (CHRYSOSTOM). In this revelation, the Word illumines the dark things in the souls of believers (CASSIAN).

45:1 To His Anointed

THOSE DESIGNATED FOR A SPECIFIC FUNCTION. THEODORET OF CYR: The divine Scripture designates under the name "anointed" not only those who are brought forward for unction but also those whom the God of the universe has singled out with a view toward [fulfilling] a required function. Thus, referring to the patriarchs who lived before the law, he has said, "Touch not my anointed ones."[1] Here, in any case, he has given to Cyrus the title "anointed," in order to announce that it is [God] who has chosen him as king in such a way as to defeat the empire of the Babylonians, to make an end to the captivity of the Jews and to [re]construct the temple of God. COMMENTARY ON ISAIAH 14.45.1.[2]

CYRUS UNKNOWINGLY FORESHADOWS THE ANOINTED ONE. CYRIL OF ALEXANDRIA: What is most clear is the power of the prophecy or the prophetic preaching. We should look at each of the lines to see clearly what seems obscure. For it calls Cyrus "Christ" and not as if he were one of the saints, who could bear this name, but it functions to mean that he bears the name as anointed by God, in that God was in the habit of anointing those called to the kingdom even if they were not

saints or worshipers. For we find the holy prophets saying to those who have received this, "The Lord has anointed you king over Israel."[3] So Cyrus is the anointed one, anticipating Christ as king. Only through God has he triumphed and been brought to this triumphal song so as to reflect that since he is called "anointed," that is, by chrism and selection, he is called by God to the kingdom . . . so that you might know. . . . "I am the Lord God who calls your name, the God of Israel, for the sake of Jacob my servant/son and Jacob my chosen. I, God alone, have called you for this, and I have honored you with radiance, that you will be civil to my servant Israel. I have called you and have crowned you with glory, even though you do not know that I am the Lord and that there is no God other than me."[4] COMMENTARY ON ISAIAH 4.2.45.1.[5]

THE FIGURE OF CYRUS FORESHADOWS THAT OF CHRIST. TERTULLIAN: "Thus says the Lord God to my Christ [the] Lord, whose right hand I have held, that the nations may hear him, 'the powers of kings will I burst asunder; I will open before him the gates, and the cities shall not be closed to him.'" This very thing we see now fulfilled. For whose right hand does God the Father hold but Christ's, his Son? All nations have heard of him, that is, people of all nations have believed. Their preachers, the apostles, are pointed to in the psalms of David: "Into the entire earth," he says, "is gone out their sound, and to the ends of the earth their words."[6] For on whom else have nations the world over believed but on the Christ who has now already come? . . . In all these places the name of the Christ has already come to reign. He is the one before whom the gates of all cities have been opened and to whom none are closed, before whom iron bars have been crumbled and brazen gates opened. There is a spiritual sense affixed to these expressions. The hearts of individuals, having been blockaded in various ways by

---

[1]Ps 105:15 (104:15 LXX). [2]ITA 668; SC 315:18. [3]Ps 45:7 (44:8 LXX). [4]Is 45:3-5. [5]PG 70:949-52. [6]Ps 19:4 (18:5 LXX); Rom 10:18.

the devil, are now unbarred by the faith of Christ. This promise has already been evidently fulfilled, inasmuch as in all these places there are people who live believing in the name of Christ. An Answer to the Jews 7.[7]

45:2 Level the Mountains

The Processes of Erosion Are Directed by God. Ambrose: I maintain in accord with the Scriptures that God can extend the low-lying regions and the open plains, as he has said, "I will go before you and make level the mountains." The very force of water can also make its bed deeper by the violent movements of the waves and by the impact of the surf of that wild element that day by day stirs up the bottom of the sea, drawing forth sands from its very depths. Six Days of Creation 3.3.15.45.1-7.[8]

The Lord Enables Cyrus's Sovereignty. Theodoret of Cyr: By all that is about to be said, he has taught that he has invested Cyrus as king, he has given him the necessary sovereignty to direct his empire with good will and so that the disposition of difficult matters is mitigated and facilitated. This is what the phrase means: "I will level mountains, and I will break to pieces brazen doors." Commentary on Isaiah 14.45.2.[9]

Death Is Not to Be Feared. Chrysostom: Let us not fear punishment. By this faith we shall escape punishment. . . . This is the correct attitude of the servants of God to be. For if those who were brought up under the old dispensation, when death was not yet slain,[10] or his "brazen gates broken down" or his "iron bars cut into pieces" so nobly encountered their end, how destitute of all defense or excuse shall we be, if, after having had the benefit of such great grace, we attain not even to the same measure of virtue as they did, now when death is only a name, devoid of reality. For death is nothing more than a sleep, a journey, a migration, a rest, a tranquil haven, an escape from trouble and a freedom from the cares

of this present life! Homilies Concerning the Statues 7.1.[11]

45:3 Giving Treasures

The Anticipation of Treasures Now Hidden. Basil the Great: To one who believes, a promise is given by God: "I will give you hidden treasures, unseen ones." When we have been deemed worthy of knowledge face to face, we shall see also the depth in the storehouses of God. Homilies on the Psalms 15.5 (Psalm 32).[12]

The Mysteries of Scripture. Origen: The higher and profounder spiritual meaning is the "hidden treasures of wisdom and knowledge,"[13] which the Holy Spirit speaking through Isaiah calls "dark and unseen and concealed treasures." These treasures require for their discovery the help of God, who alone is able to "break in pieces the gates of brass" by which they are shut in and concealed and to burst the iron bolts and bars that prevent us from entering in and reaching all those truths written in veiled language in Genesis concerning the various races of souls and the seeds and generations named there, whether closely akin to Israel or widely separated from his posterity. On First Principles 4.3.11.[14]

The Scriptures Open the Treasures of Faith. Gregory of Nazianzus: Who is the person whose heart has never been made to burn,[15] as the Scriptures have been opened, with the pure words of God that have been tried in a furnace;[16] who has not, by a triple inscription[17] of them on the breadth of his heart, attained the mind of Christ,[18] or been admitted to the treasures that to most people remain hidden, secret and dark, to gaze on the riches therein and become able to enrich others, comparing spiritual things with spiritual.[19] In Defense of His

[7]ANF 3:157-58**. [8]FC 42:78-79. [9]ITA 668; SC 315:18. [10]Hos 13:14. [11]NPNF 1 9:390**. [12]FC 46:237*. [13]Col 2:3. [14]OFP 306. [15]Lk 24:32. [16]Ps 12:6 (11:7 LXX). [17]Prov 22:20 LXX. [18]1 Cor 2:16. [19]1 Cor 2:13.

FLIGHT TO PONTUS, ORATION 2.96.[20]

THE RESTING PLACE OF ABRAHAM, ISAAC AND JACOB. CHRYSOSTOM: "I will give you the treasures of darkness." . . . This is the way [Isaiah] referred to hell. Even if it was hell, it still preserved the sacred souls and precious vessels, Abraham, Isaac and Jacob. This is why Isaiah called it a place of treasures, even if in darkness, because the Sun of justice had not yet penetrated there with its rays or with any message on the resurrection. DEMONSTRATION AGAINST THE PAGANS 4.14-15.[21]

THE WORD BRINGS SELF-KNOWLEDGE OF SECRET SIN. JOHN CASSIAN: Then the word of

God will precede us and first humble the powerful of our earth—that is, these same harmful passions that we wish to subdue and that claim dominion for themselves and a most cruel tyranny in our mortal body—and it will make them submit to our investigation and our exposure. And, breaking open the gates of ignorance and smashing the bolts of the vices that shut us out from true knowledge, it will lead us to our concealed secrets and, according to the apostle, it will, once we have been enlightened, reveal to us "the hidden things of darkness and make manifest the counsels of hearts."[22] INSTITUTES 5.2.2.[23]

---

[20]NPNF 2 7:224. [21]FC 73:208. [22]1 Cor 4:5. [23]ACW 58:117-18.

45:4-7 NO OTHER GOD

4"For the sake of my servant Jacob,
  and Israel my chosen,
I call you by your name,
  I surname you, though you do not know me.
5I am the LORD, and there is no other,
  besides me there is no God;
  I gird you, though you do not know me,

6that men may know, from the rising of the sun
  and from the west, that there is none besides
  me;
  I am the LORD, and there is no other.
7I form light and create darkness,
  I make weal and create woe,
  I am the LORD, who do all these things."

OVERVIEW: Cyrus was an instrument of God's will, even though he remained ignorant of God (ISHO'DAD, THEODORET). He could know nothing of the Son who exists together with the Father, as opposed to existing as another Father (TERTULLIAN). There is only one God, as opposed to the many false gods of the world (CHRYSOSTOM). It will be readily seen that he, and not the idols, is the immediate cause of the movement of the earth, sun and moon and of all creation (NOVATIAN).

God may use unpleasant circumstances to produce healing (CHRYSOSTOM). The reach of sin is never allowed by God to attain its full extent (AUGUSTINE). Evil has been called into existence for the sake of purifying and training obstinate souls (ORIGEN). What we receive in this life depends much on our behavior before God (EUSEBIUS). However, we should never imagine that God is the source of evil (TERTULLIAN). God sometimes sends calamities to correct and bring health to his people (CHRYSOSTOM). For our instruction, God creates both light and darkness, what seem to be good and bad events (THEODORET).

45:5 Though You Do Not Know Me

CYRUS IS UNKNOWINGLY A PART OF GOD'S DESIGN. ISHO'DAD OF MERV: "I have called you by name, I have surnamed you, though you do not know me." God addresses these words to Cyrus, so as to say, I have honored you to such an extent that, even before you were born, I had made your name illustrious and made you a part of my design to give freedom, through your hands, back to my people who are so dear to me. Even though I have honored you so much through my prophets, you were never interested in knowing me. Even though I acted, so that every nation might know me through you, you did not want to recognize me as the master and the creator of universe, but you have given the name of gods to others instead of me. COMMENTARY ON ISAIAH 45.4-6.[1]

CYRUS IS A CHOSEN INSTRUMENT. THEODORET OF CYR: [Cyrus] also was a slave to the error of idolatry. Even though he had received kingship from the God of the universe and obtained such great assistance from him, he had not known the dispenser of these benefits. God had nevertheless deemed him worthy, despite his error, of all these benefits. He had appointed him as an instrument of chastisement to the Babylonians and of the liberation of Israel. However, I have found some copies that bear this text: "Meanwhile, Israel, you have not known me." But I have not found the presence of the word *Israel*, either in the Hebrew text or with the other interpreters or in the Hexapla version [Origen's compilation] of the Septuagint. And it is justifiably so, for it is not Israel that he is accusing of scorning him, but Cyrus. Then he also indicates the cause of the liberation of the Jews. COMMENTARY ON ISAIAH 14.45.5.[2]

45:6 There Is No Other God

UNDIVIDED AND INSEPARABLE. TERTULLIAN: And inasmuch as this Son is undivided and inseparable from the Father, so is he to be reckoned as being in the Father, even when he is not named. The fact is, if he had named him expressly, he would have separated him, saying in so many words, "Beside me there is none else, except my Son." In short, he would have made his Son actually another, after excepting him from others. AGAINST PRAXEAS 18.[3]

BESIDES ME THERE IS NO GOD. CHRYSOSTOM: The prophets were not denying the Son (God forbid!), but they wished to cure the Jews of their weakness and, meanwhile, to persuade them to give up their belief in the many gods that did not exist. AGAINST THE ANOMOEANS, HOMILY 5.23.[4]

45:7 Forming Light, Creating Darkness

THE IMMEDIATE CAUSE OF LIGHT AND DARKNESS. NOVATIAN: Ever desiring to become more completely known to us and to incite our minds to his worship, he said, "I am the Lord who made the light and created the darkness," that we may not think that some other unknown One was the artificer of those alternations whereby the nights and days are regulated; but rather, and with greater truth, we may acknowledge God as their Creator. ON THE TRINITY 3.5.[5]

GOD PERMITS WHAT WE CALL EVIL FOR OUR GOOD. CHRYSOSTOM: For since we are accustomed to use the word *evil* to speak of calamities, and not only of thefts and adulteries, so the prophet allows this usage. On this basis the prophet can say, "There is no evil in the city that the Lord has not done."[6] This too, by means of Isaiah, God has made clear, when he said, "I am God who makes peace and creates evil," again

---

[1]CSCO 303(128):47. [2]ITA 670*; SC 315:20-22. [3]ANF 3:613. [4]FC 72:147*. [5]FC 67:30**. [6]Amos 3:6.

naming calamities evils. This evil also Christ hints at, thus saying to the disciples, "Sufficient for the day is the evil thereof,"[7] that is to say, the affliction, the misery. It is manifest then on all sides that he here calls punishment an evil, even as we commonly do, affirming at the same time that God brings these on us. This affords us the greatest view of his providence. For the physician is not only to be commended when he leads forth the patient into gardens and meadows, nor even into baths and pools of water, nor yet when he sets before him a well-furnished table, but when he orders him to remain without food, when he oppresses him with hunger and lays him low with thirst, confines him to his bed, making his house a prison, depriving him of the very light and shadowing his room on all sides with curtains. When he cuts, and when he cauterizes and when he brings his bitter medicines, he is equally a physician. CONCERNING THE POWER OF DEMONS 1.5.[8]

GOD MAKES THE GOOD AND ORDERS THE EVIL. AUGUSTINE: "I make good things and 'create' evil things." For to "create" means to order and arrange. And so in most manuscripts it is written, "I make good things and order evil things." To make is to give being to something that did not exist at all, but to order is to arrange something that already exists in such a way that it becomes greater and better. Thus, when God says, "I order evil things," he means those things that fall away, that tend to non-being, and not those that have attained their end. For it has been said that, owing to the divine providence, nothing is permitted to reach a state of non-being. THE CATHOLIC AND MANICHAEAN WAYS OF LIFE 2.7.9.[9]

FOR THE SAKE OF DISCIPLINE. ORIGEN: In the same way also we explain the expressions, "I, who make peace and create evil"; for he calls into existence "corporeal" or "external" evils, while purifying and training those who would not be disciplined by the word and sound doctrine. This, then, is our answer to the question, "How is it

that God created evil?" AGAINST CELSUS 6.56.[10]

ACCORDING TO OUR DESERTS. EUSEBIUS OF CAESAREA: "From my works they will learn; for when I needed to inflict pain on my people for their repentance and discipline, I gave them up to warfare as if handing them over to darkness and wrath on account of their wickedness." Once they have turned and received help, [God] will deem it right to restore them, and it follows that the light of peace and of all good things will rise on them, but in my judgment also the things of wrath. So learn this lesson from me. As I am the creator of light and the leader of peace, likewise am I of dark things and those things considered painful. The evil things have been reckoned to the many whose creator inflicts evil on them. He does so whenever his righteous judgment appoints such, according to the various ways they deserve evil as judgment on their sins. COMMENTARY ON ISAIAH 2.27.[11]

MARCION'S TWISTED LOGIC. TERTULLIAN: Now (like many other persons nowadays, especially those who have a heretical proclivity), while morbidly brooding over the question of the origin of evil, Marcion's perception became blunted by the very irregularity of his researches. When he found the Creator declaring, "I am he that creates evil," Marcion had already concluded from other arguments that satisfy only twisted minds that God is the author of evil. So Marcion now applied to the Creator the figure of the corrupt tree bringing forth evil fruit, that is, moral evil, and then presumed that there ought to be another god, after the analogy of the good tree producing its good fruit. Accordingly, finding in Christ a different disposition—one of a simple and pure benevolence, differing from the Creator—Marcion readily argued that in his Christ had been revealed a new and strange divinity; and then with a little leaven he leavened the whole

---

[7]Mt 6:34. [8]NPNF 1 9:182**. [9]FC 56:71-72*. [10]ANF 4:599. [11]GCS 57(9):289.

lump of the faith, flavoring it with the acidity of his own heresy. AGAINST MARCION 1.2.[12]

CALAMITY AND MORAL FAILURE ARE TWO DIFFERENT THINGS. CHRYSOSTOM: These things have thus been clearly shown to you to be in some cases bad, some good and some in between, . . . the inspired author is saying the in-between things are not really bad but are thought to be by the general run of people—things like captivity, servitude and exile. Now, it is necessary to explain the reason for this statement. Loving as [God] is and quick to show mercy, while slow in exercising retribution and punishment, God sent prophets so as to avoid consigning the Jews to punishment, intending to frighten them in word, so as not to punish them in deed. . . .

Observing this and wishing to undermine the reform that was the result of such a threat, the devil sent down false prophets, and in contradiction of the prophets' threats of captivity, servitude and famine, false prophets preached the opposite—peace, prosperity and enjoyment of countless good things. Hence, the genuine prophets also mocked the false by saying, "Peace, peace—and where is peace?" This every scholar knows, that everything happened just as the prophets had foretold against the false prophets, who were undermining the people's zeal. So when they undermined the people in this way and corrupted them, God said through the prophets, "I, God, am making peace and creating evils." What sort of evils? Those mentioned—captivity, servitude and the like. Not fornication, licentiousness, avarice and anything else like that. . . .

Do not let the false prophets undermine you; God can give you peace and consign you to captivity, which is the meaning of "making peace and creating evils." For you to learn that this is true, let us make a precise examination of the individual expressions. After saying before, "I am the one who brought light and darkness into being,"

he then went on to say, "making peace and creating evils." He cited two opposites first, and two opposites after that, for you to learn that he is referring not to fornication but to calamities. I mean, what is set as the opposite of peace? Clearly captivity, not licentiousness or fornication or avarice. So just as he cited two opposites first, so too in this case; the opposite of peace is not fornication, or adultery, or licentiousness or the other vices, but captivity and servitude. HOMILIES ON ISAIAH 45.6-7.[13]

LIGHT IS HAPPINESS, DARKNESS IS SADNESS. THEODORET OF CYR: He calls "light" here the happy events—the cessation of slavery, the liberation and the return—and "darkness" the sad happenings—the siege, the subjection, the enslavement. It is I, he says, who am the author of these two series of events, of these and of those. It is I who made use of Nebuchadnezzar to inflict the chastisement and who have chosen Cyrus as the instrument for the liberation. And just as I am the creator of the light and of darkness, and [just as] I have produced each of them so that they are used for humankind, I have inflicted bondage on Israel in its interest, and I have made the gift of freedom by reason of my benevolence. "Who make peace and create evil." He has clearly taught what he has meant under the name of darkness and of light: it is peace that he has called "light" and the events that seem bad "darkness." So [God] has called them evil, not because they are evil by nature but because people considered them thus. For we have the habit of saying, "Today is a bad day for me," not because the day itself is changed to some other nature but because in the course of that day some events happened that produced sorrow. COMMENTARY ON ISAIAH 14.45.7.[14]

---

[12]ANF 3:272**. [13]COTH 2:37-39**. [14]ITA 670-71*; SC 315:22.

45:8-12 THE POTTER AND HIS CLAY

[8]"Shower,* O heavens, from above,
   and let the skies rain[†] down righteousness;
let the earth open, that salvation may sprout
      forth,[e‡]
   and let it cause righteousness to spring up
      also;
   I the LORD have created it.

[9]"Woe to him who strives with his Maker,[#]
   an earthen vessel with the potter![f]
Does the clay say to him who fashions it,
   'What are you making'?
or 'Your work has no handles'?

[10]Woe to him who says to a father, 'What are
      you begetting?'
   or to a woman, 'With what are you in
      travail?'"
[11]Thus says the LORD,
   the Holy One of Israel, and his Maker:
"Will you question me[g] about my children,
   or command me concerning the work of my
      hands?
[12]I made the earth,
   and created man upon it;
it was my hands that stretched out the heavens,
   and I commanded all their host."

e One ancient Ms: Heb *that they may bring forth salvation*   f Cn: Heb *potsherds* or *potters*   g Cn: Heb *Ask me of things to come*   * Syriac (Peshitta) *Rejoice*   † Syriac (Peshitta) *and the clouds will rain*   ‡ Syriac (Peshitta) *that salvation may be multiplied*   # LXX *Will the plowman plow the earth all day?*

OVERVIEW: The clouds of righteousness that rain down from heaven are the words of absolution from the apostles and priests that water the earth by bringing justice and righteousness on the sins of the nations (EPHREM, THEODORET). This rain on the earth waters the seed that has been planted in the soil plowed and prepared by God's Servant Christ. He used the plow of the law in order not only to prepare the soil of his people's hearts but also to transform his people to a new spiritual life and worship. They, however, resisted Christ, questioning their own transformation by questioning and resisting the one who could bring it about (CYRIL). They demanded an accounting from the Creator for his deeds. But they should have realized they are only the clay issuing a challenge to their potter (THEODORET). God's long-range providence is to be learned from in all its particularity (NEMESIUS). God both did and does future things. Predestination allows for God's sovereign freedom and our responsibility for sin, and it is unfitting for the creation to ques-

tion the Creator (AUGUSTINE). God's will is unchanging, for why should God have to improve on his basic plan (FULGENTIUS)?

45:8 The Skies Rain Down Righteousness

CLOUDS OF RIGHTEOUSNESS RAIN SALVATION ON THE EARTH. EPHREM THE SYRIAN: "Rejoice, O heavens, from above," that is, rejoice over the salvation of the nations. The angels are delighted at the repentance of a single sinner. "And the clouds will rain down righteousness." The clouds, which rain down righteousness, are the apostles and the priests who justify through the absolution, which they give by means of baptism. "Let the earth open, that salvation may be multiplied." Justice, symbolized through the earth, is poured on the mind of the nations, and salvation shall multiply in every region. "And let it cause righteousness to spring up also." In the salvation of the nations also their justice is multiplied, and salvation and justice spring up and grow at the same time. COMMENTARY ON ISAIAH 45.8.[1]

"RAIN" IS THE DISCOURSE OF THE PROPHET.
THEODORET OF CYR: "And let the clouds rain righteousness." On the occasion of making previous threats, he has said, "I will command the clouds to rain no rain on it,"[2] and . . . it was the prophets who were referred to in this way. Here, therefore, the text invites the prophets to present, as a kind of rain, the discourse dealing with righteousness. In fact, those recognized as prophets after the return from exile were Haggai, Zechariah and Malachi. "And let the earth bring forth and blossom with mercy, and bring forth righteousness likewise." For it is fitting likewise that the people who benefit from such watering offer fruits in consonance with the watering. Thus, the rain provides discourse regarding righteousness; therefore, he demands from them the fruits of righteousness and mercy. For he has called the people who inhabit the earth "the earth." "I am the Lord who created you." It is I who likewise from the beginning have brought you into existence. COMMENTARY ON ISAIAH 14.45.8.[3]

45:9 Will the Plowman Plow the Earth All Day?

THE PLOW PREPARES THE SOIL. CYRIL OF ALEXANDRIA: This is a deep saying, veiled in much obscurity, yet at the same time very useful and true. I think I ought to make a brief preliminary exposition of what it is driving at. In this way my readers will find it more accessible and easier to understand. Thus the God of all things freed Israel from Egypt, rescued them from the error of polytheism and brought them by the law of Moses from the chicanery of the demons to the dawn of the true knowledge of God. He taught them to worship a single God and bow down before a single Lord. Then by means of types and shadows he wanted to raise them up to what was still better and more perfect, that is, to the things that are in Christ. For the law was a preliminary

instructor and was laid down until the time of setting aright. This came with the advent of our Savior Jesus Christ, when he set aside the shadow of the commandments of the law and the types found in the letter and introduced to those on earth the beauty of worship in spirit and in truth openly and without disguise.

But the Jews found this hard to bear, and as they were still complying with the types, they took action against Christ and accused him of breaking the Mosaic commandments.[4] . . . Therefore, since they found the benefit resulting from the preaching of the gospel unacceptable, although it was advancing them from the unprofitable shadow to spiritual fruitfulness, the prophet says to them, "Will the plowman plow the earth all day?" "O foolish people," he is saying, "a cultivator turns over the soil with the plow, but he does not go on doing it forever, nor is the whole business of cultivation taken up with plowing. For he turns over the soil not simply for the sake of doing so but in order that it might be made ready to receive the seed when he sows it and prove to be productive. Therefore I gave the hearts of all of you, which were once overgrown like wastelands, a preliminary working over, using the law of Moses as a plow, and, turning them over like a farmer, I made them suitable for sowing with good seed. Therefore accept what he offers and do not remain permanently attached to your beloved plow, which is the law." For he plowed, as I have said, not so that you should hold fast to plowing (for what would be the use of that?) but so that you should produce the fruits of truth. Since we have been spiritually refashioned in Christ, that is to say, we have been transformed, some of us from pagan error into the knowledge of the truth, and to a holy life through Christ the Savior of us all, others from Judaism into the acquisition of evangelical teachings and into a newness of worship that no longer cleaves to the dreariness of the types but instead is resplendent with the striking beauty of spiritual

[1]SESHS 2:115-117. [2]Is 5:6. [3]ITA 672-73*; SC 315:24. [4]Jn 5:18; 9:16.

worship, both we and they have been enriched with rebirth in Christ through water and the Spirit. COMMENTARY ON ISAIAH 4.2.45.9-10.[5]

45:9-10 Does the Clay Reply to the Potter?

THE POTTER SEEKS TO REFASHION HIS CLAY. CYRIL OF ALEXANDRIA: Conversely, the grace that descended on these was rejected and not accepted by the Jewish people. For they resisted, as I have said, the teachings of Christ. . . . But "I desire to refashion you," Christ is saying, "into something better, to remodel you into something finer through a spiritual birth (meaning, of course, through water and the Spirit). But you resisted my plans without understanding." Therefore, the prophet says, does the clay reproach the potter for not having an artisan's hand or for not knowing how to shape what was in his hands? Or does someone who is about to be begotten put the question to his own father, "Why are you begetting?" How do you, then, who are like clay in the potter's hands and have not knowledge at all of how your spiritual rebirth will take place, have the audacity to enter into argument? And why do you not rather understand that you should cede to the artisan and father the knowledge of how to do these things?[6] . . . It is therefore necessary to give way to what God says. He himself knows the way of his own works, and what he has fashioned is not to be curiously inquired into. It belongs to someone like ourselves to honor what transcends the human mind with an unquestioning faith.

You should also know that the prophet Jeremiah was sent to the house of the potter to watch him at work. When the pot turned out badly and the potter refashioned the clay into a new vessel, God said to him, "Can I not do with you as this potter has done, O house of Israel? Behold, like the clay in the potter's hand, so are you in my hand."[7] That we are transformed spiritually and brought to a holy and utterly good life is explained by Paul when he says, "And we all, with unveiled face, beholding the glory of the Lord, are being changed into his likeness from one degree of glory to another; for this comes from the Lord who is the Spirit."[8] Through him we are also reborn, for we no longer contain a corruptible seed but that which is sown by the word of the living God who endures forever. COMMENTARY ON ISAIAH 4.2.45.9-10.[9]

WHO DEMANDS AN ACCOUNTING FROM THE CREATOR? THEODORET OF CYR: Just as the potter models anew the vase of broken clay, [God] says, for my part, I will make you better than at first. "Will the plowman plow the earth all day?"[10] This comes back to saying it is not effective to use chastisement continually, for the cultivator does not keep tearing up the soil without ceasing. "Woe to him who disputes with the One who formed him!" "Shall the clay say to the potter, What are you doing that you do not work, nor have hands? Shall the thing formed answer him that formed it?" Since there were many in that epoch, and now likewise, who concern themselves ill-advisedly with divine providence and who attempt to study inquisitively the cause for the occurrence of wars, of periods of sterility of the soil, of premature deaths and of all the things of this nature, it is understandable that he should first of all deplore those who demand an accounting from the Creator of the universe. He, then, has skillfully closed their mouth by the image of the clay and the potter: the clay does not demand an accounting from the one who worked it regarding his rest or his work. In the same way is it no more fitting to occupy yourself rudely with divine matters, for you are precisely the clay. But there is between me and the potter the greatest difference there could be: the potter, though he is the creator of the utensil of clay, is nevertheless, on his part, the firstborn of the clay, whereas I possess an uncreated nature. Yet the clay does not say a word but supports the modeling that the

---

[5]COA 90-91; PG 70:960-61. [6]Cyril, a few pages later, cites the example of Nicodemus (Jn 3), who questioned how one could be born again of water and the Spirit. [7]Jer 18:6. [8]2 Cor 3:18. [9]COA 91-92; PG 70:961-64. [10]Is 28:24.

potter wishes to impose on it, while you pay no attention to my providence. COMMENTARY ON ISAIAH 14.45.9.[11]

PARTICULAR AND GENERAL PROVIDENCE. NEMESIUS OF EMESA: For we, who do not know at all what the future has in store and see merely our present circumstances, misjudge what will profit us. God . . . sees what is to come as if it were present. These prophecies are addressed, however, to those who make themselves God's judges. To them may also fittingly be cited those words of Scripture, "shall the clay say to the potter" and so forth.

How shall we not shun a person who legislates in opposition to the laws of God and issues decrees in opposition to the works of providence, whereas he dares not breathe a word against human laws? Therefore, leaving such exaggerations, or, to speak more truly, blasphemies, on one side, let us demonstrate the error of denying particular providence while acknowledging universal and general providence. ON THE NATURE OF MAN 44.66.[12]

GOD BOTH DID AND DOES FUTURE THINGS. AUGUSTINE: How do we think, except as in the way that the prophet also foretells of God, that he has done the things that are going to be? For he does not say, "Who *will* do the things that are going to be, but "who *did* the things that are going to be." Therefore, [God] both did them and is going to do them. For neither have they been done if he did not do them, nor are they going to be done if he will not do them. Therefore, [God] did them by predestining them; he is going to do them by working. TRACTATES ON THE GOSPEL OF JOHN 68.1.2.[13]

GOD FOREKNOWS FUTURE EVENTS. AUGUS-

TINE: By predestination God indeed foreknew that which he himself was going to do. Thus it was said, "He has made that which shall be."[14] Furthermore, [God] can foreknow even those things that he himself does not do, such as whatever sins there may be. There are certain things that are sins and at the same time punishment for sins, so that it is written, "God delivered them up to a reprobate mind, to do those things which are not fitting."[15] This is not the sin of God, however, but the judgment of God. PREDESTINATION OF THE SAINTS 10.[16]

45:11 Will You Question Me?

WHO IS QUALIFIED TO QUESTION GOD? AUGUSTINE: There is no doubt that human wills cannot resist the will of God, "who has done whatsoever he pleased in heaven and on earth,"[17] and who has even "formed the things that are to come."[18] Nor can the human will prevent [God] from doing what he wills, seeing that even with human wills, he does what he wills, when he wills to do it. ADMONITION AND GRACE 14.45.[19]

THUS SAYS THE LORD. FULGENTIUS OF RUSPE: "He who made the things that will be,"[20] therefore, the things that were to be done, he willed them to be spoken of as if done, because these things which come about changeably in time, he has made firm with the unchangeable eternity of his plan. Therefore, in those things as well, in which the effect of the work has not yet come to be, the plan of the Creator remains firm from eternity. LETTER 9.8.7.[21]

---

[11]ITA 673; SC 315:24-26. [12]LCC 4:440**. [13]FC 90:62-63**. [14]Is 45:11 LXX: *ho poiēsas ta eperchomena*. [15]Rom 1:28. [16]FC 86:241**. [17]Ps 135:6 (134:6 LXX). [18]Is 45:11 LXX. [19]FC 2:299**. [20]Is 44:24. [21]FC 95:406.

45:13-20 DIVINE INDWELLING

¹³"I have aroused him in righteousness,
    and I will make straight all his ways;
he shall build my city
    and set my exiles free,
not for price or reward,"
    says the Lord of hosts.

¹⁴Thus says the Lord:
"The wealth of Egypt and the merchandise
    of Ethiopia,
    and the Sabeans, men of stature,
shall come over to you and be yours,
    they shall follow you;
    they shall come over in chains and bow
        down to you.
They will make supplication to you, saying:
    'God is with you only, and there is no
        other,
    no god besides him.'"
¹⁵Truly, thou art a God who hides thyself,
    O God of Israel, the Savior.
¹⁶All of them are put to shame and
    confounded,
    the makers of idols go in confusion
        together.
¹⁷But Israel is saved by the Lord

with everlasting salvation;
    you shall not be put to shame or confounded
        to all eternity.

¹⁸For thus says the Lord,
who created the heavens
    (he is God!),
who formed the earth and made it
    (he established it;
he did not create it a chaos,
    he formed it to be inhabited!):
"I am the Lord, and there is no other.
¹⁹I did not speak in secret,
    in a land of darkness;
I did not say to the offspring of Jacob,
    'Seek me in chaos.'
I the Lord speak the truth,
    I declare what is right.

²⁰"Assemble yourselves and come,
    draw near together,
    you survivors of the nations!
They have no knowledge
    who carry about their wooden idols,
and keep on praying to a god
    that cannot save."

Overview: Christians read the Old Testament prophecy that "God is *in* you" as foreknowing that Christ existed as God through the full presence of God indwelling him (Eusebius, Marius, Cyril of Jerusalem). This is what the Lord has said—the one who is truly Lord, as opposed to those who apply this term to themselves but do not know what it truly means (Cyril). He is the Lord who will remake the heavens and earth after judgment (Methodius). As the recreator of all things, he does not keep himself hidden as the idols do (Theodoret), but he reveals himself clearly and mightily in order to elicit righteous living on the earth for those he has gathered together in righteousness (Cyril).

45:13 A Righteous King

The Son Is One in Being with the Father.
Eusebius of Caesarea: [The Septuagint reads],
"You are God, and we knew it not." The words
"we knew it not," spoken in the person of those of
old who did not know him, occur only in the Septuagint. The Hebrew is different and is rendered
by Aquila, "God then is strong and hidden, God
that saves Israel," and by Theodotion, "Therefore
a strong secret God preserves Israel." It is remarkable how [Isaiah] calls Christ a hidden God and
gives the reason clearly as to why he calls him
God alone among the ones begotten after the
First and Unbegotten, namely, the dwelling of the
Father in him. . . .

According to this, then, the true and only God
must be One and alone owning the name in full
right. The Second, by sharing in the being of the
true God, is thought worthy to share his name, not
being God in himself or existing apart from the
Father, but altogether being, living and existing as
God, through the presence of the Father in him.
[He is] one in being with the Father, and constituted God from him and through him, holding his
being as well as his divinity not from himself but
from the Father. Proof of the Gospel 5.4.[1]

45:14 God Is with You

The Reality of the Son's Divinity. Marius Victorinus: But consider this also in relation to the *homoousion* [that the Son is of the same
essence as the Father], how the Spirit says to Isaiah, "God is in you, and there is no God outside
of you." Against Arius 1a.27.[2]

A Testimony to Christ's Godhead. Cyril
of Jerusalem: Would you receive yet a third testimony to Christ's godhead? Hear Isaiah saying,
"Egypt has labored, and the merchandise of Ethiopia," and soon after, "In you shall they make
supplication, because God is in you, and there is
no God except you. For you are God, and we
knew it not, the God of Israel, the Savior." You

see that the Son is God, having in himself God
the Father, saying almost the very same which he
has said in the Gospels.[3] . . . And again he has not
said, "I and the Father am one" but "I and the
Father are one," that we should neither separate
them nor make a confusion of Son-Father. Catechetical Lectures 11.16.[4]

45:18 Thus Says the Lord

There Is No Other. Cyril of Alexandria:
For it says, "thus says the Lord" and not simply
an earthly "lord," for there are many in heaven
and earth that ruin this name [the Lord] by over-
using it. But he is the one who by nature and in
truth is just—he is what he is said to be and
derives no false glory from what he has ordained.
. . . For if he who made heaven and earth did not
make it in vain but to be inhabited, . . . then who
else other than him can be considered God?
Commentary on Isaiah 4.3.45.18-19.[5]

**The Creation, Old and New, Will Be
Inhabited.** Methodius: For in reality God
did not establish the universe in vain or to no
purpose but destruction, as those weak-minded
people say, but to exist and be inhabited and continue. Therefore the earth and the heaven must
exist again after the conflagration and shaking of
all things. On the Resurrection 1.8.[6]

45:19 The Lord Speaks the Truth Openly

Mocking the Delusion of Idols. Theodoret of Cyr: [Isaiah] has said this to mock the
delusion of idols. For their votaries used certain
practices of sorcery. They took darkness as an aux-
iliary for deceit and, from the bottom of some
secluded and obscure place, they said whatever
they wished and deceived their listeners, all the
while saying that it was the idols who uttered that
voice. As for me, on the contrary, he says, when I

---

[1]POG 1:244-45**. [2]FC 69:131-32. [3]Jn 14:11. [4]NPNF 2 7:68*.
[5]PG 70:977. [6]ANF 6:366.

gave the law, as whenever I prophesied, I have spoken openly. COMMENTARY ON ISAIAH 14.45.19.[7]

THE LAW REVEALED. CYRIL OF ALEXANDRIA: I drew up laws about these things for them and did not speak in riddles, nor did I speak in a weighty tone but lightly and clearly. As a result, the Lord came down on Mount Sinai in the form of fire. There were darkness, storms, smoke and the piercing sound of trumpets.[8] COMMENTARY ON ISAIAH 4.3.45.18-19.[9]

LAW AND GOSPEL AS RIGHTEOUSNESS AND TRUTH. CYRIL OF ALEXANDRIA: "I speak righteousness and proclaim truth." Righteousness, as I take it, means the law, for the law is the arbitrator of righteousness. And truth is the discipline of Christ. For there is a form of truth in the law, and the mystery of Christ lies concealed in its shadows, for Moses wrote about this. So, in speaking of righteousness, truth and power are proclaimed along with it, since it is true that the law is a shadow—and yet in it there remains a form of the truth. COMMENTARY ON ISAIAH 4.3.45.18-19.[10]

45:20 Assemble Yourselves

ASSEMBLE AND TAKE COUNSEL TOGETHER. CYRIL OF ALEXANDRIA: But Emmanuel appeared who led with courage those who were snared. He endured for us the death of the flesh so that as Isaiah says in an evangelical way, the scattered children of God would be gathered into one[11] ... to gather, that is, to be bound together in one faith and like-mindedness. [They are] gathered by God the ruler of all through holiness and righteousness ... and "brought near through the blood of Christ."[12] ... For it is through faith that understanding grows so that it is not in doubt. Even though faith might be undermined by deceit of ill counsel or led astray into ruin by ancient wickedness, we can quickly return to God and receive the light of the true divine knowledge and with a deliberation that comes from an upright mind constantly pursue the better things. Consider then and take counsel, all who have been saved from among the nations. COMMENTARY ON ISAIAH 4.3.45.20.[13]

---

[7]ITA 677*; SC 315:36. [8]Ex 19:16, 18. [9]PG 70:980. [10]PG 70:980. [11]Jn 11:52. [12]Eph 2:13. [13]PG 70:980-81.

45:21-25 SUBMISSION TO GOD

[21]"Declare and present your case;
    let them take counsel together!
Who told this long ago?
    Who declared it of old?
Was it not I, the LORD?
    And there is no other god besides me,
a righteous God and a Savior;
    there is none besides me.

[22]"Turn to me and be saved,

all the ends of the earth!
    For I am God, and there is no other.
[23]By myself I have sworn,
    from my mouth has gone forth in
        righteousness
    a word that shall not return:
'To me every knee shall bow,
    every tongue shall swear.'

[24]"Only in the LORD, it shall be said of me,

are righteousness and strength;
to him shall come and be ashamed,
  all who were incensed against him.

[25]*In the* LORD *all the offspring of Israel*
  shall triumph and glory."

OVERVIEW: God's justice and mercy demand the fitting responses of fear and love (FULGENTIUS). He invites all to hear his call (EUSEBIUS), but people often choose to follow the false prophets instead (CYRIL). He seeks to turn our attention toward helping others avoid sin and judgment, not toward judging them (AUGUSTINE). The love of Christian people is marked by their unity in submission to God (EUSEBIUS). Isaiah is speaking of both God the Father and God the Son, whose essence is identical. Only the seed of the sons of Israel who live by faith will be justified (THEODORET).

45:21 A Righteous God and Savior

FEAR AND LOVE CORRESPOND TO GOD'S JUSTICE AND MERCY. FULGENTIUS OF RUSPE: With these[1] and innumerable other texts of the same kind, in which the Lord our God is proclaimed as merciful and just, is shown how much his mercy must be loved and how much his justice must be feared. . . . Therefore, if there are those whom the pious goodness of God does not free from the domination of sin in this present world, his just severity condemns them in the future. From this it comes about that the evil ones are tirelessly admonished for their salvation by the divine words lest they remain in the servitude of sin, but they are exhorted rather to seek the mercy of a just God while they are in this life. . . . Therefore, his mercy must be loved and his justice feared by both the good and the wicked, lest either the good, loving the mercy of God, do not fear his justice and fall into the traps of the devil who seduces, or the wicked, considering only the severity of his justice, do not seek the blessing of his mercy when they can find it in their life, and so hardened, not only reject the forgiveness of sins but also do not cease to multiply sins. ON THE FORGIVENESS OF SINS 1.8.1—9.1.[2]

45:22 Turn to God and Be Saved

THE CATHOLIC KERYGMA (UNIVERSAL PROCLAMATION). EUSEBIUS OF CAESAREA: Or as Symmachus puts it: "Run to me and be saved, all the extremities of the earth." You see how he proclaims the catholic gospel to all the nations. COMMENTARY ON ISAIAH 2.29.[3]

PEOPLE FOLLOW FALSE PROPHETS. CYRIL OF ALEXANDRIA: There is among them no true knowledge of the things to come, but rather they prophesy falsely, and with clownish talk and deception and trickery and nothing else. The God of the universe responds: If they prophesy rightly, they will come close and will know at the same time. For if they are able to prophesy rightly, then they will all be brought together as one. For their oracles came from many places. But some worked others into a frenzy and honored the unclean demons who were speaking falsehood. If they had been able to prophesy rightly, they would all be aware of what is to come and who from the very start made these things to be heard. COMMENTARY ON ISAIAH 4.3.45.21-22.[4]

45:23 Every Knee Shall Bow

ALL SHALL GIVE ACCOUNT TO GOD. AUGUSTINE: For it is written, "As I live," says the Lord, "every knee shall bow to me, and every tongue shall confess to God." So then every one of us shall give account of himself to God. Let us not, therefore, judge one another any more, but judge this rather, that no one put a stumbling block, or occasion to fall, in his brother's way. THE CATHOLIC AND MANICHAEAN WAYS OF LIFE 14.32.[5]

---

[1]Ex 34:6-7; Is 45:21-22. [2]FC 95:118-19. [3]GCS 57(9):296. [4]PG 70:984. [5]NPNF 1 4:78.

UNITY IN OBEDIENCE. EUSEBIUS OF CAESAREA: The coming of our Savior Jesus Christ fulfilled the goal of this prophecy, after which, in his church, all people, who have been brought together from throughout the world, have been taught to bend their knee to God in prayer. COMMENTARY ON ISAIAH 2.29.[6]

THE PROPHETIC TEXT SPEAKS UNIVOCALLY. THEODORET OF CYR: "I am God, and there is no other God apart from me, the righteous one and savior. There is none beside me." These words clearly teach us the *homoousion*. For if the Father is God as the Son is God, the Father savior as the Son is savior, the prophetic text applies these things univocally; it makes extremely clear that their essence is identical. . . . If the Father is speaking these things, the Son is excluded from these titles and is not *homoousios*. Or the Son is the one speaking and the Father does not have

them. But if God is the Father and God is the Son and the Father is savior and the Son savior, that is why it is said in the singular that there is no other God and savior beside him. COMMENTARY ON ISAIAH 14.45.20-21.[7]

THROUGH BELIEVING JEWS' SALVATION COMES TO THE NATIONS. THEODORET OF CYR: "They will be justified in the Lord, and all the seed of the sons of Israel will be glorified in God." It does not say *all* the seed of Israel but "all the seed of the sons of Israel." The "sons of Israel" are those who are descended from Israel. Their seed is those judged worthy of salvation from among the nations. It is, indeed, thanks to those among the Jews who believed that their descendants received the seed of the teaching and harvested the fruit of salvation. COMMENTARY ON ISAIAH 14.45.25.[8]

---

[6]GCS 57(9):297. [7]SC 315:38-40. [8]SC 315:40-42.

46:1-2 GOD'S SUPERIORITY TO BABYLON'S IDOLS

[1]Bel bows down, Nebo stoops,
their idols are on beasts and cattle;
these things you carry are loaded
    as burdens on weary beasts.

[2]They stoop, they bow down together,
    they cannot save the burden,
    but themselves go into captivity.

OVERVIEW: The idols are literally being destroyed, and spiritually the heavy burdens they caused are being relieved (EUSEBIUS). Even during Old Testament times, God predicted and arranged for the overthrow of some enslaving idols (THEODORET, CYRIL). The delusion that idols might help is the heaviest part of the oppression, symbolized by their physical mass (JEROME) and their personal histories (ISHO'DAD). Such idols are not only a burden to carry (THEODORET); it is

self-contradictory, unnatural and perverse to do so, since a god that needs to be carried is no god at all (PROCOPIUS).

46:1 Bel Bows Down

THE DESTRUCTION OF IDOLS—LITERAL AND SPIRITUAL. EUSEBIUS OF CAESAREA: The prophecy has described those things concerning the conversion of the nations and those concerning the elect of the seed of the sons of Israel, and it now turns once more to address the Jews and intends the complete destruction of idolatry . . . (following Symmachus, "their idols have become the prey of animals," that is, cast aside into total destitution). According to the literal sense, this has been fulfilled among us by these very deeds, while according to a spiritual understanding it concerns the heavy and burdensome and diabolic load of deceitful idolatry that used to lie on the souls of people. COMMENTARY ON ISAIAH 2.30.[1]

THE PREDICTION OF THE IDOL'S DESTRUCTION. THEODORET OF CYR: Having discussed the Deity, displayed the believers and confounded the unbelievers, the prophetic text also predicts the destruction of the idols. Some copies carry "Dagon." That was an idol of the Allophyles [foreigners]. As for Bel, some claim that he was Kronos. Then [Isaiah] generalizes: "Their graven images are gone to the wild beasts and the cattle." For they did not only manufacture anthropomorphic idols but also idols resembling wild beasts and cattle. The Egyptians, in particular, worshiped representations of monkeys, of dogs, of lions, of farm animals and of crocodiles, whereas the Akaronites even had an image of a fly, and some others worshiped figures of bats. These are the practices that the beginning of the prophetic text has already denounced.[2] He predicts the destruction of all these idols. COMMENTARY ON ISAIAH 14.46.1.[3]

BEL BOWS DOWN. CYRIL OF ALEXANDRIA: But Bel was also honored in other cities. For they say that Bel was the mythical figure Chronos among the godless Greeks, one who was reputedly cruel and bloodthirsty and loved to slaughter humans . . . whereas the God of the universe is not pleased with such terrible impieties and through one of the holy prophets he said to those who were accustomed to doing this, "You sacrifice humans, for you have run out of cattle."[4] . . . The expression "cast down" is apt, since the prophet here speaks of a time near to his own. For we can

read in the books of the Kings that when the former people carried the divine ark to the temple of Dagon, as those worshiping the idol went in, they saw Dagon fallen down in front of the ark.[5] COMMENTARY ON ISAIAH 4.3.46.1.[6]

THE IDOLS GO INTO CAPTIVITY. JEROME: These then are imitations that cannot save those who carry them and are nothing other than burdens for the priests and weigh them down to the point of exhaustion. And when captivity came, these were carried off first of all due to the value of the metals from which they were made, and they were not able to free the souls of those carrying them. For it is not as dumb imitations they had a life and any feeling of pain, but they are figuratively ascribed soul and body parts, though having no feeling and body parts. . . . So it could be said that this error of idolatry was the greatest burden among the nations, one that pressed its worshipers down into the ground and could not save and, in fact, made their souls captive to the devil and his demons. COMMENTARY ON ISAIAH 13.6.[7]

THE ORIGIN OF THE NAMES "BEL" AND "NEBO." ISHO'DAD OF MERV: "Bel" and "Nebo" are Babylonian idols. Bel is the statue that Nebuchadnezzar erected in the plain of Dura;[8] its name derives from "Babel." Nebo was the teacher of the school for children in Mabbugh; since he was extremely stern toward the children, one of them, in order to please him, made a statue for him, and they worshiped it and so appeased his anger; and after this generation, people were seduced by that statue, and worshiped it and called it god. COMMENTARY ON ISAIAH 46.1.[9]

46:2 They Bow Down Together, Going into Captivity

IDOLS ARE A BURDEN. THEODORET OF CYR: By

---

[1]GCS 57(9):298-99. [2]See Is 2:20. [3]ITA 686*; SC 315:42. [4]Hos 13:2 LXX. [5]1 Sam 5:3-4. [6]PG 70:989. [7]AGLB 35:1385-86. [8]See Dan 3:1. [9]CSCO 303(128):48.

the same token, [Isaiah] says, as all the other burdens that are unable to walk but have to be carried, the idols, by reason of their inanimate nature, constrain their porters to toil. Their impotence is so great that they cannot even—as people do in war time—take flight. COMMENTARY ON ISAIAH 14.46.2.[10]

THE WORSHIP OF IDOLS CAUSES SPIRITUAL OPPRESSION. PROCOPIUS OF GAZA: Here [Isaiah] argues that the idols are weak since they will be carried into slavery as the cargo of elephants and even the burden of mules. And the people who carry them will bow low to put them on their shoulders. How can someone bearing God be weak like that? But these burdens are not God. Otherwise how could they be carried off as slaves

of war? How would the ones carrying such things worship them? Others say that this burden is like the solemn procession of the demons that priests carry out when they bear statues on their shoulders and process through the streets bearing their burdens.

These words also remind Israel of their enemies who led them off: just as their enemies fell down and worshiped these idols who spoke in riddles contrary to reason, so also the demons were a heavy and oppressive burden to the souls [of Israel] whenever these demons enslaved them in ungodliness as they took them prisoner and bound them with the ropes of their [own] sins. COMMENTARY ON ISAIAH 46.1-5.[11]

---

[10]ITA 686-87; SC 315:42. [11]PG 87:2437-40.

46:3-7 GOD WILL CARRY AND SAVE

[3]*Hearken to me, O house of Jacob,*
*   all the remnant of the house of Israel,*
who have been borne by me from your birth,
*   carried from the womb;*
[4]*even to your old age I am He,*
*   and to gray hairs I will carry you.*
I have made, and I will bear;
*   I will carry and will save.*

[5]*To whom will you liken me and make me*
*   equal,*

and compare me, that we may be alike?
[6]*Those who lavish gold from the purse,*
*   and weigh out silver in the scales,*
hire a goldsmith, and he makes it into a god;
*   then they fall down and worship!*
[7]*They lift it upon their shoulders, they carry it,*
*   they set it in its place, and it stands there;*
*   it cannot move from its place.*
If one cries to it, it does not answer
*   or save him from his trouble.*

OVERVIEW: Like an expectant mother, God labors to bear his children (APONIUS). The Lord provides for the remnant; he does many things to carry them to salvation (EUSEBIUS). He is faithful to his people in sustaining and guiding and com-

forting them all the way (AUGUSTINE). He even gives advance warning of his punishments (CYRIL). And so, the stupidity of idolatry is matched only by the arrogance of the idolaters (EUSEBIUS), no matter what material they use to form their gods (THEODORET).

46:3 Listen to Me

THE INTIMACY OF GOD'S RELATIONSHIP TO HUMAN NATURE. APONIUS: We hear the voice of the Holy Spirit with wonder when it tells us in many passages of Scripture that the Word of God, in an ineffable motion of love, has given human nature the names of "sister," "daughter," "bride." For example, the words in Isaiah, "Listen to me, Israel my people, the race of Abraham my friend, you whom I carry in my womb." . . . Our mind is set aflame with desire to obtain the love that burns between the Word of God and the soul, so that it can know the measure of love and give love to God in return. EXPOSITION OF SONG OF SONGS 1.1.[1]

GOD CALLS HIS PEOPLE TO CHANGE. EUSEBIUS OF CAESAREA: After your apostasies I will still continue to call you to repentance, since you are my creation. I created you; therefore I sustain you. I promise I will make atonement for your sins, if you change. COMMENTARY ON ISAIAH 2.31.[2]

46:4 Gray Hairs

GOD IN THE INMOST PART OF THE SELF. AUGUSTINE: O Lord our God, under the shadow of your wings let us hope; defend us and support us. You will bear us up when we are little, and even down to our gray hairs you will carry us. For our stability, when it is in you, is stability indeed; but when it is in ourselves, then it is all unstable. Our good lives forever with you, and when we turn from you with aversion, we fall into our own perversion. Let us now, O Lord, return that we be not overturned, because with you our good lives without blemish—for our good is you yourself. CONFESSIONS 4.15.31.[3]

46:4 I Will Carry You

GOD WILL CARRY YOU. AUGUSTINE: Woe to the audacious soul that hoped that by forsaking you it would find some better thing! It tossed and turned, on back and side and belly, but the bed is hard, and you alone give rest. Yet you are near. You deliver us from our wretched wanderings and establish us in your way. You comfort us and say, "Run, I will carry you. I will lead you home, and I will set you free." CONFESSIONS 6.16.26.[4]

GOD WARNS BEFORE GOD PUNISHES. CYRIL OF ALEXANDRIA: But since their heart was not responsive to his promptings, he predicted the evils to come so that they would be gradually troubled by these terrors and would cease their irregular and foul way of life. COMMENTARY ON ISAIAH 4.3.46.8-11.[5]

46:6 Fashioning a God

THE FOLLY OF IDOLATRY. EUSEBIUS OF CAESAREA: And despite my exhortation you delayed in expelling such blasphemy and ungodliness, daring to compare me with those who lack being and in no way have my divinity. You esteemed me as equal to soulless wood that you shaped. You added gold and silver from contributions and made a statue from human hands, and you were not ashamed to worship it. These idols were not able to walk, let alone move, but they needed to be carried on your shoulders or dragged around by others. They are unable to hear prayers or to save. COMMENTARY ON ISAIAH 2.31.[6]

GOLD AND SILVER IDOLS ARE NO MORE POWERFUL THAN WOOD. THEODORET OF CYR: [Isaiah] has clearly mocked the impotence of the idols. And since he had made mention of their creation from a piece of wood in a preceding passage,[7] but gold and silver are more precious material than wood, and many people on account of the material treated the gods of gold and of silver with the greater regard, he considers it necessary to give this instruction concerning them: people

---

[1]SC 420:140-42. [2]GCS 57(9):299. [3]LCC 7:93-94*. [4]LCC 7:133**. [5]PG 70:996. [6]GCS 57(9):299-300. [7]Is 45:20.

collect gold and silver. They hire a goldsmith, weigh the statue he has fashioned and treat it as a god. Yet it moves with the feet of others, but if they are lacking, it stands still. Moreover, it brings no help to its worshipers. After this refuta-

tion, [Isaiah] introduces an exhortation. COMMENTARY ON ISAIAH 14.46.7.[8]

---

[8]ITA 687*; SC 315:44-46.

46:8-11 REMEMBER GOD IS IN CONTROL

[8]*Remember this and consider,*
   recall it to mind,* you transgressors,
[9]*remember the former things of old;*
for I am God, and there is no other;
   I am God, and there is none like me,
[10]*declaring the end from the beginning*
   and from ancient times things not yet done,

saying, "My counsel shall stand,
   and I will accomplish all my purpose,"
[11]*calling a bird of prey from the east,*
   the man of my counsel from a far country.
I have spoken, and I will bring it to pass;
   I have purposed, and I will do it.

* LXX *return in your heart*

OVERVIEW: The heart is summoned to him who is its resting place; the believing heart has Christ there. One comes to God through the image God has placed in humanity (AUGUSTINE). We will find God's will not by wandering but by charity and goodness (CAESARIUS). It is his charity and goodness, in fact, that moves him to desire that all be saved (CASSIAN). God has full sovereignty over all the unexpected twists and turns of history (CYRIL). He is even able to direct things devoid of reason and accelerate processes and events (THEODORET). Isaiah's prophecy here of one being called from the east could apply to the Medes or the Israelites (EPHREM), while that of the counselor from far away is a reference to Christ coming from the realm of hades (EUSEBIUS).

46:8 Recall to Mind

THE HEART SUMMONED TO ITS RESTING PLACE. AUGUSTINE: Behold, there he is, wher-

ever truth is known. He is within the inmost heart, yet the heart has wandered from him. Return to your heart, O you sinners, and hold fast to him who made you. Stand with him, and you shall stand firmly. Rest in him, and you shall be at rest. CONFESSIONS 4.12.18.[1]

THE BELIEVING HEART HAS CHRIST WITHIN IT. AUGUSTINE: "Go back, therefore, to the heart," and if you are believers, you will find Christ there. He himself is speaking to you there. Yes, here am I, shouting my head off—but he, in silence, is doing more teaching. I am speaking by the sound of these words; he is speaking inwardly by the awe you feel in your thoughts. SERMON 102.2.[2]

RETURN TO THE HEART. AUGUSTINE: "Return, you transgressors, to the heart."[3] Return to the

---

[1]LCC 7:87*. [2]WSA 3 4:73-74**. [3]The LXX can be rendered either "Return in your heart" or "Return to the heart."

heart! Why do you go away from yourselves and perish from yourselves? . . . You go astray by wandering about. Return. Where? To the Lord. It is quickly done! First, return to your heart. You are wandering away. You are an exile from yourself. You do not know yourself. You ask by whom you were made! . . . Just return to your heart! See there what perhaps you perceive about God, because the image of God is there. In the inner person Christ dwells. In the inner person you are renewed according to the image of God.[4] Tractates on the Gospel of John 18.10.1-2.[5]

God Sends Us Within. Caesarius of Arles: "Return, you transgressors, to the heart." As I have already said, what the Lord repeatedly asks of us is not found in distant lands. He sends us within, into our own hearts. For he has placed within us that which he wants, in which consists the perfection of charity in the will and goodness of the soul. Sermon 37.1.[6]

46:10 My Counsel Shall Stand

The Counsel and Will of God Is That All Be Saved. John Cassian: "Your will be done on earth as it is in heaven."[7] There cannot be a greater prayer than to desire that earthly things should deserve to equal heavenly ones. For what does it mean to say "your will be done on earth as it is in heaven," if not that human beings should be like angels and that, just as God's will is fulfilled by them in heaven, so also all those who are on earth should do not their own but his will? No one will really be able to say this but one who believes that God regulates all things that are seen, whether fortunate or unfortunate, for the sake of our well-being, and that he is more provident and careful with regard to the salvation and interests of those who are his own than we are for ourselves. And of course it is to be understood in this way—namely, that the will of God is the salvation of all, according to the text of blessed Paul: "Who desires all to be saved and to come to the knowledge of truth."[8] Of this will the prophet Isa-

iah, speaking in the person of God the Father, also says, "All my will shall be done." Conference 9.20.[9]

God Declares the End from the Beginning. Cyril of Alexandria: For he says "I am the one possessing knowledge of all, and whatever happens, I give notice of it beforehand." That which is announced, I execute . . . for what the holy God wills, who will thwart it? And who will avert his hand when it is raised? . . . We take the bird that is called from the east and from a far land to be the Babylonian, who scorched all the territory of the Jews, took Jerusalem and ruined the temple. They removed both ordinary flock and the leading birds among them and forced them into the region of the Persians. They also subjected them to a yoke of harsh imprisonment. . . .

This work was done not by Israel's own hand, as if God would need a helper. For "it is I alone who save," guard and lead him on the right road, so that those who have made little progress in godliness will help the righteous ones and the humble. By these means, glory and honor are finally given to me alone, even from among wood and stones. Commentary on Isaiah 4.3.46.8-13.[10]

46:11 Calling the Bird of Prey, the Counselor

All Creatures Submit to God's Authority. Theodoret of Cyr: All is easy for the God of the universe. Not only the beings endowed with reason but even those devoid of it submit to divine authority. In addition, by the term "bird" he has clearly shown the speed of Israel's return from exile. Commentary on Isaiah 14.46.11.[11]

A Reference to the Medes or the Israelites. Ephrem the Syrian: "I call a bird of prey from the east." [Isaiah] either calls the Medes a "bird," who will destroy the Babylonians, or the

---

[4]See Eph 3:16-17; Col 3:10. [5]FC 79:134-35**. [6]FC 31:183*. [7]Mt 6:10. [8]1 Tim 2:4. [9]ACW 57:342-43*. [10]PG 70:997-1000. [11]SC 315:46.

Israelites, who, in the course of their return, destroyed the Arameans, the Greeks and the house of Gog. COMMENTARY ON ISAIAH 46.11.[12]

CHRIST THE COUNSELOR CALLED FROM HADES. EUSEBIUS OF CAESAREA: Who other can this be than his Christ, who, it says, has been called from a distant land, that is, from the innermost part of Hades? All the things I have announced before him, I will bring into action through him. COMMENTARY ON ISAIAH 2.31.[13]

[12]SESHS 2:119-21. [13]GCS 57(9):300.

46:12-13 DELIVERANCE IS NOT FAR OFF

[12]*Hearken to me, you stubborn of heart,** *
  you who are far from deliverance:
[13]*I bring near my deliverance, it is not far off,*

  and my salvation will not tarry;
I will put salvation in Zion,
  for Israel my glory.

* LXX *you who have lost heart*

OVERVIEW: The problem with the prophet's hearers is that they have stopped thinking clearly (ORIGEN). God remains faithful to his people, however, even when he is judging them. He announces hope of salvation lest his people fall into despair (CYRIL). Ultimately, everything is for God's glory, which means salvation for his people and knowledge of God for all the world (THEODORET). God reaches all humanity by working through a particular people (PROCOPIUS).

46:12 Hearken to Me

THE MIND AND THE HEART. ORIGEN: The inner person has a heart. "Hear me, you who have lost heart."[1] They possessed a physical heart, that organ of the body. It was not that heart which they lost. But when a person neglects to cultivate his intellectual life, and in consequence of much idleness his thinking capacity has atrophied, he has lost his heart, and it is to such a person that the words are added, "Here me, you who have lost your heart." DIALOGUE WITH HERACLIDES.[2]

GOD DOES NOT ABANDON HIS PEOPLE. CYRIL OF ALEXANDRIA: Again we perceive the depth of God's loving kindness, in that God mixes with the evils also the wonders, so that they are not wiped out. For he has saved them from the hand of their enemies. When Israel fell into the marsh of judgment, God dragged them out. COMMENTARY ON ISAIAH 4.3.48.5-11.[3]

HOPE COMBATS DESPAIR. CYRIL OF ALEXANDRIA: See how he once again announces salvation to them and does not allow them to despair, lest they be overwhelmed by unrestrained sorrow and be moved too far away from the hope that they will be saved, if only they stop running. For having strayed, they were disconsolate. This described their situation accurately. For what else would they feel, they who worshiped the things they themselves had made, setting up trees and stones for worship and seeking salvation from

[1]The Greek of the LXX is *apolōlekotes*, from *apollymi*, "to lose." [2]LCC 2:451. [3]PG 70:1020.

them? COMMENTARY ON ISAIAH 4.3.46.12-13.[4]

ALL WILL LEARN OF GOD'S POWER THROUGH ISRAEL. THEODORET OF CYR: For though you are unworthy of salvation, since you have distanced yourself from righteousness because of your iniquity, I will procure salvation [for you] and will inflict just chastisement on the Babylonians. "I have given salvation in Zion to Israel for my glory." For thanks to the salvation of Israel, all will learn of my power and acknowledge that I am truly God. COMMENTARY ON ISAIAH 14.46.13.[5]

46:13 It Is Not Far Off

REACHING THE UNIVERSAL THROUGH THE PARTICULAR. PROCOPIUS OF GAZA: For God did not hate those whom he took out of Israel but intended salvation for them, just like the cutting and draining done by doctors. For all punishment was carried out for their advantage. He adds to the underlying form of the particular its significance for the human race. For the salvation through Cyrus is particular. That through Christ is universal. "I will not delay" is similar to "a little time it will come and will not delay."[6] "Zion" we take to be the church, in which we receive his salvation in glory, thus being complete in the spiritual Israel; that is, we gain a mind that, seeing God, fulfills us as children according to the promises of Abraham. COMMENTARY ON ISAIAH 47.1-15.[7]

---

[4]PG 70:1000. [5]SC 315:46-48. [6]Hab 2:3. [7]PG 87:2441-44.

47:1-4 THE CALAMITY OF BABYLON

[1]*Come down and sit in the dust,*
O virgin daughter of Babylon;
sit on the ground without a throne,
  O daughter of the Chaldeans!
For you shall no more be called
  tender and delicate.
[2]*Take the millstones and grind meal,*
  put off your veil,
strip off your robe, uncover your legs,
  pass through the rivers.
[3]*Your nakedness shall be uncovered,*
  and your shame shall be seen.
I will take vengeance,
  and I will spare no man.
[4]*Our Redeemer—the LORD of hosts is his*
  name—
is the Holy One of Israel.

OVERVIEW: The temporary glory of Babylonian despots will turn into a mocking parody (ISHO'DAD). However, there is glory in enduring suffering with dignity for the children of God (JEROME). The calamity that Babylonian arrogance suffered mercifully removed it from the temptations of power (THEODORET). Yet there is something shocking about the experience of judgment (CYRIL).

47:2 Take the Millstones

THE FUTURE BONDAGE OF BABYLON. ISHO'DAD OF MERV: "Take the millstone," that is: After

---

being deprived of the glory of your sovereignty, you will adopt the apparel of slaves. The words "cut your white hair" [in the Syriac Bible, Peshitta] mean "You have grown old and decrepit in your sovereignty." COMMENTARY ON ISAIAH 47.2.[1]

THE EXAMPLE OF FABIOLA. JEROME: As Fabiola[2] was not ashamed of the Lord on earth, so he shall not be ashamed of her in heaven. She laid bare her wound to the gaze of all, and Rome beheld with tears the disfiguring scar that marred her beauty. She uncovered her limbs, bared her head and closed her mouth. She no longer entered the church of God but, like Miriam the sister of Moses, she sat apart, outside the camp, till the priest who cast her out should himself call her back. She came down like a daughter of Babylon from the throne of her daintiness, she took the millstones and ground meal, she passed barefoot through rivers of tears. LETTER 77.5.[3]

47:3 Your Shame Shall Be Seen

SHAME BRINGS ITS OWN BENEFITS. THEODORET OF CYR: "Come down, sit on the ground, virgin daughter of Babylon." Isaiah calls her "virgin" not because she was chaste—in fact she was corrupt and shameless—but because she was dressed in the manner of a virgin. "Sit down on the ground; it is not a throne." You have been deprived of royalty, he says; you have changed place with a slave. "Sink down into the shades, O daughter of the Chaldeans, for you shall no more be called tender and luxurious." You have lost your good fortune of former times; you do not revel in the misfortunes of others. . . . The one who has redeemed you has the name "the Lord of Hosts." If anyone wants to understand this passage as applying equally to Babylon, one should recognize that through its punishment it has been spared from sinning more. Because Babylon no longer was in power, it no longer sinned and gained the benefit of avoiding greater sins. COMMENTARY ON ISAIAH 14.47.1-4.[4]

THE CAPTIVE WOMEN HAD TO BARE THEIR BODIES. CYRIL OF ALEXANDRIA: "Bare your legs and cross the rivers. Your shame will be uncovered and your disgrace shown." For she was once led into captivity. She was taken from her own land into that of the victors. Being between the two rivers, they had to cross on their feet and uncover themselves. What decorum the women had was lost, and out of necessity even the private parts of their bodies were exposed to many. COMMENTARY ON ISAIAH 4.3.47.1-3.[5]

---

[1]CSCO 303(128):49. [2] Jerome speaks earlier of how Fabiola, a woman of some standing, had divorced her adulterous husband. Even though he was an adulterer, she still appeared before the church in sack cloth and made public confession of her sin. She was restored to communion in the church and lived an exemplary Christian life thereafter, selling all her possessions and founding one of the first hospitals for the poor in the city. [3]NPNF 2 6:160. [4]SC 315:48-50. [5]PG 70:1004.

47:5-7 GOD INTERVENES ON BEHALF OF HIS PEOPLE

⁵Sit in silence, and go into darkness,
    O daughter of the Chaldeans;
for you shall no more be called
    the mistress of kingdoms.
⁶I was angry with my people,
    I profaned my heritage;

I gave them into your hand,
*   you showed them no mercy;*
on the aged you made your yoke
*   exceedingly heavy.*

[7]You said, "I shall be mistress for ever,"
*   so that you did not lay these things to heart*
*   or remember their end.*

OVERVIEW: God's people were handed over in order to discipline them, but this handing over does not afford an excuse to treat them with excessive harshness (EUSEBIUS). This would mean no longer seeing the image of God and the humanity of these shamed sinners (ATHANASIUS) whom it was God's intention to restore (THEODORET). God may intervene in a violent way in order to stop greater harm befalling his creatures (CYRIL).

47:5 Mistress of the Kingdom

A WARNING AGAINST HARSHNESS. EUSEBIUS OF CAESAREA: These words are spoken by the Lord, our redeemer and the one who has freed us from a life of hard labor. . . . Or as Symmachus puts it, "You will no longer be called queenly. For I was angry with my people and harmed my inheritance." And I, for reasons of the right discipline, handed my people into your hands, as part of my taming them, but you showed fellow sufferers no kindness by treating them excessively harshly. COMMENTARY ON ISAIAH 2.32.[1]

47:6 You Showed Them No Mercy

RESPECT THE VICTIM'S HUMANITY. ATHANASIUS: But when these accursed ones obtain possession of anyone, they immediately forget not only all others but even themselves. Raising their brow in great haughtiness, they neither grasp the times and seasons nor respect human nature in those whom they injure. Like the tyrant of Babylon, they attack more furiously; they show pity to none. "For they persecute him whom you have smitten, and him whom you have wounded, they afflict still more."[2] Had they not acted in this manner, had they not driven into banishment those who spoke in my defense against their calumnies, their representations might have appeared to some persons sufficiently plausible. DEFENSE OF HIS FLIGHT 9.[3]

ISRAEL'S PUNISHMENT IS MEANT TO RESTORE. THEODORET OF CYR: For they have burned the temple of God, they have consecrated the sacred vessels to idols, and they have used cruelty against the prisoners. "I gave them into your hands." You would not have carried off the victory if I had not willed it. I delivered them [to you] because I wanted to correct them, not exterminate them. "But you did not extend mercy to them; you made the yoke of the aged very heavy." Even age did not seem to you worthy of respect. [Isaiah] has by this trait shown the extent of their hardness. COMMENTARY ON ISAIAH 14.47.6.[4]

GOD'S HARSH BUT NECESSARY INTERVENTION. CYRIL OF ALEXANDRIA: Out of love God disciplines, then, those who were thoughtless. . . . They were made docile through their trials. He did this by delivering them into the hands of their enemies or by the affliction of other pains, just as fire and iron often heal a wound where medicine fails. In the same manner our God, a lover of virtue, when he sees a soul rushing onto the rocks with the force of vast waves and getting mixed up in the ways of wickedness, restores that person through harsh punishments. COMMENTARY ON ISAIAH 4.3.47.5-7.[5]

---

[1]GCS 57(9):302. [2]Ps 69:26 (68:27 LXX). [3]NPNF 2 4:258**. [4]ITA 695*; SC 315:50. [5]PG 70:1005.

47:8-11 NO ONE SEES

⁸Now therefore hear this, you lover of
  pleasures,
  who sit securely,
who say in your heart,
  "I am, and there is no one besides me;
I shall not sit as a widow
  or know the loss of children":
⁹These two things shall come to you
  in a moment, in one day;
the loss of children and widowhood
  shall come upon you in full measure,
in spite of your many sorceries
  and the great power of your enchantments.

¹⁰You felt secure in your wickedness,
  you said, "No one sees me";
your wisdom and your knowledge led you
    astray,
and you said in your heart,
  "I am, and there is no one besides me."
¹¹But evil shall come upon you,
  for which you cannot atone;
disaster shall fall upon you,
  which you will not be able to expiate;
and ruin shall come on you suddenly,
  of which you know nothing.

OVERVIEW: Communion with demons is condemned as unnatural (PROCOPIUS). Isaiah notes, in fact, that the people cannot flourish because of their reliance on sorcery and the divine punishment that ensues because of this (EUSEBIUS). Taken literally, this prophecy speaks of the profound impact of divine judgment on the godless (EPHREM) who with their so-called knowledge are easily led astray (EUSEBIUS) but only realize how far away they have fallen when there is a sudden change of fortune (THEODORET).

47:8 Secret Thoughts

IDOLATRY LEADS TO DESTRUCTION. PROCOPIUS OF GAZA: Thinking that you would prove to be better than the Persians, you said, "I am and there is no other," and you were encouraged by the oracles of demons and astrologers. And you called on a hope that was fornication and that was far removed from God. For the association between God and all humanity by nature is very different from that between demons and humans, which provides communion through sorcery. So

Paul likens idol worship to a spell when he writes of "idol worship, sorcery."[1] But for the Babylonians and others, idolatry does not lead to pardon or deliverance but to destruction. COMMENTARY ON ISAIAH 47.1-15.[2]

47:9 Two Things Shall Come

SUDDEN EVIL WILL COME. EUSEBIUS OF CAESAREA: And what follows describes very clearly the arrogance of the kingdom of the Chaldeans and the foolishness of their royal people, in such a way that they ascribed to themselves immortal power and an indestructible rule. However, suddenly you will experience a loss of men and the destruction of your children—that is, men to rule among you, and children meaning those to be ruled. These things will come at once upon you and reveal you abandoned and childless. This will affect you not only through these things proclaimed but also through the extent of sorceries and incantations. COMMENTARY ON ISAIAH 2.32.[3]

---

[1]Gal 5:20. [2]PG 87:2445. [3]GCS 57(9):302.

You Felt Secure in Your Wickedness.
Ephrem the Syrian: "Two plagues shall come
to you in one day," because you were deceived by
the art of the Chaldeans and ignored your doom.
"The loss of children and widowhood shall come
on you," that is, sterility. The loss of children
indicates the destruction of the city; the widowhood, the privation of the kingdom. Commentary on Isaiah 47.9.[4]

47:10 Knowledge Led You Astray

**So-Called Knowledge Can Lead One
Astray.** Eusebius of Caesarea: And since Isaiah could not find one man to address, he spoke
to the daughter of the Chaldeans, promising
these things especially: The astrologers of
heaven maintained and supported you, announcing to you what was coming to you from heaven.
For in this way we are taught that what the Lord
wishes to give to each nation cannot be known
by the lovers of learning. . . . But to us each word
is gathered into two principal ones, first to the
human customs of every city and to their good
"daimons," and second to oppose any sorcerers
and deceivers and cheats, destroying and turning from the truth into the deceitfulness of

human beings. Preparation for the Gospel
6.11.[5]

47:11 Evil Shall Come on You

Unexpected Change of Fortune. Theodoret of Cyr: Suddenly, [Isaiah] says, you will
receive destruction and undergo the misfortunes
that you do not expect. "[There shall be] a pit,
and you shall fall into it; and grief shall come on
you, and you cannot be cleared." Symmachus and
Aquila have rendered the translation of this passage as follows: "And a misfortune will befall you
that you will not be able to avert," that is to say, I
will precipitate you into unavoidable misfortunes,
and you will not obtain a pardon, for you have
sinned beyond [the point] of being pardoned."
"And destruction shall come suddenly on you,
and you shall not know." For Babylon had not
been expecting a change [of fortune] and had had
no dread of seeing the situation reversed. Commentary on Isaiah 14.47.11.[6]

---

[4]SESHS 2:121. Theodoret notes, "[Isaiah] calls the loss of her royalty
'widowhood,' and the forfeiture of her subjects 'absence of children.'"
Thus, she has sustained both simultaneously (*Commentary on Isaiah*
47.9; ITA 695; SC 315:52). [5]GCS 8 1:360. [6]ITA 696*; SC 315:52.

47:12-15 JUDGMENT ON BABYLON

[12]Stand fast in your enchantments
   and your many sorceries,
   with which you have labored from your
      youth;
perhaps you may be able to succeed,
   perhaps you may inspire terror.
[13]You are wearied with your many counsels;
   let them stand forth and save you,

those who divide the heavens,
   who gaze at the stars,
who at the new moons predict
   what[h] shall befall you.

[14]Behold, they are like stubble,
   the fire consumes them;
they cannot deliver themselves

from the power of the flame.
No coal for warming oneself is this,
    no fire to sit before!
[15]*Such to you are those with whom you have*
    labored,

who have trafficked with you from your
    youth;
they wander about each in his own direction;
    there is no one to save you.

h Gk Syr Compare Vg: Heb *from what*

OVERVIEW: The prophecy addresses its audience and their reliance on idols in an ironic manner (THEODORET) since only the true God knows the future and is able to reveal these things in prophecy (CHRYSOSTOM). For those who worship idols, there will be the fire of judgment, which itself can be salutary and beneficial; there is mercy to be found even in the severest divine punishment (ORIGEN). Believers who turn to astrology and occult science for guidance should know they will be punished (EUSEBIUS). Christ as a cleansing fire is the means to avoid the final avenging fire (GREGORY OF NAZIANZUS). Thus, the ways of those who go astray is to be noted and avoided. Do the opposite if you want to avoid judgment (THEODORET).

47:12 Stand Fast

AN IRONIC ADDRESS. THEODORET OF CYR: The prophetic text addresses these words to [Babylon] in an ironic manner: stick to your habitual magic; stick to your customary incantations. It is likely that you will escape from misfortunes that besiege you! Then he proclaims the vainness of these practices. COMMENTARY ON ISAIAH 14.47.12.[1]

47:13 Let Them Stand Forth

THE DEMONS CANNOT PROVIDE RELIABLE PROPHECY. CHRYSOSTOM: [God the] Father devoted a large portion of his discourse to prophecy when he took a stand against the cult images. "Let them[2] tell the things that shall come to you"; and again, "I have declared and have saved; and

there was no strange one among you,"[3] and throughout the entire prophecy he stressed this point.[4] Prophecy is indeed especially the work of God, which the demons would not be able to imitate, even if they should strive very hard. HOMILIES ON THE GOSPEL OF JOHN 19.[5]

47:15 Benefit Can Come from the Fire of Judgment

GOD IS JUST AND GOOD. ORIGEN: And when God afflicts those who deserve punishment, how else is it intended except for their good? It is he who says to the Chaldaeans, "You have coals of fire; sit on them. They shall be a help to you."[6] Further, let them hear what is related in the seventy-seventh psalm, which is ascribed to Asaph, about those who fell in the desert. It says, "When he slew them, then they sought him."[7] It does not say that some sought him after others had been killed but that those who were slain perished in such a manner that when put to death they sought God. From all these illustrations it is plain that the just and good God of the Law and the Gospels is one and the same and that he does good with justice and punishes in kindness, since neither goodness without justice nor justice without goodness can describe the dignity of the divine nature. ON FIRST PRINCIPLES 2.5.3.[8]

THE FOOLISHNESS OF ASTROLOGY. EUSEBIUS OF CAESAREA: It is known from the writing of

[1]ITA 696; SC 315:54. [2]Astrologers. [3]Cf. Is 47:13; 43:12. [4]That only God has power to foretell the future. [5]FC 33:189. [6]Is 42:14b-15a LXX. [7]Ps 78:34 (77:34 LXX). [8]OFP 104-5*.

Daniel in what manner certain wizards and diviners and potion makers were eminent among those Chaldeans living in Babylon.[9] And they were highly regarded by the king since the kingdom was ordered by them. They did not only dabble with potions and incantations, but through the knowledge of mathematical theorems they thought to understand the heavens, predicting the movement of the stars, their effects on human destiny and their power on the present according to the season, so as to learn to distinguish the things to come. But no mighty person is able to know the future from pondering on these things. Rather, the reward of fire[10] will be received by those who pay too much attention to them. COMMENTARY ON ISAIAH 2.32.[11]

CHRIST AS A CLEANSING FIRE. GREGORY OF NAZIANZUS: For I know a cleansing fire that Christ came to send on the earth, and he himself is anagogically called a fire. This Fire takes away whatever is material and of evil habit. This [Christ] desires to kindle with all speed, for he longs for speed in doing us good, since he gives us even coals of fire to help us. ON HOLY BAPTISM, ORATION 40.36.[12]

LEARN FROM PUNISHMENT. THEODORET OF CYR: In the other nations likewise, there are people who choose an iniquitous law, he says, but not all embrace this mode of conduct. For your part, you studied iniquity and you practiced the extreme of impiety as if it were the height of piety; therefore you will not enjoy salvation. As for us, instructed by their punishment, let us procure salvation, and may their destruction turn to our advantage! Seeing what payment is reserved for malice, and taking on the opposite mode of conduct and having as a holy anchor trust in the God of the universe, we will obtain his solicitude during the present life, just as we will enjoy the eternal benefits in the life to come by the grace of Christ our Savior. Glory to the Father, together with him, in the unity of the All-Holy Spirit, now and ever and unto ages of ages. Amen. COMMENTARY ON ISAIAH 14.47.15.[13]

---

[9] See Dan 2:2. [10]1 Cor 3:15. [11]GCS 57(9):302-3. [12]NPNF 2 7:373*. [13]ITA 697*; SC 315:56.

48:1-3 ISRAEL'S OBSTINACY

[1]Hear this, O house of Jacob,
who are called by the name of Israel,
  and who came forth from the loins[i] of Judah;
who swear by the name of the LORD,
  and confess the God of Israel,
  but not in truth or right.
[2]For they call themselves after the holy city,
  and stay themselves on the God of Israel;
the LORD of hosts is his name.

[3]"The former things I declared of old,
  they went forth from my mouth and I made
    them known;
  then suddenly I did them and they came to
    pass."

i Cn: Heb *waters*

OVERVIEW: Some who confess the name of Israel are not worthy to be called by the name of Israel (EUSEBIUS). When the people fail to hear God's warning, God's action must then become the painful corrective (THEODORET). What was prophesied long ago may come to pass suddenly, and some later prophetic utterances may be contingent on previous ones (EUSEBIUS).

48:1 O House of Jacob

JEWS IN NAME ONLY. EUSEBIUS OF CAESAREA: He calls them the house of Jacob as not being worthy of the name of their forefather. Rather, "those called by the name Israel" are not really Israel, and those bearing that name are not called such here. And he adds, "and coming forth from the water of Judah." For they had nothing of the worthiness of the patriarchal soul, although they were descended from his fluid and bodily seed. For they were children only in the physical and carnal sense and not true children of the soul. But "Judah through the water"[1] means the "kingly race" from David's line that in the days of the prophets remained in Jerusalem. They were those who, being not truly worthy of these names, used "Jacob" and "Israel" and "Judah" falsely; for they were those who praised the name of the Lord and made mention of the God of Israel with only their lips and mouth. . . . For they did "not" take their oaths "in truth" if they were [at the same time] consulting oracles. But they even thought they were being loyal to the city which was dedicated to God when, in fact, they were resisting God and performing this hypocrisy. COMMENTARY ON ISAIAH 2.33.[2]

48:3 Former Things Declared

WARNING OF APPROACHING JUDGMENT. THEODORET OF CYR: The adversities that have come on you were announced by me well beforehand, in order that you would be frightened by threats and driven to repentance, so that you may steer clear of the dreadful events. But since you failed to believe my words, I will now proceed to demonstrate their truth by my actions. For you see what is added, "I acted suddenly, and the events came to pass." COMMENTARY ON ISAIAH 15.48.3.[3]

PAST PROPHECIES MAY BE FULFILLED SUDDENLY. EUSEBIUS OF CAESAREA: It is not in human nature to know things that are to come. I am the God who foretells them even now and who did so throughout former times. In addition, the predictions that previously came through the mouths of my other prophets as declarative of many things to come were reported by and complied with by those prophesying, to whom the events seemed to fit the words of the other prophets. COMMENTARY ON ISAIAH 2.33.[4]

---

[1]Connecting with the "fluid" of his bodily seed. [2]GCS 57(9):303. [3]SC 315:60. [4]GCS 57(9):303.

48:4-8 AN OBSTINATE PEOPLE

[4]*Because I know that you are obstinate,*
and your neck is an iron sinew
and your forehead brass,
[5]*I declared them to you from of old,*

before they came to pass I announced them
to you,
lest you should say, "My idol did them,
my graven image and my molten image

commanded them."

[6]*You have heard; now see all this;*
    and will you not declare it?
From this time forth I make you hear new
        things,
    hidden things which you have not known.
[7]*They are created now, not long ago;*

before today you have never heard of them,
    lest you should say, "Behold, I knew them."
[8]*You have never heard, you have never known,*
    from of old your ear has not been opened.
For I knew that you would deal very
        treacherously,
    and that from birth you were called a rebel.

OVERVIEW: Prophecy reassures us of God's active providence (EUSEBIUS). God opposes only those who oppose him (GREGORY OF NAZIANZUS). God's people will soon be caught up in events and will benefit despite their obstinacy (JEROME). Israel, in fact, had no desire to hear God's words (THEODORET), in contrast to God, whose faithfulness remains unshaken (EUSEBIUS).

COMFORT IN THE MIDST OF DESTRUCTION.
EUSEBIUS OF CAESAREA: These words would not be of any help to you if you had not been already warned. Nevertheless, dwelling in my loving-kindness, I still bear witness and distinguish you from those assembled in Babylon and the Chaldeans about to attack you. Open your eyes! As you see the foretold destruction taking hold when the warriors come from Babylon, you will know with understanding that God has told you these things would happen and you can call on his help when the predicted end strikes. These things are available to you from my words. COMMENTARY ON ISAIAH 2.33.[1]

48:4 Obstinacy and Hard Heads

GOD'S FURY. GREGORY OF NAZIANZUS: Perchance he will say to me, who am not reformed even by blows, "I know that you are obstinate and your neck is an iron sinew, the heedless is heedless, and the lawless person acts lawlessly, and for nothing comes correction from heaven and the scourges."[2] The bellows are burned, the lead is consumed, as I once reprimanded you by

the mouth of Jeremiah: "The founder melted the silver in vain; your wickednesses are not melted away."[3] . . . May it not be that I should ever, among other chastisements, be thus approached by him who is good, and yet by my own contrariness continue to walk against his goodness. This causes God to walk against me in fury. ON HIS FATHER'S SILENCE, ORATION 16.11-12.[4]

YOUR EAR HAS NOT BEEN OPENED. JEROME: Not, therefore, on account of your merit but through my mercy I have calmed my fury, lest you come near to death. For the sake of my name I will rein you in so that like a donkey you are made to follow behind the reins of a horse. Behold, I have dried you up, that is, I have tested you in the way one fires silver. Or it may be that I will test you, not in riches but in the furnace of poverty. . . . I predict to you that Babylon is to be overcome by the Medes and Persians. I will do quickly that about which I have given warning, lest when the events predicted take place, you think they have happened at the nod of the gods you worship or by fate. And I do not intimate mere knowledge of future things, but I speak for your benefit, whose heart I know to have been from the beginning unbelieving and whose neck is like iron and whose forehead like bronze. For look! You have heard all the things that are about to come, and yet you hide the truth by keeping quiet. So it does little good to relate things long

---

[1]GCS 57(9):304.　[2]Various LXX texts diverge here.　[3]Jer 6:29.
[4]NPNF 2 7:250-51.

gone by, like how I led you out of Egypt. COM-
MENTARY ON ISAIAH 13.15.[5]

SHAMELESSNESS. THEODORET OF CYR:
Instructed by this passage, the divine Stephen in
his turn says to the Jews, "You stiff-necked,
uncircumcised in heart and ears! You always
resist the Holy Spirit; as your ancestors did, so do
you."[6] And also through the mouth of the prophet
Jeremiah, the God of the universe has declared to
them, "You have had the appearance of a prostitute; you refuse to be ashamed."[7] It is this shamelessness that [Isaiah] likewise alludes to by [the
phrase] "brazen forehead." The forehead of a
brass statue does not blush. Similarly, you no
longer blush when you commit evil or when you
are confronted or chastised. . . . In this way he has
described with greater clarity their spirit of dis-

obedience. For they voluntarily refused to listen,
because they did not even desire to hear the
words of God. COMMENTARY ON ISAIAH 15.48.4-
8.[8]

48:5-8 Called from the Womb

THINGS TO COME. EUSEBIUS OF CAESAREA: In
Symmachus's translation: "And you, though
faithless to the covenant, were called from the
womb,"[9] so that not through you but through my
merciful love I foretold and showed to you the
things that would come to destroy your enemies,
hurrying to save you in every engagement with
them. COMMENTARY ON ISAIAH 2.33.[10]

---

[5]AGLB 35:1407. [6]Acts 7:51. [7]Jer 3:3. [8]SC 315:60-62. [9]LXX (Symmachus). [10]GCS 57(9):304.

48:9-11 REFINING

[9]For my name's sake I defer my anger,
   for the sake of my praise I restrain it for
     you,
   that I may not cut you off.
[10]Behold, I have refined you, but not like[j]

   silver;
   I have tried you in the furnace of affliction.
[11]For my own sake, for my own sake, I do it,
   for how should my name[k] be profaned?
   My glory I will not give to another.

j Cn: Heb *with*   k Gk Old Latin: Heb lacks *my name*

OVERVIEW: The prophetic word brings terror to
the godless but understanding to the wise (ORI-
GEN). God does not give his glory to those unpre-
pared in heart for the Messiah's coming (JEROME).
God is marvelously able to be compassionate even
in his anger (CYRIL), ultimately causing him to
spare those who deserved his just judgment
(THEODORET).

48:9 For My Name's Sake

THAT I MAY NOT DESTROY YOU. ORIGEN: But
we say that God brings fire on the world, not like
a cook [pace Celsus] but like a God who is the
benefactor of those who stand in need of the discipline of force. This is confirmed by the prophet
Isaiah. . . . Now the Scripture is appropriately
adapted to the multitudes of those who are to
peruse it, because it speaks obscurely of things
that are sad and gloomy, in order to terrify those
who cannot by any other means be saved from

the flood of their sins, although even then the attentive reader will clearly discover the end that is to be accomplished by these sad and painful punishments on those who endure them. It is sufficient, however, for the present to quote the words of Isaiah: "For my name's sake will I delay my anger, and my glory I will bring on you, that I may not destroy you." AGAINST CELSUS 5.15.[1]

I WILL NOT GIVE MY GLORY TO ANOTHER.
JEROME: "I will not give my glory to another." This means that the idols should not be thought to oppress the people of God. Or indeed when [Isaiah] says, "I will not give to another [Christ]," he shows that he has already given it to another. For "another" is used to distinguish from the first. Many of our translators . . . assert that he here prophesies about the advent of Christ that would come suddenly and unlooked for; that Christ would show his very stubborn people his presence, to those whose ears God never opened since their heart was coarse and they are hard of hearing, in that as soon as the Lord came from the virginal womb he was called "sinner" and "unrighteous" as the people sought to kill him.[2] COMMENTARY ON ISAIAH 13.15.[3]

GOD'S WRATH IS RESTRAINED. CYRIL OF ALEXANDRIA: It is a work that is necessary, and it is the fruit of admirable foresight to avoid these things that are announced and not to wait for the end of the unhappy times but to stand outside of all wrath and judgment. . . . "I have restrained my wrath for the sake of my name," and I will establish my glorious deeds over you lest you be destroyed. . . . We see in this the greatness of God's love; he mixes in with unhappy events glorious things lest they be totally destroyed. COMMENTARY ON ISAIAH 4.3.48.5-11.[4]

48:10 The Furnace of Affliction

A FURNACE OF AFFLICTION. THEODORET OF CYR: It was not a need for money that caused me to deliver you to the Babylonians but the will to make you atone for your iniquity; nevertheless, I am going to make you a gift of freedom again. For Isaiah has called the bondage a "furnace of poverty." In a furnace the fire itself remains hidden, and only the smoke released from the furnace can be seen. Likewise, prisoners of war do not dare to lament openly, but in their hearts. For they are consumed by the flame of discouragement, and their groan rises like a kind of smoke. . . . Since the enemies thought they had triumphed, not only over you but even over me, and that it was my weakness that had allowed them to dominate you, I will liberate you from this bitter slavery to the extent that even those who do not know me will hear of my might. COMMENTARY ON ISAIAH 15.48.10-11.[5]

---

[1]ANCL 23:283. [2]Cf. Mt 26:4; Lk 19:47; Jn 7:1. [3]AGLB 35:1408-9. [4]PG 70:1020. [5]SC 315:62-64.

48:12-14 THE ARTIST OF CREATION

[12]Hearken to me, O Jacob,
    and Israel, whom I called!
I am He, I am the first,
    and I am the last.

[13]My hand laid the foundation of the earth,
    and my right hand spread out the heavens;
when I call to them,
    they stand forth together.

¹⁴*Assemble, all of you, and hear!*
who among them has declared these things?
The Lord *loves him;*

he shall perform his purpose on Babylon,
and his arm shall be against the
Chaldeans.

Overview: God is the same from age to age
(Aphrahat). He has an artistic way of creating
(Isho'dad), with the Son acting as the artist's
right hand (Tertullian). But the Son as God's
right hand is also the agent of judgment (Cyril).
The overthrow of Babylon prefigures the demol-
ishing of Satan's regime through Christ (Jerome).

48:12 I Am the First

The One Same God. Aphrahat: No one
should suppose that there is another God, either
before or afterwards. He said, "From age to age,"
just as Isaiah said, "I am the first and I am the
last." And after God had brought forth Adam
from within his thought, he fashioned him, and
breathed into him of his Spirit and gave him the
knowledge of discernment so that he might discern good from evil and might know that God
made him. Demonstrations 17.7.[1]

48:13 My Right Hand

This Is the Way God Made the Heavens.
Isho'dad of Merv: "My right hand spread out
the heavens," that is, I have flung out the heavens
with my power and fixed them on high and
spread out. [These words are said] in analogy
with one who takes some clay and puts it on the
wall or the roof of a house, where it sticks. Commentary on Isaiah 48.13.[2]

**The Son Is the Hand by Which God Made
the Universe.** Tertullian: He is the Lord's
right hand, indeed his two hands, by which he
worked and constructed the universe. Against
Hermogenes 45.[3]

**The Son Is the Hand and Arm of God at
Work in Judging.** Cyril of Alexandria:
Now the hand and the right arm is what God the
Father calls his Son. And we often find him so
called throughout Scripture. The divine Moses
said, "Your right hand has been glorified in
might, your right hand has shattered the enemies,"[4] and David the blessed said, "May your
hand be strengthened, may your right arm be
lifted up."[5] Commentary on Isaiah 4.3.48.12-13.[6]

48:14 Against the Chaldeans

**God Will Perform His Purpose on Baby-
lon.** Jerome: According to the Septuagint "to
remove the seed of the Chaldeans" refers to the
person of the Lord, who was indeed beloved of
his Father and who did the will of his Father
completely and who turned over all the seed of
the Babylonians—which means the demons in
Babylon, that is, those who lead the world into
confusion. Commentary on Isaiah 13.16.[7]

---

[1]NPNF 2 13:389*. [2]CSCO 303(128):49. [3]ANF 3:502. [4]Ex 15:6.
[5]Ps 89:13 (88:14 LXX). [6]PG 70:1024. [7]AGLB 35:1412.

48:15-16 THE SENDING OF CHRIST

¹⁵*"I, even I, have spoken and called him,*
I have brought him, and he will prosper in
his way.
¹⁶*Draw near to me, hear this:*
from the beginning I have not spoken in

secret,
from the time it came to be I have been
there."
And now the Lord GOD has sent me and his
Spirit.

OVERVIEW: The Holy Spirit would be sent along behind Christ by the Father. In the economy of salvation, Christ is sent by both Father and Spirit (ORIGEN). This double sending was to help Christ in the weakness of his flesh (JEROME). This verse clearly attests the trinitarian quality of the God of the Bible (THEODORET). It is as the Servant that Christ needs the Spirit (AUGUSTINE), having humbled himself out of love in order to save his chosen people (CYRIL). God speaks directly through the prophet here (EPHREM).

48:16 Sent Me and His Spirit

THE SON AND SPIRIT ARE SENT BY THE FATHER. ORIGEN: Did the Father and the Holy Spirit send Jesus, or did the Father send both Christ and the Spirit? The latter is correct. For, because the Savior was sent, afterwards the Holy Spirit was sent also, that the prediction of the prophet might be fulfilled. AGAINST CELSUS 1.46.[1]

THE SPIRIT DOES NOT EXCEL THE SON IN NATURE. ORIGEN: According to Isaiah the Lord has sent Christ and his Spirit.... It is also possible there to allege of the Spirit that sent the Christ that he does not excel him in nature but that the Savior was made to seek greater lowliness because of the plan of the incarnation. COMMENTARY ON THE GOSPEL OF JOHN 2.79.81.[2]

THE LORD SENT ME AND HIS SPIRIT. JEROME:

When all things were made by the Father, he [the Son] was there with him, in whom the Son rejoiced when he said, I am he who always was with the Father and in the Father and never was without the Father, and who now speaks, and due to the weakness of the flesh I assumed, I say that "the Lord has sent me and his Spirit." In this short verse we are shown the mystery of the Trinity. COMMENTARY ON ISAIAH 13.16.[3]

THE CLEAR REVELATION OF THE TRIUNE GOD. THEODORET OF CYR: Since you have not believed the gloomy predictions, believe, then, at least in the prophecies of encouragement. For I do not prophesy falsely in dark, inaccessible places after the manner of the [oracles of] idols. But I know these things clearly before their occurrence since I am present to the events themselves and see each one. "And now the Lord has sent me as well as his Spirit." It is the prophet who made this declaration. He says, "I do not speak on my own authority but because the God of the universe and the holiest Spirit has sent me." Now [the text] demonstrates here that there is another person besides God, the person of the Spirit, so as to refute the Jews and the mad ravings of Sabellius. For [Isaiah] said, "The Lord sent me as well as his Spirit." For Sabellius often taught the one deity of God.... He must also teach about the particular characteristics of the persons, sometimes that of the Son and that of the Father, sometimes that of

---

[1]ANF 4:416. [2]FC 80:114-15*. [3]AGLB 35:1412-13.

the Father and that of the Holy Spirit. COMMEN-
TARY ON ISAIAH 15.48.16.[4]

**THE PAST TENSE TO INDICATE A FUTURE
EVENT.** AUGUSTINE: Now it is Jesus Christ who
is speaking here as the "Lord God"; yet this
would not have been obvious if he had not added
the final words, "And now the Lord God has sent
me and his Spirit." These words were spoken by
Christ in his "form" as a "servant."[5] He used a
verb in the past tense to indicate a future event.
CITY OF GOD 20.30.[6]

THE SON IS NOT SENT WITHOUT THE SPIRIT.
AUGUSTINE: Furthermore, he could not be sent
by the Father without the Holy Spirit. On principle, when the Father sent him, that is made him
of woman, he cannot be supposed to have done it
without the Spirit. . . . There is even a prophecy
of Isaiah in which Christ himself is understood as
saying about his future coming, "And now the
Lord and his Spirit has sent me." ON THE TRIN-
ITY 2.2.8.[7]

FOR THOSE HE LOVES. CYRIL OF ALEXANDRIA:
Those who look toward the Savior do not
attribute grace for salvation to other gods but to

him. For it is said about him that he was moved
by love, that is, he was most loving and kind to
them in that he was prepared to go all the way to
the very end, to the uprooting of the seed of the
Chaldeans, that is, those who fought against
them and perpetrated all sorts of inhuman acts.
. . . I am spurred by love for you that I will do
what is your pleasure in the land of the Babylonians, so that the seed of the Chaldeans will be
removed. For [Isaiah] speaks here about Cyrus.
COMMENTARY ON ISAIAH 4.3.48.15-16.[8]

**THE WORDS OF THE PROPHET COME FROM
GOD.** EPHREM THE SYRIAN: "From the time this
plague came to be" in all my people, "I have been
there." In order that the words he had spoken
may not be despised by the sorcerers, the text
shows that they do not belong to the prophet as
such, but to the Lord and his Spirit, who sent the
prophet to preach to them. Indeed, the prophet
clearly said as if from the person of the Lord, "I
am in all my people, and my right hand extends to
the heavens."[9] COMMENTARY ON ISAIAH 48.16.[10]

---

[4]SC 315:66-68. [5]Phil 2:7. [6]FC 24:332. [7]WSA 1 5:102. [8]PG
70:1025. [9]Is 48:13 Peshitta. [10]SESHS 2:125.

48:17-19 PEACE LIKE A RIVER

[17]*Thus says the* LORD,
   your Redeemer, the Holy One of Israel:
"*I am the* LORD *your God,*
   who teaches you to profit,
   who leads you in the way you should go.
[18]*O that you had hearkened to my*
      commandments!
   Then your peace would have been like a

   river,
   and your righteousness like the waves of
      the sea;
[19]*your offspring would have been like the sand,*
   and your descendants like its grains;
their name would never be cut off
   or destroyed from before me."

OVERVIEW: God is the ultimate reality behind all things (CYRIL). As such, he truly can promise us peace like a river, as he gives to us his Son, who is the source of the river of the Spirit that flows to us. This grace of the Spirit that flows from Christ brings us forgiveness and life as it imparts to us the benefits of Christ's passion (AMBROSE). We are also here given the promise of having offspring, set again in the context of having peace, and this can apply only to those who trust in God (JEROME). God also would have blessed the Jews materially if they had obeyed (THEODORET).

48:17 I Am the Lord

GOD AS THE UTMOST REALITY. CYRIL OF ALEXANDRIA: He says, "I AM your God." This "I AM" means "I am the beginning."[1] He explained all this to the all-wise Moses saying "I am the one who is."[2] For he as Lord is truly the God of everything. Those things that are brought into being by him are said to be "beings" also and to share in the source of being.... Again he works in them a steadfast thinking and a well-established mind that they can see God to be truly existing in nature. To these he reveals his glory so that they are not carried away by deceitful voices. COMMENTARY ON ISAIAH 4.3.48.17-19.[3]

48:18 Peace Like a River

CHRIST IS THE SOURCE OF THE PEACEFUL RIVER OF THE SPIRIT. AMBROSE: Set before yourself any river. It springs from its fountain but is of one nature, of one brightness and beauty. And you assert rightly that the Holy Spirit is of one substance, brightness and glory with the Son of God and with God the Father. I will sum up everything in the oneness of the qualities without any dispute over degrees of greatness. For in this point also Scripture has provided for us. For the Son of God says, "Whoever shall drink of the water that I will give him, it shall become in him a well of water springing up unto everlasting life."[4] This well is clearly the grace of the Spirit, a stream proceeding from the living Fountain. The Holy Spirit, then, is also the fountain of eternal life.

You observe, then, from his words that the unity of the divine greatness is pointed out and that Christ cannot be denied to be a fountain even by heretics, since the Spirit, too, is called a fountain. The Spirit is called a river, too, just as the Father said, "Behold, I come down on you like a river of peace, and like a stream overflowing the glory of the Gentiles."[5] And who can doubt that the Son of God is the river of life from whom the streams of eternal life flowed forth? ON THE HOLY SPIRIT 1.16.180-81.[6]

THE RIVER OF FORGIVENESS WASHES US CLEAN. AMBROSE: This water is good, then. I mean here the grace of the Spirit. Who will give this Fountain to my heart? Let it spring up in me, let that which gives eternal life flow on me. Let that Fountain overflow on us and not flow away. For Wisdom says, "Drink water out of your own vessels and from the fountains of your own wells, and let your waters flow abroad in your streets."[7] How shall I keep this water so that it does not seep out or glide away? How shall I preserve my vessel, lest any crack of sin penetrating it should let the water of eternal life exude? Teach us, Lord Jesus, teach us as you taught your apostles, saying, "Lay not up for yourselves treasures on the earth, where rust and moth destroy and where thieves break through and steal."[8]

Our rust is wantonness, our rust is lust, our rust is luxury, which dim the keen vision of the mind with the filth of vices. Again, our moth is Arius, our moth is Photinus, who rend the holy vesture of the church with their impiety, and desiring to separate the indivisible unity of the divine power, gnaw the precious veil of faith with

---

[1]Gk *hyparchō*. The implication is that God is the only being that subsists, having no dependence on anything else for his existence. [2]Ex 3:14. [3]PG 70:1029, 1028. [4]Jn 4:14. [5]Is 66:12 LXX. [6]NPNF 2 10:114**. [7]Prov 5:15-16. [8]Mt 6:19.

sacrilegious tooth. The water is spilled if Arius has imprinted his tooth, it flows away if Photinus has planted his sting in anyone's vessel. . . .

If you seek Jesus, forsake the broken cisterns, for Christ did not make it his custom to sit by a pool but by a well. There that Samaritan woman[9] found him, she who believed, she who wished to draw water. Although you ought to have come in early morning, nevertheless if you come later, even at the sixth hour, you will find Jesus wearied with his journey. He is weary, but it is because of you, because he has long looked for you, your unbelief has long wearied him. Yet he is not offended if you only come now. He asks to drink who is about to give. But he drinks not the water of a stream flowing by, but your salvation. He drinks your good dispositions. He drinks the cup, that is, the passion that atoned for your sins, that you, drinking of his sacred blood, might quench the thirst of this world. ON THE HOLY SPIRIT 1.16.182-84.[10]

48:19 Your Offspring

THE PROMISE OF BLESSING FULFILLED. JEROME: "Your offspring would have been like the sand and your descendants like its grains." This promise seems still to apply to the Jewish people. . . . But how can this be taken as a real promise to them since they do not have peace and justice? For he is either angry with them or pleased with them. If angry, how can their seed grow every day? If pleased, then how can they serve and yet not have peace and justice? For this becomes clear concerning the apostolic seed about which we read above, "Unless the Lord of the sabbath left us a seed we would have been like Sodom."[11] At that time it did not seem fulfilled, but in the advent of Christ it was, and before his face the seed of Israel endures. COMMENTARY ON ISAIAH 13.17.[12]

GOD'S FAITHFULNESS TO A FAITHLESS PEOPLE. THEODORET OF CYR: "I am the Lord your God. I have shown how to find my way so that you may benefit by traveling on that way." . . . But since the Jews did not desire to pay attention to these commandments, by reason of their attachment to a fleshly manner of thinking, they viewed having many children as a sign of blessing. . . . Nevertheless, although you have despised my laws, I will consider you worthy of consideration and, once again, you will be called "my people." COMMENTARY ON ISAIAH 15.48.18-19.[13]

---

[9]Jn 4:6. [10]NPNF 2 10:114-15**. [11]Is 1:9. [12]AGLB 35:1414. [13]SC 315:68.

48:20-22 LEAVING BABYLON

[20]*Go forth from Babylon, flee from Chaldea,*
declare this with a shout of joy, proclaim it,
send it forth to the end of the earth;
say, "The LORD has redeemed his servant
Jacob!"
[21]*They thirsted not when he led them through*
the deserts;
he made water flow for them from the rock;
he cleft the rock and the water gushed out.
[22]*"There is no peace," says the LORD, "for the*
wicked."

OVERVIEW: To leave Babylon means to flee from the city of the world and look toward God (AUGUSTINE, ATHANASIUS). This prophecy did have a fulfillment in the return from the exile in Babylon and is not referring just to the exodus (THEODORET). Yet the fuller accomplishment of the prophecy was when peace was added through Christ (CYRIL). The fulfillment of this happiness came with the coming of Christ (JEROME).

48:20 Go Forth from Babylon

FLEEING FROM EARTHLY THINGS. AUGUSTINE: "Come forth out of Babylon." If we take the command of the prophet in a spiritual sense, it means that we should fly from the city of this world, from the fellowship of wicked angels and wicked [people], with the feet of that faith that works through love, and we should press onward unceasingly toward the living God. CITY OF GOD 18.18.[1]

KEEP PACE WITH GOD'S GRACE. ATHANASIUS: Now my beloved, our will ought to keep pace with the grace of God and not fall short; lest while our will remains idle, the grace given us should begin to depart, and the enemy finding us empty and naked, . . . as was the case with him spoken of in the Gospel, from whom the devil went out.[2] . . . For the departure from virtue gives place for the entrance of the unclean spirit. FESTAL LETTERS 3.3.[3]

48:21 He Made Water Flow

WATER FOR THE THIRSTY. THEODORET OF CYR: The three interpreters treat this as if it were something that had already occurred: "You made water flow for them from a rock; the waters broke the hard rock and flowed out." According to the Septuagint, the text alludes to the prophetic grace the Jews enjoyed drinking in divine draughts even while in Babylon from the prophets Daniel and Ezekiel. Because they found themselves in a desert of sorts as a result of the impiety

of the Babylonians, they possessed a kind of rock in the prophecy that poured for them the drink of salvation. Further, even after the return from exile, it was Haggai, Zechariah and Malachi who presented to them these divine waters, while the admirable Zerubbabel and the high priest Joshua, the son of Jozadek, wore their piety like a necklace. They offered divine teaching to them like water to the thirsty. COMMENTARY ON ISAIAH 15.48.20-21.[4]

48:22 No Peace for the Wicked

THE EFFECTS OF CHRIST. CYRIL OF ALEXANDRIA: No one found that this happened when they came out of Babylon and went into Judah. For this is said with reference to the economy of salvation so as to show that God, who was formerly able and is still now able, being of undiminished power, to perform similar miracles with great strength, now, as if calling out, proclaims a universal law, that "there is no peace for the wicked." COMMENTARY ON ISAIAH 4.3.48.20-22.[5]

TO LEAVE BABYLON IS TO BELIEVE IN CHRIST. JEROME: Some say that so we might know that this prophecy is not about Christ but about Cyrus, the phrase is added, "there is no peace for the ungodly, says the Lord." This would mean that there will be no perfect happiness except under Christ, which is reserved for the last times. Yet those who more truly and rightly apply these words to the advent of the Savior, about whom it is said, "He has sent me to announce to the poor, to preach liberty to the captives,"[6] understand it to be an encouragement of those who preach the gospel or of the Lord and Savior, that we leave Babylon, that is, the confusion of this world, and flee the Babylonians. . . . For the Lord has redeemed his servant Jacob with his most precious blood and led him through the desert and made a way for water to come out of a rock, about

---

[1]FC 24:106. [2]Mt 12:43-45. [3]NPNF 2 4:513. [4]SC 315:70. [5]PG 70:1033. [6]Is 61:1.

which the apostle said, "The Rock was Christ."[7] . . . And lest it be thought that the prophecy is said about all the seed of Jacob, and not those only who would believe through the apostles, mention is also made concerning this: "there is no peace for the ungodly." COMMENTARY ON ISAIAH 13.18.[8]

---

[7]1 Cor 10:4. [8]AGLB 35:1415-16.

49:1-2 THE QUIVER AND THE ARROW OF THE WORD

[1]*Listen to me, O coastlands,*
and hearken, you peoples from afar.
The LORD called me from the womb,
*   from the body of my mother he named my*
*   name.*

[2]*He made my mouth like a sharp sword,*
*   in the shadow of his hand he hid me;*
he made me a polished arrow,
*   in his quiver he hid me away.*

OVERVIEW: The prophecy is meant to be heard by all those who inhabit the earth (THEODORET). The Word calls the assembly together amid conditions of persecution (CYRIL), which even he underwent when Herod tried to kill him; but he was concealed in the shadow of the Lord's arm (CYRIL OF JERUSALEM). Christ is like a sharp and bright arrow that inflicts a saving wound (ORIGEN). The quiver that is allowed to hold such a precious arrow is our faith (AMBROSE). Christ is the divine and chosen arrow hidden as in a quiver—in the flesh—aiming at salvation (JEROME). He hid me away in his quiver to be wounded by love (THEODORET). The virgin Mary supplied the quiver in which the Word was contained and hidden (CHROMATIUS). The Word became a powerful healing weapon for spiritual deliverance (CYRIL).

49:1 *Listen to Me*

ALL CALLED TO LISTEN. THEODORET OF CYR: Instead of "after a long time," Symmachus has said, "Lend your ear, O Gentiles, [who come] from afar." The text therefore calls [those of] the islands, the continents and even those who inhabit the extremities [of the earth] to listen to the prophecy. But the expression of the Septuagint, "after a long time," should be understood as follows: the Lord of the universe promised to Abraham to bless all nations in his posterity.[1] This promise he also made to Isaac and to Jacob. Jacob, in his turn, gave it to Judah as a blessing: "The scepter shall not depart from Judah, or a lawgiver from between his feet, until he comes for whom it is reserved, he who is also the expectation of nations."[2] Now, a very great number of years had passed from the promise made to Abraham until the call of the Gentiles. This is why the prophetic text says, "Listen, you Gentiles, after a long time." Then he adds, "It shall stand, says the Lord," that is, to say the word of the promise, for the promise of God is trustworthy. COMMENTARY ON ISAIAH 15.49.1.[3]

---

[1]Gen 12:3; 18:8. [2]Gen 49:10. [3]ITA 717*; SC 315:72.

Called by My Name from the Womb.
Cyril of Alexandria: He calls to "the islands,"
which we take to be the churches of Christ, just
as they are lying in the sea or the waves of this
present existence and surrounded by the insulting attacks of "the waves," or the persecutions
and afflictions that the enemies of the truth
inflict on the churches as they war against the
divine call. Concerning these islands the divinely
inspired Scripture often speaks. There the
blessed David sang a psalm and said, "The Lord
reigns, and let the earth be glad and many islands
rejoice."[4] So when Christ taking all things in his
hands reigned over it from heaven and ejected the
demons' tyranny, then did they rejoice, that is,
the churches over all the earth were filled with
happiness.... [Isaiah] promised that our Savior
Jesus Christ would be revealed to everyone and
that God as the Word would come on the earth
among them in a form "after our likeness."...
That this is so, the person of the Savior himself
attests, "Out of my mother's womb he called my
name." Mixed into these words is a deep and
great mystery that requires mystical understanding from above.... For he was and is God the
Word, equal and sharing the throne with God the
Father, coexisting and coeternal. Commentary
on Isaiah 4.4.49.1-3.[5]

The Preexistence of the Savior. Cyril of
Jerusalem: Consider how he who was not yet
born could have a people, unless he were in being
before he was born. The prophet says this in his
person, "From my mother's womb he gave me my
name"; because the angel foretold that he would be
called Jesus. Again, concerning the plots of Herod,
he says, "He . . . concealed me in the shadow of his
arm."[6] Catechetical Lectures 10.12.[7]

49:2 A Polished Arrow in His Quiver

A Wound That Saves. Origen: If anyone has
been able to hold in the breadth of his mind and
to consider the glory and splendor of all those
things created in him, he will be struck by their
very beauty and transfixed by the magnificence of
their brilliance or, as the prophet says, "by the
chosen arrow." And he will receive from him the
saving wound and will burn with the blessed fire
of his love. Commentary on the Song of
Songs, Prologue.[8]

**Fill the Quiver of Faith with Good
Deeds.** Ambrose: "In my quiver he hid me
away," Scripture declares. The quiver, then, is
your faith. Fill it with the fragrant aroma of
your virtues, that is, of chastity, compassion and
justice, and immerse yourself wholly in the
inmost mysteries of faith, which are fragrant with
the sweet odors of your significant deeds. Six
Days of Creation 5.23.80.[9]

Christ the One Choice Arrow. Jerome:
When it says "chosen arrow," it implies that God
has many arrows but not choice ones—these
arrows are the prophets and apostles, who go
shooting off around the world.... But Christ is
the one arrow chosen from many arrows and one
son from many sons, which he hid in his quiver,
that is, in his human body, so that the fullness of
divinity could dwell in him bodily and that the
faith of believers be distributed. Commentary
on Isaiah 13.19.[10]

Wounded by Love. Theodoret of Cyr: Such
is the word, the source of division that he presented to all people; likewise he declared, "I have
not come to bring peace to the earth, but a
sword."[11] And moreover, the divine apostle says,
"The Word of God is living and powerful, and
sharper than any two-edged sword."[12] ... "He has
set me like a chosen arrow and hidden me in his
quiver." Similarly, Isaiah said this metaphorically;
he speaks of an arrow that wounds the souls of
those who love him. Each cries, "I am wounded
by love."[13] The quiver represents the mystery of

---

[4]Ps 97:1 (96:1 LXX). [5]PG 70:1036. [6]Is 49:2. [7]FC 61:204. [8]OSW
223. [9]FC 42:220*. [10]AGLB 35:1419. [11]Mt 10:34. [12]Heb 4:12.
[13]Song 2:5.

---

the economy of the incarnation. COMMENTARY ON ISAIAH 15.49.2.[14]

THE ARROW THE DIVINITY, THE QUIVER THE HUMANITY OF CHRIST. CHROMATIUS OF AQUILEIA: This arrow signifies his divinity, resting in a quiver signifying the body assumed from the Virgin, in whose cloth of flesh his divinity was clothed. TRACTATE ON MATTHEW 2.4.[15]

REVELATION HID IN THE SHADOW OF GOD'S FOREKNOWLEDGE. CYRIL OF ALEXANDRIA: The name Christ is not appropriate for God the Word before the generation that, as I said, was according to the flesh. If he was then not yet anointed, how could he be called "Christ"? But when the man came forth from his mother's womb, then he received the name at the same time as the generation according to the flesh. For it says that he "set his mouth like a sharp sword" . . . for no one can overcome his all-powerful right hand, but the

Word is kept distinct from the dimensions of the humanity. For he is the Word from the Father and himself is the Lord of hosts. When he became man, the Father did not remove the power of the mystery but confirmed him in the economy of salvation. . . . There have been several arrows of God hidden in his quiver, in his foreknowledge, and brought out at the time prepared for each, but the chosen arrow above all others is the Christ hidden in the quiver or foreknowledge of God. For he was known before the creation of the world and brought forth in the middle of time when it was necessary that the earth be visited as it was falling into destruction. . . . This chosen arrow, as I said, got rid of Satan and the evil powers with him . . . yet he wounds in another way, for benefit and salvation. Thus it says in the Song of Songs, "I am wounded with love."[16] COMMENTARY ON ISAIAH 4.4.49.1-3.[17]

---

[14]SC 315:74. [15]CCL 9A:204. [16]Song 2:5. [17]PG 70:1037-40.

49:3-4 THE SERVANT SPENDS HIS STRENGTH

[3]*And he said to me, "You are my servant, Israel, in whom I will be glorified."*
[4]*But I said, "I have labored in vain, I have spent my strength for nothing and vanity; yet surely my right is with the LORD, and my recompense with my God."*

OVERVIEW: The humanity of Christ possesses royal nature though a slave-like form (THEODORET). The servant seems to question any glory coming to the Father since the people have not responded to his call (JEROME). However, it is also important to understand that he says these things only according to his human nature (THEODORET). Christ ultimately did absorb the punishment of those who did not reject him (CYRIL).

49:3 You Are My Servant

THE DIVINE AND HUMAN SON. THEODORET OF CYR: "You are my servant Israel, and I will glorify myself in you." This is to be understood according to Christ's human nature. For according to his human nature Christ is called Israel, Jacob, the son of David, the seed of Abraham, and so on. Christ is called "servant" since the servile nature

God the Word assumed was the form of a slave. For "he has given him the name above every name,"[1] that is, to be the Son. As God, Christ the master was always Son, but as man he became Son. For there is not one that is "that Son" and another that is "this Son," but the one who is God the Son also became the Son as a human being.[2] COMMENTARY ON ISAIAH 15.49.3.[3]

THE PRINCIPLE OF FREE WILL. JEROME: With the Father saying these things to me which I have registered, I replied to him, "How are you glorified in me, Father, since I have worked in the void and have not been able to summon back to you the great part of the Jewish people?" Now this reveals a universal principle, in that it shows the free will of the human being—it is for God to call and for us to believe. And if we do not believe immediately, God is not powerless but leaves his power for our will so that the will fittingly gains the award. COMMENTARY ON ISAIAH 13.19.[4]

49:4 I Have Labored in Vain

THE HUMILITY OF CHRIST. THEODORET OF

CYR: It is necessary to recognize that he says these things as a human. For in the holy Gospels Christ as a human makes a number of humble declarations. For instance, . . . "I do nothing from myself."[5] COMMENTARY ON ISAIAH 15.49.4.[6]

MY JUDGMENT IS WITH THE LORD. CYRIL OF ALEXANDRIA: For it was a labor for the Word to come among us and to surrender himself to human fragility. But "my judgment" is the punishment of the Father that I [the Savior] have turned into a feast for their salvation. For that reason the judgment was taken away from him [the servant]. Just what sort of judgment was that? [Sinners] have been cast out of his company, to be placed outside the people of God, no longer sharers in the salvation wrought by him, and they have no longer any taste of the hope of the saints, to which many of the nations have been called in their place. COMMENTARY ON ISAIAH 4.4.49.4.[7]

---

[1]Phil 2:9. [2]Theodoret, perhaps mindful of Cyril's *Epistle* 40 to Acacius (PG 77:189-193), affirms that the state of the Son of man in the incarnation is an exalted one as befits the Son of God, who he is. [3]SC 315:74-76. [4]AGLB 35:1420. [5]Jn 5:19. [6]SC 315:76. [7]PG 70:1041.

49:5-6 THE SERVANT REMOVES SERVITUDE

[5]And now the LORD says,
    who formed me from the womb to be his
        servant,
to bring Jacob back to him,
    and that Israel might be gathered to him,
for I am honored in the eyes of the LORD,
    and my God has become my strength—
[6]he says:

"It is too light a thing that you should be my
        servant
    to raise up the tribes of Jacob
    and to restore the preserved of Israel;
I will give you as a light to the nations,
    that my salvation may reach to the end of
        the earth."

Overview: Christ's human nature was created in the womb as is everyone's (Athanasius). Zerubbabel, a type of Christ, is here envisaged by the prophecy (Isho'dad). Christ is a servant according to the adoption of a body (Ambrose). Christ as servant removed servitude (Gregory of Nazianzus), freely accepting slavery (Cyril) and becoming one of us (Theodoret). His mission was to gather Israel, who is to be saved, which includes all who have faith (Cyril) in Israel and among the nations (Theodoret).

49:5 From the Womb

Christ's Humanity Created as Ours.
Athanasius: In respect of nature, [Christ] differs in nothing from us, though he precedes us in time, so long as we all consist and are created by the same hand. Defense of the Nicene Definition 3.9.[1]

Zerubbabel Prefigures Christ. Isho'dad of Merv: "Who formed me from the womb to be his servant." This is clearly said with reference to Zerubbabel and the people but was accomplished in Christ. And indeed, since Christ will descend from them, it is with good reason that what concerns him is represented in them as in a sign. Commentary on Isaiah 49.5.[2]

49:6 My Servant

The Servant Is Christ. Ambrose: It is one thing to be named Son according to the divine substance; it is another thing to be so called according to the adoption of human flesh. For, according to the divine generation, the Son is equal to God and Father, and, according to the adoption of a body, he is a servant to God the Father. "For," it says, "he took upon him the form of a servant."[3] The Son is, however, one and the same.... According to his glory, he is Lord to the holy patriarch David but David's son in the line of actual descent, abandoning nothing of his own but acquiring for himself the rights that go with

the adoption into our race. Not only does he undergo service in the character of man by reason of his descent from David, but also by reason of his name, as it is written: "I have found David my servant";[4] and elsewhere: "Behold, I will send to you my Servant, the Orient is his name."[5] And the Son himself says, "Thus says the Lord, that formed me from the womb to be his servant and said to me: It is a great thing for you to be called my servant. Behold, I have set you up for a witness to my people and a light to the Gentiles, that you may be for salvation to the ends of the earth." To whom is this said, if not to Christ? Who, being in the form of God, emptied himself and took on him the form of a servant.[6] But what can be in the form of God, except that which exists in the fullness of the godhead? On the Christian Faith 5.8.106-7.[7]

Christ as a Servant Removed Servitude.
Gregory of Nazianzus: He is called Servant and serves many well. And his being given the grand title "Child of God" agrees with this. For in truth he was subject as a servant to flesh and to birth and to the conditions of our life with a view toward our liberation. He was subject to all that he saved, held captive as we were in sin. On the Son, Theological Oration 4(30).3.[8]

The Double-Entendre of Pais (Son-Slave). Cyril of Alexandria: For a lowly appellation is given to the Word whose origin is from God, that he is called slave, that is, a household member. For such a title can sometimes indicate "son," and at other times, as we have said, "household member." In the economy of the flesh, it is appropriate to consider the Son as a slave. For he is God by nature and free as being from God the sovereign Father, yet he took the shape or form of a slave. For no one with right understanding could say that he was a slave by nature who was then able to be brought into the

[1]NPNF 2 4:155. [2]CSCO 303:49. [3]Phil 2:7. [4]Ps 89:20 (88:21 LXX). [5]Zech 3:8 Vg. [6]Phil 2:6-7. [7]NPNF 2 10:297-98*. [8]NPNF 2 7:310**.

form of a slave. Rather, he was outside of slavery and constraint, but for the sake of a sign, in the freedom of his nature, he received the shape, that is, the form of slave.... For he was Emmanuel, and he revealed to us no less in this way his freedom which was real and by nature.... For he who was God the Word dwelled in them and among us for no other reason except so that he could save Israel and gather Jacob. For he had scattered all others who were on the earth, every inventor of wickedness, into their many-colored and multifaceted vices. Commentary on Isaiah 4.4.49.5-6.[9]

The Humanity of the Son. Theodoret of Cyr: We must also understand the prophet to be speaking of Christ's humanity here, for it would be no great honor for God the Word to be called the slave of God the Father. It is not "my child" but "my slave" that both the Hebrew text and the three translators make clear to us. Commentary on Isaiah 15.49.6.[10]

Christ's Mission Is to Gather All Who Live by Faith. Cyril of Alexandria: But when Christ appeared in the world they were gathered though faith in the one straight and blameless opinion, those whom Satan once had

scattered and who formerly had deserted their love for God. They had run toward the enemy who produces and pursues sin. Those who had thrown away God's providence of good things are now with Christ at peace.... So he reveals the ministry of his incarnation, that he was formed as a slave by the Father from the womb so as to gather Israel and Jacob. If anyone says that these are the Jewish people that are meant, he has not strayed from the intention of the text. For Christ said, "I have come to save the lost sheep of Israel."[11] But if anyone decides it is all those saved by faith who are called Israel and Jacob, he is right to do so. Commentary on Isaiah 4.4.49.5-6.[12]

The Salvation of the Nations. Theodoret of Cyr: Then Isaiah predicts the disobedience of the Jews and the salvation of the nations. "Behold, I have given your race as a covenant, as a light to the nations." The Lord's race according to the flesh was the entire race of human beings, yet his own and nearest was Israel.... "And I will put an end to the arrangements that I made with their ancestors."[13] Commentary on Isaiah 15.49.6.[14]

---

[9]PG 70:1049, 1045. [10]SC 315:80. [11]Mt 15:24. [12]PG 70:1045-48. [13]Theodoret further notes the grammatical point that "the three translators render the word 'covenant' as 'arrangement.'" [14]SC 315:80-82.

49:7-10 THE TIME OF FAVOR

[7]Thus says the Lord,
   the Redeemer of Israel and his Holy One,
to one deeply despised, abhorred by the
     nations,
   the servant of rulers:
"Kings shall see and arise;
   princes, and they shall prostrate themselves;

because of the Lord, who is faithful,
   the Holy One of Israel, who has chosen
     you."

[8]Thus says the Lord:
"In a time of favor I have answered you,
   in a day of salvation I have helped you;

I have kept you and given you
*   as a covenant to the people,*
to establish the land,
*   to apportion the desolate heritages;*
⁹saying to the prisoners, 'Come forth,'
*   to those who are in darkness, 'Appear.'*
They shall feed along the ways,

*   on all bare heights shall be their pasture;*
¹⁰they shall not hunger or thirst,
*   neither scorching wind nor sun shall smite*
*   them,*
for he who has pity on them will lead them,
*   and by springs of water will guide them."*

Overview: The time of favor is fulfilled in the humbling of the Son in his cross and resurrection (Jerome). In his humiliation, Jesus retained his divine dignity at all times (Cyril). Christ's full identification with death allows us mortals to identify with him so that we too may become immortal (Augustine, Cyril), as is evidenced in the martyrs who share immediately in Christ's suffering but also in the benefits his suffering brought us (Origen). The acceptable time and day of salvation to which Isaiah refers is a reference to our justification that is attained when faith is exercised (Augustine). Paul's use of Isaiah shows us that the acceptable time for faith is now, not just some day in the past (Fulgentius).

It was the cruelty of human beings that required Christ's suffering and death, and God took account of this (Procopius). The help from God to Christ came not on the cross but two days later (Cyril). Those who come forth from the imprisonment of indebtedness have changed their creditor from the law to Christ (Ambrose). No human historical figure other than Christ has worked such liberation; those who believe in him will be divinely nourished (Theodoret). The struggle between wisdom and insensibility reached a climax in the cross, and yet life was the result. All the graces from Christ are like a banquet for our souls (Cyril) with the Old and the New Testaments serving us like springs of saving water (Eusebius).

49:7 One Deeply Despised

The Lost Inheritance Is Regained.
Jerome: Theodotion translated, "To him who despises life, who is an abomination to the people, who is a servant of princes"—which clearly suits the person of Christ. For the good Shepherd gave his life for the sheep and despised it, he who was an abomination to the nation of the Jews . . . , one who was the servant of princes and so humble that he stood before Annas and Caiaphas and was sent to be crucified to Pilate and Herod. . . . The "peaceful and opportune time" and "the day of salvation" are the Savior's passion and resurrection—when he prayed on the cross, "God, my God, why have you abandoned me?"[1] And God kept him or formed him as death was overcome and gave him to be a covenant of the people of the Jews, or at least to those of them who believed, to waken the land that was lying in the errors of idolatry and to possess the lost or deserted inheritance that did not have God living there. Commentary on Isaiah 13.21-22.[2]

The One True Source of Holiness. Cyril of Alexandria: For any powers and rational beings and also human beings on the earth who are holy—only through participation in the holy One by nature and who alone is truly holy are they called holy . . . and he who is alone holy together with God the Father and God the Holy Spirit has given from his own fullness to those sharing the holiness with him. Commentary on Isaiah 4.4.49.7.[3]

Christ Remedies Our Human Nature by

---

[1]Mt 27:46. [2]AGLB 35:1424-25, 1427-28. [3]PG 70:1052.

Assuming It. Augustine: The Son of God assumed human nature, and in it he endured all that belongs to the human condition. This is a remedy for humanity of a power beyond our imagining. Could any pride be cured, if the humility of God's Son does not cure it? Could any greed be cured, if the poverty of God's Son does not cure it? Or any anger, if the patience of God's Son does not cure it? Or any coldness, if the love of God's Son does not cure it? Lastly, what fearfulness can be cured, if it is not cured by the resurrection of the body of Christ the Lord? Let humanity raise its hopes and recognize its own nature: let it observe how high a place it has in the works of God. Do not despise yourselves, you men: the Son of God assumed manhood. Do not despise yourselves, you women: God's Son was born of a woman. But do not set your hearts on the satisfaction of the body, for in the Son of God we are "neither male nor female."[4] Do not set your heart on temporal rewards: if it were good to do so, that human nature which God's Son assumed would have set its heart on this. Do not fear insults, crosses and death: for if they did harm humanity, the humanity that God's Son assumed would not have endured. Christian Combat 11.12.[5]

The Triumph of the Savior. Cyril of Alexandria: For it is clear that Christ caused the salvation of the flesh for all those on the earth. Through his resurrection, death was destroyed and destruction was stamped out, and we are brought springing back to life, we who through Adam had been driven into opposition. So we do not say that the Savior prayed out of a sense of failure but rather on account of the plan [economy] that he carried out in order to inspire our following. . . . For he stands as an example for us in the way he showed courage before the cross. Commentary on Isaiah 4.4.49.8-12.[6]

49:8 In a Time of Favor

The Martyrs Share Immediately in His Suffering and Its Benefits. Origen: God says through the prophet, "In an acceptable time I have heard you, and in a day of salvation I have helped you." What other time, then, is more acceptable than when for piety toward God in Christ we are led under guard in procession before the world, celebrating a triumph rather than being led in triumph? For the martyrs in Christ disarm the principalities and powers with him, and they share his triumph as fellows of his sufferings, becoming in this way also fellows of the courageous deeds wrought in his sufferings.[7] These deeds include triumphing over principalities and powers, which in a short time you will see conquered and put to shame. What other day is so much a day of salvation as the one when we gain such deliverance from them? Exhortation to Martyrdom 42.[8]

In the Time of Favor. Augustine: Those who have faith by which they win justification attain by the grace of God to the law of justice. For this reason the prophet says, "In an acceptable time I have heard you, and in a day of salvation I have helped you." Letter 186.[9]

The Acceptable Time Is Now. Fulgentius of Ruspe: The blessed Paul knew the distance between the present world and the world to come. He knew that only in the present world could the blessing of salvation be acquired but that only in the world to come could a just reward be given to individuals according to the quality of their work, good or wicked. So, when he had repeated the prophetic testimony that God speaks, "In an acceptable time, I heard you, and on the day of salvation, I helped you," he immediately followed it up by adding, "Behold, now is a very acceptable time; now is the day of salvation."[10] On the Forgiveness of Sins 2.5.3.[11]

Human Wickedness Required Christ's Suffering. Procopius of Gaza: "Father, if

---

[4]Gal 3:28. [5]FC 2:329**. [6]PG 70:1056-57. [7]See Col 2:15. [8]OSW 72-73. [9]FC 30:196*. [10]2 Cor 6:2. [11]FC 95:153-54.

this is not able to pass, then let your will be done."[12] The Father received this prayer and then pointed to the time of the resurrection after death, saying, "In a time of favor I have answered you." Some dislike this interpretation and think it not persuasive, saying that the Son failed in his prayer to form a prayer that fit with God's plan. However, even before this [prayer], it was necessary that death could in no way be avoided except through him undergoing the cross and its death. Therefore, such an earnest intercession demonstrates the guilt of those Jewish leaders who exposed him to such shameful suffering against his will. For there was no previous discussion as to whether he should be given the death sentence. "For I have come down from heaven not to do my own will but the will of him who sent me."[13] So he used their cruelty as a means to an end: the salvation of the world. He also provided an example for us not to fall into temptation but to pray to God. And so these words have special meaning for those who are chosen, "In a time of favor I have answered you." For the mystery of Christ was in existence before the foundation of the world, but it was put into action for us at a time when it pleased the Almighty. So he calls the time of the incarnation "day," as does the divine apostle: "Now is the acceptable time, now is the day of salvation."[14] COMMENTARY ON ISAIAH 49.1-13.[15]

HOW AND WHEN GOD HELPED CHRIST. CYRIL OF ALEXANDRIA: It seemed right to some of the previous exegetes to make this the head of the chapter that follows. For thus says the Lord: "In due season I heard you and on the day of salvation I helped you." And they say that this is what was said by the God and Father of all to Christ our Savior. For they weave in such a sense to the words. For he prayed, saying before the precious cross, "Father, if it is possible, take away this cup from me."[16] But he was not heard, and he drank it. When he had suffered death with the Father permitting it, then the Father said to him what was necessary, "In due season I heard you, and on

the day of salvation I helped you." COMMENTARY ON ISAIAH 4.4.49.10.[17]

49:9 Come Forth

THE IMPRISONED COME FORTH. AMBROSE: [When] we have changed our creditor, we have not entirely escaped, or, rather, we have escaped, but the debt remains, while the interest is canceled, the Lord Jesus saying, "To them that are bound, come forth. And to them that are in prison, go forth," for your sins have been forgiven. He has forgiven all, and there is no one whom he has not set free. LETTER 62.[18]

GREATER THAN ZERUBBABEL. THEODORET OF CYR: To apply these words to Zerubbabel is absolute nonsense. For Zerubbabel led the Jews out of Babylon, but he did not deliver the nations from error or present the new covenant to the nations. Isaiah says these things about the Lord Christ; it is Christ who has filled the wilderness of the world with divine shoots. He has restored the ruined earth, set those trapped in sins free from chains and illuminated those sitting in darkness with the light of the knowledge of God. COMMENTARY ON ISAIAH 15.49.8-9.[19]

49:10 No Hunger or Thirst

AN ABUNDANCE OF DIVINE NOURISHMENT. THEODORET OF CYR: He has threatened Israel [with suffering] hunger for the Word and [with] a dearth of clouds: "I will send," he says, "a famine of hearing the word of the Lord,"[20] and elsewhere: "And I will command the clouds to rain no rain upon it."[21] Here, on the contrary, he promises those who have believed in him that they would have an abundance of divine nourishment and that they will have sources of salvation at their disposal forever. COMMENTARY ON ISAIAH 15.49.10.[22]

---

[12]Mt 26:39. [13]Jn 6:38. [14]2 Cor 6:2. [15]PG 87:2472. [16]Mt 26:39. [17]PG 70:1056. [18]FC 26:388*. [19]SC 315:84. [20]Amos 8:11. [21]I.e., the vineyard: Is 5:6. [22]ITA 724-25; SC 315:86-88.

THE EMBODIMENT OF GOSPEL FAITH CRUCI-FIED. CYRIL OF ALEXANDRIA: "I descended from heaven not to do my own will but the will of the one who sent me, that is, the will of the Father who sent me that I shall not lose nothing of all which he has given but raise it up on the last day."[23] For Christ appeared in the world and accomplished the gospel among those from Israel. But since they were unbelieving and obdurate, hostile and aggressive, they did not make room for faith. Instead, they sinned in many ways against it and ended up crucifying its perfect form. See in me [Christ says] the power of ineffable wisdom. For from their insensibility there came an affliction—I am referring to his death. For he clearly foretold the salvation of the flesh to everyone on the earth, and death itself suffered corruption, being destroyed through his resurrection. We, in turn, were revived to life, even we who in Adam were dragged down to its opposite. COMMENTARY ON ISAIAH 4.4.49.8-12.[24]

GRACE AND THE SPIRIT OF COMFORT. CYRIL OF ALEXANDRIA: After they were called to the light of truth, they were provided with pastures and forests that nurtured their spiritual strength and satisfied them with every good thing. God made the abundance of his grace, help and spiritual consolation available to them. "For they shall not hunger or thirst." For once they were without spiritual consolation and did not have godly law or prophet or schoolmaster or tutor or teacher, or any spring of water of understanding. After God took mercy on them, however, a feast has been prepared for them in the choir school of spiritual good things. The food there will profit their souls. For they will eat bread from heaven and drink living water, of which the Christ himself said to the Samaritan woman: "Anyone who drinks from this water will thirst again. But whoever drinks the water I give will never be thirsty."[25] COMMENTARY ON ISAIAH 4.4.49.8-12.[26]

SPRINGS OF SALVATION. EUSEBIUS OF CAESAREA: "The merciful One will encourage[27] them, and he will lead them by springs of water." For the springs of Israel and of salvation are plentiful. The springs of Israel are those of the Old Covenant, and the springs of salvation are those of the New. COMMENTARY ON ISAIAH 2.35.[28]

---

[23]Jn 6:38-39. [24]PG 70:1056-57. [25]Jn 4:13. [26]PG 70:1060. [27]Gk *parakaleō*. [28]GCS 57(9):312.

49:11-15 JERUSALEM HAS NOT BEEN FORSAKEN

[11]*"And I will make all my mountains a way,*
and my highways shall be raised up.
[12]*Lo, these shall come from afar,*
and lo, these from the north and from the
west,
and these from the land of Syenne."[l]*
[13]*Sing for joy, O heavens, and exult, O earth;*
break forth, O mountains, into singing!
for The LORD has comforted his people,

and will have compassion on his afflicted.

[14]*But Zion said, "The LORD has forsaken me*
my Lord has forgotten me."
[15]*"Can a woman forget her sucking child,*
that she should have no compassion on the
son of her womb?
Even these may forget,
yet I will not forget you."

l Cn: Heb Sinim   * LXX *the Persians*

OVERVIEW: Zion represents the communion of souls and the angelic community in the church that will ultimately become fully international as peoples come to it from the four corners of the earth (EUSEBIUS) in repentance and faith (THEODORET). They humble themselves under the yoke of Christ's kingdom and, in this way, are prepared to worship him in spirit and in truth (CYRIL). For Christians, Zion, which is Jerusalem, is a type conveying many meanings: the place of Christ's suffering, the congregation of the faithful, the angelic rule and the celestial city (JEROME). Zion may, however, think that the Lord has forgotten it in its tribulations. But we should never think there is anything that could ever have slipped his mind even for a moment (GREGORY THE GREAT). His care for us exceeds even the precious love a mother has for her children (CASSIAN, THEODORET).

49:11-12 Ease of Access to Zion

THE IDENTITY OF THE CHOSEN PEOPLE. EUSEBIUS OF CAESAREA: According to one interpretation, this refers to the lowly and Jewish people. According to another, this is the entire gathering of souls that make up the godly spiritual commonwealth. According to a still further interpretation, this is the angelic order about which the apostle says, "She is the free Jerusalem of above that is our mother,"[1] and "you have come to Zion, the mountain and city of the living God, the heavenly Jerusalem."[2] The present word is addressed to the godly communion that formerly comprised the Jews. But they were brought down and suffered a fall, forfeiting their place to the church of the Gentiles. COMMENTARY ON ISAIAH 2.35.[3]

THOSE FROM ALL DIRECTIONS. EUSEBIUS OF CAESAREA: If some come "from the north" and some "from the sea," that is, from the western parts, and others come "from the land of the Persians" (meaning the highlands), then those in the first clause who are from the land far away are called "of the midday," since the uncircumscribable southern country lies among the midday people. These people are the ones who "shall come from a distance." But the word prophesies that they will come from all over, from the four latitudes to God and will receive the promises spoken to them. COMMENTARY ON ISAIAH 2.35.[4]

49:13 His People Comforted

REJOICING IN HEAVEN. THEODORET OF CYR: It should be noted with attention that he has not made mention here either of Israel or of Jacob but that he has given the name of "people" to those he has assembled from all parts and has deemed worthy of salvation. He has again called on creation to join in the rejoicing, since even for a single sinner who repents, according to the word of the Lord, the assembly of angels rejoices.[5] COMMENTARY ON ISAIAH 15.49.13.[6]

HUMILITY PREPARES FOR WORSHIP. CYRIL OF ALEXANDRIA: We say that those humble ones who submit their necks to Christ and who do not despise the yoke of a kingdom under him, in that they welcome faith, will be fit to worship him in spirit and in truth. [They will] fulfill the worship of those who did not receive faith, those who were not humble but raised their proud horns in the air and spoke unrighteousness against him and his holy prophecies and who exulted in stretching out the neck of their understanding. These were not worthy of spiritual consolation, for they were not deserving. "For what share has faith with unbelief?"[7] as it is written. COMMENTARY ON ISAIAH 4.4.49.13.[8]

49:14 Has the Lord Forgotten Zion?

THE FULLER MEANING OF "JERUSALEM." JEROME: We have often mentioned that Jerusalem and Zion in the holy Scriptures ought to be

---

[1]Gal 4:26. [2]Heb 12:22. [3]GCS 57(9):312-13. [4]GCS 57(9):313. [5]Lk 15:7. [6]ITA 725; SC 315:88. [7]2 Cor 6:15. [8]PG 70:1064.

understood in four ways, one according to the Jews and when the Lord lamented in the Gospel, "Jerusalem, Jerusalem, who killed the prophets." . . . Second, as the congregation of the saints that in the peace of the Lord and in the mirror of virtues is rightly called Zion, about which it is said, "Your foundations are in the holy mountains, the Lord loves the gates of Zion above all the temples of Jacob."[9] For it is not the foundations of the Jewish Zion that we saw were destroyed that was loved by the Lord, as if what was loved by the Lord could be destroyed. Third, "Jerusalem" means the host of angels and rulers and powers and all that is set up for God's ministry. . . . Fourth, by "Jerusalem" is called that which the Jews and Judaizing Christians read of in the Apocalypse of John, a text they do not understand; they think of Jerusalem as golden and jeweled and coming down from the heavens, whose dimensions and enormous width are also described in the last part of Ezekiel. . . . There is no doubt that here the congregation of the saints remembers and complains in a tearful voice that it has been deserted and left destitute of the Lord's help. COMMENTARY ON ISAIAH 13.23.[10]

GOD'S REMEMBERING. GREGORY THE GREAT: For who does not know that the memory of God is not affected by forgetting or restored by recollection? But when leaving something he passes it by, so that in the manner of human minds he is said to forget, and when after a long time he looks up what he wanted, in the habit of our mutability he is said to have recollected. By what arrangement of divinity does oblivion limit the power of the one whom the very notion of memory does

not suit? For only past or absent things can be recollected. How can God remember past things, since the very things that pass in themselves are always present, standing by for his command? Or how can he recollect absent things when everything that is present to him [is present] by its essence? MORALS ON THE BOOK OF JOB 32.5.[11]

49:15 Can a Woman Forget?

CAN A WOMAN FORGET HER SUCKLING CHILD? JOHN CASSIAN: This design and love of his, which the Lord deigns with unwearying kindness to benefit us with and which he wishes to express by an act of human affection, although he discovers no such loving disposition in his creation to which he could worthily compare it, he has compared with the most tender heart of a loving mother. He uses this example because he can find nothing dearer in the nature of human beings. CONFERENCE 13.17.4.[12]

CLOSER THAN A MOTHER. THEODORET OF CYR: Only let us put the rudders of our lives in his hands, and we shall encounter an unfailing providence. God's guardianship will be surer than that of any person, for his are the words, "Can a woman forget her nursing child? Will she not have compassion on the son of her womb? Yet I will not forget you." God is nearer to us than a father and mother, for he is our Maker and Creator. LETTER 14.[13]

---

[9]Ps 87:2 (86:2 LXX). [10]AGLB 35:1432-33. [11]CCL 143B:1632. [12]ACW 57:489. [13]NPNF 2 3:255*.

49:16-17 THE PROTECTIVE WALLS

[16]*Behold, I have graven you on the palms of*
      my hands;*
   your walls are continually before me.

[17]*Your builders outstrip your destroyers,*
      and those who laid you waste go forth from
      you.

* LXX *I have painted your walls on my hands*

OVERVIEW: Christ's sufferings reinforced by the heroes of the faith are like a protective wall for the church (CYRIL). It is God who has applied virtues to the souls of believers (AMBROSE). On the literal level the prophecy here concerns the Babylonians and Persians (THEODORET), but it also spiritually foretells the change from persecution by authorities to support for the church (AUGUSTINE).

49:16 Your Walls

A PROTECTING WALL. CYRIL OF ALEXANDRIA: He bore our sins in his body on the cross, and as he lay there, we were saved, and his sufferings became for us like a safe place and a protecting wall. He suffered outside the city so that he could sanctify the people with his own blood. Therefore . . . the suffering of Christ and his precious cross and the nailing of his hands became safety and an impregnable wall without any breach for those who believe in him. Thus he says, "I have painted your walls on my hands."... And if one wants to understand this in another way, I think it makes sense to understand it that all who believe in Christ are in the hands of the Father.... The walls of the spiritual Zion are the holy prophets and apostles as ones written on his hands, set there by God and having the knowledge of him that does not fade. For their names were written in the heavens and included in the book of life. COMMENTARY ON ISAIAH 4.4.49.16-17.[1]

THE VIRTUES ADORN THE WALLS OF OUR SOUL. AMBROSE: Let us flee these evils and ele-vate our soul to the image and likeness of God. The flight from evils is the likeness of God, and the image of God is gained through the virtues. And so, like a painter, he has painted us with the colors of the virtues. "See, I have painted your walls, Jerusalem." Let us not wipe away with the brush of neglect the props of the painted walls of our soul. DEATH AS A GOOD 5.17.[2]

49:17 Builders Outstrip Destroyers

A PROPHECY OF BABYLON AND PERSIA. THE-ODORET OF CYR: It is the king of Babylon who has destroyed Jerusalem and the king of the Persians who has ordained its reconstruction. But as these last were formerly subjects of the Assyrians, they also joined with them in taking the city. Thus, he can say that the same men both destroyed the city and reconstructed it. "And they that made you desolate shall depart from you." It is to levy the punishment for their faults that they have been delivered into the hands of their enemies. But it is the demons who are the cause of their faults, those they served in giving them the name of gods. He, therefore, predicts the end of the cult of idols and the deliverance from error. COMMENTARY ON ISAIAH 15.49.17.[3]

THE BUILDERS OF THE WALLS OF JERUSALEM OUTSTRIP THE DESTROYERS. AUGUSTINE: Since by the command of the apostle we are not allowed to understand this as about the Jewish people but about Christians, what are we to

---

[1]PG 70:1068. [2]FC 65:83. [3]ITA 727; SC 315:90-92.

understand in that which Isaiah says here, "you will quickly be built up by those from whom you fled," except the kings of the earth who formerly persecuted the church and later would help it as much as previously foretold. LETTER TO THE CATHOLICS ON THE SECT OF THE DONATISTS 7.16.[4]

[4]CSEL 52:249.

49:18-20 THE BEAUTY OF THE BRIDE

[18]Lift up your eyes round about and see;
  they all gather, they come to you.
As I live, says the LORD,
  you shall put them all on as an ornament,
  you shall bind them on as a bride does.

[19]Surely your waste and your desolate places
  and your devastated land—
surely now you will be too narrow for your inhabitants,
  and those who swallowed you up will be far away.
[20]The children born in the time of your bereavement
  will yet say in your ears:
"The place is too narrow for me;
  make room for me to dwell in."

OVERVIEW: The blood of Christ washed all sins from all people (AMBROSE), cleansing the church white in order to wear it as a beautiful garment of lives well lived (BEDE, JEROME). Love for Christ receives a reward of harmony and spiritual beauty in the church (CYRIL). The preparation of beautiful deeds is a fitting way to meet Christ the groom (APONIUS) in his church, which is sewn together in Christ (GREGORY THE GREAT) as it grows so much that it can hardly fit into its boundaries (CYRIL).

49:18 Like an Ornament

AN ORNAMENT TO ZION. AMBROSE: In the passion of his body [Christ] washed the nations with his blood. Truly the mantle represents the nations, as it is written, "As I live, says the Lord, unless I shall clothe myself with them all, as with a garment," and in another passage, "Like clothing you will change them, and they will be changed."[1] And so with his own blood he cleansed not his own sins, for there were none, but the offenses that we committed. ON THE PATRIARCHS 4.24.[2]

THE CHURCH AS THE LORD'S WHITE GARMENTS. BEDE: If anyone asks what the Lord's garments, which became white as snow, represent typologically, we can properly understand them as pointing to the church of his saints. Of them Isaiah said, "You will be clothed with all of these as though with an ornament." HOMILIES ON THE GOSPELS 1.24.[3]

SPIRITUAL GRACES. JEROME: Happy are those

[1]Ps 102:26 (101:27 LXX). [2]FC 65:255. [3]CS 110:238.

ones of so great merit and so great virtue that they can be called the ornament of the church! I think that different spiritual graces are meant here, through which the display of the bride is decorated, of whom it speaks in Psalm 44. COMMENTARY ON ISAIAH 13.23.[4]

MAKE ROOM FOR GOD. CYRIL OF ALEXANDRIA: What, then, is the message promised by the divine words? Namely, the calling and assembling of those who were scattered and a return in the spirit for those who were lost and a way back for those who fled, and a return and a reawakening as well as the reward of love for Christ. . . . "And I have put them on" says the Lord, "to be the ornament of a bride." Such is the beautiful order of the churches. For it is customary in the divinely breathed Scriptures to decorate the church with gold and colors. COMMENTARY ON ISAIAH 4.4.49.18.[5]

ELEMENTARY STEPS PREPARE FOR SPIRITUAL UNION. APONIUS: Spiritual preparation produces faith in the one Lord, and this faith is the opportunity for salvation, through which there is a coming to the knowledge of God through bap-

tism and the doing of various noble works for the hope of eternal life. Their souls are compared with various choice gems, and the church is shown to be fashioned with a crown. EXPOSITION OF SONG OF SONGS 7.13.[6]

CLOTHING AS UNITY IN DIVERSITY. GREGORY THE GREAT: The clothes of the church are all who are joined to it in the unity of faith. MORALS ON THE BOOK OF JOB 27.38.[7]

49:19-20 A Promise of Repopulation

THOSE WHO ARE CALLED ARE MANY. CYRIL OF ALEXANDRIA: This means that he is teaching here about the ones who were swarming and absorbing it, those who had taken it over. For almost like wild beasts they had reduced and absorbed it. He shows here that the number of those called are so many that they are without number. For his children, it says, that you have lost have pleaded in your ear, "Make room for me." COMMENTARY ON ISAIAH 4.4.49.19-21.[8]

---

[4]AGLB 35:1435. [5]PG 70:1069-72. [6]CCL 19:160. [7]CCL 143B:1380. [8]PG 70:1073.

49:21-26 THE LORD DEFENDS HIS PEOPLE

[21]"Then you will say in your heart:
  'Who has borne me these?
I was bereaved and barren,
  exiled and put away,
  but who has brought up these?
Behold, I was left alone;
  whence then have these come?'"

[22]Thus says the Lord GOD:

"Behold, I will lift up my hand to the nations,
  and raise my signal to the peoples;
and they shall bring your sons in their bosom,
  and your daughters shall be carried on their
    shoulders.
[23]Kings shall be your foster fathers,
  and their queens your nursing mothers.
With their faces to the ground they shall bow
    down to you,

and lick the dust of your feet.
Then you will know that I am the LORD;
   those who wait for me shall not be put to
   shame."

²⁴Can the prey be taken from the mighty,
   or the captives of a tyrant^m be rescued?
²⁵Surely, thus says the LORD:
"Even the captives of the mighty shall be taken,
   and the prey of the tyrant be rescued,
for I will contend with those who contend with

you,
   and I will save your children.
²⁶I will make your oppressors eat their own
   flesh,
   and they shall be drunk with their own
   blood as with wine.
Then all flesh shall know
   that I am the LORD your Savior,
   and your Redeemer, the Mighty One of
   Jacob."

m One ancient Ms Syr Vg: Heb *righteous man*

OVERVIEW: God knows clearly what is said by people in their hearts (AMBROSE). The church serves Christ and is served by kings (JEROME). God's presence has truly touched the earth, and his power has been rendered accessible (THEODORET). Only Jesus is strong enough to snatch the prey from the demonic powers (EPHREM). The peace of Jesus is established after rescuing the prey from the devil, who snatched it (LEANDER). It was Jesus' humanity that made the difference for ours (JEROME). Christ has removed the hold of the devil over human beings by his great strength (CYRIL). God has provided for us from first to last (THEODORET). Even evil plans backfire to the benefit of the saints (ISIDORE).

49:21 Saying in Your Hearts

WHAT IS SAID IN THE HEART IS KNOWN TO GOD. AMBROSE: We are to be a model for everyone around us, not just in our actions but also in our speech, in our chastity and in our faith. Let us be what we should wish others to think us, and let us show our feelings as they really are. We should never mutter a word that is unjust, even in our own heart, thinking to ourselves that it is hidden under a veil of silence; for the One who made the secret places hears words that are spoken in secret, and the One who implanted the

power of thought in our innermost parts knows the hidden things that those innermost parts contain. So as people who live under the eyes of their Judge, let us remember that everything we do is exposed to the light, and in this way it will be manifest to all. DUTIES OF THE CLERGY 2.19.96.[1]

49:23 Licking the Dust

THE CHURCH SERVES CHRIST AND IS SERVED BY KINGS. JEROME: Then they will carry on their sides or at the breast the sons of Zion, and they will carry her daughters on their shoulders—as for Lazarus and all the saints who rest on the breast of Abraham and the souls of believers, to whom the apostle Paul said, "I have given you milk to drink."[2]

Every day the queen [church] feeds Christ's little ones and leads them to maturity; and people, no matter their age, sex and position, will adore Zion on account of him who dwells in it. For if Christ is the head of the church, the head is adored in the body. And if it can be said to some, "Exalt the Lord our God and adore his footstool,"[3] not that a footstool is to be adored but that it is a means of showing the greatness of his feet, why not adore the church, which embraces

---

¹AO 323. ²1 Cor 3:2. ³Ps 99:5 (98:5 LXX, Vg).

the whole body of Christ? "They will lick the dust of your feet." This means that kings and princes will support the church in its progress with earthly works and wipe and lap up its word. ... Through all this the church learns that it is to have no other lord than he whom they who await eternal glory will possess. COMMENTARY ON ISAIAH 13.24.[4]

A LOVE FOR HOLY PLACES. THEODORET OF CYR: And all, even to our own day, stream toward Jerusalem, driven by the desire to see the three longed-for places of the cross, the resurrection and the ascension. Thus, it is from this church, gathered from across the earth and sea, that kings have become foster fathers and rulers providers of nourishment; the first offer firstfruits and the second tithes. These kings, for their part, are even granted an allocation of food for those consecrated to the God of the universe. ... The rest of the passage teaches this with clarity. "With their faces to the earth, they prostrate themselves before you and lick the dust off your feet. You will know that I am the Lord." We see these things happening every day. In all the churches the faithful approach with their foreheads bowed to the ground and their lips on the doors to demonstrate their respect for God. COMMENTARY ON ISAIAH 15.49.22-23.[5]

49:24 Can the Prey Be Taken?

TAKEN FROM THE MIGHTY. EPHREM THE SYRIAN: "Can the prey be taken from the giant?" These words refer to Christ, who took the imprisoned nations away from the demon, a mighty giant. Therefore the prey shall be snatched away from the mighty demon. COMMENTARY ON ISAIAH 49.24.[6]

49:25 Contending with the Ravagers

RAPINE REPLACED BY PEACE. LEANDER OF SEVILLE: Well may that ancient ravager [the devil] mourn that he has lost his prey, for we see

it is fulfilled as we have heard it foretold by the prophet. "Yes," he said, "captives can be taken from a warrior and booty rescued from a tyrant." The peace of Christ has destroyed the wall of discord built by the devil, and the house that was divided into mutual slaughter is now joined by the cornerstone, which is Christ. HOMILIES ON THE TRIUMPH OF THE CHURCH.[7]

BLESSING FOR THE FLESH. JEROME: For it is not the spirit (which is incorporeal) but the flesh that is eaten, suffering the bites of savage beasts. And then let Zion learn that it is indeed all flesh that will see the salvation of God, that its Redeemer and Savior is he who wrestled with Jacob or was the helper to Jacob's strength as Christ, though overwhelmed by his crucifiers, blessed them in his suffering.[8] COMMENTARY ON ISAIAH 13.25.[9]

RESCUE FROM THE TYRANT. CYRIL OF ALEXANDRIA: Our Lord Jesus Christ came into the house of the strong man ... he raided it and, throwing away the broken chains and the bonds of dark hell, he gave him over to the judgment of the great day to be kept for punishment. ... Then Christ has conquered, and he has passed the victory on to us. ... For he is the sole cause of our salvation. Therefore, he is the boast of the might of the saints, as Paul the most wise says: "I can do all things through Christ who gives me strength."[10] ...

For Christ gave us the ability to overcome the murderous dragon so that we can take spoil from it, and we are saved from it as he sends us the victory to everlasting life for glory, praise and the kingdom of heaven. ... For Christ said, "I have given you authority to tread on snakes and scorpions and over all the power of the enemy."[11] ... This is just what we take from the strong one, that is, from Christ. Since he is the Lord of powers, we have been saved and have the victory. ...

Whoever suffers anything on account of me

[4]AGLB 35:1438-39. [5]SC 315:94-96. [6]SESHS 2:135. [7]FC 62:234. [8]See Gen 32:22-32. [9]AGLB 35:1442. [10]Phil 4:13. [11]Lk 10:19.

obtains help from me, the One who gives strength to you, Jacob, that is, all of you from the seed of Jacob. I have said how he sends them prophetic words in the mouth of the holy apostles and evangelists that they are from Jacob, which clearly relates to the flesh. And it is small wonder that Jacob was called the supplanter, that is, the supplanter of Satan and of those who casually and with youthful neglect rush into the noose of sins. COMMENTARY ON ISAIAH 4.4.49.25-26.[12]

GOD'S COMPLETE PROVISION. THEODORET OF CYR: For "it is I," he says, who "am God the first, and I am he for the things to come." It is he who has made us and judged us to be worthy of salvation, he who has freed us from the original deception, he who has promised us the kingdom of God, of which may we enjoy the grace of him

who has saved us and to whom is due glory for ages of ages. COMMENTARY ON ISAIAH 15.49.26.[13]

OPPRESSORS WILL BE DRUNK WITH THEIR OWN BLOOD. ISIDORE OF SEVILLE: In consoling his people through the prophet, God accordingly promises to judge their enemies. . . . For the wickedness of the evil ones who customarily tear at the chosen of God with their own teeth. When this happens, the life of the unrighteous is undone while that of the righteous is not, but rather it flourishes. Meanwhile, however, the evil ones are educating the righteous through the training of tribulation so that they will hate this present life and long for the life to come. THREE BOOKS OF THOUGHTS 3.57.8-9.[14]

---

[12]PG 70:1080-81. [13]SC 315:100. [14]PL 83:729.

50:1-3 ISRAEL'S SIN BRINGS CHASTISEMENT

[1]*Thus says the LORD:*
"Where is your mother's bill of divorce,
with which I put her away?
Or which of my creditors is it
to whom I have sold you?
Behold, for your iniquities you were sold,
and for your transgressions your mother was
put away.
[2]*Why, when I came, was there no man?*

When I called, was there no one to answer?
*Is my hand shortened, that it cannot redeem?**
Or have I no power to deliver?
Behold, by my rebuke I dry up the sea,
I make the rivers a desert;
their fish stink for lack of water,
and die of thirst.
[3]*I clothe the heavens with blackness,*
and make sackcloth their covering."

* Syriac (Peshitta) *Did my hand reap the crop? And did it drop?*

OVERVIEW: Israel is responsible for the infliction visited on it (ISHO'DAD), which is often the case as people who have neglected God sell themselves to the devil. But God buys back his own (ORIGEN) using the credit of Christ as collateral for our

spiritual worth (AMBROSE). He continually issues a call to us to come back to him (CYRIL), but no one listens (PROCOPIUS), choosing instead to desert him (JEROME). The metaphors Isaiah uses here allow us to have some obscure understanding of God (CYRIL). God's previous miraculous activity points to the fact that he can accomplish his will in the future (THEODORET) as he did at the crucifixion, when the heavens were clothed in darkness and our salvation was accomplished on the cross (THEODORET, JEROME).

50:1 Sold for Your Inquities

ISRAEL THE CAUSE OF ITS AFFLICTION.

ISHO'DAD OF MERV: "Did my hand reap the crop? And did it drop?" that is, Is it tired and weakened? He is inspired by what happens to the harvesters, from whose hands the ears escape. For he teaches, through these words, that it is from them that the cause of their afflictions derives and not from him. COMMENTARY ON ISAIAH 50.2.[1]

SELF-SALE INTO SIN. ORIGEN: Hear what the

prophet says: "You have been sold for your sins, and for your iniquities I sent your mother away." You see, therefore, that we are all creatures of God. But each one is sold for his own sins and, for his own iniquities, separates from his Creator. We, therefore, belong to God insofar as we have been created by him. But we have become slaves of the devil insofar as we have been sold for our sins. Christ came, however, and "bought us back"[2] when we were serving that lord to whom we sold ourselves by sinning. And so [Christ] appears to have recovered as his own those whom he created; to have acquired as people belonging to another, indeed, those who had sought another Lord for themselves by sinning. HOMILIES ON EXODUS 6.9.[3]

CHRIST'S CREDIT USED FOR OUR REDEMP-

TION. AMBROSE: Joseph was sold in Egypt because Christ was going to come to those to whom it was said, "It was for your sins that you were sold," and thus he redeemed with his own blood those who had been sold by their own sins. But Christ was sold because he took our condition on himself, not our fault. He is not held to the price of sin, because he himself did not commit sin.[4] And so he made a contract at a price for

our debt, not for money but for himself. He took away the debtor's bond,[5] set aside the moneylender, freed the debtor. He alone paid what was owed by all. JOSEPH 4.19.[6]

GOD'S PATIENT ENTREATY TO HIS PEOPLE.

CYRIL OF ALEXANDRIA: God never sends away anyone who makes his home with him, and he rejects none of those who walk uprightly. He allows them to be forever associated and firmly joined to him as a way of obtaining help. However, everyone who opposes or fights against his divine teaching falls completely away from the glory of God and shows that he is a lover of pleasure rather than a lover of God. Therefore, like one who lived with the mother of the Jews God says, "What kind of bill of divorce did your mother have when I sent her away?" For no one could prove that I hated her and despised her. Instead, he would rather have to accuse her of deserting me.... It says, "I came," that is, I took human form and appeared to those in Israel, and there was no man among them, that is, no one with a heart who was able to recognize the season of redemption. "I called, but no one listened." ... For he was in a form like ours, and yet he was God the Word, having become man by taking on flesh born of a woman. But those who knew this and were not ignorant of the depth of the mystery of his divinity knew that he was able to do all things because he was God by nature and suitable for the redemption of everyone under heaven. COMMENTARY ON ISAIAH 4.4.50.1-3.[7]

NO ONE ANSWERED HIS CALL. PROCOPIUS OF

GAZA: For he compares himself with a husband who is his wife's master and householder. For what master is obliged to let you go? But you have been transgressors from the beginning and so cast out, "sold to[8] your iniquities," enslaved by them,

---

[1]CSCO 303(128):49. [2]See Gal 3:13. [3]FC 71:295**. [4]See 2 Cor 5:21. [5]See Col 2:14. [6]FC 65:201*. [7]PG 70:1084–88. [8]The Greek dative allows the sense of "sold into [your iniquities]," although the context of the word suggests a causal sense ("because of your iniquities").

who were before independent and free. And finally, since God did not wait for you but came to you, and coming down to a lowly dignity, he became man. But no one answered him as he was calling for salvation. He adds "there was not one person," since the mass of those not answering are deemed to be as nothing. Whereas those who answered, a few out of the nations will be exempted from the fate of the nations; as with Lot in the days of Sodom, they will be brought out. For the Lord did not think fit to make the holy land available to many. And the barren fig tree was a sign of that.[9] COMMENTARY ON ISAIAH 50.1-11.[10]

50:2 No One Answered My Call

CHRIST COULD NOT AVOID THE CROSS. JEROME: So that you might know that your mother was not rejected by me but deserted of her own will, after many benefits I put on human flesh and not through any prophets but actually present myself I spoke forth: "I have come, and there was not a man" or a person. For all people, abandoning the image of humans, adopted the images of beasts and serpents. Thus it was said to Herod on account of his wickedness, "Go and tell that fox,"[11] or to the Pharisees, "brood of vipers."[12] . . . I have called them as if they were rational animals. . . . We can say that although he is the accomplisher of such great signs and he makes the sky and earth and sea to serve his uses, even he could not avoid the cross. COMMENTARY ON ISAIAH 13.26.[13]

DO NOT MISINTERPRET ISAIAH'S METAPHORS. CYRIL OF ALEXANDRIA: No one who views things correctly thinks God possesses a physical body. It is only that the holy Scriptures speak in a human fashion about him. For those of us in simple and crass bodies can think in no other way, except that these things are adapted for us by a range of metaphors, so that in the perception of visible things we are able to know in part about the divine and higher being, which is

higher than all bodily imaginings. Observe how in these words the message is adapted to human understanding. COMMENTARY ON ISAIAH 4.4.50.1.[14]

DELIVERANCE OF THE RED SEA. THEODORET OF CYR: Then he recalls for them what he has accomplished: "Behold, by my rebuke I will dry up the sea and make rivers a wilderness; and their fish shall be dried up because there is no water and shall die for thirst." Symmachus has rendered this passage as if it concerns events already accomplished: "Behold that at my rebuke I have dried up the sea, that I have made the rivers a desert and that their fish have been putrified for lack of water." Thus, the God of the universe accomplished this at the time he delivered them from the bondage of the Egyptians: it was then that he parted the Red Sea, divided the Jordan in two and revealed that the fish in its bed were dead from deprivation of its nourishing waters. If, however, one likewise understands this passage [to relate] to the future, as the Septuagint desires [to do], one will do no violence to the senses. It indicates from great miracles that he will also be able to accomplish small things: if it was easy for me to dry up the sea, he says, and to interrupt the course of rivers, it would have been much easier to annihilate an army that was marching against you. COMMENTARY ON ISAIAH 16.50.1.[15]

GOD COMES TO HIS PEOPLE AS A SERVANT. THEODORET OF CYR: I have many times endured your belief in idols and the infinite number of iniquities that you have perpetrated, but what you have dared now is not susceptible to any pardon: it is an evil that is irremediable and incurable. For I am no longer acting through the prophets as intermediaries, but I have assumed the form of a servant,[16] and I have lived among you as a man; and in spite of the frequency of my appeals and my exhortations, I have not per-

---

[9]Mt 21:19. [10]PG 87:2485. [11]Lk 13:32. [12]Mt 12:34. [13]AGLB 35:1444-45. [14]PG 70:1084. [15]SC 315:104-6. [16]Phil 2:7.

suaded you. This, in turn, is confirmed by the recital of the divine Gospels in these terms: "Jesus cried out, saying, 'If anyone thirst, let him come to me and drink,'[17] and elsewhere: "Come to me, all you who labor and are heavy laden, and I will give you rest."[18] The divine Evangelists have let us know still many other declarations of this kind. In this way, then, the prophetic text has taught us that the total destruction that they undergo in the last place has been obtained for them by their folly against the Master. Then, in interrogative form again [he declares]: "Is not my hand strong to redeem? Or do I not have the strength to protect you [from danger]?" Do you think, he says, that the adversaries have conquered me because of my weakness? Is it not possible for anyone to see how easy and convenient it is for me to make you appear superior to everyone? COMMENTARY ON ISAIAH 16.50.2.[19]

50:3 I Clothe the Heavens

DARKNESS AT THE CRUCIFIXION AND THE CONSUMMATION. THEODORET OF CYR: "I will clothe the sky with shadows, and I will change its cover to be like mourning cloth." He has done this and will do it. For he did it when he was crucified: "From the sixth hour to the ninth the shadows covered the whole earth."[20] And he will do it again at the time of the fulfillment, for it says, "The sun will be darkened, and the moon will not give off its light."[21] COMMENTARY ON ISAIAH 16.50.3.[22]

COVERED IN DARKNESS. JEROME: Everything that is above us we call "heaven," just as the winged things that are in the air are called "celestial" and the enemy powers are called "celestial" since they shuttle between heaven and earth.... Therefore, heaven is not covered up by a bag; but with the light of heaven closed off, the air that is underneath it becomes darkened with black clouds. We can interpret the heavens covered in darkness and concealed in a bag by saying that all are under sin and that the holy ones, too, need the mercy of God. COMMENTARY ON ISAIAH 13.27.[23]

---

[17]Jn 7:37. [18]Mt 11:28. [19]ITA 740*; SC 315:104. [20]Mt 27:45. [21]Mt 24:29. [22]SC 315:106. [23]AGLB 35:1447-48.

50:4-9 THE TRUE COMFORTER OF THE WEARY

[4]The Lord GOD has given me
    the tongue of those who are taught,
that I may know how to sustain with a word
    him that is weary.
Morning by morning he wakens,
    he wakens my ear
    to hear as those who are taught.
[5]The Lord GOD has opened my ear,
    and I was not rebellious,
    I turned not backward.

[6]I gave my back to the smiters,
    and my cheeks to those who pulled out the
        beard;
I hid not my face
    from shame and spitting.

[7]For the Lord GOD helps me;
    therefore I have not been confounded;
therefore I have set my face like a flint,
    and I know that I shall not be put to shame;

> ^{8}he who vindicates me is near.
> Who will contend with me?
>   Let us stand up together.
> Who is my adversary?
>   Let him come near to me.

> ^{9}Behold, the Lord GOD helps me;
>   who will declare me guilty?
> Behold, all of them will wear out like a
>   garment;
>   the moth will eat them up.

OVERVIEW: Christ knew when to speak and when to be silent (JUSTIN MARTYR) as the Word who brought new teaching to the world (EPHREM). The wise know how to keep silent and therefore know when to speak (AMBROSE). Once they have listened to the Word, they are empowered to preach (CYRIL) and to follow Christ with ears that hear what he has to say (THEODORET). The impassible Word suffered in the passible body as he gave his back to to those who whipped him (ATHANASIUS). So with master, so with servant: dignity in the face of humiliation and insult (BASIL). Christ provided a courageous example for his disciples (CYRIL OF JERUSALEM), undergoing discipline (JEROME). He teaches his disciples how to endure suffering (ATHANASIUS), setting in stark contrast his divine humility with our innate pride (MACARIUS). The passion was predicted in order to teach us his patience (THEODORET). He also let us know that the endurance of evil is limited; God's help is all-sufficient (CHRYSOSTOM). God's dignity in Christ served to overcome the power of death (CYRIL). But we also see the danger of sin that devours those who succumb to it (THEODORET, CLEMENT OF ALEXANDRIA) as a reckless conscience runs overconfidently to perdition (PROCOPIUS).

50:4 Speaking and Listening

THE TONGUE THAT KNOWS WHEN TO SPEAK. JUSTIN MARTYR: The power of his mighty word with which he always refuted the Pharisees and scribes, and indeed all the teachers of your race who disputed with him, was stopped like a full and mighty fountain whose waters have been suddenly shut off when he remained silent and would no longer answer his accusers before Pilate, as was recorded in the writings of the apostles, in order that those words of Isaiah might bear fruit in action: "The Lord gives me a tongue, that I may know when I ought to speak." And his words, "You are my God, depart not from me," teach us to put all our trust in God, the Creator of all things, and to seek aid and salvation from him alone; and not to imagine, as other [people] do, that we can attain salvation by means of birth, or wealth, or power or wisdom. DIALOGUE WITH TRYPHO 102.[1]

A TONGUE WELL TAUGHT. EPHREM THE SYRIAN: "The Lord God has given me the tongue of the doctrine." These words refer to Christ as well, who preached his new doctrine to all the peoples. And therefore all the peoples listened to it and were converted. COMMENTARY ON ISAIAH 50.4.[2]

IN SILENCE WE LEARN HOW TO SPEAK. AMBROSE: Now what ought we to learn before everything else, but to be silent that we may be able to speak? Lest my voice should condemn me before that of another acquits me, for it is written: "By your words you shall be condemned."[3] What need is there, then, that you should hasten to undergo the danger of condemnation by speaking when you can be more safe by keeping silent? How many have I seen to fall into sin by speaking, but scarcely one by keeping silent; and so it is more difficult to know how to keep silent than how to speak . . . a person is wise, then, who knows how to keep silent. Lastly, the Wisdom of

---

^{1}FC 6:307-8. ^{2}SESHS 2:135-37. ^{3}Mt 12:37.

God said, "The Lord has given to me the tongue of learning, that I should know when it is good to speak." Justly, then, is one wise who has received of the Lord to know when he ought to speak. Wherefore the Scripture says well: "A wise person will keep silence until there is opportunity."[4] DUTIES OF THE CLERGY 1.2.5.[5]

THE POWER OF HEARING. CYRIL OF ALEXANDRIA: [Ministers] who sing thankful hymns say that they have been given a tongue of discipline; that is, they are able to speak in a trained manner and expound the divine mysteries without fault and are able to speak fittingly to those who need words of encouragement.... On us the sun of righteousness has arisen and has shed its light on our mind so that we are and are known as children of light and of the day. For we, having faith in Christ, are enriched with illumination from him; that is, we have our hearing enhanced and are thus enabled to hear. COMMENTARY ON ISAIAH 4.4.50.4-5.[6]

"EARS" ARE THOSE WHO HEAR CHRIST. THEODORET OF CYR: Christ our Master says this in a human way. For the rest, we find many statements of this kind in the divine Gospels: "And Jesus increased in age," it is said, "and wisdom and grace before God and before people."[7] He calls youth "early"; thus, the prophet likewise taught this in a preceding passage. After having announced [Christ's] conception by the Virgin, he had added, "Before he [the child] shall know good or evil, he refuses evil, to choose the good."[8] The Evangelist declares something similar: "And the child grew and became strong in spirit, filled with wisdom; and the grace of God was on him."[9] As for the phrase "the instruction the Lord gives opens my ears," in my opinion, it is not pronounced regarding him but on the subject of the disciples who believed in [Christ], for he gives the name of "ears" to his hearers, that is, to those to whom he presents the divine words, that is, to those to whom he declared, as we learn it in reading the holy Gospels: "He who has ears to hear, let him hear!"[10] COMMENTARY ON ISAIAH 16.50.5.[11]

50:6 I Gave My Back to Be Beaten

HE SUFFERED, YET HE SUFFERED NOT. ATHANASIUS: And being by nature intangible, the Word yet said, "I gave my back to the stripes, and my cheeks to blows, and I hid not my face from shame and spitting." For what the human body of the Word suffered, this the Word, dwelling in the body, ascribed to himself, in order that we might be enabled to be partakers of God the Word.[12] Truly it is a mystery that it was he who suffered, and yet suffered not. He suffered, because his own body suffered, and he was in it, which thus suffered. He suffered not, because the Word, being by nature God, is impassible. And while he, the incorporeal, was in the passible body, the Body had in it the impassible Word, which was destroying the infirmities inherent in the body.[13] LETTER TO EPICTETAS 59.6.[14]

A CALL TO SELF-CONTROL. BASIL THE GREAT: If you remain unruffled, you silence your insolent assailant by giving him a practical illustration of self-control. Were you struck? So also was the Lord. Were you spat on? The Lord also suffered this, for "he did not turn his face from the shame of the spittle." ... You have not been condemned to death or crucified. HOMILY AGAINST THOSE WHO ARE PRONE TO ANGER.[15]

CHRIST THE EXAMPLE OF COURAGE. CYRIL OF JERUSALEM: [This is] as though he were to say, "Though I knew beforehand that they would strike me, I did not even turn aside my cheek; for how could I have nerved my disciples to undergo death for the truth if I had been afraid?" CATECHETICAL LECTURES 13.13.[16]

THE LEARNING THAT COMES THROUGH DISCIPLINE. JEROME: The Jews, separating this

[4]Sir 20:7. [5]NPNF 2 10:1-2*. [6]PG 70:1089. [7]Lk 2:52. [8]Is 7:16. [9]Lk 2:40. [10]Mt 11:15; 13:9; Lk 8:8. [11]ITA 742*; SC 315:106-8. [12]2 Pet 1:4. [13]Cyril Letter 39 in explicit continuity with this line of interpretation. [14]NPNF 2 4:572**. [15]FC 9:454-55. [16]FC 64:14.

chapter from what has been said previously, wish to refer it to the person of Isaiah, in that he would say that he received the word from the Lord and how he put up with a lazy and wandering people and called them back to salvation, and in the manner of small children who are trained early in the morning, Isaiah recited what he heard from the Holy Spirit. . . . But these verses should be applied to the person of the Lord in which the older book is fulfilled, since according to the dispensation of the flesh that Christ assumed, he was trained and accepted the lash of discipline so that he would know when he ought to speak and when to keep quiet. And he who in his passion was silent, through the apostles and apostolic people speaks throughout the whole world.

To Christ was added through the grace of the ear things that he did not have by nature, that we might understand that we ought to accept with the ears not of our body but of the mind. . . . The breast that contained God was beaten. . . . This discipline and training opened his ears that he was able to communicate the knowledge of the Father to us. . . . We learned more fully in the gospel that the Son, according to the flesh he took on, spoke the mystery that he had heard from the Father. COMMENTARY ON ISAIAH 14.2.[17]

THE VIRTUE OF DIGNIFIED PASSIVITY. ATHANASIUS: Our Lord and Savior Jesus Christ comes before us, when he would show [people] how to suffer, who when he was struck bore it patiently, being reviled he reviled not again, when he suffered he threatened not, but he gave his back to the smiters and his cheeks to buffetings, and he turned not his face from spitting;[18] and at last, he was willingly led to death, that we might behold in him the image of all that is virtuous and immortal, and that we, conducting ourselves after these examples, might truly tread on serpents and scorpions and on all the power of the enemy. LETTER 10.7.[19]

OUR PRIDE IN CONTRAST TO GOD'S HUMIL-

ITY. MACARIUS OF EGYPT: Now if God willed to accept and to lower Himself to such sufferings, dishonours, and humiliations, then no matter how much you humble yourself, you whose nature is mud and subject to death, you will never resemble your Lord [in this]. God for your sake humbled Himself, but you, for your own sake, do not humble yourself. You are proud and puffed up. God came and took up your burden to give you His rest, but you do not wish to endure labours and suffering. By your labours your wounds are healed. FIRST SYRIAC EPISTLES 7.[20]

PREDICTION OF CHRIST'S SUFFERING. THEODORET OF CYR: This whole recital is taught by the holy Gospels.[21] For the servant of the high priest gave [Christ] a blow on the cheek; some struck his face, saying, "Prophesy to us, Christ! Who is the one who struck you?"[22] Others spat in his face; as for Pilate, he had him scourged and delivered him to be crucified. So, all this he predicts in the prophecy to teach of his own patience. COMMENTARY ON ISAIAH 16.50.6.[23]

50:7 I Will Not Be Put to Shame

EVILS WILL QUICKLY PASS. CHRYSOSTOM: For the railings, and insults, and reproaches and gibes inflicted by enemies and their plots are compared with a worn-out garment and moth-eaten wool when God says, "Do not fear the reproach of people, neither be afraid of their revilings, for they shall grow old as does a garment, and like moth-eaten wool so shall they be consumed." Therefore, let none of these things that are happening trouble [you], but stop asking for the aid of this or that person and running after shadows (for such are human alliances); persistently call on Jesus, whom [you serve] . . . and in a moment of time all these evils will be dissolved. LETTERS TO OLYMPIAS 7.2.[24]

---

[17]AGLB 35:1451-53. [18]1 Pet 2:23; Is 50:6. [19]NPNF 2 4:530*. [20]AHSIS 457. [21]Cf. Jn 18:22; Mt 27:26. [22]Mt 26:67-68. [23]ITA 744-45; SC 315:108. [24]NPNF 1 9:290.

HUMAN AND DIVINE. CYRIL OF ALEXANDRIA: And the Father was Christ's helper. For he did not allow or concede that his own Son should be completely shamed or overwhelmed. For they were punished, those who sought to take their punishment out on me as those who dare to fight with God. . . . For though being with us, he was the only-begotten Word of God. He put on an identical human likeness, by which reason alone he was believed to be of a nature with us. For every human being is subject to faults and sins, and no one alive is completely blameless. He alone in becoming man retained the divine dignity. . . . And being Word and God, his flesh was able to shoo away destruction. Thus, the Son became a man who was fit to be accepted by the Father. For all that human beings have is God-given. For the one God and Father, through him, undid the power of death through his resurrection from the dead. . . . He was the servant of God, who while being human was yet truly the Son of God and the Father. And to hear his voice means no transgression of the law but a confirming of the law through types and shadows discerning the truth which is Christ and the prophecies of him, as Paul notes.[25] . . . His voice is the evangelical and divine preaching that calls us to the redemption that is through faith in Christ. He also calls us to a proper behavior that lives in a way that is, by far, more consistent than the way of the law. The law was given in the shadows. Faith was given in the bright and shining light. COMMENTARY ON ISAIAH 4.5.50.6-9.[26]

50:9 The Moth Will Eat Them

SIN EATS AWAY AT THOSE WHO GIVE IT ORIGIN. THEODORET OF CYR: "Behold, you will all like a garment grow old, and something like a worm will devour you." The parable is accurate, for the worm that comes from the clothes destroys them, and sin, which is born from us, ruins those who allow it to grow. COMMENTARY ON ISAIAH 16.50.7-9.[27]

DO NOT DISPARAGE PROCREATION. CLEMENT OF ALEXANDRIA: There is a person who runs down birth, describing it as subject to decay and death, who forces things and suggests that the Savior was speaking about having children in saying that we should not store treasure on earth, where it grows rusty and moth-eaten. And [this person] is not ashamed to set alongside these the prophet's words: "You shall all grow old like clothes, and the moth will feed on you." We do not contradict Scripture. Our bodies are subject to decay and are naturally unstable. Perhaps he might be prophesying decay to his audience because they were sinners. The Savior was not speaking about having children. He was encouraging sharing of resources in those who wanted only to amass vast amounts of wealth rather than offer help to those in need. STROMATEIS 3.12.86.3-4.[28]

THE MOTH DEVOURS. PROCOPIUS OF GAZA: Isaiah also gives the name "moth" to those who devour their conscience in their recklessness. . . . It might be said that the moths are their sins, which worm their way in among those they inhabit, like moths devouring clothing for food. An attitude that inclines toward having no fear is indicative of a people on their way to this kind of ruin, yet who think they are indestructible. But punishment also clearly awaits them. They will be utterly consumed by misfortune as by a moth. COMMENTARY ON ISAIAH 50.1-11.[29]

---

[25]Rom 3:31. [26]PG 70:1093-1100. [27]SC 315:110. [28]FC 85:310. [29]PG 87:2493.

50:10-11 LISTEN TO THE VOICE OF THE SERVANT

[10]Who among you fears the LORD
  and obeys the voice of his servant,
who walks in darkness
  and has no light,
yet trusts in the name of the LORD
  and relies upon his God?

[11]Behold, all you who kindle a fire,
  who set brands alight!"
Walk by the light of your fire,
  and by the brands which you have kindled!
This shall you have from my hand:
  you shall lie down in torment.

n Syr: Heb *gird yourselves with brands*

OVERVIEW: God through prophecy foretold his Son so that he could be recognized when he came to earth (TERTULLIAN). The title of Servant is applied to the Son because he took on human form (THEODORET). We should not confuse the fire of destruction, which human beings kindle for themselves, with the purifying fire that God supplies (ORIGEN). This cleansing fire can be identified with Christ (GREGORY OF NAZIANZUS).

50:10 The Voice of the Servant

PAY ATTENTION TO THE VOICE OF THE SON. TERTULLIAN: By the mouth of Isaiah also [God] has asked concerning him, "Who is there among you that hears God? Let him hear the voice of his Son."[1] When, therefore, he here presents him with the words, "This is my beloved Son,"[2] this clause is of course understood, "who I have promised." For if he once promised and afterwards says, "This is he," it is suitable conduct for one who accomplishes his purpose that he should utter his voice in proof of the promise that he had formerly made; but unsuitable in one who is amenable to the retort, "Can you, indeed, have a right to say, 'This is my son,' concerning whom you have given us no previous information, any more than you have favored us with a revelation about your own prior existence?" AGAINST MARCION 4.22.[3]

SERVANT ACCORDING TO HIS HUMAN

NATURE. THEODORET OF CYR: It is as a man that he calls himself "Servant," for "although he exists in the form of God, he has assumed the form of a servant."[4] Likewise in the divine Gospel [Christ] says that he has received instruction as to what he should say and proclaim.[5] "They walk in darkness, and there is no light for them." Although the light has risen, as for them, they have clung to the darkness. "Trust in the name of the Lord, and rely on God." [Isaiah] says, if you really put absolute and true hope in God, that will [serve to] sustain you and make you sure. COMMENTARY ON ISAIAH 16.50.10.[6]

50:11 Kindling a Fire

WHAT IS ETERNAL FIRE? ORIGEN: If then this is the character of the body that rises from the dead, let us now see what is the meaning of the threatened "eternal fire." Now we find in the prophet Isaiah that the fire by which each person is punished is described as belonging to himself. For it says, "Walk in the light of your fire and in the flame which you have kindled for yourselves." These words seem to indicate that every sinner kindles for himself the flame of his own fire and is not plunged into a fire that has been previously

---

[1]The LXX's *pais* can be understood as either "servant" or "son." [2]Mt 3:17. [3]ANF 3:384. [4]See Phil 2:6-7. [5]See Jn 12:49. [6]ITA 745*; SC 315:110-12.

kindled by someone else or that existed before him. On First Principles 2.10.4.[7]

The Flame Kindled for Yourselves. Origen: This "fire" is not "from the altar." The fire that is "from the altar" is the fire of the Lord. But that which is outside the altar is not of the Lord but is properly of each one who sins. . . . This fire is of those who have ignited it, just as it also was written in other places, "Walk in your fire and in the flame which you kindled for yourselves." But to Isaiah his own fire was not applied but the fire of the altar that "will cleanse his lips."[8] Homilies on Leviticus 9.8.1.[9]

Cleansing and Avenging Fires. Gregory of Nazianzus: One light alone let us shun: that which is the offspring of the terrible fire. Let us not walk in the light of our own fire and in the very flame we have kindled. For I know of a cleansing fire that Christ came to send on the earth, and that he himself is anagogically called a fire. This Fire takes away whatever is material and of evil habit. This he desires to kindle with all speed, for he longs for speed in doing us good, since he gives us even coals of fire to help us. I know also a fire that is not cleansing but avenging; either that fire of Sodom, which he pours down on all sinners, mingled with brimstone and storms, or that which is prepared for the devil and his angels. On Holy Baptism, Oration 40.36.[10]

---

[7]OFP 141-42. [8]Is 6:6-7. [9]FC 83:192-93. [10]NPNF 2 7:373*.

51:1-6 THE WORD THAT OUTLASTS HEAVEN AND EARTH

[1]Hearken to me, you who pursue deliverance,
*   you who seek the LORD;*
look to the rock from which you were hewn,
*   and to the quarry from which you were*
*   digged.*
[2]Look to Abraham your father
*   and to Sarah who bore you;*
for when he was but one I called him,
*   and I blessed him and made him many.*
[3]For the LORD will comfort Zion;
*   he will comfort all her waste places,*
and will make her wilderness like Eden,
*   her desert like the garden of the LORD;*
joy and gladness will be found in her,
*   thanksgiving and the voice of song.*

[4]Listen to me, my people,
*   and give ear to me, my nation;*
for a law will go forth from me,
*   and my justice for a light to the peoples.*
[5]My deliverance draws near speedily,
*   my salvation has gone forth,*
*   and my arms will rule the peoples;*
the coastlands wait for me,
*   and for my arm they hope.*
[6]Lift up your eyes to the heavens,
*   and look at the earth beneath;*
for the heavens will vanish like smoke,
*   the earth will wear out like a garment,*
*   and they who dwell in it will die like gnats;[o]*
but my salvation will be for ever,
*   and my deliverance will never be ended.*

o Or in like manner

OVERVIEW: When we look to the rock, we look to Christ, or more precisely, to his tomb. His coming forth from there changed the nations who had been deserted (JEROME), justifying them and removing from them the stain of sin as it prepared them for the honor of becoming children of God (CYRIL). When we are tempted to wander from this righteousness we have received into the darkness of sin, Scripture provides guiding lights like Abraham and Sarah to bring us back on course (GREGORY OF NYSSA). When we remember how God dealt with them, doing the impossible by bringing an entire nation from a woman who was declared barren, we come to realize that there is no obstacle that can get in the way of divine power. We see this, for instance, when those places in the western part of Jerusalem and those outside the walls, which were deserted during the time of Isaiah, became a flourishing garden of the Lord at the time of Christ, possessing the tree of life where our Lord was crucified (THEODORET).

Christ became the eternal and final law given to the inhabitants of the earth (JUSTIN) who are called to listen to him (JEROME) as he is revealed in his spiritual law of the New Testament (EPHREM). Far from destroying the law, the Savior Jesus embodied it as our righteousness who, as the Father's right arm (CYRIL), has nonetheless come to save the world in humility (THEODORET). As part of this salvation, Isaiah prophesies that the heavens will vanish. Though the heavens and the earth pass away, God and his servants endure forever (IRENAEUS). Destruction of the old really means destruction of its old form. The creation will continue but more gloriously (METHODIUS). The heavens in their new state are much more firm and everlasting (JEROME), having been recreated by the one who is all-powerful (THEODORET).

51:1 Look to the Rock

THE ROCK FROM WHICH YOU WERE CUT.

JEROME: The Jews refer this to the time of Zerubbabel, because after the devastation of Babylon Zion was restored and its temple built up and the old religion reinstated. . . . But here the Lord speaks to those who were persecuting him because he was righteous. . . . Moreover, according to the Septuagint, it is said to the persecutors of righteousness that they are to look on the hardest stone, which they cut out, and on the pit of the crater that they dug, that is, on the Lord and Savior, about whom the apostle said, "The rock was Christ."[1] We can say that the cut-out rock means the tomb of the Savior into which he was placed. When he rose from the dead, he bore innumerable children and was called Abraham, that is, the father of many nations, just as Sarah's once sterile womb means the church, which is otherwise called Zion, whom the Lord comforted and made its desert places like paradise. COMMENTARY ON ISAIAH 14.6.[2]

RUNNING TOWARD THE COMFORT OF ZION.

CYRIL OF ALEXANDRIA: "Righteous," he says, instead of "righteousness,"[3] which is through Christ through faith in him, a faith that justifies the ungodly and removes all stain from those who have been filthy, and cleanses them in the Spirit and prepares for them the shining honor of sonship. They pursue righteousness, not in the sense of driving it before them and so away from their minds, but of running toward it to take hold of it. As David said, "Seek peace and pursue it."[4] . . . The speech of the holy prophets always draws figures from the visible and the tangible things. For it has expressions that transcend reference, the senses and even the mind. In this way "Zion" is mentioned—not that we think of the earthly city but rather take it to be the spiritual one, that is, the church of the living God. Or how else would we see the words of the prophet coming true? . . .

"Worship in spirit and truth,"[5] and the power of spiritual worship gave off the pleasant spiritual fragrance and joy in the hope that is in Christ.

---

[1]1 Cor 10:4. [2]AGLB 35:1462-63. [3]LXX of v.1 has *hoi diōkontes to dikaion*, which Jerome in the previous comment takes to mean "persecute the righteous one," whereas Cyril here has it meaning "to seek righteousness." [4]Ps 34:14 (33:15 LXX). [5]Jn 4:24.

For if we trust that our body of lowliness will be transformed into the body of his glory, so we shall be with him and reign with him, assembled among the children of God and enriched with his divine and life-giving Spirit. We too bring forward the spiritual harvest to him—the confession and hymns of thanksgiving. For with such sacrifices is God well pleased. COMMENTARY ON ISAIAH 4.5.51.1-3.[6]

51:2 Look to Abraham

LOOK TO ABRAHAM AND SARAH. GREGORY OF NYSSA: For the divine voice says somewhere in the prophecy of Isaiah, "Consider Abraham, your father, and Sarah, who gave you birth." Scripture gives this admonition to those who wander outside virtue. Just as at sea those who are carried away from the direction of the harbor bring themselves back on a course by a clear sign, on seeing either a beacon light raised up high or some mountain peak coming into view, in the same way Scripture by the example of Abraham and Sarah may guide again to the harbor of the divine will those adrift on the sea of life with a pilotless mind. LIFE OF MOSES, PROLOGUE 11.[7]

AN ADDRESS TO BELIEVERS. THEODORET OF CYR: He is leaving aside the unbelievers here in order to address those who have believed: it is to them that he gives the name of enamored with God and with righteousness. He comforts them because they are few in number and invites them to turn their eyes toward their ancestors: he reminds them of Abraham and Sarah and the many thousands of descendants who came from them. This is similar to the term expressed in the divine Gospels: "Do not fear, little flock, for it is your Father's good pleasure to give you the kingdom."[8] It is the same here. COMMENTARY ON ISAIAH 16.51.1.[9]

NO OBSTACLE TO DIVINE POWER. THEODORET OF CYR: Nothing made is an obstacle to my power: not the fact that I called just one man or

that old age was on him, or that Sarah lacked the physical capability; yet his race was [indeed] increased, just as I had wished. Be unbelieving no longer, therefore, even though you are [now] easy to count; I will make you too many to number. COMMENTARY ON ISAIAH 16.51.2.[10]

51:3 Making the Wilderness Like Eden

THE CURRENT GEOGRAPHY OF ZION. THEODORET OF CYR: It is not a question of inhabited places but of desert places, not of regions situated in the east but of those in the west. Those who have seen the city with their own eyes know that the temple of the Jews was in the eastern part of the city, whereas the cross and the [place of] the resurrection were in the western part. Moreover, these places were formerly situated outside the walls. The divine apostle was witness to this when he said, "Jesus . . . suffered outside the gate. Therefore let us go forth to him outside the camp, bearing his reproach."[11] He makes this prediction accordingly: all the places of the city that were deserted and all those that were in the west will be as the garden of the Lord, for they truly possess the tree of life. "They shall find in it gladness and exultation, thanksgiving and the voice of praise." This also we still see fulfilled in our day: in place of the smoke, of the odor of fat that rises from the victims and of the cult rendered according to the law, which the Lord of the universe, even in former days, did not find agreeable, night and day Zion raises hymns in honor of the God of the universe, for it is filled with [worshipers] who chant hymns. COMMENTARY ON ISAIAH 16.51.3.[12]

51:4 Listen to Me

LISTEN TO GOD. EPHREM THE SYRIAN: "Listen to me, my people, and give ear to me, my nation;

---

[6]PG 70:1104-9. [7]GNLM 31-32. [8]Lk 12:32. [9]ITA 753; SC 315:112. [10]ITA 754-55; SC 315:114-16. [11]Heb 13:12-13. [12]ITA 755*; SC 315:116-18.

for a law will go forth from me." And how could it go forth now, if it were the same law that went forth in the days of Moses? But it is evident that here he mystically signifies the spiritual law, which is the New Testament. "And my justice is a light to the peoples," that is, my sacrament. He also means that the conscience of the Gentiles, which is now clouded by idolatry, will be enlightened after all their gods are condemned by the divine sentence. COMMENTARY ON ISAIAH 51.4.[13]

WITH BODY AND SOUL. JEROME: In the Septuagint "listen to me" is said twice to teach us that we ought to listen with the ears of our body and with the understanding of our soul.... For "tribe," as we have translated, Theodotion has "race," Symmachus "people" and the Septuagint "kings." For we are a tribe and line and a royal, priestly race of the Lord, such as was Abraham, who was called "king," and the rest of the saints, concerning whom it is written, "touch not my christs."[14] COMMENTARY ON ISAIAH 14.7.[15]

CHRIST THE ETERNAL AND FINAL LAW. JUSTIN MARTYR: The law promulgated on Horeb is now old and belongs to yourselves alone, but this is for all universality. Now, law placed against law has abrogated that which is before it, and a covenant that comes after in like manner has put an end to the previous one; and an eternal and final law—namely, Christ—has been given to us, and the covenant is trustworthy, after which there shall be no law, no commandment or ordinance. Have you not read this, which Isaiah says: "Hearken to me, hearken to me, my people; and your kings, give ear to me: for a law shall go forth from me, and my judgment shall be for a light to the nations." And Jeremiah, concerning this same new covenant, speaks this way: "Behold, the days come, says the Lord, that I will make a new covenant with the house of Israel and with the house of Judah; not according to the covenant that I made with their fathers, in the day that I took them by the hand, to bring them out of the land of Egypt."[16] DIALOGUE WITH TRYPHO 11.[17]

CHRIST, THE SUM OF THE LAW, ILLUMINES THE NATIONS. CYRIL OF ALEXANDRIA: But when the time of his incarnation unexpectedly arrived, then the shadows made way for the truth. And he said, "Listen to me, O my people." ... He is speaking here not only to those who are numbered among the people but also to the kings, because he wanted the rulers, the leaders of the people, to receive his message as well.... "The law will go forth from me, and my judgment will be a light to the nations." He refers to the divine and evangelical preaching as "law" here; it is just that it is in a different form now, just as the oracles and salvation also are new. For just as the old law was changed to something better, there has also been a transfer from those things that were provisional types to that which is the truth. For Christ said, "Do not think I have come to destroy the law."[18] ... The law in letters was given by Moses, but the preaching of salvation, which is the gospel, came through Christ.... He calls his "judgment" here something that is both sanctioned by the law of God as well as a benevolent accounting; it is the grace from him that went out to illuminate the Gentiles; they were amazed at his judgment, which was both righteous and just—truly the righteousness that is clearly made known in the gospel. COMMENTARY ON ISAIAH 4.5.51.4.[19]

51:5 The Arm of God

THE SON AS THE RIGHT ARM OF THE FATHER. CYRIL OF ALEXANDRIA: If we want to know the meaning of these words in the person of God and Father, then we say that he calls the Son "his righteousness." For we are saved in him ... through his great mercy.... He is called "righteousness" and "salvation" and rightly so. For he has removed all evil from us and, freeing us from the chains of death, has led us into eternal life....

---

[13]SESHS 2:137-39. [14]Ps 105:15 (104:15 LXX). [15]AGLB 35:1464-65. [16]Jer 31:31-32 (38:31-32 LXX). [17]ANF 1:200*. [18]Mt 5:17. [19]PG 70:1109-12.

Those who were once weak and prostrate on the ground grasp his right hand and gain the hope of an unexpected salvation. For the holy Scriptures often call the Son the right arm of the Father. For he is his power. COMMENTARY ON ISAIAH 4.5.51.5.[20]

THE HUMILITY OF GOD'S CONQUEST OF THE WORLD. THEODORET OF CYR: He calls his power "arm": that which constitutes the greatest proof of divine power is to have conquered the world by the cross, by ignominy and by death; it is to have given fishermen, publicans, shoemakers as masters to philosophers and to rhetoricians; it is to have, thanks to a dozen men, cultivated the whole world and, thanks to an equally small number of men, filled the entire earth and sea with the divine message. COMMENTARY ON ISAIAH 16.51.5.[21]

51:6 The Heavens Will Vanish

GOD AND HIS SERVANTS ENDURE. IRENAEUS: [Some malignantly assert] that if heaven is indeed the throne of God and earth his footstool,[22] and if . . . the heaven and earth shall pass away, then when these pass away, the God who sits above must also pass away, and therefore he cannot be the God who is over all. In the first place, they are ignorant what the expression means, that heaven is [his] throne and the earth [his] footstool. For they do not know what God is, but they imagine that he sits after the fashion of a person and is contained within the bounds, but nothing contains God. And they are also unacquainted with [the meaning of] the passing away of the heaven and earth; but Paul was not ignorant of it when he declared, "For the form of this world passes away."[23] In the next place, David explains their question, for he says that when the fashion of this world passes away, not only shall God remain, but his servants also, expressing himself thus in Psalm 101: "In the beginning, you, O Lord, have founded the earth, and the heavens are the works of your hands. They shall

perish, but you shall endure, and all shall grow old as a garment; and as a piece of clothing you shall change them, and they shall be changed. But you are the same, and your years shall not fail. The children of your servants shall continue, and their seed shall be established forever";[24] pointing out plainly what things they are that pass away and who it is that does endure forever—God, together with his servants. AGAINST HERESIES 4.3.1.[25]

DESTRUCTION DOES NOT MEAN THE TOTAL ABANDONMENT OF CREATION. METHODIUS: But if our opponents say, How then is it, if the universe is not destroyed, that the Lord says that "heaven and earth shall pass away," and the prophet, that "the heaven shall perish as smoke" and "the earth shall grow old as a garment"; we answer, because it is usual for the Scriptures to call the change of the world from its present condition to a better and more glorious one destruction, as its earlier form is lost in the change of all things to a state of greater splendor, for there is neither contradiction nor absurdity in the Scriptures. For not "the world" but "the fashion of this world" passes away, it is said. So it is usual for the Scriptures to call the change from an earlier form to a better and more comely state "destruction"; just as when one calls by the name of "destruction" the change from a childish form into a perfect adult, as the stature of the child is turned into mature size and beauty. ON THE RESURRECTION 1.9.[26]

THE HEAVENS WILL VANISH LIKE SMOKE. JEROME: And not only the souls of people, which are immortal, but also their bodies will be changed into a glorified substance. . . . The opinion of the world's philosophers is that all things that we can see will be destroyed by fire. . . . Just as John the apostle says, "The world and its desire will pass away,"[27] and here in Hebrew it is

---

[20]PG 70:1112-13. [21]ITA 757; SC 315:118. [22]Cf. Is 66:1; Acts 7:49. [23]1 Cor 7:31. [24]Ps 102:25-28 (101:26-29 LXX). [25]ANF 1:465**. [26]ANF 6:366*. [27]1 Jn 2:17.

said, "The sky like smoke will evaporate," or, as Aquila and Symmachus have it, "will be reduced to nothing and will be worn away." . . . Therefore I wonder at what the Septuagint wants to say when it says, "The sky like smoke has been made firm." For if we take "firmness" to be "solidity," how can what is firm be compared with smoke? Unless perhaps we can say that all the firmness and solidity and strength of the heaven that dissolves in the air is as Ecclesiastes says, the most empty wind and smoke: "Vanity of vanities, all is vanity." And that must be said that if the sky and the earth were to perish and grow old, then its inhabitants would also die and vanish, although we know that souls are everlasting and bodies are also resurrected. From this it is clear that heaven and earth do not perish and become reduced to nothing, but

they are changed into something better. COMMENTARY ON ISAIAH 14.8.[28]

GOD MADE THE HEAVENS AND THE EARTH.
THEODORET OF CYR: From the sky and the earth, from the things on high and those below, learn of my power. I produced these elements with great ease and, conversely, I can make them disappear. "But my salvation shall be for eternity, and my righteousness shall not fail." This is what the Lord has likewise said in the holy Gospels: "Heaven and earth shall pass away, but my words will by no means pass away."[29] COMMENTARY ON ISAIAH 16.51.6.[30]

---

[28]AGLB 35:1468-70. [29]Mt 24:35. [30]ITA 758*; SC 315:120.

51:7-11 NOTHING CAN STOP THE FULFILLMENT OF SALVATION

[7]"Hearken to me, you who know righteousness,
 the people in whose heart is my law;
fear not the reproach of men,
 and be not dismayed at their revilings.
[8]For the moth will eat them up like a garment,
 and the worm will eat them like wool;
but my deliverance will be for ever,
 and my salvation to all generations."

[9]Awake, awake, put on strength,
 O arm of the LORD;
awake, as in days of old,

 the generations of long ago.
Was it not thou that didst cut Rahab in pieces,
 that didst pierce the dragon?
[10]Was it not thou that didst dry up the sea,
 the waters of the great deep;
that didst make the depths of the sea a way
 for the redeemed to pass over?
[11]And the ransomed of the LORD shall return,
 and come to Zion with singing;
everlasting joy shall be upon their heads;
 they shall obtain joy and gladness,
 and sorrow and sighing shall flee away.

OVERVIEW: Having the eternal qualities of justice and righteousness, the Son is indestructible.

(CYRIL). Likewise those who suffer for the gospel should be encouraged by these words to know that they too will endure. Isaiah here invites Jerusalem to awaken to the renewal that will come to it, although we should also understand that this prophecy of Jerusalem's return from exile in Babylon was made at a different time but was put together with the other earlier ones later to form a single book (THEODORET). Isaiah's prophecy extends to every age, however, encouraging believers of any age to pray for their God to act when they are faced with spiritual trials (EUSEBIUS). This is what Israel of old did when faced with overwhelming odds against Pharaoh. God's actions then and now should instill confidence concerning the future of his people (THEODORET) as Israel's exodus symbolizes a new beginning for the church and for the soul (JEROME).

51:7-8 Do Not Fear

RIGHTEOUSNESS DOES NOT WEAR OUT.
CYRIL OF ALEXANDRIA: The Son is called "salvation" and "righteousness," as we often say, and thus his quality is declared that he has in himself, by which and in which he is Son by nature. Indeed, he is eternal and does not "wear out." Such is the difference between creator and creation, the made from the maker, which is clearly seen in this verse. COMMENTARY ON ISAIAH 4.5.51.6.[1]

THOSE WHO SUFFER FOR THE GOSPEL WILL ENDURE. THEODORET OF CYR: This is what the Lord has also said in the divine Gospels: "Do not fear those who kill the body but cannot kill the soul,"[2] and again: "Do not fear them,"[3] and: "Blessed are you when they revile and persecute you and shall say all kinds of evil against you falsely for my sake. Rejoice and be exceedingly glad, for great is your reward in heaven."[4] Similarly, here, the prophetic text has shown that people who revile and trample underfoot the heralds of truth are like garments and like wool that is eaten away by the moth, while the salvation and the righteousness of those who are being insulted has no end and escapes death. After having made

the prediction here concerning the new people, [the prophet] passes to another subject and prophesies to Jerusalem the return from exile in Babylon. One should know, however, that these announcements were not made at the same time as the others, but that the first dates from one epoch, the second from some other time, and that they were put together later to form a single book. COMMENTARY ON ISAIAH 16.51.8.[5]

51:9 Awake

AN INVITATION FOR JERUSALEM TO BE RENEWED. THEODORET OF CYR: He addresses these words as if [Jerusalem] had fallen and were prone on the ground, and he invites it to take up again its power of other times. "Awake as in the early time, as the ancient generation." Renew yourself, he says, and become again such as you were when your splendor attracted all eyes. COMMENTARY ON ISAIAH 16.51.9.[6]

THE NEED TO PRAY FOR GOD'S INTERVENTION. EUSEBIUS OF CAESAREA: According to the Hebrew, it is not Jerusalem but the arm of the Lord that has to put on strength. This relates to what we spoke about above [v. 5], about the nations hoping in "my arm." For we have said that the divinity of the Word is signified here, since he urges the people not to fear the rebuke of human beings or to be affected by their filth, and in the same way here it is right to see in the person of the people a prayer being sent to the "arm of the Lord" to rouse himself and overcome the enemies of his people. For we confess we are nothing unless you rise up and overcome on our behalf. COMMENTARY ON ISAIAH 2.39.[7]

51:10 The Sea

THE "SEA" REFERS TO EGYPTIANS OR ASSYRIANS. THEODORET OF CYR: The great number of

---

[1]PG 70:1117. [2]Mt 10:28. [3]Mt 10:26. [4]Mt 5:11-12. [5]ITA 758-59*; SC 315:120-22. [6]ITA 759*; SC 315:122. [7]GCS 57(9):323-24.

the Egyptians he calls the "sea." If, however, one wishes also to see the Assyrians under this name, the explanation would hardly stray from the truth. "[Are you not the one] who made the depths of the sea a way of passage for the delivered and redeemed?" He has said that of the Red Sea: because it was parted in two, Israel enjoyed salvation. So he is recalling these events in order to invite them to have confidence relating to future events. The ensuing passage makes this quite clear. COMMENTARY ON ISAIAH 16.51.10.[8]

A NEW BEGINNING FOR THE CHURCH AND THE SOUL. JEROME: The Hebrew gives the historical sense for the Jews [the Red Sea overcoming Pharaoh], yet this includes another sense, since the One who who did these things now also leads those redeemed and freed by your blood into Zion and into the heavenly Jerusalem—into the church that you have prepared by your blood. . . . This is what the Hebrew teaches. The rest of the meaning is found through reading the Septuagint concerning Jerusalem, that is, the sinful soul is provoked to put on the strength of God's arm and to take on the former works such as it did before the fall, when the soul was illumined. COMMENTARY ON ISAIAH 14.10.[9]

51:11 Joy and Gladness

AFRAID OF THE ENEMY, YOU FORGOT GOD. THEODORET OF CYR: "They will be gathered by the Lord, and they will arrive in Zion full of joy and an eternal cheerfulness; and on their head praise and joy will take hold of them; sadness, pain and grief will have gone." He has declared in advance the return of cheerfulness and joy, which take hold of believers after the coming as man of our Savior. . . . Then by the expression of the face he inspires confidence. . . . It is the Lord who strengthens him, the One who worked these paradoxes in former times, who delivered Pharaoh with his army into the sea, who killed the many thousands of Assyrians through one angel.[10] . . . He says, "You have worked with the enemies and have carried out their aims—you were afraid of them and forgot me who am the Creator of all things, among whom he gave a thousand pledges of power. Yet you feared a mortal and corruptible man while you have not paid attention to your own dignity and you have not sought my help." COMMENTARY ON ISAIAH 16.51.11-13.[11]

---

[8]ITA 760*; SC 315:124. [9]AGLB 35:1474. [10]Ex 14:28; Is 37:36. [11]SC 315:124-26

51:12-16 THE CREATOR'S NEW REGIME OF GRACE

[12]I, I am he that comforts you;
  who are you that you are afraid of man who dies,
  of the son of man who is made like grass,
[13]and have forgotten the LORD, your Maker,
  who stretched out the heavens
  and laid the foundations of the earth,
and fear continually all the day

because of the fury of the oppressor,
when he sets himself to destroy?
  And where is the fury of the oppressor?
[14]He who is bowed down shall speedily be released;
  he shall not die and go down to the Pit,
  neither shall his bread fail.
[15]For I am the LORD your God,

who stirs up the sea so that its waves
roar—
the LORD of hosts is his name.
[16]*And I have put my words in your mouth,*

and hid you in the shadow of my hand,
stretching out[p] the heavens
and laying the foundations of the earth,
and saying to Zion, "You are my people."

p Syr: Heb *plant*

OVERVIEW: Christ as Lord is the maker of creation and thus prior to it (ATHANASIUS). The prophet predicts Christ's having a death that did not involve corruption (JEROME). God's providential care gives good things but also sometimes causes disruption in people's lives (THEODORET). Yet built into the creating activity is God's protection of the incarnate Christ and his people the church (JEROME).

51:13 *Who Stretched Out the Heavens*

WITHOUT THE WORD, NOTHING WOULD HAVE BEEN MADE. ATHANASIUS: And David being taught this, and knowing that the Lord's hand was nothing else than Wisdom, he says in the psalm, "In wisdom you have made them all; the earth is full of your creation."[1] Solomon also received the same from God and said, "The Lord by wisdom founded the earth."[2] And John, knowing that the Word was the hand and the Wisdom, preached, "In the beginning was the Word, and the Word was with God, and the Word was God ... without him was not anything made."[3] DEFENCE OF THE NICENE DEFINITION 4.[4]

51:14 *Speedy Release and Provision*

CHRIST AS THE TRAILBLAZER. JEROME: Symmachus in this verse translated, "speedily hell will open up, and he will not remain in corruption," which indicates Christ when it says, "You will not abandon my soul to hell, nor will you give your holy one over to see corruption."[5] COMMENTARY ON ISAIAH 14.11.[6]

WHERE IS THE FURY OF THE OPPRESSOR? THEODORET OF CYR: "And his bread will not fail

because I am the Lord your God, who stirs up the sea and its waves, the Lord of hosts is my name." The phrase "and his bread will not fail" appears in the Septuagint with an asterisk.[7] The text means that in very captivity they will enjoy the divine concern since God provides generously for their need. COMMENTARY ON ISAIAH 16.51.15.[8]

51:16 *You Are My People*

I HAVE HID YOU IN THE SHADOW OF MY HAND. JEROME: For the same verse we, following the Hebrew and Aquila, translated "I have put my words in your mouth, and in the shadow of my hands I have protected you as you lay out the heavens and establish the earth and say to Zion, 'you are my people.'" Symmachus had, "I will put my words in your mouth, and in the shadow of my hand I will protect you—[the hand] with which I laid out the sky and founded the earth so that I might say to Zion, 'You are my people.'" According to the Septuagint, it is spoken to all the souls of believers because, though created towards the image and likeness of God, it was unaware of its dignity. Instead, it feared man and the son of man who can only kill the body and did not understand that it is immortal. COMMENTARY ON ISAIAH 14.11.[9]

DIVINE ACTION ATTESTS DIVINE WORDS. THEODORET OF CYR: It is by means of actions that I will teach you the truth of my words. "And I will shelter you under the shadow of my hand,

---

[1]Ps 104:24 (103:24 LXX). [2]Prov 3:19. [3]Jn 1:1-3. [4]NPNF 2 4:161*. [5]Ps 16:10 (15:10 LXX). [6]AGLB 35:1478. [7]Text that has an asterisk is text that is found in the LXX but not in the Hebrew. However, both texts affirm God's providential care for his people. [8]SC 315:126. [9]AGLB 35:1478-79.

with which I fixed the sky and founded the earth: and the Lord shall say to Zion, you are my people." It suffices to recall the creation to show the capability of his dynamic force that he has promised to convey to them; for he has indicated his dynamic force by the name "hand." COMMENTARY ON ISAIAH 16.51.16.[10]

[10]ITA 761*; SC 315:128.

51:17-23 THE CUP OF THE LORD'S WRATH

[17]*Rouse yourself, rouse yourself,*
    stand up, O Jerusalem,
you who have drunk at the hand of the LORD
    the cup of his wrath,
who have drunk to the dregs
    the bowl of staggering.
[18]*There is none to guide her*
    among all the sons she has borne;
there is none to take her by the hand
    among all the sons she has brought up.
[19]*These two things have befallen you—*
    who will condole with you?—
devastation and destruction, famine and
        sword;
    who will comfort you?[q]
[20]*Your sons have fainted,*
    they lie at the head of every street
    like an antelope in a net;
they are full of the wrath of the LORD,
    the rebuke of your God.

[21]*Therefore hear this, you who are afflicted,*
    who are drunk, but not with wine:
[22]*Thus says your Lord, the* LORD,
    your God who pleads the cause of his
        people:
"Behold, I have taken from your hand
    the cup of staggering;
the bowl of my wrath
    you shall drink no more;
[23]*and I will put it into the hand of your*
        tormentors,
    who have said to you,
    'Bow down, that we may pass over';
and you have made your back like the
        ground
    and like the street for them to pass over."

q One ancient Ms Gk Syr Vg: Heb *how may I comfort you*

OVERVIEW: The "cup of wrath" signifies chastisement; there are two calamities: falling, and being crushed (THEODORET). Although the righteous God is angry, as befits his just response to sin, nevertheless he is inclined to clemency by his mercy (GREGORY OF NAZIANZUS). God exacts different forms of punishment first for abandoning him and then further for worshiping idols (ISHO'DAD). The prophet's description here indicates Israel's laxness, not God's unfaithfulness (THEODORET). The soul has only itself to blame for being abused by the ungodly; still they too shall be punished in turn with God's wrath (JEROME). But the cup of wrath can also serve to increase the thirst for living water for those who are faithful (Cassiodorus). As God's faithful people, Israel should have sought an alliance with him instead of with their enemies. Since they did not, however, they were humbled by God's wrath (Theodoret), demonstrating that any soul that inclines toward this world instead of toward God comes readily to harm and is humiliated by its spiritual enemies (Gregory the Great).

51:17 The Cup of Wrath

The Cup of Wrath Is Chastisement. Theodoret of Cyr: He calls chastisement "the cup," because it is stupefying like drunkenness. Of this cup, the blessed David has likewise made mention in the following terms: "For there is a cup in the hand of the Lord, full strength, full of a mixture [of aromatics]; and he has turned it from side to side"—for he chastises some, now others—"but its dregs have not been wholly poured out; all the sinners of the earth shall drink them."[1] The divine Jeremiah, in turn, has mentioned this in these terms: "Thus the Lord God said, Take the cup of this undiluted wine from my hand, and you shall cause all the nations to drink, to whom I send you. And they shall drink and vomit and become mad." And to teach what he means by the name "cup," he has added, "from the face of my sword, which I shall send in the middle of them." Then he adds, "I took the cup out of the Lord's hand and caused the nations to whom the Lord sent me to drink: Jerusalem and the cities of Judea, and the kings of Judea and their princes, to make them a desert place, a desolation and a hissing," as is the case today and so on.[2] Here also, God has therefore declared through the prophet: "You have drained the cup of calamity and emptied it," that is to say, you have endured a very great chastisement, and you have had no help from the kings, the generals and the multitude of soldiers in whom you continued to put your trust. Commentary on Isaiah 16.51.18.[3]

God Moderates His Wrath with Compassion. Gregory of Nazianzus: Anger, which is called "the cup in the hand of the Lord" and "the cup of falling that is drained," is in proportion to transgressions, even though he abates to all some of what is their due and dilutes with compassion the unmixed draught of his wrath. For he inclines from severity to indulgence toward those who accept chastisement with fear, and who after a slight affliction conceive and are in pain with conversion and bring forth the perfect spirit of salvation. But he nevertheless reserves the dregs, the last drop of his anger, that he may pour it out entire on those who, instead of being healed by his kindness, grow obdurate, like the hardhearted Pharaoh. On His Father's Silence, Oration 16.4.[4]

51:19 Two Things Have Befallen You

Double Calamity and Double Chastisement. Theodoret of Cyr: By "two," he means the bravery of the adversaries and the desertion of the auxiliaries: while the former attack with courage, the others flee in a cowardly fashion. "Downfall and destruction." He has again presented two calamities: that of falling and that of being crushed. For sometimes a person falls without being struck. "Famine and sword." Again a double chastisement: if the first make a siege from the city of the outside, even harder to endure than the enemies was the famine that was within, annihilating them. Commentary on Isaiah 16.51.19.[5]

Destruction, Famine and Sword. Isho'dad of Merv: "These two things have befallen you," that is, they have befallen you because of your sins. You have abandoned God, and you have followed the idols; that is why two punishments have come over you, "famine and sword," because "devastation" comes from the

---

[1]Ps 75:8 (74:9 LXX). [2]Jer 25:15-18 (32:15-18 LXX). [3]ITA 762; SC 315:128-30. [4]NPNF 2 7:248*. [5]ITA 762-63*; SC 315:130.

sword and "destruction" from famine. COMMENTARY ON ISAIAH 51.19.[6]

51:20 Your Sons Have Fainted

INDICATIONS OF ISRAEL'S LAXNESS. THEODORET OF CYR: By the slumber, he has indicated their indolence, and by the cooked vegetables their laxness. But what he adds is even harsher than what he has said before: "They that are full of the anger of the Lord are caused to faint by the Lord God." By their iniquity they draw my anger, and by reason of my anger, they are deprived of my kind attention and despoiled of every kind of strength. COMMENTARY ON ISAIAH 16.51.20.[7]

RAW, COOKED OR HALF-COOKED BEETS. JEROME: Whoever is at any time unbelieving is called a raw beet root,[8] whereas whoever is happy in the faith of the simple, without paying attention to reflection and the truth of doctrines but who performs deeds of justice, can be called a cooked beet root; in turn, the one who floats between vices and the virtues and approaches the service of God with a mixed heart can be called semi-cooked. . . . Those who sin in the law will be judged by the law, which works the wrath of God for those who are half-hearted. . . .

Let us come, following the Septuagint, to the spiritual sense. It is said to the soul brought down by vices and the upsets of drunkenness that it may come to know the Lord its Judge as one who will give reasons for all things. And if they turn to better things, the cup will be given over to those who humiliated them. . . . It should be noted that others did not force Israel or make it, who was once upright, now bent down to the earth, but their own will was directly toward abandonment. [Israel] by its own will put its neck or back or whole body down low for those who abused it within and without. COMMENTARY ON ISAIAH 14.13-14.[9]

51:22 The Bowl of My Wrath

THE CUP OF WRATH MAKES ONE SPIRITU-

ALLY THIRSTY. CASSIODORUS: For it is the function of the blood of the Lord that as it makes drunk it heals the mind, shielding it from fancies, not leading it toward sins. This wine makes them sober; this fullness empties them of evils. One who does not become full with this cup will be rendered hungry with an eternal lack . . . Anyhow, when God bestows such things, he does so that they may draw them to the kingdom of heaven. And about this cup it is said in the Gospel, "Whoever drinks from the water that I give will never thirst and will become in them a source of water springing up for eternal life."[10] EXPOSITION OF PSALM 22.5.[11]

51:23 Bow Down

ISRAEL SHOULD HAVE REQUESTED AN ALLIANCE WITH GOD. THEODORET OF CYR: He has indicated both the arrogance of the enemies and the distress of the city. He says, If you had requested my alliance, you would have prevailed over those who waged war on you; but since you did not want to do this, you have been abased even to the level of the ground. COMMENTARY ON ISAIAH 16.51.23.[12]

THE VULNERABILITY OF THE WORLDLY SOUL. GREGORY THE GREAT: Concerning these enemies indeed it is spoken through the prophet, for they say to your soul, "Bow down that we may cross over." The sublime soul is indeed straight, standing tall, while the humbled one is bent, since through the heavenly quality of virtues and the heavenly longing it is lifted into the higher places, but when it is deflected to the love of this world, it fell to where the enemy attacked it and easily laid it waste. So they say to the souls, "bow down that we may cross over," that is, to see if they bring it down to act or think in a worldly way or infiltrate its mind with mean thoughts

---

[6]CSCO 303(128):51. [7]ITA 763*; SC 315:130-32. LXX of v. 20 has *seutlion hēmiephthon.* [9]AGLB 35:1487, 1489. [10]Jn 4:14. [11]CCL 97:213. [12]ITA 764; SC 315:134.

and upset it with the warfare of vices. From this we can learn just how far away we ought to be from worldly action, word and thought. Six

BOOKS ON 1 KINGS 5.57.[13]

---

[13]CCL 144:455.

52:1-6 SANCTIFIED JERUSALEM

[1]*Awake, awake,*
put on your strength, O Zion;
put on your beautiful garments,
    O Jerusalem, the holy city;
for there shall no more come into you
    the uncircumcised and the unclean.
[2]*Shake yourself from the dust, arise,*
    O captive[r] Jerusalem;
loose the bonds from your neck,
    O captive daughter of Zion.

[3]*For thus says the* LORD: *"You were sold for nothing, and you shall be redeemed without money.* [4]*For thus says the Lord* GOD: *My people went down at the first into Egypt to sojourn there, and the Assyrian oppressed them for nothing.* [5]*Now therefore what have I here, says the* LORD, *seeing that my people are taken away for nothing? Their rulers wail, says the* LORD, *and continually all the day my name is despised.* [6]*Therefore my people shall know my name; therefore in that day they shall know that it is I who speak; here am I."*

r Cn: Heb *sit*

OVERVIEW: Jerusalem has a special holiness that is a gift of God (JEROME). The effect of this gift does not bypass the earthly Jerusalem, but it also looks toward the heavenly Zion (THEODORET). Here in the earthly Jerusalem of the church, we are transformed by participation in Christ, having been justified by faith in the one who shelters and protects us from every assault of the devil (CYRIL). The church looks forward to the day when it will shake off its mortality and corruption at the resurrection of the dead (METHODIUS), having been reconciled by grace (JEROME) and

ransomed from captivity through the most precious blood of Christ (BASIL). Only special blood avails against sin; nothing material does (AUGUSTINE). Having been cleansed by his blood, we then are clothed with Christ (CASSIAN).

The Gentiles blaspheme the name of God because they attribute Israel's misfortune to weakness in God (THEODORET). This is why immediate repentance is so important, so that God's name is not dishonored (PSEUDO-CLEMENT). This is different from offending the world because of a faithful witness (TERTULLIAN). Repentance is important because the effects of disobedience can change from external pain to internal corruption (EUSEBIUS). When we do repent, we begin to see God more clearly. It is not that God gradually becomes holy but that his holiness is becoming more rightly perceived in us (CYRIL OF JERUSALEM). If we instead seek self-indulgence, this will only lead to pain and shame (JEROME). God wants his people to avoid such destruction and thus directs his prophecy to reach his people (AMBROSE). He did this at his incarnation as well, wanting the people to know that he was the one the prophets had foretold would speak to them directly (JEROME).

52:1 The Holy City

THE HOLY CITY. JEROME: And it is called the city of sanctuary, for *qodeš* means that quality on which the city was founded. Or it is called the city of the holy one, because of the knowledge of God, or it is called the holy city because, of all the world's cities, it alone accepted the law. Hence, after the resurrection of the Savior the bodies of many dead people appeared in the holy city,[1] which because of blasphemy and the hands laid on the Lord could not until then have been holy. COMMENTARY ON ISAIAH 14.15.[2]

THE CONTINUITY BETWEEN THE EARTHLY AND HEAVENLY CITIES. THEODORET OF CYR: He calls the lower city "Jerusalem," and the city on high "Zion," but both together are one city. This is why he promises restoration to both; and, since foreign nations crossed through it without fear when its inhabitants had been taken captive, he is promising deliverance from these foreigners. ... It is due to their sins that they have been sold, but it is by the benevolence of God that they have obtained deliverance. COMMENTARY ON ISAIAH 16.52.1-3.[3]

WHERE CHRIST CLEANS AND PROTECTS. CYRIL OF ALEXANDRIA: He calls the holy city "the church." It is sanctified not by the prescribed cultic system, for the law never perfected anyone, but it is made in the likeness of Christ and participates in his divine nature, according to the communication of the Holy Spirit, in whom we are sealed for the day of redemption, with all vileness washed and removed. ... We have been justified by faith in him, who reinforces us in all safety and shelters us in his love from every fierce attack of the devil and wild surges of enemy opposition. And so he teaches us when he says "to Zion or Jerusalem, that is, the church of the living God." COMMENTARY ON ISAIAH 5.1.52.1.[4]

52:2 Shake Yourself from the Dust

SHAKING OFF MORTALITY IN THE RESURRECTION. METHODIUS: The creation, then, after being restored to a better and more fitting state, remains, rejoicing and exulting over the children of God at the resurrection. For their sake the creation now groans and travails, waiting itself also for our redemption from the corruption of the body, that, when we have risen and shaken off the mortality of the flesh,[5] according to that which is written, "shake off the dust, and arise and sit down, O Jerusalem," and have been set free from sin, it also shall be freed from corruption and be subject no longer to vanity but to righteousness. ON THE RESURRECTION 1.8.[6]

52:3 Redeemed Without Money

GOD'S GRACE RECONCILES US. JEROME: "You shall be redeemed without money." For it is not because of merits but because of grace and the faith of Christ that we have been reconciled to God. It speaks about those souls who have lost the whiteness of their former way of life and are told, along with the apostles, to shake off the dust that has stuck to their feet. COMMENTARY ON ISAIAH 14.16.[7]

---

[1]Mt 27:52. [2]AGLB 35:1491. [3]ITA 772-73; SC 315:134. [4]PG 70:1144-45. [5]Rom 8:19-22. [6]ANF 6:366. [7]AGLB 35:1494-95.

THE NEED TO PARTICIPATE IN THE SAVIOR'S BLOOD. BASIL THE GREAT: No one is sufficient to redeem himself, unless he comes who turns away the captivity of the people, not with ransoms or with gifts, as it is written in Isaiah, but in his own blood. HOMILIES ON THE PSALMS 19.4 (PSALM 48).[8]

REDEEMED WITHOUT MONEY. AUGUSTINE: Let us all flee to Christ. Against sin let us appeal to God, the giver of freedom. Let us request to have ourselves put up for sale that we may be redeemed by his blood. For the Lord says, "You were sold for nothing, and without money you shall be redeemed." That is, without payment, without your payment, because by mine. The Lord says this, for he gave the payment himself, not silver but his own blood. For we had remained both slaves and in need. TRACTATES ON THE GOSPEL OF JOHN 41.4.3.[9]

PUT ON THE CLOTHING OF INCORRUPTION. JOHN CASSIAN: For without a doubt he will not deserve to be adorned with the garment of incorruption (concerning which the apostle commanded, "Put on the Lord Jesus Christ";[10] and again: "Clothed in the breastplate of righeousness and love";[11] and about which the Lord himself said to Jerusalem through the prophet: "Rise up, rise up, Jerusalem, put on the garments of your glory") who has been overcome by slumbering idleness and boredom and who has chosen to be clothed not by the effort of his own toil but in the rags of laziness, which he has cut off from the complete fullness of the Scriptures and from their body and which he refits into a disgraceful covering to hide his slothfulness rather than into a garment of glory and beauty. INSTITUTES 10.21.2.[12]

52:4 The People of God

IS GOD'S WEAKNESS THE CAUSE OF ISRAEL'S BAD FORTUNE? THEODORET OF CYR: His question is a matter of style meant to show the strangeness of the happening: Did you not go to

Egypt? he says. Why then have you come back from there? "Thus says the Lord, because my people was taken for nothing, you wonder and howl." You are struck with amazement, he says, in deploring the captivity, because, despite the title of "my people" that you carry, you have suffered these misfortunes. Well, do not wonder, but consider how "on account of you my name is continually blasphemed among the Gentiles."[13] The fact that you are justifiably undergoing these misfortunes is not so insupportable as the fact that I am blasphemed because of you and that the Gentiles think my weakness is the cause of the bad fortune that you have endured. COMMENTARY ON ISAIAH 16.52.5.[14]

REPENT AND WIPE AWAY YOUR SINS. PSEUDO-CLEMENT OF ROME: Therefore, brothers, let us repent immediately. Let us be clear-headed regarding the good, for we are filled with great stupidity and weakness. Let us wipe off from ourselves our former sins and be saved, repenting from the very souls of our being. And let us not seek to please people. 2 CLEMENT 13.1.[15]

52:5 My Name Is Despised

MY NAME IS BLASPHEMED. TERTULLIAN: There is indeed a blasphemy that we must avoid completely, namely, that any of us should give a pagan any cause for blasphemy by deceit or injury or insult or some other matter justifying complaint in which the Name is deservedly blamed, so that the Lord is deservedly angry. But if the words "because of you my name is blasphemed" cover every blasphemy, then we are all lost, since the whole culture assails the Name, for no fault of ours, with its wicked outcries. . . . Our name is blessed when we are cursed for keeping our discipline. ON IDOLATRY 7.14.[16]

---

[8]FC 46:318. [9]FC 88:139. [10]Rom 13:14. [11]1 Thess 5:8. [12]ACW 58:231-32. [13]Rom 2:24; Is 52:5. [14]ITA 774*; SC 315:136. [15]AF 119*. [16]LCC 5:98.

Why Was Israel Taken Captive? Eusebius of Caesarea: For he said, "I found nothing here among them," as was made clear in the earlier passage, "Why did I come, and there was no one? Why did I call, and there was none to hear?"[17] However, earlier they were violently led away as captives, first by the Egyptians and then by the Assyrians, and were given over on account of their sins. But now they have been taken away for nothing, "as a gazelle caught in a net,"[18] by hunters of souls who trap them with nets of wickedness. Commentary on Isaiah 2.40.[19]

The People Shall Know My Name. Cyril of Jerusalem: The name of God is in its nature holy, whether we say so or not; but since it is sometimes profaned among sinners, according to the words, "Through you my name is continually blasphemed among the Gentiles," we pray that in us God's name may be hallowed; not that it comes to be holy from our being holy but because it becomes holy in us, when we are made holy and do things worthy of holiness. Mystagogical Lectures 5.12.[20]

A Warning Against Self-Indulgence. Jerome: Moreover, according to the anagogical sense, we can say that the people of God go down into the Egypt of this age, when they are lovers of pleasures more than of God and do not hear that prophetic voice, "Woe to you who descend to

Egypt for help."[21] Whoever is softened with vices and lives in a place of lakes and rivers but does not have the dryness of chastity will be violently handed over to the Assyrians, and they will master him and try and convict him of sin. Commentary on Isaiah 14.17.[22]

52:6 I Who Speak

God Reaches Out in Prophecy. Ambrose: He stretched out his hands to an unbelieving and contradicting people. To save his own people, the Lord spoke directly without an envoy.[23] "I myself who spoke, I am here,"[24] and "I was made manifest to those who sought me not, I appear to those who asked me not."[25] Joseph 12.67.[26]

The Authority of Christ. Jerome: [Christ] was not speaking as a teacher but as the Lord. He was not speaking in reference to a greater authority, but he was teaching that which was his very own. Particularly, he was speaking in this manner because he who had spoken by the prophets was speaking now in person. "It is I who have foretold it, Here I am!" Homilies on Mark 76 (Mark 1.3-31).[27]

---

[17]Is 50:2. [18]Is 51:20. [19]GCS 57(9):329. [20]NPNF 2 7:155**. [21]Is 31:1. [22]AGLB 35:1500. [23]Cf. Is 65:2; Ps 28:9 (27:9 LXX). [24]Is 52:6. [25]Is 65:1. [26]FC 65:229**. [27]FC 57:139-40**.

52:7-12 HOMECOMING OF THE CAPTIVES

[7]How beautiful upon the mountains
  are the feet of him who brings good tidings,
who publishes peace, who brings good tidings of
    good,
  who publishes salvation,

who says to Zion, "Your God reigns."
[8]Hark, your watchmen lift up their voice,
  together they sing for joy;
for eye to eye they see
  the return of the Lord to Zion.

⁹Break forth together into singing,
*   you waste places of Jerusalem;*
for the Lord has comforted his people,
*   he has redeemed Jerusalem.*
¹⁰The Lord has bared his holy arm
*   before the eyes of all the nations;*
and all the ends of the earth shall see
*   the salvation of our God.*

¹¹Depart, depart, go out thence,
*   touch no unclean thing;*
go out from the midst of her, purify yourselves,
*   you who bear the vessels of the Lord.*
¹²For you shall not go out in haste,
*   and you shall not go in flight,*
for the Lord will go before you,
*   and the God of Israel will be your rear*
*   guard.*

Overview: The apostles' feet are beautiful because they touch the path the beautiful One trod (Origen). The apostles traveled throughout the world to proclaim the gospel (Eusebius). The preaching of the gospel finds those who are foreknown as children of peace. As God divided light and darkness, the brightness of those who have gone before in mission now illumine those who follow (Augustine). The gospel preaching gives protection to one's walk, as a shoe protects the foot (Cassiodorus). The apostles' feet run to proclaim the news to all the world (Jerome). The elevation of faith raises the soul above passions (Eusebius). The church, like Jerusalem, had its population decimated (Cyril), but God's universal power still can save (Theodoret).

To put oneself at a distance from the world does not imply a matter of physical space but a way of life (Origen). In fact, one has to be Christ-like and to remain near to sinners in order to make plain their sins (Augustine). In times of persecution, fleeing an area does not constitute denying the faith (Cyprian). Early Christians, based on the Savior's guidance in the prophetic text, fled before the Roman campaign against Jerusalem (Theodoret).

52:7 How Beautiful Are the Feet

The Beautiful Feet of the Apostles. Origen: "How are beautiful are the feet of those who announce good things!" Since Isaiah perceived the beautiful and opportune preaching of the apostles who follow the One who said, "I am the way,"[1] he praises the feet that proceed over the intelligible way, which is Christ Jesus, and go in to God through the door.[2] Those whose feet are beautiful announce Jesus as "good tidings." Commentary on the Gospel of John 1.51.[3]

Those Proclaiming Good News. Eusebius of Caesarea: Here [Isaiah] says very particularly that it is the feet of those who publish the good news of Christ that are beautiful. For how could they not be beautiful, which in so small, so short a time have run over the whole earth and filled every place with the holy teaching about the Savior of the world? Proof of the Gospel 3.1.[4]

The Publishers of Peace. Augustine: When they of whom it was foretold, "How beautiful on the mountains are the feet," . . . announce this gospel of peace, then each one begins to be a son of peace when he obeys and believes this gospel, and, justified by faith, begins to have peace with God. However, according to the predestination of God he already was a child of peace. For it is not said, "He on whom your peace shall have rested, he will become a child of peace." "If a child of peace is there, your peace will rest on him."[5] Admonition and Grace 15.46.[6]

Follow His Feet. Augustine: But you, "O

---

[1]Jn 14:6. [2]See Jn 10:9. [3]FC 80:44**. [4]POG 1:102. [5]Lk 10:6. [6]FC 2:302.

elect people,"[7] set in the firmament of the world, who have forsaken everything that you may follow the Lord, follow him now and confound the mighty! Follow him, O beautiful feet, and shine in the firmament, that the heavens may declare his glory, dividing the light of the perfect ones— though not yet so perfect as the angels—from the darkness of the little ones, who are nevertheless not utterly despised. CONFESSIONS 13.19.[8]

THE GOSPEL GIVES PROTECTION ON LIFE'S WALK. CASSIODORUS: We appropriately regard *shoe* as the gospel preaching, for just as the shoe's protection wards off troublesome thorns and other injuries from our feet, so the authority of the gospel protects our most glorious way of life, which is often compared with advancing on foot. So fulfilled by such kind help and with the Lord's protection we can pass through the world without suffering gashes. EXPOSITION OF PSALM 59.10.[9]

THE APOSTLES' FEET RUN TO PROCLAIM THE GOOD NEWS. JEROME: Christ brought peace to all things in heaven and earth through the blood of his cross.[10] He said to the apostles, "My peace I give to you, my peace I leave to you,"[11] and he announced good things to us, not that which is called "indifference" by philosophers, but things which are truly good, which the Father gives to those seeking him—that is all the graces of the Holy Spirit. . . .

Paul, following the sense of the Hebrew truth in the epistle to the Romans puts it, "How beautiful are the feet of those proclaiming good news, proclaiming peace,"[12] meaning the apostles whose feet the Lord washed, that they are clean and fair for preaching and to run through the world, quickly filling the globe with the doctrine of Christ. Following the Septuagint and the ambiguity of the Greek word, *hōra* means either "time" or "beauty." . . . If "beauty" is meant, then we might refer to what is said in the psalm, "Beautiful in appearance before the sons of men"[13]—for what is more beautiful than for the

form of a servant to become the form of God and to sit and reign with Christ in heaven? COMMENTARY ON ISAIAH 14.18.[14]

BREAK FORTH IN SONG. EUSEBIUS OF CAESAREA: Zion and Jerusalem, that here have the good news told them, the apostle knew to be heavenly, when he said, "But the Jerusalem that is above (that is, our mother) is free,"[15] and, "You have drawn near to Mount Zion and the city of the living God, heavenly Jerusalem and to an innumerable company of angels."[16] Zion might also mean the church established by Christ in every part of the world, and Jerusalem the godly citizenship (*politeuma*) that, once established long ago among the ancient Jews alone, was driven out to the wilderness by their impiety and then again was restored far better than before through the coming of our Savior. Therefore, the prophecy says, "Let the waste places of Jerusalem break forth into joy together, for the Lord has pitied it and saved Jerusalem."

Nor would you be wrong in calling Zion the soul of every holy and godly person, so far as it is lifted up above this life, having its citizenry in heaven and seeing things far beyond the world. For it means "a watchtower." And insofar as such a person remains calm and free from passion, you could call him Jerusalem—for Jerusalem means "vision of peace." PROOF OF THE GOSPEL 6.24.[17]

52:8-9 Its Desert Places Will Rejoice

THE CHURCH FROM THE NATIONS. CYRIL OF ALEXANDRIA: Israel was destroyed in the war with the Romans,[18] so that very few survived to remain, and the holy city was deserted. But its desert places[19] will rejoice, so it says. For the houses were mournful and filled with dejection for not having inhabitants. But they rejoice as if

[7]1 Pet 2:9. [8]NPNF 1 1:198**. [9]ACW 52:67-68. [10]Col 1:20. [11]Jn 14:27. [12]Rom 10:15. [13]Ps 45:2 (44:3 LXX). [14]AGLB 35:1503-5. [15]Gal 4:26. [16]Heb 12:22. [17]POG 2:45-46**. [18]Israel during the Maccabean period. [19]Gk *erēma*: desert places.

they have many living there. From the historical sense we can draw something that the spiritual senses can grasp. The church from the nations—that is, those believers from the nations who are called Zion and even Jerusalem—were few in the early days and the holy city of God, the church, was truly like a desert. COMMENTARY ON ISAIAH 5.1.52.9-10.[20]

52:10 The Lord's Holy Arm

THE ARM OF SALVATION. THEODORET OF CYR: The God of the universe will show his power, he says, to all the nations—for he gives to his power the name "arm"—and all people will know the Provider of salvation. COMMENTARY ON ISAIAH 16.52.10.[21]

52:11 Touch Nothing Unclean

PURIFY YOURSELVES TO BEAR VESSELS OF THE LORD. ORIGEN: It says, "you who carry the vessels of the Lord be separated and depart from their midst, says the Lord." "Separate yourself" from earthly deeds; "separate yourself" from the desire of the world.... Moreover, we say to be set apart not from places but from deeds, not from regions but from ways of life. HOMILIES ON LEVITICUS 11.5-6.[22]

TO DEPART FROM EVIL IS NOT TO ABANDON THE PEOPLE OF GOD. AUGUSTINE: What else does touching anything unclean mean, anyway, but consenting to sins? And what else does going out from there mean, but doing what is involved in rebuking the bad, to the extent that this can be done, taking account of each person's status and position, without damage to peace? It has displeased you that someone sinned; you have taken care not to touch an unclean thing. You have challenged, rebuked, warned, even administered, if the matter called for it, a suitable penalty that does no violence to unity; you have gone out from there....

When Scripture thunders at us that we must withdraw from the wicked, we are only being required to understand that we must withdraw in our hearts. Otherwise we may commit a greater evil by separating too simply the good from the bad. This is what the Donatists have done....

To understand what he said, I pay attention to what he did.... What he said was "Depart."... What I am asking is, did he depart physically from such people? I find that he did not. So he must have understood his own words differently. Because, of course, he himself would be the first to do what he commanded.... God, after all, could not blame him for his own sins, because he did not commit any; or for other people's, because he did not approve of them; or for indifference or neglect, because he did not keep quiet; or for pride, because he remained steadily in the unity of God's people. SERMON 88.23, 25.[23]

BETTER TO AVOID SIN AND LIVE FOREVER. CYPRIAN: Who is there among those destined to be born and die who will not at some point have to leave his country and suffer the loss of his estate? But by no means let Christ be forsaken. The loss of salvation and an eternal home is a much greater threat. See how the Holy Spirit cries to the prophet, "Leave. Depart. Get out of here. Do not touch any unclean thing. Get out of the middle of such things and be separate, you who bear the vessels of the Lord." And yet, those who are the vessels of the Lord and the temple of God do not go out from the middle of all this and leave so that they wouldn't have to be compelled to touch the unclean things or be polluted and corrupted with deadly food. In another place, a voice is heard from heaven, warning them ahead of time what servants of God should be doing. It says, "Come out of her,[24] my people, so that you do not become partakers of her sins and so that you do not receive her plagues."[25] The one who goes out and leaves does not become a partaker of the guilt. But whoever is found as a companion in

---

[20]PG 70:1160. [21]ITA 777*; SC 315:138-40. [22]FC 83:210. [23]WSA 3 3:434-36. [24]Babylon, personified [25]Rev 18:4.

her crimes will be wounded with the plagues. Therefore, the Lord commanded us in persecution to leave and to flee. He not only taught that this should be done; he did it himself. For just as the crown is given by the condescension of God and cannot be received unless the hour comes for accepting it, so those who remain in Christ but leave for a while do not deny their faith but instead bide their time. One who has fallen, however, after refusing to leave, remains only to deny his crown. The Lapsed 10.[26]

Flee Unbelief and Persevere in Faith. Theodoret of Cyr: When the Romans were on the point of making a campaign against Jerusalem, all those who had accepted the message exiled themselves in other cities, for they had learned of the misfortunes that would strike Jerusalem. Thus, it is the Lord in person who commanded them to do this: "But when you see Jerusalem surrounded by armies, then know that its desolation is near,"[27] and again: "Then, let those who are in Judea flee to the mountains, let him who is on the housetop not come down to take anything out of his house."[28] Therefore, because they knew these events in advance, they went out and escaped the misfortunes of the siege of the city, while the Savior in person guided them, directed their steps toward the Gentiles and assembled the church derived from the Gentiles. Since we also have learned of these events, let us, therefore, flee disbelief; let us persevere in the faith; let us guard the commandments of God and let us proceed on the right path, with the Lord Jesus to guide our way. Commentary on Isaiah 16.52.12.[29]

---

[26]ANF 5:439-40*. [27]Lk 21:20. [28]Mt 24:16-17. [29]ITA 778*; SC 315:140-42.

52:13-15 THE HUMBLE SERVANT IS EXALTED

[13]*Behold, my servant shall prosper,**
    he shall be exalted and lifted up,
    and shall be very high.
[14]*As many were astonished at him[s]—*
    his appearance was so marred, beyond
        human semblance,
    and his form beyond that of the sons of
        men[†]—

[15]*so shall he startle[t] many nations;*
    kings shall shut their mouths because of
        him;
for that which has not been told them they
        shall see,
    and that which they have not heard they
        shall understand.

s Syr Tg: Heb you   t The meaning of the Hebrew word is uncertain   * Syriac (Peshitta) shall be wise   † Even as many will be astounded at you, so your appearance will be without glory from people.

Overview: It is clear that the servant spoken of here by Isaiah is Christ, who served the Father and took a servant's form and was exalted (Ephrem). In him we see a spiritual grace that has a beauty all its own (Tertullian), despite the marring of his physical appearance by those who tortured and crucified him (Chrysostom). Christ's majesty is even now becoming obvious to all as they recognize his justice and kingship (AUGUSTINE) as even the scattered nations are brought together to acknowledge him (JEROME) and their emperors become convinced of the strange authority of the crucified one (ISHO'DAD). Faith produces an intelligence and piety beyond natural appearances (JUSTIN MARTYR). But those who are seemingly knowledgeable are ignorant of God and will be stunned into silence (THEODORET).

52:13 Behold My Servant

MY SERVANT SHALL BE EXALTED. EPHREM THE SYRIAN: "Behold, my servant shall be wise," that is, shall be illustrious; these words certainly concern our Lord. Indeed, he was called a servant by his Father, because, in the first place, he was sent by his Father in order to fulfill his will in procuring salvation for all humankind, and in the second place, because he assumed the aspect of a servant. "He shall be exalted and lifted up, and he shall be very high" through his virtues and miracles. COMMENTARY ON ISAIAH 52.13.[1]

52:14 Many Were Astonished

THE NATIONS STARTLED AT CHRIST'S SPIRITUAL GRACE. TERTULLIAN: Similarly the Father addressed the Son, "Even as many will be astounded at you, so your appearance will be without glory from people." For though, as David has it, he is timely in beauty even above the children of human beings,[2] yet this is in that allegorical state of spiritual grace, when he girds himself with the sword of the Word, which is in truth his very own form and comeliness and glory. AGAINST MARCION 3.17.[3]

MARRED BEYOND HUMAN SEMBLANCE. CHRYSOSTOM: "Even as many will be astounded at you, so your appearance will be without glory from people." For what could be equal to this insolence? Even the sea, on seeing his face, gave it reverence. Even the sun, when it beheld him on the

cross, turned away his rays. Yet on his face they did spit, and struck it with the palms of their hands, and some on the head; giving full swing in every way to their own madness. HOMILIES ON THE GOSPEL OF MATTHEW 85.1.[4]

52:15 Kings Shall Shut Their Mouths

THEY SHALL UNDERSTAND. AUGUSTINE: The Word, joined to human flesh, came forth from the virgin womb and has now strode forth like a giant and has run his course, and his exit was from the highest heaven and his return to the height of heaven. Now he has been exalted and honored, and many nations now marvel at him, and the kings stop their mouths because they have passed the cruelest laws against Christians. For, indeed, they were not told about him. Now they see, and though they did not hear, now they understand. AGAINST PHILOSOPHERS 3.[5]

THE ONENESS THAT ONLY GOD CAN BRING. JEROME: For they had the Lord as trailblazer who gathered them, the God of Israel to make one flock from the whole earth, to fulfill what the Lord said in the Gospel to his Father, "Grant that just as I and you are one, so they also may be one in us,"[6] as they in one mind and one opinion, rebutting vices and leaving behind disagreements among them, would grasp one unique virtue. For they do not run after vices and disputes, since here it only speaks about their virtues in which there is neither too much nor too little, but all is moderate. COMMENTARY ON ISAIAH 14.21.[7]

THAT WHICH THEY HAVE NOT BEEN PREVIOUSLY TOLD. ISHO'DAD OF MERV: "Kings shall shut their mouths because of him." He means that they will be troubled, after examining [his miracles]. Or, he alludes to what happened at the time of the crucifixion; the sun became obscure,

[1]SESHS 2:143-45*. [2]Ps 45:2 (44:3 LXX). [3]TAM 221-23**. [4]NPNF 1 10:506**. [5]CCL 58A:194-95. [6]Jn 17:21-22. [7]AGLB 35:1511.

and everybody stood up, being struck by stupe-faction. COMMENTARY ON ISAIAH 52.15.[8]

FAITH'S OWN INTELLIGENCE. JUSTIN MARTYR: We, indeed, have not believed in him in vain, nor have we been led astray by our teachers, but by wonderful divine providence it has been brought about that we, through the calling of the new and eternal testament (namely, Christ), should be found more understanding and more religious than you, who are reputed to be, but in reality are not, intelligent [people] and lovers of God. Isaiah, in amazement at this, said, "And kings shall shut their mouth; for they to whom it was not told of him, shall see; and they that heard not, shall understand. Lord, who has heard our report? And to whom is the arm of the Lord revealed?"[9] DIALOGUE WITH TRYPHO 118.[10]

GENTILES WILL KNOW THE MIGHT OF GOD'S POWER. THEODORET OF CYR: For not all believed, but those who did believe admired to the highest point the mystery of piety. "And kings shall keep their mouths shut." At the manifest demonstration of God's power, those who formerly persecuted him and had dared to blaspheme will restrain their tongues from slander. Then he adds in a clearer vein: "For they to whom no report was brought concerning him shall see; and they who have not heard shall consider." For those who did not receive the prophetic predictions, but who served idols, will see, thanks to the heralds of truth, the might of him who was proclaimed to them, and they will know his power. After the predictions concerning the Gentiles, he also prophesies the incredulity of the Jews. COMMENTARY ON ISAIAH 17.52.15.[11]

---

[8]CSCO 303:51.　[9]Is 52:15; 53:1.　[10]FC 6:330.　[11]ITA 781*; SC 315:146.

53:1-3 THE INHUMAN TREATMENT OF THE SERVANT

[1]*Who has believed what we have heard?*
　And to whom has the arm of the LORD
　　been revealed?
[2]*For he grew up before him like a young plant,* *
　and like a root out of dry ground;
he had no form or comeliness that we should
　look at him,

and no beauty that we should desire him.
[3]*He was despised and rejected[u] by men;*
　a man of sorrows,[v] and acquainted with
　　grief;[w]
and as one from whom men hide their faces
　he was despised, and we esteemed him not.

---

u Or *forsaken*　v Or *pains*　w Or *sickness*　* Syriac (Peshitta) *like a child*; LXX *We brought a report as of a child before him*

OVERVIEW: We still ask, with Isaiah, "Who has believed what we have heard? And to whom has the arm of the Lord been revealed?" (APOSTOLIC CONSTITUTIONS), realizing how incredible it is that the Son of God should be spoken of as having suffered these things (RUFINUS). He is the right hand or arm who works salvation. He is equal with the Father (TERTULLIAN) and was instrumental in bringing about the creation of the world (JEROME). God's right hand is the one who also has authority to judge and decide the fate of all. The Son is the mediating power of God the Father in his work (AUGUSTINE). The arm is the means of the consolation of the weary and prodigal human race (CAESARIUS). But let us also remember that the Son as the Father's arm has to be understood wisely and metaphorically (AUGUSTINE).

There was a child-like innocence about Christ and his apostles (ISHO'DAD). The Servant Messiah was not seen as beautiful in human terms (ORIGEN), having but a lowly career on earth, although his origin as well as his destiny was beyond anything of this world (IRENAEUS). The beauty of his soul is all the more profound for his despised bodily appearance (CLEMENT OF ALEXANDRIA). The lowliness of Christ in his incarnation was but a temporary measure (AMBROSE) as the incarnate Son revealed grace and beauty even when dishonored on the cross (CHRYSOSTOM). He looked miserable to those who saw him, but he was glorious in the minds of those who knew him (GREGORY OF NAZIANZUS). The humanity contained the healing power of the divine in a digestible form (ISAAC). On the cross there occurred an exchange of form for deformity (AUGUSTINE). The Word was contained in a humble form (CYRIL). His lowliness did not have to do with who he was but with what he had to do for us (ATHANASIUS).

53:1 Faith and the Arm of the Lord

MANY PEOPLE DID NOT BELIEVE. APOSTOLIC CONSTITUTIONS: Due to their exceedingly great wickedness, they would not believe in him, as the Lord shows in these words, "Who has believed our report? And to whom has the arm of the Lord been revealed?" And afterward, "Hearing you shall hear and shall not understand; and seeing you shall see and shall not perceive, for the heart of this people has become desensitized."[1] Therefore, knowledge was taken from them, because

when they saw, they overlooked, and when they heard, they heard nothing at all. CONSTITUTIONS OF THE HOLY APOSTLES 5.3.16.[2]

WONDERS FORETOLD CONFIRM FAITH. RUFINUS OF AQUILEIA: For it is incredible that God, the Son of God, should be spoken of and preached as having suffered these things. For this reason they are foretold by the prophets, lest any doubt should spring up in those who are about to believe. COMMENTARY ON THE APOSTLES' CREED 21.[3]

THE EQUALITY OF FATHER AND SON. TERTULLIAN: Now he would most certainly have said "your arm" if he had not wished us to understand that the Father is Lord and the Son also is Lord. AGAINST PRAXEAS 13.[4]

THE RIGHT HAND OR ARM IS THE SON. JEROME: May your right hand with which you fashioned the world bring light to the world. "To whom has the arm of the Lord been revealed?" May your right hand with which you formed humanity take on a human body and save human persons. HOMILIES ON THE PSALMS 67, ALTERNATE SERIES (PSALM 90).[5]

GOD'S RIGHT HAND AND ARM OF JUDGMENT. AUGUSTINE: Are we correct in understanding God's right hand to be the one of whom Isaiah says, "And the arm of the Lord, to whom has it been revealed"? That, you see, is the only Son, whom the Father did not spare "but handed him over for us all."[6] And thus he stretched out his right hand on the cross, and the earth devoured the godless, when they thought of themselves as victorious and of him as despicable in defeat. SERMON 363.2.[7]

MEDIATOR OF THE FATHER'S WILL. AUGUSTINE: If we should understand "hand" as power,

[1]Is 6:9-10. [2]ANF 7:446*. [3]NPNF 2 3:551. [4]ANF 3:607-8*. [5]FC 57:80*. [6]Rom 8:32. [7]WSA 3 10:272-73.

the power of the Father and the Son is one; but if we should understand "hand" as it was said through the prophet, "And to whom has the arm of the Lord been revealed?" the hand of the Father is the Son himself. TRACTATES ON THE GOSPEL OF JOHN 48.7.[8]

THE ARM EXECUTES THE WILL. AUGUSTINE: For just as it is your arm through which you work, so his Word was called the arm of God, because through the Word he constructed the world. For why does a person, in order to construct something, stretch out his arm except to directly execute his will? TRACTATES ON THE GOSPEL OF JOHN 53.2.[9]

THE FATHER PUTS HIS ARM AROUND PRODIGAL HUMANITY. CAESARIUS OF ARLES: God truly put his arm around the prodigal son when he clothed his Son in human flesh. Then he exclaimed and said to all, "Take my yoke on you."[10] Whoever accepts the yoke of Christ is embraced as with the arm of a father and is known to be reconciled with God. SERMON 163.2.[11]

THE SON IS THE FATHER'S ARM. AUGUSTINE: Look and see that he alone is Father and his arm is the Son, and there are not two but one, a person and his arm. Not understanding or noticing how the words of one thing are transferred to other things on account of some similarity in everyday speech concerning visible and well-known things, how much more when ineffable things are spoken in some way, which are said in such a way to be impossible [in another way]? For a person calls another person "his arm" through whom he does whatever he does. And if he is taken away, he mourns and says, "I have lost my arm." And to the one who took him away, he says, "You have taken my arm away." We can thus understand how it can be said that the Son is the arm of the Father through which the Father works all things. Failing to understand this, we remain in the shadows of error, just like those of

whom it was said, "To whom has the arm of the Lord been revealed?" TRACTATES ON THE GOSPEL OF JOHN 53.3.[12]

53:2 The Stunted Shoot

LIKE A ROOT OUT OF DRY GROUND. ISHO'DAD OF MERV: "For he grew up before him like a child," like a child dear to his Father, he says, because he will be dear to God. But "like a root out of the ground," which is deprived of water, he will also be deprived of life at the moment of the passion. In fact, God wanted these evil things to befall him. Others have seen these words as referring to the apostles who, like candid and young children, believed in him and did not refrain from knowing him, as the scribes and the Pharisees did. According to Qatraya,[13] this points to the fact that Simeon had already blessed him in the temple before God when he was yet an unborn child. Or this: The Son offered our nature before God, like a child, and made it pleasing before God. COMMENTARY ON ISAIAH 53.2.[14]

OF AVERAGE APPEARANCE. ORIGEN: There are, indeed, admitted to be recorded some statements respecting the body of Jesus having been "ill-favored"; not, however, "ignoble," as has been stated, nor is there any certain evidence that he was "little." AGAINST CELSUS 6.75.[15]

THE HUMILITY OF THE DIVINE KING. IRENAEUS: I have shown from the Scriptures that no one of the children of Adam is as to everything, and absolutely, called God, or named Lord. But that he is himself in his own right, beyond all people who ever lived, God, and Lord, and King eternal and the incarnate Word, proclaimed by all

---

[8]FC 88:233-34. [9]FC 88:290-91**. [10]Mt 11:29. [11]FC 47:386-87. [12]PL 35:1775. [13]Dadisho Qatraya (second half of the seventh century) is a fundamental figure in Syriac literature. He wrote his very refined and elegant works in the course of his monastic life. He is the author of a commentary on Isaiah, which has been partially edited and published only recently—see CSCO 326. [14]CSCO 303(128):51-52. [15]ANCL 23:418.

the prophets, the apostles and the Spirit himself, may be seen by all who have attained to even a small portion of the truth. Now, the Scriptures would not have testified these things of him if, like others, he had been a mere man. But that he had, beyond all others, in himself that preeminent birth that is from the most high Father and also experienced that preeminent generation that is from the Virgin, the divine Scriptures do in both respects testify of him: also, that he was a man without comeliness and liable to suffering; that he sat on the foal of a donkey; that he was despised among the people and humbled himself even to death; and that he is the holy Lord, the wonderful, the counselor, the beautiful in appearance and the mighty God,[16] coming on the clouds as the judge of all people[17]—all these things did the Scripture prophesy of him. AGAINST HERESIES 3.19.2[18]

BEAUTY OF SOUL AND BODY. CLEMENT OF ALEXANDRIA: The Spirit gives witness through Isaiah that even the Lord became an unsightly spectacle: "And we saw him, and there was no beauty or comeliness in him, but his form was despised and rejected by people." Yet, who is better than the Lord? He displayed not beauty of the flesh, which is only outward appearance, but the true beauty of body and soul—for the soul, the beauty of good deeds; for the body, the beauty of immortality. CHRIST THE EDUCATOR 3.1.3.[19]

HE BECAME MORE. AMBROSE: Isaiah says, "We have seen him, and he had neither appearance nor beauty." Nevertheless, from being great he became lesser, and from being lesser he became great. THE PRAYER OF JOB AND DAVID 4.4.17.[20]

NO BEAUTY THAT WE SHOULD DESIRE HIM. CHRYSOSTOM: For not by any means in working wonders only was he wonderful, but even when merely showing himself, he was full of great grace. To declare this, the prophet said, "Fair in beauty beyond the children of humankind."[21] When Isaiah says, "He had no form nor comeli-

ness," he is comparing the [embodied Son] with the glory of his godhead, which surpasses all utterance and description. Or he is speaking of what took place at his passion, the dishonor that he underwent at the season of the cross and the mean estate that throughout his life he exemplified in all respects. HOMILIES ON THE GOSPEL OF MATTHEW 27.2.[22]

THE HUMAN AND DIVINE NATURES CONTRASTED. GREGORY OF NAZIANZUS: For he whom you now treat with contempt was once above you. He who is now man was once the uncompounded. What he was he continued to be; what he was not he took to himself. In the beginning he was uncaused; for what is the cause of God? But afterwards for a cause he was born. And that cause was that you might be saved, who insult him and despise his godhead, because of this, that he took on him your denser nature, having converse with flesh by means of mind. While his inferior nature, the humanity, became God, because it was united to God and became one person because the higher nature prevailed, [this happened] in order that I too might be made God so far as he is made man. He was born—but he had been begotten. He was born of a woman—but she was a virgin. The first is human, the second divine. In his human nature he had no father, but also in his divine nature [he had] no mother. Both these belong to godhead. He dwelled in the womb—but he was recognized by the prophet [John the Baptist], himself still in the womb, leaping before the Word, for whose sake he came into being.[23] He was wrapped in swaddling clothes—but he took off the swathing bands of the grave by his rising again. He was laid in a manger—but he was glorified by angels, and proclaimed by a star and worshiped by the magi.[24] Why are you offended by what is presented to your sight, because you will not look at what is presented to your mind? He

---

[16]See Is 9:6. [17]See Dan 7:13. [18]ANF 1:449*. [19]FC 23:201. [20]FC 65:401-2. [21]Ps 45:2 (44:3 LXX). [22]NPNF 1 10:186*. [23]Lk 1:41. [24]Mt 2:1-12; Lk 2:7-16.

was driven into exile into Egypt[25]—but he drove away the Egyptian idols. He had no form or comeliness in the eyes of the Jews—but to David he is fairer than the children of humankind.[26] And on the mountain he was bright as the lightning and became more luminous than the sun,[27] initiating us into the mystery of the future. ON THE SON, THEOLOGICAL ORATION 3(29).19.[28]

AN ORDINARY AND HUMBLE FORM. ISAAC OF NINEVEH: Therefore, beloved, have in your mind God's providence (which from the beginning until now is dispensed with foreknowledge) as some excellent medicine for weakened eyes, and keep its recollection with you at all times. Ponder, consider, and be taught by these things, that you may learn to hold the remembrance of the greatness of God's honour in your soul, and thus find life eternal for your soul in Jesus Christ our Lord, Who is become "the Mediator between God and men,"[29] as being the Uniter in His two natures. The orders of the angels cannot approach the glory that surrounds the throne of His majesty, yet He has appeared in the world for our sake in a mean and humble form, as [Isaiah] said: "We beheld Him, that He had no form nor beauty." It is He that, being invisible to all created nature, put on a body and fulfilled the economy for the salvation and life of all the nations that were cleansed by Him, and to Him be glory and dominion unto the ages of ages. Amen. ASCETICAL HOMILIES 3.[30]

53:3 He Was Despised

HIS DEFORMITY REGAINS OUR ORIGINAL FORM. AUGUSTINE: Christ's deformity is what gives form to you. If he had been unwilling to be deformed, you would never have got back the form you lost. So he hung on the cross, deformed; but his deformity was our beauty. SERMON 27.6.[31]

HE SUFFERED AS WE DO. CYRIL OF ALEXANDRIA: One of the holy Evangelists[32] said that when our Lord's time of suffering drew near, he began to weep and grew sad. Yet by nature he was the only-begotten Word of the Father, being immune from sufferings and grief and the like. Nevertheless, he accommodated himself to our nature and showed himself empty of all [his divine qualities] in the face of the anxiety of the threatening onslaught of his trials. Through all these trials he declared himself to be similar to us, so that he emerges not (as some are fond of saying) as a shadow or specter seen on the earth but as a real human being. COMMENTARY ON ISAIAH 5.1.53.3.[33]

HE IS DISHONORED SO THAT WE ARE HONORED. ATHANASIUS: Nor is even his death passed over in silence: on the contrary, it is referred to in the divine Scriptures, even exceedingly clearly.... He suffers it not for his own sake but for the immortality and salvation of all, and the counsels of the Jews against him and the indignities offered him at their hands.... O marvel at the loving-kindness of the Word, that for our sakes he is dishonored, that we may be brought to honor. ON THE INCARNATION 34.1-2.[34]

---

[25]Mt 2:13-15. [26]Ps 45:2 (44:3 LXX). [27]Mt 17:2. [28]NPNF 2 7:308*. [29]1 Tim 2:5. [30]AHSIS 28. [31]WSA 3 2:107. [32]Mt 26:37. [33]PG 70:1172. [34]NPNF 2 4:54**

53:4-6 INIQUITY TAKEN AWAY FOR STRAY SHEEP

*⁴Surely he has borne our griefs*ˣ
  *and carried our sorrows;*ʸ
yet we esteemed him stricken,
  smitten by God, and afflicted.
⁵But he was wounded for our transgressions,
  he was bruised for our iniquities;
upon him was the chastisement that made us

  whole,
  and with his stripes we are healed.
⁶All we like sheep have gone astray;
  we have turned every one to his own way;
and the LORD has laid on him
  the iniquity of us all.

x Or *sicknesses*   y Or *pains*

OVERVIEW: Isaiah anticipates the full humanity of the Messiah (GREGORY THAUMATURGUS). His glory was first hidden, then revealed, to us (EUSEBIUS). He was not in himself ugly but made to look that way by human sin (JEROME). His inglorious state suited his condescension to the wretched (CYRIL). He shared fully in our human sorrows (TERTULLIAN). He bore our sins, which ultimately means he bore them away. The church leader must also bear the sins of his people (APOSTOLIC CONSTITUTIONS). In becoming sin for us, the point is not that the Lord was transmuted into flesh but that by assuming our flesh he bore our sins away (GREGORY OF NAZIANZUS). By doing this, the Son embodies conformity of the human will to the Father's on our behalf (AUGUSTINE). He saved the wandering sheep by himself becoming a sheep. He had to assume human embodiment in order to heal the human body (THEODORET). Christ's death was no accident but one he chose (PSEUDO-GREGORY THE GREAT). He did not just patch up infirmities but removed them (ATHANASIUS). The human condition when he assumed it was well beyond death (EUSEBIUS). Christ acted as if he were our debtor and received sin and dealt with it (THEODORE). Christ is the teacher who sees our sins and corrects them (CLEMENT OF ALEXANDRIA).

53:4 He Bore Our Griefs

A HUMANITY AS HUMAN AS OURS. GREGORY THAUMATURGUS: Therefore, when it is said that he was "troubled in spirit,"[1] that "he was sorrowful in soul,"[2] that "he was wounded in body," he places before us designations of susceptibilities proper to our constitution, in order to show that he was made man in the world and had his conversation with [people], yet without sin. TWELVE TOPICS ON THE FAITH 12.[3]

CHRIST'S ANONYMITY AND HIDDEN GLORY. EUSEBIUS OF CAESAREA: We did not reckon him to be much or wonder who he was then. He was, however, the Savior of our souls, the healer and purifier of all sin. Therefore it continues, "He bore our sins . . . though we reckoned him struck down by God and humiliated," as Aquila has it. . . . We like babes had this opinion of him while he suffered these things for us, so as to save us from all disgrace . . . he was wounded and became a curse for us . . . he became a peace offering . . . who was through all his life a sin offering in word and deed. COMMENTARY ON ISAIAH 2.42.[4]

GOD STOOPED LOW TO RISE ALL THE HIGHER. JEROME: Let him be understood now not as the Word of God and wisdom but as servant and boy. . . . And here there will be the

---

[1]Jn 11:33; 12:27; 13:21. [2]Mt 26:38. [3]ANF 6:52. [4]GCS 57(9):335-36.

greater miracle that his appearance will be inglorious among people, not in that it means a foul-
ness of form but that he came in lowliness and
poverty.... "He will wash many nations," cleansing them with his blood and consecrating for service in the baptism of God....

He did not have beauty or glory. His form was
base and lacking before [humanity], or as the
Hebrew has it, despised and least among people.
... How then can it be said in the psalms, "Gird
your side with your sword, O most powerful, with
your beauty and fairness"?[5] This puzzle can be easily solved. He was despised and base when he hung
on the cross and was made for us a curse and carried out sins and said to the Father, "God, my
God, why have you forsaken me?" But he was glorious *and* fair in appearance when, at his passion,
the earth trembled, rocks were split and the elements were terrified at the sun's fleeing and the
eternal night. COMMENTARY ON ISAIAH 14.21-22.[6]

GOD HAS NO NEED OF HUMAN GLORY. CYRIL
OF ALEXANDRIA: What therefore does the prophet
say in these words? ... For he confesses what we
also have announced,[7] that is, we have foretold
unceasingly that he will come in due season. But
perhaps someone shall say in response, "What
then if God who is the Word should come down
from heaven, covered in divine glory and resplendent in unapproachable light, and appear to those
on earth as one who cannot be looked at because of
his ineffable glory?" Indeed, when he visited the
earth in the form of fire on Mount Sinai it was
dark and gloomy, and storms and fire burst from
on high along with smoke, and there were many
other things that so completely terrified [the Isra-
elites] that his appearance was unbearable to those
who saw it. In fact, it was so unbearable that the
Israelites called for a mediator, saying to Moses,
"Speak to us, and do not let God speak lest we
die."[8] So, as Isaiah says, it is no wonder that the
one who shall appear should be hard to look at.
Why then do the prophets say that unbelief is
without excuse and rebellion is unjustifiable when
there is no form or glory to his appearance? For he

was not, it says, in a form or glory that befits the
divine. For he emptied himself, taking on the likeness of humanity, and being found in the appearance of a man he humbled himself.[9] And we say
this not merely from hearing the reports, but we
have gazed with our own eyes on the one proclaimed. For human things are in every way small,
cheap and worthless compared with the divine,
supreme, eminent and illustrious beauty of that
nature that is above all things. For it is said in the
Psalms, "You are the most beautiful among the
sons of men."[10] And our text here adds, "more
rejected than all people," speaking of his appearance, as if to say that there are to be seen among
people of distinction some which are distinguished
by their fine radiant appearance ... but Emmanuel
was not among them, reduced instead to someone
who was despised and lowly. This message is true,
for he did not come from the holy virgin mother in
opulence, but through all that is lowly and humble
so as to raise up the humble and to bless those who
seem worthless. And anyway, what need does God,
who is Lord and king of the universe, have of
human splendor? COMMENTARY ON ISAIAH
5.1.53.2.[11]

**NO DOUBTING THAT CHRIST HAD A HUMAN
SOUL.** GREGORY THAUMATURGUS: How could
one say that the body of the Lord [Christ] is void
of soul and understanding? For perturbation and
grief and distress are not the properties either of
a flesh void of a soul or of a soul void of understanding; nor are they the sign of the nature of
immutable divinity or the index of a mere phan-
tasm; nor do they mark the defect of human
moral weakness. But the Word exhibited in himself the exercise of the affections and susceptibilities proper to us, having endued himself with our
passibility, even as it is written, that "he has
borne our griefs and carried our sorrows." For

[5]Ps 45:3 (44:4 LXX). [6]*AGLB* 35:1512-13, 1516. [7]The *we* here refers to
the LXX rendering of v. 2, which reads in part, "We brought a report as of
a child before him," as well as carrying on the first person plural of
v. 1. [8]Ex 20:19 LXX. [9]Phil 2:7. [10]Ps 45:2 (44:3 LXX). [11]PG 70:1169-72.

perturbation and grief and distress are disorders of soul; and toil, and sleep and the body's liability to wounding are infirmities of the flesh. TWELVE TOPICS ON THE FAITH 11.[12]

HE BORE AWAY OUR SINS. TERTULLIAN: Now the Greeks are accustomed to use for "carry" a word that also signifies "to take away." . . . Whatever were the cures that Jesus effected, he is mine. AGAINST MARCION 4.8.[13]

THE DIVINE BECAME HIDDEN. THEODORET OF CYR: And next he teaches the forms of dishonor and shame, "A man being in sorrow." He points out the nature that received the suffering, for his body was nailed to the cross, but his divinity made the passion its own. "And he was familiar with sickness." This was said about his humanity. For to be courageous and philosophical touches not divine but human nature. "For his face was turned away. It was not valued or appreciated." The three translators render it this way, "And like a hiding of the face from him, he was made nothing and not appreciated." That is, he hid the divine energy and chose suffering and did not seek vengeance on others. For as he was on the cross he said, "Father, forgive them, for they do not know what they are doing." This teaches us the reasons for the passion: "He bore our sicknesses and suffered for us." Symmachus translated, "Indeed, he personally has taken on our sicknesses and endured our pains." We deserved death for those sins we had committed, and having received this penalty, he received death on our behalf. COMMENTARY ON ISAIAH 17.53.3-4.[14]

THE CROSS-BEARING LIFE OF THE SPIRITUAL LEADER. APOSTOLIC CONSTITUTIONS: [To bishops.] For as yours is the burden, so you receive as your fruit the supply of food and other necessities. For you imitate Christ the Lord; and as he "bore the sins of us all on the tree" at his crucifixion, the innocent for those who deserved punishment, so also you ought to bear the sins of the people your own. For concerning our Savior it is

said in Isaiah, "He bears our sins and is afflicted for us." . . . For do not you imagine that the office of a bishop is an easy or light burden. CONSTITUTIONS OF THE HOLY APOSTLES 2.4.25.[15]

THE WORD WAS MADE A CURSE FOR US. GREGORY OF NAZIANZUS: "He was made flesh" seems to be equivalent to that in which it is said that he was made sin or a curse for us, not that the Lord was transmuted into either of these— for how could he? But because by taking them on him he "took away our iniquities and bore our infirmities." LETTER 51(101).[16]

THE SON EMBODIES OBEDIENCE TO THE FATHER. AUGUSTINE: "But not what I will, but what you will, Father,"[17] It is not as if the Father's will was one thing and the Son's another. [Christ is referring to] the utterance of our weaknesses, however faithful, which our Head transformed into himself, when also he bore our sins. TRACTATES ON THE GOSPEL OF JOHN 111.4.[18]

53:5 Wounded for Our Transgressions

CHRIST CHOSE TO DIE. GREGORY THE GREAT: No one usually brings hardship on himself. For example, the prophet insinuates the severity of [Christ's] hardship when he says, "Surely he has borne our griefs and carried our sorrows." For dying does not [necessarily] entail suffering what a condemned nature is capable of suffering. Therefore, the severity of the hardship he brought on himself comes to the fore in that he did not have by nature[19] a body that could suffer; and yet, so that he might free us by his suffering, he humbly assumed the very thing that would allow him to suffer. SIX BOOKS ON I KINGS 4.80.[20]

HE CARRIED OUR SORROWS. ATHANASIUS: It did not say, "He remedied our infirmities," lest, as

---

[12]ANF 6:52. [13]ANF 3:354. [14]SC 315:148-50. [15]ANF 7:409*. [16]NPNF 2 7:442. [17]Mt 26:39. [18]FC 90:300*. [19]Lit. "in himself." [20]CCL 144:335.

being external to the body and only healing it, as he has always done, he should leave people subject still to death. Rather, he carries our infirmities, and he himself bears our sins, that it might be shown that he has become human for us, and that the body that in him bore them was his own body. DISCOURSE AGAINST THE ARIANS 3.31.[21]

OUR STATE WAS FULLY ROTTING. EUSEBIUS OF CAESAREA: Alone did he assume the penalties of our wicked deeds, not when we were half dead but even when already altogether foul and stinking in tombs and graves. ECCLESIASTICAL HISTORY 10.4.[22]

53:6 The Inquity of Us All

THE INIQUITY OF US ALL. THEODORE OF HERACLEA: He bore the sum of human evils and every form of transgression, as well as their recompense and punishment. And as if he were our debtor, the only-begotten Word of God, coming into the world alongside us, fulfilled every law and all righteousness and did not stumble over sin but received it willingly so as to change our punishment into peace and harmony. For undergoing temptation he carried our rebukes and punishments, and by faith we make our own his suffer-

ings, and dying together with him we are saved by grace. He was not delivered by force but as an act of obedience. FRAGMENTS ON ISAIAH.[23]

WE ALL HAD ABANDONED GOD. THEODORET OF CYR: The offenses of all were not equal, and there was not only one way of being impious; for the idols of the Egyptians and those of the Phoenicians were not the same, those of the Greeks were different, and those of the Scythians were something else. Nevertheless, although the forms of error were different, we had all in a common manner abandoned the true God, and by this we resembled sheep who have gone astray and are exposed to the wolves. COMMENTARY ON ISAIAH 17.53.6.[24]

THE PEDAGOGY OF CHRIST. CLEMENT OF ALEXANDRIA: Isaiah says [about Christ], "The Lord has laid on him the iniquity of us all," that is, to correct our iniquities and set them right. For that reason, he alone is able to forgive our sins, he who has been appointed by the Father of all as our educator, for he alone is able to separate obedience from disobedience. CHRIST THE EDUCATOR 1.8.67-68.[25]

---

[21]NPNF 2 4:411. [22]FC 29:247. [23]PG 18:1356. [24]ITA 788; SC 315:152. [25]FC 23:61.

53:7-9 THE OPPRESSION OF THE SERVANT

[7]He was oppressed, and he was afflicted,
    yet he opened not his mouth;
like a lamb that is led to the slaughter,
    and like a sheep that before its shearers is
        dumb,
    so he opened not his mouth.
[8]By oppression and judgment he was taken
        away;

    and as for his generation,* who considered
that he was cut off out of the land of the
        living,
    stricken for the transgression of my people?
[9]And they made his grave with the wicked
    and with a rich man in his death,
although he had done no violence,
    and there was no deceit in his mouth.

* LXX, Vg Who shall declare his generation?

OVERVIEW: Christ is compared with a lamb in his meekness and innocence (AMBROSE). As a lamb he is silent, yet as the Word he is proclaimed (GREGORY OF NAZIANZUS). He became a silent lamb to save other lambs (THEODORET). Even though he was God, he still endured human insult with the silence of humility (CYRIL). He needed to keep silent so that judgment would fall on him rather than on us, but he will not always be silent (AUGUSTINE). Anger would have been justified, but in his mercy he accepted the injury intended for us (CAESARIUS). Christ suffered in the flesh to slay its sinfulness (MELITO).

There is mystery in his eternal begetting and his human birth (AUGUSTINE). Both the eternal and the temporal generations are beyond words (LEO). For what happens in God is beyond humankind (ALEXANDER), and the virgin birth is of a most inconceivable manner (ATHANASIUS). The eternal generation of the Son can be understood only with the premise that the Father is eternal and the Son is eternal in terms of divine substance, as distinguished from actual birth in God (MARIUS). His human generation was mysterious enough, so how much more so would his divine generation have been (AUGUSTINE)?

Christ was able to be both shepherd and sheep (CYRIL OF JERUSALEM). His removal of the curse by taking it to himself is God's new justice (CHRYSOSTOM). Christ alone offers a righteousness that never goes out of tune (HIPPOLYTUS). The devil's wickedness, in contrast, was revealed in arranging the murder of the only innocent person in human history (THEODORE).

53:7 Like a Lamb

BEHOLD, THE LAMB OF GOD. AMBROSE: It is the price of our freedom, as Peter says, "You were redeemed with the precious blood,"[1] not of a lamb but of him who came in meekness and humility like a lamb and freed the whole world with the single offering of his body, as he himself said, "I was led like a lamb to be sacrificed," and John also said, "Behold, the lamb of God, behold the one who takes away the sins of the world."[2] LETTER 69.[3]

THE SHEPHERD OF ISRAEL LED AS A SHEEP TO THE SLAUGHTER. GREGORY OF NAZIANZUS: He prays, but he hears prayer. He weeps, but he causes tears to cease. He asks where Lazarus was laid, for he was man; but he raises Lazarus, for he was God.[4] He is sold, and very cheap, for it is only for thirty pieces of silver,[5] but he redeems the world, and that at a great price, for the price was his own blood.[6] As a sheep he is led to the slaughter, but he is the shepherd of Israel, and now of the whole world also. As a lamb he is silent, yet he is the Word and is proclaimed by the voice of one crying in the wilderness.[7] He is bruised and wounded, but he heals every disease and every infirmity. He is lifted up and nailed to the tree, but by the tree of life he restores us, yes, he saves even the robber crucified with him.[8] . . . He dies, but he gives life, and by his death, he destroys death. He is buried, but he rises again; he goes down into hell, but he brings up the souls; he ascends to heaven and shall come again to judge the living and the dead. ON THE SON, THEOLOGICAL ORATION 3(29).20.[9]

LIKE A SHEEP BEFORE ITS SHEARERS. THEODORET OF CYR: It was fitting for him to heal like by like and to recall the other wandering sheep by becoming a sheep himself. He became a sheep, without being changed into one, or without being altered or without quitting his own essence. . . . For, according to Isaiah, he was sheared as well as slaughtered. For he endured death in his humanity. But as God he remained alive and impassible and gave the fleece of his body to the shearers. ON DIVINE PROVIDENCE 10.29-30.[10]

SILENT WHEN FACED WITH HUMAN INSULT. CYRIL OF ALEXANDRIA: For the spiritually dead and unholy Caiaphas asked him, "I put you under

---

[1] 1 Pet 1:19. [2] Jn 1:29. [3] FC 26:412. [4] Jn 11:43. [5] Mt 26:15. [6] 1 Pet 1:19. [7] Jn 1:23. [8] Lk 23:43. [9] NPNF 2 7:309*. [10] ACW 49:144*.

oath to the living God to tell us if you are the Chist, the Son of God." And he answered him right away, saying, "From now on you will see the Son of man seated at the right hand of power and coming on the clouds of heaven."[11] And then Pilate asked him whether he was king of Israel, and Christ replied, "You say so."[12] Pilate was complacent with the madness of the Jews and had Jesus beaten, and he ordered his soldiers to put him between two thieves in his suffering of death on the cross. So what the prophet said was true: "Because of his affliction he did not open his mouth." But he suffered a myriad of afflictions from the time of his arrest onwards, suffered insolence and spitting and the beatings of mindless underlings and other things beside these that could be wickedly arranged, before he was brought to Pilate. COMMENTARY ON ISAIAH 5.1.53.7-8.[13]

SILENCE AS THE WAY TO ACCEPT THE JUDGMENT. AUGUSTINE: [Christ] kept silent while he was concealed, because "in humility his judgment was taken away."[14] He kept silent while he was concealed, because he was thought to be only human. But as God he will come openly; and as our God, he will not keep silent. So what about you? You were saying, "I want him to come." SERMON 299.4.[15]

SILENT ON THE CROSS, GOD WILL NOT REMAIN SILENT. AUGUSTINE: Because he has come hidden, our God, that is, Christ, will come manifest. "And he will not keep silence."[16] What does it mean, "will not keep silence"? Because he had first kept silence. When did he keep silence? He was judged in order that there might be fulfilled that which the prophet had also predicted: "As a sheep he was led to the slaughter, and as a lamb before his shearer, without voice, so he opened not his mouth." Therefore, if he were unwilling to suffer, he would not suffer. If he did not suffer, his blood would not be poured forth. If his blood would not be poured forth, the world would not be redeemed. TRACTATES ON THE GOSPEL OF JOHN 37.10.1.[17]

MERCY ACCEPTED THE INJURY. CAESARIUS OF ARLES: Though he was guilty of not even a slight sin, for no serpent could make a mark on this rock, he was condemned. He suffered with patience the insults, blows, crown of thorns, scarlet robe, and the other mockeries enumerated in the Gospel. Although guiltless, he endured it in order that filled with patience he might come to the cross "as a sheep for sacrifice." Although he could have returned the injury to his adversaries, he bore it all with kindness. SERMON 11.4.[18]

CHRIST IS THE ONE. MELITO OF SARDIS: This is the one who comes from heaven onto the earth for the suffering one, and wraps himself in the suffering one through a virgin womb, and comes as a man.

He accepted the suffering of the suffering one,
through suffering in a body that could suffer,
and set free the flesh from suffering.
Through the spirit that cannot die
he slew the manslayer death.
He is the one led like a lamb
and slaughtered like a sheep;
he ransomed us from the worship of the world
as from the land of Egypt,
and he set us free from slavery of the devil
as from the hands of Pharaoh,
and sealed our souls with his own spirit,
and the members of our body with his blood.
This is the one who clad death in shame
and, as Moses did to Pharaoh,
made the devil grieve.
This is the one who struck down lawlessness
and made injustice childless,
as Moses did to Egypt.
This is the one who delivered us
from slavery to freedom,
from darkness into light,
from death into life,
from tyranny into eternal kingdom,
and made us a new priesthood,
and a people everlasting for himself.

---

[11]Mt 26:63-64. [12]Mt 27:11. [13]PG 70:1177. [14]Is 53:7-8. [15]WSA 3 8:232*. [16]Ps 50:3 (49:3 LXX). [17]FC 88:104. [18]FC 31:65.

This is the Pascha of our salvation:
this is the one who in many people endured
    many things.
This is the one who was murdered in Abel,
tied up in Isaac,
exiled in Jacob,
sold in Joseph,
exposed in Moses,
slaughtered in the lamb,
hunted in David,
dishonored in the prophets.
This is the one made flesh in a virgin,
who was hanged on a tree,
who was buried in the earth,
who was raised from the dead,
who was exalted to the heights of heaven.
This is the lamb slain,
this is the speechless lamb,
this is the one born of Mary the fair ewe,
this is the one taken from the flock,
and led to slaughter.
Who was sacrificed in the evening,
and buried at night;
who was not broken on the tree,
who was not undone in the earth,
who rose from the dead and resurrected
    humankind from the grave below.
ON PASCHA 66-71.[19]

53:8 His Generation

HIS ETERNAL AND EARTHLY BEGETTING ARE A MYSTERY. AUGUSTINE: The Son of God, who is also the Son of man, our Lord Jesus Christ, born of the Father without mother, created every single day; born of his mother without father, he consecrated this particular day [Christmas Day]; invisible in his divine birth, visible in his human one, in each of them wonderful. Thus it is difficult to judge about which of the two the prophet is more likely to have prophesied, "Who shall tell the tale of his begetting?"—whether of that one in which, never not born, he has the Father co-eternal with himself; or of this one in which, born at a particular time, he had already made the mother of whom he would be made; whether of that one where he was always born, since he always was. Who, after all, will tell the tale of how light was born from light, and they were both one light; how God was born from God, and the number of gods did not increase? SERMON 195.1.[20]

BEYOND HUMAN TELLING. LEO THE GREAT: The birth of our Lord and Savior, whether that of his divinity from the Father or that of his flesh from his mother, surpasses the power of human eloquence. As a result, the saying ("Who will recount his generation?") may rightly be referred to either. SERMON 30.1.[21]

THE MYSTERY OF THE SON'S ETERNAL GENERATION. ALEXANDER OF ALEXANDRIA: "Who shall declare his generation?" His subsistence no nature that is begotten can investigate, even as the Father can be investigated by none. For the nature of rational beings cannot receive the knowledge of his divine generation by the Father. EPISTLES ON THE ARIAN HERESY 1.12.[22]

THE MYSTERY OF HIS EARTHLY GENERATION. ATHANASIUS: For he it is who proceeded from a virgin and appeared as man on the earth and whose generation after the flesh cannot be declared. For there is none who can tell his father after the flesh, his body not being of a man but of a virgin alone. Thus, no one can declare the corporeal generation of the Savior from a man in the same way as one can draw up a genealogy of David and Moses and of all the patriarchs. ON THE INCARNATION 37.[23]

A MIRACLE TO OUR REASONING. MARIUS VICTORINUS: Those who do not understand the manner of begetting may mislead you when they say, "Who can speak of the birth of the Lord?" First, "who" or still more "no one" does indeed seem to signify men. Only the Holy Spirit can grasp or

[19]MOP 54-56. [20]WSA 3 6:57. [21]FC 93:125. [22]ANF 6:295. [23]LCC 3:91.

explain this manner of begetting. That is why we ourselves with the permission of God the Father and of Jesus Christ our Lord have set it forth. Certainly it is not a hopeless enterprise, but we have described it as by a miracle. Next, supposing that the manner of begetting is unknown, we speak of substance when we say that the Father and Son are of the same essence (*homoousios*). ON THE NECESSITY OF ACCEPTING *HOMOOUSION* 4.[24]

BOTH GENERATIONS ARE INEFFABLE. AUGUSTINE: If you think this to be referred to the human generation by which he was born of a virgin, look into yourself and ask your soul whether the prophet would dare to declare the divine generation if words failed him for the human one. LETTER 242.[25]

WHO SHALL DECLARE HIS GENERATION? AUGUSTINE: To sum up, Christ was born both of a Father and of a mother; both without a father and without a mother; of a Father as God, of a mother as man; without a mother as God, without a Father as man.... "Who will recount his begetting," whether that one without time or this one without seed; that one without beginning or this one without precedent; that one which never was not, or this one which never was before or after that one which has no end, or this one which has its beginning in its end? SERMON 184.3.[26]

CHRIST IS BOTH SHEPHERD AND SHEEP. CYRIL OF JERUSALEM: This sheep is equally called shepherd and says "I am the good Shepherd."[27] By his manhood he is sheep; by his divine lovingkindness he is shepherd. CATECHETICAL LECTURES 10.3.[28]

53:9 He Had Done No Violence

GOD'S NEW JUSTICE. CHRYSOSTOM: In reality, the people were subject to another curse, which says, "Cursed is everyone who does not continue in all that is written in the book of the law."[29] To this curse, I say, people were subject, for no person had continued in or was a keeper of the whole law. But Christ exchanged this curse for the other, "Cursed is every one that hangs on a tree."[30] ... It was necessary for him who is about to relieve us from a curse to be himself free of it. But he received another instead of ours. Therefore Christ took on himself just such curse and thereby relieved us from the curse. It was like an innocent person deciding to die for another sentenced to death, and so rescuing him from punishment. For Christ took on him not the curse of transgression but the other curse, in order to remove that of others. For "he had done no violence, neither was any deceit in his mouth." COMMENTARY ON GALATIANS 3.[31]

HE DID NO VIOLENCE. CHRYSOSTOM: Then to show that the court was corrupt and the sentence unjust, he went on to say, "In his humiliation his legal trial was taken away," that is, no one judged justly in his case. DEMONSTRATION AGAINST THE PAGANS 4.7.[32]

NO DECEIT WAS IN HIS MOUTH. CHRYSOSTOM: And is not one ashamed to say that God is not crafty or deceitful? Concerning him, however, in respect of the flesh, it might be reasonable [to say it]. ON THE EPISTLE TO THE HEBREWS 13.7.[33]

HE MADE MUSIC OUT OF SILENCE. HIPPOLYTUS: David alone of the prophets prophesied with an instrument, called by the Greeks the "psaltery." ... But this psaltery has the source of its musical numbers above, in order that we, too, may practice seeking things above and not suffer ourselves to be borne down by the pleasure of melody to the passions of the flesh. And I think that this truth, too, was signified deeply and clearly to us in a prophetic way in the construction of the instrument, namely, that those who have souls well ordered and trained have the way ready to things above. And again, an instrument

---

[24]FC 69:309-10*. [25]FC 32:217. [26]*WSA* 3 6:18-19. [27]Jn 10:11. [28]LCC 4:132. [29]Deut 27:26. [30]Gal 3:13. [31]NPNF 1 13:27. [32]FC 73:205. [33]NPNF 1 14:430; 13.3 in Gk text.

having the source of its melodious sound in its upper parts may be taken as like the body of Christ and his saints—the only instrument that maintains rectitude; "for he did no sin, neither was guile found in his mouth."[34] This is indeed an instrument, harmonious, melodious, well-ordered, that took in no human discord and did nothing out of measure but maintained in all things, as it were, harmony toward the Father; for, as he says, "he that is of the earth is earthly and speaks of the earth; he that comes from heaven testifies of what he has seen and heard."[35] FRAGMENTS ON THE PSALMS 1.6.[36]

THE DEVIL'S WICKEDNESS AND THE SON'S INNOCENCE. THEODORE OF HERACLEA: If you wish to look at the mind behind his appearance, you will find it to be an ocean of compassion for humanity residing there. For he saved them, the most foul people who gloried in their wealth and those condemned to death from their deeds, as they trusted and received the death of the Savior which was a ransom for them, offering them, in place of the tomb and death, eternal life and incorruptible everlasting life.

This verse shows the unrighteous rage of the devil when he unleashed himself on our Savior. For although there was no sin found in his being according to the flesh, but that flesh remained

sinless, the devil as if [Christ] were a sinner killed him and in so doing manifested the totality of his wickedness. But for this very reason came salvation for those who had fallen into sin.

Receiving the sufferings due to us, [Christ] made them his own and so from a standpoint of faith it is said that he became a curse for us himself. And it is said that they make gifts not with sacrifices but with feeling and repentance, and thus they receive a spiritual healing as they trade not only their present life.

Once the only Son of God made our salvation his own prize when he took a body and endured sufferings on our behalf. And his Father rightly said that he took away [Christ's] pain as our healing and purifying, that our illumination was shown to be his light just as we grow into the knowledge of God and understanding with our behavior changed for the better and converted in the intelligence of God. Since the only-begotten Son of God acted in every way according to the paternal command and filled every thought with obedience, it was characteristic of him that the Savior should wrap a towel around himself and fill the basin with water and be of service in every way.[37] FRAGMENTS ON ISAIAH.[38]

---

[34]Is 53:9. [35]Jn 3:31. [36]ANF 5:200-201*. [37]Jn 13:1-20. [38]PG 18:1357-60.

53:10-12 THE VINDICATION OF THE SERVANT

[10]Yet it was the will of the LORD to bruise him;
    he has put him to grief;[z]
when he makes himself[a] an offering for sin,
    he shall see his offspring, he shall prolong his days;

the will of the LORD shall prosper in his hand;
    [11]he shall see the fruit of the travail of his soul and be satisfied;
by his knowledge shall the righteous one, my servant,

> make many to be accounted righteous;
>   and he shall bear their iniquities.
> [12]Therefore I will divide him a portion with
>   the great,*
>   and he shall divide the spoil with the strong;
>
> because he poured out his soul to death,
>   and was numbered with the transgressors;
> yet he bore the sin of many,
>   and made intercession for the transgressors.

z Heb *made him sick*   a Vg: Heb *thou makest his soul*   * Syriac (Peshitta) *among the many*

OVERVIEW: When the Servant's suffering finally ceased, the condemnation for our sins vanished (PROCOPIUS). But sin still remains in us, and so repentance and piety are also important if the Christian is to benefit from Christ's death (THEODORET) and see the fruit of the seed of faith sprout at the resurrection (CYRIL). Christ demonstrated a servant heart for us on the cross, so why can't we serve others? (APOSTOLIC CONSTITUTIONS). But first we must experience the burial of our heart of sin. There can be no burial without death and no removal without resurrection (TERTULLIAN).

Having been tested, Christ is given full authority in the vindication of the resurrection. He aims to take people today out of the devil's power and booty (CHRYSOSTOM). "I will divide him" thus anticipates the Eucharist as the division of Christ for the strengthening of the Christian mission in the face of the devil's opposition (EPHREM). Believers are the spoil of God's victory over the devil (THEODORE). Christ has taken the cloak of our sin and removed it forever (PROCOPIUS), having paid for crimes against God committed by all humanity (AUGUSTINE). He inspires us to become law-abiding (GREGORY OF NAZIANZUS). In his death he divides the penitent and the impenitent transgressor (CYRIL OF JERUSALEM).

53:10 Seeing Offspring and Prolonging His Days

YOUR SOUL SHALL SEE A LONG-LIVED SEED.
PROCOPIUS OF GAZA: "His soul will see his offspring grow." On the day after his suffering, the spiritual conception of that indescribable, indwell-

ing birth came. The divine power was vindicated in accordance with the promises to Abraham in the undoing of death-bearing sin and the access to redemption. And where the [LXX] text has "And the Lord wills to alleviate his soul from its suffering," Symmachus renders, "And the will of the Lord prospered in his hand." And this fits the Savior well. He gave light to himself so that others would be illuminated through his being just, but he also gave understanding. For the spirit of wisdom and understanding was resting on him to give others understanding and "to justify those worthy of being justified."[1] Others interpret in this way: the Lord wills to turn the sorrow on the cross to gladness through revealing himself to those who had once been deceived in darkness who were now being transformed into light. For as Paul said, "We who were once darkness are now light in the Lord"[2] and "recreated in understanding,"[3] as though being changed from glory into glory. . . .

God is said to have made one new humanity from two peoples, that is, to have made a transformation. For the Only Begotten considered our salvation to be his own reward. By taking a body, he thus suffered on our behalf. And so, it was necessary for the Father to make the "alleviation of suffering"—which is said about Christ—our healing and to make his light our illumination, exchanging what we had for something better as we were recreated in the understanding of God. For Christ did not come to be served but, as he

---

[1]See Gal 3:8. [2]Eph 5:8. [3]Reading, in v. 11a: *plasai tei synesei*, literally "to form in understanding." Such a translation requires an object, and Procopius finds it in the people whom God transforms as the reward of and the effect of the alleviation of the Savior's suffering.

ᐟ

said himself, to serve the working out of the plan[4] of our salvation in his incarnation. COMMENTARY ON ISAIAH 53.12.[5]

REPENTANCE AND SALVATION. THEODORET OF CYR: Having thus proclaimed in advance the iniquity of the people, he addresses to them an exhortation to repent—for he saw in advance those among them who, after these events, would have the faith. Of this number was the divine Paul; of this number were the three thousand men and the many thousands[6]—and he says, "If you can give an offering for sin, your soul shall see a long-lived offspring." If you acknowledge your impiety, and if you request salvation, you will obtain life eternal; for this is what he has called "long-lived." COMMENTARY ON ISAIAH 17.53.10.[7]

53:11 My Servant Shall See Fruit of His Suffering

THE FRUITFUL SEED THAT LEADS TO RESUR-RECTION. CYRIL OF ALEXANDRIA: He has bought us with his own blood. He endured the cross, despising its shame, so that he might win our salvation. Therefore bow your necks to his yoke. For your soul will see the fruitful seed, that is, you will be sharers in those being kept for eternal life, that is, the saints who have been enriched with the hope of eternal life. For there was no idea of the resurrection of the dead among the Greeks, and the mystery until now was not set forth. They all but said that the breath in your nostrils is smoke that is burning. All the ashes will disappear, and the spirit like a weak person will be dissolved. COMMENTARY ON ISAIAH 5.1.53.11.[8]

HE DID THIS SERVICE FOR US. APOSTOLIC CONSTITUTIONS: If the Lord of heaven and earth underwent all his sufferings for us, how then do you make a difficulty to minister to such as are in want, who ought to imitate him who underwent servitude, and want, and stripes and the cross for us? We ought therefore also to serve the brethren, in imitation of Christ. For says he,

"He who will be great among you, let him be your minister; and he who will be first among you, let him be your servant."[9] For so did he really, and not in word only, fulfill the prediction of "serving many faithfully." CONSTITUTIONS OF THE HOLY APOSTLES 3.19.[10]

NO REMOVAL WITHOUT RESURRECTION. TER-TULLIAN: However, I will show [Marcion] the death and burial and resurrection of Christ all indicated in a single sentence of Isaiah, who says, "His sepulchre was removed from the midst of them." Now there could have been no sepulchre without death and no removal of sepulchre except by resurrection. . . . "He shall divide the spoil of many, because he poured out his soul to death." For here is set forth the cause of this favor to him, even that it was to recompense him for his death. AGAINST MARCION 3.19.[11]

THE POWER AND THE AUTHORITY OF THE RESURRECTION. CHRYSOSTOM: [David] predicted that Christ would rise again. "You will not leave my soul in hell, nor will you allow your holy one to see corruption."[12] Isaiah expressed the same thing in a different way. For he said, "The Lord wishes to cleanse him from his wounds, to show him light, to justify the righteous one who served many well."

Isaiah established that the slaying of Christ was a ransom for humanity's sins when he said, "He has borne the sins of many." And he will free humankind from demons, for as Isaiah said, "He will divide the spoils of the strong." And the same prophet spoke out clearly that Christ did this through his death when he said, "Because his soul was delivered up to death." That Christ would be put in charge over the whole world he revealed by these words of his, "He shall inherit many." DEMONSTRATION AGAINST THE PAGANS 4.12-13.[13]

---

[4]Lit., "economy" (oikonomia). See Mt 20:28. [5]PG 87:2529. [6]See Acts 2:41; 21:20. [7]ITA 792; SC 315:158. [8]PG 70:1185. [9]Mt 20:26. [10]ANF 7:432*. [11]ANF 3:338**. [12]Ps 16:10 (15:10 LXX). [13]FC

53:12 *Dividing the Spoils*

HE SHALL DIVIDE THE SPOILS OF THE STRONG. CHRYSOSTOM: Hear, at least, what God says to the Jews, "As my child Isaiah walked, naked and barefoot, so shall the children of Israel walk into captivity naked and barefoot."[14] He wishes, therefore, to remind you by your appearance that the devil held sway over you, and he brings you to the recollection of how lowly born you were before regeneration. Hence, you stand not only naked and unshod, but you even stand with upturned hands to confess God's future sovereignty to which you draw near. You are all the spoils and booty of war. Isaiah mentioned these spoils long ago, before our release from troubles, when he prophesied as follows, "He shall divide the spoils of the strong." BAPTISMAL INSTRUCTIONS 10.14.[15]

A PREDICTION OF EUCHARIST AND THE HOLY APOSTLES. EPHREM THE SYRIAN: "Therefore I will divide him a portion among the many," among the many who will eat his body and will drink his blood. "And he shall divide the spoil with the strong" . . . he calls "the strong" the holy apostles, among whom he divided the nations to be ruled, which he had taken away the power of the devil. COMMENTARY ON ISAIAH 53.12.[16]

BELIEVERS ARE THE SPOIL OF GOD'S WAR WITH THE DEVIL. THEODORE OF HERACLEA: The inheritance of the Son is all those who believe in him. They are rightly called the spoil of the devil. This occurred when the only Son in his wonderful dispensation made everyone to participate in the knowledge of the Son and the Father. They were released from error and from the tyranny of the devil, whom they previously thought to be too strong. They are rightly said to have been made an inheritance, those who became a part of him when the devil was plundered. FRAGMENTS ON ISAIAH.[17]

THE JUSTIFICATION OF THE NATIONS. PROCO-

PIUS OF GAZA: For "he is justified." Either we have been made just, or he is admitted to be just by those who attacked him and enslaved him, to reveal the full injustice of their judgment at that time. . . . "Yet he bore the sins of many." . . . For taking them to himself [Christ] then took off the cloak of our sin. And in this way "he justified many," that is, the nations. For there was previously one nation, Israel, whereas those from the nations came in many shapes, whom, making his own, he calls his inheritance, saying, "The Lord said to me, You are my Son, today I have begotten you. Ask from me, and I will give you the nations as an inheritance, and the ends of the earth will be your possession."[18] COMMENTARY ON ISAIAH 53.12.[19]

WORSHIP HIM WHO WAS HANGED FOR YOU. GREGORY OF NAZIANZUS: If you are a Simon of Cyrene, take up the cross and follow. If you are crucified with him as a robber,[20] acknowledge God as a penitent robber. If even he was numbered among the transgressors for you and your sin, do you become law-abiding for his sake. Worship him who was hanged for you, even if you yourself are hanging; make some gain even from your wickedness; purchase salvation by your death; enter with Jesus into paradise,[21] so that you may learn from what you have fallen.[22] ON HOLY EASTER, ORATION 45.24.[23]

CHRIST WAS CRUCIFIED FOR OUR CRIMES. AUGUSTINE: Three men were crucified in the same place, the Lord in the middle, because "he was reckoned among the wicked." They placed the two robbers on either side, but they were not crucified for the same reason. They were flanking Christ as he hung there, but they were far removed from him in reality. They were crucified by their crimes, he by ours. SERMON 285.2.[24]

---

[14]Cf. Is 20:3. [15]ACW 31:154. [16]SESHS 2:151. [17]PG 18:1360. [18]Ps 2:7-8. [19]PG 87:2532. [20]Lk 23:42. [21]Lk 23:43. [22]Rev 2:5. [23]NPNF 2 7:431-32. [24]WSA 3 8:95*.

ONE TRANSGRESSOR WAS SAVED. CYRIL OF JERUSALEM: Concerning the robbers who were crucified with him it is written, "And he was numbered with the transgressors." Both of them were before this transgressors, but one was so no longer. For the one was a transgressor to the end, stubborn against salvation; who, though his hands were fastened, struck with blasphemy by his tongue. When the Jews passing by wagged their head, mocking the crucified and fulfilling what was written, "When they looked on me, they shook their head,"[25] he also reviled with them. But the other rebuked the reviler; and it was to him the end of life and the beginning of restoration, the surrender of his soul a first share in salvation. CATECHETICAL LECTURES 13.30.[26]

---

[25]Ps 109:25 (108:25 LXX). [26]NPNF 2 7:90*.

54:1-3 THE EXPANSIVENESS OF THE CHURCH

¹*Sing, O barren one, who did not bear;*
break forth into singing and cry aloud,
you who have not been in travail!
For the children of the desolate one will be
more
than the children of her that is married,
says the LORD.
²*Enlarge the place of your tent,*
and let the curtains of your habitations be
stretched out;
hold not back, lengthen your cords
and strengthen your stakes.
³*For you will spread abroad to the right and*
to the left,
and your descendants will possess the
nations
and will people the desolate cities.

OVERVIEW: "Rejoice, O barren one" is addressed to the church, which was barren before being given children (PSEUDO-CLEMENT). Indeed, the number of those descendants of Israel who believed was small (JUSTIN MARTYR). But when he turned toward the nations to call them, the church no longer remained barren (ORIGEN) but was blessed with an abundance of children (CHRYSOSTOM). The abundance of God's grace is what causes the church of the nations to be fertile (THEODORET). The beginning of this new faith was the end of the mission of the Savior (JEROME). Sterility from the spiritual atmosphere of idolatrous pagan sacrilege had to be removed for spiritual fertility to return (MAXIMUS). There is no rest in the Christian life until the final repose of the saints with God (JEROME). Christian leaders serve to keep the church upright and secure so that it may flourish and grow (THEODORET).

54:1 Sing, O Barren One

FROM STERILITY TO FERTILITY. PSEUDO-CLEMENT OF ROME: By saying, "Rejoice, O barren one, who did not bear" he meant us, for our church was barren before being given children. And by saying, "Cry aloud, you who have not been in travail," he means this, to offer up our prayers in simplicity to God and not grow weary like women in labor. And by saying, "For the children of the desolate one will be more than the children of her that is married," he meant that our people seemed to be abandoned by God, but now, having believed, we have become more numerous than those who seemed to have God. 2 CLEMENT 2.1-3.[1]

THE BELIEVING DESCENDANTS OF ISRAEL WERE FEW. JUSTIN MARTYR: All the Gentiles were desolate of the true God, serving the works of [human] hands. But Jews and Samaritans, having the word from God given them through the prophets and constantly looking for Christ, did not recognize him when he came, except only for a few, whose salvation the holy prophetic Spirit predicted through Isaiah. FIRST APOLOGY 53.6.[2]

CHRIST AS A FERTILE LAND. ORIGEN: So when he was not a desert or a land made dry to Israel, he was, with respect to what is particular, a desert and land made dry to the pagan nations. But when he turned away from Israel and became to that Israel like a desert and land made dry, then grace was poured forth on the pagan nations, and Jesus Christ became now to us not a desert but abundance, and not a land made dry but one that bears fruit.[3] HOMILIES ON JEREMIAH 3.3.[4]

PLENITUDE OF SPIRITUAL CHILDREN. CHRYSOSTOM: Who is this who before was "barren" and "desolate"? Clearly it is the church of the Gentiles, which was before deprived of the knowledge of God. Who is "she who has the husband"? Plainly the synagogue. Yet the barren woman surpassed her in the number of her children, for the other embraces one nation, but the children of the church have filled the country of the Greeks and of the barbarians, the earth and the sea, the whole habitable world. COMMENTARY ON GALATIANS 4.[5]

SPIRITUAL FERTILITY. THEODORET OF CYR: And through these prophecies, the God of the universe declares that in his overflowing love for

human beings he is not only "Lord" and "Father" but that he also calls himself "husband" and "groom." This prophecy teaches that the woman who was deserted produced more children than the one who had a husband. COMMENTARY ON ISAIAH 17.54.1.[6]

THE OUTWORKING OF THE CHRIST-EVENT IN THE NEW FAITH. JEROME: After the birth of the Savior and the sequence of life and miracles, the passion of the cross and the glory of resurrection, when laying down his life he saw his progeny lengthened and as righteous he justified many by his knowledge and divided the spoils of the strong and prayed for transgressors, giving a place for penance; the text then switches to the calling of the nations and describes in plain words those who would believe in him. COMMENTARY ON ISAIAH 15.2.[7]

THE CLEANSING WORK OF CHRIST. MAXIMUS OF TURIN: The church, then, is that sterile city which, because of the bad condition of the waters before the coming of Christ (that is to say, because of the sacrilege of the Gentile peoples), was unable to conceive children for God in its sterility. But when Christ came, taking on a human body like a clay vessel, he cleansed the bad condition of the waters; that is to say, he cut off the sacrileges of the peoples, and immediately the church, which used to be sterile, began to be fruitful. SERMON 84.4.[8]

54:2 The Place of Your Tent

SECURE AND PROSPEROUS LIVING. JEROME: Here is the spiritual sense. Anyone who is in a tent does not have a secure and everlasting dwelling but is always changing places and hurrying on to the next. . . . For the end of "living in tents" is the taking possession of the eternal home, whose foundations do not shift nor are moved around.

---

[1]FC 1:66**. [2]LCC 1:276-77*. [3]Cf. Jer 2:31. [4]FC 97:29. [5]NPNF 1 13:34*. [6]SC 315:164. [7]AGLB 35:1536. [8]ACW 50:203.

Those planted in the house of God, in his very atrium, flower so that from the blooms they may come to bear fruit and be able to say, "I am like an olive tree bearing fruit in God's house."[9] COMMENTARY ON ISAIAH 15.3.[10]

54:3 To the Right and to the Left

CHRISTIAN TEACHERS HOLD THE CHURCH UP. THEODORET OF CYR: He accordingly bids the barren one to fill the world with houses of prayer and to make them left and right, that is to say, in the south and the north. One is not, however, mistaken if one gives the name of "stakes" to the holy prophets, to the apostles and to the martyrs, hidden in the earth, as the tent stakes are; these are the ones who maintain the tabernacle of the church, holding it upright with their doctrines as if with ropes. They are also called "foundations."[11] COMMENTARY ON ISAIAH 17.54.2.[12]

---

[9]Ps 52:8 (51:10 LXX, Vg). [10]AGLB 35:1541. [11]Eph 2:20. [12]SC 315:166.

54:4-10 THE REINSTATED BRIDE OF THE LORD

[4]Fear not, for you will not be ashamed;
　be not confounded, for you will not be put to shame;
for you will forget the shame of your youth,
　and the reproach of your widowhood you will remember no more.
[5]For your Maker is your husband,
　the LORD of hosts is his name;
and the Holy One of Israel is your Redeemer,
　the God of the whole earth he is called.
[6]For the LORD has called you
　like a wife forsaken and grieved in spirit,
like a wife of youth when she is cast off,
　says your God.
[7]For a brief moment I forsook you,
　but with great compassion I will gather you.
[8]In overflowing wrath for a moment
　I hid my face from you,
but with everlasting love I will have compassion on you,
　says the LORD, your Redeemer.

[9]For this is like the days of Noah to me:
　as I swore that the waters of Noah should no more go over the earth,
so I have sworn that I will not be angry with you
　and will not rebuke you.
[10]For the mountains may depart
　and the hills be removed,
but my steadfast love shall not depart from you,
　and my covenant of peace shall not be removed,
　says the LORD, who has compassion on you.

OVERVIEW: The Lord has called us in grace so that we need have no fear of being ashamed, since he has saved us by his grace. He transforms us by his Spirit from the widowhood of an empty life to a life of beauty through the gospel (CYRIL). God sometimes abandons us for a short while, even as he did to Israel and the church, but he ultimately will restore us to share in his majesty (JEROME). God's goodness and glory are much more powerful than our sins (GREGORY OF NAZIANZUS), strong enough to bring us into his kingdom, where he will establish us as sons and daughters of the king (CYRIL). Baptism has an effect on the soul, and the souls of those before Christ are saved through the eternal covenant (JEROME). The covenant with Noah is a pledge of God to all humankind (THEODORET).

54:4-6 The Lord Has Called You

SAVED BY MERCY. CYRIL OF ALEXANDRIA: We have been justified in Christ, and not from works of righteousness that we have done but according to his mercy. But this is also what the supremely wise Paul has written. For we have been set free from the darkness, deceit and wickedness, which have been inherited from our ancestors. . . . [Therefore,] do not fear that you will be put to shame. For just as a parent looks after children, the Lord will look after those who fear him. Your sins will be as far removed from you as the east is from the west. How necessary is it, then, that you not stumble again but reject those same sins in fear. Remember the grace of our justifying God, and do not bear malice or demand justice from those who sin against you. COMMENTARY ON ISAIAH 5.2.54.4-5.[1]

CHANGED FOR A DIFFERENT WAY OF LIFE. CYRIL OF ALEXANDRIA: He makes clear how he makes the shame of widowhood disappear, saying that it is "the Lord who makes you, the Lord of hosts is his name." He is making you rather than creating you, transferring us into another type of citizenship and beautiful life. For we are being transformed in Christ into the newness of the holy and evangelical life, ascending to his own beautiful form through the Spirit so that others see us as different from the rest [of humanity]. COMMENTARY ON ISAIAH 5.2.54.4-5.[2]

54:7-8 I Hid My Face

THE QUEENLY JOY OF THE CHURCH. JEROME: It is clear that in no way is this said to Jerusalem, which never ruled over the whole world, but to the church of Christ whose inheritance is the whole world.

The Lord left [the church] for a brief moment, momentarily hiding his face; then he took it up in his everlasting mercy and changed its former sadness into joy. This is how it is said in the Hebrew. Yet according to the Septuagint it says that [the church] is *not* like an abandoned and faint-hearted woman summoned by God and is *not* like a wife despised from her youth, and accordingly he had left her and turned away from her only for a brief period, that he might take pity on her in eternity. If the Jews and those of a Judaizing tendency among us say that here is Israel abandoned for a brief period and that God takes pity on her in the coming of the Messiah, and understand a brief period in comparison with the whole eternity, why do they not allow us to say that the brief period is the time for which the nations were abandoned, who were rejected of God during adolescence, but who later in old age pursued his eternal mercy, especially when in the calling of the time of Israel the crowd of Gentiles were never shut out, but a door of returning was opened to them as proselytes? It appears we are excluded from their calling only for a short time, if by their eternal exclusion we are allowed a return to God. For we have spoken of an eternal exclusion if they do not act penitently. . . . The sinful soul was rejected by God, not because of God's hatred, but because of his timing, so that, weighed down with a load of evils she might return to her former husband and not despair of having lost the substance of the father's kindness. COMMENTARY ON ISAIAH 15.4-5.[3]

THE DISPROPORTIONATE KINDNESS OF GOD. GREGORY OF NAZIANZUS: I seem, indeed, to hear

---

[1]PG 70:1197. [2]PG 70:1197-1200. [3]AGLB 35:1545-47.

that voice from him who gathers together those who are broken and welcomes the oppressed. . . . The measure of his kindness exceeds the measure of his discipline. The former things were owing to our wickedness, the present things to the adorable Trinity, the former for our cleansing, the present for my Glory. THE LAST FAREWELL, ORATION 42.7.[4]

ETERNAL LOVING-KINDNESS. CYRIL OF ALEXANDRIA: "And by my eternal[5] mercy I will have mercy on you." For the season of anger is short and brief in comparison with the measure of the boundless loving-kindness given to us from God. He rescued us out of the power of darkness and transferred us to the kingdom of the Son of his love in light. It is appropriate to think greatly of the mercy that is through Christ, who cleanses us from every stain and takes away the accusation of justice. He restores us to a relationship with him through holinesss and gives the garlands of the glory of sonship to those whom he establishes in the kingdom of heaven. COMMENTARY ON ISAIAH 5.2.54.8.[6]

54:9 The Waters of Noah

THE WASHING OF BAPTISM AND THE ETERNAL COVENANT. JEROME: The sense that the Septuagint gives is confused and all things are disordered, so that what is said is hard to understand. It is not that I do not know what that very wise man[7] has said on this chapter but rather that it does not satisfy my mind. For he takes it to be about a figurative flood that means the Savior's baptism . . . that in baptism he removed all sins. . . . In this figure the water cleanses us, not washing away the dirtiness of flesh but by the appeal of a good conscience to God.[8] The mountains and the hills are those saints who were not moved in the flood of this sort, having accepted the eternal covenant, although in the previous flood they were moved, but they left their weakness behind. COMMENTARY ON ISAIAH 15.6.[9]

A SIGN OF GOD'S FAITHFULNESS. THEODORET OF CYR: He says, "Remember the covenants made with Noah and recognize their truth. I have promised never again to destroy the earth in such a way. Having the first covenant as a pledge, believe that you will always enjoy my love, and I will firmly guard your peace, and I will never dissolve this marriage." COMMENTARY ON ISAIAH 17.54.9-10.[10]

---

[4]NPNF 2 7:388. [5]Gk aiōniou: the LXX has megalou; Cyril's reading here seems idiosyncratic. [6]PG 70:1204. [7]The "very wise man" is most likely Origen. Jerome here gives us an interpretation of which he is not wholly sure. [8]1 Pet 3:21. [9]AGLB 35:1549-50. [10]SC 315:170.

54:11-17 THE FUTURE SPLENDOR OF THE CHURCH

[11]O afflicted one, storm-tossed, and not comforted,
behold, I will set your stones in antimony,*
and lay your foundations with sapphires.[b]
[12]I will make your pinnacles of agate,
your gates of carbuncles,
and all your wall of precious stones.
[13]All your sons shall be taught by the LORD,
and great shall be the prosperity of your sons.
[14]In righteousness you shall be established;
you shall be far from oppression, for you

shall not fear;
  and from terror, for it shall not come near
    you.
¹⁵If any one stirs up strife,
  it is not from me;
whoever stirs up strife with you
  shall fall because of you.
¹⁶Behold, I have created the smith
  who blows the fire of coals,[‡]
  and produces a weapon for its purpose.

I have also created the ravager to destroy;
  ¹⁷no weapon that is fashioned against you
    shall prosper,
  and you shall confute every tongue that rises
    against you in judgment.
This is the heritage of the servants of the
    LORD
  and their vindication from me, says the
    LORD.

b Or lapis lazuli   * Syriac (Peshitta) I will transform your stones into beryl   † LXX Behold, proselytes shall come to you through me and shall take refuge in you   ‡ Syriac (Peshitta): Who made the vases in his work

OVERVIEW: Isaiah compares the souls of those who resist the enemy and glorify God with precious stones (EUSEBIUS) as God transforms ordinary stones into precious jewels that build up his church (ISHO'DAD) on the tried and solid foundation of prophets and apostles (PROCOPIUS). These, in turn, find their solid foundation on Christ, the most precious stone of all (CYRIL). Plato's idea of things reflecting their true heavenly forms can be seen here (ORIGEN). The symbolism serves to remind us of spiritual graces and virtues and unity in Christ (JEROME). The inner teacher gives lessons that are to be acted on rather than cognitively grasped (AUGUSTINE). The saints' virtues are taught by the Spirit and produce peace for wandering souls (THEODORET). We are to pay utmost attention to what the Spirit has written on our heart (ISAAC) with the added benefit that obedience to God's instructions quells anxiety (EUSEBIUS). Righteousness and the overcoming of human discrimination is what keeps the city built up (PROCOPIUS).

The devil engenders a spiritual contest that makes reward by God possible (JEROME). God's door is always open to the penitent at any stage of life (FULGENTIUS). In the figurative language of Isaiah, the blacksmith is the apostle who helps arm and fortify the people of God (EPHREM). The kingdom of God is the inheritance of the righteous (THEODORET).

54:11 I Will Set Your Stones in Antimony

THE HEAVENLY STRENGTH THE CHURCH RECEIVES. EUSEBIUS OF CAESAREA: We should understand all these things of which Isaiah speaks as worthy and precious souls, with whom God commits himself to build the heavenly citizenry. He compares them with sapphire on the grounds of its likeness to the color of heaven. Their intercourse is heavenly and angelic, as Paul teaches, saying, "Our citizenship is in heaven."[1] In Ezekiel the place under the throne of God is said to be like sapphire. . . . And the parapets of this new Jerusalem would be of jasper or, in Symmachus's translation, *karchēdonion*, a special, shining stone. This means those who belong to the church, whom in a spiritual manner strengthen their faith and are like the battlements of the heavenly citizenry, destroy "every obstacle raised against the knowledge of God"[2] and refute any false opinion contrary to the truth. Since parapets are designed to resist the enemy, those who in the church are equipped with wisdom may be rightly called "parapets." Alongside these others is a comparison drawn with crystals, with which he foretells that the gates of the city will be built and denotes the clarity and purity of sure faith of those who believed the foundational and elemen-

---

[1]Phil 3:20. [2]2 Cor 10:5.

tary doctrine. Isaiah also declares that the wall of the new city of God will be made from special stone. Such are they who through their prayers surround and confirm, just like an enclosure, the city's edifice and its great, precious and worthy building. COMMENTARY ON ISAIAH 2.43.[3]

THE JOY FOR THE RETURN. ISHO'DAD OF MERV: "Behold, I will transform your stones into beryl," that is, the place is stony, and God will transform the ordinary stones into beryl, both in reality and for the fact that this is imagined as a consequence of their great joy. COMMENTARY ON ISAIAH 54.11.[4]

THE JEWELED GLORY OF THE LORD. PROCO-PIUS OF GAZA: Some think that Jesus is here called "coal" since he was placed as a foundation in Zion and those who believe in him will not be ashamed.[5] Similarly Amos calls him "adamantine" in these words, "I will place adamantine in the middle of the people of Israel."[6] And Zachariah, "Look, I will give the dawn over my servant. And the stone that I will give before the face of Joshua, on that stone there are seven eyes."[7] For Christ is the all-seeing one. This coal, he says, is also the support and the foundation stone, to which, since they approximate to it, the apostles, too, are here called "foundations" and are spoken of as marked out by the name of sapphire, as in the seventeenth psalm, which says, "The springs of waters are uncovered and the foundations of the earth are revealed at your chastisement and from the breath of your Spirit, O Lord."[8] For those in Israel were shaken by what the apostles dared to do through Christ, when purification through water first appeared. The disciples of the Savior receive this title, but the prophets are also called foundation, as Paul says, "building on the foundation of the apostles and prophets."[9] Sapphire is the color of heaven, and again Paul tells us that this denotes the citizenship of heaven.[10] ... But "anthracite" [coal], according to another interpretation that has been handed down, refers to stones that adorn, just as the sainted martyrs who have been tested by fire adorn with *stimei* [a

type of eyeliner] the eyes of the bridegroom of Christ.[11] COMMENTARY ON ISAIAH 54.1-17.[12]

FOUNDATIONS IN CHRIST. CYRIL OF ALEXAN-DRIA: "I will place you as a carbon stone." It is fitting to want to signify Jesus through this stone that was set, the Scriptures say, as the foundation of Zion. If anyone trusts in this foundation, he will not be ashamed. He calls him a foundation stone among them. And he is also mentioned by the holy prophets. For he says through the voice of Amos, "Look, I am setting a diamond[13] in the middle of my people Israel."[14] And through the voice of Zechariah, "Behold, I will bring my servant the sunrise."[15] "I have placed a stone before the face of Jesus; on the one stone there are seven eyes."[16] For the all-seeing one is Christ who is able to survey all things everywhere. For the carbon is placed to be a stone and a fixed foundation of the holy city. On it are the stones of sapphire, which perhaps signify the ranks of the apostles who are set. For they were very close to Christ, and when they followed him they became foundations in the earthly realm. COMMENTARY ON ISA-IAH 5.2.54.11-13.[17]

54:12 Pinnacles of Agate

ISAIAH TAUGHT PLATO ABOUT HEAVEN. ORI-GEN: It seems to me also that that fancy of Plato, that those stones that we call precious stones

---

[3]GCS 57(9):342-43. [4]CSCO 303(128):54. [5]Is 28:16. [6]Amos 7:8 LXX. [7]Cf. Zech 3:8 LXX. [8]Ps 18:15 (17:16 LXX). [9]Eph 2:20. [10]Phil 3:20. [11]The imagery here is of the Lord as a master builder who is rebuilding Jerusalem. Procopius, who had himself written on architecture, here melds two metaphors, that of stones which make up a building, and the eyeliner which in ancient times was made of anthracite, antimony or other charred ingredients and utilized by oriental women to bring out the whites of their eyes. The Lord, in other words, uses this cosmetic as a kind of mortar that not only binds together the building blocks of the wall he is building, but also achieves the effect of highlighting each individual block, making it appear like a beautiful woman's eye set off and apart by the use of this black cosmetic which can also be used as fuel to be burned, thus Procopius's references to the testing of the martyred saints. [12]PG 87:2541. [13]Gk *adamanta*. [14]Amos 7:8 LXX. [15]Gk *anatolē*. Cf. Zech 3:8 LXX. [16]Zech 9:16 LXX. [17]PG 70:1209.

which derive their luster from a reflection, as it were, of the stones in that better land, is taken from the words of Isaiah in describing the city of God: "I will make your battlements of jasper, your stones shall be crystal and your borders of precious stones." AGAINST CELSUS 7.30.[18]

THE SYMBOLISM OF THE BEAUTIFUL CITY.
JEROME: All except the Septuagint translate, "I will cover your stones in eye paint," in the likeness of an adorned woman who paints her eyes with mascara, thus signifying the beauty of the city . . . inducing him to come and descend in person and build on earth the heavenly Jerusalem, which in the Apocalypse of John is called "the bride and wife of the lamb,"[19] containing light like a precious stone such as jasper and crystal and a great wall. . . . "O the depth of the wisdom and knowledge of God."[20] . . . From which it is clear under the dispensation of righteousness that we ought to seek the name of virtue and also the other virtues in the building up of the church. . . . For these words illustrate that which is said in Proverbs, "More precious than all most precious stones."[21] For if Christ is the virtue of God and the wisdom of God, then it is stupid to have Christ compared with inanimate stones . . . for God is the builder and founder of the city. . . . Many Greek and Latin authors have written on the nature of the twelve stones and gems. From these I will name only two, bishop Epiphanius of holy and venerable memory . . . and Pliny the Younger. . . . Coal that is prepared or is spread out in an orderly manner seems to me to be the word of doctrine that ignites, which when error is dispelled enlightens the hearts of those who believe . . . sapphire, which is put in foundations, resembles the sky and the air above us. . . . The bulwarks of the Lord's city, that is, the pinnacles of the walls, are strengthened with jasper; these are able to destroy all pretension that raises itself against God's knowledge, to convince it and subject falsehood to truth. In such disputation the strongest bulwark of the church is reinforced with the testimonies of the holy Scriptures. . . .

We should be acquainted with the worldwide spiritual graces in the church, with which he who has them puts empty fears to flight and can say with the bride, "My kinsman is white and red."[22] . . . This city is to be sought not on earth but in heaven, which, situated on the mountain that is Christ, cannot be hidden. COMMENTARY ON ISAIAH 15.7.[23]

54:13 Taught by the Lord

THE SIGN YOU HAVE BEEN TAUGHT BY GOD.
AUGUSTINE: And the surest sign that you have been taught of God is that you put into practice what you have been taught. Of that character are all who are called according to God's purpose, as it is written in the prophets, "They shall be all taught of God." The person, however, who has learned what ought to be done but does not do it, has not yet been "taught of God" according to grace but only according to the law, not according to the Spirit but only according to the letter. There are many who appear to do what the law commands through fear of punishment, not through love of righteousness, and such righteousness as this apostle calls "his own which is after the law"[24]—a thing as it were commanded, not given. . . . When the free person keeps a commandment, he does it readily. And whosoever learns his duty in this spirit does everything that he has learned ought to be done. ON ORIGINAL SIN 1.14.[25]

THE VIRTUES OF THE SAINTS REFLECT THE DIVINE LIGHT. THEODORET OF CYR: Symmachus translated, "The Lord who takes pity on you says, lowly one, who has not been comforted, I have mercy for you. For I have seen you wandering aimlessly, as if surrounded by the spirits of deceit that have restless thoughts." . . . He calls godly public behavior a "city." The marks of the saints are various. But all are equally pleasing in God's sight. For that reason he calls them all pre-

---

[18]ANCL 23:452. [19]Rev 21:9. [20]Rom 11:33. [21]Prov 20:15. [22]Song 5:10. [23]AGLB 35:1551-62. [24]Eph 3:8-9. [25]NPNF 1 5:222-23.

cious stones, even if they have various characters. By coal is symbolized God's burning love. Sapphire represents the person who hides his virtue, for the hue of sapphire is a deep one. By "jasper" . . . is designated, I think, the luster of miracle working. . . . Then Isaiah leaves the figurative way of speaking to put things more clearly: "All your sons shall be taught of the Lord." He has called figuratively "stones," the appearance of virtue. The peace of God is here promised. Paul refers to this construction when he says, "Like a skilled architect I laid the foundation."[26] COMMENTARY ON ISAIAH 17.54.11-14.[27]

PAY ATTENTION TO THE TEACHING OF THE SPIRIT. ISAAC OF NINEVEH: In the same way He wrote through the prophets, for "He put His laws into their minds and He wrote them on their hearts,"[28] so that they should all be "taught of God."

If we now set aright our disgraceful lives with the aid of writings on account of the rationality that our nature received from the beginning, how much shall we turn aside from God if we show contempt for the natural book of the heart, the book written by Moses and the prophets, and the light of our Savior's Gospel of life! Hence we shall bring capital punishment upon ourselves if we gain no help from the hidden book, or from the visible one, or from the Gospel of the life-giving commandments of our Lord Jesus Christ.

Not even the man who toils and exerts himself in prayer, reading, divine vision, and insight, will make progress in the truth and gain an illumined intellect, unless he aims the intention of his mind toward the strength of what is written by the Spirit on the book of his heart.

The veil of the passions that overlays our heart prevents us from truly beholding that which is written on our heart by the Spirit. When we pray, read, and sing praises, we float over the surface of our heart without truly perceiving what lies within. But if we raise the veil of the passions by observing the commandments, then with the eye of the spirit we shall see the truth that is

imprinted in our heart. BOOK OF GRACE 5.74-77.[29]

54:14 *In Righteousness You Will Not Fear*

COURAGE OR FEAR. EUSEBIUS OF CAESAREA: I promised to you by grace beforehand—if you no longer struggle with these promises—that no fear of attack by war would touch you. Therefore rejoice in my commandments, for if you do so, these kinds of fears will not affect you—unless you do not guard the commandments and fall into the fear of human reproach. And so, I testify to you and say, "You will be far from oppression, and you will not fear. Terror shall not come near you." Rather, you will remain close to me and will act in a godly way according to the following words of Isaiah: "the proselytes will come to you." But they will not come apart from my will, for it says they also will come "through me." COMMENTARY ON ISAIAH 2.43.[30]

ALL ARE INVITED TO DWELL WITH GOD. PROCOPIUS OF GAZA: And then Isaiah adds, "and you will be built up in righteousness." For with the utmost rightness the architect and builder of the whole is the wisdom of God, fitting the living and smooth stones to the building. Some he uses for towers, others for foundations and others for walls; some for the building of the temple of the city and others for the surrounding area. And with the rest he builds up the rest of the city, not in the human way by discriminating between types of people or evaluating them, but allowing all in, free and slave, poor and rich, so that they whose lives were unknown receive honor. And then God promises that he will give the church further orders, to step back from evil so that terror shall not come near. He instructs them in the mystery. Formerly the bride was encouraged by the prophets to advance to communion, summoning her through holiness and righteousness. By

---

[26]1 Cor 3:10. [27]SC 315:170-74. [28]Jer 31:33. [29]AHSIS 413. [30]GCS 57(9):343.

the kisses of Christ's mouth we have been kissed. He has appeared in the flesh, speaking mouth to mouth to us. He says that no enemy will prevail against [the church] if it cultivates righteousness. Commentary on Isaiah 54.1-17.[31]

54:16 Who Blows the Fire of Coals

The Live Coals Represent the Devil. Jerome: "I, who created the smith who blows the fire of coals, that is, the devil of all evil arts, was not forced by nature to create him but freely chose to do so. I created the Adversary, not to cause people's ruin but in order to provide a moral struggle. Those who lose that struggle lie in ruins, but I reward those who triumph in the struggle." . . . Now the following seems to be the sense as the Septuagint has it: "I your creator have not made you in the way that the devil, that most evil craftsman with an unclean spirit, fills vessels of iniquity and carries them into perdition." It should be known that vessels of this kind do not have a prosperous road ahead but are destroyed en route. . . . But the inhabitants of the church will be righteous to the Lord. For everyone who does right is born of God. To them the Lord says, "Be holy, since I am holy."[32] Commentary on Isaiah 15.10.[33]

God's Delight in Showing Mercy. Fulgentius of Ruspe: Therefore, it is good for us if we flee to the mercy of him whose justice we are incapable of escaping. The justice of God is such that it condemns those who turn away and saves those who turn to him. So he says, "Be converted to me, and I will save you."[34] [God] is always delighted by our conversion, nor has he set a time

for a human being, so long as he is in this life, at which time he cannot be merciful to the one who turns to him; on the contrary, the whole time of the present life is known to have been destined for our conversion. For the blessed Peter says, "The Lord does not delay his promise as some regard 'delay,' but he is patient with you, not wishing that any should perish but that all should come to repentance."[35] Letter 13.[36]

The Blacksmith Symbolizes the Apostles. Ephrem the Syrian: "Behold, I have created the blacksmith, who made the vases in his work," that is, I elected the apostles and the disciples of the apostles, who perfectly instruct the peoples through the doctrine of truth. "I have also created the destroyer." I did not prevent the liars and the persecutors from rising against the church at the time of the apostles. Commentary on Isaiah 54.16.[37]

The Kingdom Is Given to the Righteous. Theodoret of Cyr: This the Lord has taught in turn in the holy Gospels: "Come, you blessed of my Father, inherit the kingdom prepared for you from the foundations of the world." He gives it to those who provide proof of the righteousness that he has established by his laws: "For I was hungry," he says, "and you gave me food; I was thirsty, and you gave me drink" and the rest.[38] Commentary on Isaiah 17.54.17.[39]

---

[31]PG 87:2544. [32]Lev 20:26. [33]AGLB 35:1565, 1567. [34]See Mt 11:28. [35]2 Pet 3:9. [36]FC 95:360. [37]SESHS 2:155. [38]Mt 25:34, 35. [39]ITA 810; SC 315:176.

55:1-5 A CALL TO SEEK THE LORD

¹*Ho, every one who thirsts,*
* come to the waters;*
and he who has no money,
* come, buy and eat!*
Come, buy wine and milk
* without money and without price.*
²*Why do you spend your money for that which*
* is not bread,*
* and your labor for that which does not*
* satisfy?*
Hearken diligently to me, and eat what is
* good,*
* and delight yourselves in fatness.*
³*Incline your ear, and come to me;*

* hear, that your soul may live;*
and I will make with you an everlasting
* covenant,*
* my steadfast, sure love for David.*
⁴*Behold, I made him a witness to the peoples,*
* a leader and commander for the peoples.*
⁵*Behold, you shall call nations that you know*
* not,*
* and nations that knew you not shall run to*
* you,*
because of the LORD your God, and of the
* Holy One of Israel,*
* for he has glorified you.*

OVERVIEW: The cost of the virtue of the fear of God is repentance and nothing else (ISHO'DAD). Repentance must be expressed in using money to help the poor and thereby Christ (CHRYSOSTOM). The price of God's salvation is paid for us if we know the buyer by word and blood (AMBROSE). The refreshment that comes with this salvation must be a spiritual one in which "milk" stands for the wisdom of innocents (JEROME). The Septuagint, by reading "wine and suet," also hints at the Eucharistic offering that God freely provides (EUSEBIUS). There could be no payment for such priceless things except from Christ (CYRIL). That which provides spiritual training is what Isaiah calls "good" (JEROME), and the righteousness that is in Christ Jesus is the only money that has currency in the kingdom of God (THEODORET). This is what the Lord is trying to communicate to his people, if only they will listen (THEODORE). He is telling them of the covenant to come after Isaiah that will last forever (JEROME). He speaks of the line of David from which this covenant arises (THEODORET). It is a covenant that ultimately

promises our justification through faith as we receive the life-giving power of Christ (CYRIL).

55:1 Come to the Waters

AN EXORTATION TO REPENTANCE. ISHO'DAD OF MERV: "Ho, everyone who thirsts, come to the waters," that is, you, who are deprived of any kind of good, run to the fear of God, because you will be educated through the doctrine that comes from me; even though you possess nothing better, at least pay "the price," which is repentance, and buy the virtue of the fear of God thanks to the generosity that [comes] from his mercy. This is what the words "without money and without price" mean. COMMENTARY ON ISAIAH 55.1.[1]

EXPRESS REPENTANCE WITH ALMSGIVING. CHRYSOSTOM: As long as the virtues are found before us and are sold cheaply, let us take from the munificent One, let us grasp, let us

---

[1]CSCO 303(128):55.

purchase.... As long as the festival lasts, let us buy alms, or, better yet, let us purchase salvation through almsgiving. You clothe Christ when you clothe the poor. HOMILIES ON REPENTANCE AND ALMSGIVING 7.6.22.[2]

GOD BUYS SALVATION FOR US. AMBROSE: The free person is the wise one who was bought with the price of heavenly speech, the gold and silver of God's word, bought with the price of blood (not least important is it to know the buyer), bought with the price of grace, for he heard and understood the one who said, "All you who thirst, come to the waters, and you that have no money, make haste, buy and eat and drink." LETTER 54.[3]

WISDOM HAS A LOGIC OF ITS OWN. JEROME: It is very marvelous how they can buy water without money and do not drink it but eat it. For he who came down from heaven is himself both bread and water.... We read that he mixed wine and wisdom in his bowl, telling all the fools of this age and the world who do not have wisdom to drink, that we buy not only wine but also milk, which signifies the innocence of little ones. The manner and type of this remains today in the Eastern churches, where wine and milk are given to the newborn in baptism. COMMENTARY ON ISAIAH 15.11.[4]

WE RECEIVE THE MYSTERY OF CHRIST IN THE SACRAMENTS. EUSEBIUS OF CAESAREA: Aquila translates "like wine and milk" so as to say not only water but also wine and milk are promised to the thirsty. "Water" is clearly the gospel message that flows from the spring of the Savior, but "wine and milk" hymn the mystery of the rebirth in Christ.... One should be mindful of the fact that according to the old covenant mystical milk is given to those reborn in Christ along with the body and blood of the new covenant. It is said to be kept even now as a custom in some churches, if not in a bodily at least in a spiritual way, in that the mystical blood is provided for those deemed worthy of the new life in Christ in

the form of wine and milk. If with the Septuagint we read "and suet"—the fat and richness and nourishment of the spiritual food that is in Christ is here praised, just as our Savior revealed, saying, "Unless you eat my flesh and drink of my blood, you shall not have life in you."[5] So just as in Isaiah his body is called "suet" and as the blood is called wine, we understand the suet to mean his incarnate economy and the wine to mean the mystery of his passion. COMMENTARY ON ISAIAH 2.44.[6]

55:2 Without Money

ONLY GOD CAN AFFORD THE PRICE OF HIS LIVING RESOURCES. CYRIL OF ALEXANDRIA: How can they purchase, yet receive gifts without paying? Well, because we accept the payment in faith from Christ, and we pay for none of these things with short-term or perishable goods. For it says, "I said to my Lord, 'You are my Lord since you have no need of goods from me.'"[7] By way of gifts and honor to Christ we offer to Christ the confession of faith in him. So without money and payment comes this drink and bountiful gift of spiritual charisms. For what could we offer and what price could we pay for such a drink? For those drinking the living water are those enriched with grace through the Holy Spirit through participation in him and purchasing this through faith, since they are sharers of the wine and suet, that is, of the holy body and the blood of Christ. COMMENTARY ON ISAIAH 5.2.55.1-2.[8]

THAT WHICH BRINGS SPIRITUAL BLESSING IS GOOD. JEROME: "What is good."... Abraham did not have good things because he was rich but because he used his riches well. And Lazarus,[9] who later rested on Abraham's bosom, did not suffer the pains of sickness and bear evils on the grounds of natural necessity; rather, he was pursued by evil people who thought truly good

---

[2]FC 96:104. [3]FC 26:290-91. [4]AGLB 35:1570. [5]Jn 6:53. [6]GCS 57(9):344. [7]Ps 16:2 (15:2 LXX). [8]PG 70:1220. [9]Lk 16:19-31.

things were to be found in the world. Hence, the rich man of noble standing received good things in his life—which were food to him who thought they were good. Conversely, about Lazarus it is not said, "He received his own bad things in his life," but rather "he received evil things in his life," since they were not evils to him who suffered but seemed that way to others. Blessed Job has offered us an example of each, since he neither in good things nor in bad was overcome but endured all things with firm equanimity. COMMENTARY ON ISAIAH 15.12.[10]

THE RIGHTEOUSNESS GIVEN BY GOD NOURISHES THE SOUL. THEODORET OF CYR: Behold what [Isaiah] has shown here, before indicating the road of righteousness. For it is thanks to all-holy baptism that "we are justified freely," according to the divine apostle: "by his grace through the redemption that is in Christ Jesus."[11] It is this the prophetic text likewise allows [us] to understand: "And all that have no money, go and buy, and eat and drink wine and fat without money or price." The divine Scripture often calls righteousness "money." "The oracles of the Lord are pure oracles; as silver tried in the fire, proved in a furnace of earth."[12] As for those who live with iniquity, "call them rejected silver, for the Lord has rejected them."[13] . . .

Here he rejected the sacrifices of the law. . . . The prophetic text teaches that these sacrifices gave no nourishment to the soul. COMMENTARY ON ISAIAH 17.55.1-2.[14]

55:3 Incline Your Ear

ATTENTION IS THE KEY TO THE OPERATION OF GOD'S GRACE. THEODORE OF HERACLEA: The Lord God, ever compassionate, is ready to bring people to good things, and he promises to give not only good things in the present but also the enjoyment of eternally good things in the hereafter. For he demands nothing other than a ready listener, one who takes in his words and is quick to respond willingly to his voice. To attend

with the ears in the sense of physical hearing is only what seems to be meant here. For attending with the eyes, we are not able to hear with these, and we cannot see as we listen with our ears. The same is true in the case of the other senses. From this we can assume that we pay attention with the eyes of the mind and are able to listen with the ears. For the soul is single and with one form by nature, and with one power [it] is able to listen and to see. But the mass of your sins and ungodliness constricts you and hinders you from fleeing to him. But there would be no such great obstacle if you desire that mercy beyond words; for then such evils of yours would not defeat and overcome his compassion. For God is great in pity, and he will provide forgiveness for your sins and so will show you to be pure, so that no trace of your former sins will remain. FRAGMENTS ON ISAIAH.[15]

THE ETERNAL COVENANT. JEROME: This covenant that the Lord promises will not be short-lived and for one age only, as it was of the Jewish people, but it will remain in eternity, in that the true David will come and the things promised in the gospel from the person of God will be fulfilled: "I have found my servant David, and in holy mercy I have anointed him." COMMENTARY ON ISAIAH 15.12.[16]

CONTINUITY OF COVENANTS. THEODORET OF CYR: I will fulfill these covenants that had been made to David for them, clothing the human nature from the line of David according to the promise and bringing forth the New Testament. COMMENTARY ON ISAIAH 17.55.2-3.[17]

55:5 You Shall Call the Nations

JUSTIFICATION BY THE PROMISES THROUGH FAITH. CYRIL OF ALEXANDRIA: For the law was

---

[10]AGLB 35:1573. [11]Rom 3:24. [12]Ps 12:6 (11:7 LXX). [13]Jer 6:30. [14]ITA 816-18*; SC 315:178. [15]PG 18:1360-61. [16]AGLB 35:1575. [17]SC 315:178.

not a perpetual and immoveable law, but it remained in force only as long as the time of its imposition. As the most wise Paul said, "For the former and ancient command has a gap whose filling is to be sought in the second, that is, the new has many things quite different from the old."[18] . . .

That second one is the eternal covenant, and that he fulfilled it for those approaching him by faith is confirmed when it immediately adds, "the holy trustworthy things of David." This concerns the announcements about the Savior of us all, Christ, which are declared to be given to those who are attentive among the nations, or it means the divine and sacred prophecies of Christ, who was born from the seed of David according to his humanity. These are called "holy," for they make perfect those in whom they dwell, just as the fear of God is called "pure" because it is purifying and the gospel word is called "life" because it gives life. . . . This is the power through Christ of these prophecies. . . .

For those who had never seen Christ on account of residing in gloom and darkness called on him, that is, they acknowledged Jesus as God and fled to him calling him their hope and shelter and means of salvation and called on him as God . . . for although according to the measure of humanity Christ was thought to be ignoble, he went back to that which was appropriate to him and divine and the highest glory—but not without his flesh. COMMENTARY ON ISAIAH 5.2.55.1-5.[19]

---

[18]See Heb 8:7. [19]PG 70:1221-25.

55:6-13 SINNERS IN ISRAEL MUST REPENT

[6]Seek the LORD while he may be found,
    call upon him while he is near;
[7]let the wicked forsake his way,
    and the unrighteous man his thoughts;
let him return to the LORD, that he may have
      mercy on him,
    and to our God, for he will abundantly
      pardon.
[8]For my thoughts are not your thoughts,*
    neither are your ways my ways, says the
    LORD.
[9]For as the heavens are higher than the earth,
    so are my ways higher than your ways
    and my thoughts than your thoughts.

[10]For as the rain and the snow come down
    from heaven,
    and return not thither but water the earth,
making it bring forth and sprout,
    giving seed to the sower and bread to the
      eater,
[11]so shall my word be that goes forth from my
      mouth;
    it shall not return to me empty,
but it shall accomplish that which I purpose,
    and prosper in the thing for which I sent it.

[12]For you shall go out in joy,
    and be led forth in peace;
the mountains and the hills before you
    shall break forth into singing,
    and all the trees of the field shall clap their

hands.

*[13]Instead of the thorn shall come up the
     cypress;
     instead of the brier shall come up the*

*myrtle;
and it shall be to the LORD for a memorial,
     for an everlasting sign which shall not be
     cut off.*

* LXX *For my counsels are not as your counsels*

OVERVIEW: The body can be happy only when the soul has its desires met (AUGUSTINE). Seeking God means to turn from evil and seek God in faith with the heart (JEROME). Turning to God is more than just a lifestyle change, although that is part of it (THEODORET). Finding and continuing to seek God is of the essence of the Christian life (AUGUSTINE) because sin continues to be a part of the Christian's life. And so, we continue to seek the Lord and return to him when we have sinned, whatever the extent of that sin may be (FULGENTIUS).

God works in our lives in many ways that we cannot always understand (CASSIAN). But the thoughts of his that we can understand are those given to us through Christ, God's mouthpiece (EUSEBIUS). We learn, among other things, that it is our lack of penitence, not our sins, that offends God the most (CHRYSOSTOM). And so, the divine perspective of life is worth grasping, if only for our own peace of mind (PRUDENTIUS). His Word that comes to us soaks into the spiritual earth and causes spiritual growth up to and including our resurrection to glory (APHRAHAT). In Christ, the Word came forth and returned to the Father in fulfillment of the reconciliation of the world to God (JEROME). God's love is what he opposes to our hate (THEODORET).

The pictorial language from creation helps us to understand something of the church (CYRIL) and those in it, who may for instance, be called good or bad trees by the nature of the fruit they produce (JEROME). The thorns in the church are those of a fiery nature, whereas the cypress represents those of a more moderate disposition (GREGORY THE GREAT). But the thorns, which represent sin, and the brier, which is devoid of fruit, will ultimately be replaced by the sweet-smelling cypress and the myrtle, which symbolize the actions of virtue, purity and holiness and are pleasing to God and delight him (EPHREM). And so let us strive to be these types of trees that proclaim what our God and Savior has done in our lives (THEODORET).

55:6 Seek the Lord

SEEKING GOD FOR THE SOUL'S HAPPINESS.
AUGUSTINE: How then am I to seek for you, Lord? When I seek for you, my God, my quest is for the happy life. I will seek you that "my soul may live,"[1] for my body derives life from my soul, and my soul derives life from you. . . . Is not the happy life that which all desire, which indeed no one fails to desire? CONFESSIONS 10.20.[2]

SEEKING GOD MEANS FORSAKING EVIL.
JEROME: Seek him while he can be found, while you are in the body and as long as an opportunity for penitence is provided, and seek him not in any particular place but in faith. Just how God is to be sought we learn elsewhere. . . . "Taste of the Lord in goodness, and in simplicity of heart seek him."[3] . . . For it is not enough to seek the Lord and while there is a time of penitence to find him and to call on him while he is near—unless the ungodly also leave their former ways and leave the old ways of thinking for those of the Lord. COMMENTARY ON ISAIAH 15.14.[4]

THE CIRCLE OF FORGIVENESS. THEODORET OF CYR: He says, "When you who seek have found, when you have called and have found pardon, flee the former road of ungodliness and immorality

---

[1]Is 55:3. [2]SAC 196. [3]Wis 1:1. [4]AGLB 35:1579-80.

and show God your face, not your back. For he will grant you mercy and give you forgiveness of sins." Commentary on Isaiah 17.55.7.[5]

The Journey and the Mystery Flow into Each Other. Augustine: If, therefore, he who is sought can be found, why was it said, "seek his face evermore"? Or is he perhaps still to be sought even when he is found? For so ought we to seek incomprehensible things, lest we should think that we have found nothing, who could find only how incomprehensible is the thing that we are seeking. Why, then, does he so seek if he comprehends that what he seeks is incomprehensible, unless because he knows that he must not cease as long as he is making progress in the search itself of incomprehensible things and is becoming better and better by seeking so great a good, which is sought in order to be found and is found in order to be sought? For it is sought that it may be found sweeter and is found in order that it may be sought more eagerly. On the Trinity 15.2.2.[6]

55:7 God Will Abundantly Pardon

The Immensity of God's Forgiveness. Fulgentius of Ruspe: Let the wicked forsake his own way, in which he sins; let the unrighteous abandon his thoughts with which he despairs of the forgiveness of sins and according to the prophet's statement, "return to the Lord, for he will abundantly pardon." In this "abundantly," nothing is lacking. Here mercy is omnipotent and omnipotence is merciful. For so great is the kindness in God that there is nothing that he is unable to loose for the converted person. Letter 6.[7]

55:8 My Thoughts Are Not Your Thoughts

God Works in Many Ways. John Cassian: God provides for the salvation of the human race in numberless different manners and in inscrutable ways. He inspires some, who wish it and thirst for it, to a greater ardor, while some others, who do not even wish it, he compels against their will.

Sometimes he helps to accomplish the things that he sees we desire for our own good, and at other times he inspires the beginnings of that holy desire and bestows both the commencement of a good work and perseverance in it. . . . The blessed apostle, reflecting on the manifold bounty of God's design and seeing that he has fallen into the vast and boundless sea as it were of God's goodness, exclaims, "Oh, the depth of the riches of the wisdom and knowledge of God! How unsearchable his ways! For who has known the mind of the Lord?"[8] Whoever believes that he can sound the depths of that immeasurable abyss by human reason is trying to nullify the marvelous aspect of this knowledge, then, that struck with awe the great teacher of the Gentiles. For the person who is sure that he can conceive in his mind or discuss at length the designs whereby God works salvation in human beings is certainly resisting the truth of the apostle's words and declaring with impious audacity that the judgments of God are not inscrutable and that his ways are traceable. The Lord also witnesses to this when he says, "For my thoughts are not your thoughts, neither are your ways my ways."[9] Conference 13.17.1-3.[10]

Christ Is God's Mouthpiece. Eusebius of Caesarea: He speaks these words clearly to the believers in the gospel that he delivered to the godless and lawless ones who were turning to him from the nations, presenting the word that was there in the beginning and is now coming down from the Father above like rain and snow in its descent to human beings, inasmuch as he makes their souls watered and fruit-bearing. . . . It is as though these words come out of Christ's own mouth, so that there is no need to think of the spoken word reexpressed among us, since here is a physical mouthpiece for God. Commentary on Isaiah 2.44.[11]

[5]SC 315:182. [6]FC 45:452. [7]FC 95:356-57. [8]Rom 11:33-34. [9]This last sentence is found in some manuscripts of Cassian but was not included by the editors of ACW. [10]ACW 57:488-89*. [11]GCS 57(9):347.

GOD HAS CREATED US FOR BLESSING, NOT PUNISHMENT. CHRYSOSTOM: "For my counsels are not as your counsels.". . . Now if we admit to our favor household slaves when they have offended against us, on their promising to become better, and place them again in their former position and sometimes even grant them greater freedom of speech than before, much more does God act thus. For if God had made us in order to punish us, we might well have despaired and questioned the possibility of our own salvation. But if he created us for no other reason than his own good will, and with a view to our enjoying everlasting blessings, and if he does and contrives everything for this end, from the first day until the present time, what is there which can ever cause us to doubt? Have we provoked him severely, in a way no other person did? This is just the reason why we ought specially to abstain from our present deeds and to repent for the past and exhibit a great change. For the evils we have once perpetrated cannot provoke him so much as our being unwilling to make any change in the future. For to sin may be a merely human failing, but to continue in the same sin ceases to be human and becomes altogether devilish. LETTER TO THE FALLEN THEODORE 1.15.[12]

55:9 As the Heavens Are Higher Than the Earth

DIVINE PERSPECTIVE ON LIFE. PRUDENTIUS:
"If you would," he says,
"Ascend to heaven, banish cares of earth.
For far as earth is distant from the sky
And heaven from the world below, so far
Are your vain thoughts from my eternal
  thoughts,
Ill from good, sin from virtue, dark from light.
I counsel you to shun all passing things
And deem as nought all to corruption prone,
For it is destined to return to nought.
All earth brings forth and holds, at dawn of
  time
I made; I decked with splendid ornaments

The shining world and formed the elements,
But willed that the enjoyment be confined
Within due bounds, as far as mortal frame
And fleeting human life may have the need,
Not that humanity, by unbridled passion
  ruled,
Should reckon good alone things sweet and
  vain,
Which I have preordained to pass with time.
AGAINST SYMMACHUS 2.123-40.[13]

55:10 The Rain and the Snow

THE WORD WORKS ITS POWER INTO THE WORLD. APHRAHAT: For the rain and the snow do not return to heaven but accomplish in the earth the will of him that sends them. So the word that he shall send through his Christ, who is himself the Word and the Message, shall return to him with great power. For when he shall come and bring it, he shall come down like rain and snow, and through him all that is sown shall spring up and bear righteous fruit, and the word shall return to his sender; but not in vain shall his going have been, but thus shall he say in the presence of his sender, "Behold, I and the children that the Lord has given me."[14] And this is the voice through which the dead shall live. And this is the voice of God that shall sound from on high and raise up all the dead. DEMONSTRATIONS 8.15.[15]

55:11 My Word Shall Not Return Empty

THE RELIABLE EFFICACY OF GOD'S WORD. JEROME: "For my thoughts are not like the thoughts of human beings, and as far as the heaven is from the earth, so much are my thoughts separated from the thoughts of human beings. For I am extremely gracious and very much for forgiving . . . so that once I have promised and it has come out of my mouth, it will not be void, but everything will be completed

---

[12]NPNF 1 9:106**. [13]FC 52:145. [14]Is 8:18. [15]NPNF 2 13:380.

through its efficacy." According to the anagogical sense, there is a double meaning here, because the Word of the Lord or he about whom it is written, "In the beginning was the Word, and the Word was with God, and God was the Word."[16] God's word does not return to him void, only through his doing the will of his Father as he filled all things on account of which he had become embodied and reconciled the world to God. He is the One who is said to proceed out of his mouth and out of the womb and vulva, not that God has bodily parts like that but so that we learn the nature of the Lord through our words. Or it indeed could be said that the word of gospel teaching may be called "rainstorms" and the rain that the spiritual clouds pour over the good earth, where the truth of God has reached. COMMENTARY ON ISAIAH 15.16.[17]

GOD'S LOVE AGAINST OUR HATE. THEODORET OF CYR: We stand far apart from each other, as far as the heaven is from the earth. For you hate me, while I love you. You avoid me, while I call you. You fight me, while I work for your benefit. COMMENTARY ON ISAIAH 17.55.8-9.[18]

55:12 The Mountains and Trees

THE REALITIES SYMBOLIZED BY THE NATURAL WORLD. CYRIL OF ALEXANDRIA: The mountains are the heavenly powers that are instituted in heaven by God for the sake of those who are on the earth. For they are ministering spirits sent for the service of those inheriting the future salvation.[19] And they also offer thanks for even one repentant sinner.[20] . . . Or they could be understood to be those who have a teaching practice in the church and care not for earthly things but those that are above. . . . And the trees of the field can be understood as those who are perfected among the people. For the Savior has a flowering garden. And since, indeed, it flourishes there and produces good fruit, it is written in the Song of Songs of the bride, "May my beloved come into his garden."[21] COMMENTARY ON ISAIAH 5.3.55.12-13.[22]

55:13 The Cypress

GOD MAKES OUR FREE CHOICE A REALITY. JEROME: Thus when it is said in the Gospel, "A good tree cannot bring forth bad fruit,"[23] in no way does this refer to the property of nature, as the heretics maintain, but to the will of the mind. . . . From this it is clear that each by his own will can make his soul a good or bad tree, which produced different fruit. COMMENTARY ON ISAIAH 15.17.[24]

HEAVENLY THOUGHTS GIVE CARNAL ONES NO ROOM. GREGORY THE GREAT: For in the hearts of the saints, instead of the baseness of earthly thoughts, the loftiness of heavenly contemplation rises up. Now the thorn is of a very fiery nature, while the cypress is of a moderate strength. Instead of the brier the myrtle comes up, when the minds of the righteous turn from the lasciviousness and heat of vices to the coolness and temperance of thoughts that do not desire the earthly things but with heavenly desires extinguish the flames of the flesh. MORALS ON THE BOOK OF JOB 18.20.[25]

A NEW LIFE IN THE FAITH OF CHRIST. EPHREM THE SYRIAN: "Instead of the thorn shall come up the cypress; instead of the brier shall come up the myrtle." The spiritual meaning of these words refers to the change of customs, which sprouted and rose up in the advent of Christ among those nations who embraced his faith. Instead of thorns, which represent the sins, and instead of the brier, which is devoid of fruits, the sweet-smelling cypress and the myrtle have risen, which are figures of the actions of virtue, purity and holiness and . . . are pleasing to God and delight him. COMMENTARY ON ISAIAH 55.13.[26]

---

[16]Jn 1:1. [17]AGLB 35:1583-84. [18]SC 315:182. [19]Heb 1:14. [20]Lk 15:7. [21]Song 5:1. [22]PG 70:1236-37. [23]Mt 7:18. [24]AGLB 35:1589. [25]CCL 143A:907. [26]SESHS 2:157.

LET US BE A SIGN WORTHY OF OUR GOD.
THEODORET OF CYR: He has shown by this the
change undergone by the foreign nations. For
people who formerly resembled useless and ram-
pant weeds, behold, after having had knowledge
of the Savior, they have imitated the height of the
cypress and the sweet aroma of the myrtle. They
proclaim by their deeds the power of our God
and Savior, in offering their own change as a sign
[to others] and as a miracle, great, astonishing
and lasting. Thus, this sign will be eternal and
shall not fail. . . . Let us therefore offer ourselves

[to others] as a sign worthy of our God and Savior, not only in adhering to the holy precepts but
also in embracing the mode of life corresponding
thereto, to the end that seeing our "good works"
people may "glorify your Father in heaven."[27] To
him are due all glory, honor and magnificence,
together with his only-begotten Son and the All-
Holy Spirit, now and forever and to ages of ages.
Amen. COMMENTARY ON ISAIAH 17.55.13.[28]

[27]Mt 5:16. [28]ITA 821*; SC 315:184-86.

56:1-8 SALVATION FOR OTHERS

[1]Thus says the LORD:
"Keep justice, and do righteousness,
for soon my salvation will come,
    and my deliverance be revealed.
[2]Blessed is the man who does this,
    and the son of man who holds it fast,
who keeps the sabbath, not profaning it,
    and keeps his hand from doing any evil."

[3]Let not the foreigner who has joined himself
        to the LORD say,
    "The LORD will surely separate me from his
        people";
and let not the eunuch say,
    "Behold, I am a dry tree."
[4]For thus says the LORD:
"To the eunuchs who keep my sabbaths,
    who choose the things that please me
    and hold fast my covenant,
[5]I will give in my house and within my walls

a monument and a name
    better than sons and daughters;
I will give them an everlasting name
    which shall not be cut off.

[6]"And the foreigners who join themselves to
        the LORD,
    to minister to him, to love the name of the
        LORD,
    and to be his servants,
every one who keeps the sabbath, and does
        not profane it,
    and holds fast my covenant—
[7]these I will bring to my holy mountain,
    and make them joyful in my house of
        prayer;
their burnt offerings and their sacrifices
    will be accepted on my altar;
for my house shall be called a house of prayer
    for all peoples.

⁸*Thus says the Lord God,*
  who gathers the outcasts of Israel,

I will gather yet others to him
  besides those already gathered."ᶜ

c Heb *his gathered ones*

Overview: Isaiah speaks of the blessed person as one who delights in and stays close to the Lord (Jerome) as he or she follows closely what the prophet here has written. Isaiah also points to the Master's appearing in the future (Theodoret). Christians are to do good works in offering themselves as those already saved for God's pleasure. Devotion and behavior that honor the Lord are what makes one belong to God's people (Cyril). Eunuchs for God's sake are more than, not less than, men (Jerome). God's spiritual family makes up for the loss of a natural family (Ambrose), enabling one to focus on the blessings of that life which is to come (Aphrahat), knowing there is much at stake in terms of eternal reward (Cyril). The church is comprised of foreigners whom the Lord has chosen who offer up prayers to him (Ephrem) in a confession of faith that remains one and central, even while the churches are many and scattered, sometimes because their teachers work for their own aggrandizement (Jerome). To become one in prayer and fellowship is natural; schisms are against nature (Leander). The church embraces all the people of the world who have faith in Christ (Cassiodorus). Since the coming of the gospel, prayer is a possibility for all (Augustine). God invites those of Israel who were dispersed back to him (Procopius).

56:1-2 Blessed Is the One

Staying Close to God As the Priority. Jerome: This *man* is also the son of the inner person, about which it is frequently said in Leviticus,[1] a person is blessed in that he does and understands these following things as the priority: namely, judgment, justice, and the salvation of the Lord, all of which are near and are to be revealed to all the nations. Such a person also

understands that he will not only do that which is commanded but will hold it firmly. And he will keep the sabbath so that he does not pollute it. . . . But we are called into freedom, and by this freedom Christ grants us that we do not work for food that perishes. Instead, cleaving to the Lord, let us say with the prophet, "It is good for me to stay close to God, and let us become one spirit with him, and let us fulfill the delightful sabbath, and we shall not belong to the six days in which the world was made." Commentary on Isaiah 15.19.[2]

The Moral and the Predictive Teaching. Theodoret of Cyr: The inspired prophets spoke not only of things to come but also gave dogmatic and ethical instruction. And they announced both judgment and salvation to those of former times, so that by the promise of good things and by the warning of pains they might turn them from evil and point them to virtue. One can easily learn this from the present oracle. For the prophetic word counsels Israel to be held by righteousness and to have uprightness as the soul's principle and then adds the prediction of the Savior and the revelation of mercy. For both [the moral and the predictive teaching] point to the Master's appearing. Commentary on Isaiah 18.56.1.[3]

Spiritual Works Delight God. Cyril of Alexandria: No one should be exercised by the words said to the Israelites about keeping the law, which doubtless belongs to the shadows of the world of types; for no one is justified by the law with God. . . . We should understand this spiritually; and abstaining from the care of the flesh we should offer spiritual sacrifices with the odor of a

---

[1]Lev 17:3. [2]AGLB 35:1592-93. [3]SC 315:188.

good spiritual fragrance and minister to God . . . to keep the sabbath spiritually now means for us keeping away from worldly cares . . . and with holy vigor making him glad, and offering ourselves in holy sweetness. COMMENTARY ON ISAIAH 5.3.56.1-2.[4]

56:3-4 The Eunuch and the Dry Tree

THE LORD WILL ORDER EVERYTHING. CYRIL OF ALEXANDRIA: The stranger who comes before the Lord should not say, " The Lord will surely cut me off from his people." For it will not be because he is foreign in the sense of not having Israelite blood therefore that he will be without a share in the gifts from the Lord, the intimate and spiritual relationship with him. But if he clings to the Lord in his domestic affairs and his friendships, he will be made to belong in the holy people and to the royal priesthood and to the inheritance of God. He will be numbered among the children of Abraham. For not all from Israel are Israel as most-wise Paul said: not all the progeny are the seed of Abraham, but the children of the promise are reckoned as descendants.[5] COMMENTARY ON ISAIAH 5.3.56.3-5.[6]

SPIRITUAL EUNUCHS. JEROME: This barrenness is made fruitful by virginity, this eunuch forces entry to the kingdom of God and forcefully snatches it. Who is the observer of the sabbaths that never does the works of marriage? Such a person chooses what the Lord desires and offers more than is demanded of him; he does not think about leniency but the will of his apostle. He keeps the everlasting covenant of the Lord and does not leave what he says unfulfilled and again return to his [former] self, but he knows that he will receive in the home of the Lord the best place . . . and that instead of children of the flesh he will have spiritual children. Such was the Evangelist John . . . who, while Peter was walking slowly, was flying with the wings of virginity and ran to the Lord, and who, losing himself in the secrets of the divine birth, dared to say things of which the ages were ignorant: "In the beginning was the

Word."[7] . . . Therefore, let all murmuring of the Jews end and cease to taunt that the kingdom of God is open to "half-men," since purity is not measured in the disability of the body but in the will of the mind. COMMENTARY ON ISAIAH 15.20.[8]

THE PUREST TEMPLE. JEROME: Those who please me are those who choose to be eunuchs voluntarily. . . . Who can receive this teaching, let him receive it.[9] It is a matter of great faith and great virtue to be the purest kind of temple of God, in that one dedicates oneself completely to the Lord as a burnt offering and to be holy in body as well as spirit. Those are eunuchs who, thinking themselves to be "dry trees" because of their infertility, hear through Isaiah that instead of sons and daughters they will have a place prepared in heaven. Of this sort were Ebedmelech in Jeremiah and that eunuch of Queen Candace.[10] AGAINST JOVINIANUS 1.12.[11]

56:5 Receiving a Better Name

GOD PROMISES A FAMILY TO THOSE WHO HAVE NONE. AMBROSE: The Lord says this to the eunuchs: Let not the eunuch say, "I am only a dry tree," for the Lord says to the eunuchs, "Whoever keeps my commands and chooses what I want and embraces my covenant . . . will receive a place that has a better name in my house and within my walls. I will give them the eternal name of sons and daughters." He promises others that they will not be deprived. Was anyone deprived of their own mother? Mary did not go without [a family]; the mistress of virginity did not go without, just because she was not thought able to bear a man, who had already borne God. ON THE INSTRUCTION OF VIRGINS 6.45.[12]

SINGLE-MINDED DEVOTION TO ETERNAL LIFE. APHRAHAT: All the pure virgins who are

---

[4]PG 70:1240-41. [5]Rom 9:6-7. [6]PG 70:1244. [7]Jn 1:1. [8]AGLB 35:1597-98. [9]Mt 19:12. [10]Acts 8:27. [11]PL 23:239. [12]SAEMO 14 1:144.

betrothed to Christ shall light their lamps, and with the Bridegroom they shall go into the marriage chamber.[13] All those who are betrothed to Christ are far removed from the curse of the law and are redeemed from the condemnation of the daughters of Eve. For they are not wedded to men so as to receive the curses and come into the pains of childbirth. They take no thought of death, because they do not deliver children who will die. And in place of a mortal husband, they are betrothed to Christ. And, "because they do not bear children, there is given to them the name that is better than sons and daughters." And instead of the groans of the daughters of Eve, they utter the songs of the Bridegroom. The wedding feast of the daughters of Eve continues for only seven days. But for these virgins, the Bridegroom never leaves. The adornment of the daughters of Eve is wool that wears out and perishes, but the garments of these does not wear out. Old age withers the beauty of the daughters of Eve, but the beauty of these shall be renewed at the time of the resurrection. DEMONSTRATIONS 6.6.[14]

THE REWARDS OF SELF-CONTROL. CYRIL OF ALEXANDRIA: The house and wall that are strength and security seem to describe the church that is above somewhere in the heavens, that is, over the earth. People dwell there who have grown in holiness and virtue and who shine forth and receive the honor of self-control along with a greater inheritance. They receive from God an eternal glory. There is nothing lacking of grace in them. For the rewards of self-control are great. And not only to the guileless eunuchs does he announce the provision of illustrious dignity, but he also announces it to those who keep the [new] sabbath that Christ established. For the others kept his sabbath by the law. For what was formerly in type is now illuminated in the beauty of truth. COMMENTARY ON ISAIAH 5.3.56.3-5.[15]

56:6-7 House of Prayer for All Peoples

A PREFIGURATION OF THE CHURCH OF THE

GENTILES. EPHREM THE SYRIAN: "And the sons of the foreigners who join themselves to the Lord, . . . these I will bring to my holy mountain and make them joyful in my house of prayer." These words refer to the church of the Gentiles, as the Lord himself explained to the Jews, and it is written in the Gospel, "My house shall be called the house of prayer for all nations."[16] COMMENTARY ON ISAIAH 56.7.[17]

WE FIND THE CHURCH AROUND THE WORLD. JEROME: The holy mountain or the teachings of the truth are the confession of the Trinity or the Lord himself, to whom in the last days, according to Isaiah and the prophet Micah, many nations will flood.[18] The house of prayer is the church, which is distributed across the whole globe. COMMENTARY ON ISAIAH 15.22.[19]

DO NOT TREAT MINISTRY AS A BUSINESS. JEROME: Is it not written, "He says, 'My house shall be called a house of prayer for all the nations'"? We read this in Isaiah: "But you have made it a den of thieves."[20] . . .

Where we read, "You have made it a den of thieves," John's Gospel had instead, "You have made it a house of business." Wherever there are thieves, there is a house of trafficking. Would that it were applied only to the Jews and not the Christians! We would, indeed, weep for them but rejoice for ourselves. But now, in many places, the house of God, the house of the Father, has become a place of business. . . . I who am speaking and each one of you, priest, deacon or bishop, who yesterday was a poor man, who today is a rich man in the house of God! HOMILIES ON MARK 83 (MARK 11:15-17).[21]

UNITY IS NATURAL. LEANDER OF SEVILLE: Heresies and schism spring from the source of evils and, therefore, whoever comes to unity returns

---

[13]Mt 25:1-13. [14]NPNF 2 13:367-68*. [15]PG 70:1245. [16]Mk 11:17. [17]SESHS 2:159*. [18]Mic 4:1-2. [19]AGLB 35:1599-600. [20]Lk 19:46. [21]FC 57:182-83.

from vice to nature; for just as it is natural for many to become one, so is it a vice to avoid the sweetness of brotherly love. Let us, then, with our whole hearts be lifted up in joy that Christ has restored to his friendship in a single church the people who perished from love of strife. In this church, the harmony of love will again receive them. Of this church, the prophet foretold, saying, "My house shall be called a house of prayer for all peoples." HOMILIES ON THE TRIUMPH OF THE CHURCH.[22]

THE CHURCH EMBRACES ALL HUMAN BEINGS. CASSIODORUS: As if you did not know that all human beings come from Adam and that it is written that the nations will believe in Christ, as it is said, "My house will be called a house of prayer for all nations." . . . . The saints were uncircumcised before they were circumcised, and Abraham before circumcision had faith, since there is one God who justifies a circumcision of faith. And he proclaims that each nation ought to be saved through the faith of Christ, that is, by faith in him. EXPOSITION OF ROMANS 3.[23]

THE GOSPEL MAKES PRAYER AN OPTION FOR ALL. AUGUSTINE: It is written in the prophet Isaiah, "My house will be called a house of prayer among all nations." But perhaps the Jews will say that the house of God, that is, the synagogue, is open to all. We will not argue the point, except to say that the circumcised always appeal to the law. For their law is of the manner of Abraham's circumcision. Nothing new is to be seen in what the prophet gives. But if only worthless things can be found, who will say that the prophet is speaking unnecessary and empty words? I do not know whether it is prudent to listen and not to prohibit. For since the Jewish people because of their sins, which took them away from God, were asking requests from idols, they were often rebuked by the prophets. They did not want to walk the road of penitence and return to God; to their shame he signals his house is open to all nations for prayer and that since the Jews have abandoned it, he will put others in their place. For if the nations were always being admitted to the law, as the Jews claim, how was the prophet speaking of the future, unless that signified something other than had already been commanded? For it would not be possible to speak of such things as happening every day, since they were yet to come. QUESTIONS ON THE OLD TESTAMENT 44.[24]

56:8 Gathering the Outcasts

GOD'S ENDURING LOYALTY TO HIS PEOPLE. PROCOPIUS OF GAZA: The Savior, however, is gentle not only with the nations. For he says, "I will gather the scattered of Israel." For these were far from the community in the law, being far away from Judah, and [they] were idol worshiping and teaching doctrines and precepts of human invention. Those who were thus gathered included the godly of old and even the disciples of the Savior. COMMENTARY ON ISAIAH 56.1-11.[25]

---

[22]FC 62:232-33. [23]PL 68:432. [24]PL 35:2240. [25]PG 87:2568-69.

56:9—57:2 GOD'S ACCUSATION OF THE WICKED

⁹All you beasts of the field, come to devour—
  all you beasts in the forest.
¹⁰His watchmen are blind,
  they are all without knowledge;
they are all dumb dogs,*
  they cannot bark;
dreaming, lying down,
  loving to slumber.
¹¹The dogs have a mighty appetite;
  they never have enough.
The shepherds also have no understanding;
  they have all turned to their own way,
  each to his own gain, one and all.
¹²"Come," they say, "let us^d get wine,

let us fill ourselves with strong drink;
and tomorrow will be like this day,
  great beyond measure."

57 The righteous man perishes,
  and no one lays it to heart;
devout men are taken away,
  while no one understands.
For the righteous man is taken away from
    calamity,
  ² he enters into† peace;
they rest in their beds
  who walk in their uprightness.

d One ancient Ms Syr Vg Tg: Heb *me*   * Syriac (Peshitta) *stammering dogs*   † LXX *his grave shall be in*

OVERVIEW: Those Israelites who became wild are to come back to their true owner (PROCOPIUS). The Gentiles are also his, and he summons all those who fear him (EUSEBIUS). Sometimes the Gentiles, however, despite all their education and reason, act like brute beasts (CHRYSOSTOM). Isaiah here predicts such brutishness, speaking of when the ruthless Romans came to besiege the Jews (THEODORET). The sleep of such brutes is not innocent but receptive to occult messages (ISHO'DAD). These false messages delivered to the disobedient are the source of their error (BASIL). Church leaders without courage to speak out will lack courage to guard their flock (GREGORY THE GREAT), especially during times of persecution. But martyrs will rest on an eternal throne (JEROME). It is the resurrection that gives them peace in heaven as their resting place (THEODORET). The elect deserve to escape the evils of the world but are kept there by God as motivating examples (GREGORY THE GREAT).

56:9 *All You Beasts*

AN INVITATION TO A SPIRITUAL BANQUET.
PROCOPIUS OF GAZA: "The beasts of the forest" means the nations. For a forest denotes the group of nations of different branches that he invites to the spiritual banquet. According to Aquila, he does not call them simply wild beasts, but "his wild beasts." Why "his"? Why "God's"? Because, captured by the devil, they became wild beasts under his tyranny and while alive they were hardly human. Yet God calls these as his own to his spiritual banquet, to eat the bread of life and to rejoice.... For although they were away from him for a long time, they were able through faith to come close to him and to share in the bread that strengthens the heart of humankind. COMMENTARY ON ISAIAH 56.1-11.[1]

---

[1]PG 87:2569.

EVEN THE WILD BEASTS ARE IN HIS POWER.
EUSEBIUS OF CAESAREA: We have often seen the
mass of the other nations called "the woodlands."
These are the beasts of God's calling worthy to be
called up due to their fear. Aquila has instead, "all
the beasts," "all his living beings," and then, the
second time, "all his living things." Do they
belong to someone or to God? For he does not
call them simply "beasts" but "his." Isaiah made
mention of the nations of other tribes and the
forest of beasts, and he saw in the Spirit that
these would obey the call; yet so many of the Jews
were persistent in unbelief. COMMENTARY ON
ISAIAH 2.45.[2]

ROMANS WILL ATTACK JUDEA. THEODORET OF
CYR: Having made these promises to foreigners
and eunuchs, he predicts to the Jews the last siege
that would be made by the Romans. . . . The
Roman army was gathered from diverse nations,
because they were at that time the masters of all
Europe and had conquered the larger part of Asia.
This is why the prophetic text says, "Come to
devour, all you beasts of the forest." Some, however, have related these words to Gog and Magog,[3]
without observing the fact that the latter were consumed in the mountains of Judea under the effect
of punishment coming from God, whereas those
who are now summoned are being urged to devour
other people. COMMENTARY ON ISAIAH 18.56.6-9.[4]

56:10 Dumb Dogs

THE GENTILES ARE LIKE BEASTS. CHRYSOS-
TOM: Hence even sacred Scripture, with these
sorts of disturbing passions in mind, in many
places applies the names of brutes and of wild
beasts to those gifted with reason; sometimes it
calls them "dogs" on account of their shameful
and headstrong behavior—"dumb dogs," since
they are "unable even to bark." HOMILIES ON
GENESIS 12.10.[5]

**THE PRACTICE OF IDOLATRY AND DIVINA-
TION.** ISHO'DAD OF MERV: "They are all stam-

mering dogs" who stutter the praise of God and
"cannot bark" against the idols, as against strangers. "They dream, lay down and love to slumber,"
that is, they love to sleep in the graves and in the
places where sacrifices are offered to demons, and
there they expect from them visions, dreams and
ghosts. COMMENTARY ON ISAIAH 56.10.[6]

**BE VIGILANT AGAINST A FALSE PROPHETIC
GIFT.** BASIL THE GREAT: In souls, pure and
cleansed from all defilement, the prophetic gift
shines clear. In a foul mirror you cannot see what
the reflection is, neither can a soul preoccupied
with cares of this life and darkened with the passions of the lust of the flesh receive the rays of the
Holy Spirit. Every dream is not a prophecy, as
Zechariah says, "The Lord shall make bright
clouds and give them showers of rain . . . for the
idols have spoken vanity, and the diviners have
spoken false dreams."[7] Those who, as Isaiah says,
"dream and love to sleep in their bed" forget that
an instigation of error is sent to "the children of
disobedience."[8] LETTER 210.6.[9]

56:11 Turning to Their Own Way

GUARD DOGS OF THE FLOCK. GREGORY THE
GREAT: For often church leaders do not have
foresight, and they fear to lose favor with human
beings and fear to say the right things freely and
according to the voice of truth. They in no way
act with the attention of the pastors of the flock
but are more like hired hands who flee when the
wolf approaches,[10] while they themselves quietly
hide. LETTER 1.24.[11]

57:1-2 The Righteous Man

THE SPECIAL ROYAL ROAD OF CHRIST.
JEROME: The peace of the righteous Man is coming, who, when departing from the apostles and

---

[2]GCS 57(9):350-51. [3]Ezek 38-39. [4]SC 315:192-94. [5]FC 74:162**.
[6]CSCO 303(128):55. [7]Zech 10:1-2. [8]Eph 2:2. [9]NPNF 2 8:251*.
[10]Jn 10:12-13. [11]CCL 140:25.

ascending to the Father, said, "My peace I give to you, my peace I bequeath to you."[12] And when the peace of Christ that surpasses every bodily sense arrives, his apostles will be resting in their beds, and death will become their rest. This shows that martyrs do not perish but conquer and take their rest on an eternal throne. But the Man of peace, whose apostles rest in their beds, walks his own direction, a victor ascending to the Father by the upright path. Then there is what we read in the Septuagint: "The Righteous Man is removed from the face of evil and there will be peace at his grave, which is set apart," all referring directly to the Messiah, without any admixture from the apostles. For Christ's grave is in peace and set apart, nor did his body either see corruption or remain in the tomb. He is "free among the dead,"[13] as the angel said to the women: "Jesus whom you seek is not here."[14] COMMENTARY ON ISAIAH 15.25.[15]

CROSS AND RESURRECTION. THEODORET OF CYR: He foretells here the cross of the Master; for he calls the Master Christ "righteous," he who committed no sin and in whose mouth no deceit

was found. . . . "His grave shall be in peace." For the righteous has been removed out of the way of injustice. He says this about Christ our Master and simultaneously lets us see the injustice of the murder and the victory that followed the death. For the death effected for us the reconciliation with God. He himself left his grave to ascend to the heavens. COMMENTARY ON ISAIAH 18.57.1-2.[16]

NOT ALL THE ELECT ARE REMOVED FROM THE WORLD. GREGORY THE GREAT: The malice remaining in the world deserves no better than to have those who could be of profit quickly taken away. It is to spare the elect the sight of worse evils that they are removed when the end of time approaches. . . . It is not our belief, however, that all the elect are taken out of this world, leaving only the perverse to continue on, for sinners would never turn to sorrow and repentance if there were no good examples to motivate them. DIALOGUE 3.37.[17]

---

[12]Jn 14:27. [13]Ps 88:6 (87:7 LXX, Vg). [14]Mk 16:6. [15]AGLB 35:1609-10. [16]SC 315:196-98. [17]FC 39:185.

57:3-8 IDOLATRY IS SHAMEFUL ADULTERY

[3]But you, draw near hither,
  sons of the sorceress,
  offspring of the adulterer and the harlot.
[4]Of whom are you making sport?
  Against whom do you open your mouth wide
  and put out your tongue?
Are you not children of transgression,
  the offspring of deceit,
[5]you who burn with lust among the oaks,

  under every green tree;
who slay your children in the valleys,
  under the clefts of the rocks?
[6]Among the smooth stones of the valley is your portion;
  they, they, are your lot;
to them you have poured out a drink offering,
  you have brought a cereal offering.
  Shall I be appeased for these things?
[7]Upon a high and lofty mountain

you have set your bed,
and thither you went up to offer sacrifice.
[8]*Behind the door and the doorpost*
you have set up your symbol;
for, deserting me, you have uncovered your bed,
you have gone up to it,

you have made it wide;
and you have made a bargain for yourself
with them,
you have loved their bed,
you have looked on nakedness.[e]

e The meaning of the Hebrew is uncertain

Overview: Despite the descendants of Israel being called the "children of transgression" here, the spiritual fate of the lost is not predetermined, since even the worst can and do repent (Jerome). They had abandoned God and chose instead to worship idols, which is shameful and deserving of divine anger (Cyril). God through Isaiah confronts the unfaithfulness of his people (Jerome). There is nothing but spiritual bondage in such idolatry (Theodoret). God should be enough for all we desire (Augustine).

57:4 Children of Transgression

Abandoning God Is a Moral Choice.
Jerome: Since, therefore, history is clear that those who killed Christ were the children of those who did these things,[1] the question occurs as to how they are called "children of perdition," in opposition to those who wish to be of a different nature. The former are evil and lost, unable to be saved, whereas the latter are good, unable to perish. For if, as they think, the children of perdition are worse by nature, how is it possible that one of them could be found who was previously lost? In the parable of the prodigal, moreover, both the one sheep lost out of one hundred and the one silver coin lost out of ten were found again, as was the son, about whom the father said to his elder brother: "This your brother was lost and is found again; he was dead, and now he lives!"[2] For no one perishes unless previously healthy, and no one dies unless previously alive. Therefore, those who are now called children of perdition, or children of iniquity and crime, have

failed the Lord by their own fault and thus began to be children of perdition when they were still children of the Lord, as the prophet says to these very people: "You failed the Lord and provoked the holy One of Israel to wrath."[3] We can receive this, according to the tropological sense, as applying to heretics who are children of perdition and the seed of the worst, or liars. For they were liars from the beginning, just like the devil, who is the father of their lie and the father of every lie.[4] . . . Nor is there any doubt but that such children of perdition and wicked seed will themselves have many children whom they will deceive and murder in deep valleys and in the abyss of impiety, under overhanging rocks that continuously threaten destruction, rocks that are called "many" on account of the diversity of their lies and the variety of their false doctrines. We, by contrast, have one Rock that the people of God continuously follow and from which the people of Israel formerly drank, when they enjoyed familiarity with the Lord.[5] Commentary on Isaiah 16.3.[6]

57:5 Slay Your Children

Shall God Not Be Angry? Cyril of Alexandria: This shows them to be those who detest God, having a sick hatred for him and ready to eat blood. There was nothing new in this; it was a long established custom. For you are the ones

[1]Namely, fathers of the chosen people who commingled with pagans, sacrificed their children to demons, polluted the ground with innocent blood, worshiped idols. See Ps 106:34ff. (105:34ff. LXX, Vg). [2]Lk 15:32. [3]Is 65:11. [4]Jn 8:44. [5]Ex 17:6; Num 20:11; 1 Cor 10:4. [6]AGLB 35:1631-32.

who have from long ago called on idols under a leafy tree. . . . Your guilt is that you first think to kill your firstborn and then offer libations to impure demons and soulless idols; so slaying will also be your portion and your lot. . . . Should I not be angry with these people? Is there not a good cause for my anger? COMMENTARY ON ISAIAH 5.3.57.5-7.[7]

57:8 Behind the Door

THE DECEIT OF IDOLATRY. JEROME: First we will discuss the Hebrew, which differs greatly in this location from the Septuagint. As for what it said above [Is 57:7], "You have set your bed on a high and lofty mountain," it also accuses her of behaving like a prostitute, standing behind the door to the entrance of houses and in other shadowy places, such that whoever wished to enter a room would have temptation before his eyes. Now, it blames and insults the same adulterous wife, who, while sleeping with her husband, will secretly receive an adulterer and uncover herself to him and extend her bed for him and forge an agreement with him, as though she were signing a contract. COMMENTARY ON ISAIAH 16.6.[8]

SPIRITUAL BONDAGE IN IDOLATRY. THEODORET OF CYR: "You have made a bargain for yourselves with them" means, "You have united with many demons, and you have followed their laws, and you have covenanted to serve each one." COMMENTARY ON ISAIAH 18.57.8.[9]

GOD ALONE SUFFICES. AUGUSTINE: Rightly does God through the prophet reproach the sinful soul that goes whoring away from him and say, "You thought, if you withdrew from me, you would have more?"[10] But like that younger son, why, you have ended up feeding pigs; why, you have lost all things;[11] why, you have remained in want and left it very late before you grew tired and came back. Now at last realize that what the Father gave you, he could keep for you more safely. . . . O sinful soul, filled with harlotries, turned foul and faded, turned unclean, and still loved like that! So go back to the beautiful one, in order to return to beauty; go back and speak to him who alone suffices you. . . . So lift your heart up, do not leave it on the ground, or in those beggarly treasures or in a place to rot. In Adam, too, the root of all evils was avarice. You see, he wanted more than he had received, because God had not been enough for him. SERMON 177.9.[12]

---

[7]PG 70:1260-61. [8]AGLB 36:1636-37. [9]SC 315:202-4. [10]Mk 11:17 (cf. Mt 21:13; Lk 19:46). [11]Lk 15:14-16. [12]WSA 3 5:285-86.

57:9-14 A COMPLACENT PEOPLE

[9]You journeyed to Molech[f] with oil
    and multiplied your perfumes;
you sent your envoys far off,
    and sent down even to Sheol.
[10]You were wearied with the length of your
    way,
    but you did not say, "It is hopeless";

you found new life for your strength,
    and so you were not faint.

[11]Whom did you dread and fear,
    so that you lied,
and did not remember me,
    did not give me a thought?

Have I not held my peace, even for a long time,
and so you do not fear me?
[12]I will tell of your righteousness and your
doings,
but they will not help you.
[13]When you cry out, let your collection of idols
deliver you!
The wind will carry them off,
a breath will take them away.

But he who takes refuge in me shall possess
the land,
and shall inherit my holy mountains.

[14]And it shall be said,
"Build up, build up, prepare the way,
remove every obstruction from my
people's way."

f Or *the king*

Overview: The spiritual life does not wander to far off places of the soul. Both riches and poverty are a test (Jerome). And yet, God desires to show mercy even in the face of such rebellion (Cyril, Jerome), inviting sinners instead to occupy a place of fellowship and holiness, the church, which is our prize in this life (Augustine). But no one should forget Israel's example in which judgment and harsh punishment came to them for their complacency (Ephrem).

57:9 You Journeyed

The Right Royal Way of Moderation.
Jerome: Whoever walks along the one royal way does not labor. Indeed, God issued a commandment about this through Moses: "You shall walk along the royal way and not deviate to your right or to your left."[1] The one way is the way of truth, as it says in the Gospel: "I am the way, the truth and the life."[2] But there are various ways of deception, along which Jerusalem is now demonstrated to have walked. God, who knows the difference between such ways, said earlier to those who were wandering: "Your ways are not like my way."[3] And those who trust in the Lord said, "You have caused our ways not to depart from your ways."[4] With knowledge of the one royal way, then, let us beware of deviations to the left and right, along which we are forbidden to walk. The royal way is temperance, having neither too little nor too much. For example, the royal and right

way entails prudence; we deviate to the right if we understand more than is proper for us to understand and if we prefer cleverness above prudence, by which measure the serpent was more prudent than all the animals in paradise[5] and the children of darkness are more prudent than the children of light.[6] We deviate to the left, however, when we are foolish and have less understanding than is necessary. Concerning such people, it is said, "The fool says in his heart, 'There is no God.'"[7] Commentary on Isaiah 16.7.[8]

Human Pride.
Jerome: The royal road also involves fortitude and constancy, from which the impulsive and rash deviate to the right and the timid and fearful deviate to the left. Hence, a holy person desiring to walk along the right way prays, "Lead me, Lord, on the right path,"[9] and, in another passage, "Make known to me, O Lord, the way in which I should walk, for to you I lift my eyes."[10] ... Then it continues, according to the Hebrew: "You found life by your own hand, so you did not beseech" [Is 57:10], which has the following sense and meaning: Because you were abounding in all things and flowing in riches, you neglected the Lord, whereas Solomon refused such riches precisely so that he would not forget

[1]Num 20:11. [2]Jn 14:6. [3]Is 55:8. [4]Ps 44:18 (43:19 LXX, Vg). [5]Gen 3:1. [6]Lk 16:8. [7]Ps 14:1 (13:1 LXX, Vg). [8]AGLB 36:1639-40. [9]Ps 27:11 (26:11 LXX, Vg). Cf. Ps 139:24 (138:24 LXX, Vg). [10]Ps 143:8 (142:8 LXX, Vg).

God. . . . For not only riches but poverty also tests a person, which is why it was written above: "I tested you on the road of poverty,"[11] the same road on which Lazarus the poor man was tested, who sustained debilitating illness as well as poverty.[12] Commentary on Isaiah 16.7.[13]

God's Desire to Show Mercy. Cyril of Alexandria: But how could it not have been necessary to act as a suppliant and ask God for mercy when you had dared to commit such shameful and foul deeds? For he receives those who wish to repent. He is good by nature, and he knows our substance, as it is written. For he has spoken through one of the holy prophets: "Return, my sons, return and I will heal you from what oppresses you."[14] Therefore this is a sin of their extreme lawlessness and of their total turning away and being fixed in evil things, that they refuse to seek mercy from God by confessing their sins. Commentary on Isaiah 5.3.57.10.[15]

57:11 You Do Not Remember Me

Remembrance, Trust and Fear. Jerome: "Of what are you so afraid that you would lie and neither remember me nor think of me in your heart? For I am silent, as if I do not see, and you forget me."[16] Because you put your trust in the gods whose storehouses are full, you refused to ask me and were thus fearful of many things. For you were unable to say, "The Lord is my help, and I am therefore unafraid of my enemies,"[17] or "The Lord is my light and my savior, so whom shall I fear?"[18] If at any time you chose to speak against what was in your own mind, you lied. For how would you be able to invoke me, who remember neither me nor any of my precepts, such as: "Honor the Lord and you will be strong and will fear nothing"[19]? For, according to Symmachus and Aquila, I am he who continually remained silent about your sins and pretended to ignore the crimes you committed, as though I had not seen them at all, this so that you would return to me at least for the sake of my patience,

if not because you fear me. . . . The word *mind*, which is associated with the heart in the Septuagint, is not written in the Hebrew text but is added here as though it were a gloss on how the mind ought to be identified with the heart in Scripture. Commentary on Isaiah 16.8.[20]

57:13 My Holy Mountain

The Church Is the Mountain. Augustine: This, as I have said, is obscure: "shall possess the land and inhabit my holy mountain." After all, if we take it literally and materialistically, we won't be cleansing ourselves from every defilement of flesh and spirit; and God will have procured for us to no purpose the conjunction of the end of the reading from the prophet with the beginning of the reading from the apostle, if to possess some earthly mountain we start getting ourselves ready for avarice, not for godliness. Well, but what should we understand by the mountain? It is obscure what [Isaiah] meant by "mountain."

Yes, but if God had really let us down, he would nowhere say what mountain means. Where he does tell us openly, that is where you must love the mountain. Where he openly recommends a mountain to you, and Scripture opens itself up to say what mountain means, that is where you must love it. Yes, wherever you hear such a mountain promised you, set your sights on it. . . . What sort of mountain really has been promised us? . . .

The church itself is the mountain . . . we are going to rise again, and we shall be the holy mountain of God. On this mountain dwells whoever has given himself to God. "But those who have given themselves to me shall possess the land and inhabit my holy mountain." Sermon 45.3-5.[21]

---

[11]Is 48:10. [12]Lk 16:19-31. [13]AGLB 36:1641-42. [14]Jer 3:22. [15]PG 70:1268. [16]Is 57:11. [17]Ps 118:7 (117:7 LXX, Vg). [18]Ps 27:1 (26:1 LXX, Vg). [19]See Ps 27:14 (26:14 LXX, Vg). [20]AGLB 36:1643. [21]WSA 3 2:253-55.

57:14 Remove Every Obstacle

A REFERENCE TO THE ZEALOTS. EPHREM THE SYRIAN: "And it shall be said, 'Remove every obstruction from my people's way.'" Probably he said these words with regard to the Jewish Zeal- ots, who killed their fellow citizens, because they had lapsed into idolatry and had been an obstacle for their fellows in the days of the Greeks. COM- MENTARY ON ISAIAH 57.14.[22]

[22]SESHS 2:163.

57:15-21 COMFORT FOR THE LONELY IN SPIRIT

^{15}*For thus says the high and lofty One*
  who inhabits eternity, whose name is Holy:
"I dwell in the high and holy place,
  and also with him who is of a contrite and
   humble spirit,
to revive the spirit of the humble,
  and to revive the heart of the contrite.
^{16}*For I will not contend for ever,*
  nor will I always be angry;
for from me proceeds the spirit,
  and I have made the breath of life.
^{17}*Because of the iniquity of his covetousness I*
   was angry,
  I smote him, I hid my face and was angry;
  but he went on backsliding in the way of his

  own heart.
^{18}*I have seen his ways, but I will heal him;*
  I will lead him and requite him with
   comfort,
  creating for his mourners the fruit of the
   lips.
^{19}*Peace, peace, to the far and to the near, says*
   the LORD;
  and I will heal him.
^{20}*But the wicked are like the tossing sea;*
  for it cannot rest,
  and its waters toss up mire and dirt.
^{21}*There is no peace,* says my God, for the*
   wicked."

* LXX *joy*

OVERVIEW: The God who exists by and for himself is the one who has shown mercy (CYRIL). God's discipline is disproportionate to our sins, which deserve greater punishment than they receive (THEODORE). The humble in whom Christ dwells are thereby heavenly, having the gift of the Holy Spirit who proceeds from the Father while sent by the Son (JEROME). He chooses to dwell in us even though we are undeserving (THEODORET). But it is part of God's majesty to have the mercy by which he tempers his wrath (CASSIODORUS).

No matter the depravity, the sincere penitent is accepted by God (CHRYSOSTOM). Praise comes when a penitent people are restored (ISHO'DAD). Peace inside and out should mark the Christian community (APOSTOLIC CONSTITUTIONS). One should humbly esteem one's soul and true position (CHRYSOSTOM). Life in God is the source of good and, therefore, of happiness (AUGUSTINE) because Christ chose to be alienated from the

Father in our stead and to take on our sins that ultimately drove him to mourning and death (JEROME). Only when our sorrow is heartfelt over the sins that drove him to this can the heart issue spiritual praise (THEODORET) and experience true joy, something David experienced but that the wicked could never taste (AUGUSTINE).

57:15 A Holy Name and a Humble Spirit

WORSHIP THE UNCHANGING GOD. CYRIL OF ALEXANDRIA: The blessed prophets, when the Lord of the universe promises what is great and godly to them, were filled with much wonder at his glory and clemency and, as if responding from excitement, they run to give praise. We find the prophet doing precisely that here. The Lord says these things but has to add, "the exalted," that is, he who is by nature over and above all things that have come to be. "I dwell in the high places" means again that he is in the unshakeable upper reaches and that this divine and lofty nature is in the ineffable transcendence that is above. However, I think that this, the divine nature's dwelling in the exalted places, is forever. For it exists without change in these places by itself, and there is nothing in better conditions than it is, but rather the being that is in these conditions unchangingly exists unceasingly. COMMENTARY ON ISAIAH 5.3.57.15-16.[1]

GOD'S DISCIPLINE AND PENITENCE. THEODORE OF HERACLEA: By these names the kindness of God shows that he is supreme. For those sharing in these titles have made him to be low, consorting with idols and demons. Although he is holy, these people blaspheme his name with evil desires and deeds that are not honorable. He says, I am holy, and I rejoice with the holy as I sanctify them, stirring up their power and rousing them in their attitudes, providing they show themselves to be worthy and demonstrate their wills to be contrite and penitent. For to such I will grant eternal life.

Revenge is meant in the sense that God will give sinners over to troubles so that they receive discipline. God does these things, yet also he spares our race in his compassion. God shows his compassion in these instances of recompense by only disciplining us a little, given the large amount of our sins. FRAGMENTS ON ISAIAH.[2]

THE HEAVENLY QUALITY OF THE HUMBLE. JEROME: Thus says the Lord, who is exalted and sublime, who dwells in the heights and is holy in the saints, though not as in a locality but in the merit of those in whom he lives, one of whom said in the Psalms: "I will exalt you, O Lord, for you have raised me."[3] . . . It is not to be understood from this that God is elevated by human speech but that God can be exalted also in the humble, according to what was said elsewhere: "God has become my salvation."[4] . . . Moreover, just as wisdom does not enter a wicked soul, neither does it dwell in a body subjected to sins. In this way does the holy One dwell in saints. And wherever there is filth, purity cannot live. . . . For Christ does not dwell in earthly places but in regions above the heavens, which proclaim the glory of the Lord.[5] COMMENTARY ON ISAIAH 16.11.[6]

57:16 The Spirit and the Cessation of God's Anger

GOD IS PRESENT EVERYWHERE BY HIS SPIRIT. JEROME: We certainly ought not to agree, after the Jewish custom, that God is enclosed in any place and dwells only in heaven. For God, by whom all things are held together, is present everywhere. Instead, we should understand correctly the meaning of heights and heavens and saints and virtues. . . .

Because I strike in order to correct, therefore do I kill in order to bring to life. For I have mercy on my creatures, nor will I allow those whom I

---

[1]PG 70:1273. [2]PG 18:1364. [3]Ps 30:1 (29:1 LXX, Vg). [4]Ps 118:14 (117:14 LXX, Vg). [5]See Ps 8:2 (8:3 LXX, Vg); 113:4 (112:4 LXX, Vg); 148:4. [6]AGLB 36:1648-49.

have established to perish eternally. And my Spirit that proceeds from me, or, according to the Hebrew of Aquila and Symmachus and Theodotion, that "encompasses all things" (for this is what the Greek words *perieilēthēsetai* and *periballei* signify), is the animator of all that exists. I also created the breath, or plural breaths (this is what "nasamoth" indicates), about which it is written elsewhere: "May every breath, or everything that breathes, praise the Lord."[7] . . . Some among us say that this is the Spirit[8] whereby all the world is inspired and ruled. . . . But others understand it to be the Holy Spirit who was borne above the waters in the beginning and vivified everything,[9] the Spirit who proceeds from the Father and, because of the union[10] of natures, is sent by the Son, on account of which he said: "It is expedient for you that I go away, for unless I depart, the Paraclete will not come to you. If I go, however, I will send him to you."[11] . . . Let no one be scandalized, though, if the Spirit is said to proceed from the Father, for the Son also says this about himself: "I proceeded and came from the Father; I did not come on my own, but he sent me."[12] COMMENTARY ON ISAIAH 16.11-12.[13]

THE CONDESCENSION OF A GOD WHO LOVES THE WORST. THEODORET OF CYR: He has shown the variety of types of care; although he dwells in the heavens, [God] considers lowly things, and though as holy he resides among holy ones he gives spiritual comfort to those who are spiritually weak. Those who are heartbroken he leads back to life. For he does not concern himself only with the righteous but also with those who have let themselves draw near to the abyss of evil, and he brings healing in various ways to those afflicted in soul. COMMENTARY ON ISAIAH 18.57.15.[14]

DIVINE MERCY AS MAJESTY QUALIFIES WRATH. CASSIODORUS: It is easier for the Lord to restrain his anger, which we know is remote from his tranquility; but we should believe that he is more inclined to mercy, which is never

detached from his majesty. . . . So he will not restrain his mercy in anger, but rather he will refrain from anger in mercy, as long as devoted conversion is forthcoming in this world. Remember too that in the case of the Lord anger is mentioned in a loose rather than a precise sense. EXPOSITION OF PSALM 76.10.[15]

57:18 Healing and the Fruit of the Lips

THE CASE OF EXTREME SINNERS. CHRYSOSTOM: For such is the loving-kindness of God; he never turns his face away from a sincere repentance, but if any one has pushed on to the very extremity of wickedness and chooses to return afterwards toward the path of virtue, God accepts and welcomes and does everything so as to restore him to his former position. LETTER TO THE FALLEN THEODORE 1.6.[16]

THE SALVATION OF THE PEOPLE. ISHO'DAD OF MERV: "Creating for his mourners the fruit of the lips," that is, at this stage they will not use anymore their outrages and blasphemies against me, but praises, which are convenient to these facts. Others assert, I made them live in perfect security, and this is the reason why they will be led to holiness. COMMENTARY ON ISAIAH 57.18-19.[17]

57:19 Peace

THE IMPORTANCE OF PEACE. APOSTOLIC CONSTITUTIONS: It is our duty to be at peace in our own minds, for the person who does not find any disorder in himself will not quarrel with another but will be peaceable, friendly, gathering the Lord's people and a fellow worker with him, in order to increase the number of those who shall be saved in unanimity. For those who contrive enmities, and strifes, and contests and lawsuits

[7]Ps 150:6. [8]Referring to passages quoted from Gen 2:7 and Job 27:3. [9]See Gen 1:2. [10]Lat *societatem*. [11]Jn 16:7. [12]Jn 8:42. [13]*AGLB* 36:1650-53. [14]SC 315:208. [15]ACW 52:243-44. [16]NPNF 1 9:95. [17]CSCO 303(128):56.

are wicked and aliens from God. CONSTITU-
TIONS OF THE HOLY APOSTLES 2.7.54.[18]

**A CHRISTIAN PERSPECTIVE IS NOT BASED ON
CIRCUMSTANCES.** CHRYSOSTOM: But let us
humble our own souls by almsgiving and forgiving our neighbors their trespasses, by not remembering injuries or avenging ourselves. If we
continually reflect on our sins, no external circumstances can make us elated, neither riches,
nor power, nor authority nor honor; no, even
should we sit in the imperial chariot itself, we cry
bitterly. ON THE EPISTLE TO THE HEBREWS 9.9.[19]

SEEK COMFORT IN THE TRULY GOOD LIFE.
AUGUSTINE: Through love of this true life you
ought, then, to consider yourself desolate in this
world, no matter what happiness you enjoy. For,
just as that is the true life in comparison with
which this other, which is so much loved, is not
to be called life, however pleasant and prolonged
it may be, so that is their true comfort that God
promised by the prophet saying, "I will give them
true comfort, peace on peace." Without this comfort there is no more grief than consolation to be
found in earthly comforts, whatever they may be.
... Not by such goods do we become good, but
having become good otherwise, they make these
things good by their good use of them. Therefore,
there is no true comfort in these things; rather, it
is found where true life is. A person's happiness
necessarily must come from the same source as
his goodness. LETTER 130.[20]

THE AFFLICTION OF CHRIST. JEROME: Some
understand this passage to be about the Savior in
particular, because he was deeply saddened for a
while over the sins of the world, saying, "My soul
is sorrowful to the point of death."[21] And the
Father struck him, who said through Zechariah,
"I will strike the shepherd, and the sheep will be
scattered."[22] ... God also averted his face from
the Savior, so that he could accept the "form of a
servant"[23] for a time and walk in sadness, mourning the sins of the people and deploring and

lamenting Jerusalem. Because the Father saw the
road he was traveling, he healed him who was
"forsaken among the dead."[24] COMMENTARY ON
ISAIAH 16.13.[25]

**THE IMPORTANCE OF HEARTFELT REPEN-
TANCE.** THEODORET OF CYR: Symmachus and
Aquila, instead of saying, "to the afflicted," have
said "to those who weep for him." God our Master has shown the power of repentance. For he
has seen their regret and their change of thinking
and the sadness of their expression, and he has
deemed them to be worthy of encouragement,
they and those who weep for them. Now it is the
heralds of truth who weep for them, while the
blessed Paul prayed that he might be cut off for
their sake.[26] These things he has done, God who
created fruit of the lips, that is, he who established the sacrifice of praise, rather than the cult
appointed by the law. COMMENTARY ON ISAIAH
18.57.17-19.[27]

57:21 No Joy for the Wicked

TRUE AND FALSE JOYS. AUGUSTINE: For that joy
that is after the fashion of the world is not true
joy. Hear the prophet Isaiah: "There is no joy,
says my God, to the wicked." What the wicked
call joy is not joy, such as he [David] knew, who
made no account of their joy; let us believe him,
brothers. He was a man, but he knew both kinds
of joy. He certainly knew the joys of the cup, for
he was a man; he knew the joy of the table, he
knew the joys of marriage, he knew those joys
worldly and luxurious. ... But you say, I don't see
that light which Isaiah saw. Believe and you shall
see it. For perhaps you do not have the eye to see
it. For it is a certain type of eye by which that
beauty is discerned. For just as there is an eye of
the flesh by which this light is seen, so there is an
eye of the heart by which that joy is perceived.

---

[18]ANF 7:420*. [19]NPNF 1 14:412; 9.5 in Gk text. [20]FC 18:378*.
[21]Mt 26:38. [22]Zech 13:7. [23]Phil 2:7. [24]Ps 88:6 (87:6 LXX, Vg).
[25]AGLB 36:1657. [26]2 Cor 4:11. [27]SC 315:210.

Perhaps your eye is wounded, dimmed, disturbed by passion, by greed, by indulgence, by senseless lust. Your eye is disturbed. You cannot see that light. Believe before you see. You shall be healed, and then you will see. EXPLANATIONS OF THE PSALMS 97.16.[28]

---

[28]NPNF 1 8:480*.

58:1-5 FASTING AND SABBATH

[1]*Cry aloud, spare not,*
lift up your voice like a trumpet;
declare to my people their transgression,
  to the house of Jacob their sins.
[2]*Yet they seek me daily,*
  and delight to know my ways,
as if they were a nation that did righteousness
  and did not forsake the ordinance of their
    God;
they ask of me righteous judgments,
  they delight to draw near to God.
[3]*'Why have we fasted, and thou seest it not?*
  Why have we humbled ourselves, and thou
    takest no knowledge of it?'
Behold, in the day of your fast you seek your
    own pleasure,[g]
  and oppress all your workers.
[4]*Behold, you fast only to quarrel and to fight*
  and to hit with wicked fist.
Fasting like yours this day
  will not make your voice to be heard on
    high.
[5]*Is such the fast that I choose,*
  a day for a man to humble himself?
Is it to bow down his head like a rush,
  and to spread sackcloth and ashes under
    him?
Will you call this a fast,
  and a day acceptable to the LORD?

g Or *pursue your own business*

OVERVIEW: Proclamation needs to be bold and to strike at the heart (MAXIMUS). It is the inward holiness that matters to God (CYRIL). God as truth nevertheless welcomes the liar (JEROME). God has given free will for us to consecrate to him in works and a pure conscience (ISAAC). True spirituality is about charity to the poor and cheerfulness (JEROME). Fasting should never be used to serve our own ends (EPHREM). To draw near to God occurs by refraining from sins as well as doing good works (CYRIL). Drawing near to God concerns living a life worthy of him, not just asking him to draw near in favor and providence (THEODORET). Flesh submits to spirit, which should in turn submit to God (AUGUSTINE). A fast should be characterized by humility and obedience (ATHANASIUS). Fasting should not make us think ourselves better than those who eat in moderation (JEROME). Fasting is a work that needs to be made good, not a good work in itself (CASSIAN).

58:1 A Voice Like a Trumpet

THE SHOCK TACTICS OF PROCLAMATION.
MAXIMUS OF TURIN: We are commanded then to
cry out and to cry forcefully and not to spare our
voice, lest we lose our salvation. "And do not be
sparing," he says. That is, do not pass over the
sinner's wickedness by keeping silent and by
being considerate of his shame but inconsiderate
of his well-being, for by keeping silent you have
made worse the wounds that you ought to have
healed by crying out.... We know that a trumpet
is usually not so much heard as dreaded; it is not
so much accustomed to bring pleasure as to
inspire fear. A trumpet is necessary for sinners; it
not only penetrates their ears but should strike
their heart as well; it should not delight with its
melody but chastise when it has been heard; it
should encourage the bravehearted to righteousness, while it should turn the cowardly from
their crimes. SERMON 93.1.[1]

58:2 A Nation with False Pretences

CONVERSION FROM FALSE PIETY. CYRIL OF
ALEXANDRIA: These words about the calling of
those from Israel can be transferred and come to
be understood in another good and highly useful
way.... For I think the scope of the prophecy is
to be unveiled to those who are prayerful, as will
become clear from what follows.[2] ... There were
those among them who received a reputation for
piety and behaved shamefully without being
noticed, decorating themselves on the outside
and gaining a reputation of gentleness. They
undertook fasts and made prayers, thinking that
through this they could turn aside God's anger.
... Here they learn what their sins are and that
they must turn from these if they want to be
rewarded by God and become worthy of his sparing them. COMMENTARY ON ISAIAH 5.3.58.1.[3]

GOD'S TRUTHFULNESS WELCOMES THE LIAR.
JEROME: Here, however, because they were sinners to whom it was to be proclaimed and

because they dwelled in the lowlands, the prophet
is not commanded to ascend the mountain.
Instead, he is asked only to raise his voice like a
trumpet and announce to them that wars are
coming.... For the Lord draws near to those who
draw near to him and to those who rightly follow
what is just and thus are able to say, "It is good
for me to cling to God."[4] For if Almighty God is
the Father of truth and justice, then whoever is
deceptive and unjust is unable to draw near to
God, of whom it is written: "Evil people may not
live in your presence, nor will the unjust endure
before your eyes."[5] COMMENTARY ON ISAIAH
16.14, 16.[6]

58:3 Fasting and Seeking Pleasure

FREE WILL AS THE SACRIFICE. ISAAC OF NIN-
EVEH: Ye offer [your own wills] as whole burnt
offerings unto idols; and unto the wretched
thoughts, that ye reckon in yourselves as gods, ye
daily sacrifice your free will, a thing more precious than all incense, which ye ought rather to
consecrate unto Me by your good works and your
purity of conscience. ASCETICAL HOMILIES 6.[7]

TRUE SPIRITUALITY. JEROME: The unjust accuse
the Lord of not respecting good works, and then
they offer to God only hunger pangs of the stomach but not the work of virtue. Nor do they eat
the foods that God created for believers and
those who know the truth, to be received with
thanksgiving.[8] ...

This is what follows in the Septuagint: "And
you wound all those who are subject to you," [Is
58:3] or "afflict," as in the better translation of
Theodotion and Symmachus, which we follow
with "and you are demanding of your debtors."
From this he shows that it is not without danger
to demand repayment of a poor person who is
insolvent or to refuse to return to a freezing

---

[1]ACW 50:215. [2]He refers us to Is 47:11-13. [3]PG 70:1280. [4]Ps 73:28
(72:28 LXX, Vg). [5]Ps 5:5 (5:6 LXX, Vg). [6]AGLB 36:1659, 1662.
[7]AHSIS 54. [8]See 1 Tim 4:3.

debtor the garment that you took as collateral, lest his cry reach God. For one who has mercy on the poor lends to God. In contrast, whoever demands repayment from those who have nothing violates God. . . . The servant of the Lord . . . must not be litigious but be kind and imitate him who said, "Learn from me, for I am kind and humble of heart,"[9] such that his humility would not be pretentious but of the heart, a humility that seeks the soul's conscience rather than human glory. . . .

And we say this not to reprove the practice of fasting, through which Daniel, a man of passions, came to know the future[10] and the Ninevites placated the wrath of God, and Elijah and Moses, after fasting for forty days,[11] were filled with God's friendship. The Lord, moreover, fasted for all those days of solitude in the desert in order to bequeath solemn days of fasting to us.[12] But it profits nothing to endure an empty stomach and then to do other things that are displeasing to God. . . .

Nor should they disfigure their faces but wash them with water and anoint their heads with oil, about which John the Evangelist wrote, "You also have been anointed by the holy One,"[13] through which the anointed were themselves made holy. COMMENTARY ON ISAIAH 16.16-17.[14]

IS THIS THE FAST THAT WILL PLEASE THE LORD?

EPHREM THE SYRIAN: "Fasting like yours this day will not make your voice heard on high. Is such the fast that I choose a day for a person to humble himself?" Do not fast as if with the aim to fulfill your evil intentions, as if you had made a certain vow in order to obtain one thing or another and so that misfortunes might befall your enemies. Through this kind of fasting and prayers, he says, you seek to delight your will and not mine, and, since you despise me, you say on high, "Why have we fasted, and you do not see it? Why have we humbled ourselves, and you do not notice?" COMMENTARY ON ISAIAH 58.4-5.[15]

DRAW NEAR TO GOD.

CYRIL OF ALEXANDRIA: Now fasting is a very worthwhile and excellent

thing, and prayer is most useful. And humbling oneself in God's eyes has much to commend it.[16] . . . The God of the universe says, return to me with fasting, wailing, mourning. For he readily has mercy on those doing penance through travail. But it is unusual that those wishing to receive mercy in another way should annoy the legislator and provoke him to wrath by not liking to do the things commanded. For it is necessary that all saints who wish to draw near to God not only do the good works to be done but also that they be free from all reproach. COMMENTARY ON ISAIAH 5.3.58.3-4.[17]

DRAWING NEAR TO GOD.

THEODORET OF CYR: They think that abstaining from food is the height of virtue, and they accuse me of not automatically deeming them worthy of all providence. As for the phrase "they desire to be near to God," Symmachus translates, "they wish[18] the nearness of God" and Aquila, "they will[19] the drawing near of God." The text shows that they have no desire to draw near to God, but want him to come near to them through his protection and care, even while choosing a life unworthy of him. COMMENTARY ON ISAIAH 18.58.3.[20]

THE CHAIN OF COMMAND.

AUGUSTINE: What if your flesh obeys you, and you do not obey God? Aren't you condemned by your own flesh, when it submits to you? Doesn't it bear witness against you, precisely by submitting to you? SERMON 400.7.[21]

HUMILITY AND FASTING.

ATHANASIUS: The Word blamed the children of Israel on account of such a fast as this,[22] exhorting them by Isaiah the prophet and saying, "This is not the fast or the day that I have chosen, that a person should humble his soul." That we may be able to show

[9]Mt 11:29. [10]See Dan 9:3. [11]See Ex 34:28; 1 Kings 19:8. [12]See Mt 4:2. [13]1 Jn 2:20. [14]AGLB 36:1662, 1664-65, 1667. [15]SESHS 2:165. [16]Ps 35:13 (34:13 LXX); Ps 109:24 (108:24 LXX). [17]PG 70:1281-84. [18]Gk thelousin. [19]Gk boulontai. [20]SC 315:212. [21]WSA 3 10:476. [22]See Lk 18:12.

what kind of persons we should be when we fast, and of what character the fast should be, listen again to God commanding Moses. . . . In the tenth day of this seventh month, there shall be a day of atonement; a convocation, and a holy day shall it be to you; and you shall humble your souls, and offer whole burnt offerings to the Lord.[23] And afterwards, that the law might be defined on this point, he proceeds to say, "Every soul that shall not humble itself shall be cut off from the people."[24] FESTAL LETTERS 1.4.[25]

58:5 To Humble Oneself

FASTING IS NO BASIS FOR PRIDE. JEROME: If you have fasted two or three days, do not think yourself better than others who do not fast. You fast and are angry; the other eats and wears a smiling face. You work off your irritation and hunger in quarrels. He uses food in moderation and gives God thanks. LETTER 22.37.[26]

FASTING NOT A GOOD IN ITSELF. JOHN CASSIAN: You see, then, that fasting is by no means considered an essential good by the Lord, inasmuch as it does not become good and pleasing to God by itself but in conjuction with other works. . . . By reason of accessory circumstances it might be considered not only vain but even hateful, as the Lord says: "When they fast, I will not hear their prayers."[27] CONFERENCE 21.14.7.[28]

---

[23]See Lev 23:26-32. [24]Lev 23:29. [25]NPNF 2 4:507-8**. [26]NPNF 2 6:39. [27]Jer 14:12. [28]ACW 57:731.

58:6-8 TRUE FASTING

[6]Is not this the fast that I choose:
　　to loose the bonds of wickedness,
　　to undo the thongs of the yoke,
to let the oppressed go free,
　　and to break every yoke?
[7]Is it not to share your bread with the hungry,
　　and bring the homeless poor into your
　　　　house;
when you see the naked, to cover him,

　　and not to hide yourself from your own
　　　　flesh?
[8]Then shall your light break forth like the
　　　　dawn,
　　and your healing shall spring up speedily;
your righteousness shall go before you,
　　the glory of the LORD shall be your rear
　　　　guard.

OVERVIEW: There is a spiritual fasting that is hidden and humble, a fasting from malice (CHRYSOSTOM). The spiritual benefit from giving to the poor is substantial (CAESARIUS). The gospel when lived out has one eye on the poor (JEROME). It is serious to divert energies from lawful things only in order to do forbidden things more (AUGUS-

TINE). The gospel introduces a positive righteousness for which we need to participate in Christ (CYRIL). Health is the healing of spiritual weaknesses and the easy, gracious production of goodness. Divine glory comes to accompany our good works. (THEODORET). Already in this life healing of sin's scars can occur (JEROME).

58:6 The Fast I Choose

FASTING UNSEEN. CHRYSOSTOM: Do you see, dearly beloved, what true fasting really is? Let us perform this kind and not entertain the facile notion held by many that the essence of fasting lies in going without food till evening. This is not the end in view, but that we should demonstrate, along with abstinence from food, abstinence also from whatever is harmful, and should give close attention to spiritual duties. The person fasting ought to be reserved, peaceful, meek, humble, indifferent to the esteem of this world. HOMILIES ON GENESIS 8.15.[1]

58:7 Share Your Bread

A COIN AND A KINGDOM. CAESARIUS OF ARLES: If we carefully heed the fact that Christ hungers in the person of the poor, beloved, it will be profitable for us.... Listen and see, a coin and a kingdom. What comparison is there, beloved? You give the poor a coin and receive a kingdom from Christ; you bestow a mouthful and are given eternal life; you offer clothes, and Christ grants the forgiveness of your sins. SERMON 25.2.[2]

BREAKING THE CHAINS OF INIQUITY. JEROME: But the affliction of the body entreats for the indulgence of sinners. Divine Scripture teaches us to forgive our debtors so that the heavenly Father would also forgive our debts.[3] The old history instructs in the seventh year of remission, or in the fiftieth, which is the true jubilee, to return all possessions to the Lord and to restore to one's servants their original freedom and to render void every name that was used as a warranty.[4] But if this was commanded in the law, how much more in the gospel, where all goods are doubled and where we are ordered by no means to take an eye for an eye or a tooth for a tooth but instead to offer our cheek to the assailant! ...

When you see people freezing outside the church in the frigidity of unbelief, without the warmth of faith, impoverished and homeless, lead them home into the church and clothe them with the work of incorruption, so that, wrapped in the mantle of Christ, they will not remain in the grave. COMMENTARY ON ISAIAH 16.18.[5]

THE FEAST OF THE KINDHEARTED. AUGUSTINE: He is finding fault, you see, with the fasts of the quarrelsome; he is looking for the fasts of the kindhearted. He is finding fault with those who oppress others; he is looking for those who give relief. He is finding fault with those who stir up strife; he is looking for those who set free. That is why, you see, during these days you restrain your desires for lawful things; it is in order not to commit unlawful things. If you refrain from your marriage rights during these days, then surely you should not drown yourself in wine or adultery on any day.

In this way, in humility and charity, by fasting and giving, by restraining ourselves and forgiving, by paying out good deeds and not paying back bad ones, by turning away from evil and doing good, our prayer seeks peace and obtains it. SERMON 206.3.[6]

LOVE IS THE FULFILLMENT OF THE LAW. CYRIL OF ALEXANDRIA: When you refrain from doing these things, then the things you lack will be yours. For the bearing of fruit toward the neighbor refers to the noble things of love. Love is the fulfillment of the law, as it stands written. For the fulfilling of love toward brothers and compassion are the marks of a reward with God. Seeing how to abstain from evil and doing good are not the same thing. For it does not suffice for glory with God to flee evil but to try in all ways to meet needs and do good works and hold fast to diligence in godliness ... thus the old law being a schoolmaster to Christ[7] did not introduce the fulfillment of the good for those at that time but rather taught them to restrain from evil. Thus, "do not kill, do not commit adultery, do not

[1]FC 74:114; 8.6 in Gk text. [2]FC 31:129*. [3]See Mt 6:12. [4]See Lev 25. [5]AGLB 36:1670, 1674. [6]WSA 3 6:107-8. [7]Gal 3:24.

swear"[8] have this force. But the perfect fulfillment of all goodness in the oracles is kept through Christ, through which we learn to fulfill those works of love toward God and our fellows. COMMENTARY ON ISAIAH 5.3.58.6-7.[9]

58:8 Your Light Will Break Forth

TRANSFORMING EFFECT OF DIVINE LIGHT AND HEALTH. CYRIL OF ALEXANDRIA: This oracle has great force. For it does not simply say, "Light will be given to you by God," but it will be like lightning whose course and progress is sent by God, through which is clearly shown the desire of those who pray. By saying "first light," it instructs us that it will appear before time. For God, the guardian of all things, knew, as the giver of spiritual gifts, the time suited to each person for his blessings. But if anyone is fair and good and also caring and benevolent—to that person a reward will be given as a "first thing," so that in him there will arise just like an ear of corn his health (that is, the departing of all infirmities and the returning of good health). For the one who is free of diseases is fruitful in all ways, with an easy and cheerful production of good things. So the light of the divine understanding and our healthiness both arise within us, as God removes the burden of all sickness and also sets in us in its place the will to do good works and to abound in righteousness. COM-

MENTARY ON ISAIAH 5.4.58.8.[10]

GOD GLORIFIES OUR EFFORTS. THEODORET OF CYR: The light is desirable, but more desirable still is the dawn that appears after the night. This he has called "the morning light." ... Aquila has, "Then your light will break through like the dawn." For just as the dawn tears away the curtain of the night, so, he says, the night of your misfortunes, your life lived under the law, will disperse, and the light of my providence will be supplied to you. ... "Your righteousness will go out before you, and the glory of the Lord will surround you." He makes it clear that the divine works follow our works. For with our righteousness in the vanguard, the glory of the Lord of the universe is given access, shining on us as we look for it. COMMENTARY ON ISAIAH 18.58.8.[11]

THE NEW LIFE AND THE HEALING OF SIN'S SCARS. JEROME: "And your healing," it says, "will arise quickly." Aquila translates this word for word: "And the scar of your wound will be formed quickly," so that the wounds of our sins may be closed by the quickly formed scar at the rising of the sun of justice. COMMENTARY ON ISAIAH 16.19.[12]

---

[8]Ex 20:13-16. [9]PG 70:1285-88. [10]PG 70:1288-89. [11]SC 315:216. [12]AGLB 36:1675.

58:9-12 COMPLETE RENEWAL AS THE BLESSING OF MERCY

[9]Then you shall call, and the LORD will
   answer;
   you shall cry, and he will say, Here I am.

If you take away from the midst of you the

   yoke,
   the pointing of the finger, and speaking
      wickedness,
[10]if you pour yourself out for the hungry
   and satisfy the desire of the afflicted,

then shall your light rise in the darkness
and your gloom be as the noonday.
[11]*And the* LORD *will guide you continually,*
and satisfy your desire with good things,[h]
and make your bones strong;
and you shall be like a watered garden,
like a spring of water,

whose waters fail not.
[12]*And your ancient ruins shall be rebuilt;*
you shall raise up the foundations of many
generations;
you shall be called the repairer of the breach,
the restorer of streets to dwell in.

h The meaning of the Hebrew word is uncertain

OVERVIEW: God is eager to bless our prayer requests (PSEUDO-CLEMENT). God does not wait a long time but acts immediately according to the person's need (ATHANASIUS). The believer should ask things from God when he has been obeying him (ISAAC). God is present to the believer and attends on him like the best possible parent (CHRYSOSTOM). Those who stand between God and his wrath in the world are well-esteemed (JEROME). The steward of God gives generously (GREGORY OF NAZIANZUS). God's closeness is not a vague presence but an active force to answer prayer (THEODORET). Souls nourished by God are a winning picture of his grace. Christ and reverence to God help to keep the soul established and protected (CYRIL).

58:9 Here I Am

THE READINESS OF GOD TO ANSWER OUR REQUESTS. PSEUDO-CLEMENT OF ROME: Let us, therefore, in righteousness and holiness remain true to the things we have believed, in order that we may boldly ask of God, who says, "While you are still speaking, I will say, 'Behold, I am here.' "[1] For this word is the sign of a great promise, for the Lord says he is more ready to give than the one asking is to ask. So then, since we share in such great kindness, let us not begrudge each other the gaining of such great blessings. For these words bring pleasure to those who do them to the same degree that they bring condemnation to those who disobey. 2 CLEMENT 15.3-5.[2]

GOD IS SWIFT TO ANSWER. ATHANASIUS: God is always one and the same; but people have come to be afterwards through the Word, when the Father himself willed it; and God is invisible and inaccessible to originated things, especially to people on earth. When then people in infirmity invoke him, when in persecution they ask help, when they pray as they endure injuries, then the Invisible, being a lover of people, shines forth on them with his beneficence, which he exercises through and in his proper Word. And forthwith the divine manifestation is made to every one according to his need, and is made to the sick, and to the persecuted a "refuge" and "house of defense." DISCOURSE AGAINST THE ARIANS 1.63.[3]

GROUNDING IN GOD. ISAAC OF NINEVEH: Whenever you keep the ways of the Lord and do His will, then put your hope in the Lord and call on Him. . . .

When temptation overtakes the iniquitous person, he has no confidence wherewith to call upon God, nor to expect salvation from Him, since in the days of his ease he stood aloof from God's will. ASCETICAL HOMILIES 5.[4]

GOD HEARS US THE MOMENT WE CALL. CHRYSOSTOM: Were he distant from us in place, you might well doubt, but if [God] is present everywhere, to him that strives and is in earnest

---

[1]It is the LXX (*eti lalountos sou erei idou pareimi*) that gives the sense of the divine interruption and hence anticipation that is absent in the Hebrew text. [2]AF 123. [3]NPNF 2 4:342*. [4]AHSIS 49.

he is near. . . . What father would ever be thus obedient to his offspring? What mother is there, so ready and continually standing, in case her children call her? There is not one, no father, no mother, but God stands continually waiting . . . and never, when we have called as we ought, has he refused to hear. HOMILIES ON THE GOSPEL OF MATTHEW 54.8.[5]

THE NEED FOR COMPASSIONATE MEDIATORS OF GOD. JEROME: One who is not bound by such chains of sin is found only with difficulty. And a soul is rarely discovered who does not have this extremely heavy collar around its neck, oppressing it with such terrestrial work that it cannot gaze at heaven at all, but only the earth. This also recalls the woman in the Gospel whom Satan conquered for eighteen years, keeping her bent over and unable to look toward heaven.[6] . . .

Similarly, if we refrain from doing the things just mentioned and if we accomplish the deeds that are to be outlined, so that we would give food to the hungry . . . with our very soul, helping them in whichever way we are able to help, and this "not begrudgingly or under compulsion,"[7] but giving from the soul, thus we receive more benefits than we give, for "God loves a cheerful giver."[8] This means that we should saturate the hungry or afflicted soul, instead of restoring it just partially, and if we suffer with the suffering and mourn with those who mourn, then our light will arise in the darkness, that light that said, "I am the light that came into the world so that all who believe in me would not remain in the darkness"[9] but "have the light of life."[10] For "the lamp of our body is the eye; if it is good, our entire body will be illuminated."[11] . . .

We can identify this fountain[12] with none other than that to whom it was said, "With you is the fountain of life,"[13] which irrigates his church unceasingly, along with the heart of every believer. COMMENTARY ON ISAIAH 16.20-22.[14]

58:10 Pour Yourself Out

WE ARE ONLY STEWARDS. GREGORY OF NAZIANZUS: [My father] actually treated his own property as if it were another's, of which he was but the steward, relieving poverty as far as he could and expending not only his superfluities but his necessities—a manifest proof of love for the poor, giving a portion not only to seven, according to the injunction of Solomon,[15] but if an eighth came forward, not even in his case being stingy but more pleased to dispose of his wealth than we know others are to acquire it. . . . This is what most people do: they give indeed, but without that readiness that is a greater and more perfect thing than the mere offering. For he thought it much better to be generous even to the undeserving for the sake of the deserving than from fear of the undeserving to deprive those who were deserving. And this seems to be the duty of casting our bread on the waters,[16] since it will not be swept away or perish in the eyes of the just Investigator but will arrive yonder where all that is ours is laid up and will meet with us in due time, even though we think it not. But what is best and greatest of all, [my father's] magnanimity was accompanied by freedom from ambition. ON THE DEATH OF HIS FATHER, ORATION 18.20-21.[17]

58:11 Strong Bones and a Watered Garden

GOD'S PRESENCE IS IN HIS ACTIONS. THEODORET OF CYR: As for "Here I am," this does not mean a voice but the operation through actions. For you are taught by events that the God whom you called on is with you.

You will have God present, who will offer you a share of his goodness. We think by "bones" is meant the thoughts; for these receive joy. For if anyone takes God's promise to his "bones," he

---

[5]NPNF 1 10:337*; 54.5 in Gk text. [6]See Lk 13:11. [7]2 Cor 9:7.
[8]2 Cor 9:7. [9]Jn 12:46. [10]Jn 8:12. [11]Mt 6:22. [12]Referring to the previous sentence, wherein he wrote "a fountain went forth and irrigated every face of paradise," probably from Gen 2:10: "a river flowed out of Eden [lit., "the place of desire"] to irrigate paradise." [13]Ps 36:9 (35:10 LXX, Vg). Cf. Jn 4:14. [14]AGLB 36:1678, 1680-81, 1683. [15]Eccles 11:2. [16]Eccles 11:1. [17]NPNF 2 7:260-61.

will not miss the intention[18] of the prophecy. For the body is enriched by joy in the soul. "For a joyful heart cheers the face."[19] COMMENTARY ON ISAIAH 18.58.11.[20]

THE BEAUTY OF SOULS NOURISHED BY GOD.
CYRIL OF ALEXANDRIA: Those who were of Israel by blood are written as a type when God sent down manna from heaven.[21] For this figure can be thought of as the bread of angels and as heavenly bread. For there are those in whose minds the divine light shines brightly and who work hard and irreproachably to know the holy Scriptures—we say that these people are filled and brimming with the heavenly nourishment of God. . . . Now whoever receives knowledge and is filled by his divine mysteries, that person's bones have flesh put on them. For the oracle here is constructed in fleshly terms. Their soul became like a lush garden, that is, luxuriant and tree-filled and with many types of flowers abounding and providing all sorts of fruit. For gardens that lack water are exceedingly ugly, being dry and barren of all fruit. . . . For just the hardiest among trees has the most beautiful fruit, so also fairest and finest virtues exist in God's sight among the souls of the saints. COMMENTARY ON ISAIAH 5.4.58.11.[22]

58:12 The Ancient Ruins Restored

THE SOUL AS A CITY. CYRIL OF ALEXANDRIA: The prophetic word comes to us through two further metaphors, and the beautiful form of hidden ideas is displayed. For it is about a deserted town and its defenseless state that a form of words is molded.[23] It declares, your deserts will be lived in perpetually, that is, you will not be naked of good thoughts indwelling your heart, nor will you be defenseless or unguarded and insecure. For Christ will be your enduring foundation and support, and like a city you will have countless people dwelling there. For the souls of the saints are full of holy words and thoughts. And many will come to it as the level of perfection, running up and down, declaring it to be full of good things. And you will be called a builder of walls. . . . You must know that there are evil and contrary powers invading the vulnerable soul, giving rise to awful desires and in a despotic way carrying off whatever they want and strolling round the barren garden. But they will stop this interference when a wall is erected, that is, the divine fear set up within [the soul]. COMMENTARY ON ISAIAH 5.4.58.12.[24]

---

[18]Gk *skopos*. [19]Prov 15:13. [20]SC 315:220. [21]Jn 6:31. [22]PG 70:1293-96. [23]Is 58:12. [24]PG 70:1297-1300.

58:13-14 RIGHT OBSERVANCE OF SABBATH

[13]*If you turn back your foot from the sabbath,*
from doing your pleasure[i] on my holy day,
and call the sabbath a delight
and the holy day of the LORD honorable;
if you honor it, not going your own ways,
or seeking your own pleasure,[j] or talking
idly;

[14]*then you shall take delight in the LORD,*
and I will make you ride upon the heights
of the earth;
I will feed you with the heritage of Jacob your
father,
for the mouth of the LORD has spoken.

i Or business **j** Or pursuing your own business

OVERVIEW: From honoring the sabbath, one is led to honor the whole will of God (ISHO'DAD). The true sabbath is the rested state of one's soul that will find its end in heaven (JEROME). When we, however, neglect to focus on what is above, and instead focus on what the world thinks is important, we will experience spiritual turmoil (GREGORY THE GREAT). The Jews neglected the law's higher sense and were stuck observing a means as an end (THEODORET).

58:13 The Sabbath

EXORTATION TO FOLLOW THE WILL OF GOD.
ISHO'DAD OF MERV: "If you call the sabbath a delight," in other words, you honor it for the banquets and the drinks, finding your joy on that day as if it were a party. "If you honor it, not following your will or speaking any word." Indeed, it was not forbidden to them to speak but it was forbidden to lie. And by the word *will* he does not prohibit them from doing their own will, but from acting according to a will that is contrary to the will of God. By mentioning the sabbath, he alludes to all the commandments of the law. COMMENTARY ON ISAIAH 58.13.[1]

THE SABBATH REPRESENTS THE SOUL'S FREEDOM AND ANGELIC VIRTUES. JEROME: It is commanded by the law that we do no servile work on the sabbath, that we not light a fire, that we remain seated in one place and that we perform only those works that pertain to the salvation of the soul. Yet, should we receive this according to the letter, it would not be able to be fulfilled perfectly. For who is able to do this, sitting in one place for the entire day and night without moving even slightly, lest he become a transgressor of the law? From this one commandment, therefore, which is impossible to fulfill literally, we are also compelled to understand the others in a spiritual manner, lest we destroy the liberty of the soul by doing servile work. For "whoever commits sin is a slave to sin";[2] so let us not bear a burden on the sabbath, as did the one who said, "My iniquities have been raised above

my head and are on me like an unbearable burden."[3] Neither should this iniquity that weighs more than lead have power over us, nor should the lustful desire of the body inflame us, for the hearts of all adulterers are like furnaces.[4] . . .

But this promise, "Honor your father and mother, and you will live a long life on the land,"[5] is hardly able to stand according to the letter. For many honor their parents and die quickly, whereas others who commit patricide live for a long time. But that we may know with certainty that this land of which he speaks lies above, let us recall briefly the thirty-sixth psalm, in which it is written, "The meek will possess the land and rejoice in an abundance of peace,"[6] which is followed by "Wait upon the Lord and keep his ways and he will elevate you to possess the land,"[7] about which it is sung in another place, "The just will possess the land and live on it forever."[8] But this is impossible. For even if the land in which we currently dwell passes over, how will the just live on it forever? Hence, we learn from this that the land in question must be situated above. . . .

So also in the resurrection, "they neither marry nor are given in marriage but are like the angels because they are sons of the resurrection."[9] The apostle likewise says about food and the stomach: "Food is made for the stomach and the stomach for food, but God will destroy both of them."[10] Thus, how will we, with incorrupt and spiritual and immortal bodies, seek again the vices of the former flesh, which was corrupt and mortal? We say these things not to deny the glorification of the body's substance but thoroughly to eradicate the former works of those who are like the angels. By contrast, we who imitate angelic virtues while still in this body, through fasting and continence and perpetual chastity and charity, nevertheless do not lose the substance of our bodies. COMMENTARY ON ISAIAH 16.23-24.[11]

---

[1]CSCO 303(128):57. [2]Jn 8:34. [3]Ps 38:5 (37:6 LXX, Vg). [4]See Prov 6:32; Mt 15:19. [5]Ex 20:12; cf. Deut 5:16. [6]Ps 37:11 (36:11 LXX, Vg). [7]Ps 37:34 (36:34 LXX, Vg). [8]Ps 37:29 (36:29 LXX, Vg). [9]See Lk 20:35-36. [10]1 Cor 6:13. [11]AGLB 36:1687-88, 1691-93.

58:14 Heights of the Earth

**THE HIGH RESPONSIBILITIES OF THE PAS-
TORATE.** GREGORY THE GREAT: "I will lift you up
upon the high places of the earth." For he is lifted
up on the high places of the earth who treads
under foot through looking down on them in his
mind, even the very things of the present world,
which seem lofty and glorious. But, having been
suddenly dashed from this summit of things by
the whirlwind of this trail, I have fallen into fears
and tremors, since, even though I have no fears
for myself, I am greatly afraid for those who have
been committed to me. On every side I am tossed
by the waves of business and sunk by storms, so
that I may truly say, "I am come into the depth of
the sea, and the storm has overwhelmed me."[12]
After business I long to return to my heart; but
driven from there by vain tumults of thoughts, I
am unable to return. LETTER 5.[13]

HOW WE SHOULD REST. THEODORET OF CYR:
He teaches the manner [in which it is required]
to rest: "Nor speak a word in anger out of your
mouth," he says, "and you shall trust in the Lord";
it is as though if he ordains to honor the sabbath
by making an end to bad actions and clinging to

the accomplishment of good actions. There you
see why he imposes a double duty even on priests,
for they offered double sacrifices; they were
required to sacrifice the victims and to clean the
meats, offer them on the altar, light the fire and
bring wood to the fire to feed it. Similarly, the
reading of the divine word was done in abundance, as was the chanting of hymns and the
prayer. And all that shows that the law diverted
them from practical realities to lead them to spiritual realities on the day of the Sabbath, for they
could not act continuously in such a way, given
that they lived in a too-carnal fashion and were
entirely absorbed in the cares they took with the
body. "And he shall bring you up to the good
places of the land and feed you with the heritage
of Jacob your father." And [here is] the confirma-
tion of what he has just said: "For the mouth of
the Lord has spoken it." The One who has made
the promise does not lie, he says; he will
undoubtedly grant you to take part in his beneficence, and you will enjoy the providence accorded
to your ancestors. COMMENTARY ON ISAIAH
18.58.14.[14]

---

[12]Ps 69:3 (68:3 LXX, Vg). [13]NPNF 2 12:75. [14]*ITA* 864-65*; SC
315:222-24.

59:1-4 THE WALL OF SEPARATION

[1]Behold, the LORD's hand is not shortened,
  that it cannot save,
  or his ear dull, that it cannot hear;
[2]but your iniquities have made a separation
  between you and your God,
and your sins have hid his face from you
  so that he does not hear.
[3]For your hands are defiled with blood

and your fingers with iniquity;
your lips have spoken lies,
  your tongue mutters wickedness.
[4]No one enters suit justly,
  no one goes to law honestly;
they rely on empty pleas, they speak lies,
  they conceive mischief and bring forth
  iniquity.

OVERVIEW: When we consider our sins (CYP-RIAN) only in light of the law, we can only become further enemies of God (CHRYSOSTOM). But when we remember his mercy, we do not despair (ISAAC), although we come to realize any punishment we do receive is deserved and helps in understanding our personal theodicy (CYPRIAN, FULGENTIUS), knowing that God punishes his people for their own good. Sin is a barrier that needs to be removed by repentance and faith (CHRYSOSTOM). Hatred drains energies and wastes the heart (CYRIL). Christ is behind the wall of sin waiting for the confession (APONIUS) of lips that would otherwise normally speak lies that lead to lawlessness (ATHANASIUS).

59:2 Sin and Separation

SELF-EXAMINATION. CYPRIAN: Let us consider our sins, and reviewing the secrets of our action and mind, let us weigh the merits of our conscience. THE LAPSED 21.[1]

ENMITY THROUGH THE LAW. CHRYSOSTOM: The enmity that God had both against Jews and Gentiles was, as it were, a middle wall. And this wall, while the law existed, was not only not abolished but rather was strengthened. HOMILIES ON EPHESIANS 5.[2]

REMEMBER GOD AS HE REMEMBERS YOU. ISAAC OF NINEVEH: But since we say that God is plenteous in mercy, why is it that when amidst temptations we unceasingly knock and pray, we are not heard and He disregards our prayer? This we are clearly taught by the Prophet when he says, "The Lord's hand is not little, that it cannot save; nor is He hard of hearing, that He cannot hear: but our sins have separated us from Him." ... Remember God at all times, and He will remember you whenever you fall into evils. ASCETICAL HOMILIES 5.[3]

CONTRITION BEGINS WHERE SELF-RIGHTEOUSNESS ENDS. CYPRIAN: The Lord can pro-hibit adversities, but the merits of sinners cause him to give no aid.... Therefore, let your sins and offences be numbered; let the wounds of your conscience be considered; and let each one cease to complain about God and about us, if he understands that he deserves what he suffers. To DEMETRIAN 11.[4]

GOD PRESENT WITH EVIL BY NATURE THOUGH NOT BY GRACE. FULGENTIUS OF RUSPE: Therefore, since bodies that cannot exist without a place cannot be spatially separated from God, without a doubt neither are the spirits that God created spatially separated from God.

For every spirit that God created exists in some place, and God is there. [God], through the grace by means of which he grants to whom he wishes a holy and blessed life, is not in evil spirits; still he is always in all his creatures through his natural power. Thus there is no creature than can be found in whom God is not present through his power. Therefore, that nature can be separated from God that was or is able to be subject to sin. There is no other thing that can go away from God except that substance that is able or has been able to sin with its own will. For Isaiah says, "See, the Lord's hand is not too short to save or his ear too dull to hear. Rather, your iniquities have been barriers between you and your God." BOOK TO VICTOR AGAINST THE SERMON OF FASTIDIOSUS THE ARIAN 4.1-2.[5]

THE BLESSING OF PUNISHMENT. CHRYSOSTOM: But punishments lead us back to God.... Suppose anyone has a wound, which is the more deserving of fear—gangrene or the surgeon's knife? The steel or the devouring progress of the ulcer? Sin is gangrene; punishment is the surgeon's knife. As then he who has a gangrene, although he is not lanced, has to sustain the malady and is then in the worse condition when he is not lanced, so also the sinner, though he is not pun-

---

[1]FC 36:76. [2]NPNF 1 13:72*. [3]AHSIS 46. [4]FC 36:177. [5]FC 95:396-97*.

ished, is the most wretched of people and is then especially wretched when he has no punishment and is suffering no distress. HOMILIES CONCERNING THE STATUES 6.14.[6]

SERIOUS SIN CAN STILL BE FORGIVEN. CHRYSOSTOM: Inasmuch, then, as this is the cause that puts us far from God, let us remove this obnoxious barrier that prevents any near approach being made.

But now hear how this has actually occurred in real instances. Among the Corinthians some man of mark committed a sin such as was not named even among the Gentiles.[7] This man was a believer and belonged to the household for Christ; and some say that he was actually a member of the priesthood. What then? Did Paul cut him off from the communion of those who were in the way of salvation? By no means, for he himself it is who rebukes the Corinthians countless times, backwards and forwards, because they did not bring the man to a state of repentance; he desired to prove to us that there is no sin that cannot be healed. LETTER TO THE FALLEN THEODORE 1.8.[8]

HATRED WEARIES THE HEART. CYRIL OF ALEXANDRIA: Scripture is accustomed to call hatred "toil." For the word has more than one meaning. Hatred wastes and withers up the hearts of those who receive it. Thus says the psalmist about someone or about Israel as a whole, "He conceived toil and bore iniquity."[9] COMMENTARY ON ISAIAH 5.4.59.4-5.[10]

CHRIST STANDS BEHIND THE WALL OF SIN SEPARATING US FROM GOD. APONIUS: Rising again with the same flesh as that with which he was buried, [Christ] stands behind the wall of our unbelief, the wall that as we sinned we built with our muddy, dirty works. About these works God spoke through the prophet Isaiah, "But your sins have made a wall between you and God."

Behind the wall stands Christ the Lord, and he waits to be called on by the ungodly, and he summons the sinful soul to penitence. Behind the wall where [Christ] stands,[11] he waits for the unbelieving to believe in him until such time as they reach baptism or penitence. EXPOSITION OF SONG OF SONGS 4.16.[12]

59:4 *Your Lips Have Spoken Lies*

IGNORANCE LEADS TO INIQUITY. ATHANASIUS: Now those who meditate evil, we say, do not [think] truth but falsehood, and not righteousness but iniquity, for their tongue learns to speak lies. They have done evil and have not ceased that they might repent. For, persevering with delight in wicked actions, they hasten thereto without turning back, even treading under foot the commandment with regard to neighbors, and instead of loving them, they devise evil against them, as the saint testifies, saying, "And those who seek my evil have spoken vanity and imagined deceit all the day."[13] But that the cause of such meditation is none other than the lack of instruction the divine proverb has already declared: "The son who forsakes the commandment of his father meditates evil words."[14] But such meditation, because it is evil, the Holy Spirit blames in these words and reproves too in other terms, saying, "Your hands are polluted with blood, your fingers with sins, your lips have spoken lawlessness, and your tongue imagines iniquity: no one speaks right things, nor is there true judgment." But what the end is of such perverse imagining, he immediately declares, saying, "They trust in vanities and speak falsehood, for they conceive mischief and bring forth lawlessness." FESTAL LETTERS 11.4.[15]

---

[6]NPNF 1 9:387*; 6.6 in Gk text. [7]1 Cor 5:1. [8]NPNF 1 9:96*. [9]Ps 7:14 (7:15 LXX); Job 15:35. [10]PG 70:1305. [11]Song 2:9. [12]SC 421:28. [13]Ps 38:12 (37:13 LXX). [14]Prov 19:27 LXX. [15]NPNF 2 4:534*.

59:5-15 ISRAEL BRINGS MISFORTUNE
ON ITSELF AND NEIGHBORS

⁵*They hatch adders' eggs,*
  they weave the spider's web;
he who eats their eggs dies,
  and from one which is crushed a viper is
  hatched.
⁶*Their webs will not serve as clothing;*
  men will not cover themselves with what
  they make.
Their works are works of iniquity,
  and deeds of violence are in their hands.
⁷*Their feet run to evil,*
  and they make haste to shed innocent blood;
their thoughts are thoughts of iniquity,
  desolation and destruction are in their
  highways.
⁸*The way of peace they know not,*
  and there is no justice in their paths;
they have made their roads crooked,
  no one who goes in them knows peace.

⁹*Therefore justice is far from us,*
  and righteousness does not overtake us;
we look for light, and behold, darkness,
  and for brightness, but we walk in gloom.
¹⁰*We grope for the wall like the blind,*
  we grope like those who have no eyes;
we stumble at noon as in the twilight,

among those in full vigor we are like dead
  men.
¹¹*We all growl like bears,*
  we moan and moan like doves;
we look for justice, but there is none;
  for salvation, but it is far from us.
¹²*For our transgressions are multiplied before*
  thee,
  and our sins testify against us;
for our transgressions are with us,
  and we know our iniquities:
¹³*transgressing, and denying the* LORD,
  and turning away from following our God,
speaking oppression and revolt,
  conceiving and uttering from the heart lying
  words.
¹⁴*Justice is turned back,*
  and righteousness stands afar off;
for truth has fallen in the public squares,
  and uprightness cannot enter.
¹⁵*Truth is lacking,*
  and he who departs from evil makes himself
  a prey.

The LORD *saw it, and it displeased him*
  that there was no justice.

OVERVIEW: The wicked catch the poor in their schemes but will at length be caught (ISHO'DAD). Heretical teaching is as robust and reliable as cobwebs (GREGORY OF NYSSA). Such teaching does not give shelter or remove shame but is twisted and useless (JEROME). The mind that is overrun with evil cannot see peace (THEODORET). It takes God's light to reveal the hidden mess of the human spiritual state (EPHREM). The groaning on the last day can be avoided by asking for light and eyes to see (THEODORE), as anyone reading the Scriptures with skill can attest (JEROME). Those who have given up on the Christian walk are restless as they follow the lusts of their heart (CLEMENT OF ROME). It is not that God has failed to be concerned for us but that we who choose to follow a life of sin deprive ourselves of his help (THEODORET). In the end, God sees all things and our deeds will testify against us (EPHREM). Therefore, God here provides instruction on the right ordering of repentance because a life of iniquity produces a veil of deceit that in open animosity covers the truth, but only for a time (THEODORET).

59:5 Hatching Adders' Eggs

THE MEANING OF "ADDERS' EGGS" AND "SPIDER'S WEB." ISHO'DAD OF MERV: "They will hatch adders' eggs." Also the children, whom they have generated, are evil and want to be even more harmful than their parents. "And they have woven a spider's web." As the threads woven by the spider catch the flies, so their schemes catch the poor amid the trials, which they organize arbitrarily. According to Qatraya,[1] he calls "spider's web" their faith in the idols, which is of no use for the [spiders] on the day when they are caught. Through the words "adders' eggs," he shows their venomousness and iniquity, and through "spider's web," their weakness. COMMENTARY ON ISAIAH 59.5.[2]

THE COBWEB RESEMBLES THE INSUBSTANTIALITY OF HERETICAL TEACHING. GREGORY OF NYSSA: For in the cobweb there is the appearance of something woven but no substantiality in the appearance, for he who touches it touches nothing substantial. As the spider's threads break with the touch of the finger, just such is the unsubstantial texture of idle phrases, "Not dividing his own essence by begetting and being at once begetter and begotten." . . . Who is so distracted, who is so demented, as to make the statement against which Eunomius[3] is doing battle? For the church believes that the true Father is truly Father of his own Son, as the apostle says, and not of a Son alien from him. AGAINST EUNOMIUS 2.7.[4]

THE LOSTNESS OF CHRISTLESS TEACHING. JEROME: Because Isaiah said that "they weave a spider's web," he now explains why the weaving of this web profits nothing. All of their work and teaching, he says, fails to produce either a vestment for Christ or a covering to protect the soul's nakedness, but they spend themselves in vain labor, as the same prophet says: "This people honors me with their lips, but their heart is far from me. They worship me in vain, teaching doctrines and precepts of humankind," the following of which neglects the law of God.[5] . . .

Then it continues that their ways are perverse not by nature but by their own will, for everything that is perverted and crooked has been twisted from what was right into something depraved. COMMENTARY ON ISAIAH 16.27-28.[6]

59:7 Thoughts of Iniquity

SIN BEGINS IN THE DISPOSITION. THEODORET OF CYR: They sin with all parts of the body, through hands, feet, tongue. But it is the life inside their minds that sins before all of these once it has fallen into imprudence, so that it cannot recognize the peace that is at hand. COMMENTARY ON ISAIAH 18.59.6-8.[7]

59:10 We Grope for the Wall

THE LIGHT THAT REVEALS OUR DIRT. EPHREM THE SYRIAN: At times even we, when we were in error, mired in the pride of our mind as if our feet were stuck in the mud, did not perceive our error of the divine gospel each day. We would "grope around in the dark like blind people," because our inner mind did not possess that which is necessary for discernment. Then, as if from a deep sleep, the mercy of the Most High

---

[1]Dadisho Qatraya (second half of the seventh century) wrote important and elegant works on monastic life in Syriac. He also wrote a commentary on Isaiah, which has been partially published as CSCO 326. [2]CSCO 303(128):57. [3]One of the foremost leaders of the Anomoean party within Arianism. [4]NPNF 2 5:109. [5]Mt 15:8-9; Mk 7:6-7; cf. Is 29:13. [6]AGLB 36:1698-99, 1701. [7]SC 315:228.

poured out like pure rain, was sprinkled on our drowsiness, and from our sleep we were roused and boldly took up this mirror to see our self in it. At that very moment we were convicted by our faults, and we discovered that we were barren of any good virtue and that we had become a dwelling place for every corrupting thought and a lodge and abode for every lust. LETTER TO PUBLIUS 11.[8]

THE UNIVERSALIZING OF THE MESSAGE TO INDIVIDUAL SOULS. THEODORE OF HERACLEA: This is to be understood that just as there are eyes where there is no light or there is light but not eyes to see it with, they are unable to see the matter at hand; so it is necessary that the one who wants to understand the sense must not miss what is offered as wisdom from the holy Scriptures.

There will be on that day so much groaning and howling, just as a bear when it is robbed of her cubs, or even as with doves who by nature constantly moan. FRAGMENTS ON ISAIAH.[9]

59:11 Moaning Like Doves

SCRIPTURAL MEDITATION IS MORE THAN MEMORIZING WORDS. JEROME: And we coo like meditating doves who have no sense and no understanding of the Scriptures, contemplating only those words that they sing from memory. But just as it is written of doves that "Ephraim is like a dove with no sense,"[10] and just as the innocence of doves is contrasted with the prudence of serpents in the Gospel,[11] so also innocence without prudence, which is the neighbor of foolishness, is shown in the present passage to consist of meditating on words alone. COMMENTARY ON ISAIAH 16.29.[12]

59:12 Transgressions Are Multiplied

THE RESTLESSNESS OF THOSE FAR FROM GOD. CLEMENT OF ROME: For this reason righteousness and peace are far from you, since each has abandoned the fear of God and grown blind in his faith and ceased to walk by the rules of his

precepts or to behave in a way worthy of Christ. Rather does each follow the lusts of his evil heart by reviving that wicked and unholy rivalry, by which, indeed, "death came into the world."[13] 1 CLEMENT 3.4.[14]

OUR LIFE OF INIQUITY HAS FAILED GOD. THEODORET OF CYR: It was not you who failed to be concerned for us, but it was our life of iniquity that deprived us of your care and concern. COMMENTARY ON ISAIAH 18.59.12.[15]

GOD HAS THE EVIDENCE WITH WHICH TO JUDGE. EPHREM THE SYRIAN: For just as the deeds of the wicked are their accusers before the righteous Judge, making them bend and bow down their heads silently in shame, so also their beautiful deeds plead cause for the good before the good One. For the deeds of all humankind are both silent and speak silently by their nature, yet they speak when one sees them.

In that place there is no interrogation, for [God] is the judge of knowledge; nor is there any response, for when he sees it, he hears. He hears with sight, and he sees with hearing. LETTER TO PUBLIUS 9.1-2.[16]

59:14 Righteousness Stands Far Off

THE DETAILS OF REPENTANCE. THEODORET OF CYR: The prophetic text[17] makes this statement detailed in order to invite those who desire help to appease the Lord by saying something like the following: We acknowledge our offenses, we have recognized our impiety, we have spoken falsely against you, our Master, since we promised to keep your laws and we have violated them. We have not ceased contradicting you, uttering words of unrighteousness, proposing things that are unjust, failing to dread your judgment. We have

---

[8]FC 91:348. [9]PG 18:1364. [10]Hos 7:11. [11]See Mt 10:16:"Be as prudent as serpents and as innocent as doves." [12]AGLB 36:1704. [13]Wis 2:24. [14]LCC 1:44-45. [15]ITA 876*; SC 315:230. [16]FC 91:347. [17]Theodore either paraphrases the text here or is working from a text that differs not only from the RSV but also from the LXX.

kept ourselves far from righteousness. After this, he changes the form of his statements and puts their accusation categorically: "For truth is consumed in their ways." It has vanished, he says, because deceit has veiled it. "And they could not pass by a straight path." For they have not stopped taking the opposite route. COMMENTARY ON ISAIAH 18.59.14.[18]

59:15 Truth Is Lacking

WHEN TRUTH IS TAKEN AWAY, THERE IS OPEN OPPOSITION. THEODORET OF CYR: He has shown how truth has departed: they did not want to consider their duty, he says, but they have distorted their intelligence so as not to understand what ought to be done and what is useful. "The truth in this has disappeared, and the person who turned away from evil has been besieged." They have distanced themselves so far from the truth that they openly combat those who turn away from perversity and choose the good. COMMENTARY ON ISAIAH 18.59.15.[19]

---

[18]ITA 876-77*; SC 315:230-32. [19]ITA 877*; SC 315:232.

59:16-21 THE LORD'S HELP AND THE WORLD'S IMPOTENCE

[16]He saw that there was no man,
  and wondered that there was no one to
    intervene;
then his own arm brought him victory,
  and his righteousness upheld him.
[17]He put on righteousness as a breastplate,
  and a helmet of salvation upon his head;
he put on garments of vengeance for clothing,
  and wrapped himself in fury as a mantle.
[18]According to their deeds, so will he repay,
  wrath to his adversaries, requital to his
    enemies;
  to the coastlands he will render requital.
[19]So they shall fear the name of the LORD from
    the west,

and his glory from the rising of the sun;
for he will come like a rushing stream,
  which the wind of the LORD drives.

[20]"And he will come to Zion as Redeemer,
  to those in Jacob who turn from
    transgression. ays the LORD.
[21]"And as for me, this is my covenant with
them, says the LORD: my spirit which is upon
you, and my word which I have put in your
mouth, shall not depart out of your mouth, or
out of the mouth of your children, or out of the
mouth of your children's children, says the
LORD, from this time forth and for evermore."

OVERVIEW: Discipline is part of the overall long-term plan of mercy and justice that leads to spiritual profit (THEODORET) for those clothed with the righteousness of Christ (THEODORE), who fights on behalf of his beleaguered people and comes to their defense "like a rushing river that the Spirit of the Lord drives" (JEROME). Christ, like Zorababbel, comes to Zion as its Redeemer (EPHREM), expecting to see sorrow and repentance from the people he has come to redeem with his own blood, which seals the future eternal covenant made by him (JEROME). The grace that comes from the new covenant is spread by praise and preaching like seeds (THEODORET).

59:16 God's Righteousness Upheld

MERCY AND JUSTICE ARE THE PURPOSE OF DISCIPLINE. THEODORET OF CYR: For the unjust deeds displeased the just judge so he did not call the workers of these deeds "humans," for although being in an honored place they do not understand and are comparable to the unthinking beasts and resemble them.... In place of "mercy" the three translators have rendered "justice," so as to say "he has exacted a just recompense on them." It calls the operation of God his "arm," while "mercy" teaches the usefulness of discipline. The God of all things disciplines for profit. COMMENTARY ON ISAIAH 18.59.16.[1]

59:17 He Put on Righteousness

THE GARMENT OF RIGHTEOUSNESS INCLUDES HUMAN DEEDS. THEODORE OF HERACLEA: [Isaiah] says that God shares salvation, which is exchanged for repentance and understanding with those deserving, who put on righteousness just as if it were their garment. He says nothing less than that God is girded with the righteous deeds of human beings, just like body and head armor. Such things are said with reference to God to enthuse the listeners and to raise up their thoughts as being those capable of becoming the garment of God and so sharing his righteousness. FRAGMENTS ON ISAIAH.[2]

THE SPIRIT OF THE LORD IS SIGNIFIED. JEROME: He is referring here, without doubt, to those Jews who continued in their blasphemies and to the change effected by their enemies when

the Roman army surrounded them. By their victory, the Lord is shown to have done the fighting. Indeed, this testimony was used by Paul in his letter to the Ephesians, urging us to be clothed in the armor of Christ whereby we would be enabled to repel the flaming arrows of the devil.[3] ... The author of this blessing[4] is he who will come "like a rushing river that the Spirit of the Lord drives," or, as Aquila translates it, "like a narrow river that is a sign of the Spirit of the Lord," or, as Theodotion has it, "like a warring river that the Spirit of the Lord has inscribed." Of that testimony, therefore, that the Septuagint translates as "like a violent river, the wrath of the Lord will come with fury," the last portion is not included in the Hebrew. For wrath and fury are not to be placed into the promises of God, since in the other promises that follow, blessing belongs to the future and warnings and punishments to sinners. But according to Aquila and Theodotion, it is in Christ that the Spirit of the Lord is signified, confirming what was first read in John the Evangelist: "for God the Father has set his seal on the Son of man."[5] COMMENTARY ON ISAIAH 16.31-32.[6]

59:20 To Zion as Redeemer

THE SAVIOR COMES TO HIS CHURCH. EPHREM THE SYRIAN: "And he will come to Zion as Redeemer," that is, Zerubbabel. Therefore the spiritual Zion and the hill of visions and revelations is the church. The Redeemer, who comes to it, is Christ, that great Zerubbabel. "This is my covenant with you," which I made with your ancestors on the mountain, so that my words might never be lacking from the mouths of your descendants. COMMENTARY ON ISAIAH 59.20-21.[7]

THE REQUIREMENT OF SORROW. JEROME: He continues, "The Redeemer will come to Zion and

---

[1]SC 315:232. [2]PG 18:1364-65. [3]See Eph 6:10-16. [4]Referring to "Blessed is the one who fears the Lord." See Ps 112:1 (111:1 LXX, Vg); Ps 128:1 (127:1 LXX, Vg); Sir 34:15. [5]Jn 6:27. [6]AGLB 36:1709, 1711-12. [7]SESHS 2:171.

to those who return from iniquity in Jacob, says the Lord." The Septuagint, however, translates this as follows: "He who will liberate shall come from Zion and avert impieties from Jacob." If he who averts impieties from Jacob will come from Zion, therefore, we should understand that this man is born in Zion and that the Most High established him there who averts sins from Jacob. If, however, "the Redeemer will come to Zion and to those who return from iniquity in Jacob, says the Lord," this means that Christ will redeem Zion with his own blood. Or it could be that he was begotten from the seed of Israel, for that is what "Goel" means (*Anchisteus* in Greek) according to the distinctively Hebrew, which neighbors Zion. And lest we think that all of Zion is redeemed and liberated from sin, which is flowing with the blood of the Lord, he adds significantly, "to those who return from iniquity," that is, provided that they are willing to do penance, for which persons the prayer of the Lord is completed with "Father, forgive them, for they know not what they do."[8] COMMENTARY ON ISAIAH 16.32.[9]

59:21 The Covenant with the Lord

THE PROPHETIC OFFICE. JEROME: [Verse 21] is addressed either to Isaiah, as I think, or to the Lord, as many believe. This is why the order of thought is presented thus to Isaiah: "This is the eternal covenant of the gospel, that my Spirit, which is in you, and my words, which I have put in your mouth, through which you will come to preach, will depart neither from your mouth, nor from the mouth of your children nor from the mouth of their children, so that it will be demonstrated to every generation consecutively." But the grace of the prophets will surely come to the apostles and to those who will believe through the apostles. COMMENTARY ON ISAIAH 16.32.[10]

PRAISE AND PROCLAMATION AS MARKS OF THE COVENANT. THEODORET OF CYR: He calls "mouth" that of the apostles, and "seed" of the apostles those who learn from their teaching. Thus he promises grace of the Spirit to those who believe in him. . . . Thus, we who also enjoy this grace, let us sing praises to the fount of grace to whom glory is due for the ages of ages. Amen. COMMENTARY ON ISAIAH 18.59.21.[11]

---

[8]Lk 23:34. [9]*AGLB* 36:1713-14. [10]*AGLB* 36:1714. [11]SC 315:236.

60:1-12 THE GLORY OF ZION

[1]*Arise, shine;* * *for your light has come,*
  and the glory of the LORD *has risen upon you.*
[2]*For behold, darkness shall cover the earth,*
  and thick darkness the peoples;
but the LORD *will arise upon you,*
  and his glory will be seen upon you.
[3]*And nations shall come to your light,*
  and kings to the brightness of your rising.

[4]*Lift up your eyes round about, and see;*
  they all gather together, they come to you;
your sons shall come from far,
  and your daughters shall be carried in the arms.
[5]*Then you shall see and be radiant.*
  your heart shall thrill and rejoice;[k]
because the abundance of the sea shall be turned to you,

the wealth of the nations shall come to you.
⁶A multitude of camels shall cover you,
 the young camels of Midian and Ephah;
 all those from Sheba shall come.
They shall bring gold and frankincense,
 and shall proclaim the praise of the LORD.
⁷All the flocks of Kedar shall be gathered to
  you,
 the rams of Nebaioth shall minister to you;
they shall come up with acceptance on my
  altar,
 and I will glorify my glorious house.

⁸Who are these that fly like a cloud,
 and like doves to their windows?
⁹For the coastlands shall wait for me,
 the ships of Tarshish first,
to bring your sons from far,

 their silver and gold with them,
for the name of the LORD your God,
 and for the Holy One of Israel,
 because he has glorified you.

¹⁰Foreigners shall build up your walls,
 and their kings shall minister to you;
for in my wrath I smote you,
 but in my favor I have had mercy on you.
¹¹Your gates shall be open continually;
 day and night they shall not be shut;
that men may bring to you the wealth of the
  nations,
 with their kings led in procession.
¹²For the nation and kingdom
 that will not serve you shall perish;
 those nations shall be utterly laid waste.

k Heb *be enlarged* * LXX *Enlighten yourself, enlighten yourself*

OVERVIEW: Unlike with Greek philosophy, Christian illumination is provided by the blazing of the divine Spirit (ORIGEN). The light that illumines Jerusalem is Christ (METHODIUS). Mother Zion is called to rejoice in the resurrection of Christ her Son (JOHN OF DAMASCUS). The Old Testament fulfillment of prophecy in history is the sketch to which the New Testament is the full painting (THEODORET). The glory of the Lord has risen upon the earth as the Lord shares his glory with us, ennobling our nature to be like his (CYRIL).

The inner beauty of the church is matched by God's public glorification of it (METHODIUS). This glory outshines that of the most illustrious kings in their pomp (AMBROSE). The gathering in illustrates the Jewish diaspora who believed the gospel when preached to them by the apostles (EPHREM). Or it might be understood as predicting the pilgrimages of Gentiles to the holy places where they will offer acceptable sacrifices of

praise to God (THEODORET).

Isaiah speaks of those who fly like clouds in contrast to sin and its evil forces that cannot affect those whose faith allows them to fly above such forces (GREGORY OF NYSSA). It is the thoughts of the wise, which are elevated through the heavenly things they consider (AMBROSE). It is almost as if the people of God are fitted with a homing device that keeps leading them toward their heavenly home, like doves that return to the windows from which they were let loose (ISHO'DAD). Therefore the windows of their souls are closed to bodily lusts or anything else that might lead them astray (GREGORY THE GREAT), as Isaiah here pictures the gathering home of the church of God (THEODORET).

God is glorified by the conversion of the nations (EUSEBIUS). He takes an active role in caring for his church (PROCOPIUS) but not so as to manipulate people or events (THEODORE). When Isaiah prophesies that foreigners will build up

Jerusalem's walls, this was accomplished under Cyrus, Darius and Artaxerxes, but also it has been accomplished by those teachers who came from foreign nations to build up the church, bringing to it their wealth of knowledge and instruction (THEODORET).

60:1 Your Light and the Glory of the Lord

CHRISTIAN ILLUMINATION MAKES A DIFFERENCE TO LIFESTYLE. ORIGEN: And the Logos, exhorting us to come to this light, says, in the prophecies of Isaiah, "Enlighten yourself, enlighten yourself, O Jerusalem, for your light is come, and the glory of the Lord is risen on you." Observe now the difference between the fine phrases of Plato respecting the chief good and the declarations of our prophets regarding the light of the blessed; and notice that the truth as it is contained in Plato concerning this subject did not at all help his readers to attain to a pure worship of God, or even himself, who could philosophize so grandly about the chief good, whereas the simple language of the Scriptures led to their honest readers being filled with a divine spirit; and this light is nourished within them by the oil, which as a certain parable is said to have preserved the light of the torches of the five wise virgins.[1] AGAINST CELSUS 6.5.[2]

CHRIST AS GOD IS THE LIGHT HIMSELF. METHODIUS: Hail and shine, thou Jerusalem, for thy light is come, the Light eternal, the Light forever enduring, the Light supreme, the Light immaterial, the Light of same substance with God and the Father, the Light that is in the Spirit, and that is the Father; the Light that illumines the ages; the Light that gives light to mundane and supramundane things, Christ our very God. ORATION CONCERNING SIMEON AND ANNA 13.[3]

EASTER EXULTATION IN NEW JERUSALEM. JOHN OF DAMASCUS: Shine, shine, O new Jerusalem, for the glory of the Lord has shone on you.

Rejoice and be glad, O Zion! And you, O immaculate, O Mother of God, exult with Job in the resurrection of your Son. Christ is risen, and he has crushed death and raised the dead: rejoice, therefore, O nations of the earth! Shine, shine, O new Jerusalem, for the glory of the Lord has risen over you. Cry out now and rejoice, O Zion; and you, the pure one, the Mother of God, exult in the resurrection of the One to whom you gave birth. On this day, the whole creation rejoices and exults, for Christ is risen and hades despoiled. THE CANON OF PASCHA, NINTH ODE.[4]

SKETCH AND PAINTING. THEODORET OF CYR: This prophecy has three subjects. One subject, presented as in a sketch, is the rebuilding of Jerusalem that took place at the time of Cyrus and Darius. Another is like an icon "written" or drawn with many colors as it shows more precisely the lines of truth—the shining brightness of the holy church. The third is the archetype of the icon, that is, the life to come and our citizenship in heaven. The divine Paul taught this distinction: "The law contained the shadow of things to come and not the image of the realities."[5] And he calls the things to come the immortal and pain-free existence, the life unsullied by worry; whereas the image of the realities[6] is the ecclesiastical commonwealth and its existence, which is like a model of the things to come.... For the painters have the reality that they copy to make their picture, drawing a sketch first before filling in the shadow with colors ... the prophetic words apply to the church of God, which has received the light of the knowledge of God and is encircled by the glory of the Savior. COMMENTARY ON ISAIAH 19.60.1.[7]

CHRIST SHARES HIS GLORY WITH US. CYRIL OF ALEXANDRIA: [Christ] made our poverty his own, and we see in Christ the strange and rare paradox of lordship in servant's form and divine

---

[1]Mt 25:4. [2]ANF 4:575. [3]ANF 6:392. [4]RWC 37-39; *Pente* 23-24. [5]Heb 10:1. [6]Gk *archetypoi*. [7]SC 315:238-40.

glory in human abasement. That which was under the yoke in terms of the limitations of manhood was crowned with royal dignities, and that which was humble was raised to the most supreme excellence. The Only Begotten, however, did not become man only to remain in the limits of that emptying. The point was that he who was God by nature should, in the act of self-emptying, assume everything that went along with it. This was how he would be revealed as ennobling the nature of humanity in himself by making it participate in his own sacred and divine honors. We shall find that even the saints call the Son of God the "glory" of God the Father, and King, and Lord, even when he became a man. Isaiah, for example, says in one place . . . "Shine forth, Jerusalem, for your light has come, and the glory of the Lord has risen on you. Behold, darkness and gloom may cover the earth, but over you the Lord shall be made manifest, and his glory shall be seen on you." ON THE UNITY OF CHRIST.[8]

60:3 Nations Shall Come

DIVINE LIGHT BECOMES THE OUTWARD LIFESTYLE. METHODIUS: It is the church whose children shall come to it with all speed after the resurrection, running to it from all quarters. [The church] rejoices, receiving the light that never goes down and clothed with the brightness of the Word as with a robe. For with what other more precious or honorable ornament was it becoming that the queen should be adorned, to be led as a bride to the Lord, when she had received a garment of light and therefore was called by the Father? Come then, let us go forward in our discourse and look on this marvelous woman as on virgins prepared for a marriage, pure and undefiled, perfect and radiating a permanent beauty, lacking nothing of the brightness of light; and instead of a dress, clothed with light itself; and instead of precious stones, her head adorned with shining stars. SYMPOSIUM OR BANQUET OF THE TEN VIRGINS 8.5.[9]

THEY ARE NOW CLOTHED IN MANTLES OF GLORY. AMBROSE: Prophecy did not lie, then, when it said, "Kings shall walk in thy light." They shall walk openly, and especially Gratian and Theodosius[10] before other princes, no longer protected by the weapons of their soldiers but by their own merits; clothed not in purple garments but in the mantle of glory. In this world they took delight in pardoning many. How much the more are they consoled in the other life by the remembrance of their goodness, recalling that they had spared many? They now enjoy radiant light. ON THE DEATH OF THEODOSIUS 52.[11]

60:4 They All Gather Together

A FIGURE OF THE CHURCH RECEIVING THE GENTILES. EPHREM THE SYRIAN: "Lift up your eyes round about, and see; they all gather together, they come to you; your sons shall come from far, and your daughters shall be carried in the arms. Then you shall see and be radiant, your heart shall thrill and rejoice." He says these words with regard to the righteous ones of the synagogue, who gather from every land and come to it; however, in a figurative sense, these words signify the children of the holy church, the dispersed peoples, I mean, who were quite far away and distant from God. The gospel of Christ, preached to them by the holy apostles, gathered them, so that the apostles carried them as if in their arms and introduced them into the sheepfold of the church, their mother. COMMENTARY ON ISAIAH 60.4-5.[12]

PILGRIMAGES FIND THE END OF THEIR JOURNEY IN JERUSALEM. THEODORET OF CYR: This does not easily apply to the Jews. For those who were captives did not all return. . . . But the church of God gathers its children from all the nations. And [they are] to be seen running toward Jerusalem from all the world, not in order to worship God in the temple of the Jews but that

---

[8]OUC 101. [9]ANF 6:336. [10]The last two emperors of the undivided Roman empire. [11]FC 22:330. [12]SESHS 2:173.

they might see the well-known places of the cross and the resurrection and the ascension. . . .

This does not apply to the Jews. Of what sort of nations and peoples are riches brought forth for them? But the church of God receives the gifts once offered to the demons, and the sea that was once bitter is now sweetened by the wood of the cross of the Savior, and having thus received a wonderful change it brings forth the church of God—it is especially to the city of Jerusalem they bring these, running from all lands. COMMENTARY ON ISAIAH 19.60.4-5.[13]

60:7 Rams of Nebaioth

EVEN BEASTS BRING PRAISE. THEODORET OF CYR: The text teaches that irrational beasts share in the light of the knowledge of God. And it is not thoughtless gifts that on the altar are offered, but acceptable ones that are pleasing. He says, "A sacrifice of praise will glorify me" and "Sacrifice an offering of praise to God."[14] COMMENTARY ON ISAIAH 19.60.6-7.[15]

60:8 Fly Like a Cloud

THE SEA DOES NOT DRAG THE FAITHFUL UNDER. GREGORY OF NYSSA: Typically, under the leadership of the law (for Moses was a type of the law that was coming) Israel passes dry over that sea, while the Egyptian who crosses in its track is overwhelmed. Each fares according to the disposition that he carries with him; one walks lightly enough, the other is dragged into the deep water. For virtue is a light and buoyant thing, and all who live in its way "fly like clouds," as Isaiah says, "and as doves with their young ones"; but sin is a heavy affair, "sitting," as another of the prophets says, "on a talent of lead."[16] If, however, this reading of the history appears to any forced and inapplicable and the miracle at the Red Sea does not present itself to him as written for our profit, let him listen to the apostle: "Now all these things happened to them for types, and they are written for our admonition."[17] ON VIRGINITY 18.[18]

THE THOUGHTS OF THE FREE HAVE WINGS. AMBROSE: For the soul has flights, as has been said, "Who are these that fly like clouds and like doves with their young?" You see, the soul has spiritual flights that, in a brief moment, circle the whole globe. For the thoughts of wise people are free and, insofar as they rise up from lower to higher shadows, so much and more they fly without the hindrance of any earthly weight, and they are the more carried along by the beating of spiritual wings onto that ethereal and rarefied place; [the soul] despises all worldly things. It soars above the world in its regard for eternal virtues; for justice is above the world, goodness is above the world, wisdom is above the world, even when it is found in the world, it is above the world nevertheless. ON VIRGINITY 17.108.[19]

A FIGURE OF THE RETURN. ISHO'DAD OF MERV: "Like doves to their windows." With these words he speaks of the return. As the doves, he says, know their nests, so the people hasten to Jerusalem and to their prosperity. COMMENTARY ON ISAIAH 60.8.[20]

SPIRITUAL WATCHFULNESS. GREGORY THE GREAT: For death indeed climbs in through the windows and enters houses, in that through the body's sense lust comes and enters the dwelling of the mind. Quite to the contrary is this which we have often cited from Isaiah concerning the righteous: "Who are they who fly like clouds and like doves come to their windows?" The righteous are said to be like clouds since they are raised above earthly contagions, just as doves go to their own windows, since each one does not pay much attention to their exterior senses, and fleshly lust does not catch them when they are far from home. . . . For the holy person who receiving the senses of his body like servants to help him is in control of them; and the fairest judge sees sins

---

[13]SC 315:242-44. [14]Ps 50:23 (49:23 LXX). [15]SC 315:248-50. [16]Zech 5:7. [17]1 Cor 10:11. [18]NPNF 2 5:364*. [19]AOV 48. [20]CSCO 303(128):58.

before they come and closes the windows to the plundering death of the body, saying, "I have made a covenant with my eyes, that I should not gaze at a young woman." MORALS ON THE BOOK OF JOB 21.2.[21]

THE FEAST OF THE CHURCH. THEODORET OF CYR: And what is more, they (Ethiopians, Midianites, Arabians) are also in the habit of offering these beasts as presents to the God of the universe, some, in gaining closeness to some apostle, offer them as gifts; others, in approaching a martyr, look for his intercession to reconcile themselves to God and lead [their beasts] by way of firstfruits of offerings that they have promised to make. . . . The text teaches therefore that even less intelligent people will share in the light of the knowledge of God. And indeed it did not say that irrational offerings would be made on the altar, but "acceptable" sacrifices, that is, "agreeable" sacrifices. . . .

The church of God is therefore seized with amazement in contemplating the clouds of people who hasten towards it; they resemble doves flying in the company of their little ones. However, if one desires to understand this passage exactly, let him consider what happens during public feasts of the Lord or those of holy martyrs. COMMENTARY ON ISAIAH 19.60.6-8.[22]

60:9 Foreigners Will Build

GOD'S PROVIDENTIAL CARE FOR ESTABLISHING THE CHURCH. PROCOPIUS OF GAZA: He calls the ships "from Tharsis," those that come from Tharsis in India, which is situated in the far east and puts us in mind of Jonah. These will come to Jerusalem not for its sake but for God, who wished to ratify the promise made to the ancestors through his great mercy. And next, "And strangers will build you walls." This can now be seen, for the Gentiles lead the churches and fence them round with their teachings, so that there is no place for a contrary word of counsel. "And their kings will minister to you." For

even today the leaders of the Roman administration and the fear of kings restrain those plotting against the churches. Indeed, "minister" means their subordination. For they listen to the church's holy oracles and value the gospel message with all consideration. COMMENTARY ON ISAIAH 60.1-22.[23]

THE CHURCH IS GLORIFIED BY THE CONVERSION OF THE NATIONS. EUSEBIUS OF CAESAREA: It is possible to contemplate the fulfillment of the divine word when one sees, in consequence of the conversion of the nations, such souls dedicating themselves to the message of godliness and being diligently busy in the ministry of the altar of God. It is then especially on account of the conversion of such souls and their salvation that the church of God receives glory. COMMENTARY ON ISAIAH 2.50.[24]

GOD WAITS TO SEE HOW ALL PEOPLE WILL RESPOND. THEODORE OF HERACLEA: We need to observe how the Lord, out of his benevolence, foretells all things before they happen. When he threatens doom, this is so that his servants, afraid of what might happen, will turn and repent and manage to deflect the terrible trials. Again, blessings are promised, and these promises strengthen the souls of those who act justly, providing them with hope before God. But there is never any necessity on God to carry out these things. For when people repent there is no need for anger, or, when they do not persevere in doing good, he will not [necessarily] bring to an end the promised blessings either, we ourselves being the ones who provide the reasons for God to execute the promised harm.

And these events can be discovered if one looks, for instance, at when Cyrus and then Darius rebuilt Jerusalem. Also, no less a person than Alexander was impressed by the sacred vestment and turned anger into worship.[25] FRAGMENTS ON ISAIAH.[26]

---

[21]CCL 143A:1065-66. [22]SC 315:248-50. [23]PG 87:2629. [24]GCS 57(9):373. [25]See Josephus *Antiquities* 11.8.3. [26]PG 18:1365.

60:10 *Strangers Rebuild Your Walls*

GUARDING JERUSALEM WITH PRAYER AND INSTRUCTION. THEODORET OF CYR: Cyrus ordained the reconstruction of Jerusalem, but the work remained unfinished. Under Darius, the son of Hystapis, only the temple of God was reconstructed. Under Artaxerxes the Long-armed, Nehemiah—who was not a stranger but a Jew—was engaged in the reconstruction of the walls. The money that he possessed to cover the expense was not provided from royal riches, but he had gathered it as the result of a collection; and, after the conquest of the Jews, the Roman emperors rebuilt the walls of Jerusalem. Whoever would wish, however, to understand [the text] more precisely will find that these are the teachers who have come from foreign nations who watch over it and guard it by their prayers and their instructions. "For by reason of my wrath I struck you, and by reason of mercy I loved you." That applies both to the ancient Jerusalem, which had been destroyed by reason of [their] sins, and to the reconstruction by reason of the singular [divine] benevolence, and to the church of God, which was formerly like a desert, since it did not benefit from divine solicitude but which has enjoyed the result of the Savior's providence. COMMENTARY ON ISAIAH 19.60.10.[27]

60:11-12 *Their Kings as Captives*

THE CHURCH HAS BUILT A GOOD REPUTATION IN THE WORLD. THEODORET OF CYR: Which power of the nations ran toward the former Jerusalem to worship? Which kings were led to worship the God of the universe? But the gates of the church of God are always open to receive the arrivals, and they receive also the godly kings drawn there by the teaching of the holy apostles. . . .

The Babylonians hardly idolized Jerusalem, whereas the majority of the members of the Gentiles adore the church of God and that is particularly true of their offspring. When the parents have reached the end of their life, their children, having learned the truth from them, present worship to the Savior by carrying out their acts of worship in the houses of prayer. . . . For the earthly Jerusalem received another name, when the Roman kings called it Aelia. How then can the accuracy of the prophecy be shown unless one understand "Zion" more in a spiritual sense? . . . The church of God demonstrates the truth of this prediction. It continually receives royal gifts and welcomes that which is brought forth from the nations as it sings the praises of the One who is the cause of all these. COMMENTARY ON ISAIAH 19.60.11-16.[28]

---

[27]ITA 892-93*; SC 315:252-54. [28]SC 315:254-58.

60:13-22 THE RENOVATION OF ZION

13The glory of Lebanon shall come to you,
   the cypress, the plane, and the pine,
to beautify the place of my sanctuary;
   and I will make the place of my feet
     glorious.

14The sons of those who oppressed you
   shall come bending low to you;
and all who despised you
   shall bow down at your feet;
they shall call you the City of the LORD,

the Zion of the Holy One of Israel.

¹⁵*Whereas you have been forsaken and hated,*
    with no one passing through,
I will make you majestic for ever,
    a joy from age to age.
¹⁶*You shall suck the milk of nations,*
    you shall suck the breast of kings;
and you shall know that I, the LORD, am your
    Savior
    and your Redeemer, the Mighty One of
    Jacob.

¹⁷*Instead of bronze I will bring gold,*
    and instead of iron I will bring silver;
instead of wood, bronze,
    instead of stones, iron.
I will make your overseers peace
    and your taskmasters righteousness.
¹⁸*Violence shall no more be heard in your land,*
    devastation or destruction within your
    borders;

you shall call your walls Salvation,
    and your gates Praise.

¹⁹*The sun shall be no more*
    your light by day,
nor for brightness shall the moon
    give light to you by night;[1]
but the LORD will be your everlasting light,
    and your God will be your glory.
²⁰*Your sun shall no more go down,*
    nor your moon withdraw itself;
for the LORD will be your everlasting light,
    and your days of mourning shall be ended.
²¹*Your people shall all be righteous;*
    they shall possess the land for ever,
the shoot of my planting, the work of my
    hands,
    that I might be glorified.
²²*The least one shall become a clan,*
    and the smallest one a mighty nation;
I am the LORD;
    in its time I will hasten it.

[1] One ancient Ms Gk Old Latin Tg: Heb lacks *by night*

OVERVIEW: Humility that comes from persecution is a preparation for worship. Such a humbled church is always renewed by those being joined to it (PROCOPIUS). Isaiah's promises for worldly blessing here are transposed into even better ones of spiritual rewards (ORIGEN) such as the gift of justifying faith, which in turn offers praise as its evidence (EUSEBIUS). Here in Isaiah, God also speaks of the celestial city as a place of order, beauty and joy (BASIL), having foreseen long ago the order of the church's ministry whose overseers would be peace (CLEMENT OF ROME).

The Lord needs no light but gives the righteous light from himself (ORIGEN). The Lord will guide and illuminate his people without fail from his incarnation onwards (DIDYMUS). The people

of God, as they grow, move from uncertainty to certainty (THEODORET).

60:13-14 Lebanon's Glory Comes to Jerusalem

HUMBLED MINDS PROVIDE FOR THE RENOVATION OF DIVINE WORSHIP. PROCOPIUS OF GAZA: Scripture likes to compare the multitude of the saints with trees of this kind. . . . Paul calls us in one place "the plantation of God."[1] Some interpreters say that Scripture calls the nations Lebanon (just as Carmel can mean Jerusalem, though it is a mountain in Samaria) on the grounds that it comes from another race. Accord-

---

[1] 1 Cor 3:9.

ing to the historical sense it means those trees supplied for rebuilding. But according to the spiritual sense, it means the minds of the righteous ones. These are they who submitted themselves to those persecuting the church and with this transformation of mind worship God in it. Others think that it is Jerusalem that has been humbled and sings praises to Christ. COMMENTARY ON ISAIAH 60.1-22.[2]

60:15 Glory That Lasts

NEW BLOOD IN THE MEMBERSHIP OF THE CITY OF GOD. PROCOPIUS OF GAZA: Those who are strangers to godliness are said to be cut off and hated and to have no help. But those from the wild olive branch come to take their place and are made to be joined into one people out of each. And in the Savior's power there is made the full number of those being saved, the one city out of both tribes that is called Zion, and to it is the following promise made. Some say that it has been humbled on account of its insubordination against Christ and that yet it will be saved through acknowledging this. And so the words that follow are, "I will place you in eternal gladness and joy for all ages." For this is the hope of immortality in the church of God, the everlasting life and glory and kingdom of heaven, and there is no place for shame. "And you will drink the milk of the nations." This means the ever-new sacramental mystery and the fundamental teaching of those being reborn through faith in Christ. COMMENTARY ON ISAIAH 60.1-22.[3]

60:16 Your Savior

GOD GIVES THE BEST TO THOSE SATISFIED WITH THE GOOD. ORIGEN: And they will be called the city of the Lord, Zion of holy Israel. On account of your being trapped and despised when there was no help, I will give you eternal rejoicing and joy for ages to come. And though you desire the milk of the nations and to consume the riches of kings, so that you might know that I

am the Lord who saved you and led you out of Israel, "I will render for you gold instead of brass, and silver instead of steel . . . and I will give you rulers in peace and your bishops in justice, and injustice will no longer be heard in your land." COMMENTARY ON THE GOSPEL OF JOHN 10.294.[4]

PRAISE AS THE ACTIVE SIGN OF JUSTIFYING FAITH. EUSEBIUS OF CAESAREA: Instead of "salvation," the Hebrew reading has "Jesus" in its marks and letters, by which our Savior is written there. This is the origin of the power of the name of our Savior Jesus, which serves as a partition or strong wall to those worthy of these things. Such is seen now in part, but with the new age it will come into being with the perfection of presence. . . . See how the message stops us from a more physical understanding and from falling into the obvious, literal Jewish understanding. For it calls the gates of this new Jerusalem hymn singing and praising. Thus we are instructed that the entries of the revered citizenship is to consist of those who enter singing hymns and praising God. COMMENTARY ON ISAIAH 2.50.[5]

60:17 Your Overseers

THE NATURE OF THE LEADERSHIP OF THE CHURCH. CLEMENT OF ROME: The apostles received the gospel for us from the Lord Jesus Christ; Jesus the Christ was sent forth from God. So then Christ is from God and the apostles are from Christ. Both, therefore, came of the will of God in good order. Having therefore received their orders and being fully assured by the resurrection of our Lord Jesus Christ and full of faith in the Word of God, they went forth with the firm assurance that the Holy Spirit gives, preaching the good news that the kingdom of God was about to come. So, preaching in the country and in the towns, they appointed their firstfruits, when they had tested them by the Spirit, to be bishops and deacons for the future believers. And

---

[2]PG 87:2632. [3]PG 87:2633. [4]SC 157:562-64. [5]GCS 57(9):377.

this was no new thing they did, for indeed something had been written about bishops and deacons many years ago; for somewhere thus says the Scripture, "I will appoint their bishops in righteousness and their deacons in faith."[6] 1 CLEMENT 42.1-5.[7]

60:18 Walls of Salvation and Gates of Praise

THE GLORY AND ARRANGEMENT OF THE HEAVENLY CITY. BASIL THE GREAT: Some give the definition that a city is an established community, administered according to law. And the definition that has been handed down of the city is in harmony with the celestial city, Jerusalem above. For there it is a community of the firstborn who have been enrolled in heaven,[8] and this is established because of the unchanging manner of life of the saints, and it is administered according to the heavenly law. Therefore, it is not the privilege of human nature to learn the arrangement of that city and all this adornment. Those are the things "eye has not seen or ear heard, nor has it entered into the heart of humanity, what things God has prepared for those who love him."[9] But there are myriads of angels there, and an assembly of saints and a church of the firstborn that are enrolled in heaven.... Therefore, having raised the eyes of your souls, seek, in a manner worthy of things above, what pertains to the city of God. What could anyone consider as deserving of the happiness in that city, which the river of God makes joyful and of which God is the craftsman and creator? HOMILIES ON THE PSALMS 18.4 (PSALM 45).[10]

THE CHURCH WATCHES OVER VICTIMS OF INJUSTICE. THEODORET OF CYR: Everyone will see a truer fulfillment of these promises in the future life. That life is free from all injustice. That life is adorned with the highest justice. That life is in truth without sorrow and exempt from troubles. However, one also finds, as it were, a prefigurement of a similar state of affairs even now in the church of God. It has been freed from the

error of idols, it continually extols the God of the universe in hymns and its leaders watch (insofar as it is in their power) over the interests of those who are victims of injustice. COMMENTARY ON ISAIAH 19.60.18.[11]

60:19-20 The Lord Will Be Your Everlasting Light

GOD IS THE ONLY SOURCE OF LIGHT. ORIGEN: We must keep in mind, however, that the Word promises to the righteous through the mouth of Isaiah that days will come when not the sun but the Lord will be to them an everlasting light, and God will be their glory. And it is from misunderstanding, I think, some pestilent heresy that gave an interpretation to the words "let there be light," as if they were the expression of a wish merely on the part of the Creator, that Celsus made the remark, "The Creator did not borrow light from above, like those persons who kindle lamps at those of their neighbors." AGAINST CELSUS 6.51.[12]

THE COMING OF THE LORD. DIDYMUS THE BLIND: According to the word of blessing to the one receiving illumination, "The Lord will be your everlasting light."... When this economy was reconstituted, God opened his eyes on the house of Judah, that is, the living church of God, with the Savior sent from the house of Judah to rule over it. COMMENTARY ON ZECHARIAH 4.200-201.[13]

THE CERTAIN HOPE OF A NEW LIFE TO COME. THEODORET OF CYR: This is exactly what the future life possesses. It will need neither moon nor

---

[6]This divergence in the translation "in faith" (*en pistei*) at the end of the quotation from Is 60:17 from the LXX: *kai dōsō tous archontas sou en eirēnē kai tous episkopous sou en dikaiosynē* can be explained as in the textual transmission prior to Clement. The Hebrew is more abstract, taking "peace and righteousness" to be their overseers and taskmasters: "I will make your overseers peace and your taskmasters righteousness." [7]AF 75. [8]Heb 12:23. [9]1 Cor 2:9. [10]FC 46:302-3. [11]ITA 897*; SC 315:260. [12]ANF 4:597. [13]SC 85:904.

sun, since it has the ineffable light of God. But those who believe can take advantage of it in a provisional form. Nevertheless, in a figurative sense, believers enjoy this light even now. When they are illuminated by this light, they take the road that is free from error.... And this is what is announced about the life to come. It will have immutability of thought. It will be arrayed in righteousness forever. It will have freedom from sin. It will not have an excess of either youth or age. Instead, it will have a life without end. And in that life those who are worthy will inherit the land of the living. Commentary on Isaiah 19.60.19.[14]

60:21 Preserving the Shoot of My Planting

THE GARDENER PRESERVES HIS CHURCH.
THEODORET OF CYR: From the various translations and the Septuagint we find that the author of these words, and so to speak, the gardener, is the God of the universe. For it is he who has planted his church. It is he who watches over it now. It is he who has made it grow and he who receives the glory that proceeds from it. Commentary on Isaiah 19.60.21.[15]

[14]SC 315:262. [15]ITA 898*; SC 315:264.

61:1-3 THE YEAR OF THE LORD'S FAVOR

[1]The Spirit of the Lord GOD is upon me,
  because the LORD has anointed me
to bring good tidings to the afflicted;[m]
  he has sent me to bind up the
    brokenhearted,
to proclaim liberty to the captives,
  and the opening of the prison[n] to those
    who are bound;
[2]to proclaim the year of the LORD's favor,

and the day of vengeance of our God;
  to comfort all who mourn;
[3]to grant to those who mourn in Zion—
  to give them a garland instead of ashes,
the oil of gladness instead of mourning,
  the mantle of praise instead of a faint spirit;
that they may be called oaks of righteousness,
  the planting of the LORD, that he may be
    glorified.

m Or poor   n Or the opening of the eyes: Heb the opening

OVERVIEW: The Son in his incarnate state bowed to the Holy Spirit (ATHANASIUS). Jesus' promise of a year of release from the toil of this life will be fulfilled in the age to come (EUSEBIUS). The Spirit is the essence of God who descended on the Son for our benefit (EPHREM). The Spirit sent Christ, and Christ sent the Spirit (AMBROSE). The prophet addresses his words to Christ as the antitype of Zerubbabel (ISHO'DAD). The Spirit of God rested on the perfect man (IRENAEUS). The Spirit cannot be contained in one place but now fills every creature (FULGENTIUS). The authority of Jesus' teaching was heavenly, from God (AMBROSE). Christ as God sent the Spirit and as man received it. The decisive year of the Lord has already taken place in his incarnation and in our baptism (CYRIL). The prophecy refers to his first and second advents (THEODORET) and to the fact that once Christ has come, there is no place for despair for those who are in him (ISAAC).

61:1 *The Spirit of the Lord*

JESUS AND THE SPIRIT. ATHANASIUS: What is there to wonder at, what to disbelieve, if the Lord who gives the Spirit, is here said himself to be anointed with the Spirit, at a time when, necessity requiring it, he did not refuse in respect of his manhood to call himself inferior to the Spirit? DISCOURSE AGAINST THE ARIANS 1.50.[1]

CHRIST SENDS HIS PEOPLE HOPE OF RELEASE TO COME. EUSEBIUS OF CAESAREA: "The Spirit of the Lord is on me because he has anointed me." Clearly this happened to those who thought that the Christ of God was neither a mere man nor an unfleshed and unembodied Word who did not take on a mortal nature. Instead they say he is both God and human, God in that he is the only-begotten God who was in the bosom of the Father, and man . . . from the seed of David according to the flesh.[2] Thus, God the Word, who through the prophecy has been called Lord, speaks out this prophecy that is pre-eminent among other promises: "I am the Lord, and in the right time I will draw them together." . . . Taking the chrism in the Holy Spirit, he, chosen from among all, appears as the only-begotten Christ of God. And the verse "he has sent me to proclaim good news to the poor,"[3] he fulfilled in that time when he "was preaching the kingdom of heaven" and explaining the beatitudes to the disciples by saying, "Blessed are the poor in spirit, for theirs is the kingdom of God."[4] . . . And for those nations then imprisoned in their souls by the invisible and spiritual powers he preached release to his newly encouraged disciples. . . . Therefore, he preached release to the prisoners and to those suffering from blindness who were those enslaved by the error of polytheism, and he creates a year that is acceptable, through which he made all time his own year. And from the passing years of humanity he provides days of created light for those close to him. He never kept hidden the age that is to come after the perfecting of the present. For that age will be a time much on the Lord's mind, being an age and day of requiting. For he will grant a change of fortune or a year of favor to those struggling in the present life. COMMENTARY ON ISAIAH 2.51.[5]

THE ANOINTING OF JESUS THROUGH THE HOLY SPIRIT. EPHREM THE SYRIAN: "The Spirit of the Lord God is on me, because the Lord has anointed me to bring good tidings to the afflicted," that is, God anointed him with the Holy Spirit. Therefore, after being incarnated and clothed with a human body, as is said, he has received the Spirit and has been anointed with the Spirit, because he has received the Spirit for us and has anointed us with it.

"The Spirit of the Lord is on me." That Spirit, which proceeds from the Father and is his essence, is in me, who am the Word and the Son of the Father, and through my incarnation I received the anointment of the economy of salvation. COMMENTARY ON ISAIAH 61.1.[6]

THE ANOINTING SPIRIT ON THE SON OF MAN. AMBROSE: We have shown by the clear evidence of the Scripture that the apostles and prophets were appointed, the latter to prophesy, the former to preach the gospel, by the Holy Spirit in the same way as by the Father and the Son. Now we add what all will rightly wonder at and not be able to doubt, that the Spirit was on Christ; and that as he sent the Spirit, so the Spirit sent the Son of God. For the Son of God says, "The Spirit of the Lord is on me, because he has appointed me, he has sent me to preach the gospel." And having read this from the book of Isaiah, he says in the Gospel, "Today has this Scripture been fulfilled in your ears,"[7] that he might point out that it was said of himself. ON THE HOLY SPIRIT 3.1.1.[8]

ADDRESSED TO CHRIST. ISHO'DAD OF MERV: "The Spirit of the Lord is on me," etc. These words are manifestly said with regard to Zerub-

---

[1]NPNF 2 4:335. [2]Lk 1:32. [3]Lk 4:18. [4]Mt 5:3. [5]GCS 57(9):378-80. [6]SESHS 2:179. [7]Lk 4:21. [8]NPNF 2 10:135*.

babel but actually with regard to our Lord, as he has testified by himself. "Today," he said, "that Scripture has been fulfilled at your ears."[9] COMMENTARY ON ISAIAH 61.1.[10]

THE TRINITARIAN ANOINTING. IRENAEUS: For inasmuch as the Word of God was man from the root of Jesse and son of Abraham, in this respect did the Spirit of God rest on him and anoint him to preach the gospel to the lowly. But inasmuch as he was God, he did not judge according to glory or reprove after the manner of speech. For "he needed not that any should testify to him of humanity, for he himself knew what was in humanity."[11] For he called all people who mourn, and granting forgiveness to those who had been led into captivity by their sins, he loosed them from their chains, of whom Solomon says, "Everyone shall be held with the cords of his own sins."[12] Therefore, did the Spirit of God descend on him, [the Spirit] of him who had promised by the prophets that he would anoint him, so that we, receiving from the abundance of his unction, might be saved. Such then [is the witness] of Matthew.[13] . . . In the name of Christ is implied he who anoints, he who is anointed and the unction itself with which he is anointed. And it is the Father who anoints but the Son who is anointed by the Spirit, who is the unction, as the Word declares by Isaiah: "The Spirit of the Lord is on me, because he has anointed me"— pointing out the anointing Father, the anointed Son and the unction, which is the Spirit. AGAINST HERESIES 3.9.3, 3.18.3.[14]

THE UBIQUITY OF THE SPIRIT. FULGENTIUS OF RUSPE: But afterward [the Spirit] came on him as he was baptized . . . and Jesus returned to Galilee. Considering all those things, we remember and acknowledge the Holy Spirit, who is one like the Father and the Son, without measure, and one who fills every creature and does the works that only God does, since one such cannot be sent from place to place since he is one who, we are taught, is immeasurable by nature. AGAINST FABIANUS, FRAGMENT 28.10-11.[15]

GOD'S WILL IS REVEALED IN THE TEACHING OF JESUS. AMBROSE: Here is the one who says, "My teaching is not mine but his who sent me. If anyone wants to do his will, let him know about the teaching, whether it is from God or I am speaking by my own authority."[16] For one is teaching from God, the other is human teaching. Thus, the Jews, when they asked whether his teaching was taken from people, saying, "How has he known these writings without learning them?" Jesus replied, "My teaching is not mine."[17] ON THE CHRISTIAN FAITH 2.9.79.[18]

THE TIME OF RECKONING IS THE FIRST ADVENT. CYRIL OF ALEXANDRIA: Being God by nature, the Only Begotten is the holy of holies, and he sanctifies all creation and so originates from the holy Father with the Holy Spirit proceeding from him and sending in the power from above to those on earth who recognize him. How was he sanctified? For he is God and man equally; he gives the Spirit to creation but receives the Spirit on account of being human. . . .

"Acceptable" is that year in which we were received, when we took kinship with him, having our sins washed away through holy baptism and becoming partakers of the divine nature through the sharing of the Holy Spirit. Or "acceptable" is the year in which he revealed his glory through the divine miracle attesting the message. We received the time for salvation gladly . . . the day of reckoning is none other than the time of his dwelling among us in which the reckoning has been given by him to those believing in him through the promise in hope. . . . For the Savior himself said, "Now is the judgment of this world, now is the prince of the world cast out."[19] The time of reckoning, then, is in this manner, when Christ illuminated the world. COMMENTARY ON ISAIAH 5.5.61.1-3.[20]

---

[9]Lk 4:21. [10]CSCO 303(128):59. [11]Partly from the Peshitta, partly Jn 2:25. [12]Prov 5:22. [13]Mt 3:16. [14]ANF 1:423, 446**. [15]CCL 91A:810-11. [16]Lk 4:18; Is 61:1; Jn 7:16-17. [17]Jn 7:15-16. [18]CSEL 78:85-86. [19]Jn 12:31. [20]PG 70:1349-56.

FIRST COMING AND SECOND COMING. THE-
ODORET OF CYR: After completing these predictions, Isaiah now turns the prophecy to Christ
the Master, who in the present life has given
these things to the church and has promised the
commonwealth to come. . . . We do not need
many examples to explain the meaning of this
prophecy. For the Master himself has made it
clear to us. For, entering the synagogue he took
the book, unrolled it[21] . . . and he was anointed by
the All-Holy Spirit, not as God but as man. For
we have often made this manifest already in our
other writings. . . .

Isaiah calls "poor" those who have lost heavenly riches, "broken-hearted" those who have
corrupted their reason, "blind" those who do not
know God and who worship creation, "prisoner"
those brought into the enemy's camp and who
have lost their original freedom. . . . Christ did
not only give to us the forgiveness of sins and free
us from the tyranny of the devil and reveal to us
the divine light, but he also announced the future
existence and warned of the righteous judgment.
For I think that "the year of grace" means his first
coming and "day of recompense" the day of judgment. To console all who mourn with the hope of
the resurrection, he has tempered the despair of
death. . . .

"Perfume of joy," which Theodotion and Symmachus translate by "oil of gladness," refers to the
mystical anointing through which those made
worthy receive the cloak of glory; for "cloak" must

be understood as spiritual clothing. . . .

As the blessed David says, "This is the generation that seeks the Lord."[22] The three interpreters, instead of "the generations of justice," have
"the strong ones of justice, a plantation of the
Lord for his glory." In this way, the finest generals
of godliness, as they roam the globe, remove impiety, and they plant in the desert the first planta-
tions of the Lord. COMMENTARY ON ISAIAH
19.61.1-3.[23]

DO NOT DESPAIR. ISAAC OF NINEVEH: Do not
fall into despair because of stumblings. I do not
mean that you should not feel contrition for
[your sins], but that you should not think them
incurable. For it is more expedient to be bruised
than dead. There is, indeed, a Healer for the person who has stumbled, even He Who on the
Cross asked that mercy be shown to His crucifiers, He Who pardoned His murderers while He
hung on the Cross.[24] . . . For a brief moment of
mourning He pardoned Simon, who had denied
Him. . . . Christ came in behalf of sinners, to heal
the broken of heart and to bandage their wounds.
"The Spirit of the Lord," He says, "is upon Me, to
preach good tidings to the poor." . . . And the
Apostle says in his epistle, "Jesus Christ came
into the world to save sinners."[25] ASCETICAL
HOMILIES 64.[26]

---

[21]Lk 4:16-17. [22]Ps 24:6 (23:6 LXX). [23]SC 315:264-70. [24]Lk 23:34.
[25]1 Tim 1:15. [26]AHSIS 314.

61:4-8 THE REDEEMED AS PRIESTS
OF THE LORD

[4]They shall build up the ancient ruins,
   they shall raise up the former devastations;
they shall repair the ruined cities,
   the devastations of many generations.

[5]Aliens shall stand and feed your flocks,
   foreigners shall be your plowmen and
     vinedressers;
[6]but you shall be called the priests of the

LORD,
men shall speak of you as the ministers of
our God;
you shall eat the wealth of the nations,
and in their riches you shall glory.
[7]Instead of your shame you shall have a double
portion,
instead of dishonor you[o] shall rejoice in
your[p] lot;

therefore in your[p] land you[o] shall possess a
double portion;
yours[q] shall be everlasting joy.

[8]For I the LORD love justice,
I hate robbery and wrong;[r]
I will faithfully give them their recompense,
and I will make an everlasting covenant
with them.

o Heb they   p Heb their   q Heb theirs   r Or robbery with a burnt offering

OVERVIEW: It is a spiritual reward that God's coworkers will gain (CYRIL). These words were spoken to the apostles as well, who in the face of suffering brought salvation to the nations (THEODORET). This reward will be doubled at the bodily resurrection when both soul and body will be blessed (GREGORY THE GREAT). But while still here, we should restrain the body (CASSIAN). There is no proper mercy that promotes unrighteousness (GREGORY THE GREAT).

61:4 They Shall Rebuild

GOD'S COWORKERS IN MISSION. CYRIL OF ALEXANDRIA: For the Savior cultivates us through the holy people of faith. And these are called God's coworkers.... And the gladness will be everlasting; for we do not expect the reward to be in things of this age but in exceeding hope and life without limit for those who are noble concerning thought and speech. COMMENTARY ON ISAIAH 5.5.61.4-7.[1]

SUFFERING LEADS TO THE NATIONS' SALVATION. THEODORET OF CYR: This is said to the holy apostles, "Do not be distressed when you are persecuted, tortured and disgraced among all and endure death of a thousand vanities. For through your sufferings the nations will gain salvation, and they will have a portion among those rejoicing." COMMENTARY ON ISAIAH 19.61.7.[2]

61:7 Double Portion

DOUBLE RESURRECTION: SOULS, THEN BODIES. GREGORY THE GREAT: About this twin glory it is written, "they will possess double in their own land." This is written concerning the souls of the saints, for single white cloaks are given to them, and it is said that they might have rest a short time until the number of their colleagues and brothers is filled up. So they take now single cloaks, but they will have double cloaks on the day of judgment; for the first is in the way of souls only, but later they will rejoice in the glory of souls and bodies together. DIALOGUE 4.26.3-4.[3]

61:8 The Lord Loves Justice

THE ONLY VICTIMS OF OUR FAST SHOULD BE OUR STOMACHS. JOHN CASSIAN: "If you offer rightly but do not divide rightly, have you not sinned?"[4] For the victims of fasting that we imprudently squeeze out of ourselves by violently wrenching our stomachs and that we believe we are offering rightly to the Lord are detested by him who "loves mercy and judgment"[5] when he says, "I, the Lord, love judgment, but I hate robbery in a whole burnt offering." The divine word also condemns as fraudulent workers those who offer the Lord their leavings and the smallest por-

[1]PG 70:1357, 1364. [2]SC 315:272. [3]SC 265:86. [4]Gen 4:7 LXX. [5]Ps 33:5 (32:5 LXX).

tion while keeping for the pleasure of the flesh and for their own use the best parts of their oblations—that is, their duties and acts: "Cursed is the one who does the works of the Lord fraudulently."[6] CONFERENCE 21.22.3-4.[7]

THE DISTINCTION BETWEEN MERCY AND INDULGENCE. GREGORY THE GREAT: But it is one thing to show mercy for sins, another to sin for the sake of showing mercy, which cannot really be called mercy since it does not issue in

sweet fruit, since it is embittered through the influence of a diseased root. For here the Lord rebukes such sacrifices through the prophet, saying, "I, the Lord, love justice and hate robbery with whole burnt offerings." . . . Such people also often withdraw from the poor what they give to God. But the Lord shows how strongly he disowns and censures such conduct. PASTORAL CARE 3.21.[8]

---

[6]Jer 48:10 LXX. [7]ACW 57:736. [8]NPNF 2 12:48**.

61:9-11 THE CHURCH CLOTHED WITH SALVATION

[9]Their descendants shall be known among the nations,
    and their offspring in the midst of the peoples;
all who see them shall acknowledge them,
    that they are a people whom the LORD has blessed.

[10]I will greatly rejoice in the LORD,
    my soul shall exult in my God;
for he has clothed me with the garments of salvation,

he has covered me with the robe of righteousness,
as a bridegroom decks himself with a garland,
    and as a bride adorns herself with her jewels.
[11]For as the earth brings forth its shoots,
    and as a garden causes what is sown in it
        to spring up,
so the Lord GOD will cause righteousness
        and praise
    to spring forth before all the nations.

OVERVIEW: The bride's beauty is seen in the spiritual glory of her members (EUSEBIUS). In putting on the dress of salvation, she becomes identified with Christ and like him (THEODORET). Two persons, Christ and the church, become as one, and share each other's strength (AUGUSTINE). Believers are as strong as the Groom and as fertile as the bride (CYRIL). It is the scattering of Christians who bear the Word (BEDE). The audible sign of God's redemption in Christ is the gospel; its visual equivalent is the cross (PROCOPIUS). There is joy in a determined vision of future glory for those who have put on Christ. Making room for Christ's word to bear fruit involves cooperation with the divine light in our souls (THEODORE) as we then experience the joy of the Lord, being joined to him (PROCOPIUS).

61:10 *Garments of Salvation*

THE PROMISE OF RESURRECTION GLORY.
EUSEBIUS OF CAESAREA: After these promises
that the Son of God has made concerning his first
advent, it is extremely fitting that the word here
addresses the church of God as receiving good and
blessed things in those in whom he labored. As if
receiving the appropriate items to wear, she takes
the fullness of those being saved and like a bride
she is said to consist of one fine and fair body and
to have clothed around her the beauty of her
groom. She is a monument of light, flashing forth a
body of divine resurrection that is called the body
of the Savior. For it is no longer a body of death, as
Paul confirms: "Who will save me from this body
of death?"[1] For this is salvation, to put a cloak
of salvation on one's soul and a tunic of righteousness. For each one by his deeds that are done
according to righteousness puts on his own fine
apparel. . . . For she who is the bride of the Word
receives seeds from him and returns splendid and
fresh fruit. COMMENTARY ON ISAIAH 2.52.[2]

PUTTING ON JESUS AT BAPTISM. THEODORET
OF CYR: Here in the person of the church he cries
to its benefactor, . . . "May my soul rejoice." . . .
He calls the grace of baptism "the garment of salvation" and "the cloak of joy," for "as many of you
as were baptized into Christ have put on Christ."[3]
For in the Hebrew language the garment of salvation is called the garment of "Jeshua," that is, of
Jesus, like a young groom.[4] . . . She both calls herself a bride, because she has been yoked to the
bridegroom, and a bridegroom, because she has
put on the bridegroom [Christ]. As for the mitre,
the three interpreters translate it as "crown." Of
this adornment the blessed David comments,
"The queen is here on your right, arrayed in a
multicolored golden vestment."[5] The text means
the multicolored gifts of the All-Holy Spirit.
COMMENTARY ON ISAIAH 19.61.10.[6]

IDENTIFICATION IN CHRIST. AUGUSTINE:
What is it that was said? "The two will be one

flesh. This is a great sacrament, but I am speaking
of Christ and the church."[7] . . . So that you may
realize that these are in some sense two persons
and yet again are one by the union of marriage, he
speaks as one in Isaiah: "He has bound a head-
band on me like a bridegroom and clothed me
with an ornament like a bride."[8] He called himself
a bridegroom as the head, the bride as the body.
So he speaks as one; let us hear him and let us
also speak in him. May we be in his members, so
that his voice can be ours also. EXPLANATIONS OF
THE PSALMS 74.4.[9]

**LIFE IN CHRIST AS THE GARMENT OF THE
CHURCH'S REJOICING.** CYRIL OF ALEXANDRIA:
Generously he lays his hands on them and in
order to crown with many fine gifts those peti-
tioning he says, "Everyone who sees them will
recognize that they are a seed blessed by God"
and adds, "And they will rejoice in the Lord." And
he immediately gives them joy. Here the person
of the church is introduced full of joy as it sounds
forth, "May my soul rejoice in the Lord, for he
has clothed me in a cloak of salvation and a tunic
of rejoicing." The tunic of rejoicing means our
Lord Jesus Christ.[10] . . . They who have him like a
garment gain not only salvation but also happiness and many joys. The Savior says, "The thief
only comes to steal, but I have come that they
may have life and have it abundantly."[11] . . . Christ
is, therefore, the tunic that is from heaven and
from above, which if anyone takes he or she will
be crowned with all beauty (spiritually understood) and with the distinction of good work—
like a groom wearing a mitre or as a bride clothed
in all beauty. For those in Christ, fortified for the
spiritual mastering, are well-equipped and ready
for every aspect of virtue. They are like brides on
account of their fruitfulness, with the many-
splendored beauty that comes from the brilliance

---

[1]Rom 7:24. [2]GCS 57(9):382. [3]Gal 3:27. [4]Theodoret thinks that the
"like a young groom" applies to the object of the clause, Christ. [5]See
Ps 45:9 (44:10 LXX). [6]SC 315:274-76. [7]Eph 5:31-32. [8]Is 61:10. [9]PL
36:949. [10]Rom 13:14. [11]Jn 10:10.

of virtues. Thus spoke one of the holy prophets, highlighting those who made straight the well-led life, "For the fear of you, Lord, we have conceived in the womb and labored and brought forth the spirit of salvation that you have given throughout the world."[12] Thus, the saints are compared with a bridegroom and bride on account of their fortitude and their fertility.... It shows that Christ shines out justice and gladness among the nations, just like flowers garland the earth.... For as the small and growing seed becomes a flower, just so was our Lord Jesus Christ proclaimed before the nations when it says also in the Song of Songs, "I am flower of the field, a lily of the valleys."[13] COMMENTARY ON ISAIAH 5.5.61.10-11.[14]

61:11 What Is Sown

THE WORD IS SPREAD THROUGH THE SCATTERING OF CHRISTIANS. BEDE: Therefore, those who had been scattered returned, preaching the word of God. Instead of "the dispersed," the Greek text has "disseminated," that is, scattered like seed, for they were those about whom Isaiah said, "their offspring in the midst of the peoples" and about whom the Lord in the parable of the Gospel said, "the good seed is those sons of the kingdom."[15] For this seed was disseminated throughout many regions, so that the harvest of faith that started in Jerusalem filled first Judea and Samaria and then the whole world. About these same ones, dispersed or rather disseminated through the next generations, it is said that they spoke the word not only to Jews but also to Greeks, and the noblest foundations of the new church in Antioch were planted through these. RETRACTIONS ON THE ACTS OF THE APOSTLES 8.4.[16]

THE STANDARD OF THE CHURCH IS THE GOSPEL AND THE CROSS. PROCOPIUS OF GAZA: Then Isaiah says, "Raise a standard to the nations."[17] For the Lord has made it to be heard to the end of the earth. Let no one think that this is said about the Jewish people. For he orders the standard to be raised to the ends of the earth.

The nature of this audible sign that he has raised is his making known the word of faith, which we proclaim, or perhaps it is the symbol of the suffering of the Savior. For this is contained in the confession of faith. For it should be said that the Lord Jesus believed that God raised him from the dead. Now he instructs the daughter of Zion, who is clearly the church as it awaits salvation. For it is the daughter of those among the Jews who of old were a godly community. Now he speaks of the second coming, reminding [the church] that he is the one who formerly saved it, on whose account he acted and suffered. COMMENTARY ON ISAIAH 62.1-12.[18]

THE GARMENT OF SALVATION. THEODORE OF HERACLEA: It is the custom of prophets to foresee the things to come, to mourn and lament the disasters and then from their visions of favor to tell the people the good news, even when those listening reject them, to rejoice and raise their spirits, since the prophets are those who possessed a fixed intention concerning the vision of things signified. Now the prophet looks toward Christ as he puts him on as a garment. For all who are clothed in Christ have put on the garment of salvation and beautify his holy church. And this is a fuller version of that disposition that a young man is filled with toward a virgin, rejoicing and dancing in spirit, as one united with Christ, having put him on and having him as a tunic of rejoicing. FRAGMENTS ON ISAIAH.[19]

SPIRITUAL PREPARATION. THEODORE OF HERACLEA: The text signifies the seed-like words that are planted in the soul as in earth and as seeds grow in a garden. No seed from outside or of a different sort is let in, but it is like soil that has the word and yields to Christ. Just as the eyes in the body have a close connection with the light

---

[12]See Is 26:18; 52:10. [13]Song 2:1. [14]PG 70:1365-68. [15]Mt 13:38. [16]CCL 121:136. [17]Is 62:10. [18]PG 87:2660. [19]PG 18:1365.

and when the sun rises we immediately see this link, so when the Savior will enlighten us, we will in turn illuminate that readiness for righteousness, which is mixed into us, putting aside the dark ways of our souls. FRAGMENTS ON ISAIAH.[20]

THE JOY OF THE LORD AND THOSE WHO ARE JOINED TO HIM. PROCOPIUS OF GAZA: There are some who would explain the whole passage this way. It is prophetic custom to lament the bad things but to rejoice in the good. And this is what the prophet does here. For telling forth the good news of the coming of Christ and the salvation of all things, putting on Christ and being adorned and surrounded by him, he gives praise in the spirit, having the disposition of a young man with

a virgin, as long as he is joined to Christ. And the "as the earth shoots forth its flower" represents those who receive in their souls the spermatic words that prepare the way for Christ. For their eyes have an affinity with the light. They see whenever light is present. So, too, when Christ arises we receive him through our preparedness for him and immediately turn away from darkness. It says that he appeared from the shoot of Israel as one openly rejoicing before the nations.

And lest Israel seemed abandoned, I will not abandon my plan, which was made from the beginning, nor its dignity. For first of all Christ sent his disciples to the lost sheep of Israel. COMMENTARY ON ISAIAH 62.1-12.[21]

---

[20]PG 18:1365. [21]PG 87:2661-64

62:1-5 ZION'S ELEVATION

[1]For Zion's sake I will not keep silent,
 and for Jerusalem's sake I will not rest,
until her vindication goes forth as brightness,
 and her salvation as a burning torch.
[2]The nations shall see your vindication,
 and all the kings your glory;
and you shall be called by a new name
 which the mouth of the LORD will give.
[3]You shall be a crown of beauty in the hand of
 the LORD,
 and a royal diadem in the hand of your God.

[4]You shall no more be termed Forsaken,[s]
 and your land shall no more be termed
 Desolate;[t]
but you shall be called My delight is in her,[u]
 and your land Married;[v]
for the LORD delights in you,
 and your land shall be married.
[5]For as a young man marries a virgin,
 so shall your sons marry you,
and as the bridegroom rejoices over the bride,
 so shall your God rejoice over you.

s Heb Azubah **t** Heb Shemamah **u** Heb Hephzibah **v** Heb Beulah

---

OVERVIEW: The martyrs form the crown of Christ in glory (EUSEBIUS). But God's kingdom with its righteousness and glory is promised first to the Jewish people and then beyond (PROCO-

PIUS). The people of Israel were betrothed to God, but not only Israel but the nations too now come together with him in the church as it finds itself completed in him (CYRIL). The bridal soul in baptism assumes a new name that is common to all believers (THEODORE). The church's life with God signifies the protection of the divine presence and the fact that he keeps it in holiness (PROCOPIUS). Faith means that Christ is now the head of our household (THEODORET). This faith repopulates the land as it becomes fertile once more, through the church, with its new spiritual receptivity (ISHO'DAD). The sons of this marriage are the leaders of the church: the apostles, the priests and the righteous ones (EPHREM).

62:3 A Crown of Beauty

THE MARTYRS ARE THE CROWN. EUSEBIUS OF CAESAREA: For the crown is really all those of Christ who, being set right through him, receive the diadem of the kingdom—those who sustained the struggle because of him, the holy martyrs whom the Father hand-picked to circle the crown for his son along with the royal "diadem" of honor, which is filled with the great number of those who have been saved by him. COMMENTARY ON ISAIAH 2.52.[1]

DELIGHT IN THE INEXORABLE EXPANSION OF GOD'S KINGDOM. PROCOPIUS OF GAZA: In the translators the prophet holds forth like one caught up in delight: "For Zion's sake I will not keep quiet." For I will cry to God and ask to see the perfecting of what has been said—a time when "righteousness and the salvation of Jerusalem" will enlighten all. For after this a "light to the nations" will be passed on. For the choir of apostles extended the teaching to all the kingdoms, "and the kingdoms were like a jewel in the hand of God," and so on. This was the blessing of those who fulfilled the promises first of all, that is, the community among the Jews called Jerusalem. Some call these new, for the apostles of the church were the firstfruits. "And I will not stop," therefore, until God will fulfill his promises to it, the salvation through Christ for all the earth. For God is not of Israel alone but also of the nations. Some think that the words "my righteousness

and my salvation" are actually spoken by the mouth of God promising to fulfill all these things.

Christ is righteousness and salvation, just as a light in the world, saying, "When I am in the world, I am the light of the world,"[2] which was formerly discordant in godlessness and all shadows. "Righteousness and glory" are terms that once more name Christ. For we are justified in him, and we are enriched with glory from him.

To the newness of life, in place of the synagogue is rendered the name "church" and house and city of God, in which David said, "Glorious things are said of you, city of God."[3] COMMENTARY ON ISAIAH 62.1-12.[4]

BETROTHAL AND MARRIAGE. CYRIL OF ALEXANDRIA: "You will be a crown of beauty in the hand of the Lord and a royal diadem in the hand of your God." Now this compares both each holy soul and the collective church, that is, the company of the saints, to a garland tied together from many flowers or to a royal diadem, shining with Indian jewels and with a variety of beautiful forms. For many are the noble characteristics of the saints, and there is not one type of distinction but many and various . . . and Christ himself said about his own sheep or the flock of those believing in him, "No one shall snatch them from the hand of the Father."[5] . . .

"As a young man marries a virgin." This is said to the church about the time in the beginning when it was constituted from the Jewish tribes. For the godly disciples were Jewish according to their human origin, but they stood out from the others and took the lead since they had apostolic status. Yet they retained a great love and respect for their religion, so that there seemed to be great affection toward it as a man ought to feel toward a young virgin bride when he lies with her. . . .

"The Lord will rejoice over you." . . . For the only-begotten Word of God came down from

---

[1]GCS 57(9):383. [2]Jn 9:5. [3]Ps 87:3 (86:3 LXX). [4]PG 87:2653-56. [5]Jn 10:29.

heaven to make the church fertile, which he presented to himself as a pure virgin, without spot or stain, wholly blameless.[6] She received from him the seeds of the evangelical citizenship, became pregnant and gave birth, not with blood . . . but rather as one shaped to the beauty of the truth. Commentary on Isaiah 5.5.62.3-5.[7]

The Churches' Honeymoon with the Divine Groom. Theodore of Heraclea: The new name means the names given to the Christians. For the person baptized into saving baptism is called by another name because he received a total change of condition. But the Jew fought against the new name. For that reason it says in the prophecy of Isaiah, "He put a new name on you.". . .

A garland is composed from many different flowers, and the diadem of the kingdom denotes the ranks of apostles who led the churches, being Israelites by birth, and whom the new name suited since they were in communion so as to become a people. They are called "will," those who have done his will, those who are said to love as a young man dwells with a virgin. This does not denote corruption but the blooming of her condition, for in dwelling with the virgin the groom protects her.

This indicates the present-day condition of the churches; day and night the people guard God's commands; the priests teach about God the whole night, and they praise the Lord and remember him. Fragments on Isaiah.[8]

62:4 My Delight Is in Her

The Bliss and Protection of Divine Favor. Procopius of Gaza: Because she will be adorned and established in incomparable beauty, he adds, "You will be a beautiful garland."[9] For every holy soul and the whole church must be compared with a garland put together from many flowers and a royal jewel. For David says that the church is adorned in gold-embroidered and multicolored clothing similar to what is said in our

text. "In the hand of God" means "under his shelter." For he says, "Under my hand I will shelter you." And Christ concerning his own sheep said, "No one can steal them from the Father's hand."[10] Some say that the garland of Christ are those corrected by him. And the jewel of his kingdom are those martyrs for his sake,[11] whom in his hand the Father had chosen to put round the Son, garlanding him and placing as a royal jewel, with the fullness of those who have been saved through him and by him. Among these taking a new name, she will no longer be called "she who is left deserted" but "my will," that is, according to my will. This means that she who was previously deserted[12] will be saved and placed with him, rather than deserted. . . .

He says "will," meaning those doing his will, those who love him, as a young man loves a virgin. . . . For he protects and keeps her as virgin, according to the mystery mentioned by Paul when he discusses Christ and the church.[13] He shows the present state of the churches under the guidance of the priests day and night. While the people are unconscious of God, the priests become their defending wall, unconquered and placing a faithful guard against any approach of the devil. Commentary on Isaiah 62.1-12.[14]

Sharing His Name. Theodoret of Cyr: Those who believe in the Lord received a new title; they are not called after Abraham or Israel or Judah but are named after the master, Christ. For they are called Christians by everyone, since they have put on Christ through the most holy baptism. Commentary on Isaiah 19.62.2.[15]

Israel's New Fertility. Isho'dad of Merv: "Married," since on the days of the captivity [your land] had become a widow, without kings or children; now, on the contrary, because of the return,

---

[6]Eph 5:27. [7]PG 70:1369-73. [8]PG 18:1368. [9]See Is 61:3. [10]Jn 10:28. [11]See GCS 57(9):383, for the same interpretation. [12]The Greek can mean "barren" as well as "deserted." [13]Eph 5:32. [14]PG 87:2656, 2664. [15]SC 315:276-78.

it will be a married woman and a mother of children. "Your land shall be married," that is, it will be sowed and made fertile, or it will now cooperate in its tilling and germination. COMMENTARY ON ISAIAH 62.4.[16]

62:5 Your Sons Marry You

THE SONS ARE THE APOSTLES, THE PRIESTS AND THE RIGHTEOUS ONES. EPHREM THE SYR-IAN: "For as a young man marries a virgin, so shall your sons marry you." He calls sons the apostles, the priests and the righteous ones of the church, who constitute the head of the body of the church, as the husband is the head of a woman.[17] These are like husbands to the church through its doctrine and constantly generate spiritual sons to it. COMMENTARY ON ISAIAH 62.5.[18]

---

[16]CSCO 303(128):59. [17]Eph 5:23. [18]SESHS 2:185.

62:6-12 MAKING JERUSALEM AN OBJECT OF PRAISE

[6]Upon your walls, O Jerusalem,
    I have set watchmen;
all the day and all the night
    they shall never be silent.
You who put the LORD in remembrance,
    take no rest,
[7]and give him no rest
    until he establishes Jerusalem
    and makes it a praise in the earth.*
[8]The LORD has sworn by his right hand
    and by his mighty arm:
"I will not again give your grain
    to be food for your enemies,
and foreigners shall not drink your wine
    for which you have labored;
[9]but those who garner it shall eat it
    and praise the LORD,
and those who gather it shall drink it

    in the courts of my sanctuary."
[10]Go through, go through the gates,
    prepare the way for the people;
build up, build up the highway,
    clear it of stones,
    lift up an ensign over the peoples.
[11]Behold, the LORD has proclaimed
    to the end of the earth:
Say to the daughter of Zion,
    "Behold, your salvation comes;
behold, his reward is with him,
    and his recompense before him."†
[12]And they shall be called The holy people,
    The redeemed of the LORD;
and you shall be called Sought out,
    a city not forsaken.

* LXX 6b-7 there is none like you, until he sets Jerusalem right and makes it a shining example on the earth   † LXX Behold, your Savior has come to you, having his reward and his work before his face

---

OVERVIEW: God accommodates into his plans the heartfelt prayers of his people (EUSEBIUS). He has sworn to defeat his people's enemies (CYRIL) and to guard those who are his own through his angels (THEODORET). The prophet reassures them of the preservation of their virtue by the Lord (EUSEBIUS). God will protect and keep his people (THEODORET). But we must make room in our hearts if Christ is to walk among his people (JEROME). Obstacles to the knowledge of God must and will be removed (PROCOPIUS). The glory of the Lord is revealed through his divinity and the rewards he graciously gives to the church (CYRIL). Thus Isaiah was pointing the way toward the work Christ would do (THEODORET) in calling the church to be holy (ACTS OF THE COUNCIL OF CARTHAGE) and giving hope to all who have believed (PROCOPIUS).

62:6-7 Never Be Silent Till Jerusalem Shines

GOD'S PEOPLE WILL NOT REMAIN SILENT. EUSEBIUS OF CAESAREA: Instead of "there is none like you, until he sets Jerusalem right and makes it a shining example on the earth," Symmachus has, "do not be silent and do not let him be silent until he prepares and makes Jerusalem to sing on the earth."... For with the prophetic choir asking such questions, the Holy Spirit is encouraging them and exhorting them to continue in those prayers on behalf of those mentioned. So he says, "Don't be silent and give no silence, that is, to the Lord who promises these things, until he has prepared and makes Jerusalem to sing on the earth." He provides for the intercession made by the powers of all the people, that it should not be quiet or ever fall silent, but with shouts and unrestrained cries rouse him. The people's intercession should never give God peace. COMMENTARY ON ISAIAH 2.52.[1]

GOD WILL OVERCOME HIS ENEMIES. CYRIL OF ALEXANDRIA: Jerusalem ... there is nothing like you; for there is nothing like you among us. Nevertheless, because whatever he has surpasses the human by the excess of glory, God outstrips us by the glory of his divinity in his being good and compassionate....

If you could correct yourself, Jerusalem, that

is, if you could change to spiritual worship, if you could ... take notice of the things written by Moses, if you would receive God's grace through faith and make his praise known through the earth, then you would make known the shining glory that is in Christ. This is the glory by which the Lord has sworn, since he has no one better to swear by. He has sworn "by his right arm," in that those who of old afflicted you with great injustice would no longer get in your way. COMMENTARY ON ISAIAH 5.5.62.6-9.[2]

ANGELS LEAD AND GUARD THE CHURCH. THEODORET OF CYR: Again, he gives the name Jerusalem to the bride but calls guards those who lead the godly people through city and town, those who night and day sing praises to God and guard the city. If one wants to take these as angels, one would not be far wrong. For it says, "The angel of the Lord will encircle those who are afraid and protect them."[3] COMMENTARY ON ISAIAH 19.62.6.[4]

62:8 Foreigners Shall Not Drink Your Wine

GOD'S PEOPLE WILL KEEP THE FRUIT OF THEIR LABOR. EUSEBIUS OF CAESAREA: He promises those crying out and who give unceasing praise to the Lord, "While you are still speaking, behold, I am here."[5] ... Now to those who will be worthy of the new age and involved in the things the Lord promises, he will no longer give their fruit to their enemies, but they will profit from these themselves. For they are correcting their lives in the direction of virtue and in godly manner are pursuing righteousness and enjoying their own harvest. COMMENTARY ON ISAIAH 2.52.[6]

GOD WILL PROTECT HIS PEOPLE'S WORK. THEODORET OF CYR: As you battle courageously, I will lead from the front. Since there is no one else

---

[1]GCS 57(9):384. [2]PG 70:1373-76. [3]Ps 34:7 (33:8 LXX). [4]SC 315:280. [5]Is 58:9. [6]GCS 57(9):384.

better by whom one should swear, then by my own glory and by my own power I swear, since I will guard your harvest for you and stop those who are perpetual thieves, while you will profit from your own labors. Wheat and wine and food, spiritually speaking, signify the harvest of righteousness. COMMENTARY ON ISAIAH 19.62.8-9.[7]

62:9 In the Courts of My Sanctuary

REMOVE EVERY OBSTACLE TO THE KNOWLEDGE OF GOD. PROCOPIUS OF GAZA: "They will eat and drink in the courts of my sanctuary."[8] These are the many mansions with the Father.[9] He mentions "courts," or "dwellings" as some prefer, and so consequently mentions the temple. He says, "Go out through my gates," meaning the heavenly city with its mansions and gates, which will be revealed to the saints in the future, in the place of those called. For no one will enter who is crippled by hate, or anyone who seeks to enter under false pretences. No demon will enter, or anyone who has obstructed the kingdom. "Make a road for my people," he says to the angelic powers. But some take these powers to signify the churches of the world, and that the stones in that road are snares laid by the enemy. But the guards (that is, the disciples) are told to keep those who enter on the way free from harm. For the Jews . . . like to dwell in legal figures, while Greeks stumble against the strange teaching. For they refer to words that the Jewish scribes have written. But the spiritual leaders cut down the wild thickets of scandalous unclarity and remove every obstacle to the knowledge of God. Therefore, Paul says to those from the circumcision, "There is neither circumcision nor uncircumcision"[10] but only the keeping of God's commands. COMMENTARY ON ISAIAH 62.1-12.[11]

62:10 Prepare the Way

MAKE WAY FOR THE LORD IN YOUR HEART. JEROME: "And salvation, along the way of his steps." Note the exact words, "his steps," where there are no rocks, where there are no thorns or thistles, where the path is even, where he may walk, where he cannot stumble. Let us, therefore, make way for the Lord in our heart, that way for which John [the Baptist] was giving his life's effort. . . . Although formerly we faced obstacles of thorns and thistles, although we had stones, he declares to us in Isaiah, "clear the highway of stones." He proclaims this, furthermore, lest he stumble on them when he is ready to walk in the way of our heart. Now the stones that he bids us to throw out from our way are our sins. Christ does not walk in our heart if there is any sin there. He stumbles at once against these stones. "And salvation along the way of his steps." Let us prepare the way, and Jesus will set his steps in it. HOMILIES ON THE PSALMS 17 (PSALM 85).[12]

62:11 Your Salvation Comes

THE CHURCH IS DAUGHTER OF ZION. CYRIL OF ALEXANDRIA: This forecasts the coming of the Savior and our redemption by his coming. It also foretells the granting of riches to those who believe in him. . . . Concerning that which is new, that is, the church, it may be fittingly said that it is the daughter of Zion. . . . For whom does he order to proclaim good news to Zion? Those holy spiritual guides, of course, who took on the leadership role in the church and whose job it was to open the gates and to remove the stones from their midst. And what were they to announce? "That the Savior has come bringing his own reward and his work before his face."[13] Two points are made, that which relates to his godhead and that which is a reward for us. Through both the Savior's glory becomes apparent. COMMENTARY ON ISAIAH 5.5.62.11-12.[14]

ISAIAH POINTS TO CHRIST'S WORK. THEODORET OF CYR: Thus, what God has indicated

---

[7]SC 315:282. [8]Procopius combines the eating and drinking in anticipation of the Eucharist. [9]Jn 14:2. [10]Gal 5:6. [11]PG 87:2660. [12]FC 48:134. [13]Is 62:11 LXX. [14]PG 70:1380.

to the ends of the earth is not the reconstruction of Jerusalem but the cross, the passion, the resurrection, the ascension of the Master to the heavens, the coming of the Holy Spirit and the hope of future benefits. He commands the heralds to prepare the road and to make it level . . . by removing difficulties. For he calls obstacles "stones." . . . Then, once the route has been arranged, he ordains the heralds to say to the daughter of Zion, that is, to the church extended throughout the world, "Behold, your Savior has come to you, having his reward and his work before his face." COMMENTARY ON ISAIAH 19.62.10-11.[15]

62:12 The Holy People Sought Out

THE CHURCH IS CALLED TO BE HOLY. COUNCIL OF CARTHAGE 411: Our adversaries argue against us who defend the purity of the church that it will have mixed within it at the same time good and bad up to the end of the age. For this reason we demonstrate that the church of the Lord is called nearly everywhere in the divine Scriptures "holy" and "without spot." In Isaiah, "say to the daughter of Zion, behold, your Savior comes bringing his reward and work with him,

and he will call that people holy and redeemed by the Lord; and you will be called a desired city and not an abandoned one." . . . For Paul clearly shows this: "Christ loved the church and gave himself up for it that he might sanctify it, washing it in the water of the word and joining it to himself, not having a spot or stain or anything like that, but holy and spotless."[16] ACTS OF THE COUNCIL OF CARTHAGE (411) 3.258.[17]

THE PERSONAL QUEST OF THE SAVIOR. PROCOPIUS OF GAZA: He rewarded the confession of the thief on the cross when he said, "Today you will be with me in paradise."[18] "He comes" to those who believed "and will call a people who have been ransomed by the Lord." For it was not an elder or an angel but the Lord himself who has saved us. He says "the city shall be called 'sought out,'" that is, worthy of memory. For it was formerly abandoned. So Jeremiah says, "I have abandoned my house and lost my inheritance."[19] And the Savior says, "Behold, your house will be left deserted."[20] COMMENTARY ON ISAIAH 62.1-12.[21]

---

[15]ITA 921*; SC 315:282-84. [16]Eph 5:25-27. [17]CCL 149A:244. [18]Lk 23:43. [19]Jer 12:7. [20]Mt 23:38. [21]PG 87:2661.

63:1-6 TREADING THE WINEPRESS ALONE

[1]Who is this that comes from Edom,
     in crimsoned garments from Bozrah,
he that is glorious in his apparel,
     marching in the greatness of his
          strength?

"It is I, announcing vindication,
     mighty to save."

[2]Why is thy apparel red,
     and thy garments like his that treads in the
          wine press?

[3]"I have trodden the wine press alone,
     and from the peoples no one was with me;
I trod them in my anger
     and trampled them in my wrath;

their lifeblood is sprinkled upon my garments,
*   and I have stained all my raiment.*
⁴*For the day of vengeance was in my heart,*
*   and my year of redemption*ʷ *has come.*
⁵*I looked, but there was no one to help;*
*   I was appalled, but there was no one to*
*   uphold;*

so my own arm brought me victory,
*   and my wrath upheld me.*
⁶*I trod down the peoples in my anger,*
*   I made them drunk in my wrath,*
*   and I poured out their lifeblood on the*
*   earth."*

w Or *the year of my redeemed*

OVERVIEW: The ascension and exaltation of Christ was beyond the angels' expectations (AMBROSE). The angels' question reveals they are puzzled about his essence (JEROME). Angels were just as amazed as we are at the incarnation of the Word of God, who brings his justice with him to the earth (CYRIL). He has a kingly quality as he marches (ISHO'DAD). The red garments he wears are a prediction of Christ's body, which was indeed true human flesh that could bleed (TERTULLIAN). The passion is the presupposition of the eucharistic nourishment, just as grapes have to be pressed before there can be wine (CYPRIAN). The red clothing symbolizes the shame Christ had to endure (CYRIL OF JERUSALEM). The redness has a shining quality because Christ immediately rose from death to glory (JEROME). Indeed, there is a nobility in Christ's heroism through his passion (AUGUSTINE). His glorification is the greater for having been manifested through humiliation (GREGORY OF NAZIANZUS). The power of Christ's righteousness overcame human weakness (THEODORET).

63:1-2 Who Is This Savior in Crimsoned Garments?

THE WONDER OF CHRIST'S ASCENSION AND EXALTATION. AMBROSE: The angels, too, were in doubt when Christ arose; the powers of heaven were in doubt when they saw that flesh was ascending into heaven. Then they said, "Who is this King of glory?" And yet some said, "Lift up your heads, O gates! And be lifted up, O ancient

doors! That the King of glory may come in."[1] In Isaiah, too, we find that the powers of heaven doubted. ON THE MYSTERIES 7.36.[2]

ANGELS PROCLAIM CHRIST'S BEAUTY. JEROME: Similarly, in Isaiah, "who is this that comes from Edom, in radiant garments?" Notice what the angels do; they proclaim his beauty but are silent about his essence.[3] HOMILIES ON THE PSALMS, ALTERNATE SERIES 69 (PSALM 91).[4]

WHO IS THIS WHO COMES? CYRIL OF ALEXANDRIA: The only-begotten Word of God ascended in the heavens with his flesh united to him, and this was a new sight in the heavens. The multitude of holy angels was astounded seeing the king of glory and the Lord of hosts in a form similar to ours. And they said, "Who is this that comes from Edom [that is, from earth], in crimsoned garments, from Bosor." But "Bosor" is to be interpreted as "flesh" or "anguish and affliction." LETTER 41.17.[5]

MARKS OF THE PASSION ARE SIGNS TO THE HEAVENLY POWERS. CYRIL OF ALEXANDRIA: For he appeared to the powers above not only in the form in which he came for us, that is, as a human, but also showing the signs of his passion. Thus, we say that after his resurrection from the dead the marks of the nails and the other things

---

[1]Ps 24:9 (23:9 LXX). [2]NPNF 2 10:322. [3]In Jerome and Origen (*Commentary on the Gospel of John* 6.288; FC 80:246) this verse is linked with Ps 24:7 (23:7 LXX). [4]FC 57:91. [5]FC 76:178; PG 77:216.

of his wounds were marked on the holy flesh. . . . So that the angels asking each other might say, "Who is this?" He considers and replies to them, "I speak justice and the judgment of salvation."[6] He calls "justice" the divine and good news-bearing message or every just word that the Lord speaks. And the judgment of salvation refers to the judgment we receive. He indicated the world also to Satan, who was accusing it, and he saved those burdened by terrible greed. And he expelled the rebel and foreign usurper from among them, saying, "Now is the judgment of this world."[7] COMMENTARY ON ISAIAH 5.5.63.1-7.[8]

THE ASPECT OF A WARRIOR. ISHO'DAD OF MERV: "Who is this that comes from Edom?" It seems that the prophet sees God under the aspect of a warrior who marches at the head of his people, and, after destroying the Edomites, has come back and arrives; and the prophet asks who is this that comes from Edom and Bozrah, their royal cities. COMMENTARY ON ISAIAH 63.1.[9]

HIS RED GARMENTS SYMBOLIZE CHRIST'S PASSION. TERTULLIAN: He likewise, when mentioning the cup and making the New Testament to be sealed "in his blood,"[10] affirms the reality of Christ's body. For no blood can belong to a body that is not a *body* of flesh. If any sort of body were presented to our view, which is not one of flesh, not being fleshly, it would not possess blood. In order, however, that you might discover how anciently wine is used as a figure for blood, turn to Isaiah, who asks, "Who is this that comes from Edom, from Bosor with garments dyed in red, so glorious in his apparel, in the greatness of his might? Why are your garments red, and your clothing as his who comes from the treading of the full winepress?" The prophetic Spirit contemplates the Lord as if he were already on his way to his passion, clad in his fleshly nature; and as he was to suffer therein, he represents the bleeding condition of his flesh under the metaphor of garments dyed in red, as if reddened in the treading and crushing process of the winepress, from

which the laborers descend reddened with the wine juice, like men stained in blood. AGAINST MARCION 4.40.[11]

63:3 *Treading the Winepress Alone*

NO EUCHARISTIC SALVATION WITHOUT THE PASSION. CYPRIAN: And does not also the Holy Spirit, speaking in Isaiah, testify the same thing concerning the passion of the Lord, saying, "Why are your vestments red and your garments as from treading the wine press full and well-trodden?" For can water make vestments red, or is it water that is trodden by the feet in the winepress or forced out by the press? The mention of wine is placed there, indeed, that in the wine the blood of the Lord may be known and that which was afterward manifested in the chalice of the Lord might be foretold by the prophets who announced it. The treading and pressing of the winepress are also spoken of, since wine cannot be prepared for drinking in any other way unless the cluster of grapes is first trodden and pressed. Thus, we could not drink the blood of Christ unless Christ had first been trodden on and pressed, and unless he had first drunk the chalice of which he should also give believers to drink. LETTER 63.7.[12]

THE SHAME OF THE CROSS. CYRIL OF JERUSALEM: Who is that who for shame is clothed in scarlet? For Bosra among the Hebrews has such a meaning. CATECHETICAL LECTURES 13.27.[13]

THE MYSTERY OF THE RESURRECTION REVEALED. JEROME: Edom is by interpretation either "earthy" or "bloody"; Bosor either "flesh" or "in tribulation." In a few words, [Isaiah] shows the whole mystery of the resurrection, that is, the reality of the flesh and the growth in glory. And the meaning is, Who is he that comes up from the earth, comes up from blood? According to the

---

[6]Is 63:1 LXX. [7]Jn 12:31. [8]PG 70:1381-84. [9]CSCO 303(128):59. [10]See Mt 26:28. [11]ANF 3:418. [12]FC 51:206* Epistle 62 in ANF. [13]FC 64:22.

prophecy of Jacob, he has bound his foal to the vine and has trodden the winepress alone, and his garments are red with new wine from Bosor, that is, from flesh or from the tribulation of the world, for he himself has conquered the world.[14] And, therefore, his garments are red and shining, because he is beautiful in form, more than the sons of humankind,[15] and on account of the glory of his triumph they have been changed into a white robe; and then, in truth, as concerns Christ's flesh, were fulfilled the words, "Who is this who is coming up all in white, leaning upon her beloved?"[16] And there is also that which is written in the same book, "My beloved is white and ruddy."[17] Against John of Jerusalem 34.[18]

The Noble Color of Christ's Passion. Augustine: Each quality, though, that is both beauty and strength, had been seen and understood by Isaiah, when he said, "Who is this who is arriving from Edom, the crimson of his garments from Bozrah, so handsome in the robe of his garment with strength?" So this prophet, who called him both handsome and strong, knew him as bridegroom and giant. Sermon 372.2.[19]

Marks of the Passion Adorn His Glory. Gregory of Nazianzus: And, if they marvel and say, as in Isaiah's drama, "Who is this that comes from Edom and from the things of the earth?" or "How are the garments red when he is without blood or body, as of one that treads in the full winepress?"—if they say this, then set forth the beauty of the array of the body that suffered, adorned by the passion and made splendid by the Godhead. Nothing can be lovelier or more beautiful than that.... Will you think little of him because he humbled himself for your sake? ... Do you conceive of him as less because he

girds himself with a towel and washes his disciples and shows that humiliation is the best road to exaltation?[20] On Holy Easter, Oration 45.25-26.[21]

63:4-6 Liberation Through the Lone Arm of the Lord

Liberating Divine Power. Theodoret of Cyr: They call the red land "Edom," and "Bosor" to the flesh; they were amazed at the ineffable beauty of the one wrapped in earthly and fleshly apparel, such as to drive those who looked to love. The blessed David is mindful of this beauty: "Fair and beautiful among the sons of humankind."[22] That Edom means flame-colored is affirmed in the Song of Songs by the bride, who cries, "My beloved is red and white."[23] Christ's nature is twofold. Therefore, white means the inaccessible light of divinity, red the human appearance....

For this is the time for these who were brazen to receive retribution and for those unjustly enslaved by them to get their freedom....

He calls "arm" the power of righteousness, for he guarded spotless and free from sin the nature that he assumed.... We who have benefited from this good work and have been delivered from that bitter slavery, let us sing praises to the author of these things. He was the one who underwent the battle and provided us with the gift of victory and peace. Let us hope that we can enjoy this victory until the end, by the grace of the one who has conquered. Commentary on Isaiah 19.63.1-6.[24]

---

[14]Jn 16:33. [15]Ps 45:2 (44:3 LXX). [16]Song 5:10. [17]Song 5:10. [18]NPNF 2 6:441*. See also his *Homilies on the Psalms* 7 (Psalm 68), FC 48:56. [19]WSA 3 10:317. [20]Jn 13:4. [21]NPNF 2 7:432*. [22]Ps 45:2 (44:3 LXX). [23]Song 5:10. [24]SC 315:284-90.

63:7-19 GOD'S LOYALTY TO ISRAEL

^{7}I will recount the steadfast love of the LORD,
  the praises of the LORD,
according to all that the LORD has granted us,
  and the great goodness to the house of Israel
which he has granted them according to his
      mercy,
    according to the abundance of his steadfast
      love.
^{8}For he said, Surely they are my people,
  sons who will not deal falsely;
  and he became their Savior.
^{9}In all their affliction he was afflicted,^{x}
  and the angel of his presence saved them;
in his love and in his pity he redeemed them;
  he lifted them up and carried them all the
      days of old.

^{10}But they rebelled
  and grieved his holy Spirit;
therefore he turned to be their enemy,
  and himself fought against them.
^{11}Then he remembered the days of old,
  of Moses his servant.
Where is he who brought up out of the sea
  the shepherds of his flock?
Where is he who put in the midst of them
  his holy Spirit,
^{12}who caused his glorious arm
  to go at the right hand of Moses,
who divided the waters before them
  to make for himself an everlasting name,

^{13}who led them through the depths?
Like a horse in the desert,
  they did not stumble.
^{14}Like cattle that go down into the valley,
  the Spirit of the LORD gave them rest.
So thou didst lead thy people,
  to make for thyself a glorious name.

^{15}Look down from heaven and see,
  from thy holy and glorious habitation.
Where are thy zeal and thy might?
  The yearning of thy heart and thy
      compassion
  are withheld from me.
^{16}For thou art our Father,
  though Abraham does not know us
  and Israel does not acknowledge us;
thou, O LORD, art our Father,
  our Redeemer from of old is thy name.
^{17}O LORD, why dost thou make us err from thy
      ways
  and harden our heart, so that we fear thee
      not?
Return for the sake of thy servants,
  the tribes of thy heritage.
^{18}Thy holy people possessed thy sanctuary a
      little while;
  our adversaries have trodden it down.
^{19}We have become like those over whom thou
      hast never ruled,
  like those who are not called by thy name.

x Another reading is he did not afflict

OVERVIEW: God moves in compassion to rescue the fallen (SYMEON). His last word is kindness, which qualifies his wrath (CYRIL). The retribution that Christ offers is, incredibly, mercy (THEODORET), embodied in the Son, who as divine Lord condescends to suffer the afflictions of humanity (CYRIL).

The Holy Spirit acted as God's right hand in guiding his servants in the Old Testament (CYRIL). God provides the Holy Spirit to lead his people; while in their midst the Spirit is united to the Father in his divinity (ATHANASIUS). The Holy Spirit, who is in the Father and Son together, comes down to focus and correct the minds of believers. The exaltation of Christ at the resurrection is fitting of his superiority as a human being (CYRIL). Christ released human nature from the prison of hellish bondage (THEODORET).

Moses' staff possessed extraordinary power and prefigured the cross (EPHREM). The universal and ubiquitous God is Father of the fatherless (CYRIL). God's patience makes him reluctant to exercise full discipline (THEODORET). When he does harden people's hearts, this is the result of their own preceding sin (AUGUSTINE). To feel God's discipline is a healthy sign we are not yet hardened (CAESARIUS). God drives unrepentant sinners on a course they have themselves chosen (ISIDORE).

Without Christ, our situation is like that of the Israelites in Egypt before their deliverance by Moses—a people without a name or an inheritance (EUSEBIUS, THEODORET). Those who are in the church now do have an inheritance as they reside on that "holy mountain" (CYRIL).

63:7 Recount God's Steadfast Love

THE COMPASSION OF GOD. SYMEON THE NEW THEOLOGIAN: I, wretched one, cast myself into the pit and the mud of the abyss[1] of shameful thoughts and deeds, and once I had come there, I fell into the hands of those who were concealed by the darkness. From these neither I alone, nor the whole world gathered into one, could have availed to bring me up from there and deliver me from out of their hands....

Even when I in my senselessness rejoiced in being led astray by them, you could not bear to see me led about and dragged in dishonor, but you did have compassion, O Master, and showed pity on me. It was not an angel or a man whom you sent to me, miserable sinner, but you yourself were moved by your tender goodness. DISCOURSE 36.2-3.[2]

THE GOOD AND CALM JUDGE CAN BE TRUSTED. CYRIL OF ALEXANDRIA: "For the Lord is a good judge to the house of Israel." For he is not harsh but benevolent or good. For the task of a harsh judge takes the way of interrogating those sinners like ones standing accused. The good judge has mercy on them as weak ones. Since the judge is good, he will act according to his mercy, that is, he will temper his anger and will work in mercy in making the complaint. For there is so much justice in him that he will prosecute justice to the letter. Therefore, it is fitting that he will not let Israel go unpunished, but rather he will mingle his wrath with kindness, as I said. For a remnant will be saved....

Now he will save them himself, finding nothing worthwhile in them, but only because he loved them and cared for them. This is a strong visible sign of his unequaled philanthropy and the calmness of divinity. For he saved them from the house of slavery, carried them and raised them up. This is what he was talking about at the beginning of Isaiah, "I have borne and raised sons."[3] COMMENTARY ON ISAIAH 5.5.63.7-10.[4]

63:9 God Redeemed Them

GOD'S GOOD WILL TRUMPS HIS JUSTICE. THEODORET OF CYR: For the grace of the incarnation is of mercy and good will. Aquila translates, instead of "virtues," "hymns"; Theodotion and Symmachus render it "songs of praise." For "make retribution," Symmachus has "work benefits." But the Septuagint is more accurate in putting "make retribution," since we deserved punishment but received salvation instead of punishment.... He switches us to the opposite,

[1]Ps 69:2 (68:3 LXX). [2]SNTD 369-70*. [3]Is 1:2. [4]PG 70:1385-88.

giving us good things in place of bad. . . . He does not use justice only in judging, but he moderates justice with mercy, or rather good will wins over justice. COMMENTARY ON ISAIAH 20.63.7.[5]

THE INCARNATION ENTAILS AFFLICTION.
CYRIL OF ALEXANDRIA: We say that these human things are his by an economic appropriation, along with the flesh all the things belonging to it. We recognize no other Son apart from him, for the Lord has saved us, giving his own blood as a ransom for the life of all. ON THE UNITY OF CHRIST.[6]

63:13 The Spirit in the Midst of His People

MOSES LED BY THE HOLY SPIRIT, GOD'S RIGHT HAND. CYRIL OF ALEXANDRIA: Where is he who put in them the Holy Spirit, that is, he who established the divine and saving Spirit in them? For the Spirit descended from the Lord and guided them, saying, "David divinely uttered, 'Send forth your word and heal us.'" For the Lord is the Spirit; he works through the Spirit that is of the same nature. Where then is he? For they forgot him and did not seek him, when they clearly should have remembered him and loved him. Where is he who led Moses by the right hand? Moses was great, famous and lofty in dignity. And this is shown in that it says [Moses] led them, working through [the Spirit] who is the right hand of God. COMMENTARY ON ISAIAH 5.5. 63:11-14.[7]

GOD LEADS BY HIS SPIRIT. ATHANASIUS: There can be no doubt that in refusing the accompaniment of an angel Moses was inviting God to lead them himself. God was making this promise, "This word that you have just spoken I shall accomplish, since you have found favor with me and I know you in preference to all the others."[8] It is also said in Isaiah, "the one who made the shepherd of the sheep to ascend the earth? Where is he who put the Holy Spirit in their midst, who led Moses by his right hand?"

. . . At that time God promised to lead the people himself, and now he promises to send, no longer an angel but the Spirit who is above the angels. It is he who becomes the guide of the people. He thereby shows that the Spirit is neither from among the creatures nor even an angel, but he is superior to creation, united to the divinity of the Father. LETTER TO SERAPION 1.12.[9]

THE GUIDING ROLE OF THE HOLY SPIRIT.
CYRIL OF ALEXANDRIA: Indeed just as the Lord and the Son are one, the Lord is the Father. For they come together, and the Holy Spirit both is and can be understood to be in both, and he makes sharp the straight way of truth whenever the mind of believers lacks correct thinking. On account of this being the case, the Spirit is Lord and God, as the Scriptures declare, with the great Isaiah speaking concerning the race of Israel, "The Spirit came down from the Lord and led them." ON THE HOLY AND CONSUBSTANTIAL TRINITY 7.[10]

THE UNIQUE SON. CYRIL OF ALEXANDRIA: It seems that Isaiah is making mention here of the resurrection of Christ, the Savior of us all. "He who has gone up" is said in place of "he who has risen"—from the earth—the chief shepherd of all, not just that he was rising up from the dead, but in the sense that he was clearly distinct among human beings. For he became like one of us, undergoing birth from a woman according to the flesh—he who was the only-begotten Word of the Father. COMMENTARY ON ISAIAH 5.5.63.11-14.[11]

CHRISTUS VICTOR. THEODORET OF CYR: Just as with Pharaoh and the Egyptians chasing them, the people led by Moses crossed the sea, so, too, as the devil and the demons were waging war, Christ the master shattered the gates of death, was first to go through them and took with him

---

[5]SC 315:292. [6]SC 97:456-58. [7]PG 70:1389. [8]Ex 33:12-14. [9]PG 26:560-61. [10]PG 75:1104. [11]PG 70:1389.

human nature in its entirety! COMMENTARY ON ISAIAH 20.63.11-12.[12]

63:14 Lead Your People

MOSES' STAFF PREFIGURED THE CROSS. EPHREM THE SYRIAN: "Like cattle that go down into the valley, the Spirit of the Lord gave them rest. So you did lead your people." Through all these words that the prophet speaks about the exodus of the Israelites from Egypt, he leads the mind back to the wonders that God performed by means of his servant Moses, whom he called the shepherd of his flock, and through whose right hand, which moved the staff, he divided the sea.[13] The staff, therefore, prefigured the cross of Christ, who is the hidden arm of the glory of the Father. COMMENTARY ON ISAIAH 63.14.[14]

63:15 Look Down from Heaven

GOD'S PARENTAL CARE. CYRIL OF ALEXANDRIA: Here onwards the prophet prays for every nation, and in the person of the Israelites he presents his supplication. He prays that God will withhold his wrath from them and cease rebuking them and in a forgiving manner subdue Israel's desertion; for there was no one on earth for them other than the true God, one having a glorious home in heaven, their father. Although God is said to dwell in heaven, this should not be thought of him in physical terms. For we say that God is not in a place or to be circumscribed; he is simple, and without a body he fills all things. COMMENTARY ON ISAIAH 5.5.63.15-17.[15]

63:17 Hardened Hearts

GOD'S PATIENCE. THEODORET OF CYR: Your great tolerance encouraged our shamelessness. When you did not punish our sins, we remained transgressors, disregarding your laws. In the same sense, God said to the blessed Moses, "I will harden Pharaoh's heart."[16] He used his great forbearance and tolerance and punishes Pharaoh

only with frogs and locusts and flies to begin with, and Pharaoh thought that God could not increase the level of punishment. . . . You have been patient for a long time; you have not disciplined us, seeing us transgressing without a care; we have accordingly hardened our hearts and as a consequence left the straight path. COMMENTARY ON ISAIAH 20.63.17.[17]

SIN AS PUNISHMENT OF PRECEDING SIN. AUGUSTINE: Is not sin also punishment for sin? . . . We can recount many other events clearly showing that perversity of heart comes from a hidden judgment of God, with the result that a refusal to hear the truth leads to commission of sin, and this sin is also punishment for preceding sin. AGAINST JULIAN 5.3.12.[18]

THE WORST STATE. CAESARIUS OF ARLES: Behold how a person is hardened if he does not merit to be chastised by the Lord for his correction? Moreover, what is written concerning those whom God's mercy does not even allow to become hardened? "God scourges every child whom he receives";[19] . . . and again, "For whom God loves he reproves."[20] Concerning this hardening the prophet also exclaims to the Lord in the person of the people, "Why do you harden our hearts that we fear you not?" Surely this is nothing else than, You have abandoned our heart, that we should be converted to you. SERMON 101.3.[21]

THE NEED FOR HARSH PUNISHMENT. ISIDORE OF SEVILLE: The punishment for previous sins is called "hardening" that comes from the divine righteousness. . . . While those who are righteous are in no way driven by God to become evil, nevertheless, when they are evil they are hardened so that they become worse, as the apostle says, "Since they did not receive the love of God's truth that they might be saved, God sent them a

---

[12]SC 315:296. [13]See Ex 14. [14]SESHS 2:191. [15]PG 70:1392. [16]Ex 7:3. [17]SC 315:300. [18]FC 35:254**. [19]Heb 12:6. [20]Prov 3:12. [21]FC 47:100*.

spirit of error."[22] So God made them sin. But in these cases there was so much sin that came before that they deserved to become worse. . . . Some sins come from God's anger which are balanced against the merit of other sins. THREE BOOKS OF THOUGHTS 2.19.5-6.[23]

63:19 Not Called by God's Name

THE DESERT EXPERIENCE. EUSEBIUS OF CAESAREA: And you did this on account of our turning away from you. For we are now a desert untended by your careful attention. We are now like we were in the beginning. For there was a time when we had neither prophet nor priest not king nor any of your gifts of grace—in like manner we have now come back to the desert. Such were we in Egypt frittering away time before Moses took us out of there. Neither did we have your name to adorn us when we were not called your people, and we did not have a share in your inheritance. And now we have arrived at a similar point. It is right to refer these words to the season after the arrival of our Savior, by whom all those things will in the end be put behind them, through what was dared by our Savior for them. COMMENTARY ON ISAIAH 2.54.[24]

THE CONTINUITY OF THE CHURCH WITH ISRAEL. THEODORET OF CYR: The holy of holies

of the sanctuary, which it was forbidden to touch and to which access was reserved for priests alone, has been despoiled and trampled by impious enemies. For the Babylonians were not the only impious ones; the Macedonians and the Romans were also, when they devastated Jerusalem. . . . We have resembled our ancestors who, in the time of slavery in Egypt, had not yet received the title of "your people." COMMENTARY ON ISAIAH 20.63.17-19.[25]

THE EARTHLY JERUSALEM. CYRIL OF ALEXANDRIA: The church is often called "the holy mountain" in the sacred Scriptures, and those from Israel are only a small part of it. For if they had demonstrated faith in our Lord Jesus Christ, the company of the faith would have sprung from them for the most part and the Gentiles would have been added in to complete the number. But because of the serious disobedience of the Jews, the people of the church were consequently largely drawn from the nations, and these provided the majority; the former people were few in number (for a remnant shall be saved), so only in small measure will they be called on to the holy mountain, that is, into the church. COMMENTARY ON ISAIAH 5.5.63.18-19.[26]

---

[22]2 Thess 2:10. [23]PL 83:622. [24]GCS 57(9):390-91. [25]ITA 935-36*; SC 315:302-4. [26]PG 70:1396.

64:1-12 PRAYER FOR DELIVERENCE

[1]O that thou wouldst rend the heavens and
  come down,
 that the mountains might quake at thy
  presence—
[2y]as when fire kindles brushwood
 and the fire causes water to boil—

to make thy name known to thy adversaries,
 and that the nations might tremble at thy
  presence!
[3]When thou didst terrible things which we
  looked not for,
 thou camest down, the mountains quaked

at thy presence.
⁴*From of old no one has heard*
   or perceived by the ear,
no eye has seen a God besides thee,
   who works for those who wait for him.
⁵*Thou meetest him that joyfully works*
      righteousness,
   those that remember thee in thy ways.
Behold, thou wast angry, and we sinned;
   in our sins we have been a long time, and
      shall we be saved?ᶻ*
⁶*We have all become like one who is unclean,*
   and all our righteous deeds are like a
      polluted garment.
We all fade like a leaf,
   and our iniquities, like the wind, take us
      away.
⁷*There is no one that calls upon thy name,*
   that bestirs himself to take hold of thee;
for thou hast hid thy face from us,

and hast deliveredᵃ us into the hand of our
   iniquities.

⁸*Yet, O LORD, thou art our Father;*
   we are the clay, and thou art our potter;
   we are all the work of thy hand.
⁹*Be not exceedingly angry, O LORD,*
   and remember not iniquity for ever.
   Behold, consider, we are all thy people.
¹⁰*Thy holy cities have become a wilderness,*
   Zion has become a wilderness,
   Jerusalem a desolation.
¹¹*Our holy and beautiful house,*
   where our fathers praised thee,
has been burned by fire,
   and all our pleasant places have become
      ruins.
¹²*Wilt thou restrain thyself at these things,*
   O LORD?
   Wilt thou keep silent, and afflict us sorely?

y Ch 64.1 in Heb   z Hebrew obscure   a Gk Syr Old Latin Tg: Heb *melted*   * Syriac (Peshitta) *some day we will be saved.*

OVERVIEW: Christ's personal works reveal who God is (EUSEBIUS). The incarnation gave visible form to what the Old Testament saints saw invisibly by faith but longed to see more clearly (CASSIAN). Once the church has been purified, Christ will come with clear cosmic and physical effect (THEODORET). But righteousness is required if God and the blessings of heaven are to be seen (LEO, CHRYSOSTOM). Isaiah saw the glory of God, even though it is written "no one has seen God at any time" (HILARY, JEROME). God reveals himself today to those with the eyes of faith (CYRIL) who see demonstrations of his justice but also his mercy (THEODORET). Surely our sin comes before God's punishing anger (ISHO'DAD). The sin does indeed come before God's anger but also before his saving mercy (JEROME). God speaks of his anger delivering impenitent sinners over to even more sin (CYRIL).

Righteousness without reference to Christ does not avail for eternal life (JEROME). Compared with God's righteousness the best of humanity is too earthly minded (CASSIAN). The righteous can free themselves from guilt, but only the death of Christ overcomes death (GREGORY THE GREAT). Those preoccupied with naming idols forget God's name and nature (EPHREM). God accommodates his judgment to the seriousness of our sin (DIDYMUS). Honest confession and reminding God that we sinners are still his own seems the best policy for sinners (CYRIL).

God the Trinity loves to dwell in a vice-free soul. Demonically inspired lust can corrupt religion unless God quenches its fire (JEROME). Judgment as an external catastrophe can be a clear sign of God's displeasure with sinful religion (CYRIL), which was evidenced in history by the destruction and disappearance of the temple (THEODORET).

64:1 *Come Down*

KNOWLEDGE OF GOD THROUGH CHRIST.
EUSEBIUS OF CAESAREA: This power is present
to you, that of which we did not hear from all
time, nor were we able to say (which would be
bearing false witness) that someone else was
such a God, in the way that our eyes have now
seen the effects in such works. We have neither
seen God nor divine deeds except from you—to
those waiting to see, you provide vision and
understanding, which coming from outside ourselves is set in place. . . . "For no one can see
God," and "no one can see my face and live."[1]
But it seems that the Christ of God is praised
through these things, he who talked with Moses
in the desert and was made visible to all people
through his glory appearing to all, about which
was said, "we have beheld his glory."[2] COMMEN-
TARY ON ISAIAH 2.54.[3]

A FULLER FORM OF REVELATION IN CHRIST.
JOHN CASSIAN: David also said "Lord, bend the
skies and come down," and Moses said, "Show
me your face that I might see you clearly."[4] For
no one saw more closely than Moses when
receiving the law of God. God was speaking
from the clouds, and [Moses] witnessed that
same presence of his majesty. How, since no one
saw God closer than he did, could [Moses]
demand a view that was closer still when he
said, "Show me yourself, that I might see you
clearly"?[5] Indeed, we can pray the same thing
to happen that the apostle declared already
occurred; the Lord openly revealed himself in
the flesh and clearly appeared in the world, was
openly assumed into glory; the saints saw the
things with their physical eyes that they had
previously seen with their spiritual sight. ON
THE INCARNATION OF THE LORD AGAINST
NESTORIUS 5.13.[6]

64:3 *The Mountains Quaked*

THE MOUNTAINS WILL MELT. THEODORET OF

CYR: These things we suffered were not on account of your weakness but on account of our
transgression. For when you make your personal
appearance from heaven, the mountains will melt
and dissolve like wax too near to the fire. For fire
will feast on our enemies, and your power will
become obvious to all. COMMENTARY ON ISAIAH
20.64.1.[7]

64:4 *No Eye Has Seen*

THE NEED FOR RIGHTEOUSNESS. LEO THE
GREAT: The brightness of the true light will not
be able to be seen by the unclean sight, and that
which will be happiness to minds that are bright
and clean will be a punishment to those that are
stained. Therefore, let the mists of earth's vanities
be shunned, and let your inward eyes be purged
from all the filth of wickedness, that the sight
may be free to feed on this great manifestation of
God. For to the attainment of this we understand
what follows to lead. SERMON 95.8.[8]

THE BLESSINGS OF HEAVEN. CHRYSOSTOM: Let
us scrutinize those who enjoy the good things of
the world in this present life, I mean wealth and
power and glory. Exulting with delight, they
reckon themselves as no longer being on the
earth. They act this way even though the things
that they are enjoying are acknowledged not to be
really good and do not abide with them but take
to flight more quickly than a dream. And even if
these things should even last for a little time,
their favor is displayed within the limits of this
present life and cannot accompany us further.
Now if these things uplift those who possess
them to such a pitch of joy, what do you suppose
is the condition of those souls that are invited to
enjoy the countless blessings in heaven, blessings
that are always securely fixed and stable? And not
only this, but also in their quantity and quality
heaven's blessings excel present things to such an

---

[1]Ex 33:20. [2]Jn 1:14. [3]GCS 57(9):391-92. [4]See Ex 33:18. [5]See Ex
33:18. [6]NPNF 2 11:589-90**. [7]SC 315:304. [8]NPNF 2 12:205.

extent as never entered even the heart of the human being. LETTER TO THE FALLEN THEODORE 1.13.[9]

THE PROPHET SAW THE GLORY OF GOD THE WORD. HILARY OF POITIERS:
But it may be argued that the apostle was not inspired by the Spirit of prophecy when he borrowed these prophetic words; that he was only interpreting at random the words of another man, and though, no doubt, everything the apostle says of himself comes to him by revelation from Christ, yet his knowledge of the words of Isaiah is only derived from the book. . . . Isaiah says that he has seen no God besides him. For he did actually see the glory of God, the mystery of whose taking flesh from the Virgin he foretold. And if you, in your heresy,[10] do not know that it was God the Only Begotten whom the prophet saw in that glory, listen to the Evangelist: "Isaiah said these things when he saw his glory and spoke of him."[11] The apostle, the Evangelist, the prophet combine to silence your objections. Isaiah did see God; even though it is written, "No one has seen God at any time, except for the only-begotten Son who is in the bosom of the Father; he has declared him."[12] It was God whom the prophet saw. He gazed on the divine glory, and people were filled with envy at such honor graciously granted to his prophetic greatness. For this was the reason why the Jews passed sentence of death on him. ON THE TRINITY 5.33.[13]

THINGS BEYOND OUR HEARING. JEROME:
The apostle Paul inserts a paraphrase of this passage, like a Hebrew from the Hebrews, in the original text of the letters that he wrote to the Corinthians, not rendering it word for word, which he altogether despised doing, but expressing the truth of its meaning, a practice that he used for purposes of emphasis.[14] Hence, the nonsense of the apocryphal texts,[15] which are conveyed to the churches of Christ on the occasion of this passage, fall silent. It can truly be said of these texts that the devil would sit in ambush with the riches

of the apocrypha to kill the innocent or that he would "wait in the 'apocrypha' like a lion in its lair to seize the poor."[16] For the *Ascension of Isaiah*[17] and the *Apocalypse of Elijah*[18] contain this very passage. COMMENTARY ON ISAIAH 17.34.[19]

HOW GOD IS REVEALED TODAY? CYRIL OF ALEXANDRIA:
The divine is invisible in nature. "For no one has ever seen God,"[20] as it is written. But God can be seen by the eyes of faith from those things that happen without explanation and beyond speech. For the invisible things, since the foundation of the world, are clearly understood by the things that are made, that is, his heavenly power and godhead.[21] For he is often recognized through those in whom he works the good and makes a sign of the serenity dwelling in him, marvelously saving those deprived of all hope, and he extends a saving hand from the ground to those lying on the earth. In like manner, they who make this prayer speak, "From the foundation of the world we have not heard nor have we seen such a God, except now for you and you alone. For you give mercy to those who wait for you and put their hope in you, refining and making them to fit together, those who work for your justice and who are mindful of your paths, that is, all who carry out the things you want. For we say that his commandments are the ways of the Lord." COMMENTARY ON ISAIAH 5.5.64.4-5.[22]

WITH WHAT CAN WE COMPARE SIN? THEODORET OF CYR:
He has shown the justice of mercy. For the mercy of God is not without judg-

---

[9]NPNF 1 9:102**. [10]A reference to the Arians. [11]Jn 12:41. [12]Jn 1:18. [13]NPNF 2 9:95**. [14]See 1 Cor 2:9, "no eye has seen, nor ear heard, nor the human heart conceived, what God has prepared for those who love them." [15]Jerome did not consider the apocryphal texts as canonical, nor did he think they were of much use in the church and could, in fact, be considered harmful. [16]See Ps 10:8-9 (9:29-31 LXX, Vg): "He sits in ambush in the villages; in hiding places he murders the innocent. His eyes stealthily watch for the hapless, he lurks in secret like a lion in its den; he lurks that he may seize the poor." [17]*Ascension of Isaiah* 11:34 included in the second Latin version. See Charlesworth, Vol. 2:176, note 62. [18] Cf M. R. James, *The Last Apocrypha* (London, 1920), 53. [19]AGLB 36:1805. [20]Jn 1:18. [21]Rom 1:20. [22]PG 70:1397.

ment, nor is his judgment lacking in mercy. On that account he adds the provision of his mercy to those who are patient and acting justly. . . . He compares not their sin but their righteousness with an unclean rag. Now if it is their righteousness that is compared with this, it is because their sin does not have anything with which it can be compared. COMMENTARY ON ISAIAH 20.64.4-5.[23]

64:5 We Sinned

THE WRATH AND THE MERCY OF GOD. ISHO'DAD OF MERV: "You were angry, and we sinned." This is a sentence with reversed terms, that is, since we have sinned, you were angry and had us deported; and this is analogous to the words "and they made his grave with the wicked."[24] "Some day we will be saved." With the same mercy through which you saved us once from Egypt, we will be saved from Babylon as well. COMMENTARY ON ISAIAH 64.5.[25]

HUMAN SIN COMES BEFORE DIVINE ANGER. JEROME: It is not because you are angry that we sinned, but rather it is because we sinned that you are angry. Because we sinned, you are angry with us, O Lord, for we strayed and abandoned the right path, or, according to the Hebrew text, we, who always lived in sin and are unclean in ourselves, will be saved only by your mercy. COMMENTARY ON ISAIAH 17.35.[26]

HUMAN SIN AS A SIGN OF GOD'S WRATH. CYRIL OF ALEXANDRIA: Some translators try to alter the meaning of this passage. . . . For it is not, they say, that the divine anger was the cause of their misdeeds, but that because they misbehaved, God was angry. For they are afraid lest God's anger be thought of as the effector of sins. I think it ought to be said that there is no condemning the divine anger, if those receiving it were insufficiently motivated to flee the attack of sin. As long as the Savior is pleased in us, let us flee sin and forcefully leave the filth of vices and

with increase be crowned in spiritual success. . . . For God is the Lord of powers. . . . Just as the kind clemency from above shows us how to be strong and brave for the resistance of evil, by the same reason when we fall under divine wrath, it is necessary that we bow in servile fashion. COMMENTARY ON ISAIAH 5.6.64.6-7.[27]

64:6 Like a Soiled Garment

THE RIGHTEOUSNESS OF THE LAW AND THE PURITY OF THE GOSPEL. JEROME: Whatever righteousness that we who are unclean in ourselves appear to possess may be compared with the rag of a menstruating woman, for which Theodotion uses the Hebrew word *eddim* and which Symmachus translates with the Greek term *kyēseōn*, that is, "of she who gives birth," while Aquila uses the word *martyriōn*, that is, "of the witnesses," from when a woman is proven to be a virgin by the issue of blood during her first act of marital intercourse. "And we fall," Isaiah continues, "like leaves from a tree, which are then dispersed by the wind on account of our iniquities." It must be borne in mind here that the righteousness that is in the law will be called unclean in comparison with the purity of the gospel. For what was previously glorified is no longer glorified, due to the surpassing glory of the latter.[28] Hence, the apostle Paul, who fulfilled everything according to the righteousness that is in the law, says that he considered everything as loss, or dung, in order to gain Christ, on account of the magnificent knowledge of our Lord Jesus Christ, and so that he may not be found having the righteousness in him that is from the law but the righteousness from God that comes through faith in Christ.[29] For there is a righteous person who dies in his righteousness if, after receiving the truth of the gospel, he chooses to use legal shadows and to pursue righteousness in a manner that is not righteous. COMMENTARY ON ISAIAH 17.35.[30]

---

[23]SC 315:304-6. [24]Is 53:9. [25]CSCO 303(128):60. [26]AGLB 36:1807. [27]PG 70:1400. [28]See 2 Cor 3:10. [29]See Phil 3:4-9. [30]AGLB 36:1807-8.

EARTHLY ENDEAVOR AND HEAVENLY GOOD.
JOHN CASSIAN: Finally, just as our goodness with regard to the goodness above becomes like evil, so our righteousness compared with divine righteousness is like menstrual rags. This is considered to be so by Isaiah the prophet: "All our righteousnesses are like menstrual rags." For although there is much of good works of the saints, nevertheless they are preoccupied with earthly endeavor and this holds them back and stops them from the contemplation of that higher good. CONFERENCE 23.4.[31]

THE REDEEMER OF THE HUMAN RACE. GREGORY THE GREAT: Here is what Isaiah deeply deplored by saying, "We all have fallen like leaves, and our sins have carried us off like the wind." . . . But the righteous are able, through innocence they have received, to ward off the charges of the present accusation, but they are not strong enough in their own strength to drive out the bonds of death that result. . . . The Redeemer of the human race, who became the mediator of God and humanity through the flesh, . . . alone showed himself righteous among people, yet he received the punishment of blame without blame. He convicted humanity lest it get worse and stood before God lest he smite; he offered examples of innocence and took the punishment for evil. MORALS ON THE BOOK OF JOB 9.38.[32]

64:7 No One Calls on God's Name

IDOLATRY IS THE SOURCE OF FORGETFULNESS. EPHREM THE SYRIAN: "There is no one who calls on your name." Since they worshiped the idols, they did not remember your name. "There is no one who bestirs himself to take hold of you." They certainly put all their faith in the idols. COMMENTARY ON ISAIAH 64.7.[33]

64:9 Be Not Exceedingly Angry

GOD'S ACCOMMODATING JUDGMENT. DIDYMUS

THE BLIND: The Lord gives to each person according to his deeds; against those who sin greatly and often he is very angry indeed, but he is angry in a mild way against those who do wrong in a few things and only for a short time. He has also said concerning the instruments of his wrath that are his punishments, "I was not all that angry, but they insisted on doing evil."[34] And they who charge themselves with transgressions make a loud cry to the merciful and compassionate Lord, "Do not be exceedingly angry with us." For as he "judges with justice, strength and magnanimity, without extending his wrath from day to day,"[35] he moderates his anger against those he judges, not counting up all their faults. COMMENTARY ON ZECHARIAH 2.192.[36]

BE MERCIFUL. CYRIL OF ALEXANDRIA: They entreat God insistently concerning his removal from friendship with them. Since they had come to this situation through their many sins, they wove their prayers with great skill. For since they are unable to mollify the one who could save them with their own works and blameless lives, they now take another route. They ask him as the creator of his own work to be reasonable and sparing with those who were brought into being and life by him. . . . "We are not unaware that we have offended you; we confess that we showed ourselves to deserve judgment and acted savagely towards the Son." COMMENTARY ON ISAIAH 5.6.64.8-9.[37]

64:11-12 Our Holy House Burned by Fire

THE SOUL AS GOD'S DWELLING PLACE.
JEROME: We can correlate this "temple of our sanctification and our glory, in which our ancestors praised you," with the church or to the soul of a holy person, which can rightly be called

---

[31]NPNF 2 11:521**. [32]CCL 143:500-501. [33]SESHS 2:195. [34]Zech 1:15. [35]Ps 7:11 (7:12 LXX). [36]SC 84:514-16. [37]PG 70:1401.

beautiful[38] or a vision of peace,[39] when the Father and the Son and the Holy Spirit dwell within it. Commentary on Isaiah 17.37.[40]

The Flame of Desire Rages in the Temple. Jerome: If, however, Zion is abandoned by the Lord due to wickedness, either ours or the people's, a conflagration of the devil's fiery arrows will appear immediately. For all are adulterers, with hearts like burning ovens.[41] With the frigidity of shame expelled, the flame of desire will rage in the temple of God, such that whatever within us that was once glorious and brilliant will corrupt, be destroyed and perish. Then what was said in the Psalms will be fulfilled: "They consumed your sanctuary with fire, they profaned the tabernacle of your name to the ground."[42] And this fire can be extinguished only by him from whose heart flows rivers of living water.[43] Commentary on Isaiah 17.37.[44]

A Clear Sign of God's Displeasure. Cyril of Alexandria: The defendants speak of the damage in the soul and that they have been caught in their sins; they are like leaves blown about by every wind and, scattered all over, now remember the external misfortunes that came on them. And the destruction of Jerusalem is deplored along with the temple's burning. For after the Savior's crucifixion, these things were fulfilled. Commentary on Isaiah 5.6.64.10-12.[45]

The Disappearance of the Temple. Theodoret of Cyr: If we who bear the name of "your people," he says, are unworthy of your goodwill, judge the city worthy to be spared by reason of its founder, for it has become a desert. And he makes mention of his name [David] in order to evoke mercy. . . . As for the passage, "the house, our sanctuary has become a curse," the other translators have rendered this by "[it has gone] into disappearance." However, the term "curse" offers just as well a meaning that is in accord with the misfortune suffered; for it is usual to say, "May you suffer what such a person suffered!" So the famous temple, the temple full of holiness, the temple praised by all, has been burned by the enemy's fire, and it now only serves as a formula to curse those who mock. Commentary on Isaiah 20.64.9-10.[46]

---

[38]Lat *specula*, literally "mirrors." Gregory the Great, Bede, Jerome, and others often write that Zion is said to be a *specula*, but Jerusalem a vision of peace. See Ps 50:2 (49:2 LXX, Vg); Ps 48:2 (47:3 LXX, Vg); Jer 6:2. [39]See Ezek 13:16: "The prophets of Israel saw visions of peace for Jerusalem." [40]AGLB 36:1814. [41]See Hos 7:4. [42]Ps 74:7 (73:7 LXX, Vg). [43]See Jn 7:38. [44]AGLB 36:1814-15. [45]PG 70:1404. [46]SC 315:308-10.

65:1-7 THE LORD REJECTS ISRAEL'S COMPLAINT

[1]I was ready to be sought by those who did not
    ask for me;
    I was ready to be found by those who did not
      seek me.
I said, "Here am I, here am I,"
    to a nation that did not call on my name.
[2]I spread out my hands all the day
    to a rebellious people,

who walk in a way that is not good,
    following their own devices;
[3]a people who provoke me
    to my face continually,
sacrificing in gardens
    and burning incense upon bricks;
[4]who sit in tombs,
    and spend the night in secret places;

who eat swine's flesh,
　　and broth of abominable things is in their
　　　vessels;
[5]who say, "Keep to yourself,
　　do not come near me, for I am set apart
　　　from you."*
These are a smoke in my nostrils,
　　a fire that burns all the day.
[6]Behold, it is written before me:
　　"I will not keep silent, but I will repay,

yea, I will repay into their bosom
[7]　their[b] iniquities and their[b] fathers'
　　　iniquities together,
　　　　　　　　　　　　　says the LORD;
because they burned incense upon the
　　mountains
　　and reviled me upon the hills,
I will measure into their bosom
　　payment for their former doings."

b Gk Syr: Heb your　* LXX, Vg. Do not touch me, because I am pure

---

OVERVIEW: It is faith, not physical descent, that marks out the true children of Abraham in whom God delights (JUSTIN MARTYR). Those who were without knowledge of God received his good news gladly (PSEUDO-CLEMENT). The Jews knew of him, expecting the prophet, but they did not recognize the prophet when he came and stretched out his hands on the cross (ATHANASIUS). Ultimately, however, God's revelation turned around even those who set out to oppose him (JEROME). The Messiah was provided for a people who had never thought to ask for one (THEODORE). The people of God then proceeded to ignore their Messiah, even when he humbled himself and appealed to them (THEODORET). The mercy of God led him to work to restore the divine image in humanity (LEO). And yet, those who refuse his mercy store up wrath for themselves (JEROME). It is blasphemy to think humans can arrogate God's powers to themselves (AUGUSTINE). The sobering example from the past is living memory for our instruction (THEODORE). But we cannot use the past as excuse, for instance, in blaming our parents for our sins. God wants Israel to know there is still hope since it will be saved by the grace of God, not by its own works (JEROME).

65:1 Ready to Be Sought

WE HAVE BECOME CHILDREN OF ABRAHAM.

JUSTIN MARTYR: This is really the nation promised to Abraham by God, when [God] told him that he would make Abraham a father of many nations, not saying in particular that he would be father of the Arabs, of the Egyptians or the Idumaeans.... And we shall inherit the Holy Land together with Abraham, receiving our inheritance for all eternity, because by our similar faith we have become children of Abraham.... Thus, God promised Abraham a religious and righteous nation of similar faith and a delight to the Father. DIALOGUE WITH TRYPHO 119.[1]

THOSE WHO SEEK WILL RECEIVE REVELATION. PSEUDO-CLEMENT OF ROME: But by the effect of God's providence it happened that the recognition of this good being was distributed equally to the nations. So, they who had never heard talk of [God] and had never been instructed by the prophets recognized him, whereas those who were abandoned to thinking about everyday things did not know him. Here is the prophecy accomplished among you who are here, longing to hear the doctrine of faith in him and of knowing the nature, circumstances and effects of his coming. For that is what was predicted by the prophets, that he had to be sought by those who had never heard a word about him. And that is why, seeing the prophetic words precisely realized

---

[1]FC 6:332*.

among you, you are right to believe in him alone and have reason to wait for him and to inform yourself about him. In this way you do not wait for him only, but still, by faith you receive the inheritance of his kingdom as [Christ] said himself; each one becomes the servant of the one to whom he has submitted himself.[2] RECOGNITIONS 5.12.1-4.[3]

PROPHECY DOES NOT SPEAK OF THE PROPHET. ATHANASIUS: Who then, one might say to the Jews, is he that was made manifest? For if it is the prophet, let them say just when he was hid, afterward to appear again. And what manner of prophet is this, who was not only openly made manifest from obscurity but also stretched out his hands on the cross? None surely of the righteous, save the Word of God only, who, incorporeal by nature, appeared for our sakes in the body and suffered for all. ON THE INCARNATION 38.2.[4]

THE POWER OF REVELATION TO EXCITE THE RELIGIOUS QUEST. JEROME: But what is said in Hebrew, namely, that "they will seek me who previously did not inquire about me," means that those who once had no knowledge of God later sought the Lord and came to know him by means of revelation. Indeed, the Lord revealed himself to Paul at a time when he was persecuting the church of believers. He also said to Peter the apostle: "Blessed are you, Simon bar Jonah, for flesh and blood did not reveal this to you but my Father who is in heaven."[5] And Moses was seeking the same thing when he said to God, "If I have found favor with you, show yourself to me openly, that I may behold you."[6] Anticipating the opprobrium of Christ amid the greater riches of the treasures of Egypt, Moses longed for the just rewards of things to come and contemplated the invisible God with his soul, as though he could see him. COMMENTARY ON ISAIAH 18.2.[7]

THE UNSOUGHT MESSIAH. THEODORE OF HERACLEA: ["I was ready to be sought by those who did not seek me."] These words should be understood as about the Savior, who, sent by the

Father's love and coming with his own compassionate love, was revealed to all people. He became savior of those who had not made him welcome nor had invited him. FRAGMENTS ON ISAIAH.[8]

65:2 I *Spread Out My Hands*

INGRATITUDE FOR DIVINE CARE AND CONCERN. THEODORET OF CYR: It is the nations who did not have a prophet sent to them who recognize their maker and benefactor, whereas those who received all sorts of care gained no profit but continued in their sinful habits. The phrase "all day long I have held out my hands" refers to the care for them that he gave for all that time, but the saving suffering of the cross in which he stretched out his hands is also alluded to here. COMMENTARY ON ISAIAH 20.65.2.[9]

GOD CAME TO SEEK AND RESTORE HIS IMAGE. LEO THE GREAT: If, dearly beloved, we comprehend faithfully and wisely the beginning of our creation, we shall find that humankind was made in God's image, to the end that he might imitate the Creator and that our race attains its highest natural dignity, by the form of the divine goodness being reflected in us, as in a mirror. And assuredly to this form the Savior's grace is daily restoring us, so long as that which in the first Adam fell, is raised up again in the second. And the cause of our restoration is nothing else but the mercy of God, whom we would not have loved unless he had first loved us and dispelled the darkness of our ignorance by the light of his truth. SERMON 12.1.[10]

65:4 *Those Who Sit in Tombs*

THE SHADOWS OF THE DEMONIC REALM. JEROME: But what is read in the Septuagint,

---

[2]Mt 6:24. [3]Apocr 317. [4]NPNF 2 4:56. [5]Mt 16:17. [6]See Ex 33:13-23. [7]AGLB 36:1823. [8]PG 18:1372. [9]SC 315:310-12. [10]NPNF 2 12:120-21.

namely, "to demons that are not," and is not included in the Hebrew text, must be taken to mean that no demons exist, either in the literal or in the spiritual sense; this because they have already fallen away from God, who truly is. Neither do sects of heretics that retain no truth exist, but they are transitory and die like shadows. For this reason did Esther say to the Lord, "Do not surrender your heritage to those who are not."[11] The holy one also prays in the Psalter: "Know me not, that I may find relief before I depart to exist no longer."[12] For whoever did not obtain the forgiveness of sinners while living in this body, leaving life in such a condition, also perished from God and therefore ceased existing, even though continuing in punishment. . . .

Wrath, therefore, which is desire for retribution, is not the same in God as it is in people, for its material cause lies in our sins, not in God's will. We are the ones who "store up wrath for ourselves on the day of wrath and the day of the revelation of the just judgment of God,"[13] so that the thorns and thistles and briars, which we have produced from the seed of God,[14] like the wood, hay and stubble with which we built on Paul's foundation, should be consumed by flames of wisdom.[15] And we read about this perpetual fire in the song of Moses: "A fire is kindled in my fury, and it will burn to the depths of hell and will devour the earth and its produce. It will set the foundations of the mountains ablaze, and my arrows will destroy them."[16] The meaning of this testimony is that the fire and vengeance of God will burn continually against sinners and that he will pursue them to hell. COMMENTARY ON ISAIAH 18.4, 6.[17]

65:5 Do Not Come Near Me

SPIRITUAL ARROGANCE. AUGUSTINE: So insofar as they say, "Do not touch me, because I am pure," they are like this Pharisee who had invited the Lord and who thought [the Lord] did not know the woman, just because he had not stopped her touching his feet. But in another

respect the Pharisee is better, in that while he thought Christ was only a man, he did not believe that sins could be forgiven by a man. So the Jews appear to have a better understanding than the heretics. What did the Jews say? "Who is this who even forgives sins?"[18] Does a mere man have the audacity to claim this for himself?" What . . . does the heretic say? "I forgive, I cleanse, I sanctify."[19] SERMON 99.8.[20]

THE POWER THAT AVENGES. THEODORE OF HERACLEA: Here is the power that avenges. It is said that he, hearing these things, is minded to comfort us in our ignorance. For since the memory is maintained for us from writings of actions in the past that encourage us to remember and almost bring to life in our minds those actions of long ago, this is what he teaches. Now all these things are known to God and before they happened. They were already in his mind. FRAGMENTS ON ISAIAH.[21]

65:7 The Parent's Inquities and the Child's Salvation

THE CHILDREN ARE NOT TO BLAME FOR THE SINS OF THE PARENTS. JEROME: For we are not obliged to accept as parents those whose iniquities and sins now return to us, but only those from whose seed our bodies were born. Elsewhere, Moses, who had said that the sins of the parents shall return to the third and fourth generation of those who hate God,[22] interpreted the verse that we are considering: "It is not on account of the sins of their parents that the children will die, but each one will die for his own sin,"[23] with Ezekiel confirming the same interpretation, saying that one should never repeat the proverb, "the parents ate sour grapes and the

[11]See Esther 14:11. [12]Ps 39:13 (38:14 LXX, Vg). [13]Rom 2:5. [14]See Mt 7:16-19; Heb 6:8. [15]See 1 Cor 3:10-15; Rom 15:20. [16]Gen 32:22-23. [17]AGLB 36:1828-29, 1833-34. [18]Lk 7:49. [19]Augustine is here speaking of the Donatists who focused authority on the person of the minister rather than his office. See also his Epistle 185.9.37 (NPNF 1 4:646). [20]WSA 3 4:55. [21]PG 18:1372. [22]See Ex 20:5. [23]Deut 24:16.

teeth of their children suffered," but that only the teeth of those who do the eating are affected, meaning that the sinful soul itself dies; it is not punished for sins that it did not commit.[24] From this we understand that when every individual departs this life, he or she must accept the parents who were assigned to them, either for good or otherwise. COMMENTARY ON ISAIAH 18.6.[25]

THERE IS STILL HOPE FOR ISRAEL. JEROME: But Abraham was saved by the integrity of faith from the fire of the Chaldeans.[26] Jeremiah agrees with this, speaking in the person of the Lord: "Like a hot spring in the desert, I found Israel with a deadly sword."[27] For . . . he said, All the world lay wounded by the deadly swords of idola-

try. I found Israel in Abraham to have the heat of faith, like a medic after a war who senses that some among the bodies of the dead have a vital pulse and provides care for the wounded to restore their health. But what was written, *ōs thermon*, that is, "like a hot spring," the Latin translator rendered "like a wolf," deceived as he was by ambiguous words that cause errors also among the Greeks. Nevertheless, it should be noted that in Hebrew *thoda*, which means "grace," is written in place of "heat." Indeed, Israel shall be saved by the grace of God, not by its own works. COMMENTARY ON ISAIAH 18.7.[28]

---

[24]See Ezek 18:1-4. [25]AGLB 36:1835-36. [26]See Neh 9:7. [27]See Jer 38:2 LXX. [28]AGLB 36:1838-39.

65:8-16 PRESERVATION OF THE REMNANT

[8]Thus says the LORD:
"As the wine is found in the cluster,
 and they say, 'Do not destroy it,
 for there is a blessing in it,'
so I will do for my servants' sake,
 and not destroy them all.
[9]I will bring forth descendants from Jacob,
 and from Judah inheritors of my mountains;
my chosen shall inherit it,
 and my servants shall dwell there.
[10]Sharon shall become a pasture for flocks,
 and the Valley of Achor a place for herds
  to lie down,
 for my people who have sought me.
[11]But you who forsake the LORD,
 who forget my holy mountain,
who set a table for Fortune
 and fill cups of mixed wine for Destiny;

[12]I will destine you to the sword,
 and all of you shall bow down to the
  slaughter;
because, when I called, you did not answer,
 when I spoke, you did not listen,
but you did what was evil in my eyes,
 and chose what I did not delight in."

[13]Therefore thus says the Lord GOD:
"Behold, my servants shall eat,
 but you shall be hungry;
behold, my servants shall drink,
 but you shall be thirsty;
behold, my servants shall rejoice,
 but you shall be put to shame;
[14]behold, my servants shall sing for gladness
  of heart,
 but you shall cry out for pain of heart,

and shall wail for anguish of spirit.
[15]You shall leave your name to my chosen for
  a curse,
and the Lord GOD will slay you;
  but his servants he will call by a different
  name.

[16]So that he who blesses himself in the land
  shall bless himself by the God of truth,
and he who takes an oath in the land
  shall swear by the God of truth;
because the former troubles are forgotten
  and are hid from my eyes."

OVERVIEW: God was mindful of those who were loyal among his people and of their time of penance (THEODORET). He demonstrates his overriding benevolence in not carrying out the judgment they deserved (THEODORE) and, in fact, making himself their safe haven (THEODORET). He calls them his "holy mountain," the church that is made up of Israel and the Gentiles, although the former will be smaller in number (CYRIL). There is a temptation to forsake the Lord on his holy mountain and to trust in other things, such as fate (ORIGEN) or astrology (JEROME). In contrast to those who forsake the Lord, the text here also speaks of his servants who shall eat and drink and rejoice in the coming kingdom, although this must be understood properly (JEROME). God predicts evil things for those who forsake him but promises and predestines only the good (FULGENTIUS).

Christians, although a recent phenomenon, are like the original human beings God and nature intended (EUSEBIUS). Christ condescends to lend us his glorious name (CYRIL OF JERUSALEM), providing us with a whole new identity (THEODORE), which also implies a whole new way of life (THEODORET) that will bring glory to Israel's former name (CYRIL), which evoked memories of what it had suffered; Israel's former name would be replaced by the name of Christian and the blessings that accompany this name in Christ (JEROME).

65:8 New Wine

GOD IS AWARE OF HIS PEOPLE'S CONTRITION. THEODORET OF CYR: If anyone finds one ripe grape in a bunch, he spares the whole bunch

on its account, in order to present to God the firstfruits. In the same way, since I promised to Abraham to bless all the nations in his seed, I maintained the seed of all Israel when they sinned, and I did not overlook their slavery in Egypt. For this reason, I freed them from their Babylonian captivity. . . . The "valley of Achor" is an allusion to the contrition that is among the churches. For Achar or Achor, having stolen and broken the law of the ban, was thrown into a ravine, and through this tragic example they were filled with much contrition.[1] COMMENTARY ON ISAIAH 20.65.8-10.[2]

THE OVERRIDING BENEVOLENCE OF GOD. THEODORE OF HERACLEA: Once again the richness of the loving nature of God is shown clearly in this simile. For just as mature wine is found on the vine for whose sake the whole is saved, spared and is not cut off by anyone, so too [God says], "If I find anyone serving me, I will spare them all, just as I swore to Abraham. When I was threatening judgment of Sodom, I showed my compassion even to five people."[3] He says this to establish his goodness. FRAGMENTS OF ISAIAH.[4]

65:9 An Heir from Judah

CHRIST IS THE HAVEN FOR THE SPIRITUAL. THEODORET OF CYR: Those who have attained the summit of perfection have as their harbor not life, or the resurrection or any of these admirable things but the desired One himself, for whose sake they counted misfortune a delight, and

---

[1]See Josh 7. [2]SC 315:314-18. [3]See Gen 19:29. [4]PG 18:1372.

weary toil the sweetest repose, and time spent in the desert more desirable than city life, and poverty fairer than wealth and irksome slavery sweeter than any position of authority. This is the reward awaited by the doers of virtue. "It is an inheritance for those who serve God," as the prophet Isaiah exclaims. On Divine Providence 9.11.[5]

Holy Mountains Are Peoples Brought into the Church. Cyril of Alexandria: The holy Scripture often calls the church "the holy mountain" whose lesser part came from Israel. For if Israel had received the faith that is in our Lord Jesus Christ, they would have formed the greater part of the church's composition, and the multitude of the nations would have been added to them. But because they did not believe, they became the lesser of the two. The nations became greater, while Israel became quite small. For the remnant will be saved. Therefore they inherit a small portion in the holy mountain, that is, the church. Commentary on Isaiah 5.5.65.18-19.[6]

65:11 Foresaking the Lord

Resist the Temptation to Confess Forces Other Than God. Origen: If a person, because he is too tenacious of life or too weak in the face of suffering, or because of the apparently convincing arguments of such as seek to induce us to accept the evil choice, has denied the one and only God and his Christ and borne testimony to demons[7] or goddesses of fortune, then this person must realize that in doing this he is "setting," as it were, "a table for the demon and offering libations" to Fortune, "forsaking the Lord" and "forgetting his holy mount." He will incur the reproaches written in Isaiah. Exhortation to Martyrdom 40.[8]

Beware the Teachings of Demons. Jerome: We have frequently spoken of the Lord's "holy mountain," which the people of Israel are here

said to forget, as either the Lord and Savior, who is the mountain of mountains and the saint of all saints,[9] or as Mount Zion and the heavenly Jerusalem, city of the living God.[10] . . . According to the tropological sense, it must be said that all who desert the church and forget the holy mountain of God and deliver themselves to the spirits of error and to the teachings of demons[11] thereby "prepare a table for Fortune," believing that everything is governed either by the vagaries of fortune or by the course of the stars but nothing by God. Paul rebukes these people, saying, "You cannot share in the table of the Lord and in the table of demons."[12] Commentary on Isaiah 18.9.[13]

65:13 My Servants Shall Eat

Spiritual and Physical "Last Things." Jerome: I am not unaware of how much diversity of interpretation there exists among people. Yet, I do not speak here of the mystery of the Trinity, whose proper confession is apophatic, but of other ecclesiastical doctrines concerning the resurrection, certainly, as well as concerning the state of souls and human flesh, concerning how prophecies about the future ought to be received and by what principle the Apocalypse of John should be understood, which, if interpreted literally, would involve Judaizing. . . . But, in saying that it should be interpreted spiritually, this because the kingdom of God does not consist of food and drink, nor will there be marriage in the resurrection,[14] among other reasons, I do not, thereby, remove the truth of the human body, which I profess to be raised incorruptible and immortal,[15] changing its glory, not its substance. Our interpretation, therefore, must begin on the right path, to avoid departing to the right or to the left,[16] so that we will not follow the errors of

[5]ACW 49:122. [6]PG 70:1396. [7]See 1 Jn 4:18; Heb 2:15. [8]ACW 19:183*. [9]See 2 Macc 14:36. [10]See Heb 12:22; Rev 3:12. [11]See 1 Tim 4:1. [12]1 Cor 10:21. [13]AGLB 36:1843-45. [14]See Mt 22:30. [15]See 1 Cor 15:52-54. [16]See Prov 4:27.

either the Judaizers or the heretics. . . . COMMEN-
TARY ON ISAIAH 18.1.[17]

PREDICTING AND PREDESTINING. FULGEN-
TIUS OF RUSPE: In all these things, whatever has
been predicted only, not promised, pertains to
the persons of the wicked. Nor should that which
because of the merit of wickedness, severity
threatens to be inflicted, be said to have been
promised by the generosity of goodness. If there
are things that pertain to the persons of those
who serve God, these have been both predicted
and promised.

This is also the point of the words of our Savior
where he says, "And these will go off to eternal
punishment, but the righteous to eternal life."[18] He
predicted and promised the reward that the just
would enjoy, but he did not promise but predicted
the torments with which the unjust would be punished. Not so he predestined the saints to receive
justice, because the "merciful and just Lord" could
freely deliver from depravity whomever he wished.
But he was never the doer of the depravity, because
no one was ever depraved except insofar as he went
away from God. Nor did God predestine anyone to
go away, even though by divine knowledge he foreknew that he would go away. LETTER TO MONI-
MUS 1.25.3-4.[19]

65:15 A Different Name

**CHRISTIANS ARE AS THE ORIGINAL, NATU-
RAL HUMANS.** EUSEBIUS OF CAESAREA: But
even if we are clearly something new, and this
truly recent name of Christians has only recently
been known among all the nations, our life and
manner of conduct in accordance with the very
teachings of our religion have not been recently
fashioned by us, but, as it were, from the first creation of humanity have been established by the
natural concepts of the God-favored people of
old. . . . And by deeds more manifest than words
is Abraham's manner of religion shown to be
practiced at present among Christians alone.
ECCLESIASTICAL HISTORY 1.4.[20]

THE GIFT OF A NEW NAME. CYRIL OF JERUSA-
LEM: With the ungrudging generosity of his godhead, Christ has granted to all of us to bear his
name. For whereas as human sovereigns have
some special title of sovereignty that they keep
exclusively from use by other people, Jesus
Christ, being Son of God, has deigned to bestow
on us the title of Christians. . . . But some will
say, "The name of 'Christians' is new and was
not previously in use": and new-fashioned
phrases are often objected to on the score of
strangeness. The prophet made this point safe
beforehand, saying, "But on my servants shall a
new name be called, which shall be blessed upon
the earth." CATECHETICAL LECTURES 10.16.[21]

**THE BLESSED ARE GIVEN NAMES FOR ETER-
NITY.** THEODORE OF HERACLEA: These things are
predicted to warn those not fearing the Lord and
who do not turn to him, whereas those who serve
me will not only weave another kind of outcome,
but just as with the patriarchs, they will receive a
name and on account of their deeds new names.
When the Jews were unrepentant, this name was
given to the Gentiles, a name that will stand forever, that is, the name of Christians. They no
longer glorify idols, singing hymns to them as if
to gods. Now they sing to God, their creator.
They worship him and enjoy his blessings. FRAG-
MENTS ON ISAIAH.[22]

**"CHRISTIAN" IS A NAME THAT DENOTES A
STANDARD OF LIFE.** THEODORET OF CYR: He
has already mentioned this name. It is new and
not old. For after the appearance of Christ the
master, those who believed were called Christians. They bore this in place of all approving
words. When one wished to praise, they were
accustomed to add after many kind words, "He is
a true Christian." And when on another occasion
exhorting someone, they were accustomed to say,
"Act as a Christian, do what befits a Christian."

---

[17]AGLB 36:1817-19. [18]Mt 25:46. [19]FC 95:221. [20]FC 19:51-53**.
[21]LCC 4:138. [22]PG 18:1373.

So this name is full of eulogy and blessing. COMMENTARY ON ISAIAH 20.65.15-16.[23]

GIVEN CHRIST'S NAME LIKE A CROWN. CYRIL OF ALEXANDRIA: All things have been made new in Christ: worship, life and legislation. For we do not adhere to shadows and useless types. Instead we offer adoration and worship to the God who is over all things in spirit and in truth.[24] We do not take our name like the physical descendants of Israel from one of the original ancestors, . . . such as Ephraim, or Manasseh or some other tribe, nor do we follow the path of the scribes and Pharisees, who value the antiquity of the letter above every other thing. Instead, we accept Christ in the newness of life of the gospel, and being given his name like a crown, we are called Christians. This celebrated and blessed name has indeed spread throughout the world. Since we have been blessed by Christ, we in turn strive to gladden him with blessings and endless praises. COMMENTARY ON ISAIAH 5.6.65.16-18.[25]

65:16 An Oath

FROM HAVING THE NAME WHICH IS CURSED TO A NEW NAME OF BLESSING. JEROME: For "abundance," which is *sabaa* in Hebrew, others translate "oath." But the word has many meanings, which vary in accordance with where the accent is placed, for it can be understood as "oath" or "abundance" or "sufficiency" or "plurality" or "seven," concerning which we already indicated that in the book of Genesis, as well as in the current book, seven women take one man.[26] Again, for that which the Septuagint translates as "true" and the Hebrew as "amen," Aquila renders *pepistōmenōs*, that is, "faithfully." But this is what it says: "Your name will be a curse for the benefit of my chosen who will follow in your place, that they may have you as an example of evil consequences and may detest enduring such things, and, therefore, swear this oath: 'I will not suffer what the Jewish people suffered.'" Or, perhaps your name will be "abundant," in as much as it will be spoken so frequently that the memory or mention of it will become odious to them and engorge them on it, such that they will grow nauseated. . . .

And there will be blessing, insofar as whoever is called by that name will be blessed by the Lord and will receive a sign of true circumcision: "amen," which the Lord often uses to indicate approval in the Gospel: "Amen, amen, I say to you."[27] But neither this new name nor another name is anything unless derived from the name of Christ, so that the people of God would never be called Jacob, Judas, Israel, Ephraim or Joseph, but "Christian." For "whoever swears in the land" does so not by idols or by false gods but by God, as is confirmed by the "amen" at the end of the sentence. Furthermore, the Septuagint translates "true God" in place of "amen," so that the true God may be blessed and that those "who swear in the land" would swear by the true God. But we do not follow the error of the Arians in referring this "true God" to the person of God the Father alone, of whom it is written, "that they may know you the one true God and Jesus Christ whom you have sent."[28] But we refer also to the Son, who is himself the true God, as John the Evangelist testifies: "The Son of God came to give us understanding, that we would know the true one and exist in his true Son, Jesus Christ. This is the true God and eternal life."[29] COMMENTARY ON ISAIAH 18.12.[30]

---

[23]SC 315:320-22. [24]See Jn 4:23. [25]COA 93; PG 70:1417. [26]See Is 4:1. [27]See Jn 1:51, 3:3. [28]Jn 17:3. [29]1 Jn 4:20. [30]AGLB 36:1851-54.

65:17-25 THE NEW HEAVEN AND EARTH

[17]For behold, I create new heavens
   and a new earth;
and the former things shall not be remembered
   or come into mind.
[18]But be glad and rejoice for ever
   in that which I create;
for behold, I create Jerusalem a rejoicing,
   and her people a joy.
[19]I will rejoice in Jerusalem,
   and be glad in my people;
no more shall be heard in it the sound of
   weeping
   and the cry of distress.
[20]No more shall there be in it
   an infant that lives but a few days,
   or an old man who does not fill out his days,
for the child shall die a hundred years old,
   and the sinner a hundred years old shall be
   accursed.
[21]They shall build houses and inhabit them;
   they shall plant vineyards and eat their

fruit.
[22]They shall not build and another inhabit;
   they shall not plant and another eat;
for like the days of a tree shall the days of my
   people be,
   and my chosen shall long enjoy the work of
   their hands.
[23]They shall not labor in vain,
   or bear children for calamity;[c]
for they shall be the offspring of the blessed of
   the LORD,
   and their children with them.
[24]Before they call I will answer,
   while they are yet speaking I will hear.
[25]The wolf and the lamb shall feed together,
   the lion shall eat straw like the ox;
   and dust shall be the serpent's food.
They shall not hurt or destroy
   in all my holy mountain,
            says the LORD.

c Or sudden terror

OVERVIEW: The new heaven and earth that God will provide for his people means they will have a new start, forgetting what is past (JEROME). Just how the heavens and the earth will be transformed is a mystery (ORIGEN). Newness is not a discontinuing of the old but a change into a better state (JEROME). The new heavens and earth can be understood as meaning the new spiritual life granted to the church by Christ's advent (EPHREM). Instead of former afflictions, those in the church or, perhaps, those in heaven, will find joy (CYRIL). All those in heaven, in fact, will find not only joy, but will no longer have to worry about death (JEROME).

Those saved will have the richness of full life added to them, but the sinner is judged across all his lifespan (THEODORE). "The young" is a reference to the Gentiles, who are new to the knowledge of the true God (PROCOPIUS). Spiritual diligence requires and is required for the discovery of a deeper sense of prophecies (AUGUSTINE). What is new about creation is that it is seen as the creation belonging to the Creator—with the eyes of faith (THEODORET). The prophecy does have a literal fulfillment in the events of the Maccabean times as well (ISHO'DAD).

Access to the tree of life is available for those who know their fault, unlike Adam, who ate impenitently (Jerome). Christ gives life to the church through the Scriptures (Augustine). When believers come to the cross, it offers the life-giving body to them (Theodoret). God works so that our will is strengthened and so that our labor in him is not in vain (Cassian).

It makes no sense to think of the final verse of this section as predicting a literal coexistence of real animals who are enemies of each other on Mount Zion (Jerome), although it does prophesy that the end state will be like the original state of uncorrupted paradise (Gregory of Elvira). All people in paradise will feed on the Holy Spirit's teaching without regard to rank (Theodoret).

65:17 New Heavens and a New Earth

A NEW START. Jerome: The new heavens and new earth are cause for rejoicing and for confessing the true God, because eternal amnesia follows on the former tribulations; this means that those who live therein will never be mindful of idols and previous errors but will pass from darkness into light for the enjoyment of eternal beatitude. For they will forget the former evils, not by having their memories destroyed but by receiving an inheritance of goods, in accordance with what is written: "On the day of good rewards, there will be no memory of evils,"[1] and again: "an affliction of one hour destroys the memory of pleasures."[2] Thus, to the extent that the former desires were born in tribulation, members of the new creation will never enjoy them in the wayward manner of the Epicureans. COMMENTARY ON ISAIAH 18.13.[3]

A NEW HEAVEN AND EARTH. Origen: Isaiah also, declaring prophetically that there will be a new heaven and a new earth, undoubtedly suggests a similar view. For this renewal of heaven and earth, and this transformation of the form of the present world and this changing of the heavens will undoubtedly be prepared for those who are walking along and are tending to that goal of happiness to which, it is said, even enemies themselves are to be subjected and in which God is

said to be "all in all."[4] And if anyone imagines that at the end, material, that is, bodily nature will be entirely destroyed, he cannot in any respect meet my view, how beings so numerous and powerful are able to live and to exist without bodies, since it is an attribute of the divine nature alone. . . . Another, perhaps, may say that in the end every bodily substance will be so pure and refined as to be like the ether and of a celestial purity and clearness. How things will be, however, is known with certainty to God alone and to those who are his friends through Christ and the Holy Spirit. ON FIRST PRINCIPLES 1.6.4.[5]

NEWNESS MEANS A CHANGE INTO SOMETHING BETTER. Jerome: Those who interpret the new heaven and earth to be a change for the better, rather than the destruction of the elements,[6] cite this passage: "You founded the earth in the beginning, Lord, and the heavens are the work of your hands. They will perish, but you will endure; they will grow old like a garment, and you will roll them up like cloth, and they will be changed."[7] In this psalm is demonstrated clearly a perdition and destruction that is not an annihilation but a transformation for the better. Neither does what is written elsewhere indicate that there will be a complete destruction of what was there at the beginning, but rather a transformation: "The moon will shine like the sun, and the sun's light will be strengthened sevenfold."[8] And that this may be better understood, let us use an example from our own human condition: when an infant grows into a boy, and a boy into an adolescent, and an adolescent into a man and a man into an old man, the same person continues to exist throughout his succession of ages. For he remains the same man as he was, even though it can be said that he has changed a little and that the previous ages have passed away. Understanding this truth, the apostle Paul said, "for the form

---

[1]Sir 11:27. [2]Sir 11:29. [3]AGLB 36:1855-56. [4]1 Cor 15:28. [5]ANF 4:262*. [6]See Is 66:15-16; Gal 4:3-9; Col 2:20; 2 Pet 3:10-12. [7]Ps 102:25-26 (101:26-27 LXX, Vg). [8]Is 30:26.

of this world is perishing."[9] Notice that he said "form," not "substance." COMMENTARY ON ISAIAH 18.13.[10]

A PROPHECY CONCERNING THE CHURCH.

EPHREM THE SYRIAN: "For behold, I create new heavens and a new earth." These words point to the church, referring to the heavenly and spiritual gifts that have been granted to it. Indeed, if the Lord took care of the Israelites for the earthly things promised to them, how much more will he provide for the church, thanks to the joy that peoples have experienced in their conversion to it. Therefore, he also calls new heavens and new earth the new and spiritual life granted to the church by the advent of Christ. COMMENTARY ON ISAIAH 65.17.[11]

65:18-19 Joy in Jerusalem

FINDING JOY IN THE CHURCH AND IN THE AGE TO COME.

CYRIL OF ALEXANDRIA: Instead of their former affliction, the prophet says, "they shall find in her joy and exultation." In whom or in what? In the church of Christ, it may be said without any doubt. It should be noted that some commentators refer this not to the period of our earthly life but to the period that is to come after this present age. For the prophet says that the just will find joy and exultation and will enjoy endless delight, that is, spiritual delight, when this creation has been transformed and renewed. For one of the holy apostles said, "The day of the Lord will come like a thief, and then the heavens will pass away with a loud noise, and the elements will be dissolved with fire, and the earth and the works that are on it will be burned up. But according to his promise we wait for new heavens and a new earth."[12] Choose, therefore, whichever of these interpretations appeals to you, the former or the latter. Whatever is useful to us is in no way to be rejected. COMMENTARY ON ISAIAH 5.6.65.16-18.[13]

THE FULLNESS OF AGE OF THOSE IN HEAVEN.

JEROME: Neither would it be congruous that in the city of Jerusalem and among the people of God, who will receive an eternal creation of exaltation and joy, there be heard any longer the voice of weeping and wailing, now that pain, sorrow and moaning have departed, for incompatible realities are surely unable to exist together.... In such a city, there is no difference in ages, as between the infant and the elderly, the young and the "old man who does not fulfill his days." Instead, like children of the resurrection, all "attain to the perfect person, to the measure of the stature of the fullness of Christ,"[14] such that none will either lack or exceed the life span, nor will it be the case that some persons retain their strength while others fail with age and cease to be what they were. Everyone, moreover, will reach one hundred years of age, as did Abraham, who received the promise that he would have his son Isaac at one hundred.[15] It is not necessary to recount the many praises of this particular number, lest our argument run too long. This alone will we say, that ten decades are squared and square forms possess strength. COMMENTARY ON ISAIAH 13.15.[16]

65:20 The Relativity of Age in Heaven

THE PERFECTION OF HUMANITY IN THE AGE TO COME.

THEODORE OF HERACLEA: Long age will be given generously to them with nobody who died an untimely death ... for he who has reached one hundred years will be just as the one who has died prematurely as a youth. But the sinner will be prone to judgment for his whole life and crosses into the lot of the cursed. FRAGMENTS ON ISAIAH.[17]

A PLACE IN CHRIST FOR ALL BACKGROUNDS.

PROCOPIUS OF GAZA: "The young" means the people from among the Gentiles ... and all will

---

[9]1 Cor 7:31. [10]AGLB 36:1856-57. [11]SESHS 2:199. [12]2 Pet 3:10, 13. [13]COA 94-95; PG 70:1420. [14]Eph 4:13. [15]See Gen 17:17. [16]AGLB 36:1859-60. [17]PG 18:1373.

be mature, having grown into the measure of the fullness of Christ.[18] COMMENTARY ON ISAIAH 65.13-25.[19]

PROPHETIC DISCOURSE IS MULTILAYERED.
AUGUSTINE: It is usual for the prophets thus to mingle metaphorical and literal expressions. Yet, anyone with serious purpose and a little useful and salutary effort can discern the prophet's spiritual sense; it is only a lazy and worldly person or one who is ignorant or uneducated who will rest content with the literal and superficial sense and refuse to penetrate the deeper meaning. CITY OF GOD 20.21.[20]

A CLARIFIED VISION. THEODORET OF CYR: The heaven became new and the earth new for those who once erred and divinized these things. For they recognize the Creator of these things and learn that the things are not gods but the creations of God. They are new for those who see things completely differently. Now that their error has ceased, creation appears clearly as creation and Creator as Creator. COMMENTARY ON ISAIAH 20.65.17-18.[21]

A PROPHECY CONCERNING THE TIME OF THE MACCABEES. ISHO'DAD OF MERV: "For the child shall die a hundred years old, and the sinner a hundred years old shall be accursed." Some authors understand these words as referring to the time after the return from exile. For a hundred years their prosperity lasted, and then the Macedonian kings rose against them. This is clearly explained in the book of the Maccabees. COMMENTARY ON ISAIAH 65.20.[22]

65:22 Days of a Tree

THE WORD OF GOD IS THE TREE OF LIFE.
JEROME: If, however, as in the Septuagint, we read "the days of the tree of life," which makes more sense than the Hebrew text, we should understand that it refers to the tree of life that was located in paradise, from which place Adam was

expelled so that he would be unable to extend his hand to the tree and thus live.[23] Paradise was then put under the custody of the cherubim, that is, "abundance of knowledge," and a flaming sword was established to guard the way to the tree of life, lest sinful Adam, not yet recognizing his sin, eat of the tree and die the ultimate death in a desperate state of impenitence. Solomon offered an especially lucid interpretation of this tree of life when, speaking from the wisdom of God, he said, "The tree of life is for all who approach it and rely on it as upon the sure foundation who is the Lord."[24] Neither is there any doubt whom the Word of God signifies, who is Life and Wisdom himself, as he said: "I am the Life."[25] ...

And does it not seem to you that their works daily grow old who press ahead into the future while forgetting the past? For this reason, both the Old and the New Testaments say that it is not the old that perishes but that on which nothing new succeeds. COMMENTARY ON ISAIAH 18.17.[26]

THE CHURCH IS SUSTAINED BY CHRIST.
AUGUSTINE: "As in the days of the tree of life, so shall be the days of my people." Now, anyone who has ever opened the Scriptures knows where God planted the "tree of life." It was from the fruit of this tree that God excluded Adam and Eve....

Of course, it might be argued that those "days of the tree of life" mentioned by Isaiah are the days that are now being spent by Christ's church, since the "tree of life" is simply a prophetic figure for Christ, for that Wisdom of God that Solomon had in mind when he said that Wisdom is "a tree of life to them that laid hold on it."[27] CITY OF GOD 20.26.[28]

THE CROSS AND ITS LIFE-GIVING FRUIT.
THEODORET OF CYR: For us the saving cross is the tree of life. For it received like fruit the life-

[18]Eph 4:13. [19]PG 87:2693. [20]FC 24:307. [21]SC 315:324. [22]CSCO 303(128):61. [23]See Gen 3:22f. [24]See Prov 3:18. [25]Jn 14:6. [26]AGLB 36:1867-68. [27]Prov 3:18. [28]FC 24:325.

giving body by which those who stretch out their hands and pick the fruit will live life eternally. COMMENTARY ON ISAIAH 20.65.22.[29]

65:23 No Laboring in Vain

OUR LABOR IS NOT IN VAIN. JOHN CASSIAN: When [God] notices good will making an appearance in us, at once he enlightens and encourages it and spurs it on to salvation, giving increase to what he planted and saw arise from our own efforts.... Not only does he graciously inspire holy desires, but he also arranges favorable moments in one's life and the possibility of good results, and he shows the way of salvation to those who are straying. CONFERENCE 13.8.4.[30]

65:24-25 The Wolf and the Lamb

A LITERAL INTERPRETATION PRODUCES NONSENSE. JEROME: Through all of these events is demonstrated the change of evil beings into good, who will be innocent once their old violence has been laid aside. This does not happen outside the holy mountain of the Lord, but on it, that is, in the church and within the profession of the mountain of him by whom the king of Tyre was wounded. He who was cast down from the mountain without hands "grew into a great mountain and filled the world."[31] Let us inquire of the Jews about this passage, along with all Christians who still feed on the chaff of the Scriptures, which, once separated from the grain by the Lord's winnowing fork, will be given over to wind and fire. Let us ask them: what blessedness should be attributed in the thousand-year reign to Mount Zion, Jerusalem, the city of the presiding Messiah?[32] What blessedness to the most holy temple, where the wolf and the lamb, the lion and the cow, serpents and people will eat and dwell together? Are these the only creatures that are to be judged harmless to those who will dwell on the holy mountain of the Lord? Are we to understand from this, therefore, that everything outside of the mountain is to be killed and that all the earth

will be denuded of wolves, lions, bears, panthers, serpents, with other animals, and of the immense forest and the desert of Egyptian solitude, which is fertile with poisonous animals? Are we to understand that the holy city is not only for the ultimate happiness of man, but also will be a home for beasts and serpents, such that, according to the prophecy above, "the wolf will dwell with the lamb and the leopard with the goat, and the bull and the lion and the cow and the bear will rest together, and a small child will rule them and an infant recently weaned will put his hand in the den of the asp."[33] COMMENTARY ON ISAIAH 18.17.[34]

THE WORLD TO COME IS PARADISE REGAINED. GREGORY OF ELVIRA: The earth will freely give its produce, and all evil will be removed, just as Isaiah said ... for God has refashioned such a world in his kingdom just as it had been made in the beginning before the first-made human being ruined it, who after he had disobeyed the word of God all things were spoiled and ruined and cursed by God's word: "the earth will be cursed in your works."[35] The former shape of this world will become the kingdom of the saints and the liberation of the creatures. ORIGEN'S TRACTATES ON THE BOOKS OF HOLY SCRIPTURE 5.36.[36]

SHARING IN THE FOOD THE HOLY SPIRIT PROVIDES. THEODORET OF CYR: This is a prediction Isaiah made previously after having announced the growth from the stem of Jesse.[37] Now, we see the fulfillment of this prophecy as rulers and ruled, kings and servants, wise and foolish will share a common table—that is, the teaching of the Spirit. For he calls those who live in moderation lambs, whereas those with high ambitions are wolves. The lion is the one exalted

---

[29]SC 315:328. [30]ACW 57:474. [31]Dan 2:35; cf. Ezek 28, esp. v 16. [32]Rev 20:1-3. [33]Is 11:6-8. [34]AGLB 36:1872-73. Justin Martyr in his *Dialogue with Trypho* 81 understood Isaiah's depiction here to refer to the literal thousand-year reign of Christ on earth (see ANF 1:239). [35]Gen 3:17. [36]CCL 69:42-43. [37]Is 11:6-7.

to royal status, cattle are those worthy of the priesthood, and straw is the food of cattle. The lion will no longer be a carnivore but shall share the food of the cattle. COMMENTARY ON ISAIAH 20.65.25.[38]

THE SERPENT'S DIET REMAINS THE SAME.
THEODORET OF CYR: "And the serpent shall eat dust as bread." This is the food that the righteous Judge has assigned to it from the beginning: "On your breast and belly you shall go, and you shall eat earth all the days of your life."[39] And so Isaiah

calls the common enemy of humanity a serpent. He has subjected him to the ancient curse. This is similarly indicated in the passage that follows: "They shall not injure or destroy on my holy mountains, says the Lord." All strength had been removed from him, not only from the fact that he crept on the ground but also that the saints had trampled him under foot and the wood of the cross crushed him. COMMENTARY ON ISAIAH 20.65.25.[40]

---

[38]SC 315:330. [39]Gen 3:15. [40]SC 315:330.

66:1-4 SINFUL PEOPLE CANNOT BUILD THE LORD'S HOUSE

[1]Thus says the LORD:
"Heaven is my throne
    and the earth is my footstool;
what is the house which you would build for
    me,
    and what is the place of my rest?
[2]All these things my hand has made,
    and so all these things are mine,[d]
                        says the LORD.
But this is the man to whom I will look,
    he that is humble and contrite in spirit,
    and trembles at my word.

[3]"He who slaughters an ox is like him who kills
    a man;

he who sacrifices a lamb, like him who
    breaks a dog's neck;
he who presents a cereal offering, like him who
    offers swine's blood;
he who makes a memorial offering of
    frankincense, like him who blesses an idol.
These have chosen their own ways,
    and their soul delights in their
    abominations;
[4]I also will choose affliction for them,
    and bring their fears upon them;
because, when I called, no one answered,
    when I spoke they did not listen;
but they did what was evil in my eyes,
    and chose that in which I did not delight."

d Gk Syr: Heb *came to be*

OVERVIEW: God is not to be thought of as contained in any space or place (CLEMENT OF ALEXANDRIA). If God is thought of as located in a heaven with physical dimensions, then it would be too small for him (AUGUSTINE). The human matter that the divine assumed is worthy of worship (AUGUSTINE). The footstool is to be respected, whether holy place or holy soul, but these are where God alone is worshiped (JEROME). God demands not space but moral qualities for him to dwell within (ORIGEN). The creative hand of God is the Word himself (GREGORY OF NYSSA). Tranquility and humility are closely tied together and provide a powerful example (CYPRIAN). The humble are to be affirmed, and the haughty are to be confounded in their choice of priorities (GREGORY THE GREAT). There has been through Christ and the Spirit an internalizing of the presence of God into human persons (JEROME). The true temple now is where order and virtue have been arranged to receive God (THEODORET). The Spirit who dwells in and rests on a person also works to assist. Wisdom comes from trembling at the Word (AUGUSTINE). Room has to be made, metaphorically speaking, for God's presence (CAESARIUS). God is to be found where his energy is effectively working (JOHN OF DAMASCUS).

The sacrificial system was an accommodation to human weakness (THEODORET). The way in which something is done, and its motivation, matter to God as much as what is done (PSEUDO-DIONYSIUS). Israel strayed from God's commands in this regard concerning the proper ordering of sacrifice, focusing instead on their own desires instead of God's (ATHANASIUS).

66:1 Heaven Is My Throne

GOD NOT LITERALLY LOCATED. CLEMENT OF ALEXANDRIA: He has not even built a house for himself! He has nothing to do with space. Even if it is written that "the heaven is his throne," he is not contained as the words suggest. STROMATEIS 2.2.3.[1]

GOD IS BEYOND ALL PHYSICAL MEASUREMENT. AUGUSTINE:[2] "Heaven is my throne, while the earth is my footstool." . . . Haven't you also read that other text, "Who measured the heaven with the palm of his hand?"[3] . . . Whoever sat in the palm of his own hand? . . .

Does the same heaven become wide when he is sitting in it and narrow when he is measuring it? Or is God the same size in his seat as he is in his palm? If that is the case, God did not make us in his own likeness, because we have palms that are much narrower than the part of the body we sit with. But if he is as broad in the palm as he is broad in the beam, then he made very unequal parts for us. No, that is not where the likeness lies. Such an idol should be ashamed of itself in a Christian mind.

So then, take "heaven" as standing for all the saints, since earth too stands for all who are on the earth, "Let all the earth worship you."[4] SERMON 53.13-14.[5]

WE CAN AND MUST WORSHIP CHRIST'S HUMANITY. AUGUSTINE: In hesitation I turn to Christ, since I am herein seeking him; and I discover how the earth may be worshiped without impiety, how his footstool may be worshiped without impiety. For he took on himself earth from earth, and he received flesh from the flesh of Mary. And because he walked here in very flesh and gave that very flesh to us to eat for our salvation, and no one eats that flesh unless he has first worshiped, we have found out in what sense such a footstool of our Lord may be worshiped, and not only that we do not sin in worshiping it but that we sin in not worshiping. EXPLANATIONS OF THE PSALMS 99.8.[6]

THE HOLY PLACES AND THE BELIEVING SOUL. JEROME: "And worship his footstool for it is holy."[7] What is this footstool of Jesus that is holy? We read in another place: "The heavens are my throne, the earth is my footstool"; and here, "worship his footstool." If earth is Jesus' foot-

---

[1]FC 85:161. [2]Augustine is largely following Origen here. See *Homilies in Genesis* (FC 71:64). [3]Is 40:12. [4]Ps 66:4 (65:4 LXX, Vg). [5]WSA 3 3:72-73. [6]NPNF 1 8:485**. [7]Ps 99:5 (98:5 LXX, Vg). [8]See Rom 1:25.

stool, and the psalm says worship his footstool, then is earth to be adored? How, then, do we read in the apostle[8] that we must worship the Creator, not the creature? In Scripture, adoration conveys two different notions: worship as an act toward God and worship in the sense of reverence. When we use the word *worship* in relation to God, we mean the adoration that is proper to God. When, however, we use the term with reference to a human being, as for example, Sarah worshiped[9] Abraham and Elijah worshiped Ahab—a most ungodly king—it does not mean that Elijah worshiped Ahab as if he were God but that this worship was more like a greeting.

Now, we are ready to examine the words "and worship his footstool," and [we will] see in which way the word *worship* is intended. Do we adore God's footstool just as we adore God or in the same sense that we worship and pay respect to a person? We have read in the Lamentations of Jeremiah and in another of the prophets, "How the Lord has hallowed his footstool!"[10] In this passage, his footstool is Jerusalem, or the temple. And so, the reference is historical.

We shall now consider the verse "and worship his footstool" from another point of view. If feet rest on a footstool, the words "Let us worship in the place where his feet have stood"[11] likewise refer to a footstool. In that event, we may hold to the letter and mean, for example, that place where he was born, where he was crucified, where he arose from the dead. This is the explanation for beginners. . . . [Or] Jesus' footstool is the soul of the one who believes. Happy the person in whose heart Jesus sets his feet every day! If only he would set his feet in my heart! If only his footsteps would cling to my heart forever! HOMILIES ON THE PSALMS 26 (PSALM 99).[12]

66:2 Humble and Contrite

THE HOLY SPIRIT DEPARTS FROM THE PROUD. ORIGEN: If you are not "humble and peaceful," the grace of the Holy Spirit cannot live within you, if you do not receive the divine words

with fear. For the Holy Spirit departs from the proud and stubborn and false soul. Therefore, you ought first to meditate on the law of God that, if perhaps your deeds are intemperate and your habits disordered, the law of God may correct you and reform you. HOMILIES ON LEVITICUS 6.2.5.[13]

THE HAND OF GOD. GREGORY OF NYSSA: The prophet says in the person of the Father, "My hand made all these things," meaning by "hand" in his dark saying, the power of the Only Begotten. Now the apostle says that all things are of the Father and that all things are by the Son,[14] and the prophetic spirit in a way agrees with the apostolic teaching, which itself also is given through the Spirit. AGAINST EUNOMIUS 7.1.[15]

TRANQUILITY COMES TO THOSE WHO TREMBLE AT HIS WORD. CYPRIAN: We must preserve in the straight and narrow road of praise and glory; and since peacefulness and humility and the tranquility of a good life are fitting for all Christians, according to the word of the Lord, who looks to no other person than "to him that is poor and of a contrite spirit, and that trembles at" his word, it the more behooves you confessors, who have been made an example to the rest of the brothers, to observe and fulfill this, as being those whose characters should provoke to imitation the life and conduct of all. LETTER 6.3.[16]

PRIORITIES AND VALUES. GREGORY THE GREAT: Differently to be admonished are the humble and the haughty. To the former it is to be carefully communicated how true is that excellence that they hold in hoping for it; to the latter it is to be intimated how that temporal glory is as nothing, which even when embracing it they do

---

[9]Jerome is using the Latin *adoro* in its original sense of rendering honor or respect. [10]Jerome appears to refer to Lam 2:1, although the reference there is actually negative: "He has not remembered his footstool" (Heb and LXX agree here). [11]See Ps 122:2 (121:2 LXX, Vg). [12]FC 48:208-9**. [13]FC 83:119. [14]See 1 Cor 8:6. [15]NPNF 2 5:194*. [16]ANF 5:284*.

not grasp it. Let the humble hear how eternal are the things that they long for, how transitory the things that they despise; let the haughty hear how transitory the things are that they court, how eternal the things are that they lose. PASTORAL CARE 3.17.[17]

GOD DWELLS IN THE HUMBLE, OBEDIENT ONE. JEROME: With the altar and earthly temple removed, which a human hand had built, the sacrifices of the Jews were also rightly removed, lest they say, perhaps, "We are not so foolish as to think that God can be enclosed in one place, but we will choose a different location for offering the sacrifices to God that are commanded in the law." He who sits in heaven, therefore, the very Creator of the universe, who refuses to be held in an earthly temple, willingly adopts the person as his temple who is humble and meek and trembles at his word, according to the apostle, "But you are the temple of God, and the Holy Spirit dwells in you."[18] COMMENTARY ON ISAIAH 18.19.[19]

GOD'S TEMPLE IS THE ONE WHOSE LIFE IS ORDERED AND PEACEFUL. THEODORET OF CYR: In these terms God rejects the worship that was restricted to one place and shows that he is the maker of heaven and earth, and the shaper of all things and the one who has no need of a temple made with hands. . . .

I have a true house and holy temple. It is whoever arranges his or her life according to my laws and fears and trembles at transgressing my commands. It is the person who stands out in a gentle disposition and humility of mind. COMMENTARY ON ISAIAH 20.66.2.[20]

THE SPIRIT RESTS ON THE JOYFULLY OBEDIENT. AUGUSTINE: "On whom does my Spirit rest, if not on one who is humble and quiet and who trembles at my words?"[21] So when he becomes the occupant, he fills and guides and leads the person, restrains from evil and spurs on to good, makes justice delightful, so that the person does good out of love for what is right, not out of fear

of punishment. No one is capable on their own of doing what I have said. But if you have the Holy Spirit as the occupant of your house, you will find him also assisting you in everything good. SERMON 72A.2.[22]

WISDOM OUT OF TREMBLING. AUGUSTINE: At these words Peter trembled, Plato did not; so let the fisherman keep what the great and famous philosopher ignored! "You have hidden these things from the wise and the knowing and have revealed them to the little ones."[23] SERMON 68.7.[24]

EXPELLING EVIL. CAESARIUS OF ARLES: People do not observe a spiritual sabbath unless they devote themselves to earthly occupations so moderately that they still engage in reading and prayer, at least frequently, if not always. SERMON 100.4.[25]

BE FILLED WITH GOD. CAESARIUS OF ARLES: God wishes to dwell in you. In order that you may not be unable to receive him because you are full, if you are filled elsewhere, let your heart be freed of superfluities so that it may be filled with what is necessary. Vices should be expelled, in order that there may be room for virtues; to say briefly what is useful and quite necessary, let carnal desires be rejected and charity invited. As long as we do not expel evil, we cannot be filled with the good, because jars filled with slime cannot receive and hold precious ointment. SERMON 210.5.[26]

GOD'S PLACE IS WHEREVER HE IS AT WORK. JOHN OF DAMASCUS: "For heaven is his resting place and the earth his footstool," because on the earth he conversed in the flesh with men and women. And the sacred flesh of God has been called his foot. The church, too, is called the place of God, because we have set it apart for the glori-

---

[17]NPNF 2 12:41. [18]1 Cor 3:16. [19]AGLB 36:1877. [20]SC 315:332. [21]The LXX takes the Heb as an interrogative. [22]WSA 3 3:282. [23]Mt 11:25. [24]WSA 3 3:227**. [25]FC 47:87. [26]FC 66:97.

fying of God as a sort of consecrated place wherein we also hold conversation with him. Likewise also the places in which his energy becomes manifest to us, whether through the flesh or apart from the flesh, are spoken of as the places of God. ORTHODOX FAITH 1.13.[27]

66:3 One Who Slaughters an Ox

THE SACRIFICIAL SYSTEM ACCOMODATES HUMAN WEAKNESS. THEODORET OF CYR: By these words he rejected the worship prescribed by the law by teaching this; it was for their sake that he had established this legislation from early times, not because he took pleasure in their sacrifices but because he was exercising forethought for them in their weakness. That is why he put side by side what was allowed and what was forbidden, for to sacrifice an ox or give a sheep as a burnt offering, to offer the fruit of corn and frankincense—these were in former times permitted by God, but to start a fight and lose one's tongue to blasphemy was totally forbidden. COMMENTARY ON ISAIAH 20.66.3.[28]

WORTHY THINGS MUST BE DONE IN A WORTHY MANNER. PSEUDO-DIONYSIUS: "When an impious person offers a lamb, it is as if he has killed a dog." To sum up: The perfect justice of God rejects those who break the law. . . . And so it is not permitted, according to the words of Scripture, to perform what may even be a work of justice, except worthily. Everyone must look to himself and, without thinking of more exalted or more profound tasks, he must think only about what has been assigned to his place. LETTER 8.1.[29]

GOD'S ANGER AT ISRAEL'S SELF-ABSORPTION. ATHANASIUS: He is angry with them, say-

ing by Isaiah, "Who has required these of your hands?"[30] And by Jeremiah, since they were very bold, he threatens, "Gather together your whole burnt offerings with your sacrifices, and eat flesh, for I did not speak to your ancestors or command them in the day that I brought them out of the land of Egypt, concerning whole burnt offerings and sacrifices."[31] For they did not act as was right, neither was their zeal according to law, but they rather sought their own pleasure in such days, as the prophet accuses them, beating down their bondsmen and gathering themselves together for strifes and quarrels, and they struck the lowly with the fist and did all things that tended to their own gratification. For this cause, they continue without a feast until the end, although they make a display now of eating flesh, out of place and out of season. For, instead of the legally appointed lamb, they have learned to sacrifice to Baal; instead of the true unleavened bread, "they collect the wood, and their fathers kindle the fire, and their wives prepare the dough, that they make cakes to the host of heaven and pour out libations to strange gods, that they may provoke me to anger, says the Lord."[32] . . . Therefore now, "he who among them sacrifices an ox is as he who strikes a man, and he who sacrifices a lamb is as he who kills a dog, he that offers fine flour, it is as [if he offered] swine's blood. . . ." Now these things will never please God, neither has the Word required this of them. But he says, "These have chosen their own ways, and their abominations are what their

---

[27]FC 37:197-98**. [28]ITA 980*; SC 315:332-34. [29]PDCW 274*. [30]Is 1:12. [31]Jer 7:21-22. [32]Jer 7:18. [33]NPNF 2 4:545**.

soul delights in." FESTAL LETTERS 19.2.[33]

66:5-9 THE END OF THE OLD AND BEGINNING OF NEW

[5]*Hear the word of the* LORD,
   you who tremble at his word:
"Your brethren who hate you
   and cast you out for my name's sake
have said, 'Let the LORD *be glorified,*
   that we may see your joy';
   but it is they who shall be put to shame.

[6]*"Hark, an uproar from the city!*
   A voice from the temple!
The voice of the LORD,
   rendering recompense to his enemies!

[7]*"Before she was in labor*
   she gave birth;

before her pain came upon her
   she was delivered of a son.
[8]*Who has heard such a thing?*
   Who has seen such things?
Shall a land be born in one day?
   Shall a nation be brought forth in one
      moment?
For as soon as Zion was in labor
   she brought forth her sons.
[9]*Shall I bring to the birth and not cause to*
      bring forth?
   says the LORD;
shall I, who cause to bring forth, shut the
      womb?
   says your God."

OVERVIEW: Loving and shaming hateful people can have the same positive result (ISHO'DAD). A religion that has no place for humility will suffer humiliation (JEROME), which is what happened to Israel. It was God who was behind the enemies of Israel's victories against it (CYRIL).

Christ's birth, which is spoken of here in this last chapter of Isaiah, involved God becoming man and a man becoming God (JOHN OF DAMASCUS). The virginal birth was different in the speed and pain-free nature of the labor (METHODIUS). The faithful remnant, represented by Mary, has by faith received the special grace to give birth to the Savior (JEROME). A remnant will preserve spiritual independence from captivity and will continue in Jerusalem for Christ (CYRIL).

66:5 Your Brethren Who Hate You

AN INVITATION TO HAVE MERCY OR TO CON-
DEMN. ISHO'DAD OF MERV: "Your brothers who hate you." Consider them as your brothers, he says, even though they hate you because of your faith, and lead them to the fear of God, so that "the Lord may be glorified in you." According to Henana,[1] consider them to be execrable and evil, he says, even though they are your brothers by nature. "When they are cast out for my name, the Lord will be glorified" in you, "and they will be put to shame," and maybe, he says, they will be put to shame because of that and will abstain from evil actions. COMMENTARY ON ISAIAH 66.5.[2]

THE DANGER OF MISUNDERSTANDING THE
SCRIPTURE. JEROME: This is the meaning of the

---

[1]Henana (about 545-610), a significant figure in Syriac literature, wrote many exegetical works, most of which are now lost. Portions of his work are preserved in the works of Isho'dad and other Syriac authors. [2]CSCO 303(128):62.

Hebrew text, as it appears to me: Listen, apostles, listen, my disciples, who tremble at the word of the Lord, for I will tell you what your brothers say who hate you and cast you out and judge you to be alien; this is not on account of any evil you have done but on account of my name, for they regard all from their ranks who believe in me as they do unclean Gentiles, to whom they say: "depart from me, for you are impure." . . . But then it immediately adds, "and they shall be confounded," namely, those who speak such things, who do not understand the mysteries of the Scriptures, who utilize its power for their own evil and who hold humility in contempt. Commentary on Isaiah 18.21.[3]

66:6 Rendering Recompense

God Directed the Nations' Attacks on Israel. Cyril of Alexandria: For it was the Lord's voice that said, "rendering recompense to his enemies," ordering and exhorting those who destroy to spare none of those captured, savagely attacking the enemies and not only simply with the wrath of warriors but also with the will of the Sovereign. For this was only the means of their captivity and suffering. Commentary on Isaiah 5.6.66.6.[4]

66:7 Delivered of a Son

Mary's Painless Labor. John of Damascus: Now when the fullness of time came, an angel of the Lord was sent to [Mary] with the good news of her conception of the Lord. And thus she conceived the Son of God, the subsistent power of the Father, "not of the will of the flesh or of the will of man"[5]—that is to say, not of carnal conjunction and seed—but of the good pleasure of the Father and the cooperation of the Holy Spirit. To the Creator she gave that he might be created, to the Fashioner that he might be fashioned, and to the Son of God and God that he might from her innocent and undefiled flesh and blood put on flesh and become man. And thus she paid the debt for the first mother. For as Eve was formed from Adam without carnal conjunction, so did this one bring forth the new Adam in accordance with the law of gestation but surpassing the nature of generation. Thus, he who is without a mother begotten of a father was without a father born of a woman. And because it was of a woman it was in accordance with the law of gestation; while, because it was without father, it surpassed the nature of generation. And because it was at the normal time, for having completed the nine-month period he was born at the beginning of the tenth, it was in accordance with the law of gestation, while because it was without pain it surpassed the established order of birth—for where pleasure had not preceded, pain did not follow, as the prophet said, "Before she was in labor, she brought forth," and again, "before her time came to be delivered she brought forth a man child."

And so the Son of God became incarnate and was born of her. It was not as God-bearing man that he was born of her but as God incarnate; not as a prophet anointed through the operation of the one anointing but as one anointed with the entire presence of the one anointing—so that the one anointing became man and the one anointed became God. Orthodox Faith 4.14.[6]

The Miracle of the Incarnation by a Virgin. Methodius: "Before she was in labor, she gave birth; before her pains came, she escaped and delivered a male child." Who has heard such a thing? Who has seen such things? The most holy virgin mother, therefore, escaped entirely the manner of women even before she gave birth, doubtless in order that with the Holy Spirit betrothing her to himself and sanctifying her, she might conceive without intercourse with man. She has brought forth her firstborn Son, even the only-begotten Son of God . . . who on earth, in the Virgin's nuptial chamber, joined to himself the nature of Adam, like a bridegroom, by an inalienable union, and he preserved his mother's

---

[3]AGLB 36:1885. [4]PG 70:1433. [5]Jn 1:13. [6]FC 37:364-65*.

purity incorrupt and uninjured; him in short who in heaven was begotten without corruption and on earth birthed in a manner quite unspeakable. ORATION CONCERNING SIMEON AND ANNA 3.[7]

66:8 Zion Was in Labor

THE FAITH OF THE REMNANT OF ISRAEL BORE THE MESSIAH. JEROME: Zion therefore gave birth, that is, the remnant of Israel and the faith of the believing apostles gave birth to the male Lord and Savior, who was generated at once throughout the entire universe. No one has either heard or told his story or taught it to anyone, so that all the nations might come to believe in a very short time and that there might be formed one Christian people from all the various peoples. This is what Paul was talking about when he said, "If any are in Christ, they are new creatures; the old has passed away and behold, they are made new,"[8] as it is also written elsewhere, "All the families of the nations will worship before him."[9] . . . And this people was created in one day, whom the "sun of righteousness"[10] illumined, as the Scripture says: "The Lord will be your everlasting light."[11] We can also correlate what is said here, "a people will arise as one because Zion bore and delivered her sons," to that time when, on one day, three thousand and another five thousand of the Jewish people believed.[12] Moreover, it is said in the same book of the Acts of the Apostles that there were persons in Jerusalem from all the nations under heaven, who heard one another speaking the glorious deeds of God, each in their own language.[13] . . . But the meaning of the Septu-

agint's text of this verse is that one people from the entire world shall arise in one moment to the preaching of the gospel. Or, in other words: I have repeatedly made this promise through many prophets, but you have not kept my promise in mind, O city full of crying, O temple vacated by the Lord, O people to whom I returned its own rejection. Is it not I who make fertile and make sterile? Did not she who was previously barren not later bear and deliver a child? Of this is it written in the Psalms: "He gives the barren woman a home and makes her a joyful mother of children."[14] COMMENTARY ON ISAIAH 18.23.[15]

THE REMNANT OF JERUSALEM AND THE APOSTLES. CYRIL OF ALEXANDRIA: Again Isaiah teaches that Jerusalem will not be destroyed root, branch and all. For when he foretold the complete captivity of Jerusalem, he mentioned those chosen to survive. For a not insignificant number will be saved, obviously through faith in Christ—and he wants to make this clear. But the Jews were enraged with him and killed the prince of life. But when he rose again, trampling on death, he returned to his God and Father in heaven. In the meantime, the divine apostles proclaimed him to all, and they called even those who had been enraged with him to repentance and to salvation through faith and the forgiveness of sins through baptism. COMMENTARY ON ISAIAH 5.6.66.7-9.[16]

---

[7]ANF 6:385**. [8]2 Cor 5:17. [9]Ps 22:27 (21:28 LXX, Vg). [10]Mal 4:2. [11]Is 60:19. [12]See Acts 2:41, 4:4. [13]Acts 2:5-8. [14]Ps 113:9 (112:9 LXX, Vg). [15]AGLB 36:1889-92. [16]PG 70:1436.

66:10-17 DELIVERANCE AND JUDGMENT

10"Rejoice with Jerusalem, and be glad for her,
  all you who love her;
rejoice with her in joy,
  all you who mourn over her;
11that you may suck and be satisfied
  with her consoling breasts;
that you may drink deeply with delight
  from the abundance of her glory."

12For thus says the LORD:
"Behold, I will extend prosperity to her like
    a river,
  and the wealth of the nations like an
    overflowing stream;*
and you shall suck, you shall be carried
    upon her hip,
  and dandled upon her knees.
13As one whom his mother comforts,
  so I will comfort you;
  you shall be comforted in Jerusalem.

14You shall see, and your heart shall rejoice;
  your bones shall flourish like the grass;
and it shall be known that the hand of the
    LORD is with his servants,
  and his indignation is against his enemies.

15"For behold, the LORD will come in fire,
  and his chariots like the stormwind,
to render his anger in fury,
  and his rebuke with flames of fire.
16For by fire will the LORD execute judgment,
  and by his sword, upon all flesh;
  and those slain by the LORD shall be many.

17"Those who sanctify and purify themselves to
go into the gardens, following one in the midst,
eating swine's flesh and the abomination and
mice, shall come to an end together, says the
LORD."

* LXX I will descend on them as a river of peace, and as a spring I will wash over the glory of the nations

---

OVERVIEW: Young Christian lives are protected by the rock-solid protection of their God and Father (JEROME). His overflowing riches come from the message of salvation, and Christ who stands behind that message (CYRIL). He provides us with his Holy Spirit, who is full of the generous overflowing of divine majesty that he pours on us (AMBROSE). God's fatherhood shows itself in the way he supplies help to his children in their weakness (CLEMENT OF ALEXANDRIA). Another of his gifts is the resurrection, which is of great consolation for God's people weighed down with the threat of death and the other enemies of this life (THEODORET). God opposes these, and all that is evil, in his pure spirit and energy (JEROME) as he fights like a warrior against anything or anyone who resists him in order to protect his children (CYRIL).

66:10 Rejoice with Jerusalem

THE SERPENT CANNOT REACH THE NEST OF CHRISTIANS. JEROME: Those who write of the nature of animals say that all wild creatures, beasts of burden, and sheep and birds have an innate affection for their offspring and young but that the greatest love is found among eagles, who build their nests in very high and inaccessible locations so that no serpent can harm their chicks. Also to be found among newly hatched eagles is the *aetiten* stone,[1] which overcomes all poisons. If this is true, then the eagle's affection is rightly compared with that of God for his creatures, who protects his children by taking every precaution to shatter the adversary's plots on the name of the stone that is placed in Zion's foundation,[2] lest the dragon and ancient serpent, the devil and Satan, seize his newborns.[3] And this Jerusalem, a mother by whom sons are consoled and caressed on her knees, is she of whom the apostle wrote: "But the Jerusalem above, who is the mother of us all, is free."[4] Commentary on Isaiah 18.26.[5]

66:11 Abundance of Glory

The Promise of Divine Comfort. Cyril of Alexandria: This struggle is the correction of noble good deeds in them. For their sweat is profitable, and they have youth-like endurance in order to gain not an earthly possession but rather so that they become filled with graces from God and are satisfied in every desire. To these he makes this promise, "Like infants at the breast you will be filled by the breasts of consolation." Since Isaiah has previously compared the figure of a woman with the new Zion, he remains in this way of speaking and compares this comfort with that of the breasts and milk of the Holy Spirit. For in the Song of Songs it says, "Your breasts are better than wine."[6] . . . And Scripture calls Christ "glory," for the psalmist says about him, "to prepare glory in our land."[7] This entrance is the mystery of the economy in the flesh. Being God by nature, he became man through his incarnation and in such manner came into the world. Those feed on the precise message of faith concerning him, and they learn in what way the glory, that is, Christ came into the world. And directly connected to this, the divine prophet speaks of his clear appearance in the flesh, taking on Christ's voice as he says, "I will descend on them as a river of peace, and as a spring I will wash over the glory of the nations." Commentary on Isaiah 5.6.66.10-12.[8]

66:12 Like a River

The River of the Holy Spirit. Ambrose: So, then, the Holy Spirit is the river, and the abundant river, which according to the Hebrews flowed from Jesus in the lands, as we have received it prophesied by the mouth of Isaiah. This is the great river that flows always and never fails. And not only a river but also one of the copious stream and overflowing greatness, as also David said, "The stream of the river makes glad the city of God."[9] On the Holy Spirit 1.16.177.[10]

66:13 I Will Comfort You

The Father Draws Near to Those Who Seek His Aid. Clement of Alexandria: A mother draws her children near her; we seek our mother, the church. Whatever is weak and young has an appeal and sweetness and lovableness of its own, just because in its weakness it does stand in need of assistance. But God does not withhold assistance from such an age of life. Just as the male and female parent regard their young tenderly— whether it be horses their colts, or cows their calves, or lions their cubs, or deer their fawn or men and women their children—so, too, does the Father of all draw near to those who seek his aid, giving them a new birth and making them his own adopted children. He recognizes them as his little ones, he loves only them, and he comes to the aid of such as these and defends them. That is why he calls them his children. Christ the Educator 1.5.21.[11]

66:14 Your Bones Shall Flourish

The Consolation of the Resurrection. Theodoret of Cyr: For it is not only in the present life that I provide consolation for you through my heralds, but also in the heavenly city I will fill you with manifold joys—granting you the resurrection from the dead. This is what he meant

---

[1]See Lewis and Short, 64: "A stone found in the nest of the eagle, eaglestone"; see Pliny 10.3.4, par. 12; 30.14.44, par. 130. [2]See Is 28:16. [3]See Rev 12:9. [4]Gal 4:26. [5]AGLB 36:1897-98. [6]Song 1:2. [7]Ps 85:9 (84:10 LXX). [8]PG 70:1437-40. [9]Ps 46:4 (45:5 LXX, Vg). [10]NPNF 2 10:113*. [11]FC 23:21-22*.

by comparing the growth of bones to the growth of a plant. COMMENTARY ON ISAIAH 20.66.13-14.[12]

66:15 The Lord Will Come

GOD AS A CONSUMING FIRE. JEROME: By "the Lord will come in fire and with his chariots like a tornado or storm" we should understand him to be speaking of the angelic powers, when the Lord will come in the glory of the Father with his angels to judge the living and the dead.[13] This is not to suggest, however, that the Lord himself is fire, but rather that the punishment to be sustained will feel like fire. Although Moses said and an apostle confirmed that "God is a consuming fire,"[14] the Savior expressed the very substance of his divinity when he said, "God is spirit."[15] And there is a great difference between fire and spirit, according to the corporal understanding. . . . God is called "a consuming fire," therefore, because he consumes our weaknesses, our stubble and briars and thorns, that is, the cares of this world, which cause the earth to be fruitless for the good seed,[16]

as it is said in the letter to the Hebrews: "But if it bears thorns and stubble, it is reprobate and near to being cursed, the end of which is destruction."[17] COMMENTARY ON ISAIAH 18.27.[18]

66:16 By Fire

THE REVERSE SIDE OF REJOICING IS JUDGMENT. CYRIL OF ALEXANDRIA: "For he will come like fire." . . . For he will descend from heaven in the glory of God the Father and with the angels. This is his chariot, as it is praised in the Psalms: "The chariot of the Lord is ten thousand in dimensions with thousands of those rejoicing."[19] For he will come to give judgment in anger and to cast them off with a flame of fire. For "casting off" means rejection, just as he says to those who are dead in their sins, "Depart from me, you evildoers."[20] COMMENTARY ON ISAIAH 5.6.66.15-17.[21]

---

[12]SC 315:340. [13]See Mt 16:27. [14]Deut 4:24; Heb 12:29. [15]Jn 4:24. [16]See Mt 13:1-9, 18-23. [17]Heb 6:8. [18]AGLB 36:1900-1901. [19]Ps 68:17 (67:18 LXX). [20]Mt 25:41. [21]PG 70:1441-44.

66:18-24 THE GOSPEL TO THE GENTILES

[18]For I know[e] their works and their thoughts, and I am[f] coming to gather all nations and tongues; and they shall come and shall see my glory, [19]and I will set a sign among them. And from them I will send survivors to the nations, to Tarshish, Put,[g] and Lud, who draw the bow, to Tubal and Javan, to the coastlands afar off, that have not heard my fame or seen my glory; and they shall declare my glory among the nations. [20]And they shall bring all your brethren from all the nations as an offering to the LORD, upon horses, and in chariots, and in litters, and upon mules, and upon dromedaries, to my holy mountain Jerusalem, says the LORD, just as the Israelites bring their cereal offering in a clean vessel to the house of the LORD. [21]And some of them also I will take for priests and for Levites, says the LORD.

[22]For as the new heavens and the new earth
    which I will make
shall remain before me, says the LORD;

so shall your descendants and your name
    remain.
[23]From new moon to new moon,
    and from sabbath to sabbath,

all flesh shall come to worship before me, says the LORD.

²⁴*"And they shall go forth and look on the*

dead bodies of the men that have rebelled against me; for their worm shall not die, their fire shall not be quenched, and they shall be an abhorrence to all flesh.

e Gk Syr: Heb lacks *know* f Gk Syr Vg Tg: Heb *it is* g Gk: Heb *Pul*

OVERVIEW: Believers are helped toward heaven by those stronger in the faith, who provide instruction and aid. As the new people of God, Christians are to be led by those who are chosen, not just on the basis of human descent, which happened under the old covenant (JEROME). The author of the new covenant, Christ, was opposed by many enemies, but this was all part of God's plan (EPHREM). The prophecy that details that plan is fulfilled in the future in the apostles and their preaching to the nations (THEODORET). God is well able to train for spiritual leadership those who come to him from the nations, enabling them to make progress effortlessly as they rely on his strength through good and bad times (CYRIL).

The church has light and dark times, but it will eventually have an eternal feast in the sun. The burning of those who have rebelled against Christ will be a spiritual fire—as the sins discovered sear consciences (JEROME). Whatever the exact nature of that final judgment is, Christ can save from it (CYRIL). There is another chance through Christ to receive the everlasting blessings (JUSTIN MARTYR). The warning Isaiah gives here helps believers to confirm their choice of the blissful final state (THEODORET). There will be for believers a lasting renewed glorification of human existence (AMBROSE), but while there is still time, they are also warned to seek true glory as they abandon all that is evil (CHRYSOSTOM).

66:18 To Gather All Nations

SAINTS AND ANGELS CARE FOR US. JEROME: And Zechariah saw during the night, "behold, a man mounting a red horse, who was standing between two shady mountains, and behind him

were red and white and chestnut and variously colored horses."[1] . . . John also in the Apocalypse testified that he saw this: "I saw heaven opened, and behold, a white horse, and he who sat on it was called faithful and true and a righteous judge and warrior. His eyes were like flames of fire, and on his head were many diadems, having a written name that no one knew except himself. And he was clothed in a garment sprinkled with blood and the name by which he was called was Word of God. And an army in heaven followed him on white horses, clothed in the purest white linen, and a sharp sword went forth from his mouth to strike the nations."[2] The Lord and Savior was sitting on a red horse as he assumed human nature, to whom it is asked: "Why are your garments red? And who is this who ascends from Edom with crimson garments from Bozrah?"[3] Horses of various colors followed him, moreover, either red with martyrdom or chestnut in flight or variegated with virtues or white with virginity. But he was sitting on a white horse when he assumed an immortal and uncorrupted body after the resurrection. Whoever followed him also used a white horse, incorrupt and immortal in body. If we wished to explain both texts, it would take a long time, but let me say only this, that the various vehicles by which people are led to faith are angels, or saints who have advanced from being people to being angels. Many Scripture passages teach that each of us should have angels, one of which is: "Do not despise one of these little ones, for their angels daily behold the face of the Father who is in heaven."[4] Also, when the maid Rhoda announced that it was

---

[1]Zech 1:8. [2]Rev 19:11-15. [3]Is 63:1, 2. [4]Mt 18:10. [5]See Acts 12. [6]*AGLB* 36:1916-18.

Peter at the door, others believed him to be Peter's angel.[5] COMMENTARY ON ISAIAH 18.30.[6]

66:19 I Will Send

THE PERSECUTION OF CHRIST PREFIGURED THROUGH ZERUBBABEL. EPHREM THE SYRIAN: "And from them I will send" the sign "to Tarshish, Tubal and Javan," and to all the other cities, which came to help the house of Gog in its fight against Zerubbabel, that is, against Christ, who was symbolized by Zerubbabel, the king of the people in its return from captivity to the land of the inheritance of the Lord. Therefore the revolt of the nations against Zerubbabel prefigured what the prophet foretold about Christ by saying, "The kings of the earth set themselves, and the rulers take counsel together against the Lord and against his anointed."[7] COMMENTARY ON ISAIAH 66.19.[8]

THE ACTS OF THE APOSTLES FULFILLS THIS PROPHECY. THEODORET OF CYR: It is with them [the apostles] that the prophecy found its accomplishment, because it was they who preached the gospel to all nations. COMMENTARY ON ISAIAH 20.66.19.[9]

66:21-22 For Priests and Levites

THE NEW MINISTRY IS ONE OF SPIRIT AND VIRTUE. JEROME: "'And I will take from them priests and Levites,' says the Lord," so that those who will be saved can preach to the Gentiles." Concerning this, one author said, "Thus a person should regard us as ministers of Christ and dispensers of the mysteries of God,"[10] and the Evangelist Luke wrote, "just as they delivered to us, who saw from the beginning and were ministers of the word."[11] We, too, read above about this very matter: "But you will be for me priests of the Lord."[12] For just as he who is circumcised by the Spirit is a Jew in hiding, of whom it is written "we are the circumcision who serve the Spirit of God and offer spiritual sacrifices pleasing to God and sing psalms with the Spirit and with the

mind,"[13] so also they are priests and Levites in hiding who follow not a genealogy but the order of faith. It is certain, at least, that this does not speak of the apostles or of apostolic men, who were the princes of the church from the people of the Jews, but it speaks instead of those Gentiles enumerated above, from the sea, from Africa, from Lybia, from Cappadocia, from Italy, from Greece, and from all the islands, the inhabitants of which have not yet had an opportunity to hear the Lord for the first time or to see his glory and afterward to be made priests, such that those who were the tail may become the head and those who were the head may become the tail.[14]

"For, like the new heaven and the new earth that I will cause to stand before me," says the Lord, "so shall your seed and your name stand. From month to month and from sabbath to sabbath, all flesh will come to adore the Lord in my presence in Jerusalem."[15]

When the Lord says, "I will take from them priests and Levites," he shows the old priesthood to have passed away, which was bound to the tribe of Levi, where there was no choice but only a succession by the order of nature in family posterity. For "when there is a change in the priesthood, it is necessary that there be a change in the law as well"[16] and that election to the priesthood be conferred by no means according to blood lineage but according to merits and virtues, choosing people who will come from the islands of the Gentiles and proclaim the glory of the Lord. COMMENTARY ON ISAIAH 18.31-32.[17]

GOD CAN TURN PAGANS INTO HIS SPIRITUAL LEADERS. CYRIL OF ALEXANDRIA: Christ makes here in these words something like a summary of the whole message and of the whole prophecy, and in short compass in summary form he announces the things from start to finish and the power of his economy in the flesh. He mentions

[7]Ps 2:2. [8]SESHS 2:209. [9]SC 315:344. [10]1 Cor 4:1. [11]Lk 1:2. [12]Is 61:6. [13]Phil 3:3; 1 Pet 2:5. [14]See Deut 28:13; Is 9:14-15. [15]Is 66:22-23. [16]Heb 7:12. [17]AGLB 36:1922-23.

the calling of the nations, the election of the holy apostles, and that he will be worshiped by the whole wide world. For the former law gathered one people only, that is, those from Israel, and called to those only speaking that language. But our Lord Jesus Christ did not grant the power of his economy in the flesh only to those from Israel by blood but to every nation and language. . . .

For like something consecrated to God, the host of the nations are given over to God's glory, released from all charges through faith and washed from all filth through holy baptism, like a guest's gift, as if given out of the apostolic fervor for God. On that account they rejoice, naming him their joy and crown. For that the return of the nations to God happens in an extremely comfortable fashion and without sweat and struggle is clearly declared in parabolic fashion when he speaks for our instruction, saying that "they will be led with horses, chariots, now with illuminations, now with shade. . . . And I will take from them priests and Levites." From whom? This is not yet so clear, meaning either those sent to call them out from the nations or from those who were thus called out. For the divine disciples served through Christ as priests. But many were called to the priesthood, and many are still called who are of Greek stock, once God has changed them into the newness of life and knowledge. COMMENTARY ON ISAIAH 5.6.66.18-21.[18]

66:23 New Moon

MORAL MEANING AND FULFILLMENT. JEROME: Physicists and those whose concern it is to argue about the heavens say that the moon does not have its own light but is illuminated by the sun's rays. For it always shines completely on that portion of its orb that is closest to the sun and is not obscured by the shadow of the earth, as the poet demonstrates in one verse: "Nor is the moon liable to rise in the rays of her brother."[19] If this is true, then we are also able to say tropologically that the church, which grows and declines in peace and in persecutions and receives pure light after enduring the op-

pression of dark temptations, possesses its splendor from the Sun of righteousness and is that reality that was spoken: "The moon will shine like the sun."[20] Its righteous inhabitants will also "shine like the sun in the kingdom of their Father."[21] Throughout these months, the seed of the Lord, which is established eternally, comes to his solemnities that the saint sings with a mystical mouth, saying: "I had eternal years in mind as I meditated in the night."[22] . . .

In relation to what follows, namely, "all flesh will come to adore the Lord in my presence in Jerusalem," it should be noted that "Jerusalem" is not written in the Hebrew text, thus enabling us to shake off the arrogance of the Jews, but only "in my presence," so the word of the Lord may be fulfilled by he who says in the Gospel: "Truly, truly, I say to you that the hour will come when you will worship the Father neither in this mountain nor in Jerusalem."[23] For "all flesh" signifies not the Jewish people but every human race, in accordance with what is said above: "All flesh will see your salvation."[24] This is also found in Joel: "I will pour out my Spirit on all flesh, and your sons and daughters will prophesy,"[25] and in Zechariah: "Let all flesh revere the face of the Lord,"[26] and in the Psalter: "All flesh will come to you,"[27] which another psalm expresses differently: "All the peoples whom you have made will come and worship in your presence and glorify your name, O Lord."[28] This "from month to month and from sabbath to sabbath," in which "all flesh will come to adore the Lord," is given a ridiculous interpretation by the chiliasts, however, whom we can call millenarians, such that all who are in the area come to Jerusalem each sabbath and all who are farther away come every month and those who live at a great distance come for Passover every year, this because of what was said in Zechariah: "Each one shall go up from year to year to wor-

---

[18]PG 70:1445-48. [19]Virgil Georgicon 1.396. [20]Is 30:26. [21]Mt 13:43. [22]Ps 77:5 (76:6 LXX, Vg). [23]Jn 4:21. [24]Is 40:5. [25]Joel 2:28; cf. Acts 2:17ff. [26]Zech 2:13. [27]Ps 65:2 (64:3 LXX, Vg). [28]Ps 86:9 (85:9 LXX, Vg). [29]Zech 14:16.

ship the Lord, the King of hosts, and to celebrate the feast of tabernacles."[29] Moreover, providing their audience with still further reason to laugh, because it is written in the last chapter of the same prophet that "there will be no merchants any longer in the house of the Lord of hosts,"[30] they understand this to mean that all salespersons will cease to exist for one thousand years, for everything will be generated in every location, such that we will neither be in need of a sweet pepper nor will an Indian desire a mint leaf from us. COMMENTARY ON ISAIAH 18.32.[31]

66:24 Judgment Against Rebellion

THE BURNING OF SINS. JEROME: But the worm that will not die and the fire that will not be extinguished are understood by many to be the conscience of sinners, which tortures those who are in supplications. Therefore, due to their vice and sin, they are deprived of the good of the elect, in accordance with which it is said, "I was turned to misery, as thorns pierced me,"[32] and in the Proverbs, "the worm of the bones is the envious heart."[33] . . . The Lord also says in the Gospel, "Depart into everlasting fire, which was prepared for the devil and his angels,"[34] and in another place, "Bind his hands and feet, and cast him into outer darkness."[35] If we hear "hands" and "feet" and "outer darkness," which is punishment for the eyes that are deprived of seeing the light of God, and "weeping," which belongs to those very eyes, and "gnashing of teeth," I marvel that this bronze body is to be dissolved gradually into an ethereal body, given that the Lord in the power of his majesty entered to the apostles when the door was closed.[36] . . . The fire, like the worm, must also be understood to burn as long as it has material with which the voracious flame is fed. If, therefore, anyone has weeds in his conscience, which the enemy sowed while the head of the family was asleep, this fire will burn them up, and this conflagration devour them. COMMENTARY ON ISAIAH 18.33.[37]

SUFFERING WRATH FOR AN INDEFINITE DURATION. CYRIL OF ALEXANDRIA: This is the immovable hope that Christ promises in all goodness to those who love him and who acknowledged his epiphany. As it says, "When I remake the heaven and the earth, I will allow them to remain, and no passing of time will destroy them." So your seed and your name will stand before me. For we are the new heaven and the new earth and his promised things, just as they are written about. For the hope of the saints will stand forever and endures, as Paul confirms.[38] . . .

These misfortunes piled on the Jews are meant to be the things we say happened to them at the hands of the Romans, when the temple was destroyed and all were subjected to cruel slaughter. For suffering such things they became a spectacle for all, but their suffering was not prolonged indefinitely. Yet this is what perhaps is meant when it says, "Their worm will not die nor the fire go out." Some, however, want to refer these words concerning them to the time of the end of the age. . . . In any case, Christ will deliver us from all such things, through whom and with whom may glory be to God the Father and the Holy Spirit forever. COMMENTARY ON ISAIAH 5.6.66.22-24.[39]

ADVICE FOR AVOIDING FINAL JUDGMENT. JUSTIN MARTYR: As people who have cut your souls off from this hope, it is necessary that you know how to obtain pardon of your sins and a hope of sharing in the promised blessings. There is no other way than this, that you come to know our Christ, be baptized with the baptism that cleanses you from sin (as Isaiah testified) and thus live a life free of sin. DIALOGUE WITH TRYPHO 44.[40]

AN ADMONITION TO PERSEVERANCE. THEODORET OF CYR: Just as I will transform all that is

---

[30]Zech 14:21. [31]AGLB 36:1925-28. [32]Ps 32:4 (31:4 LXX. Vg). [33]Prov 14:30. [34]Mt 25:41. [35]Mt 22:13. [36]See Jn 20:26. [37]AGLB 36:1929-30. [38]Rom 11:29. [39]PG 70:1448-49. [40]FC 6:214*.

seen and will produce a new creation, so I will guard your memory forever—and not yours alone but all those who have believed through you. . . . He mentions a description of the city and the various dwellings of which the Lord said, "With my father there are many mansions," that is, levels of worthiness. He means those continually rejoicing and singing in choirs . . . he has displayed by that the everlastingness of the chastisement, for the fire is inextinguishable and the worm immortal. With this chastisement he has threatened them, and not them alone but also those who infringe on his divine laws. Finally, therefore, so as not to partake of this chastisement with them, let us avoid partaking of their iniquity; for thus we will join the chorus of those who are in joy. COMMENTARY ON ISAIAH 20.66.23-24.[41]

WE WILL BE RENEWED. AMBROSE: If heaven and earth are renewed, how can we doubt the possibility of our renewal, for whom heaven and earth were made? If the transgressor is kept for punishment, why should not the just person be preserved for glory? If the worm of sinners does not die, how shall the flesh of the just perish? For the resurrection, as the very form of the word indicates, is this: What has fallen shall rise again, what has died shall live again. ON HIS BROTHER SATYRUS 2.87.[42]

SEEK TRUE GLORY. CHRYSOSTOM: If . . . we have any sense of our own salvation, let us, while we still have time, abandon evil ways, concern ourselves with virtue and despise vainglory. HOMILIES ON GENESIS 22.21.[43]

---

[41]SC 315:348-50. [42]FC 22:235. [43]FC 82:84-85; 22.7 in Gk text.

Early Christian Writers and the Documents Cited

The following table lists all the early Christian documents cited in this volume by author, if known, or by the title of the work. The English title used in this commentary is followed in parentheses with the Latin designation and, where available, the Thesaurus Linguae Graecae (=TLG) digital referenences or Cetedoc Clavis numbers. Printed sources of original language versions may be found in the bibliography of works in original languages.

Acts of the Council of Carthage 411 (*Gesta collationis Carthaginensis*)	Cetedoc 0724

Alexander of Alexandria

See Theodoret of Cyr, Ecclesiastical History [*Historia ecclesiastica*]	TLG 4089.003

Ambrose

Death as a Good (*De bono mortis*)	Cetedoc 0129
Duties of the Clergy (*De officiis ministrorum*)	Cetedoc 0144
Exposition of Psalm 118 (*Expositio psalmi cxviii*)	Cetedoc 0141
Expositions on the Gospel of Luke (*Expositio evangelii secundum Lucam*)	Cetedoc 0143
Joseph (*De Joseph*)	Cetedoc 0131
Letters (*Epistulae*)	Cetedoc 0160
On His Brother Satyrus (*De excessu fratris Satyri*)	Cetedoc 0157
On the Christian Faith (*De fide*)	Cetedoc 0150
On the Death of Theodosius (*De obitu Theodosii*)	Cetedoc 0159
On the Holy Spirit (*De Spiritu Sancto*)	Cetedoc 0151
On the Instruction of Virgins (*De institutione virginis*)	Cetedoc 0148
On the Mysteries (*De mysteriis*)	Cetedoc 0155
On the Patriarchs (*De patriarchis*)	Cetedoc 0132
On Virginity (*De virginitate*)	Cetedoc 0147
Six Days of Creation (*Exameron*)	Cetedoc 0123
The Prayer of Job and David (*De interpellatione Job et David*)	Cetedoc 0134

Aphrahat

Demonstrations (*Demonstrationes*)

Aponius

Exposition of Song of Songs (*In Canticum canticorum expositio*)	Cetedoc 0194

Apostolic Constitutions

Constitutions of the Holy Apostles (*Constitutiones apostolorum*)	TLG 2894.001

Athanasius

Against the Heathen *(Contra gentes)*	TLG 2035.001
Defense of His Flight *(Apologia de fuga sua)*	TLG 2035.012
Defense of the Nicene Definition *(De decretis Nicaenae synodi)*	TLG 2035.003
Discourses Against the Arians *(Orationes tres contra Arianos)*	TLG 2035.042
Festal Letters *(Epistulae festalis)*	
Letter to Epictetus *(Epistula ad Epictetum)*	TLG 2035.110
Letter to Serapion *(Epistulae quattuor ad Serapionem)*	TLG 2035.043
Life of St. Anthony *(Vita sancti Antonii)*	TLG 2035.047
On the Incarnation *(De incarnatione verbi)*	TLG 2035.002

Augustine

Admonition and Grace *(De correptione et gratia)*	Cetedoc 0353
Against Julian *(Contra Julianum)*	Cetedoc 0351
Against Philosophers *(Contra philosophos vel Altercationes christianae philosophiae [pseudo])*	Cetedoc 0360
Christian Combat *(De agone christiano)*	Cetedoc 0296
City of God *(De civitate Dei)*	Cetedoc 0313
Confessions *(Confessionum libri tredecim)*	Cetedoc 0251
Enchiridion *(Enchiridion de fide, spe et caritate)*	Cetedoc 0295
Explanations of the Psalms *(Enarrationes in Psalmos)*	Cetedoc 0283
Letters *(Epistulae)*	Cetedoc 0262
Letter to the Catholics on the Sect of Donatists *(Ad catholicos de secta Donatistarum)*	Cetedoc 0334
On Original Sin *(De gratia Christi et de peccato originali)*	Cetedoc 0349
On the Trinity *(De trinitate)*	Cetedoc 0329
Predestination of the Saints *(De praedestinatione sanctorum)*	Cetedoc 0354
Questions on the Old Testament *(Questiones veteris et novi testamenti)*	
Sermons *(Sermones)*	Cetedoc 0284
The Catholic and Manichaean Ways of Life *(De moribus ecclesiae catholicae et de moribus Manichaeorum)*	Cetedoc 0261
Tractates on the Gospel of John *(In Johannis evangelium tractatus)*	Cetedoc 0278

Basil the Great

Homilies on the Hexameron *(Homiliae in hexaemeron)*	TLG 2040.001
Homilies on the Psalms *(Homiliae super Psalmos)*	TLG 2040.018
Homily Against Those Who Are Prone to Anger *(Homilia adversus eos qui irascuntur)*	TLG 2040.026
Letters *(Epistulae)*	TLG 2040.004
On the Holy Spirit *(De spiritu sancto)*	TLG 2040.003

Bede

Retractions on the Acts of the Apostles Commentary *(Retractatio in Actus apostolorum)*	Cetedoc 1358
Homilies on the Gospels *(Homiliarum evangelii libri ii)*	Cetedoc 1367

Benedict

Rule of St. Benedict *(Regula)*	Cetedoc 1852

Caesarius of Arles

Sermons *(Sermones)* — Cetedoc 1008

Cassian, John

Conferences *(Collationes)* — Cetedoc 0512

Institutes *(De institutis coenobiorum et de octo principalium vitiorum remediis)* — Cetedoc 0513

On the Incarnation of the Lord Against Nestorius *(De incarnatione Domini contra Nestorium)* — Cetedoc 0514

Cassiodorus

Exposition of Romans *(Expositio sancti Pauli Epistulae ad Romanos)* — Cetedoc 0902

Expositions of the Psalms *(Expositio psalmorum)* — Cetedoc 0900

Chromatius of Aquila

Tractate on Matthew *(Tractatus in Matthaeum)* — Cetedoc 0218

Clement of Alexandria

Christ the Educator *(Paedagogus)* — TLG 0555.002

Exhortation to the Greeks *(Protrepticus)* — TLG 0555.001

Fragments *(Fragmenta)*

Stromateis *(Stromata)* — TLG 0555.004

Clement of Rome

1 Clement *(Epistula i ad Corinthios)* — TLG 1271.001

Constitutions of the Holy Apostles *(Constitutiones apostolorum)* — TLG 2894.001

Cyprian

Letters *(Epistulae)* — Cetedoc 0050

The Lapsed *(De lapsis)* — Cetedoc 0042

The Lord's Prayer *(De dominica oratione)* — Cetedoc 0043

To Demetrian *(Ad Demetrianum)* — Cetedoc 0046

Cyril of Alexandria

Commentary on Isaiah *(Commentarius in Isaiam prophetam)* — TLG 4090.103

Letters *(Epistulae)*

On the Holy and Consubstantial Trinity *(De sancta trinitate dialogi i-vii)* — TLG 4090.023

On the Unity of Christ *(Quod unus sit Christus)* — TLG 4090.027

Cyril of Jerusalem

Catechetical Lectures *(Catecheses ad illuminandos)* — TLG 2110.003

Mystagogical Lectures *(Mystagogiae [sp.])* — TLG 2110.002

Didache *(Didache xii apostolorum)* — TLG 1311.001

Didymus the Blind
Commentary on Zechariah (*Commentarii in Zacchariam*)   TLG 2102.010

Ephrem the Syrian
Commentary on Isaiah
Hymns on the Nativity (*Hymni de nativitate*)
Letter to Publius (*Epistula ad Publium*)

Epistle of Barnabas (*Barnabae epistula*)   TLG 1216.001

Eusebius of Caesarea
Commentary on Isaiah (*Commentarius in Isaiam*)   TLG 2018.019
Ecclesiastical History (*Historia ecclesiastica*)   TLG 2018.002
Preparation for the Gospel (*Praeparatio evangelica*)   TLG 2018.001
Proof of the Gospel (*Demonstratio evangelica*)   TLG 2018.005

Filastrius
Book of Heresies (*Diversarum hereseon liber*)   Cetedoc 0121

Fulgentius of Ruspe
Against Fabianus, Fragments (*Contra Fabianum fragmenta*)   Cetedoc 0824
Book to Victor Against the Sermon of Fastidiosus the Arian
  (*Liber ad Victorem contra sermonem Fastidiosi Ariani*)   Cetedoc 0820
Letters (*Epistulae*)   Cetedoc 0817
Letter to Monimus (*Ad Monimus libri III*)   Cetedoc 0814
On the Forgiveness of Sins (*Ad Euthymium de remissione peccatorum libri II*)
Cetedoc 0821

Gregory of Elvira
Origen's Tractates on the Books of Holy Scripture
  (*Tractatus Origenis de libris Sanctarum Scripturarum*)   Cetedoc 0546

Gregory of Nazianzus
In Defense of His Flight to Pontus, Oration 2 (*Apologetica*)   TLG 2022.016
Letters (*Epistulae theologicae*)   TLG 2022.002
On His Father's Silence, Oration 16 (*In patrem tacentem*)   TLG 2022.029
On Holy Baptism, Oration 40 (*In sanctum baptisma*)   TLG 2022.048
On Holy Easter, Oration 45 (*In sanctum pascha*)   TLG 2022.052
On the Death of His Father, Oration 18 (*Funebris oratio in patrem*)   TLG 2022.031
On the Holy Spirit, Theological Oration 5(31) (*De spiritu sancto*)   TLG 2022.011
On the Son, Theological Oration 3(29), (*De filio*)   TLG 2022.009
On the Son, Theological Oration 4(30), (*De filio*)   TLG 2022.010
The Last Farewell, Oration 42 (*Supremum vale*)   TLG 2022.050

Gregory of Nyssa

Against Eunomius (*Contra Eunomium*)	TLG 2017.030
(*Refutatio confessionis*)	TLG 2017.031
Life of Moses (*De vita Mosis*)	TLG 2017.042
On Virginity (*De virginitate*)	TLG 2017.043

Gregory Thaumaturgus

Twelve Topics on the Faith (*De fide capitula duodecim*)

Gregory the Great

Dialogues (*Dialogorum libri iv libri duo*)	Cetedoc 1713
Letters (*Registrum epistularum*)	Cetedoc 1714
Morals on the Book of Job (*Moralia in Job*)	Cetedoc 1708
Pastoral Care (*Regula pastoralis*)	Cetedoc 1712
Six Books on 1 Kings (*In librum primum Regum expositionum libri vi [Dub.]*)	Cetedoc 1719

Hilary of Poitiers

On the Trinity (*De trinitate*)	Cetedoc 0433

Hippolytus

Fragments on the Psalms (*Fragmenta in Psalmos [Sp.]*)	TLG 2115.012
On the Antichrist (*De antichristo*)	TLG 2115.003
The Refutation of All Heresies (*Refutatio omnium haeresium*)	TLG 2115.060

Irenaeus

Against Heresies (*Adversus haereses*)	Cetedoc 1154

Isaac of Nineveh

Ascetical Homilies (*De perfectione religiosa*)
Book of Grace

Isho'dad of Merv

Commentary on Isaiah (*Commentarii in Isaiam*)

Isidore of Seville

Three Books of Thoughts (*Sententiarum libri tres*)	Cetedoc 1199

Jerome

Against John of Jerusalem (*Contra Johannem Hierosolymitanum*)	Cetedoc 0612
Against Jovinianus (*Adversus Jovinianum*)	Cetedoc 0610
Against the Pelagians (*Dialogi contra Pelagianos libri iii*)	Cetedoc 0615
Commentary on Isaiah (*Commentarii in Isaiam*)	Cetedoc 0584
Homilies on John (*Homilia in Johannem evangelistam*)	Cetedoc 0597
Commentary on the Minor Prophets (*Commentarii in prophetas minores*)	Cetedoc 0589
Homilies on Mark (*Tractatus in Marci evangelium*)	Cetedoc 0594

Homilies on the Psalms (*Tractatus lix in psalmos*)   Cetedoc 0592
Homilies on the Psalms, Alternate Series (*Tractatuum in psalmos series altera*)   Cetedoc 0593
Letters (*Epistulae*)   Cetedoc 0620

John Chrysostom
Against the Anomoeans (*Contra Anomoeos*) 2 (*De incomprehensibili dei natura*)   TLG 2062.012
Baptismal Instructions (*Catechesis de juramento*)   TLG 2062.380
Commentary on Galatians (*In epistulam ad Galatas commentarius*)   TLG 2062.158
Concerning the Power of Demons (*De diabolo tentatore*)   TLG 2062.026
Demonstration Against the Pagans (*Contra Judaeos et Gentiles, Quod Christus sit Deus*)   TLG 2062.372
Homilies Concerning the Statues (*Ad populam Antiochenum homiliae [de statuis]*)   TLG 2062.024
Homilies on Ephesians (*In epistulam ad Ephesios*)   TLG 2062.159
Homilies on Genesis (*In Genesim [homiliae 1-67]*)   TLG 2062.112
Homilies on Isaiah (*In illud Isaiae: Ego dominus dues feci lumen*)   TLG 2062.148
Homilies on Repentance and Almsgiving (*De paenitentia [homiliae 1-9]*)   TLG 2062.027
Homilies on 2 Corinthians (*In epistulam ii ad Corinthios [homiliae 1-30]*)   TLG 2062.157
Homilies on the Gospel of John (*In Joannem [homiliae 1-88]*)   TLG 2062.153
Homilies on the Gospel of Matthew (*In Matthaeum [homiliae 1-90]*)   TLG 2062.152
Letter to the Fallen Theodore (*Ad Theodorum lapsum [lib. 1]*)   TLG 2062.002
Letters to Olympias (*Epistulae ad Olympiadem*)   TLG 2062.088
On the Epistle to the Hebrews (*In epistulam ad Hebraeos*)   TLG 2062.168

John of Damascus
Orthodox Faith (*Expositio fidei*)   TLG 2934.004
The Canon of Pascha (*Canon paschalis*)

Justin Martyr
Dialogue with Trypho (*Dialogus cum Tryphone*)   TLG 0645.003
First Apology (*Apologia*)   TLG 0645.001

Lactantius
Divine Institutes (*Divinae Institutiones*)   Cetedoc 0085

Leander of Seville
Homilies on the Triumph of the Church (*Homilia in laudem ecclesiae*)

Leo the Great
Sermons (*Tractatus septem et nonaginta*)   Cetedoc 1657

Macarius of Egypt
First Syriac Epistle

Marius Victorinus
Against Arius (*Adversus Arium*)   Cetedoc 0095
On the Necessity of Accepting Homoousion (*De homoousio recipiendo*)   Cetedoc 0097

Maximus of Turin
Sermons *(Collectio sermonum antiqua)*   Cetedoc 0219a

Melito of Sardis
On Pascha *(De pascha)*   TLG 1495.001

Methodius
On the Resurrection *(De resurrectione)*   TLG 2959.003
Oration Concerning Simeon and Anna *(Sermo de Symeone et Anna [Sp.])*   TLG 2959.012
Symposium *or* Banquet of the Ten Virgins *(Symposium* sive *Convivium decem virginum)*   TLG 2959.001

Nemesius of Emesa
On the Nature of Man *(De natura hominis)*   TLG 0743.001

Novatian
On the Trinity *(De Trinitate)*   Ceteodc 0071

Origen
Against Celsus *(Contra Celsum)*   TLG 2042.001
Commentary on Matthew *(Commentarium in evangelium Matthaei [lib. 10-11])*   TLG 2042.029
Commentary on the Gospel of John *(Commentarii in evangelium Joannis*
     [lib. 1, 2, 4, 5, 6, 10, 13])   TLG 2042.005
Commentary on the Song of Songs *(Commentarium in Canticum Canticorum)*   Cetedoc 0198
Dialogue with Heraclides *(Dialogus cum Heraclide)*   TLG 2042.018
Exhortation to Martyrdom *(Exhortatio ad martyrium)*   TLG 2042.007
Homilies on Exodus *(Homiliae in Exodum)*   TLG 2042.023
Homilies on Genesis *(Homiliae in Genesim)*   TLG 2042.022
Homilies on Jeremiah *(In Jeremiam [homiliae 1-11])*   TLG 2042.009
Homilies on Leviticus *(Homiliae in Leviticum)*   TLG 2042.024
Homilies on the Gospel of Luke *(Homiliae in Lucam)*   TLG 2042.016
Homily on 1 Kings 28 (1 Samuel 28) *(De engastrimytho)*   TLG 2042.013
On First Principles *(De principiis)*   TLG 2042.002

Pachomius
Instructions *(Catecheses)*

Procopius of Gaza
Commentary on Isaiah *(Catena in Isaiam)*   TLG 2598.004

Prudentius
Against Symmachus *(Contra Summachum)*   Cetedoc 1442

Pseudo-Clement of Rome
Recognitions *(Recognitiones)*   Cetedoc 0198 N (A)
2 Clement *(Epistula ii ad Corinthios [Sp.])*   TLG 1271.002

Pseudo-Dionysius

Ecclesiastical Hierarchy (*De ecclesiastica hierarchia*)   TLG 2798.002

Letters (*Epistulae*)   TLG 2798.006

Rufinus of Aquileia

Commentary on the Apostles' Creed (*Expositio symboli*)   Cetedoc 0196

Symeon the New Theologian

Discourses (*Catecheses*)

Tertullian

Against Hermogenes (*Adversus Hermogenem*)   Cetedoc 0013

Against Marcion (*Adversus Marcionem*)   Cetedoc 0014

Against Praxeas (*Adversus Praxean*)   Cetedoc 0026

An Answer to the Jews (*Adversus Judaeos*)   Cetedoc 0033

On Idolatry (*De idololatria*)   Cetedoc 0023

On the Resurrection of the Flesh (*De resurrectione mortuorum*)   Cetedoc 0019

On the Soul (*De anima*)   Cetedoc 0017

Theodore of Heraclea

Fragments on Isaiah (*Fragmenta in Isaiam*)

Theodoret of Cyr

Commentary on Isaiah (*Commentaria in Isaiam*)   TLG 4089.008

Dialogues (*Eranistes*)   TLG 4089.002

Letters (*Epistulae: Collectio Sirmondiana [1-95]*)   TLG 4089.006

On Divine Providence (*De providentia orationes decem*)   TLG 4089.032

Bibliography of Works
in Original Languages

Acts of the Council of Carthage 411. In *Gesta collations Carthaginiensis anno 411 accedit Sancti Augustini breviculas collationes cum Donatistis*. Edited by S. Lancel. CCL 149A, pp. 1-257. Turnhout, Belgium: Brepols, 1974. Cl. 0724.

Alexander of Alexandria. *See* Theodoret of Cyr. "Historia ecclesiastica." In *Theodoret: Kirchengeschichte*. 2nd ed. Edited by L. Parmentier and F. Scheidweiler. GCS 44, pp. 1-349. Berlin: Akademie-Verlag, 1954. TLG 4089.003.

Ambrose. "De bono mortis." In *Sancti Ambrosii opera*. Edited by Karl Schenkl. CSEL 32, pt. 1, pp. 701-53. Vienna, Austria: F. Tempsky; Leipzig, Germany: G. Freytag, 1897. Cl. 0129.

———. "De excessu fratris Satyri." In *Sancti Ambrosii opera*. Edited by Otto Faller. CSEL 73, pp. 207-325. Vienna, Austria: Hoelder-Pichler-Tempsky, 1895. Cl. 0157.

———. "De fide libri v." In *Sancti Ambrosii opera*. Edited by Otto Faller. CSEL 78.
Vienna, Austria: Hoelder-Pichler-Tempsky, 1962. Cl. 0150.

———. "De institutione virginis." In *Opere II/2: Verginità e vedovanza*. Edited by F. Gori. Opera omnia di Sant'Ambrogio 14.2. Milan: Biblioteca Ambrosiana; Rome: Citta nuovà, 1989. Cl. 0148.

———. "De interpellatione Job et David." In *Sancti Ambrosii opera*. Edited by Karl Schenkl. CSEL 32, pt. 2, pp. 209-96. Vienna, Austria: F. Tempsky; Leipzig, Germany: G. Freytag, 1897. Cl. 0134.

———. "De Joseph." In *Sancti Ambrosii opera*. Edited by Karl Schenkl. CSEL 32, pt. 2, pp. 71-122. Vienna, Austria: F. Tempsky; Leipzig, Germany: G. Freytag, 1897. Cl. 0131.

———. "De mysteriis." In *Sancti Ambrosii opera*. Edited by Otto Faller. CSEL 73, pp. 87-116. Vienna, Austria: Hoelder-Pichler-Tempsky, 1955. Cl. 0155.

———. "De obitu Theodosii." In *Sancti Ambrosii opera*. Edited by Otto Faller. CSEL 73, pp. 371-401. Vienna, Austria: Hoelder-Pichler-Tempsky, 1955. Cl. 0159.

———. *De officiis ministrorum*. Edited by Maurice Testard. CCL 15. Turnhout, Belgium: Brepols, 2000. Cl. 0144.

———. "De patriarchis." In *Sancti Ambrosii opera*. Edited by Karl Schenkl. CSEL 32, pt. 2, pp. 123-60. Vienna, Austria: F. Tempsky; Leipzig, Germany: G. Freytag, 1897. Cl. 0132.

———. "De spiritu sancto." In *Sancti Ambrosii opera*. Edited by Otto Faller. CSEL 79, pp. 5-222. Vienna, Austria: Hoelder-Pichler-Tempsky, 1964. Cl. 0151.

———. *De virginitate*. Edited by Ignazio Cazzaniga. Corpus Scriptorum Latinorum Paravianum. Turin: In Aedibus Io. Bapt. Paraviae et Sociorum, 1954. Cl. 0147.

———. "Epistulae extra collectionem traditae." In *Sancti Ambrosii opera*. Edited by Otto Faller and Michael Zelzer. CSEL 82. 4 vols. Vienna, Austria: F. Tempsky; Leipzig, Germany: G. Freytag, 1968-1990. Cl. 0160.

———. "Exameron." In *Sancti Ambrosii opera*. Edited by Karl Schenkl. CSEL 32, pt. 1, pp. 1-261. Vienna, Austria: F. Tempsky; Leipzig, Germany: G. Freytag, 1897. Cl. 0123.

———. *Expositio evangelii secundum Lucam*. Edited by Mark Adriaen. CCL 14. Turnhout, Belgium:

Brepols, 1957. Cl. 0143.

———. *Expositio psalmi cxviii*. Edited by Michael Petschenig. CSEL 62. Vienna, Austria: Verlag der Österreichischen Akademie der Wissenschaften, 1913. Cl. 0141.

Aphrahat. "Demonstrationes (IV)." In *Opera omnia*. Edited by R. Graffin. Patrologia Syriaca 1, cols. 137-82. Paris: Firmin-Didor, 1910.

Aponius. *In Canticum canticorum exposition*. Edited by Bernard de Vregille and Louis Neyrand. CCL 19. Turnhout, Belgium: Brepols, 1986. Cl. 0194.

Athanasius. "Apologia de fuga sua." In *Athanase d'Alexandrie: Apologie à l'empereur Constance; Apologie pour sa fuite*. Edited by Jan M. Szymusiak. SC 56, pp. 133-67. Paris: Éditions du Cerf, 1958. TLG 2035.012.

———. "Contra gentes." In *Contra gentes, and De incarnatione*, pp. 2-132. Edited by Robert W. Thompson. Oxford: Clarendon Press, 1971. TLG 2035.001.

———. "De decretis Nicaenae synodi." In *Athanasius Werke*. Vol. 2.1, pp, 1-45. Edited by Hans-Georg Opitz. Berlin: de Gruyter, 1940. TLG 2035.003.

———. "De incarnatione verbi." In *Sur l'incarnation du verbe*. Edited by C. Kannengiesser. SC 199, pp. 258-468. Paris: Éditions du Cerf, 1973. TLG 2035.002.

———. "Epistula ad Epictetum." In *Opera omnia*. PG 26, cols. 1049-70. Edited by J.-P. Migne. Paris: Migne, 1887. TLG 2035.110.

———. "Epistulae festalis." In *Sancti Athanasii: Syriace et Latine*. Edited by Leonis Allatii. NPB 6. Rome: Typis Sacri Consilii Propagando Christiano Nomini, 1853.

———. "Epistulae quattuor ad Serapionem." In *Opera omnia*. PG 26, cols. 525-676. Edited by J.-P. Migne. Paris: Migne, 1887. TLG 2035.043.

———. "Orationes tres contra Arianos." In *Opera omnia*. PG 26, cols. 813-920. Edited by J.-P. Migne. Paris: Migne, 1887. TLG 2035.042.

———. "Vita sancti Antonii." In *Opera omnia*. PG 26, cols. 835-976. Edited by J.-P. Migne. Paris: Migne, 1887. TLG 2035.047.

Augustine. "Ad catholicos de secta Donatistarum." In *Sancti Aureli Augustini opera*. Edited by Michael Petschenig. CSEL 52, pp. 231-322. Vienna, Austria: F. Tempsky, 1909. Cl. 0334.

———. *Confessionum libri tredecim*. Edited by L. Verheijen. CCL 27. Turnhout, Belgium: Brepols, 1981. Cl. 0251.

———. "Contra Julianum." In *Opera omnia*. PL 44, cols. 641-874. Edited by J.-P. Migne. Paris: Migne, 1861. Cl. 0351.

———. "Contra philosophos vel Altercationes christianae philosophiae (pseudo)." In *Aurelii Augustini opera*. Edited by Diethard Aschoff. CCL 58A. Turnhout, Belgium: Brepols, 1975. Cl. 0360.

———. "De agone christiano." In *Sancti Aureli Augustini opera*. Edited by Joseph Zycha. CSEL 41, pp. 101-38. Vienna, Austria: F. Tempsky, 1900. Cl. 0296.

———. *De civitate Dei*. In *Aurelii Augustini opera*. Edited by Bernhard Dombart and Alphons Kalb. CCL 47, 48. Turnhout, Belgium: Brepols, 1955. Cl. 0313.

———. "De correptione et gratia." In *Opera omnia*. PL 44, cols. 915-46. Edited by J.-P. Migne Paris: Migne, 1845. Cl. 0353.

———. "De gratia Christi et de peccato originali." In *Sancti Aureli Augustini*. Edited by Karl Franze Urba and Joseph Zycha. CSEL 42, pp. 125-206. Vienna, Austria: F. Tempsky; Leipzig, Germany: G. Freytag, 1902. Cl. 0349.

———. "De moribus ecclesiae catholicae et de moribus Manichaeorum." In *Opera omnia*. PL 32, cols. 1309-78. Edited by J.-P. Migne Paris: Migne, 1861. Cl. 0261.

———. "De praedestinatione sanctorum." In *Opera omnia*. PL 44, cols. 959-92. Edited by J.-P. Migne.

Paris: Migne, 1861. Cl. 0354.

—————. "De Trinitate." In *Aurelii Augustini opera*. Edited by William John Mountain. CCL 50-50A. Turnhout, Belgium: Brepols, 1968. Cl. 0329.

—————. "Enarrationes in Psalmos." In *Aurelii Augustini opera*. Edited by Eligius Dekkers and John Fraipont. CCL 38, 39 and 40. Turnhout, Belgium: Brepols, 1956. Cl. 0283.

—————. "Enchiridion de fide, spe et caritate." In *Aurelii Augustini opera*. Edited by E. Evans. CCL 46, pp. 49-114. Turnhout, Belgium: Brepols, 1969. Cl. 0295.

—————. *Epistulae 185-270*. In *Sancti Aurelii Augustini*. Edited by A. Goldbacher. CSEL 57. Vienna, Austria: F. Tempsky; Leipzig, Germany: G. Freytag, 1911. Cl. 0262.

—————. "In Johannis evangelium tractatus." In *Aurelii Augustini opera*. Edited by R. Willems. CCL 36. Turnhout, Belgium: Brepols, 1954. Cl. 0278.

—————. "Questiones veteris et novi testamenti." In *Opera omnia*. PL 35, 2213-416. Edited by J.-P. Migne. Paris: Migne, 1864.

—————. "Sermones." In *Augustini opera omnia*. PL 38 and 39. Edited by J.-P. Migne. Paris: Migne, 1844-1865. Cl. 0284.

Barnabae epistula. In *Épître de Barnabé*. Edited by Pierre Prigent and Robert A. Kraft. SC 172, pp. 72-218. Paris: Éditions du Cerf, 1971. TLG 1216.001.

Basil the Great. *De spiritu sancto*. In *Basile de Césarée: Sur le Saint-Esprit*. Edited by Benoit Pruche. SC 17. Paris: Éditions du Cerf, 2002. TLG 2040.003.

—————. "Epistulae." In *Saint Basil: Lettres*. Edited by Yves Courtonne. Vol. 2, pp. 101-218; vol. 3, pp. 1-229. Paris: Les Belles Lettres, 1961-1966. TLG 2040.004.

—————. *Homilia adversus eos qui irascuntur* TLG 2040.026

—————. "Homiliae in hexaemeron." In *Opera omnia*. PG 29, cols. 3-208. Edited by J.-P. Migne. Paris: Migne, 1857. TLG 2040.001.

—————. "Homiliae super Psalmos." In *Opera omnia*. PG 29, cols. 209-494. Edited by J.-P. Migne. Paris: Migne, 1857. TLG 2040.018.

Bede. "Homiliarum evangelii." In *Bedae opera*. Edited by David Hurst. CCL 122, pp. 1-378. Turnhout, Belgium: Brepols, 1956. Cl. 1367.

—————. "Retractatio in Actus apostolorum." In *Bedae opera*. Edited by M. L. W. Laistner. CCL 121, pp. 103-63. Turnhout, Belgium: Brepols, 1983. Cl. 1358.

Benedict (of Nursia). "Regula." In *La règle de saint Benoît*. Edited by Adalbert de Vogüè and Jean Neufville. SC 181, pp. 412-90 and SC 182, pp. 508-674. Paris: Éditions du Cerf, 1971-1977. Cl. 1852.

Caesarius of Arles. *Sermones Caesarii Arelatensis*. Edited by Germain Morin. CCL 103, 104. Turnhout, Belgium: Brepols, 1953. Cl. 1008.

Cassian, John. *Collationes xxiv*. Edited by Michael Petschenig. CSEL 13. Vienna, Austria: F. Tempsky; Leipzig, Germany: G. Freytag, 1886. Cl. 0512.

—————. "De incarnatione Domini contra Nestorium." In *Johannis Cassiani*. Edited by Michael Petschenig. CSEL 17, pp. 233-391. Vienna, Austria: F. Tempsky; Leipzig, Germany: G. Freytag, 1888. Cl. 0514.

—————. "De institutis coenobiorum et de octo principalium vitiorum remediis." In *Johannis Cassiani*. Edited by Michael Petschenig. CSEL 17, pp. 1-231. Vienna, Austria: F. Tempsky; Leipzig, Germany: G. Freytag, 1888. Cl. 0513.

Cassiodorus. *Expositio psalmorum*. Edited by Mark Adriaen. CCL 97 and 98. Turnhout, Belgium: Brepols, 1958. Cl. 0900.

—————. "Expositio sancti Pauli Epistulae ad Romanos." In *Opera omnia*. PL 68, cols. 415-506. Edited by J.-P. Migne. Paris: Migne, 1847. Cl. 0902.

Chromatius of Aquila. "Tractatus in Matthaeum." In *Chromatii Aquileiensis opera*. Edited by R. Étaix and

Joseph Lemarié. CCL 9A, pp. 391-442; CCL 9A Supplement, pp. 624-36. Turnhout, Belgium: Brepols, 1974-1977. Cl. 0218.

Clement of Alexandria. "Fragmenta." In *Clemens Alexandrinus*. Vol. 3. 2nd ed. Edited by Otto Stählin, Ludwig Früchtel and Ursula Treu. GCS 17, pp. 193-230. Berlin: Akademie-Verlag, 1970. TLG 0555.008.

———. "Paedagogus." In *Le pédagogue [par] Clement d'Alexandrie*. 3 vols. Translated by Mauguerite Harl, Chantel Matray and Claude Mondésert. Introduction and notes by Henri-Irénée Marrou. SC 70, 108, 158. Paris: Éditions du Cerf, 1960-1970. TLG 0555.002.

———. "Protrepticus." In *Clément d'Alexandrie. Le protreptique*. 2nd ed. Edited by C. Mondésert. SC 2, pp. 52-193. Paris: Éditions du Cerf, 1949. TLG 0555.001.

———. "Stromata." In *Clemens Alexandrinus*. Vol. 2, 3rd ed., and vol. 3, 2nd ed. Edited by Otto Stählin, Ludwig Früchtel and Ursula Treu. GCS 15, pp. 3-518 and GCS 17, pp. 1-102. Berlin: Akademie-Verlag, 1960-1970. TLG 0555.004.

Clement of Rome. "Epistula i ad Corinthios." In *Clément de Rome: Épitre aux Corinthiens*. Edited by Annie Jaubert. SC 167. Paris: Éditions du Cerf, 1971. TLG 1271.001.

Constitutiones apostolorum. In *Les constitutions apostoliques*. 3 vols. Edited by Marcel Metzger. SC 320, 329 and 336. Paris: Éditions du Cerf, 1985-1987. TLG 2894.001.

Cyprian. "Ad Demetrianum." In *Sancti Cypriani episcopi opera*. Edited by Manlio Simonetti. CCL 3A, pp. 35-51. Turnhout, Belgium: Brepols, 1976. Cl. 0046.

———. "De dominica oratione." In *Sancti Cypriani episcopi opera*. CCL 3A, pp. 87-113. Edited by Claudio Moreschini. Turnhout, Belgium: Brepols, 1976. Cl. 0043.

———. "De lapsis." In *Sancti Cypriani episcopi opera*. Edited by R. Weber. CCL 3, pp. 221-42. Turnhout, Belgium: Brepols, 1972. Cl. 0042.

———. *Epistulae*. Edited by Gerardus Frederik Diercks. CCL 3B, 3C. Turnhout, Belgium: Brepols, 1994-1996. Cl. 0050.

Cyril of Alexandria. "Commentarius in Isaiam prophetam." In *Opera omnia*. PG 70, cols. 9-1449. Edited by J.-P. Migne. Paris: Migne, 1864. TLG 4090.103.

———. "De sancta trinitate dialogi i-vii." In *Cyrille d'Alexandrie: Dialogues sur la Trinité*. Edited by G. M. Durand. SC 231, 237 and 246. Paris: Éditions du Cerf, 1976-1978. TLG 4090.023.

———. "Epistulae." In *Opera omnia*. PG 77, cols. 9-390. Edited by J.-P. Migne. Paris: Migne, 1864.

———. "Quod unus sit Christus." In *Cyrille d'Alexandrie: Deux dialogues christologiques*. SC 97. Paris: Éditions du Cerf, 1964. TLG 4090.027.

Cyril of Jeruslaem. "Catecheses ad illuminandos 1-18." In *Cyrilli Hierosolymorum archiepiscopi opera quae supersunt omnia.*" Vol. 1, pp. 28-320; vol. 2, pp. 2-342. Edited by Wilhelm Karl Reischl and Joseph Rupp. Munich: Lentner, 1860. Reprint. Hildesheim: Olms, 1967). TLG 2110.003.

———. "Mystagogiae 1-5 (Sp.)." In *Cyrille de Jérusalem: Catéchèses, mystagogigues*. 2nd ed. SC 126, pp. 82-174. Edited by Auguste Piédagnel. Paris: Éditions du Cerf, 1988. TLG 2110.002.

Didache xii apostolorum. In *La Didachè: Instructions des Apôtres*, pp. 226-42. Edited by Jean-Paul Audet. Paris: Lecoffre, 1958. TLG 1311.001.

Didymus the Blind. "Commentarii in Zacchariam." In *Didyme l'Aveugle sur Zacharie*. Edited by L. Doutreleau. SC 83, 84 and 85. Paris: Éditions du Cerf, 1962. TLG 2102.010.

Ephrem the Syrian. "Commentarii in Isaiam." In *ESOO 2*. Edited by J.A. Assemani. Rome: Typographia Vaticana, 1737.

———. "Epistula ad Publium." See Sebastian P. Brock, "Ephrem's Letter to Publius." *Le Muséon* 89 (1976): 261-305.

———. *Hymni de nativitate*. Edited by Edmund Beck. 2 vols. CSCO 186 and 187 (Scriptores Syri 82 and

83). Louvain: Secrétariat du Corpus, 1959.

Eusebius of Caesarea. "Commentarius in Isaiam." In *Eusebius Werke, Band 9: Der Jesajakommentar*. Edited by Joseph Ziegler. GCS 66. Berlin: Akademie-Verlag, 1975. TLG 2018.019.

———. "Demonstratio evangelica." In *Eusebius Werke, Band 6: Die Demonstratio evangelica*. Edited by Ivar A. Heikel. GCS 23. Leipzig: Hinrichs, 1913. TLG 2018.005.

———. "Historia ecclesiastica." In *Eusèbe de Césarée. Histoire ecclésiastique*. 3 vols. Edited by Gustave Bardy. SC 31, 41 and 55, pp. 1:3-215, 2:4-231, 3:3-120. Paris: Éditions du Cerf, 1952, 1955, 1958. TLG 2018.002.

———. "Praeparatio evangelica." In *Eusebius Werke, Band 8: Die Praeparatio evangelica*. Edited by K. Mras. GCS 43.1 and 43.2. Berlin: Akademie-Verlag, 1954-1956. TLG 2018.001.

Filastrius. "Diversarum hereseon liber." In *Chromatii Aquileiensis [et al.] opera*. Edited by F. Heylen. CCL 9, pp. 217-324. Turnhout, Belgium: Brepols, 1957. Cl. 0121.

Fulgentius of Ruspe. "Ad Euthymium de remissione peccatorum libri II." In *Opera*. Edited by John Fraipont. CCL 91A, pp. 649-707. Turnhout, Belgium: Brepols, 1968. Cl. 0821.

———. "Ad Monimum libri III." In *Opera*. Edited by John Fraipont. CCL 91, pp. 1-64. Turnhout, Belgium: Brepols, 1968. Cl. 0814.

———. "Contra Fabianum fragmenta." In *Opera*. Edited by John Fraipont. CCL 91A, pp. 763-866. Turnhout, Belgium: Brepols, 1968. Cl. 0824.

———. *Epistulae XVIII*. In *Opera*. Edited by John Fraipont. CCL 91, pp. 189-280, 311-12, 359-44; and CCL 91A, pp. 447-57, 551-629. Turnhout, Belgium: Brepols, 1968. Cl. 0817.

———. "Liber ad Victorem contra sermonem Fastidiosi Ariani." In *Opera*. Edited by John Fraipont. CCL 91, pp. 283-308. Turnhout, Belgium: Brepols, 1968. Cl. 0820.

Gregory of Elvira. "Tractatus Origenis de libris Sanctarum Scripturarum." In *Gregorius opera*. Edited by Vincent Bulhart. CCL 69, pp. 5-146. Turnhout, Belgium: Brepols, 1967. Cl. 0546.

Gregory of Nazianzus. "Apologetica (orat. 2)." In *Opera omnia*. PG 35, cols. 408-513. Edited by J.-P. Migne. Paris: Migne, 1857. TLG 2022.016.

———. "De filio (orat. 29)." In *Gregor von Nazianz. Die fünf theologischen Reden*, pp. 128-68. Edited by Joseph Barbel. Düsseldorf, Germany: Patmos-Verlag, 1963. TLG 2022.009.

———. "De filio (orat. 30)." In *Gregor von Nazianz. Die fünf theologischen Reden*, pp. 170-216. Edited by Joseph Barbel. Düsseldorf, Germany: Patmos-Verlag, 1963. TLG 2022.010.

———. "De spiritu sancto (orat. 31)." In *Gregor von Nazianz. Die fünf theologischen Reden*, pp. 218-76. Edited by Joseph Barbel. Düsseldorf, Germany: Patmos-Verlag, 1963. TLG 2022.011.

———. "Epistulae theologicae." In *Grégoire de Nazianze: Lettres théologiques*. Edited by P. Gallay. SC 208, pp. 36-94. Paris: Éditions du Cerf, 1974. TLG 2022.002.

———. "Funebris oratio in patrem (orat. 18)." In *Opera omnia*. PG 35, cols. 985-1044. Edited by J.-P. Migne. Paris: Migne, 1857. TLG 2022.031.

———. "In patrem tacentem (orat. 16)." In *Opera omnia*. PG 35, cols. 933-64. Edited by J.-P. Migne. Paris: Migne, 1857. TLG 2022.029.

———. "In sanctum baptisma (orat. 40)." In *Opera omnia*. PG 36, cols. 360-425. Edited by J.-P. Migne. Paris: Migne, 1858. TLG 2022.048.

———. "In sanctum pascha (orat. 45)." In *Opera omnia*. PG 36, cols. 624-64. Edited by J.-P. Migne. Paris: Migne, 1858. TLG 2022.052.

———. "Supremum vale (orat. 42)." In *Opera omnia*. PG 36, cols. 457-92. Edited by J.-P. Migne. Paris: Migne, 1858. TLG 2022.050.

Gregory of Nyssa. "De virginitate." In *Grégoire de Nysse. Traité de la virginité*. Edited by Michel Aubineau. SC 119, pp. 246-560. Paris: Éditions du Cerf, 1966. TLG 2017.043.

————. "Contra Eunomium." In *Gregorii Nysseni opera*. 2 vols. Vol. 1.1, pp. 3-409; vol. 2.2, pp. 3-311. Edited by Werner William Jaeger. Leiden: Brill, 1960. TLG 2017.030.

————. "De vita Mosis." In *Grégoire de Nysse. La vie de Moïse*. Edited by J. Danielou. 3rd ed. SC 1, pp. 44-326. Paris: Éditions du Cerf, 1968. TLG 2017.042.

————. "Refutatio confessionis Eunomii." In *Gregorii Nysseni opera*. Vol. 2.2, pp. 312-410. Edited by W. Jaeger. Leiden: Brill, 1960. TLG 2017.031.

Gregory Thaumaturgus. "De fide capitula duodecim." In *Excavations at Nessana, vol. 2: Literary Papyri*, pp. 155-58. Edited by L. Casson and E.L. Hettich. Princeton, N.J.: Princeton University Press, 1950.

Gregory the Great. "Dialogorum libri iv." In *Dialogues*. Edited by Paul Antin and Adalbert de Vogüé. SC 251, 260, 265. Paris: Éditions du Cerf, 1978-1980. Cl. 1713.

————. *In librum primum Regum expositionum libri vi (Dub.)* Cl. 1719.

————. *Moralia in Job*. Edited by Mark Adriaen. CCL 143, 143A and 143B. Turnhout, Belgium: Brepols, 1979-1985. Cl. 1708.

————. *Registrum epistularum*. 2 vols. Edited by Dag Norberg. CCL 140 and 140A. Turnhout, Belgium: Brepols, 1982. Cl. 1714.

————. *Regula pastoralis*. Edited by Floribert Rommel and R. W. Clement. CCL 141. Turnhout, Belgium: Brepols, 1953. Cl. 1712.

Hilary of Poitiers. *De trinitate*. Edited by Pieter F. Smulders. CCL 62 and 62A. Turnhout, Belgium: Brepols, 1979-1980. Cl. 0433.

Hippolytus. "De antichristo." In *Hippolyt's kleinere exegestische und homiletische Schriften*. Edited by H. Achelis. GCS 1.2, pp. 1-47. Leipzig: Hinrichs, 1897. TLG 2115.003.

————. "Fragmenta in Psalmos (Sp.)." In *Hippolyt's kleinere exegestische und homiletische Schriften*. Edited by H. Achelis. GCS 1.2, pp. 131-53. Leipzig: Hinrichs, 1897. TLG 2115.012.

————. "Refutatio omnium haeresium." In *Hipplytus: Refutatio omnium haeresium*. Edited by M. Marcovich. Patristische Texte und Studien 25, pp. 53-417. Berlin: de Gruyter, 1986. TLG 2115.060.

Irenaeus. "Adversus haereses, livres 1-5." In *Contre les hérésies*. Edited by Adelin Rousseau, Louis Doutreleau and Charles A. Mercier. SC 34, 100, 152, 153, 210, 211, 263, 264, 293 and 294. Paris: Éditions du Cerf, 1952-82. Cl. 1154 f.

Isaac of Nineveh. "De perfectione religiosa." In *Mar Isaacus Ninivita: De perfectione religiosa*, pp. 1-99. Edited by Paul Bedjan. Paris, 1966.

Isho'dad of Merv. "Commentarii in Isaiam." In *Commentaire d' Isho'dad de Merv sur l'Ancien Testament, IV. Isaïe et les Douze*. Edited by C. Van Den Eynde. CSCO 303 (Scriptores Syri 128). Louvain: Secrétariat du Corpus, 1969.

Isidore of Seville. "Sententiarum libri tres.î In *Opera omnia*. PL 83, cols. 537-738. Edited by J.-P. Migne. Paris: Migne, 1862. Cl. 1199.

Jerome. "Adversus Jovinianum." In *Opera omnia*. PL 23, cols. 211-338. Edited by J.-P. Migne. Paris: Migne, 1865. Cl. 0610.

————. *Commentarii in Isaiam*. Edited by Mark Adriaen. CCL 73 and 73A. Turnhout, Belgium: Brepols, 1963. Cl. 0584.

————. *Commentarii in prophetas minores*. Edited by Mark Adriaen. CCL 76 and 76A. Turnhout, Belgium: Brepols, 1969-1970. Cl. 0589.

————. *Dialogus adversus Pelagianos*. Edited by Claudio Moreschini. CCL 80. Turnhout, Belgium: Brepols, 1990. Cl. 0615.

————. *Contra Johannem Hierosolymitanum*. PL 23, cols. 371-412. Edited by J.-P. Migne. Paris: Migne, 1845. Cl. 0612.

————. *Epistulae*. Edited by I. Hilberg. CSEL 54, 55 and 56. Vienna, Austria: F. Tempsky; Leipzig, Germany: G. Freytag, 1910-1918. Cl. 0620.

————."Homilia in Johannem evangelistam (1:1-14)." In *Opera, Part 2*. Edited by Germain Morin. CCL 78, pp. 517-23. Turnhout, Belgium: Brepols, 1958. Cl. 0597.

————. "Tractatus in Marci evangelium." In *Opera*. Edited by Germain Morin. CCL 78, pp. 449-500. Turnhout, Belgium: Brepols, 1958. Cl. 0594.

————. "Tractatus lix in psalmos." In *S. Hieronymi Presbyteri opera*. Edited by Germain Morin. CCL 78, pp. 3-352. Turnhout, Belgium: Brepols, 1958. Cl. 0592.

————. "Tractatuum in psalmos series altera." In *S. Hieronymi Presbyteri opera*. Edited by Germain Morin. CCL 78, pp. 355-446. Turnhout, Belgium: Brepols, 1958. Cl. 0593.

John Chrysostom. "Ad populam Antiochenum homiliae (de statuis)." In *Opera omnia*. PG 49, cols. 15-222. Edited by J.-P. Migne. Paris: Migne, 1862. TLG 2062.024.

————. "Ad Theodorum lapsum (lib. 1)." In *Jean Chrysostome: A Théodore*. Edited by J. Dumortier. SC 117, pp. 80-218. Paris: Éditions du Cerf, 1966. TLG 2062.002.

————. "Catechesis de juramento." In *Varia Graeca sacra*, pp. 154-66. Edited by A. Papadopoulos-Kerameus. St. Petersburg: Kirschbaum, 1909. Reprint. Leipzig: Zentralantiquariat der DDR, 1975. TLG 2062.380.

————. "Contra Anomoeos (homilia 11): De incomprehensibili dei natura. In *Opera omnia*. PG 48, cols. 795-802. Edited by J.-P. Migne. Paris: Migne, 1862. TLG 2062.012.

————. "Contra Judaeos et Gentiles, Quod Christus sit Deus." In *Opera omnia*. PG 48, cols. 811-38. Edited by J.-P. Migne. Paris: Migne, 1862. TLG 2062.372.

————. "De diabolo tentatore." In *Opera omnia*. PG 49, cols. 241-76. Edited by J.-P. Migne. Paris: Migne, 1862. TLG 2062.026.

————. "De paenitentia (homiliae 1-9)." In *Opera omnia*. PG 49, cols. 277-348. Edited by J.-P. Migne. Paris: Migne, 1862. TLG 2062.027.

————. "Epistulae ad Olympiadem." In *Jean Chrysostome: Lettres à Olympias*. 2nd ed. Edited by A.-M. Malingrey. SC 13. Paris: Éditions du Cerf, 1968. TLG 2062.088.

————. "In epistulam ad Galatas commentarius." In *Opera omnia*. PG 61, cols. 611-82. Edited by J.-P. Migne. Paris: Migne, 1862. TLG 2062.158.

————. "In epistulam ad Ephesios." In *Opera omnia*. PG 62, cols. 9-176. Edited by J.-P. Migne. Paris: Migne, 1862. TLG 2062.159.

————."In epistulam ad Hebraeos (homilae 1-34)." In *Opera omnia*. PG 63, cols. 9-236. Edited by J.-P. Migne. Paris: Migne, 1862. TLG 2062.168.

————."In epistulam ii ad Corinthios (homiliae 1-30)." In *Opera omnia*. PG 61, cols. 381-610. Edited by J.-P. Migne. Paris: Migne, 1862. TLG 2062.157.

————. "In Genesim (homiliae 1-67)." In *Opera omnia*. PG 53 and 54, cols. 385-580. Edited by J.-P. Migne. Paris: Migne, 1859-1862. TLG 2062.112.

————."In illud Isaiae: Ego dominus dues feci lumen." In *Opera omnia*. PG 56, cols. 141-52. Edited by J.-P. Migne. Paris: Migne, 1862. TLG 2062.148.

————."In Joannem (homiliae 1-88)." In *Opera omnia*. PG 59, cols. 23-482. Edited by J.-P. Migne. Paris: Migne, 1862. TLG 2062.153.

————. "In Matthaeum (homiliae 1-90)." In *Opera omnia*. PG 57, 58. Edited by J.-P. Migne. Paris: Migne, 1862. TLG 2062.152.

John of Damascus. "Canon paschalis." In *Chronologie des Mittelalters und der Neuzeit*, pp. 168-69. Edited by F. Rühl. Berline: Reuther and Reichard, 1897.

————."Canon paschalis." In *Pentekostarion*. Orthodox Eastern Church. Athens: Ekdosis ts Apostoliks Diakonias ts Ekklsias ts Hellados, 1959.

————."Expositio fidei." In *Die Schriften des Johannes von Damaskos*, 2:3-239. Edited by Bonifatius Kotter. Patistische Texte und Studien 12. Berlin: de Gruyter, 1973. TLG 2934.004.

Justin Martyr. "Apologia." In *Die ältesten Apologeten*, pp. 26-77. Edited by E. J. Goodspeed. Göttingen, Germany: Vandenhoeck & Ruprecht, 1915. TLG 0645.001.

————."Dialogus cum Tryphone." In *Die ältesten Apologeten*, pp. 90-265. Edited by E.J. Goodspeed. Göttingen, Germany: Vandenhoeck & Ruprecht, 1915. TLG 0645.003.

Lactantius. "Divinae Institutiones." In *L. Caeli Firmiani Lactanti Opera omnia*. Edited by Samuel Brandt. CSEL 19, pp. 1-672. Vienna, Austria: F. Tempsky; Leipzig, Germany: G. Freytag, 1890. Cl. 0085.

Leander of Seville. "Homilia in laudem ecclesiae." In *Pelagii II, Joannis III, Benedicti I summorum pontificum opera omnia*. PL 72, cols. 893-98. Edited by J.-P. Migne. Paris: Migne, 1849.

Leo the Great. *Tractatus septem et nonaginta*. Edited by Antonio Chavasse. CCL 138 and 138A. Turnhout, Belgium: Brepols, 1973. Cl. 1657.

Macarius of Egypt. "First Syriac Epistle." In *Die syrische Überlieferung der Schriften des Makarios*, 1:132-52. Edited by Werner Strothmann. Göttinger Oreintforschungen. I. Rehihe, Syriaca 22. Wiesbaden: Harrassowitz, 1981.

Marius Victorinus. "Adversus Arium." In *Marii Victorini Opera*. Edited by Paul Henry and Pierre Hadot. CSEL 83.1, pp. 54-277. Vienna, Austria: Hoelder-Pichler-Tempsky, 1971. Cl. 0095.

————."De homoousio recipiendo." In *Marii Victorini Opera*. Edited by Paul Henry and Pierre Hadot. CSEL 83.1, pp. 278-84. Vienna, Austria: Hoelder-Pichler-Tempsky, 1971. Cl. 0097.

Maximus of Turin. *Collectio sermonum antiqua*. Edited by A. Mutzenbecher. CCL 23. Turnhout, Belgium: Brepols, 1962. Cl. 0219a.

Melito of Sardis. "De Pascha." In *Sur la pâque: et fragments*. Edited by Othmar Perler. SC 123, pp. 60-127. Paris: Éditions du Cerf, 1966. TLG 1495.001.

Methodius. "De Resurrectione." In *Methodius*. Edited by G. Nathanael Bonwetsch. GCS 27, pp. 226-420 passim. Leipzig: Hinrichs, 1917. TLG 2959.003.

————. *Sermo de Symeone et Anna (Sp.)*. In *Opera omnia*. PG 18, cols. 348-81. Edited by J.-P. Migne. Paris: Migne, 1857. TLG 2959.012.

————."Symposium *sive* Convivium decem virginum." In *Opera omnia*. PG 18, cols. 27-220. Edited by J.-P. Migne. Paris: Migne, 1857. TLG 2959.001.

Nemesius of Emesa. "De natura hominis.î In *Nemesius of Emesa* (typescript), pp. 35-368. Edited by B. Einarson. Corpus medicorum Graecorum (in press). Berlin. TLG 0743.001.

Novatian. "De Trinitate." In *Opera*. Edited by Gerardus Frederik Diercks. CCL 4, pp. 11-78. Turnhout, Belgium: Brepols, 1972. Cl. 0071.

Origen. "Commentarium in Canticum Canticorum." In *Origenes Werke*, vol. 8. Edited by William A. Baehrens. GCS 33, pp. 61-241. Leipzig: Teubner, 1925. Cl. 0198.

————."Commentaria in evangelium secundum Matthaeum." In *Opera omnia*. PG 13, cols. 829-1600. Edited by J.-P. Migne Paris: Migne, 1862. TLG 2042.029.

————. "Commentarii in evangelium Joannis (lib. 1, 2, 4, 5, 6, 10 and 13)." In *Origene. Commentaire sur saint Jean*, 3 vols. Edited by Cécil Blanc. SC 120, 157 and 222. Paris: Éditions du Cerf, 1966-1975. TLG 2042.005.

————. "Contra Celsum." In *Origène Contre Celse*. Edited by Marcel Borret. SC 132, 136, 147 and 150. Paris: Éditions du Cerf, 1967-1969. TLG 2042.001.

————."De engastrimytho." In *Origenes Werke*, vol. 3. Edited by Erich Klostermann. GCS 6, pp. 283-94. Leipzig: Teubner, 1901. TLG 2042.013.

————."De principiis." In *Origenes vier Bücher von den Prinzipien*, pp. 462-560, 668-764. Edited by Herwig Görgemanns and Heinrich Karpp. Darmstadt, Germany: Wissenschaftliche Buchgesellschaft,

1976. TLG 2042.002.

———. "Dialogus cum Heraclide." In *Entretien d'Origene avec Héraclide*. Edited by J. Scherer. SC 67, pp. 52-110. Paris: Éditions du Cerf, 1960. TLG 2042.018.

———. "Exhortatio ad martyrium." In *Origenes Werke*, vol. 1. Edited by Paul Koetschau. GCS 2, pp.3-47. Leipzig: Hinrichs, 1899. TLG 2042.007.

———. "Homiliae in Exodum." In *Origenes Werke*, vol. 6. Edited by Willem A. Baehrens. GCS 29, pp. 217-30. Leipzig: Hinrichs, 1920. Cl. 0198/TLG 2042.023.

———. "Homiliae in Genesim." In *Origène: Homélies sur la Genèse*. Edited by Henri de Lubac and Louis Doutreleau. 2nd ed. SC 7. Paris: Éditions du Cerf, 2003. Cl. 0198/TLG 2042.022.

———. "Homiliae in Leviticum." In *Origenes Werke*, vol. 6. Edited by Willem A. Baehrens. GCS 29, pp. 332-34, 395, 402-7, 409-16 Leipzig: Teubner, 1920. TLG 2042.024.

———.Migne, 1862. TLG 2042.016.

———. "In Jeremiam (homiliae 1-11)." In *Origenes Werke*, vol. 8. Edited by William A. Baehrens. GCS 33, pp. 290-317. Leipzig: Tuebner, 1925. TLG 2042.009.

Pachomius. "Catechesis." In *Oeuvres de s. Pachôme et de ses disciples*. Edited by L.-Th. Lefort. CSCO 159 (Scriptores Coptica 23-24), pp. 1-26. Louvain: Imprimerie Orientaliste, 1956.

Procopius of Gaza. "Catena in Isaiam." In *Opera omnia*. PG 87.2, cols. 1817-2717. Edited by J.-P. Migne. Paris: Migne, 1860. TLG 2598.004.

Prudentius. "Contra Summachum." In Aurelius Prudentius Clemens. Edited by Maurice P. Cunningham. CCL 126, pp. 182-250. Turnhout, Belgium: Brepols, 1966. Cl. 1442.

Pseudo-Clement of Rome. "Recognitiones." In *Rekognitionen*. Edited by Bernhard Rehm. GCS 51, pp. 6-371. Berlin: Akademie-Verlag, 1965. Cl. 0198 N (A).

———. "Epistula ii ad Corinthios." In *Die apostolischen Väter*, pp. 71-81. 3rd ed. Edited by Karl Bihlmeyer and Wilhelm Schneemelcher. Tubingen: Mohr, 1970. TLG 1271.002.

Pseudo-Dionysius. "De ecclesiastica hierarchia." In *Corpus Dionysiacum ii: Pseud-Dionysius Areopagita*. Edited by G. Heil and A.M. Ritter. Patristische Texte und Studien 36, pp. 63-132. Berlin: de Gruyter, 1991. TLG 2798.002.

———. "Epistulae." In *Corpus Dionysiacum ii: Pseud-Dionysius Areopagita*. Edited by G. Heil and A.M. Ritter. Patristische Texte und Studien 36, pp. 155-210. TLG 2798.006.

Rufinus of Aquileia. "Expositio symboli." In *Opera*. Edited by Manlio Simonetti. CCL 20, pp. 125-82. Turnhout, Belgium: Brepols, 1961. Cl. 0196.

Symeon the New Theologian. "Catecheses." In *Catéchèses: 23-24*. Edited by Basile Krivochéine. SC 113. Paris: Éditions du Cerf, 1965.

Tertullian. "Adversus Hermogenem." In *Opera*. Edited by E. Kroymann. CCL 1, pp. 397-435. Turnhout, Belgium: Brepols, 1954. Cl. 0013.

———. "Adversus Judaeos." In *Opera*. Edited by E. Kroymann. CCL 2, pp. 1339-96. Turnhout, Belgium: Brepols, 1954. Cl. 0033.

———. "Adversus Marcionem." In *Opera*. Edited by E. Kroymann. CCL 1, pp. 437-726. Turnhout, Belgium: Brepols, 1954. Cl. 0014.

———. "Adversus Praxean." In *Opera*. Edited by E. Kroymann and E. Evans. CCL 2, pp. 1159-205. Turnhout, Belgium: Brepols, 1954. Cl. 0026.

———. "De anima." In *Opera*. Edited by E. Kroymann and E. Evans. CCL 2, pp. 781-869. Turnhout, Belgium: Brepols, 1954. Cl. 0017.

———. "De idololatria" In *Opera*, vol. 2. Edited by August Reifferscheid and George Wissowa. CCL 2, pp. 1101-24. Turnhout, Belgium: Brepols, 1954. Cl. 0023.

———. "De resurrectione mortuorum." In *Opera*. Edited by J.G. Ph. Borleffs. CCL 2, pp. 919-1012.

Turnhout, Belgium: Brepols, 1954. Cl. 0019.

Theodore of Heraclea. "Fragmenta in Isaiam." In *Methodii Opera omnia*. PG 18, cols. 1307-78. Edited by J.-P. Migne. PG 57 and 58. Paris: Migne, 1857.

Theodoret of Cyr. *Commentaria in Isaiam*. In *Théodoret de Cyr: Commentaire sur Isaïe*. Edited by J.-N. Guinot. SC 276, 295 and 315. Paris: Éditions du Cerf, 1980-1984. TLG 4089.008.

———. "De providentia orationes decem." In *Opera omnia*. PG 83, cols. 555-774. Edited by J.-P. Migne. Paris: Migne, 1859. TLG 4089.032.

———. "Eranistes." Pages 61-266 In *Theodoret of Cyrus: Eranistes*. Edited by Gérard H. Ettlinger. Oxford: Clarendon Press, 1975. TLG 4089.002.

———. "Epistulae: Collectio Sirmondiana (1-95)." In *Théodoret de Cyr: Correspondance II*. SC 98, pp. 20-248. Edited by Y. Azema. Paris: Éditions du Cerf, 1964. TLG 4089.006.

Bibliography of Works in English Translation

Alexander of Alexandria. "Epistles on the Arian Heresy." In *Gregory Thaumaturgus, Dionysius the Great, Julius Africanus, Anatolius and Minor Writers, Methodius, Arnobius.* Edited by James Donaldson. ANF 6. Edited by Alexander Roberts and James Donaldson. 10 vols. 1885-1887. Reprint, Peabody, Mass.: Hendrickson, 1994.

Ambrose. *Funeral Orations by Saint Gregory Nazianzen and Saint Ambrose.* Translated by Leo P. McCauley et al. FC 22. Washington, D.C.: The Catholic University of America Press, 1953.

———. *Letters.* Translated by Mary Melchior Beyenka. FC 26. Washington, D.C.: The Catholic University of America Press, 1954.

———. *Select Works and Letters.* Translated by H. De Romestin. NPNF 10. Series 2. Edited by Philip Schaff and Henry Wace. 14 vols. 1886-1900. Reprint, Peabody, Mass.: Hendrickson, 1994.

———. *Seven Exegetical Works.* Translated by Michael P. McHugh. FC 65. Washington, D.C.: The Catholic University of America Press, 1972.

———. "Six Days of Creation." In *Hexameron, Paradise, and Cain and Abel*, pp. 3-283. Translated by John J. Savage. FC 42. Washington, D.C.: The Catholic University of America Press, 1961.

———. *On Virginity.* Translated by Daniel Callam. Toronto: Peregrina Publishing Co., 1996.

Aphrahat. "Select Demonstrations." In *Gregory the Great, Ephraim Syrus, Aphrahat*, pp. 345-412. Translated by James Barmby. NPNF 13. Series 2. Edited by Philip Schaff and Henry Wace. 14 vols. 1886-1900. Reprint, Peabody, Mass.: Hendrickson, 1994.

Athanasius. "Life of St. Anthony." In *Early Christian Biographies*, pp. 133-216. Translated by Mary Emily Keenan. FC 15. Washington, D.C.: The Catholic University of America Press, 1952.

———. *Selected Works and Letters.* Translated by Archibald Robertson. NPNF 4. Series 2. Edited by Philip Schaff and Henry Wace. 14 vols. 1886-1900. Reprint, Peabody, Mass.: Hendrickson, 1994.

Augustine. *Against Julian.* Translated by Matthew A. Schumacher. FC 35. Washington, D.C.: The Catholic University of America Press, 1957.

———. *City of God: Books XVII-XXII.* Translated by Gerald G. Walsh and Daniel J. Honan. FC 24. Washington, D.C.: The Catholic University of America Press, 1954.

———. *Confessions.* Translated by Henry Chadwick. New York: Oxford University Press, 1991.

———. *Confessions and Enchiridion.* Translated by Albert C. Outler. LCC 7. London: SCM Press, 1955.

———. "Confessions." In *The Confessions and Letters of Augustin, with a Sketch of His Life and Work*, pp. 27-207. Translated by J. G. Pilkington. NPNF 1. Series 1. Edited by Philip Schaff. 14 vols. 1886-1889. Reprint, Peabody, Mass.: Hendrickson, 1994.

———. *Expositions on the Book of Psalms.* Edited from the Oxford translation by A. Cleveland Coxe. NPNF 8. Series 1. Edited by Philip Schaff. 14 vols. 1886-1889. Reprint, Peabody, Mass.: Hendrickson, 1994.

———. *Letters.* Vols. 2, 4 and 5. Translated by Wilfred Parsons. FC 18, FC 30 and FC 32. Washington, D.C.: The Catholic University of America Press, 1953-1956.

———. "On Original Sin." in *Anti-Pelagian Writings*, pp. 237-55. Translated by Peter Holmes and Robert Ernest Wallis. NPNF 5. Series 1. Edited by Philip Schaff. 14 vols. 1886-1889. Reprint, Peabody,

Mass.: Hendrickson, 1994.

————. *The Trinity*. Translated by Stephen McKenna. FC 45. Washington, D.C.: The Catholic University of America, 1963.

————. "Predestination of the Saints." In *Four Anti-Pelagian Writings: On Nature and Grace, On the Preceedings of Pelagius, On the Predestination of the Saints, On the Gift of Perseverance*, pp. 218-70. Translated by John A. Mourant and William J. Collinge. FC 86. Washington, D.C.: The Catholic University of America Press, 1992.

————. *Saint Augustine*. Translated by John Courtney Murray. FC 2. Washington, D.C.: The Catholic University of America Press, 1947.

————. *Sermons*. Translated by Edmund Hill. WSA 1-11. Part 3. Edited by John E. Rotelle. New York: New City Press, 1990-1997.

————. *The Catholic and Manichaean Ways of Life*. Translated by Donald A. Gallagher and Idella J. Gallagher. FC 56. Washington, D.C.: The Catholic University of America Press, 1966.

————. *Tractates on the Gospel of John, 1-111*. Translated by John W. Rettig. FC 78, 79, 88 and 90. Washington, D.C.: The Catholic University of America Press, 1988-1994.

Basil the Great. *Exegetic Homilies*. Translated by Agnes Clare Way. FC 46. Washington, D.C.: The Catholic University of America Press, 1963.

————. "Homily Against Those Who Are Prone to Danger." In *Ascetical Works*, pp. 447-61. Translated by M. Monica Wagner. FC 9. New York: Fathers of the Church, Inc., 1950.

————. *Letters and Select Works*. Translated by Blomfield Jackson. NPNF 8. Series 2. Edited by Philip Schaff. 14 vols. 1886-1889. Reprint, Peabody, Mass.: Hendrickson, 1994.

————. *Letters: Volume 2*. Translated by Agnes Clare Way, with notes by Roy J. Deferrari. FC 28. Washington, D.C.: The Catholic University of America Press, 1955.

————. *On the Holy Spirit*. Translated by D. Anderson, Crestwood, N.Y.: St. Vladimir's Seminary Press, 1980.

Bede. *Homilies on the Gospels*. Translated by Lawrence T. Martin and David Hurst. 2 vols. CS 110 and 111. Kalamazoo, Mich.: Cistercian Publications, 1991.

Benedict. "Rule of St. Benedict." In *Western Asceticism*, pp. 290-37. Edited and translated by Owen Chadwick. LCC 12. Philadelphia: Westminster Press, 1958.

Caesarius of Arles. *Sermons*. 3 vols. Translated by Mary Magdeleine Mueller. FC 31, 47 and 66. Washington, D.C.: The Catholic University of America Press, 1956-64.

Cassian, John. *The Conferences*. Translated and annotated by Boniface Ramsey. ACW 57. New York: Paulist Press, 1997.

————. *The Institutes*. Translated by Boniface Ramsey. ACW 58. New York: Newman Press, 2000.

————. *The Works of Sulpicius Severus, Vincent of Lerins, John Cassian*. Translated by Edgar C. S. Gibson. NPNF 11. Series 2. Edited by Philip Schaff and Henry Wace. 14 vols. 1886-1900. Reprint, Peabody, Mass.: Hendrickson, 1994.

Cassiodorus. *Explanation of the Psalms*. 3 vols. Translated by P. G. Walsh. ACW 51, 52 and 53. New York: Paulist Press, 1990-1991.

Clement of Alexandria. *Christ the Educator*. Translated by Simon P. Wood. FC 23. Washington, D.C.: The Catholic University of America Press, 1954.

————. "Clement of Alexandria." In *Fathers of the Second Century*. 10 vols. Edited by A. Cleveland Coxe, Alexander Roberts and James Donaldson. 1885-1887. Reprint, Peabody, Mass.: Hendrickson, 1994.

————. *Stromateis: Books 1-3*. Translated by John Ferguson. FC 85. Washington, D.C.: The Catholic University of America Press, 1991.

Clement of Rome. "Clement's First Letter." In *Early Christian Fathers*, pp. 43-73. Translated by Cyril C.

Richardson. LCC 1. Philadelphia: Westminster Press, 1953.

———. "1 Clement." See "The Letter to the Corinthians." In *The Apostolic Fathers*, pp. 1-64. Translated by Francis X. Grimm. FC 1. Washington, D.C.: The Catholic University of America Press, 1947.

"Constitutions of the Holy Apostles." In *Lactantius, Venantius, Asterius, Victorinus, Dionysius, Apostolic Teaching and Constitutions, 2 Clement, Early Liturgies*, pp. 385-508. Edited by James Donaldson. ANF 7. Edited by Alexander Roberts and James Donaldson. 10 vols. 1885-1887. Reprint, Peabody, Mass.: Hendrickson, 1994.

Cyprian. *Hippolytus, Cyprian, Caius, Novatian*, pp. 267-596. Translated by Ernest Wallis. ANF 5. Edited by Alexander Roberts and James Donaldson. 10 vols. 1885-1887. Reprint, Peabody, Mass.: Hendrickson, 1994.

———. *Letters 1-81*. Translated by Rose Bernard Donna. FC 51. Washington, D.C.: The Catholic University of America Press, 1964.

———. *Treatises*. Translated by Roy J. Deferrari. FC 36. Washington, D.C.: The Catholic University of America Press, 1958.

Cyril of Alexandria. "Commentary on Isaiah." In *Cyril of Alexandria*, passim. Translated by Norman Russell. The Early Church Fathers. London: Routledge, 2000.

———. "Commentary on Isaiah." In *St. Cyril of Alexandria: Interpreter of the Old Testament*, passim, by Alexander Kerrigan. AnBib 2. Rome: Pontifical Biblical Institute, 1952.

———. *Letters: 1-50*. Translated by John I. McEnerney. FC 76. Washington, D.C.: The Catholic University of America Press, 1987.

———. *On the Unity of Christ*. Translated by John A. McGuckin. Crestwood, N.Y.: St. Vladimir's Seminary Press, 2000.

Cyril of Jerusalem. "Catechetical Lectures." In *Cyril of Jerusalem and Nemesius of Emesa*, pp. 64-192. Translated by William Telfer. LCC 4. Philadelphia: Westminster Press, 1955.

———. "Catechetical Lectures." In *The Works of Saint Cyril of Jerusalem*. Translated by Leo P. McCauley. FC 61. Washington, D.C.: The Catholic University of America Press, 1969.

———. "Mystagogical Lectures." In *The Works of Saint Cyril of Jerusalem*. Translated by Leo P. McCauley and Anthony A. Stephenson. FC 64. 2:153-203. Washington, D.C.: The Catholic University of America Press, 1970.

———. *S. Cyril of Jerusalem, S. Gregory Nazianzen*. Translated by Edward Hamilton Gifford et al. NPNF 7. Series 2. Edited by Philip Schaff and Henry Wace. 14 vols. 1886-1900. Reprint, Peabody, Mass.: Hendrickson, 1994.

Didache. In *AF*, pp. 251-69. Translated by J. B. Lightfoot and J. R. Harmer. Edited by M. W. Holmes. 2nd ed. Grand Rapids, Mich.: Baker, 1989.

Ephrem the Syrian. "Commentary on Isaiah." In *St. Cyril of Alexandria: Interpreter of the Old Testament*, passim, by Alexander Kerrigan. AnBib 2. Rome: Pontifical Biblical Institute, 1952.

———. "Hymns on the Nativity." In *Gregory the Great, Ephraim Syrus, Aphrahat*, pp. 223-62. Translated by J. B. Morris. NPNF 13. Series 2. Edited by Philip Schaff and Henry Wace. 14 vols. 1886-1900. Reprint, Peabody, Mass.: Hendrickson, 1994.

———. "Letter to Publius." In *St. Ephrem the Syrian: Selected Prose Works*, pp. 333-55. Translated by Edward G. Mathews Jr. and Joseph P. Amar. FC 91. Washington, D.C.: The Catholic University of America Press, 1994.

Epistle of Barnabas. In *The Apostolic Fathers*, pp. 133-56. 2nd edition. Translated by J. B. Lightfoot and J. R. Harmer. Edited by M. W. Holmes. Grand Rapids, Mich.: Baker, 1989.

Eusebius of Caesarea. "Commentary on Isaiah." In *St. Cyril of Alexandria: Interpreter of the Old Testament*, passim, by Alexander Kerrigan. AnBib 2. Rome: Pontifical Biblical Institute, 1952.

———. *Ecclesiastical History: Books 1-10.* 2 vols. Translated by Roy J. Deferrari. FC 19 and 29. Washington D.C.: The Catholic University of America Press, 1953-1955.

———. *Proof of the Gospel.* 2 vols. Translated by W. J. Ferrar. London: SPCK, 1920. Reprint, Grand Rapids, Mich.: Baker, 1981.

Fulgentius of Ruspe. *Selected Works.* Translated by Robert B. Eno. FC 95. Washington D.C.: The Catholic University of America Press, 1997.

Gregory of Nazianzus. *Cyril of Jerusalem, Gregory Nazianzen.* Translated by Charles Gordon Browne, Edwin Hamilton Gifford and James Edward Swallow. NPNF 7. Series 2. Edited by Philip Schaff and Henry Wace. 14 vols. 1886-1900. Reprint, Peabody, Mass.: Hendrickson, 1994.

———. *Faith Gives Fullness to Reasoning: The Five Theological Orations of Gregory Nazianzen.* Introduction and commentary by F. W. Norris. Leiden and New York: E. J. Brill, 1990.

Gregory of Nyssa. *The Life of Moses.* Translated by A. J. Malherbe and E. Ferguson. The Classics of Western Spirituality. New York: Paulist Press, 1978.

———. *Select Writings and Letters of Gregory, Bishop of Nyssa*, pp. 33-248. Translated by William Moore and Henry Austin Wilson. NPNF 5. Series 2. Edited by Philip Schaff and Henry Wace. 14 vols. 1886-1900. Reprint, Peabody, Mass.: Hendrickson, 1994.

Gregory Thaumaturgus. "Twelve Topics on the Faith." In *Gregory Thaumaturgus, Dionysius the Great, Julius Africanus, Anatolius and Minor Writers, Methodius, Arnobius*, pp. 50-53. Arranged by A. Cleveland Coxe. ANF 6. Edited by Alexander Roberts and James Donaldson. 10 vols. 1885-1887. Reprint, Peabody, Mass.: Hendrickson, 1994.

Gregory the Great. *Dialogues.* Translated by John Zimmerman. FC 39. Washington D.C.: The Catholic University of America Press, 1959.

———. *Leo the Great, Gregory the Great.* Translated by Charles Lett Feltoe. NPNF 12. Series 2. Edited by Philip Schaff and Henry Wace. 14 vols. 1886-1900. Reprint, Peabody, Mass.: Hendrickson, 1994.

Hilary of Poitiers. "On the Trinity." In *Hilary of Poitiers, John of Damascus*, pp. 40-233. Translated by E. W. Wastson et al. NPNF 9. Series 2. Edited by Philip Schaff and Henry Wace. 14 vols. 1886-1900. Reprint, Peabody, Mass.: Hendrickson, 1994.

Hippolytus. *Hippolytus, Cyprian, Caius, Novatian, Appendix.* Arranged by A. Cleveland Coxe. ANF 5. Edited by Alexander Roberts and James Donaldson. 10 vols. 1885-1887. Reprint, Peabody, Mass.: Hendrickson, 1994.

Irenaeus. "Against Heresies." In *The Apostolic Fathers with Justin Martyr and Irenaeus*, pp. 309-567. Translated by A. Cleveland Coxe. ANF 1. Edited by Alexander Roberts and James Donaldson. 10 vols. 1885-1887. Reprint, Peabody, Mass.: Hendrickson, 1994.

Isaac of Nineveh. *The Ascetical Homilies of Saint Isaac the Syrian.* Boston, Mass.: Holy Transfiguration Monastery, 1984.

Jerome. *Homilies.* Translated by Sister Marie Liguori Ewald. FC 48 and 57. Washington, D.C.: The Catholic University of America Press, 1964-1966.

———. *Letters and Select Works.* Translated by W. H. Fremantle. NPNF 6. Series 2. Edited by Philip Schaff and Henry Wace. 14 vols. 1886-1900. Reprint, Peabody, Mass.: Hendrickson, 1994.

———. "The Dialogue Against the Pelagians." In *Dogmatic and Polemical Works*, pp. 221-378. Translated by John N. Hritzu. FC 53. Washington, D.C.: The Catholic University of America Press, 1965.

John Chrysostom. *Baptismal Instructions.* Translated by Paul W. Harkins. ACW 31. New York: Newman Press, 1963.

———. "Demonstrations Against the Pagans." In *Apologists*, pp. 187-262. Translated by Paul W. Harkins. FC 73. Washington, D.C.: The Catholic University of America Press, 1985.

———. *Homilies on Galatians, Ephesians, Philippians, Colossians, Thessalonians, Timothy, Titus and Philemon.*

Translated by Gross Alexander et al. NPNF 13. Series 1. Edited by Philip Schaff. 14 vols. 1886-1889. Reprint, Peabody, Mass.: Hendrickson, 1994.

———. "Homilies on Genesis." In *Homilies on Genesis and Exodus*, pp. 45-224. Translated by Ronald E. Heine. FC 74. Washington, D.C.: The Catholic University of America Press, 1982.

———. *Homilies on Genesis 18-45.* Translated by Robert C. Hill. FC 82. Washington, D.C.: The Catholic University of America Press, 1990.

———. "Homilies on Isaiah." COTH 2:20-113. Translated by Robert Charles Hill. Brookline, Mass.: Holy Cross Orthodox Press, 2003.

———. *On Repentance and Almsgiving.* Translated by Gus George Christo. FC 96. Washington, D.C.: The Catholic University of America Press, 1998.

———. *Homilies on 1 and 2 Corinthians.* Translated by Talbot W. Chambers. NPNF 12. Series 1. Edited by Philip Schaff. 14 vols. 1886-1889. Reprint, Peabody, Mass.: Hendrickson, 1994.

———. *Homilies on the Gospel of John.* Translated by Thomas Aquinas Goggin. FC 33. Washington, D.C.: The Catholic University of America Press, 1957.

———. *Homilies on the Gospel of Saint John and the Epistle to the Hebrews.* NPNF 14. Series 1. Edited by Philip Schaff. 14 vols. 1886-1889. Reprint, Peabody, Mass.: Hendrickson, 1994.

———. *Homilies on the Gospel of Saint Matthew.* Translated by George Prevost. Revised by M. B. Riddle. NPNF 10. Series 1. Edited by Philip Schaff. 14 vols. 1886-1889. Reprint, Peabody, Mass.: Hendrickson, 1994.

———. *On the Incomprehensible Nature of God.* Translated by Paul W. Harkins. FC 72. Washington, D.C.: The Catholic University of America Press, 1984.

———. *On the Priesthood, Ascetic Treatises, Select Homilies and Letters, Homilies on the Statues.* Translated by W. R. W. Stephens et al. NPNF 9. Series 1. Edited by Philip Schaff. 14 vols. 1886-1889. Reprint, Peabody, Mass.: Hendrickson, 1994.

John of Damascus. "An Exact Exposition of the Orthodox Faith." In *Writings*, pp. 165-406. Translated by Frederic H. Chase. FC 37. Washington, D.C.: The Catholic University of America Press, 1958.

———. "Orthodox Faith." In *Hilary of Poitiers, John of Damascus*, pp. 1-101 (part 2). Translated by S. D. F. Salmond. NPNF 9. Series 2. Edited by Philip Schaff and Henry Wace. 14 vols. 1886-1900. Reprint, Peabody, Mass.: Hendrickson, 1994.

———. "The Canon of Pascha." In *RWC*, passim. Edited by Hugh Wybrew. London: SPCK, 2001.

Justin Martyr. "Dialogue with Trypho." In *Writings of Saint Justin Martyr*, pp. 147-366. Translated by Thomas B. Falls. FC 6. New York: Christian Heritage, 1948.

———. "First Apology." In *Early Christian Fathers*, pp. 242-89. Translated by Edward Rochie Hardy. LCC 1. Philadelphia: Westminster Press, 1953.

———. *The Apostolic Fathers with Justin Martyr and Irenaeus.* Arranged by A. Cleveland Coxe. ANF 1. Edited by Alexander Roberts and James Donaldson. 10 vols. 1885-1887. Reprint, Peabody, Mass.: Hendrickson, 1994.

Lactantius. *The Divine Institutes: Books I-VII.* Translated by Sister Mary Francis McDonald. FC 49. Washington, D.C.: The Catholic University of America Press, 1964.

Leander of Seville. "Homilies on the Triumph of the Church." In *Iberian Fathers*, 1:229-35. Translated by Claude W. Barlow. FC 62. Washington, D.C.: The Catholic University of America Press, 1969.

Leo the Great. *Sermons.* Translated by Jane Freeland et al. FC 93. Washington, D.C.: The Catholic University of America Press, 1996.

———. "The Letters and Sermons of Leo the Great, Bishop of Rome." In *Leo the Great, Gregory the Great*, pp. 1-205. Translated by Charles Lett Feltoe. NPNF 12. Series 2. Edited by Philip Schaff and Henry Wace. 14 vols. 1886-1900. Reprint, Peabody, Mass.: Hendrickson, 1994.

Macarius of Egypt. "First Syriac Epistles." In *AHSIS*, pp. 451-59. Boston, Mass.: Holy Transfiguration Monastery, 1984.

Marius Victorinus. *Theological Treatises on the Trinity*. Translated by Mary T. Clark. FC 69. Washington, D.C.: The Catholic University of America Press, 1981.

Maximus of Turin. *The Sermons of St. Maximus of Turin*. Translated and annotated by Boniface Ramsey. ACW 50. Mahwah, N.J.: Paulist Press, 1989.

Melito of Sardis. *On Pascha: With the Fragments of Melito and Other Material Related to the Quartodecimans*. Translated by Alistair Stewart-Sykes. Crestwood, N.Y.: St. Vladimir's Seminary Press, 2001.

Methodius. "Extracts from the Work on Things Created." In *Gregory Thaumaturgus, Dionysius the Great, Julius Africanus, Anatolius and Minor Writers, Methodius, Arnobius*, pp. 379-81. Translated by William R. Clark. ANF 6. Edited by Alexander Roberts and James Donaldson. 10 vols. 1885-1887. Reprint, Peabody, Mass.: Hendrickson, 1994.

Nemesius of Emesa. "On the Nature of Man." In *Cyril of Jerusalem and Nemesius of Emesa*, pp. 224-453. Edited by William Telfer. LCC 4. Philadelphia: Westminster Press, 1955.

Novatian. "On the Trinity," in *Novatian: The Trinity, The Spectacles, Jewish Foods, In Praise of Purity, Letters*, pp. 23-111. Translated by Russel J. DeSimone. FC 67. Washington, D.C.: The Catholic University of America Press, 1974.

Origen. "Against Celsus." Vol. 2 in *The Writings of Origen*. Translated by Frederick Crombie. ANCL 23. Edinburgh, Scotland: T. and T. Clark, 1894.

———. "Commentary on Matthew." In *The Gospel of Peter, The Diatessaron of Tatian, The Apocalypse of Peter, The Vision of Paul, The Apocalypses o f the Virgin and Sedrach, The Testament of Abraham, The Acts of Xanthippe and Polyxena, The Narrative of Zosimus, The Apology of Aristides, The Epistles of Clement (Complete Text), Origen's Commentary on John, Bokks 1-10, and Commentary on Matthew, Books 1, 2, and 10-14*, pp. 409-512. Translated by John Patrick. ANF 9. Edited by Alexander Roberts and James Donaldson. 10 vols. 1885-1887. Reprint, Peabody, Mass.: Hendrickson, 1994.

———.. *Commentary on the Gospel of John*. Translated by Ronald Heine. FC 80 and 89. Washington, D.C.: The Catholic University of America Press, 1989-1993.

———. "Dialogue with Heraclides." In *Alexandrian Christianity*, pp. 437-55. Translated by John Ernest Leonard Oulton and Henry Chadwick. LCC 2. Philadelphia: Westminster Press, 1954.

———. "Exhortation to Martyrdom." In *Prayer; Exhortation to Martyrdom*, pp. 141-96. Translated by John J. O'Meara. ACW 19. Westminster, Md.: Newman Press, 1954.

———. *Homilies on Jeremiah, Homily on 1 Kings 28*. Translated by John Clark Smith. FC 97. Washington, D.C.: The Catholic University of America Press, 1998.

———. *Homilies on Genesis and Exodus*. Translated by Ronald E. Heine. FC 71. Washington, D.C.: The Catholic University of America Press, 1982.

———. *Homilies on Leviticus: 1-16*. Translated by Gary Wayne Barkley. FC 83. Washington, D.C.: The Catholic University of America Press, 1990.

———. "Homilies on the Gospel of Luke." In *Origen: Homilies on Luke, Fragments on Luke*, pp. 3-162. Translated by Joseph T. Lienhard. FC 94. Washington, D.C.: The Catholic University of America Press, 1996.

———. *On First Principles*. Translated by G. W. Butterworth. London: SPCK, 1936. Reprint, Gloucester, Mass.: Peter Smith, 1973.

———. *Origen: An Exhortation to Martyrdom, Prayer and Selected Writings*. Translated by Rowan A. Greer with preface by Hans Urs von Balthasar. The Classics of Western Spirituality. New York: Paulist Press, 1979.

———. *Tertullian (IV); Minucius Felix; Commodian; Origen (I and III)*. Translated by Frederick Combie. ANF 4. Edited by Alexander Roberts and James Donaldson. 10 vols. 1885-1887. Reprint, Peabody, Mass.: Hendrickson, 1994.

Pachomius. "Instructions." In *Pachomian Koinonia*. 3:13-49. Translated by Armand Veilleux. CS 47. Kalamazoo, Mich.: Cistercian Publications, 1982.

Prudentius. "Against Symmachus." In *The Poems of* Prudentius, 2:113-76. Translated by M. Clement Eagan. FC 52. Washington, D.C.: The Catholic University of America Press, 1965.

Pseudo-Clement of Rome. *2 Clement* in *AF*, pp. 43-52. Translated by J. B. Lightfoot and J. R. Harmer. Edited by M. W. Holmes. 2nd ed. Grand Rapid, Mich.: Baker Book House, 1989.

———. *2 Clement*. In *The Apostolic Fathers*, pp. 65-79. Translated by Francis X. Glimm. FC 1. Washington, D.C.: The Catholic University of America Press, 1947.

Pseudo-Dionysius. *Pseudo-Dionysius: The Complete Works*. Translated by Colm Luibheid. The Classics of Western Spirituality. New York: Paulist Press, 1987.

Rufinus of Aquileia. "Commentary on the Apostles' Creed." In *Theodoret, Jerome, Gennadius, Rufinus: Historical Writings, etc.*, pp. 541-63. Translated by William Henry Fremantle. NPNF 3. Series 2. Edited by Philip Schaff and Henry Wace. 14 vols. 1886-1900. Reprint, Peabody, Mass.: Hendrickson, 1994.

Symeon the New Theologian *The Discourses*. Translated by C. J. de Catanzaro. The Classics of Western Spirituality. New York: Paulist Press, 1980.

Tertullian. *Latin Christianity: Its Founder, Tertullian*. Arranged by A. Cleveland Coxe.

ANF 3. Edited by Alexander Roberts and James Donaldson. 10 vols. 1885-1887. Reprint, Peabody, Mass.: Hendrickson, 1994.

———. "On Idolatry." In *Early Latin Theology*, pp. 83-110. Translated by S. L. Greenslade. LCC 5. Philadelphia: Westminster Press, 1956.

———. *Tertullian: Adversus Marcionem*. 2 vols. Edited and translated by Ernest Evans. Oxford Early Christian Texts. Oxford: Clarendon Press, 1972.

Theodoret of Cyr. "Commentary on Isaiah." In *Isaiah Through the Ages*, passim. Compiled and edited by Johanna Manly. Menlo Park, Calif.: Monastery Books, 1995.

———. *Eranistes*. Translated by Gerard H. Ettlinger. FC 106. Washington, D.C.: The Catholic University of America Press, 2003.

———. "Letters." In *Theodoret, Jerome, Gennadius, Rufinus: Historical Writings, Etc.*, pp. 250-348. Translated by Blomfield Jackson. NPNF 3. Series 2. Edited by Philip Schaff and Henry Wace. 14 vols. 1886-1900. Reprint, Peabody, Mass.: Hendrickson, 1994.

———. *Theodoret of Cyrus: On Divine Providence*. Translated by Thomas Halton. ACW 49. New York: Newman Press, 1988.

See the volume *Commentary Index and Resources* for a collection of supplemental ACCS material, including a comprehensive Scripture index and authors/writings index.

Subject Index